Praise for the Photoshop Bibles and Deke McClelland

You're probably thinking that if someone has the gall to call his book a Bible, it had better be pretty good. If you're not thinking that, it's probably because you've already experienced the Photoshop Bible *and you know it's good.*
— **Los Angeles Times**

Say goodbye to those dull and dusty step-by-step tutorials now that Deke McClelland, the Digital Guru of computer graphics, has updated his international bestseller, the Macworld Photoshop 5 Bible.
— **Adobe.com**

A great program deserves a great book. Photoshop has one in this mammoth paperback (Photoshop Bible).
— **Cincinnati Enquirer**

I've been involved with Photoshop for over seven years, and for as long as I can remember, I've had Deke looking over my shoulder. Deke takes you through Photoshop and covers a lot of areas with impressive depth.
— **Mark Hamburg**, Adobe Principal Scientist and Architect for Photoshop

It's always nice to see something that was very good become great — bigger and better than its predecessor (which was already quite good), the Macworld Photoshop 5 Bible *kicks some serious butt: it's simply outstanding.*
— **PhotoBooks.com**

The Photoshop Bible *is a must have encyclopedia of Photoshop info. It's a tribute to Deke's Photoshop knowledge that even the most veteran Photoshop users find the "Bible" required reading.*
— **Jeff Schewe**, Imaging Artist and Author

(Photoshop Bibles) *show you the ins and outs of this fascinating program, with step-by-step instructions for both everyday techniques and unusual but useful tricks.*
— **Houston Chronicle**

This is an excellent book. I believe you will use it for years.
— **Space Coast PC Journal**

[In Photoshop Studio Secrets] McClelland takes you step by step through every stage of the design, from concept to execution. This is the book you need if you're more interested in the artwork than in the tools.
— **Los Angeles Times**

With Photoshop expert Deke McClelland at the steering wheel, how can you go wrong!
— **The Design & Publishing Center**

The Photoshop 5 Bible by Deke McClelland sits proudly on my desk and is a constant source of information and assistance as I confidently create with Adobe Photoshop 5. McClelland's complete understanding of Adobe's suite of imaging software is only surpassed by his ability to teach. He may be my favorite author!
— **Susanne York,** *Houston, TX*

I gotta tell you — the Photoshop Bible has saved me many times. There is nothing more a designer needs (except for coffee) sitting beside his Mac than the Photoshop Bible.
— **Jason K. Jennings,** *Nashville, TN*

While it may theoretically be possible to use Photoshop without the Photoshop Bible, I can't imagine why anyone would want to try.
— **Tim Wilson,** *Keys Entertainment*

McClelland offers tons of tips, tricks and procedures. There are more insights than any one person will likely be able to digest, but even a few will prove invaluable for getting more out of the program... . One advantage of such a large book is that complicated subjects can be dealt with at length. McClelland takes full advantage of this in the special effects section, detailing how the different filters work, what the effects of the filters are, and how users can better control the results... Macworld Photoshop Bible succeeds as a valuable tome for users of all levels. It will be helpful for beginners and relevant to advanced users.
— **Communication Arts**

This was the best computer book I've ever read.
— **SM,** *Boulder, CO*

This Author's style is inviting and comfortable. He explains complex concepts in a very simple, familiar manner. Nothing else comes close.
— **TG,** *North Hollywood, CA*

I read this book on vacation — and still had a good time!
— **DLG,** *Vanderbilt, Mississippi*

This book has the most extensive coverage of Adobe Photoshop I've seen! Thanks for helping me realize the limitless potential of Photoshop!
— **DG,** *Big Sandy, Texas*

...this encyclopedic effort ought to help both new and experienced users unleash the power of this multidimensional program. Nearly every feature is explored in detail — in McClelland's conversational style…. One imaging topic of importance among Photoshop disciples — Unsharp Making— gets no less than seven pages in the Bible. It's as clear an explanation of USM as has ever been published, backed up with examples showing the effects achieved by varying the Amount, Radius, and Threshold settings. In fact, if you're looking for only one comprehensive Photoshop book, this may be the one.
— *Photo District News*

It's a must have for every professional Photoshop user.
— *RC,* London, England

I teach Photoshop; there would be no way for me to survive my first class without this book! Deke McClelland incorporates a funny way of explaining things, he's very thorough and tells you about "real-life" situations, not just what Adobe wants its customers to know.
— *CD,* Addison, Texas

I thought I was an expert Photoshop user, but you should see how many pages I've marked in this book. Deke's presentation is one of the clearest and most accurate I've seen.
— *CS,* Fullerton, California

This book puts the Photoshop user manual to shame!
— *DB,* Toronto, Ontario, Canada

Deke is humorous, not a self-righteous "know everything" author. This book cuts straight to the usable information, without the typical hype or fluff of the manufacturer manuals.
— *EV,* Somerset, New Jersey

I'm able to do more than I thought possible with Photoshop using this guide.
— *DH,* Lincoln, Nebraska

I like the clear, concise, and practical application of each process in Photoshop. Especially the use of layers! WOW!
— *MRB,* Langley, Washington

I have every Photoshop book and this one is the best. It is the one I go to when I need an answer.
— *EF,* Boulder Colorado

What I really like about the book is that Deke McClelland starts at the basics and takes you step by step as if you knew nothing about scanning or images. He takes nothing for granted, explaining in the introduction such fundamentals as when to use Photoshop and when to use a drawing program…So what does Photoshop do and how does this book help you in doing it? Mr. McClelland will answer both questions and every other question you can think of within the confines of the Macintosh and Photoshop.
*— **Work Place**, University College, Dublin, Ireland*

No other book about Photoshop is as good as this one. It's the best!
*— **JO**, Garsfontein, South Africa*

A truly wonderful book, jam packed with useful hints, tricks and basic procedures in Photoshop.
*— **TW**, Dubuque, Iowa*

I had tough deadlines and had never used Photoshop before. This book added years to my life!
*— **RB**, Green Bay, Wisconsin*

Great job McClelland! Many books are dull, but this one made me laugh out loud. **It** *was easy to read the whole thing.*
*— **PM**, Vallejo, California*

I am laughing all day thinking about and reading this book.
*— **SA**, Barcelona, Spain*

Given the technical nature of the topic and the depth of coverage, you might expect the writing to be rather dry — somewhat less than inspiring. Fortunately, Deke McClelland is as accomplished a writer as he is a Photoshop guru. He has managed to keep a potentially heavy topic from becoming too great a burden on the reader, while maintaining a strong flow of information. His wit and style show through repeatedly in every chapter. I strongly recommend this book to anyone who uses Adobe Photoshop on the Mac or PC.
*— **Flash***

It has an answer waiting for every question I could possibly have about Photoshop.
*— **TL**, Corona, California*

This "Bible" brings all the comfort that the King James Version no longer does — it's my new "Linus Blanket!" I have yet to go find a topic that I can think of that isn't covered by the book, and it is stuffed full of topics that wouldn't have occurred to me.
*— **NC**, London, England*

I learn something new every time I open it.
*— **SFJ**, Billerica, Massachusetts*

It's a great book...definitely every Photoshop user's dream.
— CT, *Brisbane, Australia*

I like Deke McClelland's sense of humor! Plus I loved all the information he poured forth about every feature of Photoshop. I just think this book is excellent!
— TC, *Augusta, Georgia*

I think I love you, Deke McClelland! Thank you for continuing my ongoing quest!
— KW, *Ocoee, Florida*

This is a great book. I know Photoshop but I never realized you could do so much with it until I read this book.
— TLS, *Whitestone, New York*

It is easily understandable and very easy reading with as much information put together as I thought possible. It has everything!
— GKP, *Eugene, Oregon*

This book helped me to understand the thought processes the developers went through to build the program, which helps me to be a better user.
— JD, *Arkansas City, Kansas*

The best Photoshop book I've seen — I know: I'm a sixteen-year professional.
— CD, *Hazelwood, Missouri*

While reading this book, it felt like a good friend was sitting over my shoulder letting me in on all the tips and tricks no one else would tell me about or knew about. Thanks!
— JO, *San Marcos, Texas*

Anyone involved with design knows about this book.
— TS, *Philadelphia, Pennsylvania*

This book has information on all aspects of Photoshop in non-technical, everyday language. It was enjoyable to read and I learned a lot.
— NI, *Fairlawn, New Jersey*

I selected Macworld Photoshop 4.0 Bible *for my digital imaging course because I was impressed with its thoroughness and with the fact that it's very appropriate for beginning through advanced-level students...a very comprehensive text!*
— Thomas Shirley, *Faculty member, Digital Imaging, Columbia College, IL*

Photoshop® 6 for Windows® Bible

Photoshop® 6 for Windows® Bible

Deke McClelland

IDG Books Worldwide, Inc.
An International Data Group Company

Foster City, CA ✦ Chicago, IL ✦ Indianapolis, IN ✦ New York, NY

Photoshop® 6 for Windows® Bible

Published by
IDG Books Worldwide, Inc.
An International Data Group Company
919 E. Hillsdale Blvd., Suite 300
Foster City, CA 94404
www.idgbooks.com (IDG Books Worldwide Web site)

Copyright © 2001 IDG Books Worldwide, Inc. All rights reserved. No part of this book, including interior design, cover design, and icons, may be reproduced or transmitted in any form, by any means (electronic, photocopying, recording, or otherwise) without the prior written permission of the publisher.

ISBN: 0-7645-3491-2

Printed in the United States of America

10 9 8 7 6 5 4 3 2 1

1B/RT/RR/QQ/FC

Distributed in the United States by IDG Books Worldwide, Inc.

Distributed by CDG Books Canada Inc. for Canada; by Transworld Publishers Limited in the United Kingdom; by IDG Norge Books for Norway; by IDG Sweden Books for Sweden; by IDG Books Australia Publishing Corporation Pty. Ltd. for Australia and New Zealand; by TransQuest Publishers Pte Ltd. for Singapore, Malaysia, Thailand, Indonesia, and Hong Kong; by Gotop Information Inc. for Taiwan; by ICG Muse, Inc. for Japan; by Intersoft for South Africa; by Eyrolles for France; by International Thomson Publishing for Germany, Austria, and Switzerland; by Distribuidora Cuspide for Argentina; by LR International for Brazil; by Galileo Libros for Chile; by Ediciones ZETA S.C.R. Ltda. for Peru; by WS Computer Publishing Corporation, Inc., for the Philippines; by Contemporanea de Ediciones for Venezuela; by Express Computer Distributors for the Caribbean and West Indies; by Micronesia Media Distributor, Inc. for Micronesia; by Chips Computadoras S.A. de C.V. for Mexico; by Editorial Norma de Panama S.A. for Panama; by American Bookshops for Finland.

For general information on IDG Books Worldwide's books in the U.S., please call our Consumer Customer Service department at 800-762-2974. For reseller information, including discounts and premium sales, please call our Reseller Customer Service department at 800-434-3422.

For information on where to purchase IDG Books Worldwide's books outside the U.S., please contact our International Sales department at 317-572-3993 or fax 317-572-4002.

For consumer information on foreign language translations, please contact our Customer Service department at 800-434-3422, fax 317-572-4002, or e-mail rights@idgbooks.com.

For information on licensing foreign or domestic rights, please phone +1-650-653-7098.

For sales inquiries and special prices for bulk quantities, please contact our Order Services department at 800-434-3422 or write to the address above.

For information on using IDG Books Worldwide's books in the classroom or for ordering examination copies, please contact our Educational Sales department at 800-434-2086 or fax 317-572-4005.

For press review copies, author interviews, or other publicity information, please contact our Public Relations department at 650-653-7000 or fax 650-653-7500.

For authorization to photocopy items for corporate, personal, or educational use, please contact Copyright Clearance Center, 222 Rosewood Drive, Danvers, MA 01923, or fax 978-750-4470.

Library of Congress Cataloging-in-Publication Data

McClelland, Deke, 1962–
 Photoshop 6 for Windows Bible / Deke McClelland.
   p.   cm.
 ISBN 0-7645-3491-2 (alk. paper)
 1. Computer graphics. 2. Adobe Photoshop.
I. Title.
T385 .M3779964   2000
006.6'869--dc21   00-046186

LIMIT OF LIABILITY/DISCLAIMER OF WARRANTY: THE PUBLISHER AND AUTHOR HAVE USED THEIR BEST EFFORTS IN PREPARING THIS BOOK. THE PUBLISHER AND AUTHOR MAKE NO REPRESENTATIONS OR WARRANTIES WITH RESPECT TO THE ACCURACY OR COMPLETENESS OF THE CONTENTS OF THIS BOOK AND SPECIFICALLY DISCLAIM ANY IMPLIED WARRANTIES OF MERCHANTABILITY OR FITNESS FOR A PARTICULAR PURPOSE. THERE ARE NO WARRANTIES WHICH EXTEND BEYOND THE DESCRIPTIONS CONTAINED IN THIS PARAGRAPH. NO WARRANTY MAY BE CREATED OR EXTENDED BY SALES REPRESENTATIVES OR WRITTEN SALES MATERIALS. THE ACCURACY AND COMPLETENESS OF THE INFORMATION PROVIDED HEREIN AND THE OPINIONS STATED HEREIN ARE NOT GUARANTEED OR WARRANTED TO PRODUCE ANY PARTICULAR RESULTS, AND THE ADVICE AND STRATEGIES CONTAINED HEREIN MAY NOT BE SUITABLE FOR EVERY INDIVIDUAL. NEITHER THE PUBLISHER NOR AUTHOR SHALL BE LIABLE FOR ANY LOSS OF PROFIT OR ANY OTHER COMMERCIAL DAMAGES, INCLUDING BUT NOT LIMITED TO SPECIAL, INCIDENTAL, CONSEQUENTIAL, OR OTHER DAMAGES. FULFILLMENT OF EACH COUPON OFFER IS THE RESPONSIBILITY OF THE OFFEROR.

Trademarks: Photoshop is a registered trademark of Adobe Systems Inc. and Windows is a registered trademark of Microsoft Corporation, in the United States and other countries. All other trademarks are property of their respective owners. IDG Books Worldwide is not associated with any product or vendor mentioned in this book.

is a registered trademark or trademark under exclusive license to IDG Books Worldwide, Inc. from International Data Group, Inc. in the United States and/or other countries.

IDG BOOKS WORLDWIDE

ABOUT IDG BOOKS WORLDWIDE

Welcome to the world of IDG Books Worldwide.

IDG Books Worldwide, Inc., is a subsidiary of International Data Group, the world's largest publisher of computer-related information and the leading global provider of information services on information technology. IDG was founded more than 30 years ago by Patrick J. McGovern and now employs more than 9,000 people worldwide. IDG publishes more than 290 computer publications in over 75 countries. More than 90 million people read one or more IDG publications each month.

Launched in 1990, IDG Books Worldwide is today the #1 publisher of best-selling computer books in the United States. We are proud to have received eight awards from the Computer Press Association in recognition of editorial excellence and three from Computer Currents' First Annual Readers' Choice Awards. Our best-selling ...For Dummies® series has more than 50 million copies in print with translations in 31 languages. IDG Books Worldwide, through a joint venture with IDG's Hi-Tech Beijing, became the first U.S. publisher to publish a computer book in the People's Republic of China. In record time, IDG Books Worldwide has become the first choice for millions of readers around the world who want to learn how to better manage their businesses.

Our mission is simple: Every one of our books is designed to bring extra value and skill-building instructions to the reader. Our books are written by experts who understand and care about our readers. The knowledge base of our editorial staff comes from years of experience in publishing, education, and journalism — experience we use to produce books to carry us into the new millennium. In short, we care about books, so we attract the best people. We devote special attention to details such as audience, interior design, use of icons, and illustrations. And because we use an efficient process of authoring, editing, and desktop publishing our books electronically, we can spend more time ensuring superior content and less time on the technicalities of making books.

You can count on our commitment to deliver high-quality books at competitive prices on topics you want to read about. At IDG Books Worldwide, we continue in the IDG tradition of delivering quality for more than 30 years. You'll find no better book on a subject than one from IDG Books Worldwide.

John J. Kilcullen
John Kilcullen
Chairman and CEO
IDG Books Worldwide, Inc.

*Eighth Annual
Computer Press
Awards ≥1992*

WINNER
*Ninth Annual
Computer Press
Awards ≥1993*

*Tenth Annual
Computer Press
Awards ≥1994*

WINNER

WINNER
*Eleventh Annual
Computer Press
Awards ≥1995*

IDG is the world's leading IT media, research and exposition company. Founded in 1964, IDG had 1997 revenues of $2.05 billion and has more than 9,000 employees worldwide. IDG offers the widest range of media options that reach IT buyers in 75 countries representing 95% of worldwide IT spending. IDG's diverse product and services portfolio spans six key areas including print publishing, online publishing, expositions and conferences, market research, education and training, and global marketing services. More than 90 million people read one or more of IDG's 290 magazines and newspapers, including IDG's leading global brands — Computerworld, PC World, Network World, Macworld and the Channel World family of publications. IDG Books Worldwide is one of the fastest-growing computer book publishers in the world, with more than 700 titles in 36 languages. The "...For Dummies®" series alone has more than 50 million copies in print. IDG offers online users the largest network of technology-specific Web sites around the world through IDG.net (http://www.idg.net), which comprises more than 225 targeted Web sites in 55 countries worldwide. International Data Corporation (IDC) is the world's largest provider of information technology data, analysis and consulting, with research centers in over 41 countries and more than 400 research analysts worldwide. IDG World Expo is a leading producer of more than 168 globally branded conferences and expositions in 35 countries including E3 (Electronic Entertainment Expo), Macworld Expo, ComNet, Windows World Expo, ICE (Internet Commerce Expo), Agenda, DEMO, and Spotlight. IDG's training subsidiary, ExecuTrain, is the world's largest computer training company, with more than 230 locations worldwide and 785 training courses. IDG Marketing Services helps industry-leading IT companies build international brand recognition by developing global integrated marketing programs via IDG's print, online and exposition products worldwide. Further information about the company can be found at www.idg.com.   1/26/00

Credits

Acquisitions Editor
Michael Roney

Project Editors
Amy Thomas Buscaglia
Sharon Eames

Technical Editor
Marc Pawliger

Copy Editors
Laura Stone
Lane Barnholtz
KC Hogue
Julie Campbell Moss
Nancy Rapoport

Proof Editor
Patsy Owens

Project Coordinators
Danette Nurse
Joe Shines

Graphics and Production Specialists
Robert Bihlmayer
Jude Levinson
Michael Lewis
Ramses Ramirez
Victor Pérez-Varela

Quality Control Technician
Dina F Quan

Permissions Editor
Carmen Krikorian

Media Development Specialist
Angela Denny

Media Development Coordinator
Marisa Pearman

Book Designer
Drew R. Moore

Illustrators
Gabriele McCann
Angela F. Hunckler

Proofreading and Indexing
York Production Services

Cover Illustrator
Peter Kowaleszyn

About the Author

In 1985, **Deke McClelland** oversaw the implementation of the first personal computer-based production department in Boulder, Colorado. He later graduated to be artistic director for Publishing Resources, one of the earliest all-PostScript service bureaus in the United States.

These days, Deke is the author of the award-winning titles *Photoshop for Windows Bible* and *Macworld Photoshop Bible* (both published by IDG Books Worldwide), now in their eighth year with more copies in print than any other guides on computer graphics.

Other best-selling titles include *Photoshop For Dummies, Photoshop Studio Secrets, Web Design Studio Secrets* (all IDG Books Worldwide), *Real World Illustrator 9,* and *Real World Digital Photography* (both Peachpit Press). He also serves as host to several entertaining and educational video training series, including *Total Photoshop, Total InDesign,* and *Total Illustrator* (all Total Training).

In 1989, Deke won the Benjamin Franklin Award for Best Computer Book. Since then, he has received honors from the Society for Technical Communication (once in 1994 and twice in 1999), the American Society of Business Press Editors (1995), the Western Publications Association (1999), and the Computer Press Association (1990, 1992, 1994, 1995, 1997, and twice in 1999). In 1999, Book Bytes named Deke its Author of the Year.

Deke is presently working on his new visual learning series, *Look & Learn,* which is slated to include *Look & Learn Photoshop* and *Look & Learn Flash* (IDG Books Worldwide). He is a contributing editor for *Macworld* magazine.

To my mad little Max, and the woman who created him.

Two sweeter people you never did see.

To see these two people is sweetness indeed.

Foreword

If you are reading this foreword, it probably means that you've purchased a copy of Adobe Photoshop 6.0, and for that I and the rest of the Photoshop team at Adobe thank you.

If you own a previous edition of the *Photoshop Bible*, you probably know what to expect. If not, then get ready for an interesting trip.

A lot of attention in various forums has been given to the fact that the year 2000 marks the ten-year anniversary of Adobe Photoshop. Unless you buy this book almost immediately after it comes out, I will also have been working on Photoshop for ten years, so this seems like a good time to do a little looking back.

When I joined the Photoshop team, my first task was to start adding vector drawing capabilities to a program that even in 1.0 could lay claim to being the leading desktop raster editing program. In other words, I was to implement a Bézier pen tool that as initially planned was little more than a glorified lasso tool. Ten years later, Photoshop 6 is now taking vectors on in earnest. I trust that doesn't mean that we sat still for the 9+ years between Photoshop 2.0 and Photoshop 6.0. It certainly doesn't feel that way.

If we had done so, I suspect that we would have heard from Deke McClelland since he's been watching over our shoulders for almost as long as I can remember.

While Photoshop 6 probably provides more instant gratification features than any previous version, at its core it offers a broad collection of basic and not so basic tools for building and manipulating images. Becoming a skilled Photoshop user involves getting to know those tools, how they interact, and when to use them. The best way I've found to do that is through use, exploration, and play. On the other hand, since Photoshop allows one to do so much, it can be difficult to know where to begin. It's like opening a watch maker's tool chest: The screwdrivers are pretty obvious, but what about all these other strange and mysterious instruments?

This is where Deke comes in. In Deke's hands, Photoshop goes from being just a toolbox to being a strange and wonderful land all its own. The *Photoshop Bible* is a guided tour through that land with a guide who has been over the territory many times.

Deke takes you through most of Photoshop and covers a lot of areas in impressive depth. Not only does he show you the features in Photoshop — after all, you've got the manual to do that—he shows you how to use them to address issues that look almost like real world problems. This is the *Photoshop Bible* not the *Photoshop Encyclopedia* and hence it tells stories rather than just presenting information.

A second thing that you'll get from this book is a lot of commentary. Deke isn't shy about letting you know how he feels about various features. I don't always agree with Deke's opinions on these matters, but I think his openness about his opinions makes the book much richer. If you become a routine user of Photoshop, you will almost certainly develop your own opinions, some of which will probably match Deke's and some of which probably won't. It's valuable to get his opinions during the tour, however, because, even if you end up disagreeing with them, they give you more to think about.

Finally, the most invigorating aspect of this book is the enthusiasm Deke brings to the tour. You'll note that I included "play" in my list of strategies for coming to know Photoshop, and I think just having fun with the program is really one of the best things you can do when starting out. Deke almost relentlessly conveys that sense of excitement and fun, and for that I thank him.

So, fasten your seat belts, put on your pith helmets, and get ready. It's a fascinating trip ahead.

Mark Hamburg
Principal Scientist and Architect for Adobe Photoshop
Adobe Systems Incorporated
September 2000

Preface

I have no idea where you are as you read this. You might be sitting in front of your computer, lounging on a beach in Martinique, or curled up under the covers with a flashlight. But there's a chance you're standing in a bookstore with a clerk behind you asking if you need any help. If so, you're at what we in the book biz like to call the "point of purchase" (POP). From my perspective, the POP is a dangerous place, fraught with ambiguities and temptations. There's a chance — however infinitesimal — that you might put this book back where you found it and buy a competing title. I shudder to think of it.

So for the benefit of you POPers, I'm about to lay it on a bit thick.

This book is not only the number-one selling guide to Adobe Photoshop, but one of the two or three most successful books on any electronic publishing topic ever printed. You can find dozens of localized translations throughout the world. The Dutch translation has been known to come out before the English edition, and I just received an e-mail from my German translator urging me to get her manuscript ASAP. The *Photoshop Bible* is the most widely accepted textbook for college courses. It is also the only third-party book that has been edited from cover to cover for technical accuracy by members of Photoshop's programming team (for which I am duly grateful).

Now, we all know "bestseller" doesn't necessarily translate to "best" — I needn't remind you that pet rocks were once hotter than Pokémon. But the *Photoshop Bible* seems to have touched a chord. Based on the letters I've received over the years, most readers find the book informative, comprehensive, and entertaining. (Okay, one woman summed it up as "violent, satanic, and blasphemous" — cross my heart, it's true — but now that we've removed all the backward lyrics, I think we've addressed that problem.) Knowing that people not only buy the book, but actually *read* it and find it pleasurable, gives me more satisfaction than I can say.

The driving philosophy behind *Photoshop 6 for Windows Bible* is a simple one: Even the most intimidating topic can be made easy if it's explained properly. This goes double when the subject of the discussion is something as modest as a piece of software. Photoshop isn't some remarkable work of nature that defies our comprehension. It's nothing more that a commercial product designed by a bunch of regular people like you for the express purpose of being understood and put to use by a bunch of regular people like you. If I can't explain something that's inherently so straightforward, then shame on me.

I've made it my mission to address every topic head-on—no cop-outs, no apologies. Everything's here, from the practical benefits of creating accurate masks to the theoretical wonders of designing your own custom layer styles. I wasn't born with this knowledge, and there are plenty of times when I'm learning with you. But when I don't know how something works, I do the research and figure it out, sometimes discussing features directly with the programmers, sometimes taking advantage of other sources. My job is to find out the answers, make sure those answers make sense, and pass them along to you as clearly as I can.

I also provide background, opinions, and a few feeble attempts at humor. A dry listing of features followed by ponderous discussions of how they work doesn't mean squat unless I explain why the feature is there, where it fits into your workflow, and—on occasion—whether or not it's the best solution. I am alternatively cranky, excited, and just plain giddy as I explain Photoshop, and I make no effort to contain my criticisms or enthusiasm. This book is me walking you through the program as subjectively as I would explain it to a friend.

But before I brag any more about the book, it's possible you're not even sure what Photoshop is, much less why you'd need a book on the subject. Just so we're all clear, let's take a peek at the program.

What Is Photoshop?

Photoshop 6 is a professional-level image editor that runs on a Power Macintosh computer running OS 8.5 or later; or a Pentium-based PC equipped with any of several versions of Microsoft Windows. By *image editor,* I mean that Photoshop enables you to edit photos and artwork scanned to disk. You can then post the resulting images on the Internet or print them on paper.

Here's an example: Your job is to take a picture of your company's high-and-mighty CEO, touch up the crow's feet, fix the hair, and publish the Chief's smiling face on the cover of the annual report. No problem. Just shoot the photo, have it scanned to disk, open Mr. or Mrs. CEO inside Photoshop, and away you go. Photoshop arms you with all the digital wrinkle cream, toupee relaxer, jowl remover, and tooth polisher that you could ask for. The head honcho looks presentable no matter how badly the company is doing.

Photoshop, then, is about changing reality. It follows in the footsteps of a rich procession of after-camera tools. Despite all the hand-wringing you may have heard about the veracity of photographs in the digital age, image editing has been around almost as long as photography itself. Witness the editorial image below, lifted from the hallowed pages of a 1917 issue of *The Geographic* (predecessor to *National Geographic*). The men on the left are authentic, but I'm a bit skeptical about that fellow inside the van. Today's editing techniques may be more sophisticated, but they're hardly anything new.

Photograph by Paul Thompson

A WAGON-LOAD OF HELMETS OR CASQUES FOR FRENCH
SOLDIERS LEAVING THE FACTORY

In 1917, *The Geographic* tendered this image as a genuine photograph,
and very likely many readers thought nothing of it. One day, future
generations will think the same of our work.

Photoshop goes beyond just reducing the distance between two Giza pyramids on
the cover of *National Geographic* or plopping a leaning Tom Cruise, photographed
in Hawaii, onto the supportive shoulder of Dustin Hoffman, photographed in New
York, for a *Newsweek* spread (both duller-than-fiction applications of image-editing
software). Photoshop brings you full-tilt creativity. Picture the head of an eagle on
the body of a lion with the legs of a spider and the wings of a dove. Picture yourself
in a boat on a river with tangerine trees and marmalade skies. Whether your inspi-
rations are original or derivative, Photoshop lets you paint snapshots from your
dreams. If you can picture it in your head, you can paint it in Photoshop.

About This Book

If you're familiar with previous editions of this book, this one represents your
everyday average exhaustive renovation. As is often the case, I am assisted by Julie
PhotoDeluxe For Dummies King and Amy *InDesign For Dummies* Thomas Buscaglia,
long-time contributors to the *Bible*. (Julie has been adding her touch since the very
first *Bible;* Amy has been on board for the last seven renditions.) With their help,
I've added detailed discussions on the subjects of layers, blending options, styles,

vector-based shapes, color management, object-oriented text, the expanded TIFF and PDF file formats, free-form distortions, and the usual plethora of interface enhancements. As always, we've reworked the structure of the book to suit the newest version of Photoshop, creating new parts, rehashing every chapter without exception, and rewriting several chapters from the ground up. In short, we've deprived ourselves of sleep and sanity to make you happy.

If you're new to the *Bible,* I urge you to take a brief moment and make sure you have the right one before you pay the clerk and take it home. You are currently holding the *Photoshop 6 for Windows Bible,* designed specifically for folks who own PCs equipped with Microsoft Windows. If you use a Apple Macintosh or iMac instead, put this book down and request a copy of the *Macworld Photoshop 6 Bible,* which is far more likely to suit your needs.

That silver Frisbee on the back cover

In the back of this book, you'll find a CD-ROM. It contains Photoshop plug-ins and several high-resolution pieces of stock photography in full, natural color. I've included many of the pivotal images from this book so that you can follow along with my examples as you see fit.

The *Bible* is nothing if not comprehensive. To bolster this claim, I've included a few additional chapters as PDF files on the CD-ROM. Assuming you have Adobe Acrobat Reader (which you can download at *www.adobe.com*), you can open the chapters, read them on screen, and print them at your leisure. Among these on-disk chapters are two collections of Photoshop shortcuts — the most extensive of their kind — one for Macintosh users (Chapter C) and one for Windows (Chapter D). This way, even if you unknowingly purchased the wrong version of the book, you have all the shortcuts you need. The CD also includes PDF copies of all the printed chapters in this book, perfect for those times you want to print an additional copy of a chapter to highlight, underline, or paper the birdcage. Bear in mind, however, that I provide these PDFs for your personal use only. If you distribute them to friends and family, you're breaking all kinds of federal codes, interstate treaties, and Geneva Convention ordinances. If you're unlucky enough to get caught, the FBI will raid your house and make you sit in the corner and write bad checks. Okay, I made that up. All I can really do is tell you I'd rather you didn't share the PDF chapters and hope you don't. I'm powerless; pity me.

As an extra special bonus, you'll find several QuickTime movie tutorials that explain how to use some of Photoshop's most challenging features. These are excerpted from my video training series, *Total Photoshop,* from Total Training (*www.totaltraining.com*).

Cross-Reference

Perhaps best of all, the CD is cross-platform, so you can open it on a Mac or PC. Read the appendix, "Using the CD-ROM," for a complete listing of the contents of the CD.

Conventions

Every computer book seems to conform to a logic all its own, and this one's no exception. Although I try to avoid pig latin — ellway, orfay hetay ostmay artpay — I do subscribe to a handful of conventions that you may not immediately recognize.

Vocabulary

Call it computerese, call it technobabble, call it the synthetic jargon of propeller heads. The fact is, I can't explain Photoshop in graphic and gruesome detail without reverting to the specialized language of the trade. However, to help you keep up, I can and have italicized vocabulary words (as in *random-access memory*) with which you may not be familiar or which I use in an unusual context. An italicized term is followed by a definition.

If you come across a strange word that is *not* italicized (that bit of italics was for emphasis), look it up in the index to find the first reference to the word in the book.

Commands and options

To distinguish the literal names of commands, dialog boxes, buttons, and so on, I capitalize the first letter in each word (for example, *click on the Cancel button*). The only exceptions are option names, which can be six or seven words long and filled with prepositions like *to* and *of.* Traditionally, prepositions and articles (*a, an, the*) don't appear in initial caps, and this book follows that time-honored rule, too.

When discussing menus and commands, I use an arrow symbol to indicate hierarchy. For example, *Choose File ➪ Open* means to choose the Open command from the File menu. If you have to display a submenu to reach a command, I list the command used to display the submenu between the menu name and the final command. *Choose Image ➪ Adjust ➪ Invert* means to choose the Adjust command from the Image menu and then choose the Invert command from the Adjust submenu.

Version numbers

A new piece of software comes out every 15 minutes. That's not a real statistic, mind you, but I bet I'm not far off. As I write this, Photoshop has advanced to Version 6.0. But by the time you read this, the version number may be seven hundredths of a percentage point higher. So know that when I write *Photoshop 6*, I mean any version of Photoshop short of 7.

Similarly, when I write *Photoshop 5,* I mean Versions 5.0, 5.0.2, and 5.5; *Photoshop 4* means Versions 4.0 and 4.0.1; *Photoshop 3* means Versions 3.0, 3.0.1, 3.0.3, 3.0.4, and 3.0.5; you get the idea.

Icons

Like just about every computer book currently available on your greengrocer's shelves, this one includes alluring icons that focus your eyeballs smack-dab on important information. The icons make it easy for folks who just like to skim books to figure out what the heck's going on. Icons serve as little insurance policies against short attention spans. On the whole, the icons are self-explanatory, but I'll explain them anyway.

The Caution icon warns you that a step you're about to take may produce disastrous results. Well, perhaps "disastrous" is an exaggeration. Inconvenient, then. Uncomfortable. For heaven's sake, use caution.

The Note icon highlights some little tidbit of information I've decided to share with you that seemed at the time to be remotely related to the topic at hand. I might tell you how an option came into existence, why a feature is implemented the way it is, or how things used to be better back in the old days.

The Photoshop 6 icon explains an option, command, or other feature that is brand-spanking new to this latest revision. If you're already familiar with previous versions of Photoshop, you might just want to plow through the book looking for Photoshop 6 icons and see what new stuff is out there.

This book is bursting with tips and techniques. If I were to highlight every one of them, whole pages would have light-bulbs popping out all over the place. The Tip icon calls attention to shortcuts that are specifically applicable to the Photoshop application. For the bigger, more useful power tips, I'm afraid you'll have to actually read the text.

The Cross-Reference icon tells you where to go for information related to the current topic. I included one a few pages back and you probably read it without thinking twice. That means you're either sharp as a tack or an experienced computer-book user. Either way, you won't have any trouble with this icon.

I thought of including one more icon that alerted you to every new bit of information—whether Photoshop 6–dependent or not—that's included in this book. But I found myself using it every other paragraph. Besides, that would have robbed you of the fun of discovering the new stuff.

How to Bug Me

Even in its sixth edition, scanned by the eyes of hundreds of thousands of readers and scrutinized intensely for months at a time by myself and my editors, I'll bet someone, somewhere will still manage to locate errors and oversights. If you notice those kinds of things and you have a few spare moments, please let me know. I always appreciate readers' comments.

If you want to share your insights, comments, or corrections, please visit my Web site, the infamous *http://www.dekemc.com*. There you'll find news and excerpts about my books, tips for various graphics products, and other goofy online stuff. Let me know what you think. To e-mail me, click on the Contact Deke button. Don't fret if you don't hear from me for a few days, or months, or ever. I read every letter and try to implement nearly every constructive idea anyone bothers to send me. But because I receive hundreds of reader letters a week, I can respond to only a small percentage of them.

Note

Please, do not write to ask me why your copy of Photoshop is misbehaving on your specific computer. I was not involved in developing Photoshop, I am not employed by Adobe, and I am not trained in product support. Adobe can answer your technical support questions way better than I can, so I leave it to the experts.

Now, without further ado, I urge you to turn the page and advance forward into the great untamed frontier of image editing. But remember, this book can be a dangerous tool if wielded unwisely. Don't set it on any creaky card tables or let your children play with it without the assistance of a stalwart adult, preferably an All-Star Wrestler or that guy who played the Incredible Hulk on TV. And no flower pressing. The little suckers would be pummeled to dust by this monstrously powerful colossus of a book.

Contents at a Glance

Contents

● ●

Part V: Color for Print and the Web   725

Chapter 16: Essential Color Management 727

Chapter 17: Mapping and Adjusting Colors 755

Bonus Chapters   On the CD-ROM

Chapter A: Constructing Homemade Effects

Chapter B: Actions and Other Automations

Chapter C: Macintosh Shortcuts

Chapter D: Windows Shortcuts

Welcome to Photoshop 6

What's Up with Photoshop 6?

What Is Photoshop?

Adobe Photoshop is the most popular image-editing application available for use on Macintosh and Windows-based computers. Despite hefty competition over the years from a diverse variety of programs ranging in price from virtually free to a few thousand dollars each, Adobe once reported that Photoshop's sales account for more than 80 percent of the image-editing market, with the number still rising. This makes Photoshop four times more popular than all its competitors combined. Where professional image editing is concerned, Photoshop's not just the market leader, it's the only game in town.

Photoshop's historically lopsided sales advantage provides Adobe with a clear incentive to reinvest in Photoshop and regularly enhance — even overhaul — its capabilities. Meanwhile, other vendors have had to devote smaller resources to playing catch-up. Although competitors have historically provided some interesting and sometimes amazing capabilities, the sums of their parts have typically fallen well short of Photoshop's.

As a result, Photoshop rides a self-perpetuating wave of industry predominance. It hasn't always been the best image editor, nor was it the earliest. But its deceptively straightforward interface combined with a few terrific core functions made it a hit from the moment of its first release. More than a decade later — thanks to substantial capital injections and highly creative programming on the part of Adobe's staff and Photoshop originator Thomas Knoll — it has evolved into the most popular program of its kind.

If you're already familiar with Photoshop and you just want to scope out its new capabilities, skip to the section "Fast Track to Version 6."

Image-Editing Theory

Like any *image editor,* Photoshop enables you to alter photographs and other scanned artwork. You can retouch an image, apply special effects, swap details between photos, introduce text and logos, adjust color balance, and even add color to a grayscale scan. Photoshop also provides the tools you need to create images from scratch. These tools are fully compatible with pressure-sensitive tablets, so you can create naturalistic images that look for all the world like watercolors and oils.

Bitmaps versus objects

Image editors fall into the larger software category of *painting programs.* In a painting program, you draw a line, and the application converts it to tiny square dots called pixels. The painting itself is called a *bitmapped image,* but bitmap and image are equally acceptable terms.

Note

Photoshop uses the term *bitmap* exclusively to mean a black-and-white image, the logic being that each pixel conforms to one *bit* of data, 0 or 1 (off or on). In order to avoid awkward syllabic mergers such as *pix-map* — and because forcing a distinction between a painting with exactly two colors and one with anywhere from four to 16 million colors is entirely arbitrary — I use the term bitmap more broadly to mean any image composed of a fixed number of pixels, regardless of the number of colors involved.

What about other graphics applications, such as Adobe Illustrator? Illustrator, Macromedia FreeHand, CorelDraw, and others fall into a different category of software called *drawing programs.* Drawings comprise *objects,* which are independent, mathematically defined lines and shapes. For this reason, drawing programs are sometimes said to be *object-oriented.* Some folks prefer the term *vector-based,* but I shy away from it because *vector* implies the physical components direction and magnitude, which generally are associated with straight lines. Besides, my preference suggests an air of romance, as in, "One day, I'm going to shake off the dust of this three-horse town and pursue a life of romantic adventure in the Object Orient!"

Photoshop 6

Photoshop 6 introduces object-oriented layers, which permit you to add high-resolution text and shapes to your photographic images, all inside a single piece of artwork. In that regard, the program has become a kind of painting and drawing hybrid. These features don't altogether take the place of a drawing program, they merely help to make Photoshop that much more flexible and capable.

The ups and downs of painting

Painting programs and drawing programs each have their strengths and weaknesses. The strength of a painting program is that it offers an extremely straightforward approach to creating images. For example, although many of Photoshop's features are complex — *exceedingly* complex on occasion — its core painting tools are as easy to use as a pencil. You alternately draw and erase until you reach a desired effect, just as you've been doing since grade school. (Of course, for all I know, you've been using computers since grade school. If you're pushing 20, you probably managed to log in many happy hours on paint programs in your formative years. Then again, if you're under 20, you're still in your formative years. Shucks, we're *all* in our formative years. Wrinkles, expanding tummies, falling arches, longer nose hairs . . . if that's not a new form, I don't know what is.)

In addition to being simple to use, each of Photoshop's core painting tools is fully customizable. It's as if you have access to an infinite variety of crayons, colored pencils, pastels, airbrushes, watercolors, and so on, all of which are entirely erasable. Doodling on the phone book was never so much fun.

The downside of a painting program is that it limits your *resolution* options. Because bitmaps contain a fixed number of pixels, the resolution of an image — the number of pixels per inch — is dependent upon the size at which the image is printed, as demonstrated in Figure 1-1. Print the image small, and the pixels become tiny, which increases resolution; print the image large, and the pixels grow, which decreases resolution. An image that fills up a low-resolution screen (640 × 480 pixels) prints with smooth color transitions when reduced to, say, the size of a business card. But if you print that same image so it fills an 8½-by-11-inch page, you'll probably be able to distinguish individual pixels, which means you can see jagged edges and blocky transitions. The only way to remedy this problem is to increase the number of pixels in the image, which increases the size of the file on disk.

 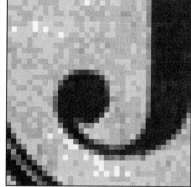

Figure 1-1: When printed small, a painting appears relatively smooth (left). But when printed large, it appears jagged (right).

Bear in mind that this is a very simplified explanation of how images work. For a more complete description that includes techniques for maximizing image performance, refer to "How Images Work" at the outset of Chapter 3.

The downs and ups of drawing

Painting programs provide tools reminiscent of traditional art tools. A drawing program, on the other hand, features tools that have no real-world counterparts. The process of drawing might more aptly be termed *constructing,* because you actually build lines and shapes point by point and stack them on top of each other to create a finished image. Each object is independently editable — one of the few structural advantages of an object-oriented approach — but you're still faced with the task of building your artwork one chunk at a time.

Nevertheless, because a drawing program defines lines, shapes, and text as mathematical equations, these objects automatically conform to the full resolution of the *output device,* whether it's a laser printer, imagesetter, or film recorder. The drawing program sends the math to the printer and the printer *renders* the math to paper or film. In other words, the printer converts the drawing program's equations to printer pixels. Your printer offers far more pixels than your screen — a 300-dots-per-inch (dpi) laser printer, for example, offers 300 pixels per inch (dots equal pixels), whereas most screens offer 72 pixels per inch. So the printed drawing appears smooth and sharply focused regardless of the size at which you print it, as shown in Figure 1-2.

Figure 1-2: Small or large, a drawing prints smooth, but it's a pain to create. This one took more than an hour out of my day, and, as you can see, I didn't even bother with the letters around the perimeter of the design.

Another advantage of drawings is that they take up relatively little room on disk. The file size of a drawing depends on the quantity and complexity of the objects the drawing contains. Thus, the file size has almost nothing to do with the size of the printed image, which is just the opposite of the way bitmapped images work. A **thumbnail** drawing of a garden that contains hundreds of leaves and petals consumes **several** times more disk space than a poster-sized drawing that contains three **rectangles.**

When to use Photoshop

Thanks **to** their specialized methods, painting programs and drawing programs fulfill **distinct** and divergent purposes. Photoshop and other painting programs are best suited to creating and editing the following kinds of artwork:

✦ Scanned photos, including photographic collages and embellishments that originate from scans

✦ Images captured with any type of digital camera

✦ Still frames scanned from videotape or film

✦ Realistic artwork that relies on the play between naturalistic highlights, **midrang**es, and shadows

✦ Impressionistic-type artwork and other images created for purely personal or aesthetic purposes

✦ Logos and other display type featuring soft edges, reflections, or tapering shadows

✦ Special effects that require the use of filters and color enhancements you simply can't achieve in a drawing program

When to use a drawing program

You're probably better off using Illustrator, CorelDraw, or some other drawing program if you're interested in creating more stylized artwork, such as the following:

✦ Poster art and other high-contrast graphics that heighten the appearance of reality

✦ Architectural plans, product designs, or other precise line drawings

✦ Business graphics, such as charts and other "infographics" that reflect data or show how things work

✦ Traditional logos and text effects that require crisp, ultrasmooth edges

✦ Brochures, flyers, and other single-page documents that mingle artwork, logos, and standard-sized text (such as the text you're reading now)

If you're serious about computer graphics, you should own at least one painting program and one drawing program. If I had to rely exclusively on two graphics applications, I would probably choose Photoshop and Illustrator. Adobe has done a fine job of establishing symmetry between the two programs, so that they share common interface elements and keyboard shortcuts. Learn one and the other makes a lot more sense.

Cross-Reference

For those who are interested, I write a cradle-to-grave guide to Illustrator called *Real World Illustrator*, published by Peachpit Press. (Occasionally a reader asks me why I didn't write IDG Books' *Illustrator Bible*, perhaps hoping for a salacious insight into the publishing world. Sadly, the reason is mundane: I already had a signed contract with Peachpit when IDG offered the *Bible* to me. Fortunately for IDG Books and the industry at large, a talented first-time author named Ted Alspach stepped in. Adobe has since snatched up Ted and made him the Illustrator 9 product manager. As IDG likes to say, that'll teach me to go writing books for other publishers.) I'm also the host of a handful of video training series, including *Total Photoshop* and *Total Illustrator,* both produced by Total Training (*www.totaltraining.com*).

The Computer Design Scheme

If your aspirations go beyond image editing into the larger world of computer-assisted design, you'll soon learn that Photoshop is just one cog in a mighty wheel of programs used to create artwork, printed documents, and presentations.

The natural-media paint program Corel Painter emulates real-world tools such as charcoal, chalk, felt-tip markers, calligraphic pen nibs, and camel-hair brushes as deftly as a synthesizer mimics a thunderstorm. Three-dimensional drawing applications enable you to create hyper-realistic objects with depth, lighting, shadows, surface textures, reflections, refractions — you name it. These applications can import images created in Photoshop as well as export images you can then enhance and adjust with Photoshop.

Page-layout programs such as Adobe InDesign and QuarkXPress let you integrate images into newsletters, reports, books (such as this one), and just about any other kind of document you can imagine. If you prefer to transfer your message to slides, you can use Microsoft PowerPoint to add impact to your images through the use of charts and diagrams. Or publish an electronic document to the Web using Adobe Acrobat.

With Adobe Premiere and After Effects, you can merge images with video sequences recorded in the QuickTime format. You even can edit individual frames in Premiere movies with Photoshop. Macromedia's Director Shockwave Studio makes it possible to combine images with animation, QuickTime movies, and sound to create multimedia presentations you can show on screen or record on videotape.

Finally, you can publish your images over the World Wide Web. You can code HTML and JavaScript in any word processor, or mock up pages in a page editor such as Microsoft FrontPage or Macromedia Dreamweaver. You can even integrate images into simple GIF animations using any number of shareware programs available over the Internet. In fact, the Web is single-handedly breathing new life and respectability into low-resolution images, as I explore in Chapter 19.

Photoshop Scenarios

All the programs I mentioned previously are well-known industry standards. But they also cost money — sometimes lots of money — and they take time to learn. The number of programs you decide to purchase and how you use them is up to you. The following list outlines a few specific ways to use Photoshop alone and in tandem with other products:

✦ After scanning and adjusting an image inside Photoshop, use InDesign or QuarkXPress to place the image into your monthly newsletter and then print the document from the page-layout program.

✦ After putting the finishing touches on a lovely tropical vista inside Photoshop, import the image for use as an eye-catching background inside PowerPoint. Then save the document as a self-running screen presentation or print it to overhead transparencies or slides from the presentation program.

✦ Capture an on-screen image by pressing the Print Screen key or using a screen capture utility. Then create a new image in Photoshop and paste the screen image from the Clipboard. That's how the screens in this book were produced.

✦ If you want to annotate the image, import it into Illustrator or CorelDraw, add arrows and labels as desired, and print it from the drawing program.

✦ Paint an original image inside Photoshop using a pressure-sensitive tablet. Use the image as artwork in a document created in a page-layout program or print it directly from Photoshop.

✦ Snap a photo with a digital photograph. As I write this, the best midrange cameras come from Olympus, Nikon, and Kodak. Correct the focus and brightness in Photoshop (as explained in Chapters 10 and 17). Then add the photo to your personal Web site or print it out from a color printer.

✦ Scan a surface texture such as wood or marble into Photoshop and edit it to create a fluid repeating pattern (as explained in Chapter 7). Import the image for use as a texture map in a three-dimensional drawing program. Render the 3D graphic to an image file, open the image inside Photoshop, and retouch as needed.

✦ Create a repeating pattern, save it as a BMP file, and apply it to the Windows desktop using the Display control panel.

✦ Take a problematic drawing that keeps generating errors and save it as an EPS file. Then open the file inside Photoshop to render it as a high-resolution bitmap. Place the image in a document created in a page-layout program or print it directly from Photoshop.

✦ Start an illustration in a drawing program and save it as an EPS file. Open the file in Photoshop and use the program's unique tools to add textures and tones that are difficult or impossible to create in a vector-based drawing program.

✦ Record a QuickTime movie in Premiere and export it to the FilmStrip format. Open the file inside Photoshop and edit it one frame at a time by drawing on the frame or applying filters. Finally, open the altered FilmStrip file in Premiere and convert it back to the QuickTime format.

Obviously, few folks have the money to buy all these products and even fewer have the energy or inclination to implement every one of these ideas. But quite honestly, these are just a handful of projects I can list off the top of my head. There must be hundreds of uses for Photoshop that involve no outside applications whatsoever. In fact, so far as I've been able to figure, there's no end to the number of design jobs you can handle in whole or in part using Photoshop.

Photoshop is a versatile and essential product for any designer or artist who owns a personal computer. Simply put, this is the software around which virtually every other computer-graphics program revolves. I, for one, wouldn't remove Photoshop from my hard drive for a thousand bucks. (Of course, that's not to say I'm not willing to consider higher offers. For $1,500, I'd gladly swap it to a Jaz cartridge.)

Fast Track to Version 6

If it seems like you've been using Photoshop for the better part of your professional career and you're itching to put a leash around the program's neck and take it for a walk, the following list explains all. Here I've compiled a few of the most prominent features that are new to Photoshop 6, in rough order of importance. I also point you to the chapter where you can sniff around for more information:

✦ **Object-oriented type (Chapter 15):** Every update to Photoshop features some kind of improvement to type, but somehow it's never quite perfect. Now it is. In Photoshop 6, type is fully editable, it outputs at the full resolution of your printer, and it wraps automatically from one line to the next. In other words, type finally works the way you'd expect! You can even apply leading, tracking, paragraph spacing, justification, and hyphenation, just as in QuarkXPress and Illustrator. The only feature missing is support for tabs.

✦ **High-resolution lines and shapes (Chapter 14):** Can you name a graphics program that's nearly 10 years old and can't draw a rectangle? If you guessed Photoshop 5.5, stick a gold star on your forehead. But don't guess Photoshop 6. It can draw not only rectangles, but also ovals, polygons, and custom shapes. Like text, Photoshop renders these vector shapes at the full resolution of the printer. What's more, you can fill them with gradients, patterns, and photographic images.

✦ **Revamped color management (Chapter 16):** Photoshop 5 introduced profile-based color management; Photoshop 6 makes it better. For one thing, Adobe has made a serious effort to standardize color management across both Photoshop and Illustrator 9, so you can get the two programs to match more easily. Second, you can work in multiple color environments at a time, so that one RGB image is calibrated for the Web and another for your printer. CMS remains highly complex, but its ability to deliver reliable color is downright extraordinary.

✦ **Layers sets (Chapter 12):** This seemingly minor feature makes a big difference in the way you work. Photoshop 6 lets you organize layers into folders called *sets,* great for making sense of complex compositions. You can also assign colors to both layers and sets in the Layers palette, wonderful for identifying layers at a glance. Sets are also powerful grouping tools, permitting you to move, transform, blend, and mask several layers at once.

✦ **Custom layer styles (Chapter 14):** Photoshop 6 has revamped layer effects such as drop shadow, glow, and bevel; as well as added new ones such as satin and stroke. As before, you can access all effects from a single dialog box, but you can also hide, show, and edit individual effects from the Layers palette. Best of all, you can save a combination of settings as a custom style available from the Styles palette. From then on, it takes just one click to apply a bunch of effects at once.

✦ **Advanced blending (Chapter 13):** Double-click a layer in the Layers palette to bring up the revised and vastly more complicated Blend Options dialog box. In addition to allowing you to blend and hide portions of a layer, you can blend a layer's pixels independently of drop shadows, glows, and other effects. You can also hide the layer in one or more color channels and control how a layer interacts with one or several layers below.

✦ **Preset manager (Chapter 5):** Photoshop 6 introduces a whole new category of preference settings called *presets.* These include predefined brushes, color swatches, and gradients, all of which you could create in Photoshop 5.5 and earlier. But they also include patterns (you used to be limited to one), layer styles, and object-oriented shapes. While presets aren't as easy to use as they should be, they make it possible to organize a variety of image attributes at the same time.

✦ **Options bar (Chapter 2):** The old Options and Brushes palettes are gone, replaced by the horizontal Options bar under the menu bar. The bar makes many features more accessible than before, and even offers a few options that were previously available only by choosing a command or pressing a key on the keyboard. As you'd expect, the Options bar changes to accommodate the active tool or operation.

✦ **Liquify command (Chapter 11):** Distortions have long been a weak spot in Photoshop. You could tug an image by one of four corner points, but aside from simple perspective effects, there was little you could do. Photoshop 6 adds the Liquify command, which permits you to paint and erase distortions inside a separate window. While you can't zoom or scroll the image—both significant disadvantages—the command provides a wide variety of tools and a lightning-fast preview.

✦ **Text warping (Chapter 15):** Artists have long requested that Photoshop add text on a curve, a common function inside Illustrator and other object-oriented programs. Instead, we get something that is at once worse and better. The Warp Text option lets you arc, wave, bulge, and twirl type, while keeping it 100 percent editable. Unlike true text on a curve, you can't draw custom paths and position the type on the path. However, you can apply an array of dazzling distortions that fall well outside the capabilities of Illustrator. My biggest complaint: You can't warp shapes or images. My one question: Why the heck not?

✦ **Image slicing (Chapter 19):** Because Photoshop is a pixel-based program and the World Wide Web is a pixel-based environment, most Web artists mock up pages inside Photoshop. Before you can incorporate text, buttons, and other links, you have to split up the page into lots of smaller images that you later reassemble with HTML. Photoshop's slicing tools automate this process, permitting you to break a composition into pieces and even generate the necessary HTML table automatically. You still have to adjust the code, but it's a heck of a time saver.

✦ **Position printed images (Chapter 18):** As I hasten to remind folks, I don't work for Adobe and I have nothing to do with the creation of Photoshop. In the interest of remaining a relatively unbiased outsider, I'm not even part of the Alpha Team, a small cluster of five or six elite users who test each version of the program a year or more before it comes out. However, I do occasionally have a direct impact on the program, and this, dear readers, is my big addition to Photoshop 6. I remember the meeting like it was yesterday. I said something like, "Gee, fellas, every time you print an image from Photoshop, it just gets plopped onto the middle of the page." One of the programmers asked, "Pardon me, did you say something?" To which I rejoined, "Well, I'd like to have control over positioning it. Like, maybe move it to the upper left corner or something. You know, if it's not, like, a big hassle or anything." Then someone said, "Oh, dry up, McClelland." Someone else said, "I'll have the salmon," and everyone ordered lunch. Now whenever you choose File ➪ Print Options, think of me and that fateful day I breathed new life into a tired old program.

✦ **Text and audio notations (Chapter 3):** In the interest of facilitating communications between artists, art directors, bosses, and clients, Photoshop 6 lets you add little sticky notes to your images. You can even record an audio annotation. Save the image as a PDF file, and you can open it in Adobe Acrobat or the free Acrobat Reader.

✦ **Save layers to TIFF and PDF formats (Chapter 3):** Photoshop 6 supports more than a dozen standardized file formats. However, prior to Version 6, the only format that supported layers was the native Photoshop (PSD) format. Now you can save layers with TIFF and PDF documents. As I write this, Photoshop is the only program that can read layered TIFF and PDF files, but other programs will likely follow suit in the years to come.

✦ **Apply JPEG to layers (Chapter 3):** When you save an image to the TIFF format, you can now have the option to apply three varieties of compression: LZW, ZIP, or JPEG. This means, for the first time, you can apply JPEG compression to a layered file, resulting in smaller compositions than ever before.

✦ **Improved Extract command (Chapter 9):** The Extract command has been improved since its introduction in Version 5.5. The Smart Highlighter check box helps you trace around the exact outline of an image element. Two new tools let you clean up the edges after Photoshop generates its automatic outline. Best of all, you can press Ctrl+Z to undo the last operation.

✦ **Dockable palettes (Chapter 2):** Photoshop 6 enables you to attach the top of one palette to the bottom of another, an operation known as *docking*. You can likewise drop palettes into a *docking well* at the far right side of the Options bar.

✦ **Actions as droplets (Chapter B on the CD-ROM):** ImageReady has long permitted you to save actions as independent files on disk called *droplets*. Now Photoshop does too. If you drag an image file and drop it onto the droplet at the desktop level, Photoshop automatically plays the saved action on the file. Note that to save space — this book is getting too big! — actions are discussed in Chapter B on the CD-ROM at the back of this book.

For those of you who hopped to the new version from Photoshop 5.0 or 5.0.2, you also have all the new Internet and masking functions introduced in Version 5.5. You can create better GIF images, preview the effects of JPEG compression, dial in hexadecimal color values, and optimize an image to a specific file size, all of which I discuss in Chapter 19. The magic and background erasers make quick work of isolating a foreground element from an image (Chapter 7). Use the art history brush to selectively revert an image and apply creative effects (Chapter 7). There are also minor enhancements to the TIFF format (Chapter 3), color correction (Chapter 17), and contact sheets (Chapter 18).

This is Photoshop's second aggressive whole-number upgrade in a row, right on the heels of the feature-rich Version 5. If you ask me, I'll tell you Photoshop 5 was more dramatic. After all, can you imagine working without multiple undos, layer effects, editable text, and the revolutionary profile-based color management system that made the entire industry sit up and take notice? Assuming your response is "No way," permit me to join in with a hardy "Me neither!" Still, Photoshop 6 is sufficiently impressive that I imagine some will argue that it's the best upgrade of them all. Of course, those people will be wrong—I mean, I just said Photoshop 5 was better—but their argument has some merit. Photoshop 6 is what we in the business like to call Seriously Good Software.

A big upgrade means big work for me. Nevertheless, I've risen to the challenge, making every effort to document the new features with clarity and in their proper context. Just remember to keep an eye peeled for the Photoshop 6 icon and you'll be over the hump and back into the image-editing groove in no time.

✦   ✦   ✦

Inside Photoshop

A First Look at Photoshop 6

These days, most computer applications speak a common graphical language, and Photoshop is no exception. It subscribes to the basic structure of on-screen nouns and verbs proposed and first spoken by the operating system. As a result, Photoshop may seem tolerably comprehensible the first time you meet it. Without any prior knowledge of its origins or behavior, you should be able to pick up a paintbrush and specify a color in a matter of a few seconds, simply based on the rudimentary vocabulary that you've picked up from other programs. After years of staring into cathode ray tubes, you can't help but get the picture.

But Photoshop has its own special dialect, one that differs from every other program out there. The dialect is so distinct that it's only peripherally understood by other applications, including those from Adobe, the very siblings that Photoshop grew up with. Photoshop has its own way of turning a phrase, it speaks its words in a different order than you might expect, and yes, it uses a lot of strange and sometimes unsettling jargon that it has picked up on the street. Photoshop is always and will forever be a foreigner unnaturally introduced to your hard drive. For all you may think you share in common, it doesn't know you and you don't know it.

Even you experienced users — you hearty few who have carried on more conversations with Photoshop than you have with most of your friends and family — may find yourselves stumbling when negotiating with Version 6. The program speaks differently every time it upgrades. In fact, it's wrong to think of Photoshop 6 as an older, wiser version of its former self. This is a completely new beast, bearing about as much resemblance to Photoshop 1.0 as you bear to a fellow human located on the exact opposite end of the earth.

So in this chapter, I introduce to you the Sixth Beast, insubordinate child of its ancestors, spoiler of photographic traditions, and speaker of the new language that you now have to learn. These pages represent a low-level primer you need to ingest before you can utter so much as a coherent "gack!" Granted, it comes to you second hand—I am a non-native myself, with my own peculiar dialect as you'll discover—but given that Photoshop 6 itself is the only native speaker on the planet, this foreigner's perspective will have to do.

See Photoshop Run

Shortly after you launch Photoshop, the splash screen appears. Shown at the top of Figure 2-1, the splash screen explains the launching process by flashing the names of plug-in modules as they load and listing the various initialization procedures.

You can access the splash screen by choosing Help ➪ About Photoshop. To make the splash screen go away, just click it.

Splash screen tricks

In a typical program, there isn't much reason to revisit the splash screen. But Photoshop 6 offers a few splash screen–related tips and tricks:

✦ Press Alt while choosing the About Photoshop command to display Photoshop team member Mike Shaw's highly disciplined secret Venus In Furs screen, pictured at the bottom of Figure 2-1.

✦ After a few seconds, the list of programmers and copyright statements at the bottom of the screen starts to scroll. Press the Alt key to make the list scroll more quickly.

✦ Photoshop 3 introduced us to Adobe Transient Witticisms—a series of arbitrary gags invented by Photoshop's sleep-deprived, espresso-swilling programmers—and they've been a staple ever since. To see the Witticisms, wait for the credit messages to scroll by one complete cycle. Then Ctrl-click the eye in the standard splash screen or the Venus In Furs screen.

Ctrl-click for witticisms

Figure 2-1: Photoshop 6 splash screens feature genuine Adobe Transient Witticisms and more.

Online studios resource

Click the icon at the top of the toolbox or choose Help ⇨ Adobe Online to open yet another variation on the splash screen titled Adobe Online. Pictured in Figure 2-2, this screen provides access to Adobe's Internet-based resources, which include technical support, tips and tricks, and information about upgrades and related products. You also can choose one of the other commands on the Help menu to link directly to a few specific areas of the online resources.

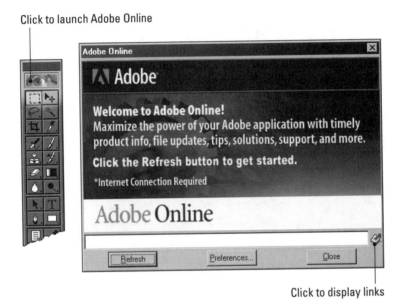

Click to launch Adobe Online

Click to display links

Figure 2-2: Adobe offers a series of online support options for Photoshop 6.

To tell Photoshop how you want your online help delivered—including whether you want Adobe to automatically download and install product updates—click the Preferences button to display the Preferences dialog box. If you're unsure what each option means, click the Setup button, which launches a wizard that spells the options out more clearly. After setting your preferences, click OK and then click the Refresh button to launch your Internet browser and hightail it to the Photoshop area of the Adobe Web site. (If you have problems, connect to the Internet, start your browser as you usually do, and then return to Photoshop and click Refresh again.)

Alternatively, click the links icon in the lower-right corner of the dialog box (see Figure 2-2) to display a list of links that take you directly to pages related to specific topics. If you have a cable modem or other setup that provides a sustained Internet connection, click the Refresh button every now and then to keep the links current. You can instruct Photoshop to update the links automatically in the Preferences dialog box, but I for one am not crazy about Photoshop using my modem without my permission.

The Photoshop Desktop

After the launch process is complete, the Photoshop desktop consumes the foreground. Figure 2-3 shows the Photoshop 6 desktop as it appears when an image is open and all palettes are visible.

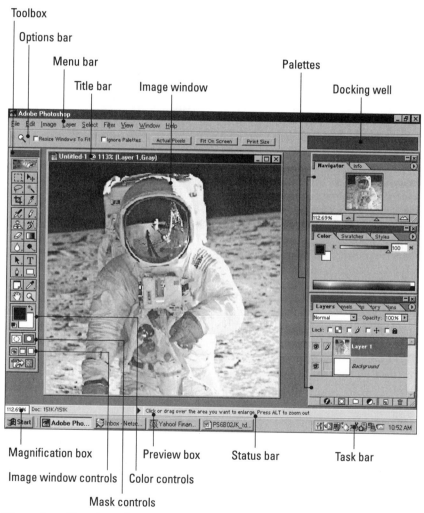

Figure 2-3: The Photoshop 6 desktop as it looks on a 17-inch screen.

Many of the elements that make up the Photoshop desktop are well known to folks familiar with the Windows environment. For example, the menu bar provides access to menus and commands. You can drag the title bar to move the image window. And the scroll bars let you look at hidden portions of the image.

Other potentially less familiar elements of the Photoshop desktop work as follows:

✦ **Image window:** Like any halfway decent product, Photoshop lets you open multiple images at a time. Each open image resides inside its own window.

✦ **Status bar:** Just above the Windows taskbar sits Photoshop's status bar, which provides running commentary on the active tool and image. (If the Status bar doesn't appear on your screen, choose Window ➪ Show Status Bar.) The left end of the status bar features two special boxes. The magnification box tells you the current view size, and the preview box lists how much room the image takes up in memory.

For complete information on the magnification box, read the "Navigating in Photoshop" section later in this chapter. The very next section explains the preview box.

✦ **Toolbox:** The toolbox icons provide one-click access to the various Photoshop tools. To select a tool, click its icon. Then use the tool by clicking or dragging with it inside the image window.

Photoshop 6 not only offers several new tools, but new tool groupings. The crop tool, for example, now has its own apartment instead of sharing quarters with the marquee tools. For a summary of these changes, read "The tools," later in this chapter.

The bottom four rows of the toolbox contains controls for changing your paint colors, entering and exiting the quick mask mode, changing the screen area available for image display, and switching to Adobe ImageReady (which ships with Photoshop).

✦ **Floating palettes:** Photoshop 6 offers a total of 12 palettes, one more than Version 5. (This number excludes the toolbox and the new Options bar, which are technically palettes as well.) Each palette is said to be "floating," which means that it's independent of the image window and of other palettes. Palettes can be grouped together or dragged apart to float separately according to your tastes.

Two palettes found in earlier versions of Photoshop, the Options palette and Brushes palette, take on a new look in Version 6. Controls formerly contained in the palettes now appear on the Options bar, labeled in Figure 2-3.

For more information on the Options bar and other palettes, see the upcoming section "The floating palettes."

✦ **Docking well:** The gray bar at the end of the Options bar is the docking well, another window item new to Photoshop 6. You can drag palettes to the well to save screen space but still keep the palettes easily accessible. For more information, see "Rearranging and docking palettes" later in this chapter.

Unfortunately, the docking well is only visible if you use a screen resolution with a horizontal pixel display of more than 800 pixels.

The preview box

The preview box is Photoshop's way of passing you a memo marked FYI. No biggie, nothing to fret about, just a little bit of info you might want to know. As an unusually obliging piece of software, Photoshop likes to keep its human masters informed on the latest developments.

Document size

By default, the preview box contains two numbers divided by a slash. The first number is the size of the base image in memory. The second number takes into account any additional layers in your image.

Photoshop calculates the first value by multiplying the height and width of the image (both in pixels) by the *bit depth* of the image, which is the size of each pixel in memory. Consider a typical full-color, 640×480-pixel image. A full-color image takes up 24 bits of memory per pixel (which is why it's called a 24-bit image). There are 8 bits in a byte, so 24 bits translates to 3 bytes. Multiply that by the number of pixels and you get $640 \times 480 \times 3 = 921,600$ bytes. Because there are 1,024 bytes in a kilobyte, 921,600 bytes is exactly 900K. Try it yourself—open a 640×480-pixel RGB image and you'll see that the first number in the preview box reads 900K. Now you know why.

But it's the second value, the one that factors in the layers, that represents the real amount of memory that Photoshop needs. If the image contains one layer only, the numbers before and after the slash are the same. Otherwise, Photoshop measures the opaque pixels in each layer and adds approximately 1 byte of overhead per pixel to calculate the transparency. The second number also grows to accommodate paths, masks, spot-color channels, undoable operations, and miscellaneous data required by the image cache.

Now obviously, it's not necessary that you be able to predict these values (which is lucky, because predicting the second value is virtually impossible). Photoshop asks no help when calculating the values in the preview box and will summarily ignore any help you might care to offer. But it's a good idea to know what's going on as you start piling layers on top of an image. The larger the preview numbers grow, the more work Photoshop has to do and the slower it's likely to perform.

Image position

A welcome new print feature, called Print Options, enables you to position a picture precisely on a page before printing. You can find Print Options on the File menu, near the other printing commands; skip to Chapter 18 for details on using this tool.

To get a rough idea of the current image position, however, click and hold on the preview box. Photoshop displays a pop-up window showing the size and placement of the image in relation to the paper. The preview also shows the approximate placement of crop marks and other elements requested in the Page Setup dialog box (File ⇨ Page Setup).

Tip

Press Alt and mouse down on the preview box to view the size and resolution of the image.

You can also Ctrl-click the preview box to see the tile sizes. Photoshop uses *tiles* to calculate pixel manipulations. If you confine your work to a single tile, it will probably go faster than if you slop a little over into a second tile. But who cares? Unless you're some kind of tile-reading robot, this technical information is rarely of any practical use.

Click the right-pointing arrowhead next to the preview box to display a pop-up menu of six options. The first option — Document Sizes — is selected by default. This option displays the image-size values described in the previous section. You can find out what information the other choices provide in the next few sections.

Tip

The prefix displayed before the values in the preview box indicates which of the options is active: Doc shows that Document Sizes is selected; Scr, Scratch Sizes; and Eff, Efficiency. When the Timing option is active, an *s* appears after the numerical value. If a tool name appears in the preview box, you know the final option, Current Tool, is active. Similarly, if you see a color profile statement, such as "untagged RBG," the Document Profile setting, new to Version 6, has the floor.

Image color profile

If you work regularly with many different color profiles, you may find the new Document Profile option handy. When you select this option, the name of the current color profile appears in the preview box.

Adobe changed several other features related to color profiles, too; Chapter 16 tells you what you need to know.

Memory consumption and availability

When you select Scratch Sizes, Photoshop changes the values in the preview box to represent memory consumption and availability. The first value is the amount of room required to hold the currently open images in RAM. The second value indicates the total amount of RAM that Photoshop has to work with. For the program to run at top efficiency, the first number must be smaller than the second.

In the old days, the number before the slash was generally equal to between three and five times the size of all open images, including layers. But thanks to the advent of multiple undos, this value can grow to more than one hundred times as big as any one image. This is because Photoshop has to store each operation in memory on the off chance that you may want to undo to a previous point in time. For each and every action, Photoshop nudges the first value upward until you reach the ceiling of undoable operations.

The second value is simply equal to the amount of memory available to your images after the Photoshop application itself has loaded. For example, suppose you've assigned 100MB of RAM to Photoshop. The code that makes up the Photoshop application consumes about 15MB, so that leaves 85MB to hold and edit images.

If the second value is bigger than the first, then all is happiness and Photoshop is running as fast as your particular brand of computer permits. But if the first value is larger, Photoshop has to dig into its supply of *virtual memory,* a disk-bound adjunct to RAM. Virtual memory makes Photoshop run more slowly because the program must swap portions of the image on and off your hard disk. The simple fact is, disks have moving parts and RAM does not. That means disk-bound "virtual" memory is slower than real memory.

To increase the size of the value after the slash, you have to get more RAM to your images in one of the following ways:

✦ Purchase more RAM. Installing an adequate supply of memory is the single best way to make Photoshop run more quickly.

✦ Quit other applications so that only Photoshop is running.

✦ Quit Photoshop and remove any filters that you don't need from the Plug-Ins folder (which resides in the same folder as the Photoshop 6 application). Don't throw the filters away, just move them to a location outside the Plug-Ins folder so they won't load into RAM when you launch Photoshop.

✦ Choose Edit ⇨ Preferences ⇨ Memory and Image Cache and increase the Physical Memory Usage value as explained later in this chapter.

Operating efficiency

When you select the Efficiency option, Photoshop lists the amount of time it spends running operations in RAM compared with swapping data back and forth between the hard disk. A value of 100 percent is the best-case scenario. It means Photoshop never has to rely on scratch files. Low values indicate higher reliance on the hard disk and, as a result, slower operations. Adobe recommends that if the value falls below 75 percent, you should either assign more memory to Photoshop or purchase more RAM for your computer.

The Efficiency option is a reality check. If it seems Photoshop is dragging its feet, and you hear it writing a little too often, you can refer to the Efficiency rating to see if performance is as bad as you suspect. Keep in mind, hearing Photoshop occasionally write to disk is not, in and of itself, cause for concern. All versions of Photoshop since 3.0 automatically copy open images to a disk buffer in case virtual memory is later warranted. In fact, this is the reason Adobe added the Efficiency option to Version 3.0.1—to quash fears that a few sparks from your hard drive indicated anything less than peak performance.

Photoshop operations timing

If you select Timing, the preview box tells how long Photoshop took to perform the last operation (including background tasks, such as transferring an image to the system Clipboard). Adobe may have added this option to help testing facilities run their Photoshop tests. But built-in timing helps you as well.

For example, suppose you're trying to decide whether to purchase a new computer. You read a magazine article comparing the newest super-fast system. You can run the same filters with the same settings on your computer and see how much slower your results are, all without picking up a stopwatch.

At the risk of starting interoffice feuding, the Timing option also provides you with a mechanism for testing your computer against those of coworkers and friends. The Timing option serves as a neutral arbitrator, enabling you and an associate to test identical operations over the phone. Like Efficiency, Timing is a reality check. If you and your associate own similarly configured computers and your Timing values are vastly different, something's wrong.

The active tool

Choose Current Tool, and Photoshop displays the name of the active tool. Why do you need such a condescending option? Surely you're not so far gone that you need Photoshop telling you what you already know. Adobe's intention is not to drum you over the head with redundant information, but to offer a helping hand if you find the tool configuration confusing. Also, the tool name serves as a companion to the tool description to the right of it in the status bar. Now you see not just what the tool does, but what the tool is.

Still, my guess is that this option will prove as rarely useful to everyday image editing as Timing. Use it if you're having problems when first using Photoshop 6 and then set it back to Document Sizes, Scratch Sizes, or Efficiency. The original three options continue to be the best.

The tools

Photoshop 6 brings with it many changes, including some significant revamping of the toolbox. Here's a quick summary:

✦ Adobe added a row of icons to the toolbox, and the new shape tools and annotation tools quickly set up housekeeping therein.

✦ The crop tool left the digs that it shared with the marquee tools and took up residence on its own nearby.

✦ The measure tool moved in with the eyedroppers, the paintbrush shacked up with the pencil, and the line tool got kicked out on the street. Fortunately, the new shape tools welcomed it as one of their own.

✦ The magnetic pen, type mask, vertical type, and vertical type mask tools fled the toolbox and hid away on the Options bar. You now access the magnetic pen by selecting a check box on the Options bar when the freeform pen is active. Similarly, you bring the type mask, vertical type, and vertical type mask tools into the open by clicking Options bar icons when the type tool is selected.

✦ Clicking the gradient tool icon no longer displays a choice of gradient styles; you now select those styles from the Options bar. The gradient tool rented out the room formerly occupied by the gradient styles icons to the paint bucket.

Finally, when multiple tools share a single toolbox slot, you select the tool you want from a menu-style list, as shown in Figure 2-4, rather than a horizontal pop-out row of tool icons as in previous editions. A tiny, right-pointing triangle in the lower-right corner of an icon indicates that more tools lurk beneath the surface. You can click the triangle and then click the name of the tool you want to use. Or, to get the job done with one less click, just drag from the icon onto the name of the tool and then release the mouse button.

Tip

You can cycle between the tools in the pop-up menu by Alt-clicking a tool icon. Pressing the key that appears to the right of the tool names also does the trick — however, depending on a tool setting that you establish in the Preferences dialog box, you may need to press Shift with the key. (See the upcoming section "General preferences.")

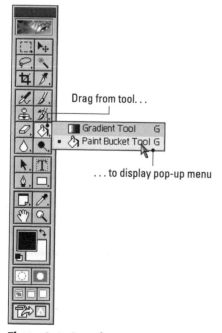

Drag from tool. . .

Gradient Tool   G

■   Paint Bucket Tool G

. . . to display pop-up menu

Figure 2-4: Drag from any tool icon with a triangle to display a pop-up menu of alternate tools.

Also, when you hover your cursor over a tool, Photoshop tells you the name of the tool and how to select it from the keyboard. I explain more about keyboard short-cuts in Chapters D and E on the CD-ROM. If you find the tool tips irritating, turn to "General preferences" to find out how to turn them off.

Note

I've catalogued each tool in the following lengthy list, with tool icons, pithy sum-maries, and the chapter to which you can refer for more information. No need to read the list word for word; just use it as a reference to get acquainted with the new program. The list presents the tools in the order that they appear in the toolbox. Incidentally, unless otherwise noted, each of the following descriptions tells how to use the tool inside the image window. For example, if an item says drag, you click the tool's icon to select the tool and then drag in the image window; you don't drag on the tool icon itself.

Rectangular marquee (Chapter 8): Drag with this tool to enclose a por-tion of the image in a rectangular marquee, which is a pattern of moving dash marks indicating the boundary of a selection.

Shift-drag to add to a selection; Alt-drag to delete from a selection. The same goes for the other marquee tools, as well as the lassos and magic wand.

As an alternative to using these time-honored shortcuts, you can click mode icons on the Options bar to change the behavior of the selection tools.

Elliptical marquee (Chapter 8): Drag with the elliptical marquee tool to enclose a portion of the window in an oval marquee.

Single-row marquee (Chapter 8): Click with the single-row marquee to select an entire horizontal row of pixels that stretches all the way across the image. You can also drag with the tool to position the selection. You rarely need it, but when you do, here it is.

Single-column marquee (Chapter 8): Same as the single-row marquee, except the single-column marquee selects an entire vertical column of pixels. Again, not a particularly useful tool.

Move (Chapter 8): Drag to move a selection or layer. In fact, the move tool is the exclusive means for moving and cloning portions of an image. (You can also Ctrl-drag selections with any tools except the shape, path, and slicing tools, but only because Ctrl temporarily accesses the move tool.)

Lasso (Chapter 8): Drag with the lasso tool to select a free-form portion of the image. You can also Alt-click with the lasso to create a straight-sided selection outline.

Polygonal lasso (Chapter 8): Click hither and yon with this tool to draw a straight-sided selection outline (just like Alt-clicking with the standard lasso). Each click sets a corner point in the selection.

Magnetic lasso (Chapter 8): As you drag with the magnetic lasso tool, the selection outline automatically sticks to the edge of the foreground image. Bear in mind, however, that Photoshop's idea of an edge may not jibe with yours. Like any automated tool, the magnetic lasso sometimes works wonders, other times it's more trouble than it's worth.

Tip

The magnetic lasso automatically lays down points as you drag. If you don't like a point and you want to get rid of it, press the Backspace or Delete key.

Magic wand (Chapter 8): Click with the magic wand tool to select a contiguous area of similarly colored pixels. To select discontiguous areas, click in one area and then Shift-click in another. Deselect the Contiguous tool option and click once to select similar colors throughout the image.

Crop (Chapter 3): Drag with the crop tool to enclose the portion of the image you want to retain in a rectangular boundary. Photoshop now tints areas outside the boundary to help you better see which image areas will go and which will stay when you apply the crop. The crop boundary sports several square handles you can drag to resize the cropped area. Drag outside the boundary to rotate it; drag inside to move it. Press Enter to apply the crop or Escape to cancel.

Slice tool (Chapter 19): The slice tool and its companion, the slice select tool, come into play when you're creating Web graphics. You can cut images into rectangular sections — known as slices — so that you can apply Web effects, such as links, rollovers, and animations, to different areas of the same image. Drag with the slice tool to define the area that you want to turn into a slice.

Slice select tool (Chapter 19): If you don't get the boundary of your slice right the first time, click the slice with this tool and then drag one of the side or corner handles that appear. Or drag inside the boundary to relocate it.

Press Ctrl when the slice tool is active to temporarily access the slice select tool, and vice versa.

Airbrush (Chapter 5): Drag with the airbrush tool to spray diffused strokes of color that blend into the image, just the thing for creating shadows and highlights.

Paintbrush (Chapter 5): Drag with the paintbrush tool to paint soft lines, which aren't as jagged as those created with the pencil, but aren't as fluffy as those created with the airbrush.

Pencil (Chapter 5): Drag with the pencil tool to paint jagged, hard-edged lines. It's main purpose is to clean up individual pixels when you're feeling fussy.

Rubber stamp (Chapter 7): The rubber stamp tool copies one portion of the image onto another. Alt-click the part of your image you want to clone, and then drag to clone that area to another portion of the image.

Pattern stamp (Chapter 7): The rubber stamp tool lets you paint with a pattern. Define a pattern using Edit ⇨ Define Pattern and then paint away.

History brush (Chapter 7): Remember how you used to be able to revert an image to its saved or snapshot appearance using the rubber stamp? Well, no more. Now you have a dedicated history brush that reverts the image to any of a handful of previous states throughout the recent history of the image. To specify the state that you want to revert to, click in the first column of the History palette. It's like an undo brush, except way, way better.

Art history brush (Chapter 7): Like the history brush, the art history brush paints with pixels from a previous image state. But with this brush, you get a variety of brush options that create different artistic effects.

Eraser (Chapter 7): Drag with the eraser tool to paint in the background color or erase areas in a layer to reveal the layers below. Alt-drag to switch to the Erase to History mode, which reverts the image to a previous state just as if you were using the history brush. (In the old days, people referred to this particular eraser mode as the "magic" eraser, which can be confusing because Photoshop 5.5 introduced an official magic eraser – one that deletes pixels rather than reverting them. For clarity's sake, I reserve the term magic eraser for the official tool.)

Background eraser (Chapter 7): Introduced in Version 5.5, the background eraser rubs away the background from an image as you drag along the border between the background and foreground. If you don't wield this tool carefully, though, you wind up erasing both background and foreground.

Magic eraser (Chapter 7): Also new in Version 5.5, the magic eraser came from the same gene pool that produced the magic wand. When you click with the magic wand, Photoshop selects a range of similarly colored pixels; click with the magic eraser, and you erase instead of select.

In case you nodded off a few paragraphs ago, this magic eraser works differently than the eraser that you get when you Alt-drag with the standard eraser, which sometimes goes by the nickname magic eraser when used with the Alt key.

Gradient (Chapter 6): Drag with this tool to fill a selection with a gradual transition of colors, commonly called a *gradient*. In Photoshop 5, you selected different gradient tools to create different styles of gradients; now you click the single gradient icon in the toolbox and select a gradient style from the Options bar.

Paint bucket (Chapter 6): Click with the paint bucket tool to fill a contiguous area of similarly colored pixels with the foreground color or a predefined pattern.

Blur (Chapter 5): Drag with the blur tool to diffuse the contrast between neighboring pixels, which blurs the focus of the image. You can also Alt-drag to sharpen the image.

Sharpen (Chapter 5): Drag with this tool to increase the contrast between pixels, which sharpens the focus. Alt-drag when this tool is active to blur the image.

Smudge (Chapter 5): The smudge tool works just as its name implies; drag with the tool to smear colors inside the image.

Dodge (Chapter 5): Drag with the dodge tool to lighten pixels in the image. Alt-drag to darken the image.

Burn (Chapter 5): Drag with the burn tool to darken pixels. Press Alt to temporarily access the dodge tool and lighten pixels.

Sponge (Chapter 5): Drag with the sponge tool to decrease the amount of saturation in an image so the colors appear more drab, and eventually gray. You can also increase color saturation by changing the setting in the Sponge Options palette from Desaturate to Saturate.

Path component selection (Chapter 8): Click anywhere inside a path to select the entire path. If you click inside a path that contains multiple subpaths, Photoshop selects the subpath under the tool cursor. Shift-click to select additional paths or subpaths. You also use this tool and the direct selection tool, described next, to select and manipulate lines and shapes drawn with the shape tools.

Direct selection (Chapter 8): To select and edit a segment in a selected path or shape, click it or drag over it with this tool. Press Shift while using the tool to select additional segments. Or Alt-click inside a path or shape to select and edit the whole object.

Type (Chapter 15): Click with the type tool to add text to your image. In Photoshop 6, you enter and edit text directly in the image window—no more fooling around with the Type Tool dialog box. This change is one of many to the type tool; explore Chapter 15 to discover all your new type options.

After selecting the type tool, you can create a type-based selection outline by switching from regular type mode to mask type mode via a button on the Options bar. You also can choose to enter either horizontal or vertical rows of type. You no longer use separate tools for different type operations.

Pen (Chapter 8): Click and drag with the pen tool to set points in the image window. Photoshop draws an editable path outline—much like a path in Illustrator—that you can convert to a selection outline or stroke with color.

Freeform pen (Chapter 8): Drag with this tool to draw freehand paths or vector masks. Photoshop automatically adds points along the path as it sees fit.

If you select the Magnetic check box on the Options bar, the freeform pen morphs into the magnetic pen introduced in Version 5.5. Deselect the check box to return to the freeform pen.

Add anchor point (Chapter 8): To insert a point in a path, click a path segment with this tool.

Delete anchor point (Chapter 8): Click a point to remove the point without interrupting the outline of the path. Photoshop automatically draws a new segment between the neighboring points.

Convert point (Chapter 8): Points in a path come in different varieties, some indicating corners and others indicating smooth arcs. The convert point tool enables you to change one kind of point to another. Drag a point to convert it from a corner to an arc. Click a point to convert it from an arc to a sharp corner.

Rectangle (Chapter 14): One of the five new vector drawing tools provided by Photoshop 6, this tool draws rectangles filled with the foreground color. Just drag to create a rectangle; Shift-drag to draw a square.

Rounded rectangle (Chapter 14): Prefer your boxes with nice, curved corners instead of sharp, 90-degree angles? Drag or Shift-drag with the rounded rectangle tool.

You can opt to create rasterized shapes and lines with the rectangle, rounded rectangle, ellipse, polygon, line, and custom shape tools. See Chapter 14 for details.

Ellipse (Chapter 14): You look pretty smart to me, so you probably already figured out that you drag with this tool to draw an ellipse and Shift-drag to draw a circle.

Polygon (Chapter 14): By default, dragging with this tool creates a 5-sided polygon. Controls available on the Options bar enable you to change the number of sides or set the tool to create star shapes.

Line (Chapter 14): Drag with the line tool to create a straight line. But before you do, travel to the Options bar to set the line thickness and specify whether you want arrowheads at the ends of the line.

Custom shape (Chapter 14): After you draw a shape with one of the other drawing tools, you can save it as a custom shape. Thereafter, you can recreate that shape by selecting it from the Options bar and then dragging with the custom shape tool. You also can choose from a variety of predefined shapes when working with the custom shape tool.

Notes (Chapter 3): This tool brings an annotation feature from Adobe Acrobat to Photoshop. Use the tool to create a little sticky note on which you can jot down thoughts, ideas, and other pertinent info that you want to share with other people who work with the image – or that you simply want to remember the next time you open the image. After you create the note, Photoshop displays a note icon in the image window; double-click the icon to see what you had to say.

Audio annotation (Chapter 3): If you prefer the spoken word to the written one, you can annotate your images with an audio clip, assuming that you have a microphone and sound card for your computer. As with the notes tool, an audio icon appears in the image window after you record your message. Clicking the icon plays the audio clip.

Measure (Chapter 12): The measure tool lets you measure distances and directions inside the image window. Just drag from one point to another and note the measurement data in the Info palette or the Options bar. You can also drag the endpoints or your line to take new measurements. And by Alt-dragging an endpoint, you can create a sort of virtual protractor that measures angles.

Eyedropper (Chapter 4): Click with the eyedropper tool on a color in the image window to make that color the foreground color. Alt-click a color to make that color the background color.

Color sampler (Chapter 4): Click as many as four locations in an image to evaluate the colors of those pixels in the Info palette. After you set a point, you can move it by dragging it to a different pixel.

Hand (Chapter 2): Drag inside the image window with the hand tool to scroll the window so you can see a different portion of the image. Double-click the hand tool icon to magnify or reduce the image so it fits on the screen in its entirety.

When the hand tool is active, you can click buttons on the Options bar to display the image at the actual-pixels, fit-on-screen, or print-size view sizes.

Zoom (Chapter 2): Click with the zoom tool to magnify the image so you can see individual pixels more clearly. Alt-click to step back from the image and take in a broader view. Drag to enclose the specific portion of the image you want to magnify. And, finally, double-click the zoom tool icon inside the toolbox to restore the image to 100-percent view size.

You can modify the performance of any tool but the measure tool by adjusting the settings on the Options bar. To change the unit of measurement used by the measure tool, choose Edit ➪ Preferences ➪ Units and Rulers and select the unit from the Rulers pop-up menu. Or, even quicker, right-click the ruler or click the plus sign in the lower-left corner of the Info palette and select a measurement unit from the resulting pop-up menu.

The toolbox controls

Well, that pretty much wraps it up for the Photoshop 6 tools. It was a breathtakingly dull tale, but one that had to be told. But the excitement isn't over yet. Gather the kittens and hold onto your mittens as we explore the ten controls that grace the lower portion of the toolbox:

■ **Foreground color:** Click the foreground color icon to bring up the Color Picker dialog box. Select a color and press Enter to change the foreground color, which is used by the pencil, paintbrush, airbrush, gradient, and shape tools.

I'm not sure why, but many users make the mistake of double-clicking the foreground or background color icons when they first start using Photoshop. A single click is all that's needed. Experienced users don't even bother with the Color Picker — they stick to the more convenient Color palette.

□ **Background color:** Click the background color icon to display the Color Picker and change the background color, which is used by the eraser and gradient tools. Photoshop also uses the background color to fill a selected area on the background layer when you press the Backspace or Delete key.

↰ **Switch colors:** Click the switch colors icon to exchange the foreground and background colors.

■ **Default colors:** Click this icon to return to the default foreground and background colors — black and white, respectively.

At any time, you can quickly make the foreground color white by clicking the default colors icon and then clicking the switch colors icon. Or just press D (for default colors) and then X (for switch colors).

▫ **Marching ants:** Click this icon to exit Photoshop's quick mask mode and view selection outlines as animated dotted lines that look like marching ants, hence the name. (Adobe calls this the "standard" mode, but I think marching ants mode better describes how it works.)

● **Quick mask:** Click here to enter the quick mask mode, which enables you to edit selection boundaries using painting tools. The marching ants vanish and the image appears half covered by a translucent layer of red, like a rubylith in traditional paste-up. The red layer covers the deselected — or masked — portions of the image. Paint with black to extend the masked areas, thereby subtracting from the selection. Paint with white to erase the mask, thereby adding to the selection.

The quick mask mode is too complex a topic to sum up in a few sentences. If you can't wait to find out what it's all about, check out Chapter 9.

Standard window: Click this icon to display the foreground image in a standard window, as shown earlier in Figure 2-3. Every image appears in the standard window mode when you first open it.

Full screen with menu bar: If you can't see enough of your image inside a standard window, click this icon. The title bar and scroll bars disappear, as do all background windows and the Windows taskbar, but the menu bar and palettes remain visible, as shown in Figure 2-5. (You can still access other open images by choosing their names from the Window menu.) A light gray background fills any empty area around the image.

This is similar to the effect that you get when you click the maximize button in the upper-right corner of the image window. However, you probably want to avoid maximizing images; use the toolbox controls instead. Photoshop has a habit of resizing a maximized window whenever you zoom with the commands under the View menu. If you use the toolbox controls, you don't have that problem.

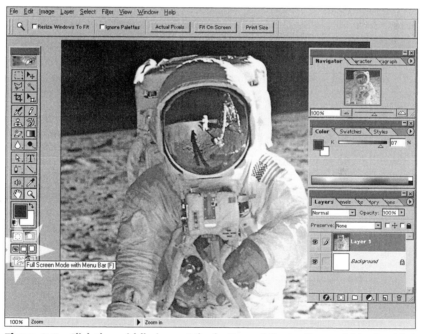

Figure 2-5: Click the middle icon at the bottom of the toolbox to hide the title bar and scroll bars.

When the image doesn't consume the entire image window, the empty portion of the window appears gray when you're working in the standard window or full screen with menu bar modes. To change it to a different color — such as black — select a color and Shift-click in the gray area with the paint bucket tool.

☐ **Absolute full screen:** If you still can't see enough of your image, click the rightmost of the image window controls to see the photo set against a neutral black background. (You can't change the color of this backdrop — it's always black.) The menu bar disappears, limiting your access to commands, but you can still access many commands using keyboard shortcuts. Only the toolbox and palettes remain visible.

If you need access to a menu command when working in the absolute full screen mode, press Shift+F to display the menu bar. Press Shift+F again to hide it.

 If Photoshop's screen elements interfere with your view of an image, you can hide all palettes — including the toolbox and Options bar — by pressing the Tab key. To bring the hidden palettes back into view, press Tab again.

 You can hide the palettes but leave the toolbox and Options bar on screen by pressing Shift+Tab. Press Shift+Tab again to bring the palettes back. (Pressing Tab while the standard palettes are gone hides the toolbox and Options bar.) If the rulers are turned on, they remain visible at all times. Press Ctrl+R to toggle the ruler display off and on.

 Here's one more tip for good measure: Shift-click the icon for absolute full screen to switch the display mode for all open images. Then press Ctrl+Tab to cycle through the open images. This same trick works for the standard and full screen with menu bar modes.

The new Options bar

Spanning the width of the Photoshop window, the new Options bar (labeled back in Figure 2-3) contains the major tool controls formerly found in the Options and Brushes palettes. The interface change enables you to keep all the vital tool settings displayed while using a minimum of screen space.

You establish tool settings by selecting check boxes, clicking icons, and choosing options from pop-up menus on the bar. In other words, think of the Options bar as just another floating palette, albeit a long, skinny one. However, you use different tactics to hide, display, and relocate the Options bar than you do a regular palette:

◆ Choose View ⇨ Show Options or double-click any tool icon in the toolbox to display the Options bar. Choose View ⇨ Hide Options to make the bar disappear. You also can press Tab to toggle the display of the Options bar and all other palettes on and off.

◆ By default, the Options bar is docked at the top of the program window. Drag the vertical handle at the left end of the bar to relocate it. If you drag the bar to the top or bottom of the window, it becomes docked again.

◆ Unfortunately, you can't change the size or shape of the Options bar.

You can attach regular palettes to the Options bar by dragging them onto the docking well at the right end of the bar. The upcoming section "Rearranging and docking palettes" tells all.

The floating palettes

In addition to the Options bar, Photoshop 6 sports two new text-related palettes, the Character and Paragraph palettes. These two palettes don't display automatically when you first launch Photoshop; you must choose Show Character or Show Paragraph from the Window menu or click the Palettes button on the Options bar while the type tool is active. Other than that, these new palettes look and behave just like the other palettes, which look and behave much like they have since Version 3. Each palette contains most or all of the elements labeled in Figure 2-6. Some palettes lack scroll bars, others lack size boxes, but that's just to keep you from getting too stodgy.

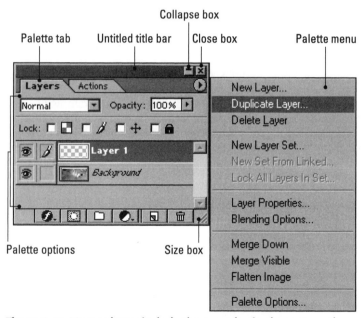

Figure 2-6: Most palettes include the same basic elements as the Layers palette, shown here.

Many palette elements are miniature versions of the elements that accompany any window. For example, the close button and title bar work identically to their image-window counterparts. The title bar lacks a title—I have a lobbyist in Washington working on getting the name changed to "untitled bar" as we speak—but you can still drag it to move the palette to a different location on screen.

Tip   Photoshop automatically snaps palettes into alignment with other palettes. To snap a palette to the edge of the screen, Shift-click its title bar. You can also Shift-drag the title bar to move the palette around the perimeter of the screen, or to snap the palette from one edge of the screen to the other. (This tip also works with the toolbox.)

Four elements are unique to floating palettes:

✦ **Palette options:** Each floating palette offers its own collection of options. These options may include icons, pop-up menus, slider bars, you name it.

✦ **Palette menu:** Click the right-pointing arrowhead to display a menu of commands specific to the palette. These commands enable you to manipulate the palette options and adjust preference settings.

✦ **Palette tabs:** Click a palette tab to move it to the front of the palette group. (You can also select the palette commands from the Window menu, but it's more convenient to click a tab.)

✦ **Collapse button:** Click the collapse button to decrease the amount of space consumed by the palette. If you previously enlarged the palette by dragging the size box, your first click reduces the palette back to its default size. After that, clicking the collapse button hides all but the most essential palette options.

Tip   In most cases, collapsing a palette hides all options and leaves only the tabs visible. But in the case of the Color and Layers palettes, clicking the collapse button leaves a sliver of palette options intact, as demonstrated in the middle example of Figure 2-7. To eliminate all options — as in the last example — Alt-click the collapse button. You can also double-click one of the tabs or in the empty area to the right of the tabs. These tricks work even if you've enlarged the palette by dragging the size box.

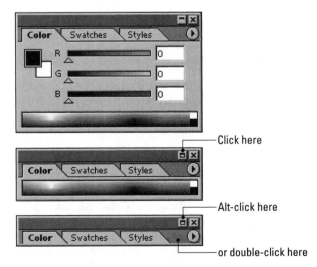

Figure 2-7: The Color palette shown at full size (top), partially collapsed (middle), and fully collapsed (bottom)

Rearranging and docking palettes

In the past, you've been able to regroup palettes to suit the way you work. Now you also can dock palettes to each other or to the Options bar. You're king of the palette hill, as it were.

To attach a floating palette to the Options bar, as shown in Figure 2-8, drag the palette tab to the docking well. After you dock the palette, you see just the palette tab on the Options bar. Click the tab to display the palette, as shown in the figure. When you click outside the palette, the palette closes automatically.

If you don't see the docking well, you need to raise your monitor resolution. The docking well isn't accessible at monitor resolutions of less than 800 pixels wide. Also, if you undock the Options bar, any palettes attached to it hide themselves. To redisplay a hidden palette, choose its name from the Window menu.

Docking well

Figure 2-8: Attach palettes to the Options bar by dragging them to the docking well.

In addition to docking palettes in the Options bar, you can dock palettes to each other. Drag a palette tab to the bottom of another palette and release the mouse button when the other palette appears highlighted, as shown in the left side of Figure 2-9. The dragged palette grabs hold of the other palette's tail and doesn't let go. Now you can keep both palettes visible but move, close, collapse, and resize the two as a single entity, as shown in the right half of the figure.

When you dock a resizable palette to another resizable palette, you can resize the palettes like so:

✦ Place your cursor over the border between two stacked palettes until you see the double-headed arrow cursor. Then drag down to enlarge the upper palette and shrink the lower one. Drag up to enlarge the lower palette and shrink the upper one. The overall size of the docked palettes doesn't change.

✦ Alt-drag the border to resize the upper palette only.

Still not happy with your palette layout? You can shuffle palettes at will, moving a single palette from one group to another or giving it complete independence from any group. To separate a palette from the herd, drag its tab away from the palette group, as demonstrated in the left column in Figure 2-10. To add the palette to a palette group, drag its tab onto the palette group, as shown in the **middle column**. The right column shows the results of the two maneuvers I made **in the first two** columns.

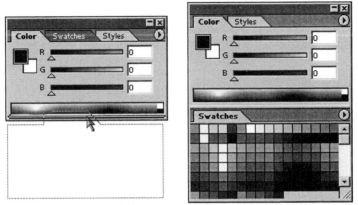

Figure 2-9: Drag a palette tab to the bottom of another palette (left) to dock the two palettes together (right).

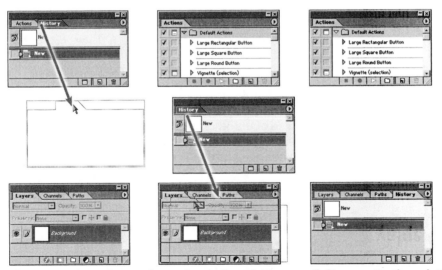

Figure 2-10: Dragging a palette tab out of a palette group (left) separates **the** palette from its original family (middle). Dragging a palette tab onto another **palette** group (middle) adds that palette to the group (right).

If you ever completely muck up the palettes — or a palette someh**ow gets** stuck under the menu bar — choose Window ➪ Reset Palette Locations.

Tabbing through the options

I mentioned earlier that you can hide the palettes by pressing Shift+Tab and that you can hide the palettes, toolbox, and Options bar by pressing Tab. But this keyboard trick doesn't work if an option box is active.

For example, suppose you click inside the R option box in the Color palette. This activates the option. Now press Tab. Rather than hiding the palettes, Photoshop advances you to the next option box in the palette, G. To move backward through the options, press Shift+Tab. This trick applies to the Options bar as well as to the standard palettes.

To apply an option box value and return focus to the image window, press Enter. This deactivates the palette options. If an option box remains active, certain keyboard tricks — such as pressing a key to select a tool — won't work properly. Photoshop either ignores the shortcut or beeps at you for pressing a key the option box doesn't like. For more information on shortcuts, read Chapter D on the CD-ROM.

While you're working in the image window, you can return focus to the Options bar from the keyboard. When you press Enter, Photoshop displays the Options bar, if it's not already visible. If the Options bar offers an option box for the active tool, Photoshop highlights the contents of the option box. You can then tab around to reach the option you want to change, enter a new value, and press Enter to get out.

Navigating in Photoshop

All graphics and desktop publishing programs provide a variety of navigational tools and functions that enable you to scoot around the screen, visit the heartlands and nether regions, examine the fine details, and take in the big picture. And Photoshop is no exception. In fact, Photoshop's navigation tools would make Magellan drool (were he inclined to edit an image or two).

The view size

You can change the view size — the size at which an image appears on screen — so you can either see more of an image or concentrate on individual pixels. Each change in view size is expressed as a zoom ratio, which is the ratio between screen pixels and image pixels. Photoshop displays the zoom ratio as a percentage value in the title bar as well as in the magnification box. The 100-percent zoom ratio shows one image pixel for each screen pixel (and is therefore equivalent to the old 1:1 zoom ratio in Photoshop 3 and earlier). A 200 percent zoom ratio doubles the size of the image pixels on screen, and so on.

Actual pixels

Photoshop calls the 100-percent zoom ratio the *actual-pixels* view. This is the most accurate view size because you can see the image as it really is. Reduced view sizes drop pixels; magnified view sizes stretch pixels. Only the actual-pixels view displays each pixel without a trace of screen distortion.

You can switch to this most accurate of view sizes at any time using one of the following techniques:

✦ Choose View ➪ Actual Pixels.

✦ Press Ctrl+Alt+0. (That's a zero, not the letter *O*.)

✦ Double-click the zoom tool icon in the toolbox.

✦ Click the Actual Pixels button, which appears on the Options bar when the zoom tool is selected.

Fit on screen

When you first open an image, Photoshop displays it at the largest zoom ratio (up to 100 percent) that permits the entire image to fit on screen. Assuming you don't change the size of the image, you can return to this "fit-on-screen" view size in one of the following ways:

✦ Choose View ➪ Fit on Screen.

✦ Press Ctrl+0.

✦ Double-click the hand tool icon in the toolbox.

✦ Select the zoom tool and then click the Fit on Screen button on the Options bar.

Strangely, any of these techniques may magnify the image beyond the 100-percent view size. When working on a very small image, for example, Photoshop enlarges the image to fill the screen, even if this means maxing out the zoom to 1,600 percent. Personally, I prefer to use the fit-on-screen view only when working on very large images.

Well, actually, I almost never use the fit-on-screen view because it's too arbitrary. Photoshop does the best job of previewing an image when you can see all pixels — that is, at 100-percent view size. Short of that, you want the screen pixels to divide evenly into the image pixels. This means view sizes like 50 percent or 25 percent, but not 75 percent or 66.7 percent. And you never know what it's going to be with the fit-on-screen view.

Print size

You can switch to yet another predefined view size by choosing View ➪ Print Size. This command displays the image on screen at the size it will print. (You set the print size using Image ➪ Image Size, as I explain in Chapter 3.)

When the zoom tool is active, you also can click the Print Size button on the Options bar to turn on the print-size view.

In practice, "print-size" view isn't particularly reliable. Photoshop assumes that your monitor displays exactly 72 pixels per inch, even on the PC, where the accepted screen resolution is 96 pixels per inch. But it's all complete nonsense, whatever the assumption. Monitor resolutions vary all over the map. And high-end monitors let you change screen resolutions without Photoshop even noticing.

The long and the short is this: Don't expect to hold up your printed image and have it exactly match the print-size view on screen. It's a rough approximation, designed to show you how the image will look when imported into QuarkXPress, PageMaker, InDesign, or some other publishing program — nothing more.

The zoom tool

Obviously, the aforementioned zoom ratios aren't the only ones available to you. You can zoom in as close as 1,600 percent and zoom out to 0.2 percent.

The easiest way to zoom in and out of your image is to use the zoom tool:

✦ Click in the image window with the zoom tool to magnify the image in preset increments — from 33.33 percent to 50 to 66.67 to 100 to 200 and so on. Photoshop tries to center the zoomed view at the point where you clicked (or come as close as possible).

✦ Alt-click with the zoom tool to reduce the image incrementally — 200 to 100 to 66.67 to 50 to 33.33 and so on. Again, Photoshop tries to center the new view on the click point.

✦ Drag with the zoom tool to draw a rectangular marquee around the portion of the image you want to magnify. Photoshop magnifies the image so the marqueed area fits just inside the image window. (If the horizontal and vertical proportions of the marquee do not match those of your screen — for example, if you draw a tall, thin marquee or a really short, wide one — Photoshop favors the smaller of the two possible zoom ratios to avoid hiding any detail inside the marquee.)

✦ If you want Photoshop to resize the window when you click with the zoom tool, select the Resize Windows to Fit check box on the Options bar. The check box appears only when the zoom tool is the active tool.

✦ Turn off the Ignore Palettes check box on the Options bar if you want Photoshop to stop resizing the window when the window bumps up against a palette that's anchored against the side of the program window. Turn the option on to resize the window regardless of the palettes. The palettes then float over the resized window.

Tip

To access the zoom tool temporarily when some other tool is selected, press and hold the Ctrl and spacebar keys. Release both keys to return control of the cursor to the selected tool. To access the zoom out cursor, press Alt with the spacebar. These keyboard equivalents work from inside many dialog boxes, enabling you to modify the view of an image while applying a filter or color correction.

The zoom commands

You can also zoom in and out using the following commands and keyboard shortcuts:

✦ Choose View ➪ Zoom In or press Ctrl+plus (+) to zoom in. This command works exactly like clicking with the zoom tool except you can't specify the center of the new view size. Photoshop merely centers the zoom in keeping with the previous view size.

✦ Choose View ➪ Zoom Out or press Ctrl+minus (–) to zoom out.

The General panel of the Photoshop 6 Preferences dialog box (Ctrl+K) includes an option called Keyboard Zoom Resizes Windows. If you select this option, Photoshop resizes the image window when you use the Zoom commands. (Despite the setting's name, it applies when you choose the zoom commands from the menu as well as when you use the keyboard shortcuts.) To override the setting temporarily, press Alt as you press the keyboard shortcut or select the menu command. Similarly, if you deselect the option in the Preferences dialog box, you can add the Alt to turn window-zooming on temporarily.

Tip

If Photoshop is unresponsive to these or any other keyboard shortcuts, it's probably because the image window has somehow become inactive. (It can happen if you so much as click the taskbar.) Just click the image-window title bar and try again.

The magnification box

Another way to zoom in and out without changing the window size is to enter a value into the magnification box, located in the lower-left corner of the Photoshop window. Select the magnification value, enter a new one, and press Enter. Photoshop zooms the view without zooming the window. (Neither the Resize Windows to Fit check box on the Options bar nor the Keyboard Zoom Resizes Windows option in the Preferences dialog box affect the magnification box.)

In Figure 2-11, I started with a specially sized window at actual-pixels view. I then entered two different zoom ratios into the magnification box — 156.7 percent and 60.4 percent — alternately enlarging and reducing the image within the confines of a static window.

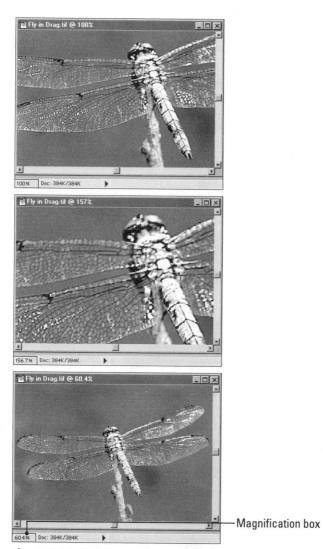

Magnification box

Figure 2-11: To zoom an image without changing the window size, enter a zoom ratio into the magnification box and press Enter. Alternatively, deselect the Resize Windows to Fit check box on the Options bar when working with the zoom tool.

You might like to know more about the magnification box:

> ✦ You can enter values in the magnification box as percentages, ratios, or "times" values. To switch to a zoom value of 250 percent, for example, you can enter *250%*, *5:2*, or *2.5x*.
>
> ✦ You can specify a zoom value in increments as small as 0.01 percent. So if a zoom value of 250.01 doesn't quite suit your fancy, you can try 250.02. I seriously doubt you'll need this kind of precision, but isn't it great to know it's there?

When you press Enter after entering a magnification value, Photoshop changes the view size and returns focus to the image window. If you aren't exactly certain what zoom ratio you want to use, press Shift+Enter instead. This changes the view size while keeping the magnification value active; this way you can enter a new value and try again.

Creating a reference window

In the ancient days, paint programs provided a cropped view of your image at the actual-pixels view size to serve as a reference when you worked in a magnified view. Because it's so doggone modern, Photoshop does not, but you can easily create a second view of your image by choosing View ➪ New View, as in Figure 2-12. Use one window to maintain a 100-percent view of your image while you zoom and edit inside the other window. Both windows track the changes to the image.

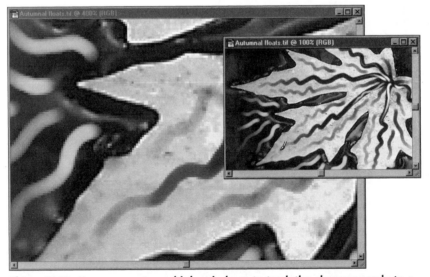

Figure 2-12: You can create multiple windows to track the changes made to a single image by choosing the New View command from the View menu.

Scrolling inside the window

In the standard window mode, you have access to scroll bars, just as you do in just about every other major application. But as you become more proficient with Photoshop, you'll use the scroll bars less and less. One way to bypass the scroll bars is to use the keyboard equivalents listed in Table 2-1.

Table 2-1 Scrolling from the Keyboard	
Scrolling Action	*Keystroke*
Up one screen	Page Up
Up slightly	Shift+Page Up
Down one screen	Page Down
Down slightly	Shift+Page Down
Left one screen	Ctrl+Page Up
Left slightly	Ctrl+Shift+Page Up
Right one screen	Ctrl+Page Down
Right slightly	Ctrl+Shift+Page Down
To upper-left corner	Home
To lower-right corner	End

I've heard tales of artists who use the Page Up and Page Down shortcuts to comb through very large images at 100-percent view size. This way, they can make sure all their pixels are in order before going to print.

Personally, however, I don't use the Page key tricks very often. I'm the kind of merry lad who prefers to scroll by hand. Armed with the grabber hand — as old timers call it — you can yank an image and pull it in any direction you choose. A good grabber hand is better than a scroll bar any day.

To access the hand tool temporarily when some other tool is selected, press and hold the spacebar. Releasing the spacebar returns the cursor to its original appearance. This keyboard equivalent even works from inside many dialog boxes.

The Navigator palette

I saved the best for last. Shown in Figure 2-13, the Navigator palette is the best thing to happen to zooming and scrolling since Photoshop was first introduced. If you routinely work on large images that extend beyond the confines of your relatively tiny screen, you'll want to get up and running with this palette as soon as possible.

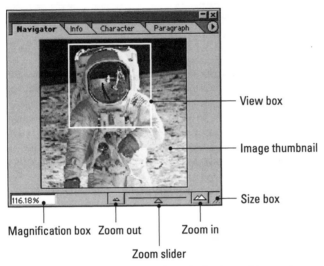

View box

Image thumbnail

Size box

Magnification box Zoom out Zoom in

Zoom slider

Figure 2-13: The Navigator palette is the best thing to happen to zooming and scrolling since Photoshop 1.0.

If the Navigator palette isn't visible, choose Window ↪ Show Navigator. You can then use the palette options as follows:

+ **View box:** Drag the view box inside the image thumbnail to reveal some hidden portion of the photograph. Photoshop dynamically tracks your adjustments in the image window. Isn't it great?

   But wait, it gets better. Press Ctrl to get a zoom cursor in the Navigator palette. Then Ctrl-drag to resize the view box and zoom the photo in the image window.

   You can also Shift-drag to constrain dragging the view box to only horizontal or vertical movement.

+ **Box color:** You can change the color of the view box by choosing the Palette Options command from the palette menu. My favorite setting is yellow, but it ultimately depends on the colors in your image. Ideally, you want something that stands out. To lift a color from the image itself, move the cursor outside the dialog box and click in the image window with the eyedropper.

✦ **Magnification box:** This value works like the one in the lower-left corner of the Photoshop window. Just enter a new zoom ratio and press Enter.

✦ **Zoom out:** Click the zoom out button to reduce the view size in the same predefined increments as the zoom tool. This button doesn't alter the size of the image window, regardless of any window resizing options you set for the other zoom controls.

✦ **Zoom slider:** Give the slider triangle a yank and see where it takes you. Drag to the left to zoom out; drag right to zoom in. Again, Photoshop dynamically tracks your changes in the image window. Dang, it's nice to zoom on the fly.

✦ **Zoom in:** Click the big mountains to incrementally magnify the view of the image without altering the window size.

✦ **Size box:** If you have a large monitor, you don't have to settle for that teeny thumbnail of the image. Drag the size box to enlarge both palette and thumbnail to a more reasonable size.

Customizing the Interface

Every program gives you access to a few core settings so you can modify the program to suit your personal needs. These settings are known far and wide as *preferences.* Photoshop ships with certain recommended preference settings already in force — known coast to coast as *factory defaults* — but just because these settings are recommended doesn't mean they're right. In fact, I disagree with quite a few of them. But why quibble when you can change the preferences according to your merest whim?

You can modify preference settings in two ways: You can make environmental adjustments using File ➪ Preferences ➪ General, or you can change the operation of specific tools by adjusting settings in the Options bar. Photoshop remembers environmental preferences, tool settings, and even the file format under which you saved the last image by storing this information to a file each time you exit the program.

To restore Photoshop's factory default settings, delete the Adobe Photoshop 6 Prefs.psp file when the application is *not* running. The next time you launch Photoshop, it creates a new preferences file automatically. You can find the preferences file in the Windows/Application Data/Adobe/Photoshop/6.0/Adobe Photoshop 6 Settings folder. (Adobe relocated the preferences file to accommodate the multiple-user features of Windows 98. Depending on your system setup, the program may choose a different storage folder. If you don't see the file in the location I specified here, keep reading for another way to trash your preferences file.)

You also can dump the preferences file using this trick: Close the program and then relaunch it. Immediately after you launch the program, press and hold Ctrl+Shift+Alt. Photoshop displays a dialog box asking for your okay to delete the preferences file. Click Yes. Continue to hold down Ctrl+Shift+Alt to display dialog boxes for changing the plug-ins folder and scratch disk settings (I discuss both topics later in this chapter).

Deleting the preferences file is also a good idea if Photoshop starts acting funny. Photoshop's preferences file has always been highly susceptible to corruption, possibly because the application writes to it so often. Whatever the reason, if Photoshop starts behaving erratically, trash that preferences file. You'll have to reset your preferences, but a smooth-running program is worth the few minutes of extra effort.

Photoshop saves actions, color settings, custom shapes, contours, and the like separately from the Prefs file. This means that you can delete your Prefs file without any worry about harming your scripts, color conversions, and other custom settings.

After you get your preferences set as you like them, you can prevent Photoshop from altering them further by locking the file. In Windows Explorer, right-click the Adobe Photoshop 6 Prefs.psp file and choose Properties from the pop-up menu. Then select the Read Only check box in the Properties dialog box and press Enter. From now on, Photoshop will start up with a consistent set of default settings.

That's a good tip, and I include it in the name of comprehensive coverage. But personally, I don't lock my Prefs file because I periodically modify settings and I want Photoshop to remember the latest and greatest. Instead, I make a backup copy of my favorite settings. After a few weeks of working in the program and customizing it to a more or less acceptable level, copy the preferences file to a separate folder on your hard disk (someplace you'll remember!). Then if the preferences file becomes corrupt, you can replace it quickly with your backup.

The preference panels

Adobe shuffled some menu commands when developing Photoshop 6, including the all-important Preferences command, which now appears on the Edit menu. Choosing the command displays a long submenu of commands, but you needn't ever use them if you remember a simple keyboard shortcut: Ctrl+K.

This shortcut brings up the Preferences dialog box, which provides access to eight panels of options, representing every one of the Edit ➪ Preferences commands. Select the desired panel from the pop-up menu in the upper-left corner of the dialog box, as demonstrated in Figure 2-14. Or press the Ctrl key equivalent for the panel as listed in the pop-up menu. You can also click the Prev and Next buttons (or press Alt+P and Alt+N, respectively) to cycle from one panel to the next.

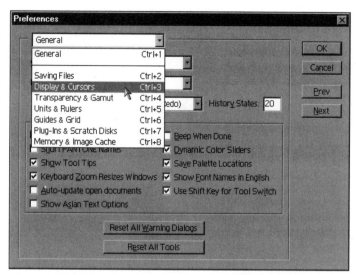

Figure 2-14: Select a panel of options from the pop-up menu, or click the Prev and Next buttons to advance from one panel to the next.

Tip

Photoshop always displays the first panel, General, when you press Ctrl+K. If you prefer to go to the panel you were last using, press Ctrl+Alt+K.

To accept your settings and exit the Preferences dialog box, press Enter. Or press Escape to cancel your settings. Okay, so you already knew that, but here's one you might not know: Press and hold the Alt key to change the Cancel button to Reset. Then click the button to restore the settings that were in force before you entered the dialog box.

The following sections examine all but two of the Preferences panels, in the order they appear in the Figure 2-14 pop-up menu. I explain how each option works, and include what I consider the optimal setting in parentheses. (The figures, however, show the default settings.) Out of context like this, Photoshop's preference settings can be a bit confusing. In later chapters, I try to shed some additional light on the settings you may find most useful.

The options on the Adobe Online panel are the same ones you get if you click the Preferences button in the Adobe Online splash screen, shown in Figure 2-2. I discuss this toward the beginning of this chapter, so no need to travel that road again.

General preferences

The General panel, shown in Figure 2-15, contains a miscellaneous supply of what are arguably the most important Preferences options.

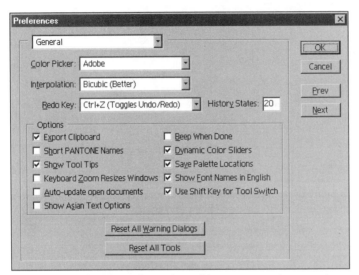

Figure 2-15: The General panel provides access to the most important environmental preference settings. I agree with many, but not all, of the default settings shown here.

✦ **Color Picker (Adobe):** When you click the foreground or background color control icon in the toolbox, Photoshop displays any color picker plug-ins that you may have installed plus one of two standard color pickers: the Adobe color picker or the one provided by the operating system. If you're familiar with other Windows graphics programs, the system's color picker may at first seem more familiar. But Photoshop's color picker is substantially more versatile.

✦ **Interpolation (Bicubic):** When you resize an image using Image ⇨ Image Size or transform it using Layer ⇨ Free Transform or one of the commands in the Layer ⇨ Transform submenu, Photoshop has to make up — or *interpolate* — pixels to fill in the gaps. You can change how Photoshop calculates the interpolation by choosing one of three options from the Interpolation submenu.

If you select Nearest Neighbor, Photoshop simply copies the next-door pixel when creating a new one. This is the fastest setting, but it invariably results in jagged effects.

The second option, Bilinear, smoothes the transitions between pixels by creating intermediate shades. Photoshop averages the color of each pixel with four neighbors — the pixel above, the one below, and the two to the left and right. Bilinear takes more time but, typically, the softened effect is worth it.

Still more time intensive is the default setting, Bicubic, which averages the color of a pixel with its eight closest neighbors — one up, one down, two on the sides, and four in the corners. The Bicubic setting boosts the amount of contrast between pixels to offset the blurring effect that generally accompanies interpolation.

Tip

The moral is this: Select Bicubic to turn Photoshop's interpolation capabilities on, and select Nearest Neighbor to turn them off. The Bilinear setting is a poor compromise between the two — too slow for roughing out effects, but too remedial to waste your time.

Photoshop 6

✦ **Redo Key (Ctrl+Z):** This option enables you to change the keyboard shortcuts assigned to the Undo, Redo, Step Back, and Step Forward commands. It's ultimately a personal preference, but I discourage you from changing this option from its default. Selecting something other than Ctrl+Z makes Photoshop appear to match other programs that feature multiple undos — such as Adobe Illustrator and Macromedia FreeHand — but any resemblance is purely coincidental. The wonders of the History palette notwithstanding, Photoshop relies on a single-level Undo command. Setting it to match other programs' multilevel undos is misleading. If you haven't the vaguest idea of what I'm talking about, check out Chapter 7, "Retouching, Repeating, and Restoring."

✦ **History States:** This value controls how many steps you can undo via the History palette. The right value depends on the amount of RAM you're willing to devote to Photoshop. If you're working with limited memory — 32MB or less — I suggest that you lower the value to 5 or 10. Otherwise, raise the value as you see fit, remembering that the more states the program retains, the more you strain your system.

✦ **Export Clipboard (off):** When selected, this option tells Photoshop to transfer a copied image from the program's internal clipboard to the operating system's clipboard whenever you switch applications. This enables you to paste the image into another running program. Turn this option off if you plan to use copied images only within Photoshop and you want to reduce the lag time that occurs when you switch from Photoshop to another program. Even with this option off, you can paste images copied from other programs into Photoshop.

✦ **Short PANTONE Names (off):** As most digital artists are already aware, Pantone is a brand name assigned to a library of premixed spot-color printing inks. Photoshop supports the most recent Pantone naming conventions. Most modern publishing programs support these longer color names, but a few older versions do not. If you run into problems separating spot-color Photoshop images when printing from another program, turn this option on. Otherwise, leave it off, as by default. (When you export straight grayscale, RGB, or CMYK images, this check box is irrelevant.)

✦ **Show Tool Tips (on):** When on, this option displays little labels and keyboard shortcuts when you hover your cursor over a tool or palette option. The tool tips don't impede Photoshop's performance, so I see no reason to turn off this option.

✦ **Keyboard Zoom Resizes Windows (on):** Select this option to force Photoshop to resize the image window when you zoom in or out on your image by selecting a Zoom command from the View menu or by using the keyboard shortcuts, Ctrl+plus and Ctrl+minus. This one's really a matter of personal choice—I leave the option on, but you'll do no harm to yourself or the planet if you turn it off. Either way, you can temporarily choose the opposite setting by pressing Alt as you choose the Zoom command.

✦ **Auto-update Open Documents (on):** This option creates and maintains a link between an open image and the image file on disk. Any time the image on disk updates, Photoshop updates the image on screen in kind. This feature is an amazing help when you're editing images with another artist over a network. Imagine that you and a coworker each have the same server file open in separate copies of Photoshop. Your coworker makes a change and saves it. Seconds later, your copy of Photoshop automatically updates the image on your screen. Then you make a change and save it, and Photoshop relays your modifications to your coworker's screen.

So what happens if you're both editing the image simultaneously? Whoever saves first gets the glory. If your coworker saves the image before you do, any changes that you haven't saved are overwritten by the other person's work.

However, you can snatch victory from the jaws of defeat simply by pressing Ctrl+Alt+Z, which undoes your coworker's edits and retrieves yours. Quickly save your image to lob your changes over the net. Ooh, psych! With any luck, your coworker won't understand Photoshop well enough to know that your changes can be undone just as easily. But just to be safe, better hide this book from prying eyes.

✦ **Show Asian Text Options (off):** This option determines whether the Character and Paragraph palettes include options related to working with Chinese, Japanese, and Korean type. My recommendation here assumes that you're not adding text in those languages to your images.

✦ **Beep When Done (off):** You can instruct Photoshop to beep at you whenever it finishes an operation that displays a Progress window. This option may be useful if you doze off during particularly time-consuming operations. But I'm a firm believer that computers should be seen and not heard.

✦ **Dynamic Color Sliders (on):** When selected, this option instructs Photoshop to preview color effects within the slider bars of the Color palette. When the option is turned off, the slider bars show the same colors regardless of your changes. Unless you're working on a slow computer, leave this option on. On a fast machine, Photoshop takes a billionth of a second longer to calculate the color effects and it's well worth it.

✦ **Save Palette Locations (on):** When this option is selected, Photoshop remembers the location of the toolbox and floating palettes from one session to the next. If you turn off this check box, Photoshop restores the default palette positions the next time you restart the program.

✦ **Show Font Names in English (on):** Check this box, and Photoshop displays foreign fonts in intelligible names in the Font menu on the Options bar and in the Character palette—well, assuming that English is intelligible to you, anyway.

✦ **Use Shift Key for Tool Switch (off):** When two or more tools share the same slot in the toolbox, you can press the keyboard shortcut associated with the tools to cycle through the tools. This Preferences option determines whether you must press Shift along with the shortcut. I recommend that you turn this option off—one extra keystroke per function adds up over the course of a day, you know.

In this book, I assume that you have this option turned off when I present tool shortcuts.

✦ **Reset All Warning Dialogs:** Every now and then, Photoshop displays a warning dialog box to let you know that the course you're on may have consequences you hadn't considered. Some dialog boxes include a check box that you can select to tell Photoshop that you don't want to see the current warning any more. If you click the Reset All Warning Dialogs button in the Preferences dialog box, Photoshop clears all the "don't show this warning again" check boxes so that you once again get all available warnings. Photoshop responds to your click of the reset button by displaying a warning dialog box that says that all warning dialog boxes will be enabled if you go forward. Don't ponder the irony too long before you click OK.

✦ **Reset All Tools:** Click this button to reset all of Photoshop's tools to their factory default settings. You also can click the tool's icon on the Options bar and choose Reset All Tools from the resulting pop-up menu. Choose Reset Tool to restore the defaults for the current tool only.

Saving Files

When in the Preferences dialog box, press Ctrl+2 to advance to the Saving Files panel, shown in Figure 2-16. Every one of these options affects how Photoshop saves images to disk. The following list explains how the options work and the recommended settings:

✦ **Image Previews (Ask When Saving):** When Always Save is active (as by default), Photoshop saves a postage-stamp preview so that you can see what an image looks like before opening or importing it. This preview appears when you select the image in the Open dialog box.

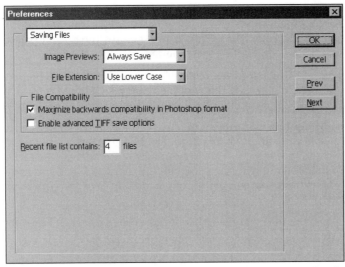

Figure 2-16: I prefer to set the Image Previews option to Ask When
Saving. And by all means, turn that first File Compatibility check box off!

The problem with previews is that they slightly increase the size of the file.
This is fine when doing print work — a little thumbnail isn't going to add that
much — but when creating Web graphics, every byte counts. That's why I prefer to select Ask When Saving from the Image Previews pop-up menu. This
option makes the preview option available in the Save dialog box so that you
can specify whether you want previews on a case-by-case basis when you
save your images.

Tip

✦ **File Extension (Use Lower Case):** This option decides whether the three-
character extensions at the end of file names are upper- or lowercase. Lower
is the better choice because it ensures compatibility with other platforms,
particularly Unix, the primary operating system for Web servers. (Unix is
case-sensitive, so a file called *Image.psd* is different than *Image.PSD*.
Lowercase extensions eliminate confusion.)

✦ **Maximize backwards compatibility in Photoshop format (OFF!):** This option
is pure evil. If you never change another preference setting, you should turn
this one off. I know, I know, if it was so awful, Adobe wouldn't have it on by
default. But believe me, this option should be named Double My File Sizes
Because I'm an Absolute Fool, and even Adobe's designers will tell you that
you probably want to go ahead and turn it off.

Okay, so here's the long tragic story: The check box ensures backward compatibility between Photoshop 6 and programs that support the Photoshop file

format but don't recognize layers. It's a nice idea, but it comes at too steep a price. In order to ensure compatibility, Photoshop has to insert an additional flattened version of a layered image into every native Photoshop file. As you can imagine, this takes up a considerable amount of disk space, doubling the file size in the most extreme situations.

So turn this check box off. And when you want cross-application compatibility, save an extra TIFF version of your file (as explained in Chapter 3).

Actually, there is one instance when you might find this option useful. It permits After Effects 3 or Illustrator 9 to open files that contain layer effects that were added to Photoshop after those products shipped.

✦ **Enable advanced TIFF save options (on):** When turned on, this check box permits you to save all data, including layers and annotations, with a TIFF image. It also lets you choose to apply JPEG or ZIP compression instead of the usual LZW. No doubt about it, turn this option on.

✦ **Recent file list contains (4) Files (Your call):** This option determines how many file names appear when you choose the new Open Recent command, which displays a list of the images that you worked on most recently. You can simply click an image name to open the image. The default number of file names is four, but you can raise it to 30. Raising the value doesn't use resources that would otherwise be useful to Photoshop, so enter whatever value makes you happy.

Display & Cursors

Press Ctrl+3 to sidle up to the Display & Cursors options, which appear in Figure 2-17. These options affect the way colors and cursors appear on screen. Here's how the options work, along with recommended settings:

✦ **Color Channels in Color (off):** An individual color channel contains just 8 bits of data per pixel, which makes it equivalent to a grayscale image. Photoshop provides you with the option of colorizing the channel according to the primary color it represents. For example, when this option is turned on, the red color channel looks like a grayscale image viewed through red acetate. Most experts agree the effect isn't helpful, though, and it does more to obscure your image than make it easier for you to see what's happening. Leave this check box turned off and read Chapter 16 for more information.

✦ **Use Diffusion Dither (on):** Here's an option for you folks working on 8-bit screens that display no more than 256 colors at a time. To simulate the 16-million-color spectrum on a 256-color screen, Photoshop automatically jumbles colored pixels using a technique called *dithering*. This option controls the pattern of dithered pixels. Photoshop offers a naturalistic "diffusion" dither that looks nice on screen. But because the diffusion dither follows no specific pattern, you sometimes see distinct edges between selected and deselected portions of your image after applying a filter or some other effect. You can eliminate these edges and resort to a more geometric dither pattern by turning off this check box.

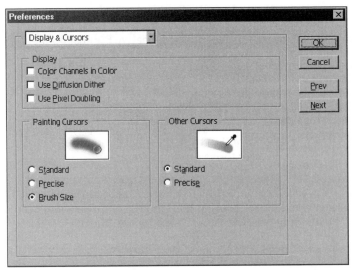

Figure 2-17: The Display & Cursors options control the way images and cursors look on screen. Shown here are the default settings, but I turn on Use Diffusion Dither.

Turning off the Use Diffusion Dither check box is an awfully drastic (not to mention ugly) solution, though. The better way to eliminate the occasional visual disharmony is to force Photoshop to redraw the entire image. You can press Ctrl+Alt+0 or perform some other zoom function.

Note that a related option found in earlier versions of Photoshop, Use System Palette, is gone. When you set your monitor to display 256 colors or less, this option let you specify whether you wanted Photoshop to use the default monitor palette or to adjust the palette constantly to best suit your image. The latter choice is no longer available.

✦ **Use Pixel Doubling (off):** This option can help speed up operations when you're editing huge images on a less-than-robust computer, but not by much. When you select the option, Photoshop displays selected areas using a low-resolution proxy. Although the option previously was connected just to moving layers, it now affects selections, too.

✦ **Painting Cursors (Brush Size):** When you use a paint or edit tool, Photoshop can display one of three cursors. The default Standard cursor looks like a paint-brush, airbrush, finger, or whatever tool you are using. These cursors are great if you have problems keeping track of what tool you selected, but otherwise they border on childish.

The Precise and Brush Size options are more functional. The Precise option displays a cross-shaped cursor — called a crosshair — regardless of which tool is active. The crosshair is great because it prevents the cursor from blocking your view as you edit. Meanwhile, the Brush Size option shows the actual size and shape of the active brush in the Brushes palette. Most artists prefer this final setting to the others because it comes the closest to showing the cursor the way it really is.

Tip

When Standard or Brush Size is selected, you can access the crosshair cursor by pressing the Caps Lock key. When Precise is selected from the Painting Cursors options, pressing Caps Lock displays the brush size.

✦ **Other Cursors (Standard):** Again, you can select Standard to get the regular cursors or Precise to get crosshairs. I prefer to leave this option set to Standard because you can easily access the crosshair cursor by pressing Caps Lock. The Precise option locks you into the crosshair whether or not you like it.

Transparency & Gamut

Press Ctrl+4 to switch to the Transparency & Gamut panel shown in Figure 2-18. The options in this panel change how Photoshop displays two conceptual items — transparent space behind layers and RGB colors that can't be expressed in CMYK printing.

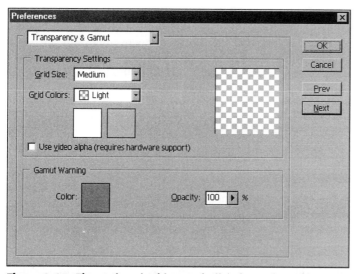

Figure 2-18: The options in this panel affect how Photoshop represents transparency and out-of-gamut colors. For the most part, you just want to select colors that you don't often see inside your images.

The options are arranged into two groups — Transparency Settings and Gamut Warning — as explained in the following sections.

Transparency Settings

Just as the Earth spins around in empty space, a Photoshop image rests on a layer of absolute transparency. By default, Photoshop represents this transparency as a gray checkerboard pattern. (What better way to demonstrate nothingness? I might have preferred a few lines from a Jean-Paul Sartre play, but no matter.) You may get a brief glimpse of this checkerboard when you first open an image or switch to Photoshop from another application.

When you view a layer independently of others, Photoshop fills the see-through portions of the layer with the checkerboard. So having the checkerboard stand out from the layer itself is essential. You can customize the size of the checkers and the color of the squares using the Grid Size and Grid Colors pop-up menus. You can also click the color swatches to define your own colors.

To lift colors from the image window, move your cursor outside the Preferences dialog box to get the eyedropper. Click a color to change the color of the white checkers; Alt-click to change the gray ones.

If you own a TrueVision NuVista+ board or some other 32-bit device that enables chroma keying, you can select the Use Video Alpha check box to view a television signal in the transparent area behind a layer. Unless you work in video production, you needn't worry about this option.

Gamut Warning

If Photoshop can display a color on screen but can't accurately print the color, the color is said to be *out of gamut*. You can choose View ➪ Gamut Warning to coat all out-of-gamut colors with gray. I'm not a big fan of this command — View ➪ Proof Colors (Ctrl+Y) is much more useful — but if you use View ➪ Gamut Warning, you don't have to accept gray as the out-of-gamut coating. Change the color by clicking the Gamut Warning Color swatch, and lower the Opacity value to request a translucent coating.

Units & Rulers

The Units & Rulers panel is the fifth panel in the Preferences dialog box; hence, you reach the panel by pressing Ctrl+5. Shown in Figure 2-19, this panel offers options that enable you to change the predominant system of measurement used throughout the program.

Whenever the rulers are visible, the Units & Rulers panel is only a double-click away. Choose View ➪ Show Rulers (Ctrl+R) to see the rulers on screen and then double-click either the horizontal or vertical ruler.

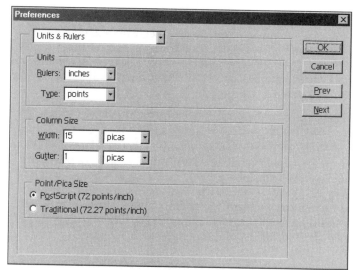

Figure 2-19: Go to the Units & Rulers panel to change the column and pica settings; to set the unit of measurement, right-click the ruler to display a pop-up menu of choices. I prefer to use Pixels as opposed to Inches.

Rulers

You can set the unit of measurement via the Units option in the Preferences dialog box. But in Version 6, there's an easier way: Just right-click anywhere on the ruler to display a pop-up menu of unit options and then click the unit you want to use. You can display the same pop-up menu by clicking the plus sign in the lower-left corner of the Info palette.

When you're first learning Photoshop, going with inches or picas is tempting, but experienced Photoshop artists use pixels. Because you can change the resolution of an image at any time, the only constant is pixels. An image measures a fixed number of pixels high by a fixed number of pixels wide — you can print those pixels as large or as small as you want. (To learn more about resolution, read Chapter 3.)

Type

Photoshop 6 enables you to set the unit of measure used for the type tool and its palettes independently of the ruler units. You can work in points, pixels, and millimeters; select your unit of choice from the Type pop-up menu. Check out Chapter 15 for more good news about type in this version of Photoshop.

Column Size

The Column Size options enable you to size images according to columns in a newsletter or magazine. Enter the width of your columns and the size of the gutter into the Width and Gutter option boxes. Then use File ⇨ New or Image ⇨ Image Size to specify the number of columns assigned to the width of the image. I explain these commands in more detail in Chapter 3.

Point/Pica Size

The last option in the Units & Rulers panel may be the most obscure of all Photoshop options. In case you aren't familiar with points and picas, exactly 12 points are in a pica, and about 6.06 picas are in an inch.

Well, because picas are almost evenly divisible into inches, the folks who came up with the PostScript printing language decided to bag the difference and to define a pica as exactly ⅙ inch. This makes a point exactly $\frac{1}{72}$ inch.

But a few purists didn't take to it. They found their new electronic documents weren't quite matching their old paste-up documents and, well, I guess life pretty much lost its meaning. So Adobe had to go back and add the Traditional (72.27 points/inch) option to keep everyone happy.

I prefer the nontraditional PostScript definition of points. This way, a pixel on screen translates to a point on paper when you print an image at 72 ppi (the standard screen resolution). Call me a soulless technodweeb, but computer imaging makes more sense when you can measure points and pixels without resorting to a calculator. The old ways are dead; long live the $\frac{1}{72}$-inch point!

Guides & Grid

Someone at Adobe said, "Let the preference settings continue." And, lo, there is Guides & Grid, which can be accessed by all who press Ctrl+6 and viewed by all who cast an eye on Figure 2-20. This panel lets you modify the colors of the guides and specify the size of the grid.

Tip   You can display the Preferences dialog box and go directly to the Guides & Grid panel by double-clicking a guide with the move tool or Ctrl-double-clicking with another tool. (To create a guide, drag from the horizontal or vertical ruler into the image.)

I explain these options in more detail in Chapter 12 but, for the moment, here are some brief descriptions.

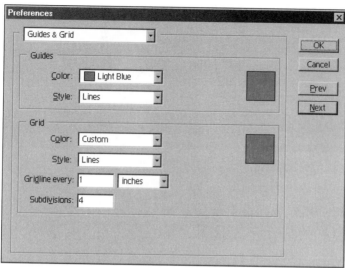

Figure 2-20: Use these options to adjust the size of the grid and change the way both the grid and ruler guides appear on screen.

Guides

Select a color for horizontal and vertical ruler guides from the Color pop-up menu. To lift a color from the image, move your cursor outside the Preferences dialog box and click in the image window with the eyedropper. You can also view guides as solid lines or dashes by selecting an option from the Style pop-up menu.

Grid

Select a color for the grid from the Color menu, or Alt-click in the image window to lift a color from the image. Then decide how the grid lines look by selecting a Style option. The Dots setting is the least intrusive.

The "Gridline every" value determines the increments for the visible grid marks on screen. But the Subdivisions value sets the real grid. For example, if you request a grid mark every one inch with four subdivisions — as in Figure 2-20 — Photoshop snaps selections and layers in quarter-inch increments (one inch divided by four).

Plug-Ins & Scratch Disk

Press Ctrl+7 to advance to the panel shown in Figure 2-21. Each time you launch Photoshop, the program searches for plug-in modules and identifies one or more scratch disks. You have to tell Photoshop where to find the plug-ins and where the temporary scratch files should go.

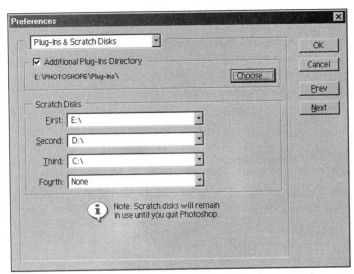

Figure 2-21: Tell Photoshop where to find plug-ins and where to put scratch files using these options.

Additional Plug-Ins Directory

By default, the plug-ins are located in a folder called Plug-Ins, which resides in the same folder as the Photoshop application. But you can tell Photoshop to also look for plug-ins in some other folder — a handy option if you install all your third-party plug-ins to some central location outside the Photoshop folders. To specify the second plug-ins location, select the check box and then click Choose to select the folder.

Scratch disks

By default, Photoshop assumes you have only one hard disk, so Photoshop stores its temporary virtual memory documents — called *scratch files* — on the same disk that contains your system software. If you have more than one drive available, though, you might want to tell Photoshop to look elsewhere. In fact, Photoshop can use up to four drives.

For example, one of my computers is equipped with two internal hard drives:

✦ A 2GB drive, C:, contains the system and most of the workaday documents I create.

✦ The other drive is a 4GB device partitioned into two 2GB segments. These are formatted as the D: and E: drives. D: contains all my applications while E: remains largely empty except for a few large miscellaneous files — QuickTime movies, digital camera snapshots, weird plug-ins — that I haven't gotten around to backing up yet.

E: has the most free space, so I set it as the First scratch disk. On the off chance that my images get so huge that Photoshop fills up E: and has to look elsewhere for scratch space, I select D: from the Second pop-up menu and my main system drive, C:, from the Third. That's the end of my drives, so Fourth remains set to None.

Adobe advises against using removable media — such as SyQuest, MO, and Zip drives — as a scratch disk. Removable media is typically less reliable and slower than a permanent drive. (A Jaz cartridge is more stable than Zip or the others, but still not as reliable as a fixed hard drive.) Using a removable drive on an occasional basis isn't the end of the world, but if you use it regularly you may end up crashing more often, in which case you'll probably want to add a new hard drive.

Changes affect the next session

As the note at the bottom of the Plug-ins & Scratch Disks panel warns, the settings in this panel don't take effect until the next time you launch Photoshop. This means you must quit Photoshop and restart the program.

There's nothing more frustrating than knowing that the options in this dialog box are set incorrectly before you've even started up Photoshop. It means you have to launch Photoshop, change the settings, quit Photoshop, and launch the program again. What a waste of time!

That is, it *would* be a waste of time if there wasn't a workaround. Fortunately, you can access the plug-ins and scratch disk settings during the launch cycle. After double-clicking on the Photoshop application icon or choosing Photoshop from the Start menu, press and hold the Ctrl and Alt keys. After a few seconds, a screen of the scratch disk options appears. Specify the disks as desired and press Enter. Your new settings now work for the current session — no restarting necessary.

Image Cache

Ever since Photoshop 3 came out, Adobe has received a fair amount of flack from high-end users who demand faster image handling. Programs such as Live Picture and xRes take seconds to apply complex operations to super-huge photographs, while Photoshop putters along for a minute or more. Granted, Live Picture and xRes aren't nearly as capable as Photoshop, but they are faster.

The good news is that Photoshop sports a caching scheme that speeds operations at reduced view sizes. You can adjust this feature by pressing Ctrl+8 in the Preferences dialog box. This displays the Memory & Image Cache panel, shown in Figure 2-22.

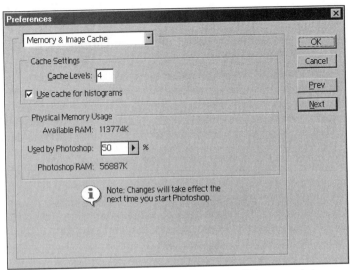

Figure 2-22: Photoshop's new caching capabilities speed the processing of very large images. This is also where you specify how much memory goes to Photoshop.

Cache Levels

Photoshop has been criticized for its lack of a "pyramid-style" file format, such as Live Picture's IVUE or xRes's LRG. Both IVUE and LRG store an image several times over at progressively smaller and smaller image sizes, called *downsamplings*. For example, the program would save a full view of the image, a 50 percent view, a 25 percent view, and so on. Live Picture or xRes can then load and edit only the portion of the image visible on screen, greatly accelerating functions.

Photoshop's alternative is image caching. Rather than saving the downsamplings to disk, Photoshop generates the reduced images in RAM. By default, the Cache Levels value is set to 4, the medium value. This means Photoshop can cache up to four downsamplings — at 100, 50, 25, and 12.5 percent — which permits the program to apply operations more quickly at reduced view sizes. For example, if you choose a color correction command at the 50 percent view size, it previews much faster than normal because Photoshop has to modify a quarter as many pixels on screen.

However, Photoshop must cache downsamplings in RAM, which takes away memory that could be used to hold the image. If you have lots of RAM (128MB or more) and you frequently work on large images (20MB or larger), you'll probably want to raise the value to the maximum, 8. The lost memory is worth the speed boost. If you have little RAM (say, 16MB or less) and you usually work on small images or Web graphics (4MB or smaller), you may want to reduce the Cache Levels value to 1 or 2. When files are small, RAM is better allocated to storing images rather than caching them.

Use cache for histograms

The "Use cache for histograms" check box tells Photoshop whether to generate the histograms that appear in the Levels and Threshold dialog boxes based on the cached sampling or the original image. As I explain in Chapter 17, a *histogram* is a bar graph of the colors in an image. When you choose a command such as Image ➪ Adjust ➪ Levels, Photoshop must spend a few seconds graphing the colors. If you turn the Use Cache for Histograms check box on, Photoshop graphs the colors in the reduced screen view, which takes less time, but is also less accurate. Turn the check box off for slower, more accurate histograms.

Generally speaking, I say leave the option on. A histogram is merely a visual indicator and most folks are unable to judge the difference between a downsampled histogram and a fully accurate one.

Again, if you're working in very large images and you have the Cache Levels value maxed out at 8, you should probably leave this check box selected. But if you have to reduce the Cache Levels value, turn off the check box. Histograms are the first thing that can go.

Note

This option is *not* responsible for the histogram irregularities that popped up in Photoshop 4. The fact that the Threshold dialog box sometimes lifted its histogram from the active layer only was a bug, not a function of Use cache for histograms. Even so, this option has received a lot of flack it did not deserve. My opinion is that, on balance, this is a positive feature that should be left on.

Physical memory usage

Windows 95, NT 4, and later offer dynamic memory allocation, which means that each application gets the memory it needs as it needs it. But Photoshop is something of a memory pig and has a habit of using every spare bit of RAM it can get its hands on. Left to its own devices, it might gobble up all the RAM and bleed over into Windows' virtual memory space, which is less efficient than Photoshop's own scratch disk scheme.

The Physical Memory Usage option helps you place some limits on Photoshop's ravenous appetites. The option lists the amount of RAM available to all applications after the operating system loads into memory. You can then decide how much of that memory should go to Photoshop. If you like to run lots of applications at the same time — your word processor, Web browser, spreadsheet, drawing program, and Photoshop, for example — then set the Used by Photoshop value to 50 percent or lower. But if Photoshop is the only program running — and if you have less than 32MB of RAM — raise the value to 70 to 80 percent.

I recommend against taking the Used by Photoshop value any higher than 80 percent, particularly on a low-capacity machine (32MB or less). Doing so permits Photoshop to fill up RAM that the operating system might need, which makes for a less stable working environment. As I've said before, if Photoshop is going too slow for you and hitting scratch disk too often, buy more RAM — don't play dangerous games with the little RAM you do have.

✦   ✦   ✦

Image Fundamentals

How Images Work

Think of a bitmapped image as a mosaic made from square tiles of various colors. When you view the mosaic up close, it looks like something you might use to decorate your bathroom. You see the individual tiles, not the image itself. But if you back up a few feet, the tiles lose their definition and merge to create a recognizable work of art, presumably Medusa getting her head whacked off or some equally appetizing thematic classic.

The colored pixels that make up an *image* work much like the tiles in a mosaic. If you enlarge the pixels, they look like an unrelated collection of colored squares. Reduce the size of the pixels, and they blend together to form an image that looks to all the world like a standard photograph. Photoshop deceives the eye by borrowing from an artistic technique older than Mycenae or Pompeii.

Of course, there are differences between pixels and ancient mosaic tiles. Pixels come in 16 million distinct colors. Mosaic tiles of antiquity came in your basic granite and sandstone varieties, with an occasional chunk of lapis lazuli thrown in for good measure. Also, you can resample, color separate, and crop electronic images. We know from the timeworn scribblings of Dionysius of Halicarnassus that these processes were beyond the means of classical artisans.

But I'm getting ahead of myself. I won't be discussing resampling, cropping, or Halicarnassus for several pages. First I address the inverse relationship between image size and resolution.

Size versus resolution

If you haven't already guessed, the term *image size* describes the physical dimensions of an image. *Resolution* is the number of pixels per linear inch in the final printed image. I say linear because you measure pixels in a straight line. If the resolution of an image is 72 *ppi* — that is, pixels per inch — you get 5,184 pixels per square inch (72 pixels wide × 72 pixels tall = 5,184).

Assuming the number of pixels in an image is fixed, increasing the size of an image decreases its resolution and vice versa. An image that looks good when printed on a postage stamp, therefore, probably looks jagged when printed as an 11 × 17-inch poster.

Figure 3-1 shows a single image printed at three different sizes and resolutions. The smallest image is printed at twice the resolution of the medium-sized image; the medium-sized image is printed at twice the resolution of the largest image.

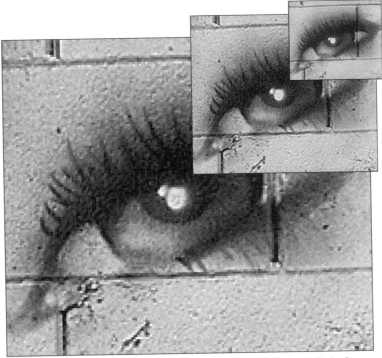

Figure 3-1: These three images contain the same number of pixels, but are printed at different resolutions. Doubling the resolution of an image reduces it to 25 percent of its original size.

One inch in the smallest image includes twice as many pixels vertically and twice as many pixels horizontally as an inch in the medium-sized image, for a total of four times as many pixels per square inch. Therefore, the smallest image covers one-fourth the area of the medium-sized image.

The same relationships exist between the medium-sized image and the largest image. An inch in the medium-sized image comprises four times as many pixels as an inch in the largest image. Consequently, the medium-sized image consumes one-fourth the area of the largest image.

Changing the printing resolution

When printing an image, a higher resolution translates to a sharper image with greater clarity. Photoshop lets you change the resolution of a printed image in one of two ways:

✦ Choose Image ➪ Image Size to access the controls that enable you to change the pixel dimensions and resolution of an image. Then enter a value into the Resolution option box, either in pixels per inch or pixels per centimeter.

A good idea (although not essential) is to turn off the Resample Image check box, as demonstrated in Figure 3-2. If you leave it on, Photoshop may add or subtract pixels, as discussed in the "Resampling and Cropping" section later in this chapter. By turning it off, you instruct Photoshop to leave the pixels intact but merely change how many of them print per inch.

✦ Alternatively, you can ask Photoshop to scale an image during the print cycle. In Version 6, you hand down this edict in the new Print Options dialog box. Choose File ➪ Print Options or press Ctrl+Alt+P to open the dialog box. You can enter specific Width and Height values or enter a percentage value into the Scale option box. Lower values reduce the size of the printed image and thereby increase the resolution; higher values lower the resolution. (Chapter 18 contains more information about scaling images as well as the other settings in the Print Options dialog box.)

Photoshop saves the Resolution setting with the image; the scale settings in the Print Options box affect the current print job only. Together, the two determine the printed resolution. Photoshop divides the Resolution value in the Image Size dialog box by the Scale percentage from the Page Options dialog box. For example, if the image resolution is set to 72 ppi and you reduce the image to 48 percent, the final printed image has a resolution of 150 ppi (72 divided by 0.48).

At the risk of boring some of you, I briefly remind the math haters in the audience that whenever you use a percentage in an equation, you first convert it to a decimal. For example, 100 percent is 1.0, 64 percent is 0.64, and 5 percent is 0.05.

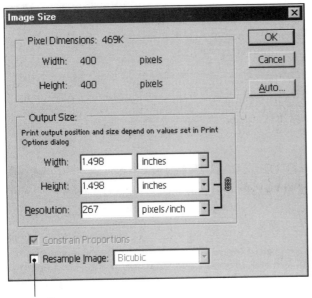

Turn off

Figure 3-2: Turn off the Resample Image check box to maintain a constant number of pixels in an image and to change only the printed resolution.

Tip

To avoid confusion, most folks rely exclusively on the Resolution value and leave the Page Options dialog box Scale value set to 100 percent. The only exception is when printing tests and proofs. Because ink-jet and other consumer printers offer lower-resolution output than high-end commercial devices, you may find it helpful to proof images larger so you can see more pixels. Raising the Scale value lets you accomplish this without upsetting the Resolution value. Just be sure to restore the value to 100 percent after you make your test print.

Changing the page-layout resolution

The Scale value in the Print Options dialog box value has no effect on the size and resolution of an image imported into an object-oriented application, such as QuarkXPress or Illustrator. But these same applications do observe the Resolution setting from the Image Size dialog box.

Specifying the resolution in Photoshop is a handy way to avoid resizing operations and printing complications in your page-layout program. For example, I preset the resolution of all the images in this book so the production team had only to import the images and print away.

Tip

Always remember: Photoshop is as good or better at adjusting pixels than any other program with which you work. So prepare an image as completely as possible in Photoshop before importing the image into another program. Ideally, you should never have to resize, rotate, or crop an image in any other program.

That tip is so important I'm going to repeat it: *Never* resize, rotate, or crop an image in Illustrator, FreeHand, CorelDraw, PageMaker, InDesign, or QuarkXPress. Get your image fully ready to go in Photoshop and then place it in the drawing or page-layout program, position it on the page, and leave it alone.

So what's the perfect resolution?

After all this explanation of pixels and resolution, you might be thinking, "Okay, this is all very interesting, but what's my bottom line? What Resolution value should I use?" The answer is frustrating to some and freeing to others: Any darn resolution you like. It's true—there is no right answer, there is no wrong answer. The images in this book vary from 100 ppi for screen shots to 300 ppi for color plates. I've seen low-resolution art that looks great and high-resolution art that looks horrible. As with all things, quality counts for more than quantity. You take the pixels you're dealt and make the best of them.

That said, I'll share a few guidelines, but only if you promise to take them with a grain of salt:

✦ Most experts recommend that you set the Resolution value to somewhere between 150 percent and 200 percent of the screen frequency of the final output device. The *screen frequency* is the number of halftone dots per linear inch, measured in *lpi* (short for *lines per inch*). So ask your commercial printer what screen frequency he uses—generally 120 lpi to 150 lpi—and multiply that times 1.5 or 2.

✦ Want to be more specific? For high-end photographic print work, it's hard to go wrong with a Resolution value of 267 ppi. That's 200 percent of 133 lpi, arguably the most popular screen frequency. When in doubt, most professionals aim for 267 ppi.

✦ If you're printing on a home or small-office printer, the rules change slightly. Different manufacturers recommend different optimum resolutions for their various models, but the average is 250 to 300 ppi. Experiment to see how low you can go, though—sometimes you can get by with fewer pixels than the manufacturer suggests. And don't forget that the quality of the paper you use may be more to blame than a lack of pixels for a lousy print.

✦ What if you don't have enough pixels for 267 ppi? Say that you shoot a digital snapshot that measures 768 × 1024 pixels and you want to print it at 6 × 8 inches. That works out to a relatively scant 128 ppi. Won't that look grainy? Probably. Should you add pixels with Image Size or some other command? No, that typically won't help. You have a finite number of pixels to work with, so you can print the image large and a little grainy, or sharp and small. The choice is yours.

✦ What if you have a photograph or slide and you can scan it at any resolution you want? Flat-bed scanners typically offer two maximum resolutions, a true optical maximum and an interpolated digital enhancement. The lower of the two values is invariably the true optical resolution. Scan at this lower maximum setting. Then use Image ➪ Image Size to resample the image down to the desired size and resolution, as explained in the "Resampling and Cropping" section near the end of this chapter.

Orson Welles claimed that he relied on his inexperience when creating *Citizen Kane*. He didn't know the rules of filmmaking, so they couldn't hamper him. When his assistants and technicians told him, "You can't do that," he ignored them because he didn't know any better.

I feel the same about resolution. Take the pixels you have and try to make them look the best you can. Then print the image at the size you want it to appear. If you focus on the function of your image first and fret about resolution and other technical issues second, you'll produce better art.

The Resolution of Screen Images

Regardless of the Resolution and Scale values, Photoshop displays each pixel on screen according to the zoom ratio (covered in Chapter 2). If the zoom ratio is 100 percent, for example, each image pixel takes up a single screen pixel. Zoom ratio and printer output are unrelated.

This same rule applies outside Photoshop as well. Other programs that display screen images — including multimedia development applications, presentation programs, and Web browsers — default to showing one image pixel for every screen pixel. This means that when you're creating an image for the screen, the Resolution value has no effect whatsoever. I've seen some very bright people recommend that screen images should be set to 72 ppi on the Mac or 96 ppi for Windows, and while there's nothing wrong with doing this, there's no benefit either. When publishing for the screen, the Resolution value is ignored.

So all that counts is the 100-percent view. That means you want the image to fit inside the prospective monitor when you choose View ➪ Actual Pixels (Ctrl+Alt+zero) inside Photoshop. I say *prospective* monitor because although you may use a 17-inch monitor when you create the image, you most likely need the final image to fit on a 13-inch display. So even though your monitor probably displays as many as 1,024 × 768 pixels, most Web and screen artists prepare for the worst-case scenario, 640 × 480 pixels. This is the 13-inch VGA standard, shared by some of the first color Macs and PCs, most laptops, an endless array of defunct computers, and even televisions.

Caution

Of course, a 640 × 480-pixel image would consume an entire 13-inch screen. If you want the image to share the page with text and other elements, the image needs to be smaller than that. A typical screen image varies from as small as 16 × 16 pixels for icons and buttons to 320 × 240 pixels for a stand-alone photograph. Naturally, these are merely guidelines. You can create images at any size you like.

For more information on creating images specifically for the World Wide Web, read Chapter 19.

How to Open, Duplicate, and Save Images

Before you can work on an image in Photoshop — whether you're creating a brand-new document or opening an image from disk — you must first load the image into an image window. Here are the four basic ways to create an image window:

✦ **File ➪ New:** Create a new window by choosing File ➪ New (Ctrl+N). After you fill out the desired size and resolution specifications in the New dialog box, Photoshop confronts you with a stark, white, empty canvas. You then face the ultimate test of your artistic abilities — painting from scratch. Feel free to go nuts and cut off your ear.

✦ **File ➪ Open:** Choose File ➪ Open (Ctrl+O) to open images scanned in other applications, images purchased from stock photo agencies, slides and transparencies digitized to a Kodak Photo CD, or an image you previously edited in Photoshop.

A variation on the Open command, Open Recent, displays a list of the images that you recently opened. Click an image name to crack open the image file without taking that tedious trip to the Open dialog box.

✦ **Edit ➪ Paste:** Photoshop automatically adapts a new image window to the contents of the Clipboard (provided those contents are bitmapped). So if you copy an image inside a different application or in Photoshop and then choose File ➪ New, Photoshop enters the dimensions and resolution of the image into the New dialog box. You can just accept the settings and choose Edit ➪ Paste (Ctrl+V) to introduce the image into a new window. Photoshop pastes the Clipboard contents as a new layer. This technique is useful for editing screen shots captured to the Clipboard or for testing effects on a sample of an image without harming the original.

✦ **File ➪ Import:** If you own a scanner or a digital camera, it may include a plug-in module that lets you transfer an image directly into Photoshop. Just copy the module into Photoshop's Plug-Ins folder and then run or relaunch the Photoshop application. To initiate a scan or to load an image into Photoshop, choose the plug-in module from the File ➪ Import submenu.

After you choose the command, Photoshop launches the device's download software. If you're scanning, select the scanner settings and initiate the scan as usual; the scanned picture appears in a new image window inside Photoshop. If you're transferring images from a digital camera, the camera software typically creates thumbnail previews of images in the camera's memory so that you can select the ones you want to transfer to Photoshop, as I'm doing in Figure 3-3.

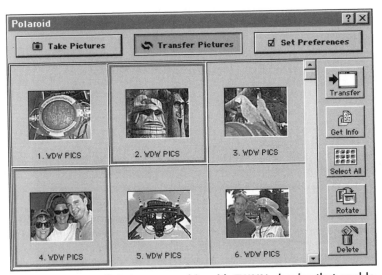

Figure 3-3: Most digital cameras ship with TWAIN plug-ins that enable you to view images stored in the camera's memory and open them up directly inside Photoshop.

Tip   Save your images to disk immediately after you scan or download them; unlike some other programs, Photoshop doesn't automatically take this step for you. Also, if your digital camera stores images on removable memory cards (Compact Flash, SmartMedia, Memory Stick, and the like), do yourself a favor and invest in a card reader or adapter that enables your computer to see the memory card as just another hard drive. Then you can just drag and drop images from the memory card to your computer's hard drive—a much faster and more convenient option than transferring images via a cable connection. You'll spend between $10 and $75, depending on what type of reader or adapter you buy, but trust me, even if you wind up at the high end of that price range, you'll never regret the purchase.

Creating a new image

Whether you're creating an image from scratch or transferring the contents of the Clipboard to a new image window, choose File ➪ New or press Ctrl+N to bring up the New dialog box shown in Figure 3-4. If the Clipboard contains an image, the

Width, Height, and Resolution option boxes show the size and resolution of this image. Otherwise, you can enter your own values in one of five units of measurement: pixels, inches, centimeters, picas, or points. If you're uncertain exactly what size image you want to create, enter a rough approximation. You can always change your settings later.

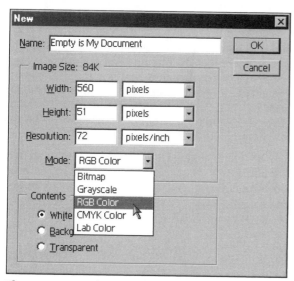

Figure 3-4: Use the New dialog box to specify the size, resolution, and color mode of your new image.

Tip

Although Photoshop matches the contents of the Clipboard by default, you can also match the size and resolution of other images:

✦ Press Alt when choosing File ⇨ New, or press Ctrl+Alt+N to override the contents of the Clipboard. Photoshop displays the size and resolution of the last image you created, whether or not it came from the Clipboard. Use this technique when creating many same-sized images in a row.

✦ You can also match the size and resolution of the new image to any other open image. While the New dialog box is open, choose the name of the image you want to match from the Window menu. It's that simple.

Units of measure

The Width and Height pop-up menus contain the five common units of measure mentioned earlier: pixels, inches, centimeters, points, and picas. But the Width pop-up menu offers one more, called Columns. If you want to create an image that fits exactly within a certain number of columns when it's imported into a desktop publishing program, select this option. You can specify the width of a column and the gutter between columns by pressing Ctrl+K and Ctrl+5 to display the Units & Rulers preferences. Then enter values into the Column Size option boxes.

The Gutter value affects multiple-column images. Suppose you accept the default setting of a 15-pica column width and a 1-pica gutter. If you specify a one-column image in the New dialog box, Photoshop makes it 15 picas wide. If you ask for a two-column image, Photoshop adds the width of the gutter to the width of the two columns and creates an image 31 picas wide.

The Height pop-up menu in the New dialog box lacks a Column option because vertical columns have nothing to do with an image's height.

You can set the default unit of measurement for the Width and Height pop-up menus in the Units & Rulers panel of the Preferences dialog box. (Select the value from the Rulers pop-up menu; the Type menu sets the measurement unit for text-related controls.) But if the dialog box isn't already open, here are two quicker options:

+ Press Ctrl+R to display the rulers and then right-click anywhere in the rulers to display a pop-up menu of units. Click the unit you want to use.

+ Display the same pop-up menu by pressing F8 to display the Info palette and then clicking or dragging on the cross icon (next to the X and Y coordinate values) in the palette's lower-left corner. Again, just click the unit you prefer.

New image size

In most cases, the on-screen dimensions of an image depend on your entries in the Width, Height, and Resolution option boxes. If you set both the Width and Height values to 10 inches and the Resolution to 72 ppi, the new image will measure 720 × 720 pixels. The exception occurs if you choose pixels as your unit of measurement. In this case, the on-screen dimensions depend solely on the Width and Height options, and the Resolution value determines the size at which the image prints.

Color mode

Use the Mode pop-up menu to specify the number of colors that can appear in your image. Choose Bitmap to create a black-and-white image and choose Grayscale to access only gray values. RGB Color, CMYK Color, and Lab Color all provide access to the full range of 16 million colors, although their methods of doing so differ.

RGB stands for red-green-blue, CMYK for cyan-magenta-yellow-black, and Lab for luminosity and two abstract color variables: a and b. To learn how each of these color modes works, read the "Working in Different Color Modes" section of Chapter 4.

Background color

The New dialog box also provides three Contents radio buttons that enable you to change the color of the background for the new image. You can fill the new image with white, with the current background color (assuming, of course, that the background color is something other than white), or with no color at all. This last setting, Transparent, results in a floating layer with no background image whatsoever, which can be useful when editing one layer independently of the rest of an image or when preparing a layer to be composited with an image. (For an in-depth examination of the more nitty-gritty aspects of layering, see Chapter 12.)

If you do select a transparent background, you must later flatten the layer by choosing Layer ➪ Flatten Image if you want to save the image to a format that doesn't support layers (see the upcoming discussion "Saving an image to disk" for information about new options for retaining layers when saving). The advantage of the Transparent setting, however, is that Photoshop doesn't create a new layer when you press Ctrl+V to paste the contents of the Clipboard. In the long run, you don't gain much—you still must flatten the image before you save it to some formats—but at least you needn't fuss with two layers, one of which is completely empty.

Incidentally, just because you create an image with a transparent background doesn't mean that you can automatically import a free-form image with transparency intact into an object-oriented program such as Illustrator or QuarkXPress. To carve a transparent area out of the naturally rectangular boundaries of an image, you have to use the pen tool to create a clipping path. I explain how in the "Retaining transparent areas in an image" section of Chapter 8.

Naming the new image

The New dialog box provides a Name option. If you know what you want to call your new image, enter the name now. Or don't. It doesn't matter. Either way, when you choose File ➪ Save, Photoshop asks you to specify the location of the file and confirm the file's name. So don't feel compelled to name your image anything. The only reason for this option is to help you keep your images organized on screen. Lots of folks create temporary images they never save; Photoshop offers a way to assign temporary images more meaningful names than *Untitled-4*, *Untitled-5*, *Untitled-6*, and so on.

Unlike some traditionalists, I whole-heartedly endorse using long files names under Windows 95, NT 4, and later. But naturally you should be aware of the implications. If you send a file to someone using Windows 3.1, DOS, or some other ancient operating system, the long file name gets truncated to eight characters with a tilde symbol (~) and number. (You can view the truncated DOS-style name at the desktop by right-clicking on the file and choosing Properties.) This can also happen when exchanging files with Macintosh users, depending on how you do it. If you give a Mac artist a PC-formatted floppy disk, Zip disk, or the like, the file names get the ax when the disk is popped into the Mac. But if you network your PC to a Mac using Miramar Systems' (*www.miramarsys.com*) PC MACLAN or the like, the long file names come through swimmingly. In fact, this is precisely how I exchange files over my own cross-platform Ethernet LAN.

Opening an existing image

Photoshop 6 provides a new File menu command, Open Recent, which displays a list of the images you worked on in recent Photoshop sessions. Click the name of the image you want to open. You set the number of files that appear on the list by entering a value in the Recent File List Contains option box, found on the Saving Files panel of the Preferences dialog box (Ctrl+K and then Ctrl+2). The maximum value is 30.

Of course, you can always open images the old-fashioned way, by choosing File ⇨ Open or pressing its keyboard shortcut, Ctrl+O, to display the Open dialog box. You also can double-click an empty spot in the Photoshop program window to open the dialog box.

The Open dialog box behaves just like the ones in other Windows applications, with a folder bar at top, a scrolling list of files, and the usual file management and navigation options. You can also open multiple files at one time. To select a range of files, click the first file name and Shift-click the last file in the range. Ctrl-click to add a single file to the group you want to open. Ctrl-click again to deselect a file from the group.

The Photoshop Open dialog box also includes a few controls that most other programs lack. You can read about these options in the next sections. But first, two other brief notes about opening files in Version 6:

✦ When you choose File ⇨ Open, Photoshop displays the folder that contained the last file you opened. Similarly, when you save a file, the folder to which you saved last is selected automatically.

✦ When you open an image, Photoshop may display a dialog box telling you that the color profile of the image doesn't match the default color profile you've established. You have the option of converting the image to the default profile or leaving well enough alone. See Chapter 16 for help with this issue.

Viewing the thumbnail

To help you assess an image before you open it, Photoshop displays a thumbnail preview of the selected file at the bottom of the Open dialog box, as shown in Figure 3-5. In Version 6, Photoshop displays thumbnails for any files saved in the native format (PSD). If you're running Windows 98 or Windows 2000, the operating system may generate thumbnails for files saved in other formats.

To generate thumbnails when saving images in Photoshop, press Ctrl+K, Ctrl+2 to display the Saving Files panel of the Preferences dialog box. Then set the Image Previews pop-up menu to Always Save or Ask When Saving, as discussed in Chapter 2. If you select Ask When Saving, Photoshop gives you the option of adding a thumbnail to the image inside the Save dialog box.

Note   If you've received images from Macintosh users in the past, you've probably wondered why the heck they saved their files without previews. The truth is, they couldn't. See, Photoshop for the Mac saves thumbnails in the so-called resource fork of the file, but Windows programs can't even see the resource fork, much less translate it. Fortunately for all, both versions of Photoshop can save Windows thumbnails. On the Mac, the Saving Files panel of the Preferences dialog box contains a check box called Windows Thumbnail. When turned on, a thumbnail is added to the data fork of the file, which translates to Windows fully intact.

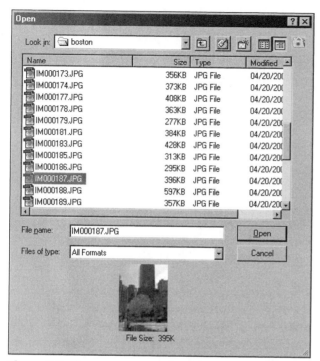

Figure 3-5: You can see a preview of an image if you previously saved it in Photoshop with the thumbnails option enabled.

Sadly, thumbnails don't work in the other direction. Because Windows doesn't recognize the resource fork, Photoshop for Windows can't save a Macintosh-style thumbnail. And because Photoshop on the Mac relies on Apple's QuickTime to interpret thumbnails, it can't see data-fork thumbnails. Dang.

Previewing outside Photoshop

Tip

Under Windows 95 and later, the Open dialog box isn't the only place you can preview an image before you open it. In fact, provided you save the image in the native Photoshop (.psd) format, you can peek at an image without even opening the program.

Right-click a file with a .psd extension — either at the desktop, in a folder window, or in Windows Explorer — and choose Properties from the pop-up menu. When the Properties dialog box opens, click the Photoshop Image tab to look at your image, as shown in Figure 3-6. Again, you must have saved a thumbnail preview along with the image for this feature to work.

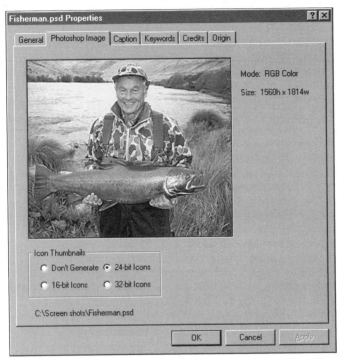

Figure 3-6: Under Windows 95 and later, you can preview files saved in the native .psd format from the Properties dialog box.

You can also see a tiny thumbnail in the General panel of the Properties dialog box. This same thumbnail appears at the desktop level, assuming that the folder is set to View ➪ Large Icons. Using the other tabs in the Properties dialog box, you can view the caption, keywords, credits, and other information created using Photoshop's File ➪ File Info command (covered at the end of Chapter 2).

Unfortunately, this trick works only for images saved in the native Photoshop format. TIFF, JPEG, GIF, and other images can be previewed only from inside Photoshop's Open dialog box. Even so, it's a heck of a trick and — if you need some ammunition — it's something your friends on the Mac can't do.

Opening elusive files

The scrolling list in the Open dialog box contains the names of just those documents that Photoshop recognizes it can open. If you can't find a desired document, it may be because the Files of Type pop-up menu is set to the wrong file format. To view all supported formats, either select All Formats from the Files of Type pop-up or enter *.* into the File Name option box and press Enter.

If a file lacks any form of extension whatsoever, the Open dialog box won't be able to identify it. This unusual situation may arise in one of two ways. On rare occasions, a file transmitted electronically (via the Internet, for example) loses its extension en route. But more likely, the file comes from a Macintosh computer. The Mac doesn't need file extensions — the file type identification resides in that resource fork I was telling you about — therefore, many Mac users never give a thought to three-character extensions.

You can solve this problem either by renaming the file and adding the proper extension, or by choosing File ➪ Open As (Ctrl+Alt+O). If you choose Open As, Photoshop shows you all documents in a directory, whether it supports them or not. Just click the extension-less file and select the correct file format from the Open As pop-up menu. Provided that the image conforms to the selected format option, Photoshop opens the image when you press Enter. If Photoshop gives you an error message instead, you need to either select a different format or try to open the document in a different application.

Duplicating an image

Have you ever wanted to try an effect without permanently damaging an image? Photoshop offers multiple undos, and you'll get a kick out of using the History palette to see before and after views of your image (as I explain in Chapter 7). But what if you want to apply a series of effects to an image independently and compare them side by side? And save the variations as separate files? Or perhaps even merge them? This is a job for image duplication.

To create a new window with an independent version of the foreground image, choose Image ➪ Duplicate. A dialog box appears, requesting a name for the new image. Just like the Name option in the New dialog box, the option is purely an organizational tool you can use or ignore. If your image contains multiple layers, Photoshop will, by default, retain all layers in the duplicate document. Or you can merge all visible layers into a single layer by selecting the Merged Layers Only check box. (Hidden layers remain independent.) Press Enter to create your new, independent image. Bear in mind that this image is unsaved; you need to choose File ➪ Save to save any changes to disk.

If you're happy to let Photoshop automatically name your image and you don't care what it does with the layers, press and hold the Alt key and choose Image ➪ Duplicate. This bypasses the Duplicate Image dialog box and immediately creates a new window.

Saving an image to disk

The first rule of image editing is to save the file to disk frequently. If your computer or Photoshop crashes while you're working on an image, all edits made during the current editing session are lost.

To save an image for the first time, choose File ➪ Save (Ctrl+S) to display the Save dialog box. Name the image, select the drive and folder where you want to store the image file, select a file format, and press Enter.

After you save the image once, choosing the Save command updates the file on disk without bringing up the Save dialog box. To save the image with a different name, location, or format, choose File ➪ Save As.

You also can issue the Save As command by pressing Ctrl+Shift+S. As for the Save a Copy command found in earlier versions of Photoshop, that function is now provided through the As a Copy check box in the Save As dialog box. By the way, if your only reason for using Save As is to change the file format, it's perfectly acceptable to overwrite (save over) the original document, assuming you no longer need the previous copy of the image. Granted, your computer could crash during the Save As operation, but because Photoshop actually creates a new file during any save operation, your original document should survive the accident. Besides, the chance of crashing during a Save As is extremely remote—no more likely than crashing during any other save operation.

Tip

To speed the save process, I usually save an image in Photoshop's native format until I've finished working on it. Then, when the file is all ready to go, I choose File ➪ Save As and save the image in the compressed TIFF or JPEG format. This way, I compress each image only once during the time I work on it.

When you close an image after saving it, you may be startled by the appearance of a dialog box asking whether you want to save the image again. Assuming that you haven't made any changes to your image since the last save, the dialog box indicates that the image incorporates features that the format you saved in doesn't support—layers, alpha channels, and so forth. If you want to save a copy of the image that retains all those features, click Yes. Photoshop displays a modified version of the Save dialog box and selects the Photoshop native format for you. Give your image a name and proceed as usual.

If you have multiple files open, you can close them in one step by choosing Window ➪ Close All or pressing Ctrl+Shift+W. Photoshop prompts you to save any images that haven't yet been saved and closes the others automatically.

Saving previews

In Chapter 2, I recommended that you set the Image Previews option in the Saving Files preferences panel (Ctrl+K, Ctrl+2) to Ask When Saving. If you followed this sage advice, the Save dialog box offers a Thumbnail check box. For print work, I generally select this option. The preview consumes extra disk space, but it's well worth it in exchange for being able to see the file before opening it.

The only reason *not* to save a thumbnail with an image is if you plan to post the picture on the Web. In that case, the file has to be as streamlined as possible, and that means shaving away the preview.

Choosing other save options

Certain save options that once were available only via the Save a Copy command now appear in the Save dialog box all the time. You also get access to these options when you choose Save As or press its keyboard shortcut, Ctrl+Shift+S. Figure 3-7 shows the dialog box.

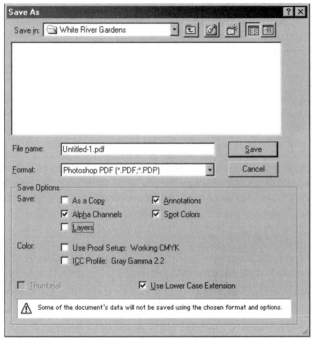

Figure 3-7: A look at the Version 6 Save dialog box, which incorporates the former Save a Copy command as a save option.

Some of these options, outlined in the upcoming list, are old friends with new names. But a few controls make their first appearance in Version 6. Note that the options you can select vary depending on the image file and the selected file format. If an option is grayed out, it either doesn't apply to your image or isn't supported by the file format you chose. And if your image includes features that won't be saved if you go forward with the current dialog box settings, Photoshop gives you the heads up by displaying a warning message at the bottom of the dialog box, as shown in Figure 3-7.

   ✦ **As a Copy:** Select this check box to save a copy of the image while leaving the original open and unchanged — in other words, to do what the Save a Copy command did in earlier versions of Photoshop. The result is the same as duplicating an image, saving it, and closing the duplicate all in one step.

The whole point of this option is to enable you to save a flattened version of a layered image or to dump other extraneous data, such as masks. Just select the file format you want to use and let Photoshop do the rest for you.

✦ **Annotations:** Select this check box to include any annotations that you created using the Version 6 notes and audio annotation tools. You can find out how to annotate your images in the section "Adding file information and annotations," later in this chapter.

✦ **Alpha Channels:** If your image contains an alpha channel—Photoshop's techy name for an extra channel, such as a mask (discussed in Chapter 9)—select the Alpha check box to retain the channel. Only a few formats—notably Photoshop, PDF, PICT, PICT Resource, TIFF, and DCS 2.0—support extra channels.

✦ **Spot Colors:** Did you create an image that incorporates spot colors? If so, select this option to retain the spot color channels in the saved image file. You must save the file in the native Photoshop, PDF, TIFF, or DCS 2.0 format to use this option.

✦ **Layers:** In Version 6, TIFF and PDF can retain independent image layers, as can the native Photoshop format. Select the check box to retain layers; deselect it to flatten the image.

If you're working with a layered image and select a file format that doesn't support layers, a cautionary message appears at the bottom of the dialog box. However, Photoshop doesn't prevent you from going through with the save as in past editions of the program, so be careful. All layers are automatically merged together when you save the file in a non-layer format. However, when you close the file, Photoshop reminds you that you haven't saved a version of the image that retains all data and gives you the opportunity to do so.

✦ **Use Proof Setup:** This option relates to Photoshop's color profile options. If the current view's proof setup is a "convert to" proof, Photoshop converts the image to the selected proofing space when saving.

✦ **ICC Profile:** If you're saving your image in a file format that supports embedded ICC profiles, selecting this option embeds the profile. The current profile appears next to the option name. See Chapter 16 for advice about working with color profiles.

File Format Roundup

Photoshop 6 supports more than 20 file formats from inside its Open and Save dialog boxes. It can support even more through the addition of plug-in modules, which attach commands to the File ➪ Save As, File ➪ Import, and File ➪ Export submenus.

File formats represent different ways to save a file to disk. Some formats provide unique image-compression schemes, which save an image in a manner that consumes less space on disk. Other formats enable Photoshop to trade images with different applications running under Windows or some other platform.

The native format

Like most programs, Photoshop offers its own native format — that is, a format optimized for Photoshop's particular capabilities and functions. This .psd format saves every attribute that you can apply in Photoshop — including layers, extra channels, file info, and so on — and is compatible with Versions 3 and later of the program. Of course, when you open files in earlier versions of Photoshop, you lose file attributes related to Version 6 features, such as annotations, color proof options, and so on.

Perhaps not surprisingly, Photoshop can open and save more quickly in its native format than in any other format. The native format also offers image compression. Like TIFF's compression, the Photoshop compression scheme does not result in any loss of data. But Photoshop can compress and decompress its native format much more quickly than TIFF, and the compression scheme is better able to minimize the size of mask channels (as explained in Chapter 9).

The downside of the Photoshop format is that relatively few applications other than Photoshop support it, and those that do don't always do a great job. Some applications such as CorelPhoto-Paint and Adobe After Effects can open a layered Photoshop image and interpret each layer independently. But most of the others limit their support to flat Photoshop files. To accommodate these programs, you can either (1) deselect the Layers check box in the Save dialog box to save a flat-tened version of the image or (2) activate the Maximize Backward Compatibility check box in the Preferences dialog box.

However, I intensely dislike both of these options. (In fact, you should be sure to turn off File Compatibility, for reasons explained in Chapter 2.) The native .psd format was never intended to function as an interapplication standard; it was meant for Photoshop alone. So use it that way. If you want to trade a flattened image with some other program, use TIFF, JPEG, or one of the other universal formats explained over the course of this chapter.

One exception: If you're creating a grayscale image for use with Filter ➪ Distort ➪ Displace, you have to create a Photoshop 2.0–compatible file. The best bet is to save the image in the Photoshop 2.0 format. Otherwise the Displace filter won't see the grayscale image. I tell you more about this filter in Chapter A on the CD-ROM that accompanies this book.

Special-purpose formats

With 20 file formats to choose from, you can imagine that most are not the kinds you'll be using on a regular basis. In fact, apart from the native Photoshop format, you'll probably want to stick with TIFF, JPEG, and GIF for Web images and EPS when preparing images for placement into QuarkXPress, PageMaker, and others.

Many of the other formats are provided simply so you can open an image created on another platform, saved from some antiquated paint program, or downloaded from the Web. In the spirit of sweeping away the chaff so we can move on to the good stuff, I cover these special-purpose formats first.

Notice that I lump Web standards GIF and PNG in with the special-purpose formats. The reason is simple—if you don't design for the Web, you rarely need them. On the other hand, if you do design for the Web, the formats take on special significance, which is why I cover them in depth in Chapter 19.

Microsoft Paint's BMP

BMP (*Windows Bitmap*) is the native format for Microsoft Paint (included with Windows) and is supported by a variety of Windows and DOS applications. Photoshop supports BMP images with up to 16 million colors. You also can use RLE (*Run-Length Encoding*), a lossless compression scheme specifically applicable to the BMP format.

The term *lossless* refers to compression schemes that conserve space on disk without sacrificing any data in the image, such as BMP's RLE and TIFF's LZW (*Lempel-Ziv-Welch*). The only reasons not to use lossless compression are that it slows down the open and save operations and it may prevent less-sophisticated applications from opening an image. (Lossy compression routines, such as JPEG, sacrifice a user-defined amount of data to conserve even more disk space, as I explain later.)

The most common use for BMP is to create images for use in help files and Windows wallpaper. In fact, rolling your own wallpaper is a fun way to show off your Photoshop skills, which is exactly what I did in Color Plate 3-1. For the best results, make sure you set your image to exactly the same pixel dimensions as your screen (which you can check from the Settings panel in the Display control panel). To conserve memory, you may want to reduce the number of colors in your wallpaper image to 256 using Image ⇨ Mode ⇨ Indexed Color. Although Color Plate 3-1 may look quite colorful, I did in fact reduce the palette to a bare-bones 256 colors. See Chapter 19 for the complete lowdown on indexed color.

When you save the wallpaper image, Photoshop displays the options shown in Figure 3-8. Generally, you'll want to select the Windows and Compress (RLE) options, but it really doesn't matter when creating wallpaper. Don't mess with the Depth options. Either you reduced the bit depth using the Indexed Color command as I directed previously or you didn't. There's no sense in changing the colors during the save process.

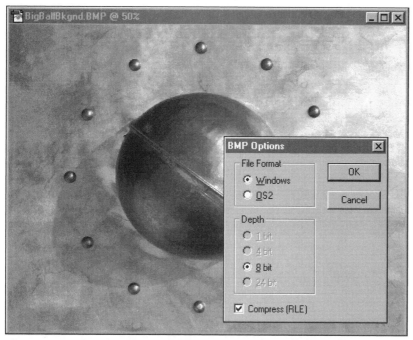

Figure 3-8: Select the options shown here when saving a BMP image for use as a desktop background. Leave the Depth setting alone.

To load the wallpaper onto your desktop, right-click anywhere on the desktop and choose the Properties command. This brings up the Display Properties dialog box shown in Figure 3-9. Click the Browse button and locate your BMP image on disk. Then click the apply button to see how it looks.

CompuServe's GIF

In the old days, the CompuServe online service championed GIF (short for *Graphics Interchange Format*) as a means of compressing files so you could quickly transfer photographs over your modem. Like TIFF, GIF uses LZW compression, but unlike TIFF, GIF is limited to just 256 colors.

With the advent of the World Wide Web, the GIF format has grown slightly more sophisticated. Two varieties of GIF currently exist, known by the helpful codes 87a and 89a. GIF87a supports strictly opaque pixels; GIF89a permits some pixels to be transparent. To open either kind of image, choose File ➪ Open.

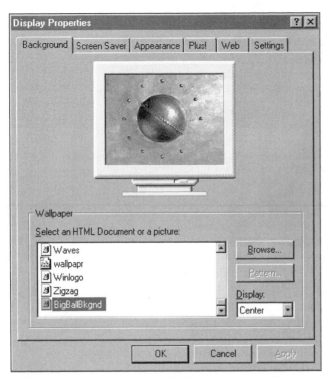

Figure 3-9: You can load a BMP file as desktop wallpaper using the Display Properties control panel provided with Windows 95 and later.

You can save an image with or without transparency by choosing File ➪ Save and selecting CompuServe GIF from the Format pop-up menu. When you index (reduce) the image to 256 colors — which you can do either before or during the file save process — select the Transparency check box in the Indexed Color dialog box if you want any areas of the image that are transparent to remain transparent when you view the image file in a Web browser. Chapter 19 explores this and other issues related to GIF transparency in detail.

If you're resistant to change and want to create GIFs with transparency via the old Export ➪ GIF89A command, you can; Adobe includes the command as an optional plug-in on the program CD just for old fogeys like you. But you'll save yourself time and trouble if you get acquainted with the new method: PC Paintbrush's PCX

PCX doesn't stand for anything. Rather, it's the extension PC Paintbrush assigns to images saved in its native file format. Although the format is losing favor, many PCX images are still in use today, largely because PC Paintbrush is the oldest painting program for DOS. Photoshop supports PCX images with up to 16 million colors. You can find an enormous amount of art, usually clip art, in this format. However, don't save files to PCX unless a client specifically demands it. Other formats are better.

Adobe's paperless PDF

The *Portable Document Format* (PDF) is a variation on the PostScript printing language that enables you to view electronically produced documents on screen. This means you can create a publication in QuarkXPress or PageMaker, export it to PDF, and distribute it without worrying about color separations, binding, and other printing costs. Using a program called Adobe Acrobat, you can open PDF documents, zoom in and out of them, and follow hypertext links by clicking highlighted words. Adobe distributes Mac, Windows, and UNIX versions of the Acrobat Reader for free, so almost anyone with a computer can view your stuff in full, natural color.

PDF files come in two flavors: those that contain just a single image and those that contain multiple pages and images. Photoshop can save only single-image PDF files, but it can open multipage files. The program rasterizes both types of files when it opens them.

You open PDF files in different ways depending on what elements of the file you want to access:

✦ Use File ⇨ Open to open a particular page in a multipage PDF file. After selecting the page you want to view, you can set the image size and resolution of the rasterized file. You also can choose File ⇨ Place to add a page as a new layer to an open image; in this case, you can't control size and resolution before adding the page. However, you can scale the page after the fact as you can any layer.

✦ Select Import ⇨ PDF Image to bring up a dialog box that enables you to open a particular image in the PDF file.

✦ Choose Automate ⇨ Multi-Page PDF to PSD to turn each page in the PDF file into a separate Photoshop image file.

The real question, however, is why would you *want* to open or place a PDF file in Photoshop instead of viewing it in Acrobat, which provides you with a full range of document viewing tools not found in Photoshop? Furthermore, because you can save only single-page PDF files, why on earth would you save to PDF in Photoshop?

I can think of two scenarios where Photoshop's PDF functions may come in handy:

✦ You want to see how images in a PDF document will look when printed on a high-resolution printer. Open the PDF file using File ⇨ Open, set the resolution to match that of the output device, and eyeball those images on-screen. This "soft-proofing" technique enables you to spot defects that may not be noticeable in draft proofs that you output on a low-res printer.

✦ You need a convenient way to distribute images for approval or input. You can save an image as a PDF file and send it to clients and colleagues, who can view the image in Acrobat if they don't have Photoshop. In Photoshop 6, you can even add text or voice annotations to your PDF file. In addition to annotations, Photoshop PDF supports layers, transparency, embedded color profiles, spot colors, duotones, and more. This enables you to route an image for approval without having to flatten the image or otherwise strip it of its Photoshop 6 features. Of course, features not supported by Acrobat aren't accessible to the viewer.

When you save to PDF in Photoshop, you have a choice of two encoding options. Choose ZIP only for images that feature large expanses of a single color; otherwise, opt for JPEG. Keep the Quality option set to Maximum to maintain the best print quality, just as you do for regular JPEG files. Select the Include Vector Data and Embed Fonts check boxes to retain any vector graphics and font data, respectively. Alternatively, you can select the Use Outlines for Text to save text as character outlines that are editable in the PDF file. The final option, Image Interpolation, enables other programs to interpolate the image when resampling to another size.

If you select JPEG encoding, you need a PostScript Level 2 or later printer to output your PDF file. Also be aware that separating files into individual plates can be problematic.

Apple's PICT

PICT (*Macintosh Picture*) is the Macintosh system software's native graphics format. Based on the QuickDraw display language that the system software uses to convey images on screen, PICT handles object-oriented artwork and bitmapped images with equal aplomb. It supports images in any bit depth, size, or resolution. PICT even supports 32-bit images, so you can save a fourth masking channel when working in the RGB mode.

PICT is obviously popular with the Macintosh crowd, especially folks who don't know much about graphics. So if you share a lot of files with Mac-type people, you may occasionally be asked to supply images in the PICT format. If you're trying to save an image in a format that your mom can open on her Mac, for example, PICT may be a better choice than JPEG. Heck, you can open PICT files inside a word processor, including everything from SimpleText to Microsoft Word. Just be sure mom has QuickTime loaded on her machine.

When you save a PICT image, Photoshop lets you set the bit depth. You should always stick with the default option, which is the highest setting available for the particular image. Don't mess around with these options; they apply automatic pattern dithering, which is a bad thing.

On the flip side, you may need to open a PICT file a Mac friend sends you. Photoshop can do this, but one problem may trip you up: On the Mac, you have the option of saving PICT files with a variety of JPEG compressions supplied by Apple's QuickTime. Unless you have QuickTime installed on your PC — which you might if you do a lot of surfing on the Web — you won't be able to open compressed PICT images.

Pixar workstations

Pixar has created some of the most memorable computer-animated movies and commercials in recent memory. Examples include the desk lamps playing with a beach ball from *Luxo, Jr.,* the run-amok toddler from the Oscar-winning *Tin Toy,* and the commercial adventures of a Listerine bottle that boxes gingivitis one day and swings Tarzan-like through a spearmint forest the next. But Pixar really made the grade with the feature-length *Toy Story,* which provided Disney with enough merchandising options to last a lifetime.

Pixar works its 3D magic using mondo-expensive workstations. Photoshop enables you to open a still image created on a Pixar machine or to save an image to the Pixar format so you can integrate it into a 3D rendering. The Pixar format supports grayscale and RGB images.

PNG for the Web

Pronounced *ping,* the PNG format enables you to save 16 million color images without compression for use on the Web. As I write this, neither Netscape Navigator nor Microsoft Internet Explorer support PNG without the help of a special plug-in. But for those folks who want full-color images without the pesky visual compression artifacts you get with JPEG, PNG may well be a big player in the future. (Of course, I wrote this same paragraph two years ago, so there's always the chance PNG will never gain acceptance.)

Cross-Reference

PNG was invented for the Web and I've never seen anyone use it for a purpose other than the Web. Find more information about PNG in Chapter 19, which covers Web issues in detail.

Scitex image-processors

Some high-end commercial printers use Scitex printing devices to generate color separations of images and other documents. Photoshop can open images digitized with Scitex scanners and save the edited images to the *Scitex CT (Continuous Tone)* format. Because you need special hardware to transfer images from the PC to a Scitex drive, you'll probably want to consult with your local Scitex service bureau technician before saving to the CT format. The technician may prefer that you submit images in the native Photoshop, TIFF, or JPEG format. The Scitex CT format supports grayscale, RGB, and CMYK images.

TrueVision's TGA

TrueVision's Targa and NuVista video boards enable you to overlay computer graphics and animation onto live video. The effect is called *chroma keying* because, typically, a key color is set aside to let the live video show through. TrueVision designed the TGA (*Targa*) format to support 32-bit images that include 8-bit alpha channels capable of displaying the live video. Support for TGA is widely implemented among professional-level color and video applications on the PC.

Interapplication formats

In the name of interapplication harmony, Photoshop supports a few software-specific formats that permit you to trade files with popular object-oriented programs such as Illustrator and QuarkXPress. Every one of these formats is a variation on EPS (*Encapsulated PostScript*), which is based in turn on Adobe's industry-standard PostScript printing language. You can use Photoshop to edit frames from a QuickTime movie created with Adobe Premiere.

Rasterizing an Illustrator or FreeHand file

Photoshop supports object-oriented files saved in the EPS format. EPS is specifically designed to save object-oriented graphics that you intend to print to a PostScript output device. Just about every drawing and page-layout program on the planet (and a few on Mars) can save EPS documents.

Prior to Version 4, Photoshop could interpret only a small subset of EPS operations supported by Illustrator (including the native *.ai* format). But then Photoshop 4 came along and offered a full-blown EPS translation engine, capable of interpreting EPS illustrations created in FreeHand, CorelDraw, Deneba's Canvas, and more. You can even open EPS drawings that contain imported images, something else Version 3 could not do.

When you open an EPS or native Illustrator document, Photoshop *rasterizes* (or *renders*) the artwork—that is, it converts the artwork from a collection of objects to a bitmapped image. During the open operation, Photoshop presents the Rasterize Generic EPS Format dialog box (see Figure 3-10), which enables you to specify the size and resolution of the image, just as you can in the New dialog box. Assuming the illustration contains no imported images, you can render it as large or as small as you want without any loss of image quality.

Tip

If the EPS illustration does contain an imported image or two, you need to know the resolution of the images and factor this information into the Rasterize Generic EPS Format dialog box. Select anything but Pixels from both the Width and Height pop-up menus, and leave the suggested values unchanged. Then enter the setting for the highest-resolution imported image into the Resolution option box. (If all the images are low-res, you may want to double or triple the Resolution value to ensure that the objects render smoothly.)

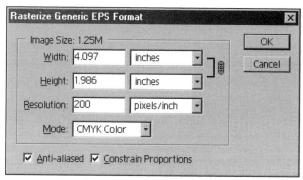

Figure 3-10: You can specify the size and resolution at which Photoshop renders an EPS illustration.

You should always select the Anti-aliased check box unless you're rendering a very large image — say, 300 ppi or higher. *Antialiasing* blurs pixels to soften the edges of the objects so they don't appear jagged. When you're rendering a very large image, the difference between image and printer resolution is less noticeable, so antialiasing is unwarranted.

Photoshop renders the illustration to a single layer against a transparent background. Before you can save the rasterized image to a format other than native Photoshop, you must eliminate the transparency by choosing Layer ➪ Flatten Image. Or save a flattened version of the image to a separate file by choosing the As a Copy option in the Save dialog box.

Tip

Rendering an EPS illustration is an extremely useful technique for resolving printing problems. If you regularly work in Illustrator or FreeHand, you no doubt have encountered *limitcheck errors,* which occur when an illustration is too complex for an imagesetter or other high-end output device to print. If you're frustrated with the printer and tired of wasting your evening trying to figure out what's wrong (sound familiar?), use Photoshop to render the illustration at 300 ppi and print it. Nine times out of ten, this technique works flawlessly.

If Photoshop can't *parse* the EPS file — a techy way of saying Photoshop can't break down the individual objects — it attempts to open the PICT (Mac) or TIFF (Windows) preview. This exercise is usually futile, but occasionally you may wish to take a quick look at an illustration to, say, match the placement of elements in an image to those in the drawing.

Placing an EPS illustration

If you want to introduce an EPS graphic into the foreground image rather than to render it into a new image window of its own, choose File ➪ Place. Unlike other File menu commands, Place supports only EPS illustrations and PDF files.

After you import the EPS graphic, it appears inside a box—which Photoshop calls a *bounding box*—with a great big X across it. You can move, scale, and rotate the illustration into position before rasterizing it to pixels. Drag a corner handle to resize the image; drag outside the image to rotate it. You can also nudge the graphic into position by pressing the arrow keys. When everything is the way you want it, press Enter or double-click inside the box to rasterize the illustration. If the placement isn't perfect, not to worry. The graphic appears on a separate layer, so you can move it with complete freedom. To cancel the Place operation, press Escape instead of Enter.

Saving an EPS image

When preparing an image for placement inside a drawing or page-layout document that will be printed to a PostScript output device, many artists prefer to save the image in the EPS format. Converting the image to PostScript up front prevents the drawing or page-layout program from doing the work. The result is an image that prints more quickly and with less chance of problems. (Note that an image does not *look* any different when saved in EPS. The idea that the EPS format somehow blesses an image with better resolution is pure nonsense.)

A second point in the EPS format's favor is clipping paths. As explained graphically at the end of Chapter 8, a clipping path defines a free-form boundary around an image. When you place the image into an object-oriented program, everything outside the clipping path becomes transparent. While some programs—notably InDesign and PageMaker—recognize clipping paths saved with a TIFF image, many programs acknowledge a clipping path only when saved in the EPS format.

Third, although Illustrator has remedied the problems it had importing TIFF images, it still likes EPS best, especially where screen display is concerned. Thanks to the EPS file's fixed preview, Illustrator can display an EPS image on screen very quickly compared with other file formats. And Illustrator can display an EPS image both in the preview mode and in the super-fast artwork mode.

So if you want to import an image into Illustrator, QuarkXPress, or another object-oriented program, your best bet is EPS. On the downside, EPS is an inefficient format for saving images thanks to the laborious way that it describes pixels. An EPS image may be three to four times larger than the same image saved to the TIFF format with LZW compression. But this is the price we pay for reliable printing.

Absolutely avoid the EPS format if you plan on printing your final pages to a non-PostScript printer. This defeats the entire purpose of EPS, which is meant to avoid printing problems, not cause them. When printing without PostScript, use TIFF or JPEG.

To save an image in the EPS format, choose Photoshop EPS from the Format pop-up menu in the Save dialog box. After you press Enter, Photoshop displays the dialog box shown in Figure 3-11. The options in this dialog box work as follows:

✦ **Preview:** Technically, an EPS document comprises two parts: a pure PostScript-language description of the graphic for the printer and a bitmapped preview so you can see the graphic on screen. Select the TIFF (8 bits/pixel) option from the Preview pop-up menu to save a 256-color TIFF preview of the image. The 1-bit option provides a black-and-white preview only, which is useful if you want to save a little room on disk. Select None to include no preview and save even more disk space.

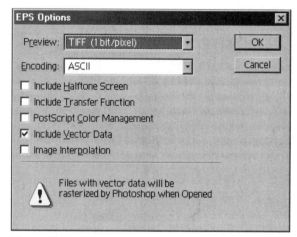

Figure 3-11: When you save an image in the EPS format, you can specify the type of preview and tack on some printing attributes.

✦ **Encoding:** If you're saving an image for import into Illustrator, QuarkXPress, or some other established program, select the Binary encoding option (also known as *Huffman encoding*), which compresses an EPS document by substituting shorter codes for frequently used characters. The letter *a*, for example, receives the 3-bit code 010, rather than its standard 8-bit ASCII code, 01100001 (the binary equivalent of what we humans call 97).

Sadly, some programs and printers don't recognize Huffman encoding, in which case you must select the less efficient ASCII option. ASCII stands for *American Standard Code for Information Interchange*, which is fancy jargon for text-only. In other words, you can open and edit an ASCII EPS document in a word processor, provided you know how to read and write PostScript.

Actually, this can be a useful technique if you have a Mac file that won't open, especially if the file was sent to you electronically. Chances are that a Mac-specific header got into the works. Open the file in a word processor and look at the beginning. You should see the four characters *%!PS.* Anything that comes before this line is the Macintosh header. Delete the garbage before *%!PS,* save the file in text format, and try again to open the file in Photoshop.

The remaining Encoding options are JPEG settings. JPEG compression not only results in smaller files on disk but also degrades the quality of the image. Select JPEG (Maximum Quality) to invoke the least degradation. Better yet, avoid the JPEG settings altogether. These options work only if you plan to print your final artwork to a PostScript Level 2 or Level 3 device. Earlier PostScript printers do not support EPS artwork with JPEG compression and will choke on the code.

So to recap, ASCII results in really big files that work with virtually any printer or application. Binary creates smaller files that work with most mainstream applications but may choke some older-model printers. And the JPEG settings are compatible exclusively with Level 2 and later PostScript printers.

✦ **Include Halftone Screen:** Another advantage of EPS over other formats is that it can retain printing attributes. If you specified a custom halftone screen using the Screens button inside the Page Setup dialog box, you can save this setting with the EPS document by selecting the Include Halftone Screen check box. But be careful—you can just as easily ruin your image as help it. Read Chapter 18 before you select this check box.

✦ **Include Transfer Function:** As described in Chapter 18, you can change the brightness and contrast of a printed image using the Transfer button inside the Page Setup dialog box. To save these settings with the EPS document, select the Include Transfer Function check box. Again, this option can be dangerous when used casually. See Chapter 18 for more details.

✦ **PostScript Color Management:** Like JPEG compression, this check box is compatible with Level 2 and 3 printers only. It embeds a color profile, which helps the printer to massage the image during the printing cycle to generate more accurate colors. Unless you plan on printing to a Level 2 or later device, leave the option off. (For more information about color profiles, read Chapter 16.)

✦ **Include Vector Data:** Select this option if your file contains vector objects, including shapes, non-bitmap type, and layer clipping paths. Otherwise, Photoshop rasterizes the objects during the save process. When you select the option, Photoshop displays a warning in the dialog box to remind you that if you reopen the file in Photoshop, you rasterize any vector objects that you saved with the file.

✦ **Transparent Whites:** When saving black-and-white EPS images in Photoshop, the four check boxes previously discussed drop away, replaced by Transparent Whites. Select this option to make all white pixels in the image transparent.

Although Photoshop EPS is the only format that offers the Transparent Whites option, many programs — including Illustrator and InDesign — treat white pixels in black-and-white TIFF images as transparent as well.

✦ **Image Interpolation:** Turn on this option if you want another program to be able to interpolate the image when resampling it to another size. For example, suppose you import an EPS image into InDesign and scale it to 400 percent. If Image Interpolation is turned off, then InDesign just makes pixels in the image four times larger, as if you had used the nearest neighbor interpolation inside Photoshop. If you turn Image Interpolation on, however, InDesign applies bicubic interpolation in order to generate new pixels. (For details on nearest neighbor and bicubic interpolation, see the "General Preferences" section in Chapter 2.) Unless you have a reason for doing otherwise, turn this option on.

QuarkXPress DCS

Quark developed a variation on the EPS format called Desktop Color Separation (DCS). When you work in QuarkXPress, PageMaker, and other programs that support the format, DCS facilitates the printing of color separations. Before you can use DCS, you have to convert your image to the CMYK color space using Image ⇨ Mode ⇨ CMYK Color. (DCS 2.0 also supports grayscale images with spot-color channels.) Then bring up the Save dialog box and select Photoshop DCS 1.0 or 2.0 from the Format pop-up menu.

Photoshop 5 introduced support for DCS 2.0 to accommodate images that contain extra spot-color channels, as explained in Chapter 18. If you add a Pantone channel to an image, DCS 2.0 is the only PostScript format you can use. If your image doesn't contain any extra channels beyond the basic four required for CMYK, DCS 1.0 is the safer and simpler option.

After you press Enter, Photoshop displays an additional pop-up menu of DCS options, which vary depending on whether you've selected DCS 1.0 or 2.0, as shown in Figure 3-12. The DCS 1.0 format invariably saves a total of five files: one master document (which is the file that you import into QuarkXPress) plus one file each for the cyan, magenta, yellow, and black color channels (which are the files that get printed). The DCS 2.0 format can be expressed as a single file (tidier) or five separate files (better compatibility).

Either way, the DCS pop-up menu gives you the option of saving a 72-ppi PostScript composite of the image inside the master document. Independent from the bitmapped preview — which you specify as usual by selecting a Preview option — the PostScript composite makes it possible to print a low-resolution version of a DCS image to a con-sumer-quality printer. If you're using a black-and-white printer, select the 72 pixel/inch grayscale option; if you're using a color printer, select the final option. Be forewarned, however, that the composite image significantly increases the size of the master document on disk.

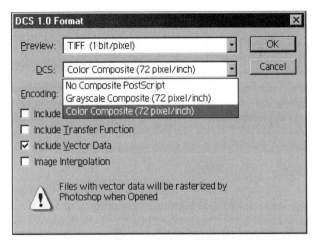

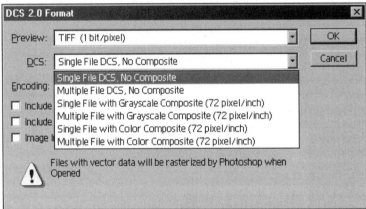

Figure 3-12: The extra options for the DCS 1.0 format (top) and those for the DCS 2.0 format (bottom).

Notice the two new options at the bottom of the options dialog boxes for DCS 1.0 and 2.0: Include Vector Data and Image Interpolation. These options work just as described earlier for the Photoshop EPS format.

Premiere Filmstrip

Adobe Premiere is a popular QuickTime movie-editing application for both Macs and PCs. The program is a wonder when it comes to fades, frame merges, and special effects, but it offers no frame-by-frame editing capabilities. For example, you can neither draw a mustache on a person in the movie nor can you make brightly colored brush strokes swirl about in the background—at least, not inside Premiere.

You can export the movie to the Filmstrip format, though, which is a file-swapping option exclusive to Photoshop and Premiere. A Filmstrip document organizes frames in a long vertical strip, as shown on the left side of Figure 3-13. The right side of the figure shows the movie after I edited each individual frame in ways not permitted by Premiere. A boring movie of a cat stuck in a bag becomes an exciting movie of a cat-stuck-in-a-bag flying. If that doesn't sum up the miracle of digital imaging, I don't know what does.

Figure 3-13: Four frames from a QuickTime movie as they appear in the Filmstrip format before (left) and after (right) editing the frames in Photoshop.

A gray bar separates each frame. The number of each frame appears on the right; the Society of Motion Picture and Television Engineers (SMPTE) time code appears on the left. The structure of the three-number time code is minutes:seconds:frames, with 30 frames per second.

Caution

If you change the size of a Filmstrip document inside Photoshop in any way, you cannot save the image back to the Filmstrip format. Feel free to paint and apply effects, but stay the heck away from the Image Size and Canvas Size commands.

Tip

I don't really delve into the Filmstrip format anywhere else in this book, so I want to pass along a few quick Filmstrip tips right here and now:

✦ First, you can scroll up and down exactly one frame at a time by pressing Shift+Page Up or Shift+Page Down, respectively.

✦ Second, you can move a selection exactly one frame up or down by pressing Ctrl+Shift+up arrow or Ctrl+Shift+down arrow.

✦ If you want to clone the selection as you move it, press Ctrl+Shift+Alt+up arrow or Ctrl+Shift+Alt+down arrow.

And finally — here's the great one — you can select several sequential frames and edit them simultaneously by following these steps:

STEPS: Selecting Sequential Frames in a Movie

1. **Select the first frame you want to edit.** Select the rectangular marquee tool by pressing the M key. Then drag around the area you want to edit in the movie. (This is the only step that takes any degree of care or coordination whatsoever.)

2. **Switch to the quick mask mode by pressing the Q key.** The areas around the selected frame are overlaid with pink.

3. **Set the magic wand Tolerance value to 0.** Double-click the magic wand tool icon in the Toolbox to display the Magic Wand Options palette. Enter 0 for the Tolerance value and deselect the Anti-aliased check box.

4. **Click inside the selected frame (the one that's not pink) with the magic wand tool.** This selects the unmasked area inside the frame.

5. **Press Ctrl+Shift+Alt+down arrow to clone the unmasked area to the next frame in the movie.** When you exit the quick mask mode, both this frame and the one above it will be selected.

6. **Repeat several times.** Keep Ctrl+Shift+Alt+down arrowing until you're rid of the pink stuff on all the frames you want to select.

7. **Exit the quick mask mode by pressing the Q key again.** All frames appear selected.

8. **Edit the frames to your heart's content.**

If you're new to Photoshop, half of these steps, if not all of them, probably sailed over your head like so many low-flying cats stuck in bags. If you want to learn more about selections and cloning, see Chapter 8. In Chapter 9, I explore the quick mask mode and other masking techniques. After you finish reading those chapters, return to this section to see if it doesn't make a little more sense. Or don't. It's entirely up to you.

The process of editing individual frames as just described is sometimes called *rotoscoping,* named after the traditional technique of combining live-action film with animated sequences. You also can try out some scratch-and-doodle techniques, which is where an artist scratches and draws directly on frames of film. If this isn't enough, you can emulate *xerography,* in which an animator makes Xerox copies of photographs, enhances the copies using markers or whatever else is convenient, and shoots the finished artwork, frame by frame, on film. In a nutshell, Photoshop extends Premiere's functionality by adding animation to its standard supply of video-editing capabilities.

You can save an image in the Filmstrip format through the Save dialog box. But remember, you can save in this format only if you opened the image as a Filmstrip document and did not change the size of the image.

The mainstream formats

The formats discussed so far are mighty interesting and they all fulfill their own niche purposes. But two formats — JPEG and TIFF — are the all-stars of digital imagery. You'll use these formats the most because of their outstanding compression capabilities and almost universal support among graphics applications.

JPEG

The JPEG format is named after the folks who designed it, the Joint Photographic Experts Group. JPEG is the most efficient and essential compression format currently available and is likely to be the compression standard for years to come. JPEG is a lossy compression scheme, which means it sacrifices image quality to conserve space on disk. You can control how much data is lost during the save operation, however.

When you save an image in the JPEG format, you're greeted with the JPEG Options dialog box (see Figure 3-14), which grew to include some new options in Version 5.5. (Chapter 19 covers the various dialog box components in detail.) But the most vital option is the Quality option, which determines how much compression Photoshop applies to your image.

Select an option from the Quality pop-up menu or drag the slider triangle from 0 to 12 to specify the quality setting. Of the named options, Low takes the least space on disk, but distorts the image rather severely; Maximum retains the highest amount of image quality, but consumes more disk space. Of the numbered options, 0 is the most severe compressor and 12 does the least damage.

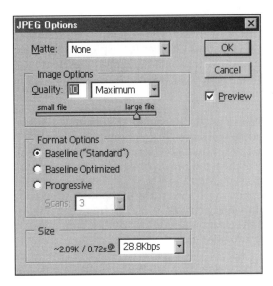

Figure 3-14: The JPEG Options dialog box provides a total of 12 compression settings, ranging from 0 (heaviest compression) to 12 (best quality).

JPEG evaluates an image in 8×8-pixel blocks, using a technique called *Adaptive Discrete Cosine Transform* (or ADCT, as in "Yes, I'm an acronym ADCT"). It averages the 24-bit value of every pixel in the block (or 8-bit value of every pixel in the case of a grayscale image). ADCT then stores the average color in the upper-left pixel in the block and assigns the remaining 63 pixels smaller values relative to the average.

Next, JPEG divides the block by an 8×8 block of its own called the *quantization matrix*, which homogenizes the pixels' values by changing as many as possible to zero. This process saves the majority of disk space, but loses data. When Photoshop opens a JPEG image, it can't recover the original distinction between the zero pixels, so the pixels become the same, or similar, colors. Finally, JPEG applies lossless Huffman encoding to translate repeating values to a single symbol.

In most instances, I recommend you use JPEG only at the Maximum quality setting (10 or higher), at least until you gain some experience with it. The smallest amount of JPEG compression saves more space on disk than any non-JPEG compression format and still retains the most essential detail from the original image. Figure 3-15 shows a grayscale image saved at each of the four compression settings.

The samples are arranged in rows from highest image quality (upper left) to lowest quality (lower right). Below each sample is the size of the compressed document on disk. Saved in the only moderately compressed native Photoshop format, the image consumes 116K on disk. From 116K to 28K — the result of the lowest-quality JPEG setting — is a remarkable savings, but it comes at a price.

I've taken the liberty of sharpening the focus of strips in each image so you can see more easily how JPEG averages neighboring pixels to achieve smaller file sizes. The first strip in each image appears in normal focus, the second strip is sharpened once by choosing Filter ➪ Sharpen ➪ Sharpen More, and the third strip is sharpened twice. I also adjusted the gray levels to make the differences even more pronounced. You can see that although the lower-image quality setting leads to a dramatic saving in file size, it also excessively gums up the image. The effect, incidentally, is more obvious on screen. Believe me, after you familiarize yourself with JPEG compression, you can spot other people's overly compressed JPEG images a mile away. This isn't something you want to exaggerate in your images.

Maximum 66K High 50K

Medium 33K Low 28K

Figure 3-15: Four JPEG settings applied to a single image, with the highest image quality setting illustrated at the upper left and the lowest at the bottom right.

To see the impact of JPEG compression on a full-color image, check out Color Plate 3-2. The original image consumes 693K in the native Photoshop format, but 116K when compressed at the JPEG module's Maximum setting. To demonstrate the differences between different settings better, I enlarged one portion of the image and oversharpened another.

JPEG is a *cumulative compression scheme,* meaning that Photoshop recompresses an image every time you save it in the JPEG format. No disadvantage exists to saving an image to disk repeatedly during a single session, because JPEG always works from the on-screen version. But if you close an image, reopen it, and save it in the JPEG format, you inflict a small amount of damage. Use JPEG sparingly. In the best of all possible worlds, you should save to the JPEG format only after you finish all work on an image. Even in a pinch, you should apply all filtering effects before saving to JPEG, because these have a habit of exacerbating imperfections in image quality.

JPEG is best used when compressing continuous-tone images (images in which the distinction between immediately neighboring pixels is slight). Any image that includes gradual color transitions, as in a photograph, qualifies for JPEG compression. JPEG is not the best choice for saving screen shots, line drawings (especially those converted from EPS graphics), and other high-contrast images. These are better served by a lossless compression scheme such as TIFF with LZW. The JPEG format is available when you are saving grayscale, RGB, and CMYK images.

Occupying the bottom half of the JPEG Options dialog box are three radio buttons, designed primarily to optimize JPEG images for the Web. Progressive isn't applicable to print images, and the Baseline options don't affect print images enough to make any difference. For now, just select the first option, Baseline ("Standard"), and be done with it. If you want to learn more about the remaining options, read the "Saving JPEG Images" section of Chapter 19.

TIFF

Developed by Aldus in the early days of the Mac to standardize an ever-growing population of scanned images, TIFF (*Tagged Image File Format*) is the most widely supported image printing format across both the Macintosh and PC platforms. Unlike EPS, it can't handle object-oriented artwork, and it doesn't support lossy compression like JPEG. But, otherwise, it's unrestricted. In fact, TIFF offers a few tricks of its own that make it very special.

In Photoshop, the TIFF format supports up to 24 channels, the maximum number permitted in any image. In fact, TIFF is the only format other than DCS 2.0, "raw," and the native Photoshop format that can save more than four channels. To save a TIFF file without extra mask channels, deselect the Alpha check box in the Save dialog box. (For an introduction to channels, read Chapter 16.)

Even more impressive, TIFF supports multiple layers in Photoshop 6. If you want layers to remain independent when you save the file, select the Layers check box in the Save dialog box. (See the earlier section "Choosing other save options" for a look at all the new controls in the dialog box.)

When you save an image as a TIFF file, Photoshop displays the TIFF Options dialog box (see Figure 3-16), which offers expanded controls in Version 6:

✦ **Compression:** Formerly, you could apply only one form of compression to TIFF files — LZW (Lempel-Ziv-Welch) compression. You now can apply JPEG and ZIP compression in addition to LZW.

• **LZW:** Like Huffman encoding (previously described in the "Saving an EPS image" section), LZW digs into the computer code that describes an image and substitutes frequently used codes with shorter equivalents. But instead of substituting characters, as Huffman does, LZW substitutes strings of data. Because LZW doesn't so much as touch a pixel in your image, it's entirely lossless. Most image editors and desktop publishing applications — including Illustrator, FreeHand, PageMaker, InDesign, and QuarkXPress — import LZW-compressed TIFF images, but a few still have yet to catch on.

• **ZIP:** The problem with LZW (from a programming perspective) is that it's regulated by a patent. And whenever a bit of technology costs money to use, you can bet somebody out there is trying to come up with a free equivalent. Hence ZIP, a competing lossless compression scheme used in PDF documents. Why use it? Theoretically, it's a bit smarter than LZW and can on occasion deliver smaller image files. On the other hand, Photoshop is currently one of the few programs to support ZIP compression in a TIFF file. So unless you discover big savings when using ZIP, I'd stick with LZW until ZIP support becomes more widespread.

• **JPEG:** If two lossless compression schemes aren't enough, the TIFF format also permits you to apply lossy JPEG compression. Long-time Photoshop users may balk at JPEG compression inside TIFF options. After all, one of the major benefits of TIFF is that it ensures optimum image quality; by applying JPEG compression, which results in loss of image data, you defeat the purpose. But now that TIFF supports layers, JPEG inside TIFF permits you a unique opportunity to cut the size of your layered images files in half. My experience shows that JPEG in TIFF results in only modest loss of data. And because the JPEG does not affect the transparency mask — which defines the outlines of the layers — the layers continue to exhibit nice, sharp edges.

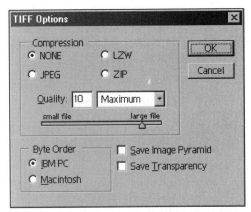

Figure 3-16: Photoshop 6 offers a choice of compression schemes for a TIFF file as well as the option to write the file as an image pyramid.

If names such as Huffman, LZW, and ZIP ring a faint bell, it may be because these are the same compression schemes used by PKzip, WinZIP, and other file compression utilities. For this reason, using an additional utility to compress a TIFF image that you've already compressed using LZW, ZIP, or JPEG makes no sense. Neither do you want to compress a standard JPEG image, because JPEG takes advantage of Huffman encoding. You may shave off a few K, but this isn't enough space to make it worth your time and effort.

Also be aware that some programs may gag on compressed TIFF files, regardless of which compression scheme you apply. If an application balks at opening your Photoshop TIFF file, try resaving the file with no compression.

✦ **Byte Order:** Every once in a while, Photoshop chooses to name a straightforward option in the most confusing way possible. Byte Order is a prime example. No, this option doesn't have anything to do with how you eat your food. Instead, there are two variations of TIFF, one for the PC and the other for the Mac. I'm sure this has something to do with the arrangement of 8-bit chunks of data, but who cares? You want PC or you want Mac? It's that simple.

✦ **Save Image Pyramid:** Choose this option to save *tiled* TIFF files. This variation of the standard TIFF file-saving algorithm divides your image into tiles and then stacks the tiles in a pyramid. Each level of the pyramid represents your image at a different resolution, with the highest-resolution version serving as the base of the pyramid. The idea is that an application can use the low-resolution tiles to perform certain image-processing tasks and dig down to the high-resolution version only when absolutely necessary. When you're working with very large image files, this approach not only speeds up certain editing tasks but also puts less strain on your computer's resources. (If you're familiar with the FlashPix format, the concept is the same.)

Unless you're saving your image for use in a program that you know supports tiled TIFF images, however, turn this option off. Photoshop itself can't take advantage of the tiled technology, and many applications can't open tiled images at all.

✦ **Save Transparency:** If the image contains transparent areas, select this check box to retain the transparency. Otherwise, transparent areas become white.

If you've been working with Photoshop for a few years, you may be wondering what happened to the File ⇨ Import ⇨ QuickEdit command. This feature enabled you to open and edit just a small portion of a large TIFF file. QuickEdit can't deal with compressed TIFF files or properly process edits that you make to a layered TIFF file. So Adobe no longer provides QuickEdit on the Photoshop CD and strongly advises against using it to edit Photoshop 6 TIFF files.

The oddball formats

Can you believe it? After plowing through a half-million formats, I still haven't covered them all. The last three are the odd men out. One format has a purpose so specific that Photoshop can open files saved in the format but it can't save to the format. The second is a new format that, while moderately promising, is not implemented thoroughly enough inside Photoshop to provide much benefit. And the last is less a format than a manual can opener that may come in handy for jimmying open a file from an unknown source.

Photo CD YCC images

Photoshop can open Eastman Kodak's Photo CD and Pro Photo CD formats directly. A Photo CD contains compressed versions of every image in each of the five scan sizes provided on Photo CDs — from 128×192 pixels (72K) to $2,048 \times 3,072$ pixels (18MB).

The Pro Photo CD format can accommodate each of the five sizes included in the regular Photo CD format, plus one additional size — $4,096 \times 6,144$ pixels (72MB) — that's four times as large as the largest image on a regular Photo CD. As a result, Pro Photo CDs hold only 25 scans; standard Photo CDs hold 100. Like their standard Photo CD counterparts, Pro Photo CD scanners can accommodate 35mm film and slides. But they can also handle 70mm film and 4×5-inch negatives and transparencies. The cost might knock you out, though. While scanning an image to a standard Photo CD costs between $1 and $2, scanning it to a Pro Photo CD costs about $10. This goes to show you, once you gravitate beyond consumerland, everyone expects you to start coughing up the big bucks.

Both Photo CD and Pro Photo CD use the YCC color model, a variation on the CIE (Commission Internationale de'Eclairage) color space, which I discuss in the next chapter. YCC provides a broader range of color — theoretically, every color your eye can see. By opening Photo CD files directly, you can translate the YCC images directly to Photoshop's Lab color mode, another variation on the CIE color space that ensures no color loss. When you open a Photo CD image, Photoshop displays the dialog box shown in Figure 3-17.

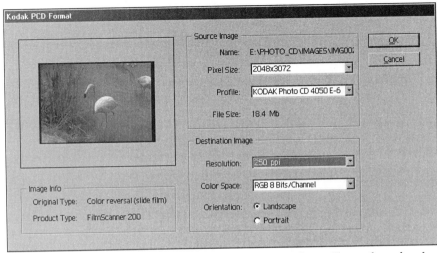

Figure 3-17: Use these options to select a resolution and to calibrate the colors in the Photo CD image.

Note   Finding your photos on a Photo CD is a little harder than it should be. Look inside the Images folder in the Photo_CD folder. The files have friendly names such as Img0017.pcd.

The newly redesigned Photo CD dialog box is divided into three main sections: Image Info, Source, and Destination. The Image Info section simply tells you the type of film on which the image was shot and the type of scanner used to scan the image to CD. Selections that you make in the Source and Destination areas tell Photoshop how you want it to open the image. Here's what you need to know:

✦ **Pixel Size:** Select which of the available image sizes you want to use from this pop-up menu.

✦ **Profile:** Use this pop-up menu to select the kind of film from which the original photographs were scanned. You can select from one of the variations on Kodak's film brands — E-6 for Ektachrome or K-14 for Kodachrome — or settle for the generic Color Negative V3.0 Film option. Your selection determines the method Photoshop uses to transform the colors in the image.

✦ **Resolution:** This setting determines the output resolution and size at which Photoshop opens the image. You get the same number of image pixels no matter what — that's controlled by the Pixel Size option. In other words, changing this value is no different than changing the Resolution value in the Image Size dialog box with Resample Image turned off.

✦ **Color Space:** Select an option from this pop-up menu to specify the color model you want to use. Select RGB to open the image in the RGB mode; select LAB to open the image in the Lab mode. You can also select from 8 Bits/Channel to edit the image in 24-bit color or 16 Bits/Channel to open the image in 48-bit color.

✦ **Orientation:** The preview in the left side of the dialog box shows you the original orientation of the image. If you want to change that orientation, click the other Orientation radio button. The preview updates to show you the new orientation.

Photoshop cannot save to the Photo CD format. And frankly, there's little reason you'd want to do so. Photo CD is strictly a means for transferring slides and film negatives onto the world's most ubiquitous and indestructible storage medium, the CD-ROM.

Note

Kodak also offers a product called Picture CD, which is quite different from Photo CD—don't get the two confused. With Picture CD, consumers can drop off rolls of undeveloped film and receive both traditional prints and a CD containing scanned versions of their pictures. Picture CD images are provided in the JPEG format, so none of the Photo CD file-opening features discussed here apply. You open Picture CD images like any other JPEG file.

Opening raw documents

A *raw document* is a plain binary file stripped of all extraneous information. It contains no compression scheme, specifies no bit depth or image size, and offers no color mode. Each byte of data indicates a brightness value on a single color channel, and that's it. Photoshop offers this function specifically so you can open images created in undocumented formats, such as those created on mainframe computers.

To open an image of unknown origin, choose File ⇨ Open As. Then select the desired image from the scrolling list and choose Raw (*.*raw*) from the Open As pop-up menu. After you press Enter, the dialog box shown in Figure 3-18 appears, featuring these options:

✦ **Width, Height:** If you know the dimensions of the image in pixels, enter the values in these option boxes.

✦ **Swap:** Click this button to swap the Width value with the Height value.

✦ **Count:** Enter the number of color channels in this option box. If the document is an RGB image, enter 3; if it is a CMYK image, enter 4.

✦ **Interleaved:** Select this value if the color values are stored sequentially by pixels. In an RGB image, the first byte represents the red value for the first pixel, the second byte represents the green value for that pixel, the third the blue value, and so on. If you turn this check box off, the first byte represents the red value for the first pixel, the second value represents the red value for the second pixel, and so on. When Photoshop finishes describing the red channel, it describes the green channel and then the blue channel.

✦ **Depth:** Select the number of bits per color channel. Most images contain 8 bits per channel, but scientific scans from mainframe computers may contain 16.

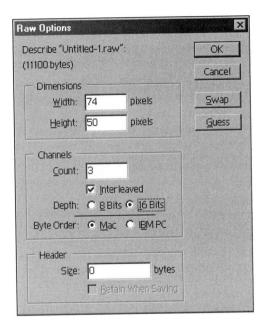

Figure 3-18: Photoshop requires you to specify the size of an image and the number of color channels when you open an image that does not conform to a standardized file format.

✦ **Byte Order:** If you specify 16 bits per channel, you must tell Photoshop whether the image comes from a Mac or a PC.

✦ **Header:** This value tells Photoshop how many bytes of data at the beginning of the file comprise header information it can ignore.

✦ **Retain When Saving:** If the Header value is greater than zero, you can instruct Photoshop to retain this data when you save the image in a different format.

✦ **Guess:** If you know the Width and Height values, but you don't know the number of bytes in the header — or vice versa — you can ask Photoshop for help. Fill in either the Dimensions or Header information and then click the Guess button to ask Photoshop to take a stab at the unknown value. Photoshop estimates all this information when the Raw Options dialog box first appears. Generally speaking, if it doesn't estimate correctly the first time around, you're on your own. But hey, the Guess button is worth a shot.

Tip

If a raw document is a CMYK image, it opens as an RGB image with an extra masking channel. To display the image correctly, choose Image ➪ Mode ➪ Multichannel to free the four channels from their incorrect relationship. Then recombine them by choosing Image ➪ Mode ➪ CMYK Color.

Saving a raw document

Photoshop also enables you to save to the raw document format. This capability is useful when you create files you want to transfer to mainframe systems or output to devices that don't support other formats, such as the Kodak XL7700.

Caution
Do not save 256-color indexed images to the raw format or you will lose the color lookup table and, therefore, lose all color information. Be sure to convert such images first to RGB or one of the other full-color modes before saving.

When you save an image in the raw document format, Photoshop presents the dialog box shown in Figure 3-19. The dialog box options work as follows:

✦ **File Type:** This option is a carry-over from the Macintosh, where it defines information for the resource fork. In Windows, the option is always dimmed. Feel free to ignore.

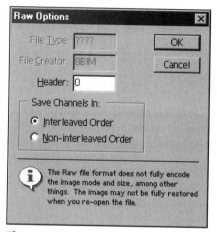

Figure 3-19: When saving a raw document, ignore the file type and creator codes and specify the order of data in the file.

✦ **File Creator:** Ditto. The default code 8BIM is selected for you and the option is dimmed.

✦ **Header:** Enter the size of the header in bytes. If you enter any value but zero, you must fill in the header using a data editor such as Norton Disk Editor.

✦ **Save Channels In:** Select the Interleaved Order option to arrange data sequentially by pixels, as described earlier. To group data by color channel, select Non-interleaved Order.

Still can't get that file open?

File format specs are continually evolving. As a result, programs that provide support for a particular format may not support the specific version of the format used to save the file you're trying to open. For example, JPEG is notorious for causing problems because there were several private implementations in the early days. As a result, some JPEG files can only be read by the originating application.

If you can't open a file in Photoshop, you may have another program that can read and write the problem format. Try the problem file in every program you have — and every program your friends have. After all, what are friends for?

You may also want to try a program such as HiJaak or TransverterPro. And Windows has recently been blessed by DeBabelizer Pro from Equilibrium (*www.equilibrium. com*). Absolutely the best format converter bar none, DeBabelizer handles every format Photoshop handles, as well as Dr. Halo's CUT, Fractal Design Painter's RIFF, the animation formats PICS, FLI, and ANM, as well as UNIX workstation formats for Silicon Graphics, Sun Microsystems, and others.

Still out of it? Go online and check out such forums as ADOBEAPPS on CompuServe. The Usenet newsgroups *comp.graphics.apps.photoshop* and *rec.photo.digital* are other good resources. Post a question about your problem; chances are good someone may have an answer for you.

Adding file information and annotations

On top of pixels, alpha channels, color profiles, and all the other image data you can cram into your image files, you can add a variety of reference information — where you shot the picture, who owns the image copyright, and so on. In Version 6, this extra data can take the form of cataloging information that you enter in the File Info dialog box or text and audio annotations that you can view and play right from the image window. The next few sections explain these options.

Recording file information

If you work for a stock agency or distribute your work by some other means, you may be interested in Photoshop's File ⇨ File Info command. Using this command, you can record captions, credits, bylines, photo location and date, copyright, and other information as prescribed by the Newspaper Association of America (NAA) and the International Press Telecommunications Council (IPTC). We're talking official worldwide guidelines here.

After you choose the File Info command, you see the six-paneled File Info dialog box, shown in Figure 3-20. You switch from one panel to another by pressing Ctrl+1 through Ctrl+6 or choosing the panel name from the Section pop-up menu. Alt+N and Alt+P also go to the next and previous panel, respectively. The first panel, the Caption panel, appears in Figure 3-20.

Although sprawling with options, this dialog box is pretty straightforward. For example, if you want to create a caption, travel to the Caption panel and enter your caption into the Caption option box, which can hold up to 2,000 characters. If you select Caption in the Page Setup dialog box, the caption appears underneath the image when you print it from Photoshop.

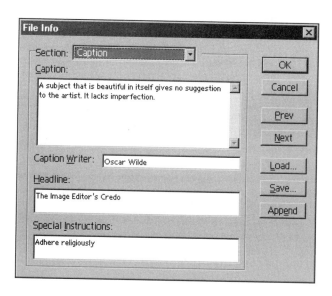

Figure 3-20: You can document your image in encyclopedic detail using the wealth of options in the File Info dialog box.

The Keywords panel enables you to enter a list of descriptive words that will help folks find the image if it's part of a large electronic library. Just enter the desired word and press Enter (or click the Add button) to add the keyword to the list. Or you can replace a word in the list by selecting it, entering a new word, and pressing Enter (or clicking Replace). Likewise, you can delete a selected keyword by clicking Delete. Browser utilities enable you to search images by keyword, as do some dedicated image servers.

The Categories panel may seem foreign to anyone who hasn't worked with a news service. Many large news services use a system of three-character categories to file and organize stories and photographs. If you're familiar with this system, you can enter the three-character code into the Category option box and even throw in a few supplemental categories up to 32 characters long. Finally, use the Urgency pop-up menu to specify the editorial timeliness of the photo. The High option tells editors around the world to hold the presses and holler for their copy boys. The Low option is for celebrity mug shots that can be tossed in the morgue to haul out only if the subject of the photograph decides to do something diverting, like lead police on a nail-biting tour of the Los Angeles freeway system.

The Copyright & URL panel enables you to add a copyright notice to your image. If you check the Mark as Copyrighted check box, a copyright symbol (©) will appear in the window title bar and in the preview box in the status bar along the bottom of the screen. This symbol tells people viewing the image they can go to the Copyright & URL panel to get more information about the owner of the image copyright.

You can also include the URL for your Web site, if you have one. Then, when folks have your image open in Photoshop, they can come to this panel and click the Go to URL button to launch their Web browsers and jump to the URL.

Because only people who open your image in Photoshop have access to the information in the File Info dialog box, you may want to embed a digital watermark into your image as well. Many watermarking programs exist, ranging from simple tools that merely imprint copyright data to those that build in protection features designed to prevent illegal downloading and reproduction of images. Photoshop provides a watermarking utility from Digimarc as a plug-in on the Filters menu; before using the plug-in, visit the Digimarc Web site (*www.digimarc.com*) to find out which, if any, of the Digimarc watermarking schemes best suits the type of work you do.

File information is only saved in file formats that support saving extra data with the file. This includes the native Photoshop (.psd) format, Encapsulated PostScript (.eps), PDF (.pdf), JPEG (.jpg), and TIFF (.tif). Because you cannot format the text in the File Info dialog box, it consumes little space on disk — 1 byte per character — meaning that you can fill in every option box without adding 1K.

You can also save the information from the File Info dialog box by clicking the Save button. Or open information saved to disk previously by clicking Load. To add the information from a saved file to the information you've already entered into the File Info dialog box, click the Append button.

Using the Actions palette, you can create an action that adds your specific copyright, byline, and URL to an image. After recording the action, you can automatically add the information to an entire folder of files using File ➪ Automate ➪ Batch. For more information on the Actions palette and Batch command, read the last half of Chapter B on this book's CD-ROM.

Taping notes to your image

Photoshop 6 enables you to slap the digital equivalent of a sticky note onto your image. The notes can be viewed in Adobe Acrobat (assuming that you save the image in the PDF format) as well as in Photoshop 6. You can jot down ideas that you want to remember later, for example. Or, if you're routing an image for approval, you can ask questions about a certain image element — or, more likely, explain why a part of the picture looks the way it does and why changing it would be an absolute *travesty* and *total* abdication of your artistic integrity.

The Photoshop notes tool works like its counterpart in Adobe Acrobat: Click in the image window to display a blank note, as shown in Figure 3-21, or drag to create a custom-sized note. If you don't see your name in the Author box on the Options bar, double-click the box and type your name. (By default, Photoshop displays the user name you entered when you installed the program.) Type your comments — all the standard text-editing techniques apply — and then click the close box in the upper-left corner of the note window. Your note shrinks to a little note icon, as shown in the figure. Double-click the icon to redisplay the note text.

Note icon

Open note

Figure 3-21: After adding text-based notes or audio comments to an image, save the file in the PDF format so that others can access the annotations when viewing the image in Adobe Acrobat.

When you save your image, be sure to save in the Photoshop native format or PDF and select the Annotations check box in the Save dialog box. Otherwise, you lose all your notes. For information on how to delete individual notes in an open image and how to customize and import notes, skip to the section "Managing annotations."

Voicing your opinions

If you like to speak your mind rather than put your thoughts in writing, check out the audio annotation tool. This tool works like the notes tool except that it inserts an audio recording of your voice rather than a text message into the file. Of course, you need a microphone, speakers, and a sound card installed in your computer to use this feature. Also, Photoshop retains audio annotations only when you save the image file using the Photoshop native format or PDF, as with text notes. Be aware, too, that audio files increase file size significantly.

The audio annotation tool shares quarters with the notes tool in the toolbox. Press N to toggle between the two tools (or Shift+N, depending on the preference you established in the General panel of the Preferences dialog box). Click in your image at the spot where you want the icon representing your message to appear.

When the Audio Annotation dialog box appears, click Start to begin your recording and then talk into the microphone. Click Stop when you've said all you have to say.

Photoshop represents your audio message with a little speaker icon in the image window. Double-click the icon to play the message.

Managing annotations

If you're a solo artist and the only approval of your work you need is your own, you may not have much reason to use the notes or audio annotation tools. Then again, you may be an easily distracted sort and find annotations a terrific way to remind yourself exactly what you're trying to accomplish in an image. And who's to say that your friends won't love being able to hear an audio clip of your dog Binky yapping at the vacuum cleaner when they view his picture in Acrobat?

Whether you're using annotations for fun or profit, use the following strategies to manage audio and text annotations:

✦ Use the Font and Size controls on the Options bar to change the font and type size in an open note.

✦ Click the Color icon to change the color of the icon and title bar for any new note you create. This option comes in handy if several people will be reviewing the image and putting in their two cents' worth. You can assign a different color to each author. To change the color of an existing note, open the note and click the Color icon. This time, you affect only the open note — other notes by the same author don't change.

✦ You can move and copy annotations between image windows. Just click the icon and use the Cut, Copy, and Paste commands as you do to move and copy any selection.

✦ If an icon blocks your view of the image, you can drag it out of the way. However, when you open the note, its window appears in the icon's original location. Drag the size box in the lower-right corner of an open note to shrink the window if necessary.

✦ Choose View ➪ Show ➪ Notes to toggle the display of annotation icons on and off. Alternatively, choose View ➪ Hide All and View ➪ Show All to hide and display icons and other interface elements such as selection marquees, guides, and so on.

✦ To delete a single annotation, click its icon and press Delete. Or right-click the icon and choose Delete Note. If you want to delete all annotations, choose Delete All Notes or click the Clear All button on the Options bar.

Tip

If you send out several copies of the same image for approval, you don't have to open each copy individually to read the annotations. Instead, open just one copy and then import the annotations from the other files. Choose File ➪ Import ➪ Annotations, select the files containing the annotations, and click Open. Photoshop gathers up all the annotations and dumps them into your open image.

Caution Remember to save your image in the PDF or Photoshop 6 file format to retain annotations in a file. And if you're sending an annotated file to other people for viewing, tell them that they need to use Adobe Acrobat 4.0 or higher to access the annotations.

Resampling and Cropping

After you bring up an image — whether you created it from scratch or opened an existing image stored in one of the five billion formats discussed in the preceding pages — its size and resolution are established. Neither size nor resolution is set in stone, however. Photoshop provides two methods for changing the number of pixels in an image: resampling and cropping.

Resizing versus resampling

Typically, when folks talk about *resizing* an image, they mean enlarging or reducing it without changing the number of pixels in the image, as demonstrated back in Figure 3-1. By contrast, *resampling* an image means scaling it so the image contains a larger or smaller number of pixels. With resizing, an inverse relationship exists between size and resolution — size increases when resolution decreases, and vice versa. But resampling affects either size or resolution independently. Figure 3-22 shows an image resized and resampled to 50 percent of its original dimensions. The resampled and original images have identical resolutions, but the resized image has twice the resolution of its companions.

Resizing an image

To resize an image, use one of the techniques discussed in the "Changing the printing resolution" section near the beginning of this chapter. To recap briefly, the best method is to choose Image ➪ Image Size, turn off the Resample Image check box, and enter a value into the Resolution option box. See Figure 3-2 to refresh your memory.

Resampling an image

You also use Image ➪ Image Size to resample an image. The difference is that you leave the Resample Image check box turned on, as shown in Figure 3-23. As its name implies, the Resample Image check box is the key to resampling.

When Resample Image is selected, the Resolution value is independent of both sets of Width and Height values. (The only difference between the two sets of options is that the top options work in pixels and the bottom options work in relative units of measure such as percent and inches.) You can increase the number of pixels in an image by increasing any of the five values in the dialog box; you can decrease the number of pixels by decreasing any value. Photoshop stretches or shrinks the image according to the new size specifications.

Original

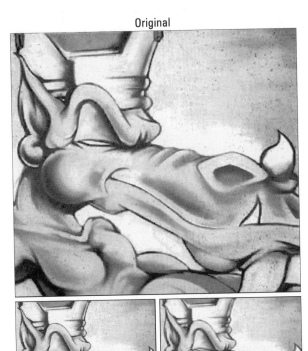

Resized   Resampled

Figure 3-22: An image (top) resized (bottom left) and resampled (bottom right) down to 50 percent. The resized image sports a higher resolution; the resampled one contains fewer pixels.

At all times, you can see the new number of pixels Photoshop will assign to the image, as well as the increased or decreased file size. In Figure 3-23, for example, I've changed the first Width value to 56 percent. The Pixel Dimensions value at the top of the dialog box reflects my change by reading *5.12M (was 16.3M),* which shows that the file size has decreased.

To calculate the pixels in the resampled image, Photoshop must use its powers of interpolation, as explained in the "General preferences" section of Chapter 2. The interpolation setting defaults to the one chosen in the Preferences dialog box. But you can also change the setting right inside the Image Size dialog box. Simply select the desired method from the Resample Image pop-up menu. Bicubic results in the smoothest effects. Bilinear is faster. And Nearest Neighbor turns off interpolation so Photoshop merely throws away the pixels it doesn't need or duplicates pixels to resample up.

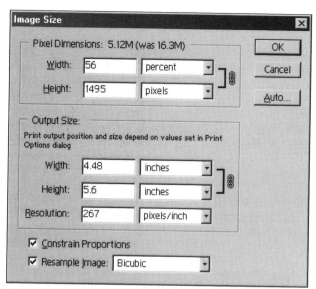

Figure 3-23: With the Resample Image check box turned on, you can modify the number of pixels in your image.

Here are a few more random items you should know about resampling with the Image Size dialog box:

✦ This may sound odd, but you generally want to avoid adding pixels. When you resample up, you're asking Photoshop to make up details from thin air, and the program isn't that smart. Simply put, an enlarged image almost never looks better than the original; it merely takes up more disk space and prints slower.

✦ Resampling down, on the other hand, is a useful technique. It enables you to smooth away photo grain, halftone patterns, and other scanning artifacts. One of the most tried-and-true rules is to scan at the maximum resolution permitted by your scanner and then resample the scan down to, say, 72 or 46 percent (with the interpolation set to Bicubic, naturally). By selecting a round value other than 50 percent, you force Photoshop to jumble the pixels into a regular, homogenous soup. You're left with fewer pixels, but these remaining pixels are better. And you have the added benefit that the image takes up less space on disk.

✦ To make an image tall and thin or short and fat, you must first turn off the Constrain Proportions check box. This enables you to edit the two Width values entirely independently of the two Height values.

Tip

✦ You can resample an image to match precisely the size and resolution of any other open image. While the Image Size dialog box is open, choose the name of the image you want to match from the Window menu.

✦ If you need help resampling an image to the proper size for a print job, choose Help ➪ Resize Image to bring up the Resize Image Wizard. The dialog box walks you through the process of resampling step by step. It's really for rank beginners, but you might find it helpful when you want to turn the old brain off and set Photoshop to autopilot. (Note that Adobe uses the word "resize" simply because it's friendlier than "resample." Whatever it's called, this command does indeed resample.)

If you ever get confused inside the Image Size dialog box and you want to return to the original size and resolution settings, press the Alt key to change the Cancel button to Reset. Then click the Reset button to start from the beginning.

Caution

Photoshop remembers the setting of the Resample Image check box and uses this same setting the next time you open the Image Size dialog box. This can trip you up if you record an action for the Actions palette, as discussed in Chapter B on this book's CD-ROM. Suppose that you create an action to resize images, turning Resample Image off. If you later resample an image — turning on Resample Image — the check box stays selected when you close the dialog box. The next time you run the action, you end up resampling instead of resizing. Always check the status of the check box before you apply the Image Size command or run any actions containing the command.

Cropping

Another way to change the number of pixels in an image is to *crop* it, which means to clip away pixels around the edges of an image without harming the remaining pixels. (The one exception occurs when you rotate a cropped image or use the new perspective crop feature, in which case Photoshop has to interpolate pixels to account for the rotation.)

Cropping enables you to focus on an element in your image. For example, Figure 3-24 shows a bit of urban graffiti from a Digital Stock CD. I like this fellow's face — good chiaroscuro — but I can't quite figure out what's going on with this guy. I mean, what's with the screw? And is that a clown hat or what? That's the problem with graffiti — no art direction. Luckily, I can crop around the guy's head to delete the extraneous image elements and hone in on his sleepy features, as shown in Figure 3-25.

Version 6 offers several new, cutting-edge cropping options — har har — including the capability to crop nonrectangular selections, automatically trim away transparent areas from the borders of an image, and correct perspective effects while cropping. You can read about all these features in the upcoming sections.

Figure 3-24: This image contains too much extraneous information. Where should my eye go? I'm so confused.

Figure 3-25: Cropping enables you to clean up the background junk and focus on the essential foreground image.

Changing the canvas size

One way to crop an image is to choose Image ⇨ Canvas Size, which displays the Canvas Size dialog box shown in Figure 3-26. The options in this dialog box enable you to scale the imaginary canvas on which the image rests separately from the image itself.

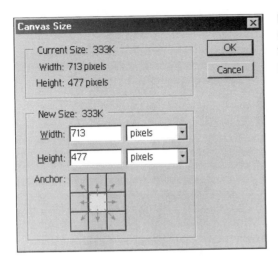

Figure 3-26: Choose Image ⇨ Canvas Size to crop an image or to add empty space around the perimeter of an image.

If you enlarge the canvas, Photoshop surrounds the image with a white background (assuming the background color is white). If you reduce the canvas, you crop the image.

Click inside the Anchor grid to specify the placement of the image on the new canvas. For example, if you want to add space to the bottom of an image, enlarge the canvas size and then click inside the upper-middle square. If you want to crop away the upper-left corner of an image, create a smaller canvas size and then click the lower-right square. The Anchor grid offers little arrows to show how the canvas will shrink or grow.

To shrink the canvas so that it exactly fits the image, don't waste your time with the Canvas Size dialog box. Using a nifty new command, Image ⇨ Trim, you can automatically clip away empty canvas areas on the outskirts of your image. When you choose the command, the dialog box shown in Figure 3-27 appears. To snip away empty canvas, select the Transparent Pixels radio button. Then specify which edges of the canvas you want to slice off by using the four Trim Away check boxes. Alternatively, you can tell Photoshop to trim the image based on the pixel color in the top-left corner of the image or the bottom-right corner — just click the appropriate Based On radio button. For example, if you have a blue stripe running down the left edge of your image and you select the Top Left Pixel Color radio button, Photoshop clips away the stripe. No trimming occurs unless the entire edge of the image is bounded by the selected color.

Tip

When you want to enlarge the canvas but aren't concerned with making it a specific size, try this time-saving trick: Drag with the crop tool to create a crop marquee and then enlarge the crop marquee beyond the boundaries of the image (see the next section if you need help). When you press Enter to apply the crop, the canvas grows to match the size of the crop marquee.

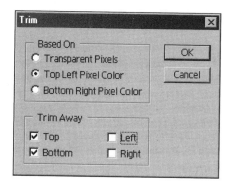

Figure 3-27: To quickly snip away transparent areas from the edges of an image, use the new Image ⇨ Trim command.

Using the crop tool

Generally speaking, the Canvas Size command is most useful for enlarging the canvas or shaving a few pixels off the edge of an image. If you want to crop away a large portion of an image, using the crop tool is a better choice.

Press C or click the crop icon in the toolbox to activate the tool. The crop tool regains its own slot in the toolbox in Version 6, which means that you no longer have to slog through the marquee flyout menu to select the tool. And that's just the beginning of the changes to the crop tool. You still drag with the tool to create a rectangular marquee that surrounds the portion of the image you want to retain. But you can control what happens during and after you crop in two important ways:

✦ To help you distinguish the borders of the crop marquee, Photoshop displays a colored, translucent overlay on the area outside the crop box — similar to the way it indicates masked versus unmasked areas when you work in the quick mask mode. Hate the overlay? Deselect the Shield Cropped Area check box on the Options bar. You also can click the neighboring color box to change the overlay and set the overlay opacity through the Opacity pop-up menu. Note that these controls don't appear on the Options bar until after you create your initial crop marquee.

✦ You now have the option of permanently discarding the pixels you crop or simply hiding them from view. Before you drag with the crop tool, click the Delete or Hide radio button on the Options bar to signify your preference. If you choose Hide, you can bring the hidden regions back into view by enlarging the canvas or by using the new Image ⇨ Reveal All command.

Tip   As you drag, you can press the spacebar to move the crop boundary temporarily on the fly. To stop moving the boundary and return to resizing it, release the spacebar.

If you don't get the crop marquee right the first time, you can move, scale, or rotate it at will. Here's what you do:

✦ Drag inside the crop marquee to move it.

✦ Drag one of the square handles to resize the marquee. You can Shift-drag a handle to scale the marquee proportionally (the same percentage vertically and horizontally).

✦ Drag outside the crop marquee to rotate it, as explained in the next section. This may strike you as weird at first, but it works wonderfully.

✦ Drag the origin point (labeled in Figure 3-28) to change the center of a rotation.

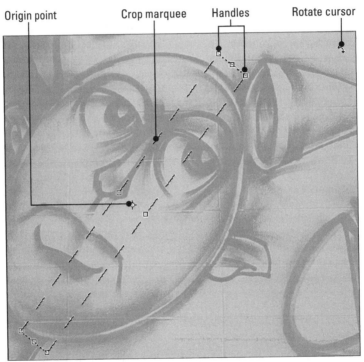

Figure 3-28: Align the crop marquee with an obvious axis in your image to determine the proper angle of rotation.

✦ Select the Perspective check box on the Options bar, and you can drag corner handles to distort the image. What's the point? Well, the primary reason to use this option is to correct convergence problems that often occur when you take pictures using a wide-angle lens. Vertical structures along the edges of the image tend to lean one way or another due to the design of the lens.

The problem is, you can't preview the results of your drags or undo the distortion, which makes correcting convergence with the crop tool a hit-or-miss proposition. So I suggest that you tackle convergence problems using the Free Transform command, covered in Chapter 12, and do your cropping afterwards.

When the marquee surrounds the exact portion of the image you want to keep, apply the crop by pressing Enter or double-clicking inside the marquee. You also can click the OK button on the Options bar, which is the giant check mark at the right end of the bar.

If you change your mind about cropping, you can cancel the crop marquee by pressing Escape or clicking the Cancel button, the big X next to the check mark on the Options bar.

Rotating the crop marquee

As I said, you can rotate an image by dragging outside the crop marquee. Straightening a crooked image, however, can be a little tricky. I wish I had a certified check for every time I thought I had the marquee rotated properly, only to find the image was still crooked after I pressed Enter. If this happens to you, choose Edit ⇨ Undo (Ctrl+Z) and try again. Do not try using the crop tool a second time to rotate the already rotated image. If you do, Photoshop sets about interpolating between already interpolated pixels, resulting in more lost data. Every rotation gets farther away from the original image.

Tip

A better solution is to do it right the first time. Locate a line or general axis in your image that should be straight up and down. Rotate the crop marquee so it aligns exactly with this axis. In Figure 3-28, I rotated my crop marquee so one edge bisects the graffiti guy's egg-shaped head. Don't worry, this isn't how you want to crop the image — you're just using the line as a reference. After you arrive at the correct angle for the marquee, drag the handles to size and position the boundary properly. As long as you don't drag outside the marquee, its angle remains fixed throughout.

Yet another solution is to use the measure tool. Just drag with the tool along the axis you want to make vertical and note the angle (A:) value in the Info palette. I don't like this technique as much because it requires you to do some unnatural math — depending on how you drag, you may have to subtract 90 degrees from the A: value or subtract the A: value from 90 degrees. Then you keep an eye on the Info palette and rotate until you get an A: value that matches the answer to the previous equation. If you like math, great. If not, it's much simpler to use the technique I suggested in the preceding paragraph.

Cropping an image to match another

There are two ways to crop an image so it matches the size and resolution of another image:

✦ Bring the image you want to crop forward and choose Image ⇨ Canvas Size. Then, while inside the Canvas Size dialog box, select the name of the image you want to match from the Window menu.

This method doesn't give you much control when cropping an image, but it's a great way to enlarge the canvas and add empty space around an image.

✦ Better yet, use the crop tool in its fixed-size mode. This feature works differently than in versions past, so pay attention: First, bring the image you want to match to the front. Then select the crop tool and click the Front Image button on the Options bar. (Don't waste time looking for the old Fixed Target Size option — it's gone. The tool automatically shifts into fixed-size mode when you click the Front Image button.) The Width, Height, and Resolution options automatically update to show the size and resolution of the front image.

Now bring the image you want to crop to the front and drag with the crop tool as normal. Photoshop constrains the crop marquee to the proportions of the targeted image. After you press Enter, Photoshop crops, resamples, and rotates the image as necessary.

The next time you select the crop tool, it starts out in fixed-size mode. To return the tool to normal, click the Clear button on the Options bar.

Cropping a selection

Another way to crop an image is to create a selection and then choose Image ⇨ Crop. As with the Version 6 crop tool, the Crop command gives you the option of permanently eliminating cropped pixels or simply hiding them in the image file. You can bring back hidden pixels at any time by choosing Image ⇨ Reveal All or simply enlarging the canvas. (If you save the image in a file format other than the native Photoshop format, however, hidden pixels are abandoned forever.)

One advantage of the Crop command is that you needn't switch back and forth between the marquee and crop tools. One tool is all you need to select and crop. (If you're as lazy as I am, the mere act of selecting a tool can prove more effort than it's worth.) And, as with the crop tool, you can now press the spacebar while you draw a marquee to move it on the fly. It's no trick to get the placement and size exactly right — the only thing you can't do is rotate.

Another advantage of the Crop command is flexibility. With the Crop command, you get all the following options:

✦ After drawing a selection, you can switch windows, apply commands, and generally use any function you like prior to choosing Image ➪ Crop. The crop tool, by contrast, is much more limiting. After drawing a cropping marquee, you can't do anything but adjust the marquee until you press Enter to accept the crop or Escape to dismiss it.

✦ You can use the Crop command on selections of any shape, even feathered selections and multiple discontiguous selections. Of course, your image canvas remains rectangular no matter what the selection shape. Photoshop simply crops the canvas to the smallest size that can hold all selected areas.

✦ Finally, Image ➪ Crop lets you crop the canvas to the boundaries of an image pasted from the Clipboard or dragged and dropped from another image window. As long as the boundaries of the pasted image are rectangular, as in the case of an image copied from a different application, you can choose Edit ➪ Paste, Ctrl-click the new layer in the Layers palette to regain the selection outline, and then choose Image ➪ Crop. Photoshop replaces the former image and crops the window to fit the new image.

✦   ✦   ✦

Painting and Retouching

Defining Colors

Selecting and Editing Colors

Occasionally, the state of computer graphics technology reminds me of television in the early 1950s. Only the upper echelon of Photoshop artists can afford to work exclusively in the wonderful world of color. The rest of us have to be prepared to print many or even most of our images in black and white.

Cross-Reference

Some of you might be thinking, "Wait a second, what about the equalizing force of the Internet? It brings color to all of us!" Well, I concur wholeheartedly. Nearly everyone owns a color monitor, so we can all share color images freely. If this appeals to you, advance to Chapter 19 and learn how you can reduce color palettes and otherwise prepare your images for the bold new challenges of the Technicolor Web.

Regardless of who you are — print person or Web head — color is a prime concern. Even gray values, after all, are colors. Many folks have problems accepting this premise — I guess we're all so used to separating the worlds of grays and other colors in our minds that never the two shall meet. But gray values are only variations on what Noah Webster used to call "The sensation resulting from stimulation of the retina of the eye by light waves of certain lengths." (Give the guy a few drinks and he'd spout off 19 more definitions, not including the meanings of the transitive verb.) Just as black and white represent a subset of gray, gray is a subset of color. In fact, you'll find that using Photoshop involves a lot of navigating through these and other colorful subsets.

Specifying colors

First off, Photoshop provides four color controls in the toolbox, as shown in Figure 4-1. These icons work as follows:

✦ **Foreground color:** The foreground color icon indicates the color you apply when you use the type, paint bucket, line, pencil, airbrush, or paintbrush tool, or if you Alt-drag with the smudge tool. The foreground color also begins any gradation created with the gradient tool (assuming that you create a custom gradient, not one of the prefab gradients available through the gradient styles pop-up menu).

Photoshop fills any shapes you create with the new shape tool with the foreground color. You can apply the foreground color to a standard selection by choosing Edit ➪ Fill or Edit ➪ Stroke or by pressing Alt+Backspace.

To change the foreground color, click the foreground color icon to display the Color Picker dialog box, select a new color in the Color palette, or click an open image window with the eyedropper tool. You also can set the foreground color by clicking a swatch in the Swatches palette (both explained later in this chapter).

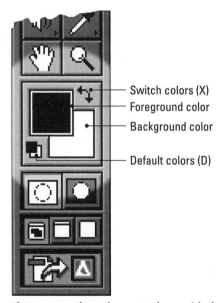

Switch colors (X)
Foreground color
Background color

Default colors (D)

Figure 4-1: The color controls provided with Photoshop (along with keyboard shortcuts in parentheses, where applicable).

✦ **Background color:** The active background color indicates the color you apply with the eraser tool. The background color also ends any custom gradation created with the gradient tool. To change the background color, click the background color icon to display the Color Picker dialog box. Or define the color by using the Color palette, clicking a swatch in the Swatches palette, or Alt-clicking any open image window with the eyedropper tool.

You can apply the background color to a selection by pressing Backspace or Delete. But if the selection is floating or exists on any layer except the background layer, Backspace actually deletes the selection instead of filling it. For complete safety, avoid the Backspace key and use Ctrl+Backspace to fill a selection with the background color instead.

✦ **Switch colors:** Click this icon (or press X) to exchange the foreground and background colors.

✦ **Default colors:** Click this icon (or press D) to make the foreground color black and the background color white, according to their factory default settings. If you're editing a layer mask or an adjustment layer, the default colors are reversed, as explained in Chapter 12.

Using the Color Picker

When you click the foreground or background color icon in the toolbox or the Color palette, Photoshop displays the Color Picker dialog box. (This assumes that Adobe is the active option in the Color Picker pop-up menu in the General Preferences dialog box. If you select the Windows option, the generic Windows Color Picker appears; see Chapter 2 on why you shouldn't select this option.) Figure 4-2 labels the wealth of elements and options in the Color Picker dialog box, which work as follows:

✦ **Color slider:** Use the color slider to home in on the color you want to select. Drag up or down on either of the slider triangles to select a color from a particular 8-bit range. The colors represented inside the slider correspond to the selected radio button. For example, if you select the H (Hue) radio button, which is the default setting, the slider colors represent the full 8-bit range of hues. If you select S (Saturation), the slider shows the current hue at full saturation at the top of the slider, down to no saturation—or gray—at the bottom of the slider. If you select B (Brightness), the slider shows the 8-bit range of brightness values, from solid color at the top of the slider to absolute black at the bottom. You also can select R (Red), G (Green), or B (Blue), in which case the top of the slider shows you what the current color looks like when subjected to full-intensity red, green, or blue (respectively), and the bottom of the slider shows every bit of red, green, or blue subtracted.

Cross-Reference

For a proper introduction to the HSB and RGB color models, including definitions of specific terms such as hue, saturation, and brightness, read the "Working in Different Color Modes" section later in this chapter.

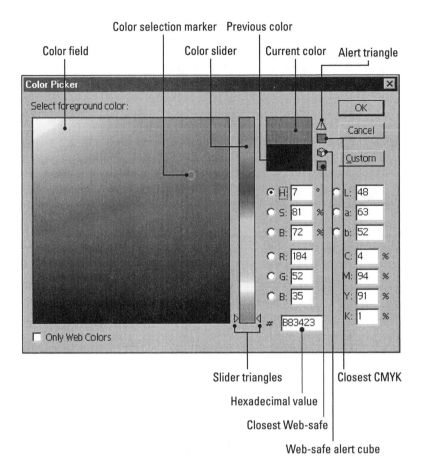

Figure 4-2: Use the elements and options in the Color Picker dialog box to specify a new foreground or background color from the 16-million-color range.

✦ **Color field:** The color field shows a 16-bit range of variations on the current slider color. Click inside it to move the color selection marker and, thereby, select a new color. The field graphs colors against the two remaining attributes not represented by the color slider. For example, if you select the H (Hue) radio button, the field graphs colors according to brightness vertically and saturation horizontally, as demonstrated in the first example of Figure 4-3. The other examples show what happens to the color field when you select the S (Saturation) and B (Brightness) radio buttons.

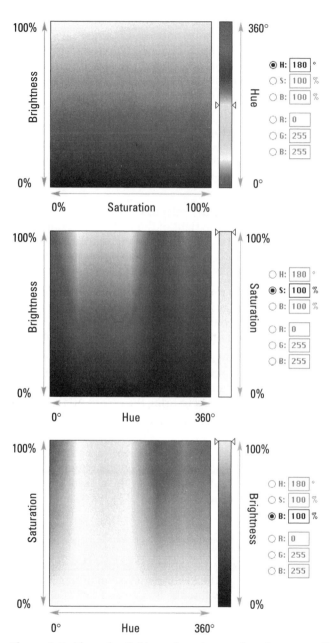

Figure 4-3: The color field graphs colors against the two attributes not represented in the slider. Here you can see how color is laid out when you select (top to bottom) the H (Hue), S (Saturation), and B (Brightness) radio buttons.

Likewise, Figure 4-4 shows how the field graphs colors when you select the R (Red), G (Green), and B (Blue) radio buttons. Obviously, it would help to see these images in color, but you probably couldn't afford this big, fat book if we'd printed it in full color. So I recommend you experiment with the Color Picker inside your version of Photoshop or refer to Color Plate 4-1 to see how the dialog box looks when the H (Hue), S (Saturation), and B (Brightness) options are selected.

Note

Slider and field always work together to represent the entire 16 million color range. The slider displays 256 colors, and the field displays 65,000 variations on the slider color; 256 times 65,000 is 16 million. No matter which radio button you select, you have access to the same colors; only your means of accessing them changes.

✦ **Current color:** The color currently selected from the color field appears in the top rectangle immediately to the right of the color slider. Click the OK button or press Enter to make this the current foreground or background color (depending on which color control icon in the Toolbox you originally clicked to display the Color Picker dialog box).

✦ **Previous color:** The bottom rectangle to the right of the color slider shows how the foreground or background color — whichever one you are in the process of editing — looked before you displayed the Color Picker dialog box. Click the Cancel button or press Escape to leave this color intact.

✦ **Alert triangle:** The alert triangle appears when you select a bright color that Photoshop can't print using standard process colors. The box below the triangle shows the closest CMYK equivalent, invariably a duller version of the color. Click either the triangle or the box to bring the color into the printable range.

✦ **Web-safe alert cube:** Added in Version 5.5, the little cube appears if you select a color that's not included in the so-called Web-safe palette, a 216-color spectrum that's supposedly ideal for creating Web graphics. You can get my take on this palette in Chapter 19; for now, just know that if you click either the cube or the swatch below, Photoshop selects the closest Web-safe equivalent to the color you originally selected.

Entering numeric color values

In addition to selecting colors using the slider and color field, you can enter specific color values in the option boxes in the lower-right region of the Color Picker dialog box. Novices and intermediates may find these options less satisfying to use than the slider and field. These options, however, enable artists and print professionals to specify exact color values, whether to make controlled adjustments to a color already in use or to match a color used in another document. The options fall into one of four camps:

✦ **HSB:** These options stand for hue, saturation, and brightness. Hue is measured on a 360-degree circle. Saturation and brightness are measured from 0 to 100 percent. These options permit access to more than 3 million color variations.

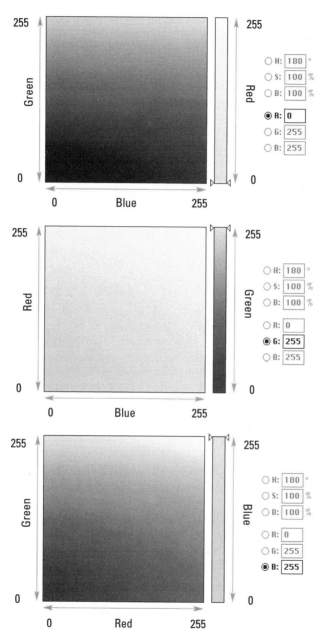

Figure 4-4: The results of selecting (top to bottom) the R (Red), G (Green), and B (Blue) radio buttons.

✦ **RGB:** You can change the amount of the primary colors red, green, and blue by specifying the brightness value of each color from 0 to 255. These options enable access to more than 16 million color variations.

✦ **Lab:** This acronym stands for luminosity, measured from 0 to 100 percent, and two arbitrary color axes, a and b, whose brightness values range from –120 to 120. These options enable access to more than 6 million color variations.

✦ **CMYK:** These options display the amount of cyan, magenta, yellow, and black ink required to print the current color. When you click the alert triangle, these are the only values that don't change, because they make up the closest CMYK equivalent.

At the bottom of the dialog box, the value next to the pound sign (#) shows you the hexadecimal value for the chosen color (see Figure 4-2). This value comes into play only if you're creating Web graphics — and maybe not even then.

In Web-land, every color is assigned a numeric value based on the hexadecimal numbering system. Each value includes a total of three pairs of numbers or letters, one pair each for the R, G, and B values. When you create a color tag in HTML code, you enter the hexadecimal value for the color you want to use. Fortunately, you can now create a Web page without having to write your own HTML code; today's page-creation programs do the work for you. But if you prefer to do your own coding — you lovable geek, you — make note of the hexadecimal value in the Color Picker dialog box.

Tip

This option can also come in handy if you want to precisely match a color on an existing Web page. Just look at the HTML coding for the page, note the hexadecimal value in the appropriate color tag, and enter that value in the Color Picker dialog box.

In my opinion, the numerical range of these options is bewildering. For example, numerically speaking, the CMYK options enable you to create 100 million unique colors, whereas the RGB options enable the standard 16 million variations, and the Lab options enable a scant 6 million. Yet Lab is the largest color space, theoretically encompassing all colors from both CMYK and RGB. The printing standard CMYK provides by far the fewest colors, the opposite of what you might expect. What gives? Misleading numerical ranges. How do these weird color models work? Keep reading and you'll find out.

Working in Different Color Modes

The four sets of option boxes inside the Color Picker dialog box represent color models — or, if you prefer, color modes (one less letter, no less meaning, perfect for you folks who are trying to cut down in life). *Color models* are different ways to define colors both on screen and on the printed page.

Outside the Color Picker dialog box, you can work inside any one of these color models by choosing a command from the Image ➪ Mode submenu. In doing so, you generally change the colors in your image by dumping a few hundred, or even thousand, colors with no equivalents in the new color model. The only exception is Lab, which in theory encompasses every unique color your eyes can detect.

Rather than discuss the color models in the order in which they occur in the Mode submenu, I cover them in logical order, starting with the most common and widely accepted color model, RGB. Also, note that I don't discuss the duotone or multi-channel modes now. Image ➪ Mode ➪ Duotone represents an alternative method for printing grayscale images, so it is discussed in Chapter 18. The multichannel mode, meanwhile, is not even a color model. Rather, Image ➪ Mode ➪ Multichannel enables you to separate an image into independent channels, which you then can swap around and splice back together to create special effects. For more information, see the "Using multichannel techniques" section later in this chapter.

RGB

RGB is the color model of light. RGB comprises three primary colors — red, green, and blue — each of which can vary between 256 levels of intensity (called brightness values, as discussed in previous chapters). The RGB model is also called the *additive primary model,* because a color becomes lighter as you add higher levels of red, green, and blue light. All monitors, projection devices, and other items that transmit or filter light — including televisions, movie projectors, colored stage lights, and even stained glass — rely on the additive primary model.

Red, green, and blue light mix as follows:

✦ **Red and green:** Full-intensity red and green mix to form yellow. Subtract some red to make chartreuse; subtract some green to make orange. All these colors assume a complete lack of blue.

✦ **Green and blue:** Full-intensity green and blue with no red mix to form cyan. If you try hard enough, you can come up with 65,000 colors in the turquoise/jade/sky blue/sea green range.

✦ **Blue and red:** Full-intensity blue and red mix to form magenta. Subtract some blue to make rose; subtract some red to make purple. All these colors assume a complete lack of green.

✦ **Red, green, and blue:** Full-intensity red, green, and blue mix to form white, the absolute brightest color in the visible spectrum.

✦ **No light:** Low intensities of red, green, and blue plunge a color into blackness.

As far as image editing is concerned, the RGB color model is ideal for editing images on screen because it provides access to the entire range of 24-bit screen colors.

Furthermore, you can save an RGB image in every file format supported by Photoshop except GIF and the two DCS formats. As shown in Table 4-1, grayscale is the only other color mode compatible with a wider range of file formats.

| Table 4-1 | | | | | | | |
File-Format Support for Photoshop 6 Color Models							
	Bitmap	*Grayscale*	*Duotone*	*Indexed*	*RGB*	*Lab*	*CMYK*
Photoshop	Yes	Yes	Yes	Yes	Yes	Yes	Yes
BMP	Yes	Yes	No	Yes	Yes	No	No
DCS 1.0	No	No	No	No	No	No	Yes
DCS 2.0	Yes	Yes	Yes*	No	No	No	Yes
EPS	Yes	Yes	Yes	Yes	Yes	Yes	Yes
GIF	Yes	Yes	No	Yes	No	No	No
JPEG	No	Yes	No	No	Yes	No	Yes
PCX	Yes	Yes	No	Yes	Yes	No	No
PDF	Yes	Yes	No	Yes	Yes	Yes	Yes
PICT	Yes	Yes	No	Yes	Yes	No	No
PNG	Yes**	Yes	No	Yes	Yes	No	No
Scitex CT	No	Yes	No	No	Yes	No	Yes
TIFF	Yes	Yes	No	Yes	Yes	Yes	Yes

Note

Table 4-1 lists color models in the order they appear in the Image ➪ Mode submenu. Again, I left out the multichannel mode because it is not a true color model. The one exception is with duotones. Notice how I've included an asterisk (*) to DCS 2.0 support for duotones. This is because you can save a duotone in DCS 2.0 only after first converting the image to the multichannel mode. For more information, consult Chapter 18. As for the double asterisk with PNG in the Bitmap column: PNG supports Bitmap mode only on the Mac OS.

On the negative side, the RGB color model provides access to a wider range of colors than you can print. If you are designing an image for full-color printing, therefore, you can expect to lose many of the brightest and most vivid colors in your image. The only way to avoid any color loss whatsoever is to have a professional scan your image to CMYK and then edit it in the CMYK mode, but then you're working inside a limited color range. Colors can get clipped when you apply special effects, and the editing process can be exceptionally slow. The better solution is to scan your images to RGB and edit them in the Lab mode, as explained in the upcoming "CIE's Lab" section.

HSB

Back in Photoshop 2, the Modes menu provided access to the HSB — hue, saturation, brightness — color model, now relegated to the Color Picker dialog box and the Color palette (discussed later in this chapter). *Hue* is pure color, the stuff rainbows are made of, measured on a 360-degree circle. Red is located at 0 degrees, yellow at 60 degrees, green at 120 degrees, cyan at 180 degrees (midway around the circle), blue at 240 degrees, and magenta at 300 degrees. This is basically a pie-shaped version of the RGB model at full intensity.

Saturation represents the purity of the color. A zero saturation value equals gray. White, black, and any other colors you can express in a grayscale image have no saturation. Full saturation produces the purest version of a hue.

Brightness is the lightness or darkness of a color. A zero brightness value equals black. Full brightness combined with full saturation results in the most vivid version of any hue.

CMYK

In nature, our eyes perceive pigments according to the *subtractive color model.* Sunlight contains every visible color found on Earth. When sunlight is projected on an object, the object absorbs (subtracts) some of the light and reflects the rest. The reflected light is the color you see. For example, a fire engine is bright red because it absorbs all non-red — meaning all blue and green — from the white-light spectrum.

Pigments on a sheet of paper work the same way. You can even mix pigments to create other colors. Suppose you paint a red brush stroke, which absorbs green and blue light, over a blue brush stroke, which absorbs green and red light. You get a blackish mess with only a modicum of blue and red light left, along with a smidgen of green because the colors weren't absolutely pure.

But wait — every child knows red and blue mix to form purple. So what gives? What gives is that what you learned in elementary school is only a rude approximation of the truth. Did you ever try mixing a vivid red with a canary yellow only to produce an ugly orange-brown glop? The reason you didn't achieve the bright orange you wanted is because red starts out darker than bright orange, which means you must add a great deal of yellow before you arrive at orange. And even then, the yellow had better be an incredibly bright lemon yellow, not some deep canary yellow with a lot of red in it.

Commercial subtractive primaries

The subtractive primary colors used by commercial printers — cyan, magenta, and yellow — are for the most part very light. Cyan absorbs only red light, magenta absorbs only green light, and yellow absorbs only blue light. On their own, these colors unfortunately don't do a good job of producing dark colors. In fact, at full intensities, cyan, magenta, and yellow all mixed together don't get much beyond a muddy brown. That's where black comes in. Black helps to accentuate shadows, deepen dark colors, and, of course, print real blacks.

In case you're wondering how colors mix in the CMYK model, it's basically the opposite of the RGB model. Because pigments are not as pure as primary colors in the additive model, though, some differences exist:

✦ **Cyan and magenta:** Full-intensity cyan and magenta mix to form a deep blue with a little violet. Subtract some cyan to make purple; subtract some magenta to make a dull medium blue. All these colors assume a complete lack of yellow.

✦ **Magenta and yellow:** Full-intensity magenta and yellow mix to form a brilliant red. Subtract some magenta to make vivid orange; subtract some yellow to make rose. All these colors assume a complete lack of cyan.

✦ **Yellow and cyan:** Full-intensity yellow and cyan mix to form a bright green with a hint of blue. Subtract some yellow to make a deep teal; subtract some cyan to make chartreuse. All these colors assume a complete lack of magenta.

✦ **Cyan, magenta, and yellow:** Full-intensity cyan, magenta, and yellow mix to form a muddy brown.

✦ **Black:** Black pigmentation added to any other pigment darkens the color.

✦ **No pigment:** No pigmentation results in white (assuming white is the paper color).

Editing in CMYK

If you're used to editing RGB images, editing in the CMYK mode can require some new approaches, especially when editing individual color channels. When you view a single color channel in the RGB mode (as discussed in the following chapter), white indicates high-intensity color, and black indicates low-intensity color. It's the opposite in CMYK. When you view an individual color channel, black means high-intensity color, and white means low-intensity color.

This doesn't mean RGB and CMYK color channels look like inverted versions of each other. In fact, because the color theory is inverted, they look much the same. But if you're trying to achieve the full-intensity colors mentioned in the preceding section, you should apply black to the individual color channels, not white as you would in the RGB mode.

Should I edit in CMYK?

RGB doesn't accurately represent the colors you get when you print an image because the RGB color space contains many colors—particularly very bright colors—that CMYK can't touch. This is why when you switch from RGB to CMYK, the colors appear duller. (If you're familiar with painting, RGB is like oils and CMYK is like acrylics. The latter lacks the depth of color provided by the former.)

For this reason, many folks advocate working exclusively in the CMYK mode, but I do not. Although working in CMYK eliminates color disappointments, it is also much slower because Photoshop has to convert CMYK values to your RGB screen on the fly.

Furthermore, your scanner and monitor are RGB devices. No matter how you work, a translation from RGB to CMYK color space must occur at some time. If you pay the extra bucks to purchase a commercial drum scan, for example, you simply make the translation at the beginning of the process — Scitex has no option but to use RGB sensors internally — rather than at the end. Every color device on Earth, in fact, is RGB except the printer.

You should wait to convert to the CMYK mode until right before you print. After your artwork is finalized, choose Image ➪ Mode ➪ CMYK and make whatever edits you deem necessary. For example, you might want to introduce a few color corrections, apply some sharpening, and even retouch a few details by hand. Photoshop applies your changes more slowly in the CMYK mode, but at least you're only slowed down at the end of the job, not throughout the entire process.

Before converting an image to the CMYK color space, make certain Photoshop is aware of the monitor you're using and the printer you intend to use. These two items can have a pronounced effect on how Photoshop generates a CMYK image. I discuss how to set up your personal RGB and CMYK color spaces in the "Creating Color Separations" section of Chapter 18.

Previewing the CMYK color space

While you're editing in RGB mode, you can *soft proof* your image — display a rough approximation of what the image will look like when converted to CMYK and printed. Version 6 offers a few new options in this regard and changes the implementation of some old ones. To display colors in the CMYK color space, you now choose View ➪ Proof Colors. You also can press the old CMYK preview keyboard shortcut, Ctrl+Y.

But before you do either, select the output you want to preview from the View ➪ Proof Colors submenu. Photoshop creates the proof display based on your selection. You can preview the image using the current CMYK working space, choose Custom to specify a particular outptut device, or preview the individual cyan, magenta, yellow, and black plates. The plates appear as grayscale images unless you colorize them by selecting the Color Channels in Color option in the Preferences dialog box (Ctrl+K, Ctrl+3). If you work with an older model color ink-jet printer that prints using just cyan, magenta, and yellow, you can choose the working CMY Plates option to see what your image will look like when printed without black ink.

View ➪ Gamut Warning (Ctrl+Shift+Y) is a companion to Photoshop's CMYK preview commands that covers so-called out-of-gamut colors — RGB colors with no CMYK equivalents — with gray. I find this command less useful because it demonstrates a problem without suggesting a solution. You can desaturate the grayed colors with the sponge tool (which I explain in Chapter 5), but this accomplishes little that Photoshop won't do automatically. A CMYK preview is much more serviceable and representative of the final CMYK image.

CIE's Lab

RGB isn't the only mode that responds quickly and provides a bountiful range of colors. Photoshop's Lab color space comprises all the colors from RGB and CMYK and is every bit as fast as RGB. Many high-end users prefer to work in this mode, and I certainly advocate this if you're brave enough.

Whereas the RGB mode is the color model of your luminescent computer screen and the CMYK mode is the color model of the reflective page, Lab is independent of light or pigment. Perhaps you've already heard the bit about how, in 1931, an international color organization called the Commission Internationale d'Eclairage (CIE) developed a color model that, in theory, contains every single color the human eye can see. (Gnats, iguanas, fruit bats, go find your own color models; humans, you have CIE. Mutants and aliens — maybe CIE, maybe not, too early to tell.) Then, in 1976, the significant birthday of our nation, the CIE celebrated by coming up with two additional color systems. One of those systems was Lab, and the other was shrouded in secrecy. Well, at least I don't know what the other one was. Probably something that measures how, when using flash photography, the entire visible spectrum of color can bounce off your retina and come out looking the exact shade of red one normally associates with lab (not Lab) rabbits. But this is just a guess.

The beauty of the Lab color model is it fills in gaps in both the RGB and CMYK models. RGB, for example, provides an overabundance of colors in the blue-to-green range but is stingy on yellows, oranges, and other colors in the green-to-red range. Meanwhile, the colors missing from CMYK are enough to fill the holes in the Albert Hall. Lab gets everything right.

Understanding Lab anatomy

The Lab mode features three color channels, one for luminosity and two others for color ranges, known simply by the initials *a* and *b*. (The Greeks would have called them alpha and beta, if that's any help.) Upon hearing luminosity, you might think, "Ah, just like HSL." Well, to make things confusing, Lab's *luminosity* is like HSB's brightness. White indicates full-intensity color.

Meanwhile, the *a* channel contains colors ranging from deep green (low-brightness values) to gray (medium-brightness values) to vivid pink (high-brightness values). The *b* channel ranges from bright blue (low-brightness values) to gray to burnt yellow (high-brightness values). As in the RGB model, these colors mix together to produce lighter colors. Only the brightness values in the luminosity channel darken the colors. So you can think of Lab as a two-channel RGB with brightness thrown on top.

To get a glimpse of how it works, try the following simple experiment.

STEPS: Testing Out the Lab Mode

1. **Create a new image in the Lab mode — say, 300 × 300 pixels, setting the Contents option to White.**

2. **Press D to return the default colors to the Toolbox.** The foreground color is now black and the background color is white.

3. **Press Ctrl+2. This takes you to the *a* channel.**

4. **Click the gradient tool in the Toolbox.** Or press Enter. In the Options bar, select the Foreground to Background option from the gradient pop-up menu, select the Linear gradient style, and select Normal from the Mode pop-up menu. (See Chapter 6 if you need help using these controls on the Options bar.)

5. **Shift-drag with the gradient tool from the top to the bottom of the window.** This creates a vertical black-to-white gradation.

6. **Press Ctrl+3. This takes you to the *b* channel.**

7. **Shift-drag from left to right with the gradient tool.** Photoshop paints a horizontal gradation.

8. **Press Ctrl+tilde (~) to return to the composite display.** Now you can see all channels at once. If you're using a 24-bit monitor, you should be looking at a window filled with an incredible array of super bright colors. In theory, these are the brightest shades of all the colors you can see. In practice, however, the colors are limited by the display capabilities of your RGB monitor.

Using Lab

Because it's device independent, you can use the Lab mode to edit any image. Editing in the Lab mode is as fast as editing in the RGB mode and several times faster than editing in the CMYK mode. If you plan on printing your image to color separations, you may want to experiment with using the Lab mode instead of RGB, because Lab ensures no colors are altered when you convert the image to CMYK, except to change colors that fall outside the CMYK range. In fact, any time you convert an image from RGB to CMYK, Photoshop automatically converts the image to the Lab mode as an intermediate step.

Tip

If you work with Photo CDs often, open the scans directly from the Photo CD format as Lab images. Kodak's proprietary YCC color model is nearly identical to Lab, so you can expect an absolute minimum of data loss; some people claim no loss whatsoever occurs.

Grayscale

Grayscale is possibly my favorite color mode. Grayscale frees you from all the hassles and expense of working with color and provides access to every bit of Photoshop's power and functionality. Anyone who says you can't do as much with grayscale as you can with color missed out on *Citizen Kane, Grapes of Wrath, Manhattan*, and *Raging Bull*. You can print grayscale images to any laser printer, reproduce them in any publication, and edit them on nearly any machine. Besides, they look great, they remind you of old movies, and they make a hefty book such as this one affordable. What could be better?

Other than extolling its virtues, however, there isn't a whole lot to say about grayscale. You can convert an image to the grayscale mode regardless of its current mode, and you can convert from grayscale to any other mode just as easily. In fact, choosing Image ➪ Mode ➪ Grayscale is a necessary step in converting a color image to a duotone or black-and-white bitmap.

Search your channels before converting

When you convert an image from one of the color modes to the grayscale mode, Photoshop normally weights the values of each color channel in a way that retains the apparent brightness of the overall image. For example, when you convert an image from RGB, Photoshop weights red more heavily than blue when computing dark values. This is because red is a darker-looking color than blue (much as that might seem contrary to popular belief).

Tip

If you choose Image ➪ Mode ➪ Grayscale while viewing a single color channel, though, Photoshop retains all brightness values in that channel only and abandons the data in the other channels. This can be an especially useful technique for rescuing a grayscale image from a bad RGB scan.

So before switching to the grayscale mode, be sure to look at the individual color channels — particularly the red and green channels (the blue channel frequently contains substandard detail) — to see how each channel might look on its own. To browse the channels, press Ctrl+1 for red, Ctrl+2 for green, and Ctrl+3 for blue. Or Ctrl+1 for cyan, Ctrl+2 for magenta, Ctrl+3 for yellow, and Ctrl+4 for black. Or even Ctrl+1 for luminosity, Ctrl+2 for *a*, and Ctrl+3 for *b*. Chapter 16 describes color channels in more detail.

Black and white (bitmap)

Choose Image ➪ Mode ➪ Bitmap to convert a grayscale image to exclusively black-and-white pixels. This may sound like a boring option, but it can prove useful for gaining complete control over the printing of grayscale images. After all, output devices, such as laser printers and imagesetters, render grayscale images as a series of tiny dots. Using the Bitmap command, you can specify the size, shape, and angle of those dots.

When you choose Image ➪ Mode ➪ Bitmap, Photoshop displays the Bitmap dialog box, shown in Figure 4-5. Here you specify the resolution of the black-and-white image and select a conversion process. The options work as follows:

✦ **Output:** Specify the resolution of the black-and-white file. If you want control over every single pixel available to your printer, raise this value to match your printer's resolution. As a rule of thumb, try setting the Output value somewhere between 200 to 250 percent of the Input value.

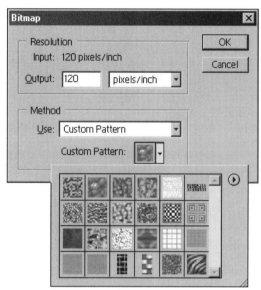

Figure 4-5: The Bitmap dialog box converts images from grayscale to black and white.

✦ **50% Threshold:** Select this option from the Use pop-up menu to change every pixel that is darker than 50 percent gray to black and every pixel that is 50 percent gray or lighter to white. Unless you are working toward some special effect — for example, overlaying a black-and-white version of an image over the original grayscale image — this option most likely isn't for you. (And if you're working toward a special effect, Image ➪ Adjust ➪ Threshold is the better alternative.)

✦ **Pattern Dither:** To *dither* pixels is to mix them up to emulate different colors. In this case, Photoshop mixes up black and white pixels to produce shades of gray. The Pattern Dither option dithers an image using a geometric pattern. Unfortunately, the results are pretty ugly, as demonstrated in the top example in Figure 4-6. And the space between dots has a tendency to fill in, especially when you output to a laser printer.

✦ **Diffusion Dither:** Select this option from the Use pop-up menu to create a mezzotint-like effect, as demonstrated in the second example in Figure 4-6. Again, because this option converts an image into thousands of stray pixels, you can expect your image to darken dramatically when output to a low-resolution laser printer and when reproduced. So be sure to lighten the image with something like the Levels command (as described in Chapter 17) before selecting this option.

Figure 4-6: The results of selecting the Pattern Dither option (top) and the much more acceptable Diffusion Dither option (bottom).

✦ **Halftone Screen:** When you select this option from the Use pop-up menu and press Enter, Photoshop displays the dialog box shown in Figure 4-7. These options enable you to apply a dot pattern to the image, as demonstrated in Figure 4-8. Enter the number of dots per inch in the Frequency option box and the angle of the dots in the Angle option box. Then select a dot shape from the Shape pop-up menu. Figure 4-8 shows examples of four shapes, each with a frequency of 24 lines per inch.

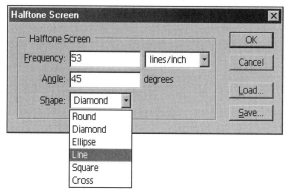

Figure 4-7: This dialog box appears when you select the Halftone Screen option in the Bitmap dialog box.

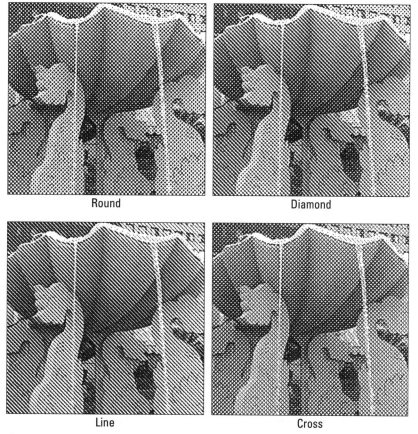

Round   Diamond

Line   Cross

Figure 4-8: Four random examples of halftone cell shapes. In all cases, the Frequency value was set to 24.

I cover screen patterns and frequency settings in more depth in the "Changing the halftone screen" section of Chapter 18.

✦ **Custom Pattern:** If you've defined a repeating pattern using Edit ⇨ Define Pattern, you can use it as a custom dither pattern. Figure 4-9 shows two custom examples. I created the first pattern using the Twirl Pattern file, which is stored in the Displacement Maps folder in the Plug-Ins folder. I created the second pattern manually using the Add Noise, Emboss, and Ripple filters (as discussed in the "Creating texture effects" section of Chapter A on the CD-ROM for this book).

Figure 4-9: Two examples of employing repeating patterns (created with Edit ⇨ Define Pattern) as custom halftoning patterns.

For a complete guide to creating and defining patterns in Photoshop, see the "Applying Repeating Patterns" section of Chapter 7.

To use a custom pattern, open the Custom Pattern palette in the Bitmap dialog box, as shown in Figure 4-5. Click the icon for the pattern you want to use. If you don't feel like creating your own patterns, use one of the preset patterns that ship with Photoshop 6. A number of these patterns appear by default in the palette; to access additional patterns, choose Load from the palette menu (click the right-pointing triangle in the upper-right corner of the palette to display the menu). You can find the patterns in the Patterns folder, which lives inside the Presets folder. To delete a pattern from the palette, click its icon and choose Delete from the palette menu.

Photoshop lets you edit individual pixels in the so-called bitmap mode, but that's about the extent of it. After you go to black-and-white, you can neither perform any serious editing nor expect to return to the grayscale mode and restore your original pixels. So be sure to finish your image editing before choosing Image ➪ Mode ➪ Bitmap. Even more important, make certain to save your image before converting it to black-and-white. Frankly, saving is a good idea prior to performing any color conversion.

Using Photoshop's Other Color Selection Methods

In addition to the Color Picker dialog box, Photoshop provides a handful of additional techniques for selecting colors. The sections that finish out this chapter explain how to use the Custom Colors dialog box, the Colors palette, and the eyedropper tool. None of this information is terribly exciting, but it will enable you to work more efficiently and conveniently.

Predefined colors

If you click the Custom button inside the Color Picker dialog box, Photoshop displays the Custom Colors dialog box shown in Figure 4-10. In this dialog box, you can select from a variety of predefined colors by choosing the color family from the Book pop-up menu, moving the slider triangles up and down the color slider to specify a general range of colors, and ultimately, selecting a color from the color list on the left. If you own the swatchbook for a color family, you can locate a specific color by entering its number on the keyboard.

The color families represented in the Book pop-up menu fall into seven brands: ANPA (now NAA, as I explain shortly), DIC, Focoltone, HKS, Pantone, Toyo, and Trumatch, all of which get a big kick out of capitalizing their names in dialog boxes. I honestly think one of these companies would stand out better if its name weren't capitalized. Anyway, at the risk of offending a few of these companies, you're likely to find certain brands more useful than others. The following sections briefly introduce the brands in order of their impact on the American market — forgive me for being ethnocentric in this regard — from smallest to greatest impact.

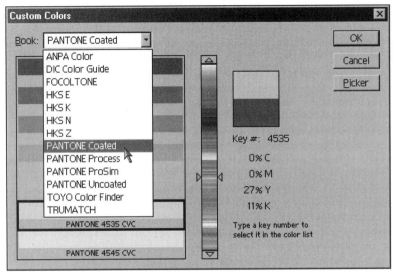

Figure 4-10: The Custom Colors dialog box enables you to select predefined colors from brand-name libraries.

The color families represented in the Book pop-up menu fall into seven brands: ANPA (now NAA, as I explain shortly), DIC, Focoltone, HKS, Pantone, Toyo, and Trumatch, all of which get a big kick out of capitalizing their names in dialog boxes. I honestly think one of these companies would stand out better if its name weren't capitalized. Anyway, at the risk of offending a few of these companies, you're likely to find certain brands more useful than others. The following sections briefly introduce the brands in order of their impact on the American market — forgive me for being ethnocentric in this regard — from smallest to greatest impact.

Tip

The number-one use for predefined colors in Photoshop is in the creation of duotones, tritones, and quadtones (described in Chapter 18). You can also use predefined colors to match the colors in a logo or some other important element in an image to a commercial standard. And you can add an independent channel for a predefined color and print it to a separate plate, as discussed later in this chapter.

Focoltone, DIC, Toyo, and HKS

Focoltone, Dianippon Ink and Chemical (DIC), Toyo, and HKS fall into the negligible impact category. All are foreign color standards with followings abroad. Focoltone is an English company; not English speaking (although they probably do), but English living, as in commuting-to-France-through-the-Channel England. DIC and Toyo are popular in the Japanese market, but have next to no subscribers outside Japan. HKS formerly was provided only in the German and French versions of Photoshop, but enough people asked for it to be included in other languages that it now is available in all versions of the program.

Newspaper Association of America

American Newspaper Publishers Association (ANPA) recently changed its name to NAA, which stands for Newspaper Association of America, and updated its color catalog. NAA provides a small sampling of 45 process colors (mixes of cyan, magenta, yellow, and black ink) plus 5 spot colors (colors produced by printing a single ink). The idea behind the NAA colors is to isolate the color combinations that reproduce most successfully on inexpensive newsprint and to provide advertisers with a solid range of colors from which to choose, without allowing the color choices to get out of hand. You can purchase a swatch book from NAA for $35. Members pay $25.

Trumatch

Trumatch remains my personal favorite process-color standard. Designed entirely using a desktop system and created especially with desktop publishers in mind, the Trumatch Colorfinder swatchbook features more than 2,000 process colors, organized according to hue, saturation, and brightness. Each hue is broken down into 40 tints and shades. Reducing the saturation in 15-percent increments creates tints; adding black ink in 6-percent increments creates shades. The result is a guide that shows you exactly which colors you can attain using a desktop system. If you're wondering what a CMYK blend will look like when printed, you need look no further than the Trumatch Colorfinder.

As if the Colorfinder weren't enough, Trumatch provides the ColorPrinter Software utility, which automatically prints the entire 2,000-color library to any PostScript-compatible output device. The utility integrates EfiColor and PostScript Level 2, thereby enabling design firms and commercial printers to test the entire range of capabilities available to their hardware. Companies can provide select clients with swatches of colors created on their own printers, guaranteeing what you see is darn well what you'll get.

Pantone

On the heels of Trumatch, Pantone released a 3,006-color Process Color System Guide (labeled Pantone Process in the Book pop-up menu) priced at $79. Pantone also produces the foremost spot color swatchbook, the Color Formula Guide. Then there's the Solid to Process Guide, which enables you to figure out quickly if you can closely match a Pantone spot color using a process-color blend or if you ought to give it up and stick with the spot color.

Pantone spot colors are ideal for creating duotones and adding custom colors to an image for logos and the like, both discussed in Chapter 18. Furthermore, Pantone is supported by every computer application that aspires to the color prepress market. As long as the company retains the old competitive spirit, you can, most likely, expect Pantone to remain the primary color printing standard for years to come.

The Color palette

Another means of selecting colors in Photoshop is to use the Color palette, shown in Figure 4-11. The Color palette is convenient, it's always there, and it doesn't hog your screen like the Color Picker dialog box. Frankly, this is the tool I use most often to select colors in Photoshop.

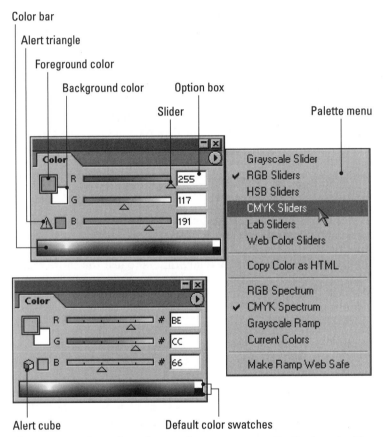

Figure 4-11: The Color palette as it appears normally (top) and with the Web Color Sliders option selected (bottom).

To display the palette, choose Window ➪ Show Color or press the F6 key. If you want, you can dock the palette in the Options bar palette well. For details on that intriguing offer, flip back to Chapter 2. Either way, you use the elements and options inside the palette as follows:

✦ **Foreground color/background color:** Click the foreground or background color icon in the Color palette to specify the color you want to edit. If you click the foreground or background color icon when it's already highlighted — as indicated by a double-line frame — Photoshop displays the Color Picker dialog box.

✦ **Sliders:** Drag the triangles in the slider controls to edit the highlighted color. By default, the sliders represent the red, green, and blue primary colors when a color image is open. You can change the slider bars by choosing a different color model from the palette menu.

✦ **Option boxes:** Alternatively, you can enter numerical values into the option boxes to the right of the sliders. Press Tab to advance from one option box to the next; press Shift+Tab to go to the previous option.

✦ **Alert triangle and cube:** Photoshop displays the alert triangle when a color falls outside the CMYK color gamut. The color swatch to the right of the triangle shows the closest CMYK equivalent. Click the triangle or the color swatch to replace the current color with the CMYK equivalent.

If you select the Web Color Sliders option from the palette menu, the alert cube appears to indicate colors that aren't included in the Web-safe palette. The palette also displays the hexadecimal values for the color, as shown in Figure 4-11. And as you drag the sliders, they automatically snap to Web-safe hues. To limit the palette so that it displays Web-safe colors only, choose Make Ramp Web Safe from the palette menu.

Tip

After you define a Web color, choose Copy Color as HTML from the palette menu to save the hexadecimal code for the color to the Clipboard. You can then paste the code into an HTML file by choosing Edit ➪ Paste in the Web application.

✦ **Color bar:** The bar along the bottom of the Color palette displays all colors contained in the CMYK spectrum. Click or drag inside the color bar to lift a color and make it the current foreground or background color (depending on whether the foreground or background icon is selected above). The sliders update as you drag. Alt-click or drag to lift the background color if the foreground icon is selected or the foreground color if the background color is selected.

You needn't accept the CMYK spectrum in the color bar, however. To change to a different spectrum, just choose the spectrum from the palette menu. Or Shift-click the color bar to cycle through the available spectrums. You can opt for the RGB spectrum, a black-to-white gradation (Grayscale Ramp), or a gradation from the current foreground color to the current background color (Current Colors). The color bar continuously updates to represent the newest foreground and background colors.

Notice the black and white squares at the right end of the color bar? You can click 'em to set a color to absolute black or white. But if all you want to do is set the foreground color to black, don't bother with the Color palette — just press D. For white, press D and then X. The first shortcut restores the foreground and background colors to black and white, respectively; pressing X swaps the colors to make white the foreground color and black the background color.

The Swatches palette

Shown in Figure 4-12, the Swatches palette enables you to collect colors for future use, sort of like a favorite color reservoir. You can use the palette also to set the foreground and background colors.

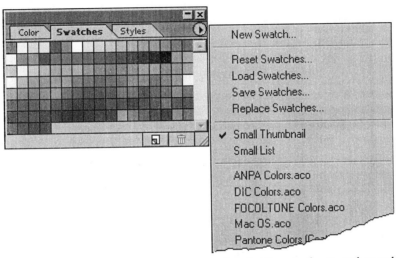

Figure 4-12: You can create custom swatch collections in the Swatches palette or in the new Preset Manager dialog box.

Here's how to take advantage of the Swatches palette:

✦ Click a color swatch to make that color the foreground color. Alt-click to set the background color.

✦ To add the current foreground color to the reservoir, Shift-click an existing color swatch to replace the old color or click an empty swatch to append the new color. In either case, your cursor temporarily changes to a paint bucket. After you click, you're asked to give the swatch a name. Type the name and click OK. If you later want to change the name, just double-click the swatch to redisplay the name dialog box.

Tip

You can bypass the dialog box and add an unnamed color to the palette by Ctrl+Alt-clicking an empty swatch.

✦ To insert a color anywhere in the palette, Shift+Ctrl-click a swatch. The other colors scoot over to make room.

✦ To delete a color from the panel, Ctrl-click a color swatch. Your cursor changes to a pair of scissors and cuts the color away.

✦ The Swatches palette in Photoshop 6 includes a new icon and trash icon, similar to those you find in the Layers palette. The icons provide alternative methods of adding and deleting colors: Click the new icon to add a new swatch in the current foreground color; Alt-click to display the name dialog box and then add the color. Drag a swatch to the trash icon to delete it from the palette.

You can also save and load color palettes on disk using options in the pop-up menu. Load Swatches appends swatches stored in a swatches file to the current set of swatches; Replace Swatches replaces the current swatches with the ones in the file. Save Swatches lets you create a new swatch collection and save it to disk.

The Presets folder, located inside the main Photoshop folder, contains folders for all the available preset items, color swatches being one of them. The Color Swatches folder, found inside the Photoshop Only folder of the Presets folder, contains palettes for the major color libraries from Pantone, Trumatch, and others. In Version 6, you can load these palettes by simply selecting them from the palette pop-up menu. You're then given the choice of appending the swatches to the existing swatches or replacing the current swatches altogether. Custom swatch sets that you create also appear on the palette menu, but only after you close and restart Photoshop.

Tip

When a color library palette is loaded, positioning your cursor over a color swatch displays a tool tip showing the name of that color. If you prefer to select colors by using the color names, select Small List from the palette menu. Now you see a scrolling list of colors instead of just the swatches.

Swatches presets

You can also create and manage swatch collections using the new Preset Manager. Choose View ➪ Presets and then select Swatches from the Preset Type pop-up menu (or press Ctrl+2) to display the Swatches presets panel, shown in Figure 4-13. The presets panel shows the current swatch set.

Many functions in the Swatches panel duplicate those offered by the Swatches palette. If you click the arrow to the left of the Done button (see the figure), you display a pop-up menu that's nearly identical to the Swatches palette menu. You can choose the Replace Swatches command on the pop-up menu to replace the current swatch collection with another or choose Reset Swatches to return to the default swatch collection. To append a collection, click the Load button. Alternatively, click a collection name in the pop-up menu, in which case you have the choice of appending or replacing the current collection with the new one.

In addition, you can click a swatch and then click Delete to remove the swatch or Rename to change the color's name. If you want to dump or rename a bunch of swatches, Shift-click them and then click Delete or Rename. To select all swatches, press Ctrl+A. You can also display the scissors cursor and then click a swatch to delete it — but for some reason, you press Alt to get the scissors cursor in the Preset Manager, not Ctrl as you do in the Swatches palette.

Click for palette menu

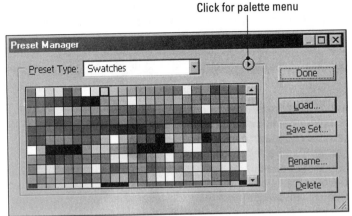

Figure 4-13: To easily create a new swatch collection using just some colors from an existing collection, head for the Preset Manager.

Aside from being able to delete or rename a batch of swatches at one time, the best reason for bothering with the Preset Manager—as opposed to working in the Swatches palette—is to create a new swatch collection out of colors from an existing set or sets. Load the collection(s) that you want to use as a basis for the new set. Then Shift-click to select swatches for the new set—or press Ctrl+A to select all swatches—and click Save Set. Give the collection a name and store it in the Color Swatches folder.

Note that wherever you do your swatch set editing, you can't overwrite any existing preset files. Also, after you add a new swatch, you must save it as part of a swatch collection, either via the palette pop-up menu or the Preset Manager. Otherwise, Photoshop deletes the swatch if you replace the current swatch collection with another.

The eyedropper tool

The eyedropper tool—which you can select by pressing I—provides the most convenient and straightforward means of selecting colors in Photoshop. This is so straightforward, in fact, it's hardly worth explaining. But quickly, here's how the eyedropper tool works:

✦ **Selecting a foreground color:** To select a new foreground color, click the desired color inside any open image window with the eyedropper tool. (This assumes the foreground icon in the Color palette is selected. If the background icon is selected, Alt-click with the eyedropper tool to lift the foreground color.) You can even click inside a background window to lift a color without bringing that window to the foreground.

✦ **Selecting a background color:** To select a new background color, Alt-click the desired color with the eyedropper tool. (Again, this assumes the foreground icon is selected in the Color palette. If the background icon is selected, click with the eyedropper to lift the background color.)

✦ **Skating over the color spectrum:** You can animate the foreground color control box by dragging with the eyedropper tool in an image window or along the color bar in the Color palette. As soon as you achieve the desired color, release your mouse button. To animate the background color icon, Alt-drag with the eyedropper tool. The icon color changes as you move the eyedropper tool. Again, swap these procedures if the background color icon is selected in the Color palette.

✦ **Sampling multiple pixels:** Normally, the eyedropper tool selects the color from the single pixel on which you click. If you prefer to average the colors of several neighboring pixels, however, choose either the 3 by 3 Average or 5 by 5 Average option from the Sample Size pop-up menu on the Options bar. Or right-click with the eyedropper to display a pop-up menu of sampling options near the cursor. In this case, you get one additional choice, Copy Color as HTML, which works just as it does when you select it from the Color palette pop-up menu. Photoshop determines the hexadecimal code for the color and sends the code to the Clipboard so that you can use Edit ⇨ Paste to dump the code into an HTML file.

Tip

To access the eyedropper tool temporarily when using the type, paint bucket, gradient, line, pencil, airbrush, or paintbrush tool, press Alt. The eyedropper cursor remains in force for as long as the Alt key is down. The eyedropper lifts whatever color is active in the Color palette (foreground or background). To lift the other color, switch to the eyedropper tool by pressing the I key and then Alt-click in an image window.

The color sampler tool

Found in the same toolbox flyout as the eyedropper, the color sampler tool looks like the eyedropper with a little crosshair target. But where the eyedropper lifts foreground and background colors, the color sampler merely measures the colors of pixels so that you can monitor how the pixels react to various color changes.

Select the color sampler and click somewhere inside the image window. Photoshop adds a crosshair target to indicate the point you clicked. The program also brings up the Info palette (if it isn't up already) and adds a new color measurement item labeled #1. This item corresponds to the target in the image, which is likewise labeled #1. Click again and you add a second target and a corresponding item #2 in the Info palette. You can add up to four targets to an image, as demonstrated in Figure 4-14.

Figure 4-14: The color sampler tool lets you measure the colors of four points in your image, as indicated by the black arrows. You can also measure a fifth point by merely moving the cursor around, as indicated by the white arrow.

The color sampler is primarily intended for printers and technicians who want to monitor the effects of color corrections on specific points in an image. If you apply Image ⇨ Adjust ⇨ Levels, for example, Photoshop constantly updates the items in the Info palette to reflect your changes (as I explain in more detail in Chapter 17). But you can also sample points in an image to monitor the effects of filters (Chapters 10 and 11, as well as Chapter A on the CD-ROM), blend modes (Chapter 13), and edit tools such as dodge and burn (Chapter 5). The color sampler is just another way to monitor changes to an image.

Here are a few more techniques of interest when color sampling:

✦ Photoshop limits you to four color targets. If you try to create a fifth one, the program generates an error message. If you want to measure a different point in the image, you can either hover your cursor over the point and note the top set of color values in the Info palette (as in Figure 4-14) or move one of the targets.

✦ To move a target inside the image window, drag it with the color sampler tool. You can also move a target by Ctrl-dragging it with the eyedropper tool.

✦ To delete a target, Alt-click it.

✦ The Info palette grows to more than twice its normal size when you start clicking with the color sampler. To hide the sampler information without deleting targets, click the Info palette's collapse box or choose Hide Color Samplers from the palette menu. If you go the second route, you have to choose Show Color Samplers to bring the samples back.

✦ By default, the sampler items in the Info palette measure colors in the active color space. If you want to track a target in a different color space, click the item's eyedropper icon in the Info palette or right-click the target in the image window. Either way, you get a pop-up menu of color space alternatives, including Grayscale, RGB, and several others that you may recall from previous explanations in this chapter.

Tip

To select the color sampler, press Shift+I when the eyedropper is active or Alt-click the eyedropper icon. Or press I repeatedly to cycle between the eyedropper, color sampler, and measure tool (add Shift if you activated the Use Shift Key for Tool Switch option in the Preferences dialog box). You can also temporarily access the color sampler any time the eyedropper is active by pressing Shift. This little trick also works when a color correction dialog box such as Levels or Curves is open, as explained in Chapter 17. It's just the ticket when you're in the middle of an adjustment and you need to know how it's affecting specific portions of the image.

Introducing Color Channels

After I've droned on for pages about color in Photoshop, it might surprise you when I say that Photoshop is at its heart a grayscale editor. Oh sure, it offers an array of color conversion features and it displays and prints spectacular full-color images. But when it comes to editing the image, everything happens in grayscale.

This is because Photoshop approaches every full-color image not as a single collection of 24-bit pixels, but as three or four bands of 8-bit (grayscale) pixels. An RGB file contains a band of red, a band of green, and a band of blue, each of which functions as a separate grayscale image. A Lab image likewise contains three bands, one corresponding to luminosity and the others to the variables *a* and *b*. A CMYK file contains four bands, one for each of the process-color inks. These bands are known as *channels*.

Channels frequently correspond to the structure of an input or output device. Each channel in a CMYK image, for example, corresponds to a different printer's plate when the document goes to press. The cyan plate is inked with cyan, the magenta plate is inked with magenta, and so on. Each channel in an RGB image corresponds to a pass of the red, green, or blue scanner sensor over the original photograph or artwork. Only the Lab mode is device independent, so its channels don't correspond to any piece of hardware.

Why you should care

But so what, right? Who cares how many planes of color an image comprises? You want to edit the photograph, not dissect it. "Dammit, Jim, I'm an artist, not a doctor!" Well, even if you don't like to rebuild car engines or poke preserved frog entrails with sharp knives, you'll get a charge out of editing channels. The fact is, channels provide you with yet another degree of selective control over an image.

Consider this example: Your client scanned a photograph of his gap-toothed daughter that he wants you to integrate into some goofy ad campaign for his car dealership. Unfortunately, the scan is downright rotten. You don't want to offend the guy, so you praise him on his fine offspring and say something to the effect of, "No problem, boss." But after you take it back to your office and load it into Photoshop, you break out in a cold sweat. You try swabbing at it with the edit tools, applying a few filters, and even attempting some scary-looking color correction commands, but the image continues to look like the inside of a garbage disposal. (Not that I've ever seen the inside of a garbage disposal, but it can't be attractive.)

Suddenly, it occurs to you to look at the channels. What the heck, it can't hurt. With very little effort, you discover that the red and green channels look okay, but the blue channel looks like it's melting. Her mouth is sort of mixed in with her teeth, her eyes look like an experiment in expressionism, and her hair has taken on a slightly geometric appearance. (If you think that this is a big exaggeration, take a look at a few blue channels from a low-end scanner or digital camera. They're frequently rife with tattered edges, random blocks of color, stray pixels, and other so-called digital artifacts.)

The point is, you've located the cancer. You don't have to waste your time trying to perform surgery on the entire image; in fact, doing so may very well harm the channels that are in good shape. You merely have to fix this one channel. A wave of the Gaussian Blur filter here, an application of the Levels command there, and some selective rebuilding of missing detail borrowed from the other channels — all of which I'll get to in future sections and chapters — result in an image that resembles a living, breathing human being. Granted, she still needs braces, but you're an artist, not an orthodontist.

How channels work

Photoshop devotes 8 bits of data to each pixel in each channel, thus permitting 256 brightness values, from 0 (black) to 255 (white). Therefore, each channel is actually an independent grayscale image. At first, this may throw you off. If an RGB image is made up of red, green, and blue channels, why do all the channels look gray?

Photoshop provides an option in the Display & Cursors panel of the Preferences dialog box (Ctrl+K, Ctrl+3) called Color Channels in Color. When selected, this function displays each channel in its corresponding primary color. But although this feature can be reassuring—particularly to novices—it's equally counterproductive.

When you view an 8-bit image composed exclusively of shades of red, for example, it's easy to miss subtle variations in detail that may appear obvious when you print the image. You may have problems accurately gauging the impact of filters and tonal adjustments. I mean, face it, red isn't a friendly shade to stare at for a half hour of intense editing. So leave the Color Channels in Color option off and temporarily suspend your biological urge for on-screen color. With a little experience, you'll be able to better monitor your adjustments and predict the outcome of your edits in plain old grayscale.

Images that include 256 or fewer colors can be expressed in a single channel and therefore do not include multiple channels that you can edit independently. A grayscale image, for example, is just one channel. A black-and-white bitmap permits only one bit of data per pixel, so a single channel is more than enough to express it.

You can add channels above and beyond those required to represent a color or grayscale image for the purpose of storing masks, as described in Chapter 9. But even then, each channel is typically limited to 8 bits of data per pixel—meaning that it's just another grayscale image. Mask channels do not affect the appearance of the image on screen or when it is printed. Rather, they serve to save selection outlines, as Chapter 9 explains.

How to switch and view channels

To access channels in Photoshop, display the Channels palette by choosing Window ⇨ Show Channels. Every channel in the image appears in the palette—including any mask channels—as shown in Figure 4-15. Photoshop even shows little thumbnail views of each channel so that you can see what it looks like.

To switch to a different channel, click a channel name in the Channels palette. The channel name becomes gray—like the Blue channel in Figure 4-15—showing that you can now edit it independently of other channels in the image.

To edit more than one channel at a time, click one channel name and then Shift-click another. You can also Shift-click an active channel to deactivate it independently of any others.

When you select a single channel, Photoshop displays just that one channel on screen. However, you can view additional channels beyond those that you want to edit. To specify which channels appear and which remain invisible, click in the far-left column of the Channels palette. Click an eyeball icon to make it disappear and hence hide that channel. Click where there is no eyeball to create one and thus display the channel.

Eyeball icon

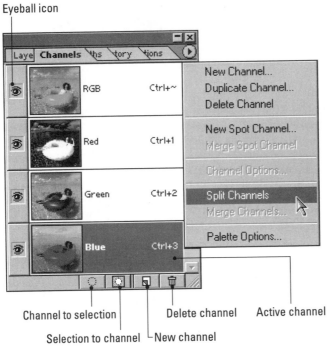

Channel to selection   Delete channel   Active channel

Selection to channel   New channel

Figure 4-15: Photoshop displays tiny thumbnails of each color channel in the Channels palette.

When only one channel is visible, that channel appears as a grayscale picture in the image window (possibly colorized in accordance with the Color Channels in Color check box in the Preferences dialog box). However, when more than one channel is visible, you always see color. If both the blue and green channels are visible, for example, the image appears blue-green. If the red and green channels are visible, the image has a yellow cast, and so on.

In addition to the individual channels, Photoshop provides access to a *composite view* that displays all colors in an RGB, CMYK, or Lab image at once. (The composite view does not show mask channels; you have to specify their display separately.) The composite view is listed first in the Channel palette and is displayed by default. Notice that when you select the composite view, all the names of the individual color channels in the Channels palette turn gray along with the composite channel. This shows that all the channels are active. The composite view is the one in which you will perform the majority of your image editing.

Press Ctrl plus a number key to switch between color channels. Depending on the color mode you're working in, Ctrl+1 takes you to the red (RGB), cyan (CMYK), or luminosity (Lab) channel; Ctrl+2 takes you to the green, magenta, or *a* channel; and Ctrl+3 takes you to the blue, yellow, or *b* channel. In the CMYK mode, Ctrl+4 displays the black channel. Other Ctrl+key equivalents — up to Ctrl+9 — take you to mask or spot-color channels (if there are any). To go to the composite view, press Ctrl+tilde (~). Tilde is typically the key to the left of 1, or on some keyboards, to the right of the spacebar.

When editing a single channel, you may find it helpful to monitor the results in both grayscale and full-color views. Choose View ➪ New View to create a new window for the image, automatically set to the color composite view. Then return to the first window and edit away on the individual channel. One of the amazing benefits to creating multiple views in Photoshop is that the views may show entirely different channels, layers, and other image elements.

The shortcuts are slightly different when you're working on a grayscale image. You access the image itself by pressing Ctrl+1. Ctrl+2 and higher take you to extra spot-color and mask channels.

Trying Channels on for Size

Feeling a little mystified? Need some examples? Fair enough. Color Plate 4-2 shows a woman in a bright yellow swimsuit on a bright red floatation device set against a bright green ocean beneath a bright blue sky. These colors — yellow, red, green, and blue — cover the four corners of the color spectrum. Therefore, you can expect to see a lot of variation between the images in the independent color channels.

RGB channels

Suppose that the sunbathing woman is an RGB image. Figure 4-16 compares a grayscale composite of this same image (created by choosing Image ➪ Mode ➪ Grayscale) compared with the contents of the red, green, and blue color channels from the original color image. The green channel is quite similar to the grayscale composite because green is an ingredient in all colors in the image, except for the red of the raft. The red and blue channels differ more significantly. The pixels in the red channel are lightest in the swimsuit and raft because they contain the highest concentrations of red. The pixels in the blue channel are lightest in the sky and water because — you guessed it — the sky and water are rich with blue.

Grayscale composite   Red

Green   Blue

Figure 4-16: A grayscale composite of the image from Color Plate 4-2 followed by the contents of the red, green, and blue color channels.

Notice how the channels in Figure 4-16 make interesting grayscale images in and of themselves? The red channel, for example, looks like the sky is darkening above our bather, even though the sun is blazing down.

I mentioned this as a tip in the previous chapter, but it bears a bit of casual drumming into the old noggin. When converting a color image to grayscale, you have the option of calculating a grayscale composite or simply retaining the image exactly as it appears in one of the channels. To create a grayscale composite, choose Image ➪ Mode ➪ Grayscale when viewing all colors in the image in the composite view, as usual. To retain a single channel only, switch to that channel and then choose Image ➪ Mode ➪ Grayscale. Instead of the usual *Discard color information?* message, Photoshop displays the message *Discard other channels?* If you click the OK button, Photoshop chucks the other channels into the electronic abyss.

When the warning dialog box appears, select the Do not show again check box if you don't want Photoshop to ask for permission to dump color information or channels when you convert to grayscale. If you miss the warning, click the Reset All Warning Dialogs button on the General panel of the Preferences dialog box.

CMYK channels

In the name of fair and unbiased coverage, Figures 4-17 and 4-18 show the channels from the image after it was converted to other color modes. In Figure 4-17, I converted the image to the CMYK mode and examined its channels. Here, the predominant colors are cyan (sky and water) and yellow (in the swimsuit and raft). Because this color mode relies on pigments rather than light, as explained in the "CMYK" section earlier in this chapter, dark areas in the channels represent high color intensity. For that reason, the sky in the cyan channel is dark, whereas it's light in the blue channel back in Figure 4-16.

Cyan   Magenta

Yellow   Black

Figure 4-17: The contents of the cyan, magenta, yellow, and black channels from the image shown in Color Plate 4-2.

Notice how similar the cyan channel in Figure 4-17 is to its red counterpart in Figure 4-16. Same with the magenta and green channels, and the yellow and blue channels. The CMY channels have more contrast than their RGB pals, but the basic brightness distribution is the same. Here's another graphic demonstration of color theory. In a perfect world, the CMY channels would be identical to the RGB channels — one color model would simply be the other turned on its head. But because this is not a perfect world (you might have noticed that as you've traveled life's bitter highway), Photoshop has to boost the contrast of the CMY channels and throw in black to punch up those shadows.

Lab channels

To create Figure 4-18, I converted the image in Color Plate 4-2 to the Lab mode. The image in the luminosity channel looks very similar to the grayscale composite because it contains the lightness and darkness values for the image. The *a* channel maps the greens and magentas, while the *b* channel maps the yellows and blues, so both channels are working hard to provide color information for this photograph. Certainly there are differences — the *a* channel is hotter in the raft, while the *b* channel offers more cloud detail — but the two channels carry roughly equivalent amounts of color information.

Grayscale composite   Luminosity

a (black is green; white is magenta)   *b* (black is blue; white is yellow)

Figure 4-18: The grayscale composite followed by the contents of the luminosity channel and the *a* and *b* color channels after converting the image shown in Color Plate 4-2 to the Lab mode.

You can achieve some entertaining effects by applying commands from the Image ⇨ Adjust submenu to the *a* and *b* color channels. For example, if I go to the *a* channel in Figure 4-18 and reverse the brightness values by choosing Image ⇨ Adjust ⇨ Invert (Ctrl+I), the water turns a sort of salmon red and the raft turns green, as demonstrated in the first example of Color Plate 4-3. If I apply Image ⇨ Adjust ⇨ Auto Levels (Ctrl+Shift+L) to the *b* channel, the sky lights up with brilliant blue without altering so much as a color in the woman or her raft, as in the second example. The third example in Color Plate 4-3 shows what happens when I apply both Invert and Auto Levels to both the *a* and *b* channels. Now there's the way I want to vacation — on a different planet!

Other Channel Functions

In addition to viewing and editing channels using any of the techniques discussed in future chapters of this book, you can choose commands from the Channels palette menu and select icons along the bottom of the palette (labeled back in Figure 4-15). The following items explain how the commands and icons work.

You'll notice that I say "see Chapter 9" every so often when explaining these options, because many of them are specifically designed to accommodate masks. This list is designed to introduce you to *all* the options in the Channels palette, even if you'll need more background to use a few of them. After I introduce the options, we'll revisit the ones that have a direct effect on managing the colors in your image.

   ✦ **Palette Options:** Even though this is the last command in the menu, it's the easiest, so I'll start with it. When you choose Palette Options, Photoshop displays four Thumbnail Size radio buttons, enabling you to change the size of the thumbnail previews that appear along the left side of the Channels palette. Figure 4-19 shows the four thumbnail settings — nonexistent, small, medium, and large.

   Have you ever wondered what those thumbnail icons in the Palette Options dialog box are supposed to show? They're silhouettes of tiny Merlins on a painter's palette. How do I know that? Switch to the Layers palette and choose Palette Options and you'll see them in color. But how do I know they're specifically Merlins? Press Alt when choosing Palette Options to see the magician up close. We're talking vintage Easter egg, here — circa Photoshop 2.5.

   ✦ **New Channel:** Choose this command to add a mask channel to the current image. The Channel Options dialog box appears, requesting that you name the channel. You also can specify the color and translucency that Photoshop applies to the channel when you view it with other channels. I explain how these options work in the "Changing the red coating" section of Chapter 9. An image can contain up to 24 total channels, regardless of color mode.

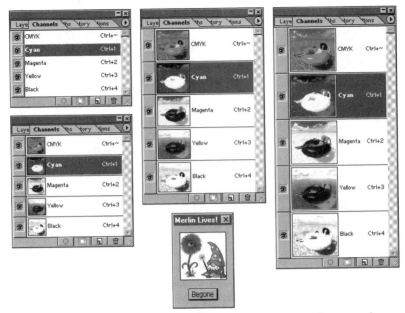

Figure 4-19: The Palette Options command lets you select between four thumbnail preview options and a Merlin.

Tip

You can also create a new channel by clicking on the new channel icon at the bottom of the Channels palette. (It's the one that looks like a little page.) Photoshop creates the channel without displaying the dialog box. To force the dialog box to appear on screen, Alt-click the page icon.

✦ **Duplicate Channel:** Choose this command to create a duplicate of the selected channel, either inside the same document or as part of a new document. (If the composite view is active, the Duplicate Channel command is dimmed, because you can only duplicate one channel at a time.) The most common reason to use this command is to convert a channel into a mask. Again, you can find real-life applications in Chapter 9.

Tip

You can also duplicate a channel by dragging the channel name onto the new channel icon. No dialog box appears; Photoshop merely names the channel automatically. To copy a channel to a different document, drag the channel name and drop it into an open image window. Photoshop automatically creates a new channel for the duplicate.

✦ **Delete Channel:** To delete a channel from an image, click the channel name in the palette and choose this command. You can delete only one channel at a time. The Delete Channel command is dimmed when any essential color channel is active, or when more than one channel is selected.

Tip

If choosing a command is too much effort, just drag the channel onto the delete channel icon (which is the little trash icon in the lower right corner of the Channels palette). Or you can just click the trash icon, in which case Photoshop asks you if you really want to delete the channel. To bypass this warning, Alt-click the trash icon.

✦ **New Spot Channel:** Photoshop lets you add spot color channels to an image. Each spot color channel prints to a separate plate, just like spot colors in Illustrator or QuarkXPress. When you choose the New Spot Color command, Photoshop asks you to specify a color and a Solidity. Click the color square to bring up the Custom Colors dialog box, from which you can select a Pantone or other spot color (see Figure 4-20). The Solidity option lets you increase the opacity of the ink, perfect for Day-Glo fluorescents and metallic inks.

Tip

To create a spot color channel without choosing a command, Ctrl-click the page icon at the bottom of the Channels palette. For more information on spot-color channels, read the "Spot-Color Separations" section at the end of Chapter 18.

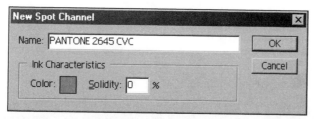

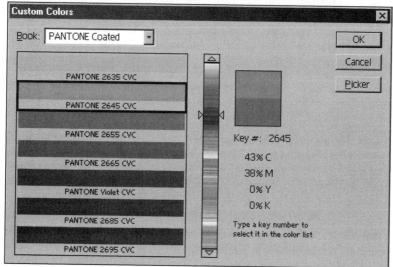

Figure 4-20: When creating a spot-color channel, Photoshop asks you to select a color and specify the degree to which the spot color will cover up other inks in the printed image.

✦ **Merge Spot Channel:** Select a spot-color channel and choose this command to merge the spot color in with the RGB, Lab, or CMYK colors in the image. Most spot colors don't have precise RGB or CMYK equivalents, so you will lose some color fidelity in the merge. Adobe includes this command to enable you to proof an image to a typical midrange color printer.

✦ **Channel Options:** Choose this command or double-click the channel name in the palette's scrolling list to change the settings assigned to a spot-color or mask channel. The Channel Options command is dimmed when a regular, everyday color channel is active.

✦ **Split Channels:** When you choose this command, Photoshop splits off each channel in an image to its own independent grayscale image window. As demonstrated in Figure 4-21, Photoshop automatically appends the channel color to the end of the window name. The Split Channels command is useful as a first step in redistributing channels in an image prior to choosing Merge Channels, as I will demonstrate later in this same chapter.

Figure 4-21: When you choose the Split Channels command, Photoshop relocates each channel to an independent image window.

✦ **Merge Channels:** Choose this command to merge several images into a single multichannel image. The images you want to merge must be open, they must be grayscale, and they must be absolutely equal in size — the same number of pixels horizontally and vertically. When you choose Merge Channels, Photoshop displays the Merge Channels dialog box, shown in Figure 4-22. It then assigns a color mode for the new image based on the number of open grayscale images that contain the same number of pixels as the foreground image.

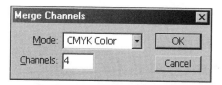

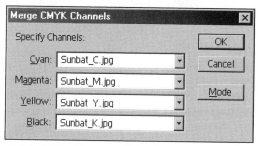

Figure 4-22: The two dialog boxes that appear after you choose Merge Channels enable you to select a color mode for the merged image (top) and to associate images with color channels (bottom).

You can override Photoshop's choice by selecting a different option from the Mode pop-up menu. (Generally, you won't want to change the value in the Channels option box because doing so causes Photoshop to automatically select Multichannel from the Mode pop-up menu. I explain multichannel images in the upcoming "Using multichannel techniques" section.)

After you press Enter, Photoshop displays a second dialog box, which also appears in Figure 4-22. In this dialog box, you can specify which grayscale image goes with which channel by choosing options from pop-up menus. When working from an image split with the Split Channels command, Photoshop automatically organizes each window into a pop-up menu according to the color appended to the window's name. For example, Photoshop associates the window Sunbat_C.jpg with the Cyan pop-up menu.

Color Channel Effects

Now that you know how to navigate among channels and apply commands, permit me to suggest a few reasons for doing so. The most pragmatic applications for channel effects involve the restoration of bad color scans. If you use a color scanner, know someone who uses a color scanner, or just have a bunch of color scans lying around, you can be sure that some of them look like dog meat. (Nothing against dog meat, mind you. I'm sure that Purina has some very lovely dog meat scans in their advertising archives.) With Photoshop's help, you can turn those scans into filet mignon — or at the very least, into an acceptable Sunday roast.

Improving the appearance of color scans

The following are a few channel-editing techniques you can use to improve the appearance of poorly scanned full-color images. Keep in mind that these techniques don't work miracles, but they can retrieve an image from the brink of absolute ugliness into the realm of tolerability.

Note

Don't forget that you can choose View ➪ New View to maintain a constant composite view. Or you can click the eyeball icon in front of the composite view in the Channels palette to view the full-color image, even when editing a single channel.

✦ **Aligning channels:** Every so often, a scan may appear out of focus even after you use Photoshop's sharpening commands to try to correct the problem, as discussed in Chapter 10. If, on closer inspection, you can see slight shadows or halos around colored areas, one of the color channels probably is out of alignment. To remedy the problem, switch to the color channel that corresponds to the color of the halos. Then select the move tool (by pressing V) and use the arrow keys to nudge the contents of the channel into alignment. Use the separate composite view (created by choosing View ➪ New View) or click the eyeball in front of the composite channel to monitor your changes.

✦ **Channel focusing:** If all channels seem to be in alignment (or, at least, as aligned as they're going to get), one of your channels may be poorly focused. Use the Ctrl+key equivalents to search for the responsible channel. When and if you find it, use the Unsharp Mask filter to sharpen it as desired. You may also find it helpful to blur a channel, as when trying to eliminate moiré patterns in a scanned halftone. (For a specific application of these techniques, see the "Cleaning up Scanned Halftones" section in Chapter 10.)

✦ **Bad channels:** In your color channel tour, if you discover that a channel is not so much poorly focused as simply rotten to the core — complete with harsh transitions, jagged edges, and random brightness variations — you may be able to improve the appearance of the channel by mixing other channels with it.

Suppose that the blue channel is awful, but the red and green channels are in fairly decent shape. The Channel Mixer command lets you mix channels together, whether to repair a bad channel or achieve an interesting effect. Choose Image ➪ Adjust ➪ Channel Mixer and press Ctrl+3 to switch to the blue channel. Then raise the Red and Green values and lower the Blue value to mix the three channels together to create a better blue. To maintain consistent brightness levels, it's generally a good idea to use a combination of Red, Green, and Blue values that adds up to 100 percent, as in Figure 4-23. If you can live with the inevitable color changes, the appearance of the image should improve dramatically.

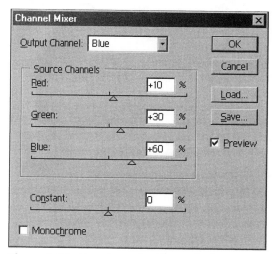

Figure 4-23: Here I use the Channel Mixer command to repair the blue channel by mixing in 10 percent of the red channel and 30 percent of the green channel. The red and green channels remain unaffected.

Note that Channel Mixer is also a great command for creating custom grayscale images. Rather than choosing Image ➪ Mode ➪ Grayscale and taking what Photoshop gives you, you can choose the Channel Mixer command and select the Monochrome check box. Then adjust the Red, Green, and Blue values to mix your own grayscale variation.

Incidentally, the Constant slider simply brightens or darkens the image across the board. Usually, you'll want to leave it set to 0. But if you're having problems getting the color balance right, give it a tweak.

Although Image ⇨ Adjust ⇨ Channel Mixer didn't arrive until Photoshop 5, I've been including my own channel mixing filter with the Photoshop Bible for better than three years now. Created in Photoshop's Filter Factory (see Chapter A on the CD-ROM), this filter coincidentally went by the name . . . *Channel Mixer!* I submit Figure 4-24 as Exhibit A. "But Deke," you say, "Your filter doesn't look anything like Adobe's Channel Mixer, and your sliders don't make nearly as much sense." Yes, I imagine that's precisely what they want you to think. Perhaps now you're beginning to understand how diabolically crafty these Photoshop programmers can be.

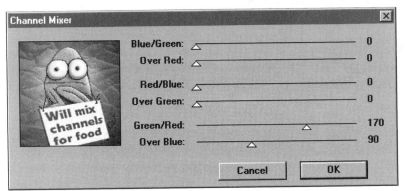

Figure 4-24: An early version of the Channel Mixer invented by yours truly. Has Adobe gone and swiped my visionary idea? You be the judge.

Using multichannel techniques

The one channel function I've so far ignored is Image ⇨ Mode ⇨ Multichannel. When you choose this command, Photoshop changes your image so that channels no longer have a specific relationship to one another. They don't mix to create a full-color image; instead, they exist independently within the confines of a single image. The multichannel mode is generally an intermediary step for converting between different color modes without recalculating the contents of the channels.

For example, normally when you convert between the RGB and CMYK modes, Photoshop maps RGB colors to the CMYK color model, changing the contents of each channel as demonstrated back in Figures 4-16 and 4-17. But suppose, just as an experiment, that you want to bypass the color mapping and instead transfer the exact contents of the red channel to the cyan channel, the contents of the green channel to the magenta channel, and so on. You convert from RGB to the multichannel mode and then from multichannel to CMYK as described in the following steps.

STEPS: Using the Multichannel Mode as an Intermediary Step

1. **Open an RGB image.** If the image is already open, make sure that it is saved to disk.

2. **Choose Image ⇨ Mode ⇨ Multichannel.** This eliminates any relationship between the formerly red, green, and blue color channels.

3. **Click the new channel icon at the bottom of the Channels palette.** Or choose the New Channel command from the palette menu and press Return to **accept** the default settings. Either way, you add a mask channel to the image. **This** empty channel will serve as the black channel in the CMYK image. (Photoshop won't let you convert from the multichannel mode to CMYK with less than four channels.)

4. **Press Ctrl+I.** Unfortunately, the new channel comes up black, which would make the entire image black. To change it to white, press Ctrl+I or choose Image ⇨ Adjust ⇨ Invert.

5. **Choose Image ⇨ Mode ⇨ CMYK.** The image looks washed out and a tad bit dark compared to its original RGB counterpart, but the overall color scheme of the image remains more or less intact. This is because the red, green, and blue color channels each have a respective opposite in the cyan, magenta, and yellow channels.

6. **Press Ctrl+Shift+L.** Or choose Image ⇨ Adjust ⇨ Auto Levels. This punches up the color a bit by automatically correcting the brightness and contrast.

7. **Convert the image to RGB, and then back to CMYK again.** The problem with the image is that it lacks any information in the black channel. So although it may look okay on-screen, it will lose much of its definition when printed. To fill in the black channel, choose Image ⇨ Mode ⇨ RGB Color, and then choose Image ⇨ Mode ⇨ CMYK Color. Photoshop automatically generates an image in the black channel in keeping with the standards of color separations (as explained in Chapter 18).

Keep in mind that these steps are by no means a recommended procedure for converting an RGB image to a CMYK image. Rather, they are merely intended to suggest one way to experiment with channel conversions to create a halfway decent image. You can likewise experiment with converting between the Lab, multichannel, and RGB modes, or Lab, multichannel, and CMYK.

Replacing and swapping color channels

If you truly want to abuse the colors in an RGB or CMYK image, there's nothing like replacing one color channel with another to produce spectacular effects. Color Plate 4-4 shows a few examples applied to an RGB image.

✦ In the first example, I used the Channel Mixer to replace the red channel with the blue. I did this by setting the Output Channel to Red, changing the Red value to 0 percent and the Blue value to 100 percent. The result is a green woman floating in a green sea under a purple sky.

✦ To achieve the next example, I again started from the original RGB image and used Channel Mixer to replace the green channel with the red. The result this time is a yellow woman against a deep blue background.

✦ To create the purple woman in a green world on the right side of Color Plate 4-4, I replaced the blue channel with the red.

You can create more interesting effects by using Color Mixer to swap the contents of color channels. For example, in the lower left example of Color Plate 4-4, I swapped the contents of the red and blue channels to create a blue woman on a green sea under an orange sky. To accomplish this, I set the Output Channel to Red, set the Red value to 0 and the Blue to 100. Then I switched to the Blue channel (Ctrl+3) and set the Red value to 100 and the Blue to 0.

The next two examples along the bottom of Color Plate 4-4 show the results of swapping the red and green channels (for a bright green woman) and the green and blue channels. Because the green and blue channels contain relatively similar data, this produces the subtlest effect, chiefly switching the sea and sky colors and turning the swimsuit pink.

✦   ✦   ✦

Painting and Editing

Paint and Edit Tool Basics

Here it is, Chapter 5, and I'm finally getting around to explaining how to use Photoshop's painting tools. You must feel like you're attending some kind of martial arts ritual where you have to learn to run away, cry, beg, and attempt bribery before you get to start karate-chopping bricks and kicking your instructor. "The wise person journeys through the fundamentals of image editing before painting a single brushstroke, Grasshoppa." *Wang, wang, wang.* (That's a musical embellishment, in case you didn't recognize it. Man, I hate to have to explain my jokes. Especially when they're so measly.) Now that you've earned your first belt or tassel or scouting patch or whatever it is you're supposed to receive for slogging this far through the book, you're as prepared as you'll ever be to dive into the world of painting and retouching images.

You might think these tools require artistic talent. In truth, each tool provides options for almost any level of proficiency or experience. Photoshop offers get-by measures for novices who want to make a quick edit and put the tool down before they make a mess of things. If you have a few hours of experience with other painting programs, you'll find Photoshop's tools provide at least as much functionality and, in many cases, more. (The one exception is Painter, which is several times more capable than Photoshop in the painting department.) And if you're a professional artist — well, come on now — you'll have no problems learning how to make Photoshop sing. No matter who you are, you'll find electronic painting and editing tools more flexible, less messy, and more forgiving than their traditional counterparts.

Cross-Reference If you screw something up in the course of painting your image, stop and choose Edit ➪ Undo (or press Ctrl+Z). If this doesn't work, press Ctrl+Alt+Z to step back through your paint strokes. (These shortcuts assume that you haven't changed the default Redo Key setting in the Preferences dialog box; see Chapter 2 for more information.) You also can select a previous state in the History palette, as explained in Chapter 7. The History palette lists brushstrokes and other changes according to the tool you used to create them.

Meet your tools

Photoshop provides three paint tools: pencil, paintbrush, and airbrush. You also get six edit tools: smudge, blur, sharpen, burn, dodge, and sponge. Figure 5-1 shows all the tools along with the keyboard shortcuts for selecting them.

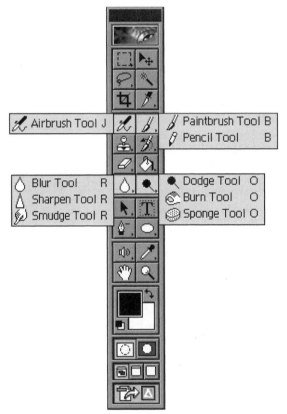

Figure 5-1: The three paint tools and six edit tools; note that the pencil and paintbrush now share a toolbox slot and a keyboard shortcut.

When two or more tools share a slot in the toolbox, click or drag on the arrow in the lower corner of the tool icon to display a flyout menu of all the tools, as shown in Figure 5-1. Or you can just press the keyboard shortcut listed in the menu to cycle through the tools. However, if you turn on the Use Shift Key for Tool Switch option in the General panel of the Preferences dialog box (Ctrl+K), you must press Shift and the shortcut to switch tools.

You can vary the performance of the paint and edit tools by using the controls on the new Options bar, which contains tool settings formerly accessed through the Options palette and the Brushes palette. If you don't see the Options bar, shown in Figure 5-2, double-click any tool icon or just press Enter to display it. You also can choose Windows ➪ Show Options. If you want to keep other palettes close by, you can dock them in the Options bar, which appears if you set your monitor's screen resolution to display more than 800 pixels horizontally. Just drag the palette tab to the docking well, labeled in Figure 5-2. Upcoming sections in this chapter explain all the ways to adjust the paint and edit tools. Check out Chapter 2 for more details about the Options bar.

If you want to return a tool to its default settings, click the tool's icon at the left end of the Options bar and choose Reset Tool from the pop-up menu. Click Reset All Tools to return every tool back to its original state.

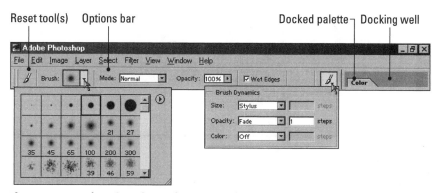

Figure 5-2: Tool settings formerly contained in the Options and Brushes palettes now hang out in the Options bar.

In addition to the paint and edit tools, Photoshop 6 provides a set of tools for drawing vector objects. I cover these tools in Chapter 14.

The paint tools

The paint tools apply paint in the foreground color. In this and other **respects**, they work like their counterparts in other painting programs, but there **are** a few exceptions:

✦ **Pencil:** Unlike pencil tools found in most other painting programs — which paint lines 1 pixel thick — Photoshop's pencil paints a hard-edged line of any thickness you specify. Figure 5-3 compares the default 1-pixel **pencil line** with **a** fatter pencil line, a paintbrush line, and an airbrush line.

If you're used to selecting the pencil tool by pressing P (as in Photoshop 3), Y (as in Version 4), or N (as in Version 5), prepare for yet another change. The new pencil tool shortcut is B, same as for the paintbrush. Toggle back and forth between the two tools by pressing B repeatedly (or Shift+B, depending on your Preferences setting for keyboard tool switches).

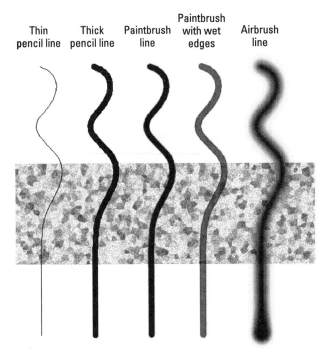

Figure 5-3: Five lines painted in black with the pencil, paintbrush, and airbrush tools. The Wet Edges option (second from right) causes the line to appear translucent. I held the airbrush tool in place for a few moments at the end of the line located at the far right.

✦ **Paintbrush:** The paintbrush works like the pencil tool, except it **paints** an *antialiased* (softened) line that blends in with its background.

When you select the Wet Edges check box on the Options bar, the paintbrush creates a translucent line with darkened edges, much as if you were painting with watercolors. Soft brush shapes produce more naturalistic effects. Figure 5-3 shows an example of this effect.

✦ **Airbrush:** Dismissing Photoshop's airbrush tool as a softer version of the paintbrush is tempting because it uses a softer brush shape by default. Photoshop's default airbrush settings also call for a lighter pressure, so the airbrush paints a translucent line. But unlike the paintbrush, which applies a continuous stream of color and stops applying paint when you stop dragging, the airbrush applies a series of colored dollops and continues to apply these dollops as long as you press the mouse button. Figure 5-3 shows the dark glob of paint that results from pressing the mouse button while holding the mouse motionless at the end of the drag.

The edit tools

The edit tools don't apply color; rather, they influence existing colors in an image. Figure 5-4 shows each of the six edit tools applied to a randomized background. Future sections cover the tools in more detail, but here's a brief introduction:

✦ **Blur:** The first of the two focus tools, the blur tool blurs an image by lessening the amount of color contrast between neighboring pixels.

✦ **Sharpen:** The second focus tool selectively sharpens by increasing the contrast between neighboring pixels. Generally speaking, both the blur and sharpen tools are less useful than their command counterparts in the Filters menu. They provide less control and usually require scrubbing at an image. Maybe I've been using a computer too long, but my wrist starts to ache when I use these tools. If, unlike me, you like the basic principle behind the tools, but you want to avoid carpal tunnel syndrome, you can achieve consistent, predictable results without scrubbing by using the tools in combination with the Shift key, as described in the next section, "Basic techniques."

✦ **Smudge:** The smudge tool smears colors in an image. The effect is much like dragging your finger across wet paint.

✦ **Dodge:** The first of three toning tools, the dodge tool lets you lighten a portion of an image by dragging across it. Named after a traditional film exposure technique, the dodge tool is supposed to look like a little paddle thingie — you know, like one of those spoons you put over your eye at the optometrist's — that you wave over photographic paper to cast a shadow and thereby lighten the exposure. Thank golly we no longer have to wave little paddle thingies in our modern age.

✦ **Burn:** The burn tool lets you darken a portion of an image by dragging over it. The effect is similar to burning a film negative, which you apparently do by holding your hand in a kind of O shape in an effort to focus the light, kind of like frying a worker ant using a magnifying glass (except not quite so smelly). At least, that's what they tell me. Sadly, I've never had the pleasure of trying it.

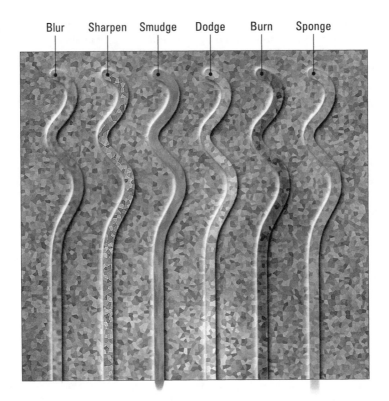

Figure 5-4: Dragging with Photoshop's edit tools creates these effects. The boundaries of each line are highlighted so that you can clearly see the distinctions between line and background.

Tip

If you're like most folks, you have difficulty remembering which tool lightens and which one darkens. So here's a little tip: That little hand icon looks like it could be holding a piece of toast, and when you burn toast, it gets darker. Hand, toast, burn, darker. That other tool, the eye doctor paddle, is not holding toast, so it must lighten. You'll never have problems again.

✦ **Sponge:** The final toning tool, the sponge tool, robs an image of both saturation and contrast. Or you can set the tool so it boosts saturation and adds contrast. For more information, stay tuned for the upcoming section "Mopping up with the sponge tool."

To access the sharpen tool temporarily when the blur tool is selected, press and hold Alt while using the tool. The sharpen tool remains available only as long as you press Alt. You also can press Alt to access the blur tool when the sharpen tool is selected, to access the burn tool when the dodge tool is selected, and to access the dodge tool when the burn tool is selected. (If the sponge tool is active, pressing Alt has no effect, except maybe to give your finger a cramp.)

Tip

You can replace the blur tool with the sharpen tool in the toolbox by Alt-clicking on the tool's icon. Alt-click again to select the smudge tool and yet again to cycle back to the blur tool. Likewise, you can Alt-click the dodge tool icon to cycle between the dodge, burn, and sponge tools.

As explained in Chapter 2, the keyboard shortcuts also toggle between the tools. When the blur tool is selected, press R to switch to the sharpen tool. Repeated pressings of R take you to the smudge tool and back to the blur tool. When the dodge tool is selected, press O to toggle to the burn tool; press O again to get the sponge.

If these shortcuts don't work for you, head for the General panel of the Preferences dialog box (Ctrl+K). Chances are, the Use Shift for Tool Switch check box is selected, which means that you have to press Shift plus the keyboard shortcut to cycle through tools. Turn the check box off to give your Shift finger a rest.

Basic techniques

I know several people who claim that they can't paint, and yet they create beautiful work in Photoshop. Even though they don't have sufficient hand-eye coordination to write their names on screen, they have unique and powerful artistic sensibilities, and they know many tricks that enable them to make judicious use of the paint and edit tools. I can't help you in the sensibilities department, but I can show you a few tricks to boost your ability and inclination to use the paint and edit tools.

Painting a straight line

You probably already know that you can draw a straight line with the line tool. And you may be wondering why I don't include the line tool in my discussion of painting tools. Well, the reason is that as a painting tool, the line tool is pretty limited in its usefulness.

In the line tool's defense, it has evolved in Version 6. You now can draw either vector lines or raster lines using the tool, and you also can set the tool to create a work path. You set the tool's function through the trio of icons on the left end of the Options bar. Click the first button to create a vector shape on a new layer, as discussed in Chapter 14; click the middle button to create a work path, a topic I cover in Chapter 9; and click the third button to paint a regular, pixel-based line.

About the only reason I ever use the line tool in painting mode is to create arrows. (I explain how in the "Applying Strokes and Arrowheads" section of Chapter 8.) If you don't want arrows, you're better off using Photoshop's other means for creating straight lines: the Shift key. Using this method, you can paint with different brushes and access other options not available when you work with the line tool.

To paint a straight line with any of the paint tools, click at one point in the image and then press Shift and click at another point. Photoshop connects the start and end points with a straight stroke of paint. Use this same technique to apply an edit tool in a straight line.

To create free-form polygons, continue to Shift-click with the tool. Figure 5-5 features a photograph and a tracing I made on a separate layer (covered in Chapter 12) exclusively by Shift-clicking with the paintbrush tool. As an academic exercise, I never dragged with the tool, I never altered the brush size, and I used just two colors: black and gray.

Figure 5-5: Starting from an image by photographer Barbara Penoyar (left), I created a stylized tracing (right) by clicking and Shift-clicking with the paintbrush tool on a separate layer.

Tip

The Shift key makes the blur and sharpen tools halfway useful. Suppose that you want to edit the perimeter of the car shown in Figure 5-6. The arrows in the figure illustrate the path your Shift-clicks should follow. Figure 5-7 shows the effect of Shift-clicking with the blur tool; Figure 5-8 demonstrates the effect of Shift-clicking with the sharpen tool.

Figure 5-6: It takes one click and 24 Shift-clicks to soften or accentuate the edges around this car using the blur or sharpen tool.

Figure 5-7: These are the results of blurring the car's perimeter with the pressure set to 50 percent (top) and 100 percent (bottom). Set the pressure by using the Pressure pop-up menu in the Options bar.

Figure 5-8: The results of sharpening the car with the pressure set to 50 percent (top) and 100 percent (bottom).

Painting a perpendicular line

To create a perpendicular line — either a vertical or a horizontal line — with any of the paint tools, press and hold the mouse button, press Shift, and begin dragging in a vertical or horizontal direction. Don't release Shift until you finish dragging or until you want to change the direction of the line, as shown in Figure 5-9. Press Shift in mid-drag to snap the line back into perpendicular alignment. Again, these techniques work with the edit tools as well as the paint tools.

One way to exploit the Shift key's penchant to snap to the perpendicular is to draw "ribbed" structures. Being left-handed, I dragged from right to left with the paintbrush to create both of the central outlines around the skeleton that appears at the top of Figure 5-10. I painted each rib by pressing and releasing Shift as I dragged with the paintbrush tool. Pressing Shift snapped the line to the horizontal axis, whose location was established by the beginning of the drag.

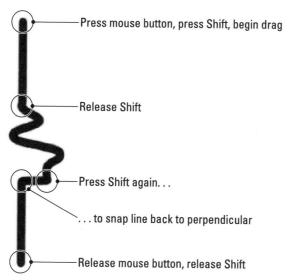

Press mouse button, press Shift, begin drag

Release Shift

Press Shift again...

... to snap line back to perpendicular

Release mouse button, release Shift

Figure 5-9: Pressing Shift after you start to drag with a paint or edit tool results in a perpendicular line for as long as the key is pressed.

In the figure, I represented the axis for each line in gray. After establishing the basic skeletal form, I added some free-form details with the paintbrush and pencil tools, as shown in the middle image in Figure 5-10. I then selected a general area around the image and chose Filter ⇨ Stylize ⇨ Emboss to create the finished fossil image. Nobody's going to confuse my painting with a bona fide fossil, but it's not bad for a cartoon.

It's no accident Figure 5-10 features a swordfish instead of your everyday round-nosed carp. To snap to the horizontal axis, I had to establish the direction of my drag as being more horizontal than vertical. If I had instead dragged in a fish-faced convex arc, Photoshop would have interpreted my drag as vertical and snapped to the vertical axis.

Painting simple shapes with the drawing tools

As I alluded to a section or two ago, you can use the new shape tools to create raster — that is, pixel-based — objects, as well as vector objects (see Chapter 3 if you need a refresher course on the difference). After selecting the rectangle, rounded rectangle, ellipse, polygon, line, or custom shape tool, click the Fill Region icon on the Options bar, labeled in Figure 5-11. Then use the tools as described in Chapter 14 to create your shapes, which Photoshop fills with the foreground color.

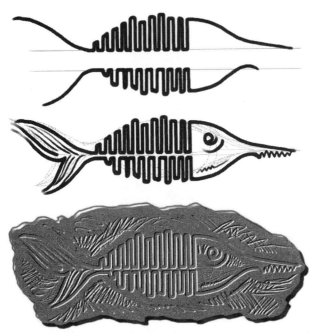

Figure 5-10: To create the basic structure for our bony pal, I periodically pressed and released Shift while dragging with the paintbrush (top). Then I embellished the fish using the paintbrush and pencil (middle). Finally, I applied the Emboss filter to transform fish into fossil (bottom).

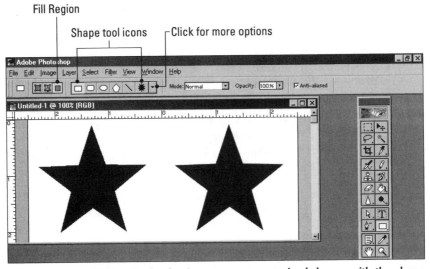

Figure 5-11: Click the paint bucket icon to create rasterized shapes with the shape tools (line, rectangle, ellipse, polygon, and custom shape).

When Fill Region is selected, you can adjust the opacity and blend mode of your paint strokes through the Opacity and Mode menus on the Options bar. You also can select the Anti-aliased check box to soften the transition between a shape and its surroundings. I created the left star in the figure with Anti-aliased turned off; the right star shows the same shape painted with the check box turned on. If you click the down-pointing triangle at the end of the strip of tool icons, you display additional options for the selected tool.

Painting with the smudge tool

Many first-time Photoshop artists misuse the smudge tool to soften color transitions. In fact, softening is the purpose of the blur tool. The smudge tool *smears* colors by shoving them into each other. The process bears more resemblance to the finger painting you did in grade school than to any traditional photographic-editing technique.

In Photoshop, the performance of the smudge tool depends in part on the settings of the Pressure and Finger Painting controls on the Options bar, which you access by pressing Enter when the smudge tool is active. Here's what you need to know about these options:

✦ **Pressure:** Measured as a percentage of the brush shape, this option determines the distance the smudge tool drags a color. Higher percentages and larger brush shapes drag colors farthest. A Pressure setting of 100 percent equates to infinity, meaning the smudge tool drags a color from the beginning of your drag until the end of your drag, regardless of how far you drag. Cosmic, Daddy-O.

✦ **Finger Painting:** The folks at Adobe used to call this effect *dipping*, which I think more accurately expressed how the effect works. When you select this option, the smudge tool begins by applying a smidgen of foreground color, which it eventually blends in with the colors in the image. It's as if you dipped your finger in a color and then dragged it through an oil painting. Use the Pressure setting to specify the amount of foreground color applied. If you turn on Finger Painting and set the Pressure to 100 percent, the smudge tool behaves exactly like the paintbrush tool.

Tip You can reverse the Finger Painting setting by Alt-dragging. If the option is off, Alt-dragging dips the tool into the foreground color. If Finger Painting is turned on, Alt-dragging smudges normally.

For some examples of the smudge tool in action, look at Figure 5-12. The figure shows the effects of using the smudge tool set to four different Pressure percentages and with the Finger Painting option both off and on. In each instance, the brush shape is 13 pixels in diameter and the foreground color is set to black.

The Use All Layers option (previously called Sample Merged) instructs the smudge tool to grab colors in all visible layers and smudge them into the current layer. Whether the option is on or off, only the current layer is affected; the background and other layers remain intact.

For example, suppose the inverted eyes of the woman at the top of Figure 5-13 are on a different layer than the rest of the face. If I use the smudge tools on the eyes layer with Use All Layers turned off, Photoshop ignores the face layer when smudging the

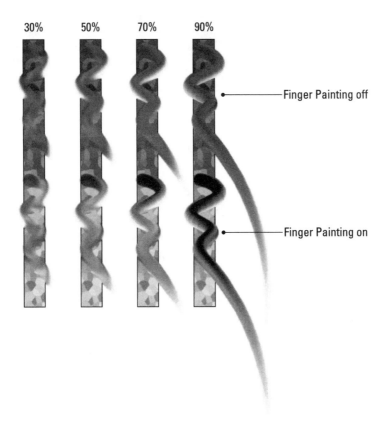

Figure 5-12: Eight drags with the smudge tool subject to different Pressure and Finger Painting settings.

eyes. As a result, details such as the nose and teeth remain unsmudged, as you can see in the lower-left example. If I turn Use All Layers on, Photoshop lifts colors from the face layer and mixes them in with the eyes layer, as shown in the lower-right example.

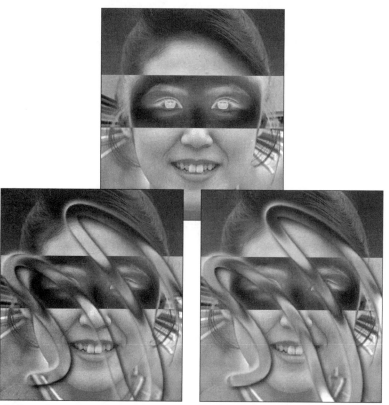

Figure 5-13: The original image (top) features inverted eyes on a layer above the rest of the face. I first smudged the eyes with Use All Layers turned off (lower left) and then with the option turned on (lower right).

Note that all this activity occurs exclusively on the eyes layer. To give you a better look, the two lower examples on the eyes layer are shown independently of those on the face layer in Figure 5-14. You can now clearly see the proliferation of face details mixed into the eyes in the right example. Meanwhile, the face layer remains absolutely unaffected.

Figure 5-14: The eyes layer from the previous figure shown by itself.

In Version 6, you can further vary the smudge tool effects through the Brush and Brush Dynamics palettes. The upcoming section "Brush Shape and Opacity" explores these options, so I won't waste space repeating everything here. For now, just know that you can set the smudge tool to create gradually tapering and/or fading strokes — and you can now use your mouse as well as a pressure-sensitive tablet to generate these effects.

Mopping up with the sponge tool

The sponge tool is actually a pretty simple tool, hardly worth expending valuable space in a book as tiny as this one. But I'm a compulsive explainer, so here's the deal: Press Enter when the sponge tool is active or double-click the tool icon in the toolbox to display the sponge tool controls on the Options bar. Then select either Desaturate or Saturate from the Mode pop-up menu to create one of the following results:

✦ When set to Desaturate, the tool reduces the saturation of the colors over which you drag. When you're editing a grayscale image, the tool reduces contrast.

✦ If you select Saturate, the sponge tool increases the saturation of the colors over which you drag or increases contrast in a grayscale image.

You can switch between the Desaturate and Saturate modes from the keyboard. Press Shift+Alt+D to select the Desaturate option. Press Shift+Alt+S for Saturate.

No matter which mode you choose, higher Pressure settings produce more dramatic results. Your settings in the Brushes and Brush Dynamics palettes also affect the sponge tool's performance; see the next section, "Brush Shape and Opacity," for more information.

Tip

Color Plate 5-1 shows the sponge tool in action. The upper-left example shows the original PhotoDisc image. The upper-right example shows the result of applying the sponge tool set to Desaturate. I dragged with the tool inside the pepper and around the corn area. The Pressure was set to 100 percent. Notice that the affected colors are on the wane, sliding toward gray. In the lower-right example, the effect is even more pronounced. I applied the sponge tools here with great vim and vigor two additional times. Hardly any hint of color is left in these areas now.

To create the lower-left example in Color Plate 5-1, I applied the sponge tool set to Saturate. This is where the process gets a little tricky. If you boost saturation levels with the sponge tool in the RGB or Lab color modes, you can achieve colors of absolutely neon intensity. However, these high-saturation colors don't stand a snowball's chance in a microwave of printing in CMYK. So, use View ⇨ Proof Colors (Ctrl+Y) to preview your image in CMYK before boosting saturation levels with the sponge tool. This way, you can accurately view the results of your edits. (Adobe changed the CMYK preview features in Version 6; Chapter 16 explains the new preview options if you need help figuring them out.)

Figure 5-15 shows the yellow channel from each of the images in Color Plate 5-1. Because yellow is the most prevalent primary color in the image, it is the most sensitive to saturation adjustments. When I boosted the saturation in the lower-left example, the yellow brightness values deepened, adding yellow ink to the CMYK image. When I lessened the saturation in the two right examples, the amount of ink diminished.

One of Adobe's recommended uses of the sponge tool is to reduce the saturation levels of out-of-gamut RGB colors before converting an image to the CMYK mode. I'm not too crazy about this technique because it requires a lot of scrubbing. Generally, selecting the out-of-gamut area and reducing the colors using more automated controls is easier (as discussed in Chapter 11). You might prefer to use the sponge tool, however, when a more selective, personal touch is required, as when curbing a distracting color that seems to leap a little too vigorously off the screen or boosting the saturation of a detail in the CMYK mode.

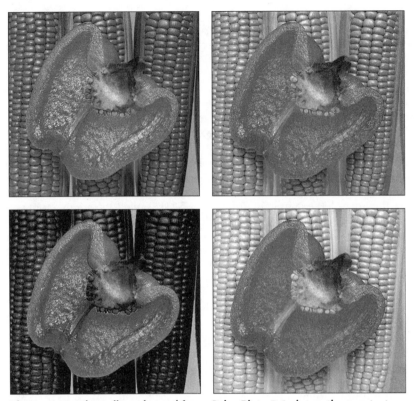

Figure 5-15: The yellow channel from Color Plate 5-1 shows the greatest a mount of variation when reducing and boosting the saturation with the sponge tool.

Brush Shape and Opacity

So far, I mentioned the words *brush shape* several times, and I have yet to explain what the Sam Hill I'm talking about. Luckily, it's simple. The brush shape is the size and shape of the tip of your cursor when you use a paint or edit tool. A big, round brush shape paints or edits in broad strokes. A small, elliptical brush shape is useful for performing hairline adjustments.

By default, your cursor outline reflects the selected brush shape. If your cursor instead looks like a crosshair or tool icon, press Ctrl+K to bring up the Preferences dialog box and press Ctrl+3 for the Display & Cursors panel. Then select Brush Size from the Painting Cursors radio buttons. Now you can create a brush as big as 999 pixels in diameter and have your cursor grow accordingly.

Tip
When you use a very small brush, four dots appear around the cursor perimeter, making the cursor easier to locate. If you need a little more help, press the Caps Lock key to access the more obvious crosshair cursor.

The Brushes palette

Unless you were completely asleep at the wheel when you launched Photoshop 6 for the first time, you no doubt noticed the Options bar stretching across the top of the program window. In computer lingo, the Options bar is known as a context-sensitive toolbar, meaning that the options on the bar change depending on what tool you're using. When you work with the paint and edit tools, the Options bar gives you access to a choice of brush shapes. To browse through the available brushes, open the Brush palette by clicking the triangle next to the brush icon, as shown in Figure 5-16.

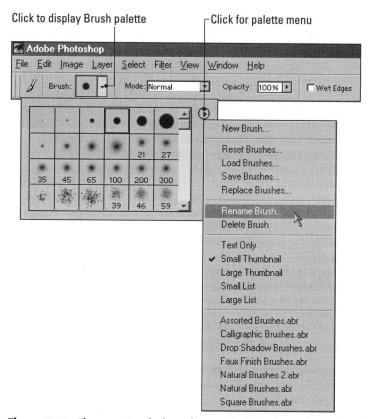

Figure 5-16: The new Brush drop-down palette looks and acts like the old Brushes palette in some regards, but can't be freed from the confines of the Options bar or grouped with other palettes.

Adobe refers to the Brush palette as the Brush menu, but I'm going to be contrary and go with "drop-down palette." For the most part, the Brush menu looks and works like the old Brushes palette. You can resize it by dragging the size box. And clicking the triangle in the upper-right corner displays a submenu, just as in a palette. Because I can't bring myself to refer to this submenu as the "Brush menu menu," I'm sticking with Brush drop-down palette. Sometimes I may even get really bold and just use "palette." I trust you will not be too distressed by the court's ruling on this matter.

That said, this Brush palette does differ from a regular palette in a few important ways. You can't tear it away from the Options bar or combine it with other palettes, as you can with the "real" palettes (Layers, Channels, and other palettes listed on the Window menu). Furthermore, the old shortcut for displaying the Brushes palette, F5, has absolutely no effect on the new Brush palette. You have to press Enter with a paint or edit tool active, double-click the tool's icon in the toolbox, or choose Window ➪ Show Options to display the Options bar and all its drop-down palettes.

You can switch brush shapes without opening the Brush palette by pressing the left-bracket key and right-bracket key, as in previous editions of Photoshop. But if you're in the habit of using these shortcuts, listen up, because the bracket keys work differently now: Each press of the left bracket decreases the diameter of the active brush by 10 pixels. Pressing the right bracket increases the brush diameter by 10 pixels. The brush icon on the Options bar shows the current diameter.

If all you want to do is move from one brush in the palette to another, use the arrow keys. For example, press the up-arrow key to select the brush that's immediately above the current brush. You have to use this technique if you want to switch from a hard brush to a soft one using the keyboard. Unfortunately, the old shortcut for selecting the first brush and the last brush, Shift and the bracket keys, no longer has any effect.

If you haven't altered the current brush—changing its softness, for example—you can also use these shortcuts: Press the comma key to toggle to the previously selected brush. Press the period key to go the other direction. You also can press the greater than key (Shift plus the period key) to select the last brush in the palette; press the less than key (Shift plus the comma key) to select the first brush in the palette.

Editing and creating brush shapes

To edit the shape of the currently selected brush, click the brush icon in the Options bar to display the brush options shown in Figure 5-17. (Be sure to click the icon and not the adjacent triangle; otherwise, you display the Brush palette.) After you select your brush settings, press Enter, click an empty area of the program window, or just begin working with the tool to close the dialog box. If you change your mind and decide to leave the brush alone, press Esc or click the brush icon again to close the dialog box.

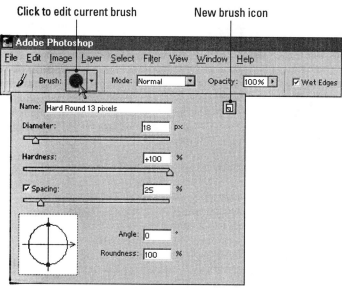

Figure 5-17: To change the size, shape, and hardness of the current brush, click its icon in the Options bar.

If you want to create a new brush shape, choose New Brush from the palette menu or click an empty brush slot in the palette. Photoshop displays the New Brush dialog box, which is just like the dialog box in Figure 5-17 except that it has a title bar. Whether you're editing an existing brush or creating a new one, you have the following options at your disposal:

✦ **Name:** You now can give your custom brushes a name to help you keep track of them. If you don't enter a name, Photoshop labels the brushes **Brush 1,** **Brush 2,** and so on. If you later want to rename a brush, just double-click its icon in the Brush drop-down palette.

✦ **Diameter:** This option determines the width of the brush shape. If the brush shape is elliptical instead of circular, the Diameter value determines the longest dimension. You can enter any value from 1 to 999 pixels. Brush shapes with diameters of 30 pixels or higher are too large to display accurately in the Brush drop-down palette and instead appear as circles with inset Diameter values.

✦ **Hardness:** Except when you use the pencil tool, brushes are always antialiased. You can further soften the edges of a brush, however, by dragging the Hardness slider bar away from 100 percent. The softest setting, 0 percent, gradually tapers the brush from a single solid color pixel at its center to a ring of transparent pixels around the brush's perimeter. Figure 5-18 demonstrates how low Hardness percentages expand the size of a 100-pixel brush beyond the Diameter value (as demonstrated by the examples set against black). Even a 100-percent hard brush shape expands slightly because it is antialiased. The Hardness setting is ignored when you use the pencil tool.

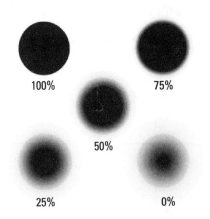

Figure 5-18: A 100-pixel diameter brush shown as it appears when set to a variety of Hardness percentages. I changed the background pixels below from white to black so that you can see the actual diameter of each brush shape. The tick marks indicate 10-pixel increments.

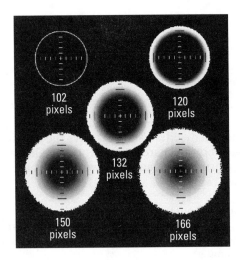

✦ **Spacing:** The Spacing option controls how frequently a tool affects an image as you drag, measured as a percentage of the brush shape. Suppose the Diameter of a brush shape is 12 pixels and the Spacing is set to 25 percent (the setting for all default brush shapes). For every 3 pixels (25 percent of 12 pixels) you drag with the paintbrush tool, Photoshop lays down a 12-pixel wide spot of color. A Spacing of 1 percent provides the most coverage but may also slow down the performance of the tool. If you deselect the Spacing check box, the effect of the tool is wholly dependent on the speed at which you drag; this can be useful for creating splotchy or oscillating lines. Figure 5-19 shows examples.

✦ **Angle:** This option enables you to pivot a brush shape on its axes. Unless the brush is elliptical, though, this won't make a difference in the appearance of the brush shape.

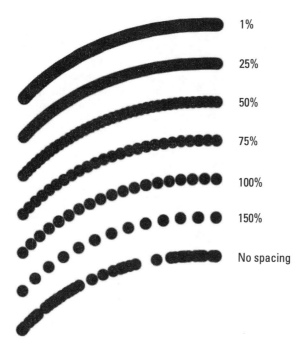

1%

25%

50%

75%

100%

150%

No spacing

Figure 5-19: Examples of lines drawn with different brush Spacing values. Gaps or ridges generally begin to appear when the Spacing value exceeds 30 percent. The final line was created by turning off the Spacing option.

✦ **Roundness:** Enter a value of less than 100 percent into the Roundness option to create an elliptical brush shape. The value measures the width of the brush as a percentage of its height, so a Roundness value of 5 percent results in a long, skinny brush shape.

You can adjust the angle of the brush dynamically by dragging the gray arrow inside the box to the left of the Angle and Roundness options. Drag the handles on either side of the black circle to make the brush shape elliptical, as demonstrated in Figure 5-20. And try this trick: Click anywhere in the white box to move the arrow to that point.

I heartily recommend that you take a few moments soon to experiment at length with the available brush options. By combining paint and edit tools with one or more specialized brush shapes, you can achieve artistic effects unlike anything permitted by traditional techniques. Starting with a PhotoDisc image lightened and filtered to serve as a template, I painted Figure 5-21 using the flat, 45-pixel brush shape shown in the dialog box. No other brush shape or special effect was applied. Think of what you can accomplish if you don't limit yourself as ridiculously as I did.

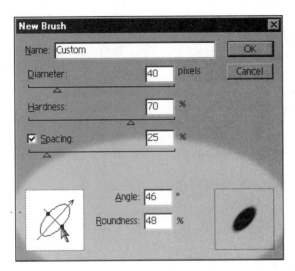

Figure 5-20: Drag the gray arrow or the black handles to change the angle or the roundness of a brush, respectively. The Angle and Roundness values update automatically, as does the preview of the brush in the lower-right corner of the dialog box.

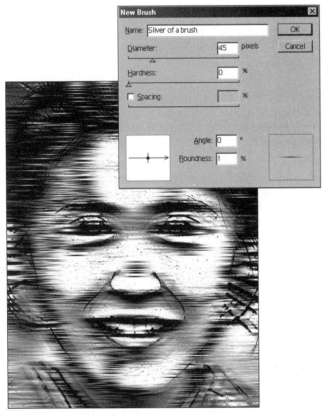

Figure 5-21: Just to show off, I painted over a scanned image with the paintbrush tool, using the brush shape shown in the dialog box at the top.

After you edit a brush, you can click the new brush icon, labeled in Figure 5-17, to save it as a new brush. Photoshop stores the brush as part of your program preferences so that it's preserved between editing sessions. Note that if you delete the preferences file (discussed in Chapter 2), you lose your custom brushes.

Creating and using custom brushes

In addition to creating ordinary custom brushes, as described in the preceding section, "Editing and creating brush shapes," you can turn an element in your image into a brush. This process works a tad differently in Version 6 than in previous versions. After you select the area that you want to use as a brush, you now choose Define Brush from the Edit menu instead of from the palette menu. You're invited to give your brush a name; if you're not feeling inspired, just press Enter and accept the default, Sampled Brush 1.

The size of your custom brush mirrors the size of the selection. That is, if you select an area that's 20 pixels wide by 10 pixels tall, you get a 20 × 10-pixel rectangular brush. Because you can't resize a custom brush as you can a regular brush, check the pixel population of the selection and adjust the image accordingly before choosing Define Brush.

You can modify your custom brush as follows:

✦ **Brush options:** After you press Enter, Photoshop displays a variation of the New Brush dialog box. You can change the spacing of the brush shape and specify whether Photoshop antialiases the edges or leaves them as is. If the brush is sufficiently large, the Anti-aliased check box appears dimmed. All custom brushes are hard-edged when you use the pencil tool.

When you display a drop-down dialog box like the one shown in Figure 5-22, you close the dialog box by either pressing Enter or by clicking an empty area in the program window. You also can simply start using the tool in the image window. Press Escape to close the dialog box without making any changes. Also remember that if you want your custom brush to take up permanent residence in the Brush drop-down palette, you must save the brush as outlined in the next section, "Saving, loading, and editing brush sets."

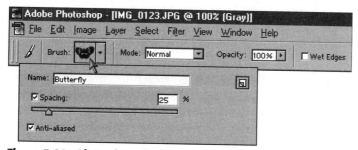

Figure 5-22: After using Edit ➪ Define Brush to create a custom brush, click the brush icon to display these additional brush options.

✦ **Brush color:** The foreground color affects a custom brush just as it does a standard brush shape. To find out more about setting the foreground color, see Chapter 4.

✦ **Opacity and brush modes:** The settings of the Opacity slider bar and the Mode pop-up menu, both now located on the Options bar, also affect the application of custom brushes, as do the choices you make in the Brush Dynamics drop-down palette. For more information on these options, keep reading this chapter.

You can achieve some unusual and, sometimes, interesting effects by activating the smudge tool's Finger Painting option and painting in the image window with a custom brush. At high Pressure settings, say 80 to 90 percent, the effect is rather like applying oil paint with a hairy paintbrush, as illustrated in Figure 5-23.

Figure 5-23: I created this organic, expressive image by combining the smudge tool's dipping capability with four custom brushes. I don't know what those finger-like growths are, but they'd probably feel right at home in an aquarium.

Tip   In addition to giving you the flexibility to create a brush from some element in your image, Photoshop ships with a file called Assorted Brushes, which contains all kinds of little symbols and doodads you can use as brush shapes. The next section explains how to load these brushes; Figure 5-24 shows an inspirational image I created using brushes in the Assorted Brushes collection.

Figure 5-24: Yes, it's Boris, the sleeping custom-brush guy. If you suspect this image is meant to suggest custom brushes are more amusing than utilitarian, you're right. The brushes from the Assorted Brushes file appear on the right.

Saving, loading, and editing brush sets

After you define a custom brush, you must save it if you want it to last forever — or at least until you decide that you can live without it. In Photoshop, you can preserve a custom brush by clicking the new brush icon in the brush options dialog boxes (shown in Figures 5-17 and 5-22) or by saving it as part of a brush set. The program ships with a default brush set plus four additional sets, found in the Presets/Brushes folder in the main Photoshop folder. Brush sets have the file extension .abr. You also can create your own custom brush collections. This option comes in handy if you need to share custom brushes with a fellow Photoshop user. Just create a new brush set containing your custom brushes and then give your colleague the brush set file. (Note that earlier versions of Photoshop can't load Version 6 brush presets.) Also, if you find that you never use certain brushes in a set, you can create a new set that doesn't contain those brushes. By limiting the number of brushes in the Brush drop-down palette, you make the job of hunting down the brush you want easier.

You can save brush sets — as well as load and edit them — either by choosing commands on the palette menu in the Brush drop-down palette (see Figure 5-16, earlier in this chapter) or via the Brushes panel of the Preset Manager dialog box, new to Photoshop 6. To check out the dialog box, choose Edit ⇨ Preset Manager. Figure 5-25 gives you a look at the Preset Manager with the Brushes panel at the forefront. If you're already working in the Preset Manager, you can press Ctrl+1 to get to the Brushes panel.

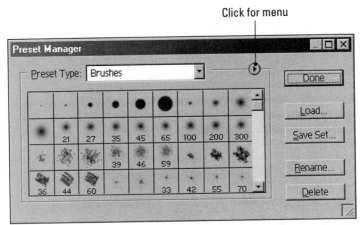

Figure 5-25: You can load, save, and edit brush sets here or in the Brush drop-down palette on the Options bar.

By default, the Brush drop-down palette displays the basic Photoshop brush set, which features a selection of round and square brushes. You can't delete this brush set, but you can prevent brushes you don't use from taking up space in the palette. You also can load or create a different set, combine two or more sets, and add or delete brushes from your custom brush sets. Here's the drill:

✦ **Save a brush set:** To save all brushes currently displayed in the Brush palette, choose Save Brushes from the palette menu. If you want to save only some of the brushes as a set, however, open the Preset Manager dialog box. Shift-click the icons of the brushes you want to save and then click Save Set. I suppose you could also delete the brushes you don't want to save from the Brush palette and save the file through the palette menu, but the Preset Manager provides a more convenient option.

Regardless of where you initiate the save, Photoshop takes you to the Save dialog box, where you can name your brush set. By default, brushes are saved in the Presets/Brushes folder, which is a darn good place for them. The next time you start Photoshop, your new brush set appears on the Brush palette menu along with other available sets.

✦ **Use a different brush set:** If you want to put the current brush set away and use a different set, choose Replace Brushes from the Brush palette menu and select the brush set you want to use. Alternatively, click the arrow at the top of the scrolling list of icons in the Preset Manager dialog box (I labeled it in Figure 5-25) to display a similar menu, and then choose Replace Brushes from that menu.

✦ **Load multiple brush sets:** You can keep multiple brush sets active if you want. After loading the first set, choose Load Brushes from the Brush palette menu or click Load in the Preset Manager dialog box. Photoshop appends the second brush set onto the first. If you want to keep using the two sets together, you should save them as a new, custom brush set.

✦ **Delete a brush:** To delete a brush from the current brush set, Ctrl-click its icon in the Brush drop-down palette. When you press Ctrl, your cursor changes to a little scissors icon, indicating that you're about to snip away a brush. You also can delete a brush by clicking its icon in the palette and choosing Delete Brush from the palette menu.

Want to give a bunch of brushes the boot? Do the job in the Preset Manager dialog box. Shift-click the brushes you no longer want and then click the Delete button.

✦ **Restore default brushes:** To return to the default Photoshop brush set, choose Reset Brushes from the menu in the palette or the dialog box. You then have the option of either replacing the existing brushes with the default brushes or simply adding the default brushes to the end of the palette.

✦ **Rename a brush:** If you ever want to rename a brush, select it in the Preset Manager dialog box and click Rename. Or, even easier, click the brush icon on the Options bar (as shown earlier, in Figure 5-22) or double-click the icon in the Brush drop-down palette. Then enter the new brush moniker in the Name option box and press Enter.

Caution

If you want your new brush names to live in perpetuity, resave the brush set. Otherwise, the names revert to their original labels if you replace the brush set, as is the case with all changes you make to brush characteristics.

Opacity, pressure, and exposure

Another way to change the performance of a paint or an edit tool is to adjust the Pressure, Opacity, or Exposure value, depending on what tool you're using. In Version 6, the controls appear on the Options bar, which replaces the former Options palette. Regardless of which setting you want to change, you click the triangle to display a slider bar, drag the slider to raise or lower the value, and then press Enter. Alternatively, you can double-click the option box, type a value, and press Enter.

Here's a look at how these options work:

✦ **Opacity:** The Opacity value determines the translucency of colors applied with the paint bucket, gradient, line, pencil, paintbrush, eraser, or rubber stamp tools. At 100 percent, the applied colors appear opaque, completely covering the image behind them. (The one exception is the paintbrush with Wet Edges active, which is always translucent.) At lower settings, the applied colors mix with the existing colors in the image.

Tip

You can change the opacity of pixels that you just altered by choosing Edit ⇨ Fade (Ctrl+Shift+F) and dragging the Opacity slider in the Fade dialog box. While you're in the dialog box, you can apply one of Photoshop's brush modes to further change how the edited pixels blend with the originals. Chapter 10 discusses the Fade command in detail; you can get an introduction to brush modes at the end of this chapter in the "Brush Modes" section.

✦ **Pressure:** The Pressure value affects different tools in different ways. When you use the airbrush tool, the Pressure value controls the opacity of each spot of color the tool delivers. The effect appears unique because the airbrush lays each spot of color onto the previous spot, mixing them together. This results in a progressive effect. Meanwhile, the paintbrush and pencil tools are not progressive, so their spots blend to form smooth lines.

When you use the smudge tool, the Pressure value controls the distance the tool drags colors in the image. And in the case of the blur, sharpen, or sponge tool, the value determines the degree to which the tool changes the focus or saturation of the image, 1 percent being the minimum and 100 percent being the maximum.

✦ **Exposure:** Available when you select the dodge or burn tool, Exposure controls how much the tools lighten or darken the image, respectively. A setting of 100 percent applies the maximum amount of lightening or darkening, which is still far short of either absolute white or black.

The factory default setting for all Exposure and Pressure values is 50 percent; the default setting for all Opacity values is 100 percent.

Tip

As long as one of the tools listed in this section is selected, you can change the Opacity, Pressure, or Exposure setting in 10-percent increments by pressing a number key on the keyboard or keypad. Press 1 to change the setting to 10 percent, press 2 for 20 percent, and so on, all the way up to 0 for 100 percent.

Want to change the Opacity, Pressure, or Exposure setting in 1-percent increments? No problem—just press two keys in a row. Press 4 twice for 44 percent, 0 and 7 for 7 percent, and so on. This tip and the preceding one work whether or not the Options bar is visible. Get in the habit of using the number keys and you'll thank yourself later.

Brush Dynamics

Photoshop 6

In previous versions of Photoshop, you've been able to apply paint and edit effects in strokes that varied in size, opacity, pressure, or color along the length of your drag. But to take advantage of some of these options, you needed a pressure-sensitive drawing tablet. Photoshop 6 enables mouse users to enjoy the same flexibility as their stylus-wielding colleagues. Whether you use the mouse, a stylus, or even a finger on a laptop trackpad, these options introduce an element of spontaneity into what seems at times like an absolute world of computer graphics.

Exploring the Brush Dynamics palette

The Brush Dynamics drop-down palette, shown in Figure 5-26, holds the secret to plying the paint and edit tools in strokes that vary from one end to the other. Click the brush icon at the right end of the Options bar to display the palette.

Figure 5-26: Click the brush icon to display the Brush Dynamics palette, the key to creating fading and tapered lines.

You get different options depending on the active tool; you can read about the options for the paint and edit tools in the next few sections. (Also see Chapter 7, which covers certain other tools affected by these settings.) But all the options have the same purpose: to enable you alter the effect of a tool as you drag. And in all cases, you can select one of three settings:

✦ **Off:** If you choose this option, the tools apply paint or edit effects consistently throughout the entire length of your drag.

✦ **Fade:** Select Fade to change the effect of a paint or edit tool gradually over the course of the drag. Enter a value in the option box to specify the distance over which the fading should occur. (More about that topic in the next section.)

The tool attributes that you can fade depend on the tool. For the paintbrush and pencil, you can vary brush size, opacity, and color. When working with the airbrush, you can adjust pressure and opacity. For the edit tools discussed in this chapter (dodge, burn, sponge, sharpen, blur, and smudge), you can alter pressure and brush size. And for the eraser, rubber stamp, history brush, art history brush, and pattern stamp, all covered in Chapter 7, you can adjust size and opacity.

No matter what tool you're using, Photoshop applies it initially at the setting you established elsewhere on the Options bar and then gradually reduces the value to the lowest possible value as you drag. For example, if you set the Opacity slider on the Options bar to 70 and select Fade from the Opacity pop-up menu in the Brush Dynamics palette, dragging with the paintbrush gives you a stroke that fades from 70 percent opacity to full transparency. And if you select a 100-pixel brush and drag with the Size option set to Fade, your paint stroke tapers from 100 pixels wide at the start to 1 pixel at the end.

✦ **Stylus:** If you use a pressure-sensitive tablet with Photoshop, the paint and edit tool effects vary according to the amount of pressure you apply as you draw on the tablet. The upcoming section "Setting up pressure-sensitive tablets" provides some additional information on working with a tablet.

The next sections explain how the Brush Dynamics settings affect the paint and edit tools, and these sections also give you a real-life example to inspire your own investigation of these options.

Fading the paint (and other effects)

In earlier versions of Photoshop, you could create a fading paint stroke by selecting the Fade check box in the Options palette and then specifying whether you wanted the stroke to fade from the foreground color to the background color or to transparency. In Version 6, you have the same choices, but they're handled a little differently.

When you work with the paintbrush or pencil, setting the Color option in the Brush Dynamics palette to Fade enables you to paint a line that fades from the foreground color to the background color. Choosing Fade from the Opacity pop-up menu, on the other hand, paints lines that fade to transparency. This option also enables you to create gradually disappearing strokes with the rubber stamp, pattern stamp, eraser, art history brush, and history brush.

If you're using the airbrush, you fade paint to transparency by setting the Pressure option in the Brush Dynamics palette to Fade. Similarly, you set the Pressure option to Fade to apply less and less pressure as you drag with the burn, dodge, sponge, blur, sharpen, and smudge tools.

To try your hand at fading lines, select the paintbrush or pencil and select Fade from the Opacity pop-up menu in the Brush Dynamics palette. Then enter a value in the corresponding option box to specify the distance over which you want the fading to occur. The fading begins at the start of your drag and is measured in brush shapes.

For example, assume that the foreground color is black. If you enter 40 into the Fade option box—as in Figure 5-27—Photoshop paints 40 brush shapes, the first in black and the remaining 39 in increasingly lighter shades of gray.

Note

The physical length of a fading line is dependent both on the Fade value you enter in the Brush Dynamics palette and on the Spacing value entered in the Brush Options dialog box, discussed in "Editing a brush shape," earlier in this chapter. To recap, the Spacing value determines the frequency with which Photoshop lays down brush shapes, and the Fade value determines the number of brush shapes laid down. Therefore, as demonstrated in Figure 5-28, a high Fade value combined with a high Spacing value creates the longest line.

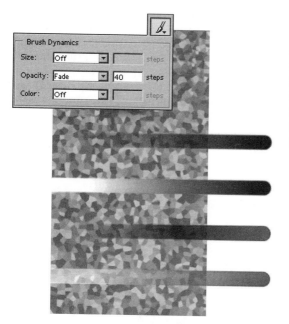

Figure 5-27: The top and middle strokes show examples of fading strokes that you can create by selecting Fade from the Opacity pop-up menu in the Brush Dynamics palette. For the other two strokes, I set the Opacity option to Off and set the Color option to Fade.

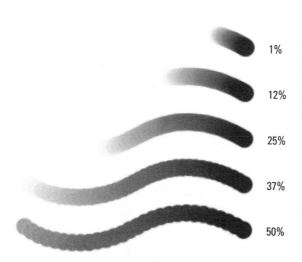

Figure 5-28: Here are five fading lines drawn with the paintbrush tool. In each case, I set the Opacity option in the Brush Dynamics palette to Fade and entered 36 as the Fade value. I changed the Spacing value incrementally from 1 to 50 percent, as labeled.

Creating sparkles and comets

Fading lines may strike you as pretty ho-hum, but they enable you to create some no-brainer, cool-mandoo effects, especially when combined with the Shift key techniques discussed earlier, in the "Painting a straight line" section.

Figures 5-29 and 5-30 demonstrate two of the most obvious uses for fading straight lines: creating sparkles and comets. The top image in Figure 5-29 features two sets of sparkles, each made up of 16 straight lines emanating from the sparkle's center. I created these lines by setting the Opacity slider on the Options bar to 100 percent and then selecting Fade from the Opacity pop-up menu in the Brush Dynamics palette. For the smaller sparkle on the right, I set the Fade value to 60 and drew each of the four perpendicular lines with the paintbrush tool. I changed the value to 36 before drawing the four 45-degree diagonal lines. The eight very short lines that occur between the perpendicular and diagonal lines were drawn with a Fade value of 20, and I created the larger sparkle on the left by periodically adjusting the Fade value, this time from 90 to 60 to 42.

Figure 5-29: I drew the sparkles in the top image using the paintbrush tool. The second image features a reflection applied with the Lens Flare filter (upper-left corner) and two dabs of a custom brush shape (right edge of the bumper).

For comparison's sake, I used different techniques to add a few more sparkles to the bottom image in Figure 5-29. To achieve the reflection in the upper-left corner of the image, I chose Filter ⇨ Render ⇨ Lens Flare and selected 50–300mm Zoom from the Lens Type options. (Lens Flare works exclusively in the RGB mode, so I had to switch to RGB to apply the filter, even though Figure 5-29 is a grayscale image.)

I created the two tiny sparkles on the right edge of the bumper using a custom brush shape. I merely selected the custom brush, set the foreground color to white, and clicked once with the paintbrush tool in each location. So many sparkles make for a tremendously shiny image.

In Figure 5-30 — a nostalgic tribute to the days when gas was cheap and the whole family would pile in the Plymouth for a Sunday drive through space — I copied the car and pasted it on top of a NASA photograph of Jupiter. I then went nuts clicking and Shift-clicking with the paintbrush tool to create the comets — well, if you must know, they're actually cosmic rays — you see shooting through and around the car. It's so real, you can practically hear the in-dash servo unit warning, "Duck and cover!"

Figure 5-30: To create the threatening cosmic rays, I set the Fade value to 110 and then clicked and Shift-clicked on opposite sides of the image with the paintbrush tool.

After masking portions of the image (a process described at length in Chapter 9), I drew rays behind the car and even one ray that shoots up through the car and out the spare tire. The three bright lights in the image — above the left fin, above the roof, and next to the right-turn signal — are more products of the Lens Flare filter in the RGB mode.

Note   I drew all the fading lines in Figures 5-29 and 5-30 with the paintbrush tool, using a variety of default brush shapes. Because I didn't edit any brush shape, the Spacing value for all lines was a constant 25 percent.

Creating tapered strokes

Available for any tool that uses a brush, the Size option in the Brush Dynamics palette tapers your paint or edit strokes when set to Fade. As with the other palette options, the Fade value that you enter determines how quickly the stroke tapers to nothingness.

Figure 5-31 shows examples of four tapering strokes created by setting the Size option to Fade and using different Fade values. In all cases, I used a 19-pixel hard brush and left the brush Spacing value at its default, 25 percent. (See the previous section for details about how the Spacing value comes into play when you create fading or tapering strokes.)

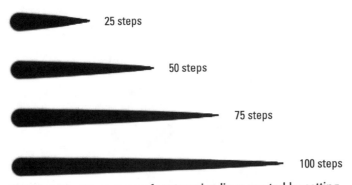

Figure 5-31: Here you see four tapering lines created by setting the Size option to Fade and using different Fade values. I used a 19-pixel hard brush and the default Spacing value for all four lines.

Setting up pressure-sensitive tablets

In Photoshop 6, you can use a mouse to create fading and tapering lines, but you can go in only one direction. You can make a line fade or taper into nothingness, but you can't make a thin, faint line get fatter and more opaque as you drag. Nor can you fade or taper a single stroke by varying amounts along the course of your drag. But with a pressure-sensitive tablet, you can dynamically adjust the thickness of lines and the opacity of colors by changing the amount of pressure you apply to the *stylus,* the pen-like input device that takes the place of the mouse when you work with a graphics tablet.

Photoshop
6

If you're an artist and you've never experimented with a pressure-sensitive tablet, I recommend that you do so soon. You'll be amazed at how much it increases your range of artistic options, not only because you have access to options like the ones I just mentioned, but also because drawing and editing with a stylus is much easier than working with a clunky old mouse. Thirty minutes after I installed my first tablet back in 1990, I had executed the cartoon you see in Figure 5-32. Whether you like the image or not — I'll admit there's a certain troglodyte quality to the slope of his forehead, and that jaw could bust a coconut — it shows off the tablet's capability to paint tapering lines and accommodate artistic expression.

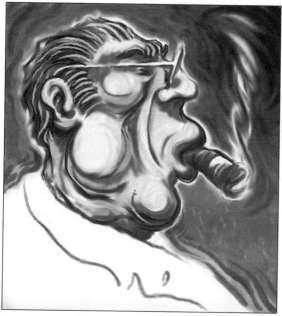

Figure 5-32: Although I painted this caricature years ago, it still demonstrates the range of artistic freedom provided by a pressure-sensitive tablet.

Pressure-sensitive options

As I mentioned a few pages ago, you control Photoshop's reaction to stylus pressure using the options in the Brush Dynamics drop-down palette. When you select Stylus from any of the palette pop-up menus, the program responds to changes in stylus pressure by varying your paint or edit strokes as follows:

✦ **Size:** Select Stylus from the Size pop-up menu, as shown in Figure 5-33, if you want Photoshop to change the thickness of the line according to stylus pressure. The more pressure you apply, the thicker the line. Figure 5-34 shows three paintbrush lines drawn using this feature. I drew the first line using a hard brush, the second with a soft brush, and the third with a hard brush and with the Wet Edges check box selected.

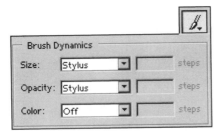

Figure 5-33: When you work with a pressure-sensitive tablet, select Stylus from any pop-up menu in the Brush Dynamics palette to vary your paint and edit strokes according to stylus pressure.

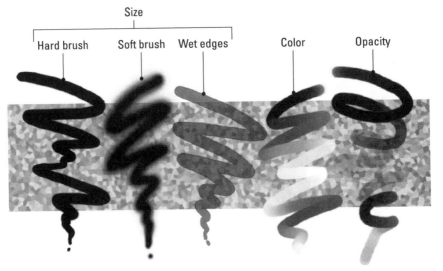

Figure 5-34: The effects of the Size, Color, and Opacity options on lines drawn with the paintbrush tool and a pressure-sensitive tablet

✦ **Color:** With Stylus selected for the Color option, the paintbrush, pencil, and airbrush lay down the foreground color at full pressure, the background color at slight pressure, and a mix of the two at medium pressure.

✦ **Opacity:** When you work with the pencil or the paintbrush, this option paints an opaque coat of foreground color at full pressure that dwindles to transparency at slight pressure. Similarly, varying stylus pressure adjusts the opacity of strokes that you paint with the rubber stamp, pattern stamp, eraser, history brush, and art history brush.

✦ **Pressure:** Here's one that I think you could probably figure out for yourself, but just in case: If you set the Pressure option to Stylus, changes in stylus pressure alter the pressure setting of the airbrush, dodge, burn, sponge, smudge, sharpen, and blur tools. Heavier stylus pressure increases the tool pressure.

Because Photoshop presents these options individually, you can select more than one at a time. For example, you can select both Size and Color to instruct Photoshop to change both the thickness and color of a line as you bear down or lift up on the stylus.

Undoing pressure-sensitive lines

In the old days, pressure-sensitive lines were a pain to undo. Because a stylus is so sensitive to gradual pressure, you can unwittingly let up and repress the stylus during what you perceive as a single drag. If, after doing so, you decide you don't like the line and press Ctrl+Z (Edit ⇨ Undo), Photoshop deletes only the last portion of the line because it detected a release midway.

This is why it's a good idea to get in the habit of using Ctrl+Alt+Z, if you haven't already. Each time you press this shortcut, you take another step back in the history of your image, permitting you to eliminate every bit of a line regardless of how many times you let up on the stylus. (See Chapter 7 for more information on Photoshop's multiple undos.) Note that the shortcuts I mention here assume that you set the Redo Key option on the General panel of the Preferences dialog box to its default setting, Ctrl+Z. Check out Chapter 2 for more information on your other Redo Key options.

Tip

Better yet, create a new layer before you paint with or without a stylus. Then you can refine your lines and erase them without harming the original appearance of your image. (You can do this without layers using the history brush, again explained in Chapter 7, but a relatively old-fashioned layer tends to be less hassle.)

Brush Modes

When certain painting or editing tools are active, the Options bar provides access to Photoshop's brush modes, which control how the colors applied by the tools affect existing colors in the image. Figure 5-35 shows which brush modes are available when you select various tools.

With the exception of the specialized modes available for the dodge, burn, and sponge tools, these brush modes are merely variations on the blend modes described in Chapter 13. Read this section to get a brief glimpse of brush modes; read Chapter 13 for a more detailed account that should appeal to brush-mode aficionados.

Tip

You can change brush modes from the keyboard by pressing Shift+plus (+) or Shift+minus (–). Shift+plus takes you to the next brush mode listed in the pop-up menu; Shift+minus selects the previous blend mode. It's a great way to cycle through the brush modes without losing your place in the image.

Figure 5-35: The available brush modes vary depending on which tool is active.

The 19 paint tool modes

Photoshop offers 19 brush modes when you use the pencil, paintbrush, airbrush, or any of the other tools shown along the left side of Figure 5-35. (An additional mode, Threshold, is an alternative to Normal in certain color modes.) To show you what these brush modes look like when applied to an image, Color Plates 5-2, 5-3, and 5-4 illustrate 18 modes, minus only Threshold. In each case, I used the paintbrush tool to apply a bit of green graffiti to a work of fourteenth-century religious iconography. Who among us hasn't been tempted with the primal urge to paint "Kilroy" on something old and priceless? Now, thanks to the miracle of digital imagery, you need resist this temptation no longer.

Just as you can cycle from one brush mode to the next from the keyboard, you can jump directly to a specific brush mode as well. Just press Shift+Alt and a letter key. For example, Shift+Alt+N selects the Normal mode, Shift+Alt+C selects the Color mode. I list the letter key for each brush mode in parentheses along with its description:

✦ **Normal (N):** Choose this mode to paint or edit an image normally. A paint tool coats the image with the foreground color, and an edit tool manipulates the existing colors in an image according to the Opacity or Pressure value.

✦ **Threshold (L):** Two color modes prevent Photoshop from rendering soft or translucent edges. The black-and-white and indexed modes (Image ➪ Mode ➪ Bitmap and Image ➪ Mode ➪ Indexed Color) simply don't have enough colors to go around. When painting in such a low-color image, Photoshop replaces the Normal brush mode with Threshold, which results in harsh, jagged edges, just like a stroke painted with the pencil tool. You can alternatively dither the soft edges by selecting the Dissolve mode, as described next.

✦ **Dissolve (I):** This mode and the six that follow are not applicable to the edit tools (though I wonder why — the Dissolve mode would be especially useful with the smudge tool). Dissolve scatters colors along the edge of a brushstroke randomly throughout the course of your drag. The Dissolve mode produces the most pronounced effects when used with soft brushes and the airbrush tool.

✦ **Behind (Q):** This one is applicable exclusively to layers with transparent backgrounds. When Behind is selected, the paint tool applies color behind the image on the active layer, showing through only in the transparent and translucent areas. In Color Plate 5-2, for example, I painted over the Madonna's head, and yet the brushstroke appears behind her head because she is positioned on an independent layer. When you're working on an image without layers or on the background layer of a multilayered image, the Behind mode is dimmed.

✦ **Multiply (M):** The Multiply mode combines the foreground color with an existing color in an image to create a third color, darker than the other two. Using the multiply analogy, red times white is red, red times yellow is orange, red times green is brown, red times blue is violet, and so on. As discussed in Chapter 4, this is subtractive (CMYK) color theory at work. The effect is almost exactly like drawing with felt-tipped markers, except the colors don't bleed. Check out the first Kilroy in Color Plate 5-3 to see the Multiply mode in action.

The multiply mode has no effect on the paintbrush when it's set to Wet Edges; the Wet Edges brush setting already multiplies.

✦ **Screen (S):** The inverse of the Multiply mode, Screen combines the foreground color with each colored pixel you paint over to create a third color, lighter than the other two. Red on white is white, red on yellow is off-white, red on green is yellow, and red on blue is pink. The Screen mode uses additive (RGB) color theory. If the effect has a traditional counterpart, it's like some impossibly bright, radioactive Uranium-238 highlighter, hitherto used only by G-men to mark the pant cuffs of Communist sympathizers.

Because the Wet Edges option always multiplies, combining it with the Screen mode must render the brush invisible. If the paintbrush tool isn't working, this could be your problem.

✦ **Overlay (O):** Overlay, Soft Light, and Hard Light are cousins. Each mode multiplies the dark pixels in an image and screens the light pixels as you lay down color with a paint tool. But although related, the three modes are not variations on an identical theme. In other words, you can't emulate the Soft Light mode by simply applying the Hard Light mode at 70 percent or some similar opacity.

Of the three modes, Overlay is the kindest. Overlay always enhances contrast and boosts the saturation of colors in an image. In fact, Overlay works rather like a colored version of the sponge tool set to Saturate. It mixes the colors in the image with the foreground color to come up with a vivid blend that is almost always visually pleasing. Overlay may be the most interesting and downright useful brush mode of the bunch.

✦ **Soft Light (F):** This mode applies a subtle glazing of color to an image. In fact, Soft Light is remarkably similar to painting a diluted acrylic wash to a canvas. Soft Light never completely covers the underlying detail—even black or white applied at 100 percent Opacity does no more than darken or lighten the image—but it does slightly diminish contrast.

✦ **Hard Light (H):** This mode might better be named *Obfuscate*. It's as if you were applying a thicker, more opaque wash to the image. You might think of Hard Light as Normal with a whisper of underlying detail mixed in.

For examples of Overlay, Soft Light, and Hard Light, check out the middle brushstrokes in Color Plate 5-3.

✦ **Color Dodge (D):** This brush mode lightens the pixels in an image according to the lightness or darkness of the foreground color. Color Dodge produces a harsher, chalkier effect than the Screen mode and is designed to act like a dodge tool that also adds color. At 100 percent Opacity, even painting with black has a lightening effect.

✦ **Color Burn (B):** If Color Dodge is like drawing with chalk, Color Burn is like drawing with coal. It darkens pixels according to the lightness or darkness of the foreground color and is designed to simulate a colored version of the burn tool. For examples of Color Dodge and Color Burn, look to the last two Kilroys in Color Plate 5-3.

✦ **Darken (K):** Ah, back to the old familiars. If you choose the Darken mode, Photoshop applies a new color to a pixel only if that color is darker than the present color of the pixel. Otherwise, the pixel is left unchanged. The mode works on a channel-by-channel basis, so it might change a pixel in the green channel, for example, without changing the pixel in the red or blue channel. I used this mode to create the first brushstroke of Color Plate 5-4.

✦ **Lighten (G):** The opposite of the preceding mode, Lighten ensures that Photoshop applies a new color to a pixel only if the color is lighter than the present color of the pixel. Otherwise, the pixel is left unchanged. On or off—either you see the color or you don't.

✦ **Difference (E):** When a paint tool is set to the Difference mode, Photoshop subtracts the brightness value of the foreground color from the brightness value of the pixels in the image. If the result is a negative number, Photoshop simply makes it positive. The result of this complex-sounding operation is an inverted effect. Black has no effect on an image; white inverts it completely. Colors in between create psychedelic effects. For instance, in the third example of Color Plate 5-4, the Difference mode inverts the green paint to create a red brushstroke.

Because the Difference mode inverts an image, it results in an outline around the brushstroke. You can make this outline thicker by using a softer brush shape. For a really trippy effect, select the paintbrush tool, turn on Wet Edges, and apply the Difference mode with a soft brush shape.

✦ **Exclusion (X):** When I first asked Mark Hamburg, lead programmer for Photoshop, for his definition of Exclusion, he kindly explained, "Exclusion applies a probabilistic, fuzzy-set-theoretic, symmetric difference to each channel." Don't think about it too long—your frontal lobe will turn to boiled squash. After Mark remembered he was communicating with a lower life form, he told me (very slowly) that Exclusion inverts an image in much the same way as Difference, except colors in the middle of the spectrum mix to form medium gray. Exclusion typically results in high-contrast effects with less color saturation than Difference. My suggestion is to try the Difference mode first. If you're looking for something a little different, press Ctrl+Z and try Exclusion instead. (Both Difference and Exclusion brushstrokes appear in Color Plate 5-4.)

✦ **Hue (U):** Understanding this and the next few modes requires a color theory recap. Remember how the HSL color model calls for three color channels? One is for hue, the value that explains the colors in an image; the second is for saturation, which represents the intensity of the colors; and the third is for luminosity, which explains the lightness and darkness of colors. If you choose the Hue brush mode, therefore, Photoshop applies the hue from the foreground color without changing any saturation or luminosity values in the existing image.

None of the HSL brush modes—Hue, Saturation, Color, or Luminosity—are available when painting within grayscale images.

✦ **Saturation (T):** If you choose this mode, Photoshop changes the intensity of the colors in an image without changing the colors themselves or the lightness and darkness of individual pixels. In Color Plate 5-4, Saturation has the effect of breathing new life into those ancient egg-tempura colors.

✦ **Color (C):** This mode might be more appropriately titled *Hue and Saturation*. Color enables you to change the colors in an image and the intensity of those colors without changing the lightness and darkness of individual pixels.

Tip

The Color mode is most often used to colorize grayscale photographs. Open a grayscale image and then choose Image ⇨ Mode ⇨ RGB Color to convert the image to the RGB mode. Then select the colors you want to use and start painting. The Color mode ensures that details in the image remain completely intact.

✦ **Luminosity (Y):** The opposite of the Color mode, Luminosity changes the lightness and darkness of pixels, but leaves the hue and saturation values unaffected. Frankly, this mode is rarely useful. But its counterpart—the Luminosity blend mode—is exceptionally useful when applied to layers. Read Chapter 13 to find out more.

The three dodge and burn modes

Phew, that takes care of the brush modes available to the paint tools, the smudge tool, and the two focus tools. I already explained the Desaturate and Saturate modes available to the sponge tool (in the "Mopping up with the sponge tool" section of this chapter). That leaves the three brush modes available to the dodge and burn tools.

You now access these modes from the Range pop-up menu on the Options bar. As with other brush modes, you can select the dodge and burn modes from the keyboard. Just press Shift+Alt and the letter in parentheses as follows:

✦ **Shadows (S):** Along with the Midtones and Highlights modes (described next), Shadows is unique to the dodge and burn tools. When you select this mode, the dodge and burn tools affect dark pixels in an image more dramatically than they affect light pixels and shades in between.

✦ **Midtones (M):** Select this mode to apply the dodge or burn tools equally to all but the very lightest or darkest pixels in an image.

✦ **Highlights (H):** When you select this option, the dodge and burn tools affect light pixels in an image more dramatically than they affect dark pixels and shades in between.

Selecting Shadows when using the dodge tool or selecting Highlights when using the burn tool has an equalizing effect on an image. Figure 5-36 shows how using either of these functions and setting the Exposure slider bar to 100 percent lightens or darkens pixels in an image to nearly identical brightness values.

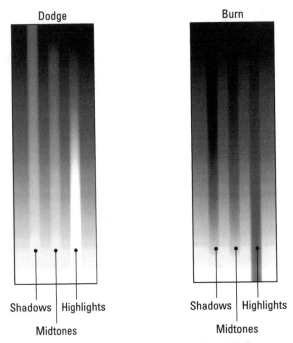

Figure 5-36: The dodge and burn tool applied at 100-percent Exposure settings subject to each of the three applicable brush modes.

✦   ✦   ✦

Filling and Stroking

Filling Portions of an Image

No explanation of filling and stroking would be complete without a definition, so here goes: To *fill* a selection or a layer is to
put color inside it; to *stroke* a selection or a layer is to put color
around it. Some folks prefer the term *outline* to *stroke,* but I defer
to PostScript terminology because that's where this whole desktop graphics thing started. Besides, when I think outline, I think
perimeter, boundary, enclosure, prison, let me out of here.
Stroke is more like brush, caress, pet, puppy, warm fire, glad
heart. I'm a joker, I'm a smoker, I'm a midnight stroker. I'd rather
be stroking. Stop me before I stroke again. And, that timeless
favorite, keep on strokin'. So you see, people who prefer the
word "outline" have no soul.

But whatever you call them, Photoshop's fill and stroke functions
are so straightforward that you may have long since dismissed
them as wimpy little tools with remarkably limited potential. But
the truth is, you can do a world of stuff with them. In this chapter, for example, I show you how to fill selections using nifty keyboard shortcuts, how to create an antique framing effect, how to
make the most of Photoshop's new gradient options, and how to
add an arrowhead to a curving line—all in addition to the really
basic stuff every Photoshop user needs to know.

As the poet said, "Teacher don't you *fill* me up with your
rules, I know *strokin's* not allowed in school." I'd love to share
the entire transcript from "Strokin' in the Boy's Room," but
this is, after all, a family book.

Filling Selections with Color or Patterns

You can fill an area of an image in the following ways:

✦ **The paint bucket tool:** Also known as the fill tool, the paint bucket now resides in the same flyout as the gradient tool in the toolbox. You can apply the foreground color or a repeating pattern to areas of related color in an image by clicking in the image window with the tool. For example, if you want to turn all midnight blue pixels in an image into red pixels, set the foreground color to red and then click one of the blue pixels. Note that you can't use this tool on images that you converted to Bitmap mode.

✦ **The Fill command:** Choose Edit ➪ Fill to fill a selection with the foreground color or a repeating pattern. In Photoshop 6, you don't need to select a portion of the image to access the Fill command. If you choose the command while no selection is active, Photoshop fills the entire layer.

To choose the Fill command without so much as moving the mouse, press Shift+Backspace.

✦ **Backspace key techniques:** After selecting part of a single-layer image — or part of the background layer in a multi-layered image — you can fill the selection with the background color by pressing Backspace or Delete. On any other layer, press Ctrl+Backspace. To fill the selection with the foreground color, press Alt+Backspace.

✦ **The gradient tool:** Drag across a selection with a gradient tool to fill it with a multi-color gradation in one of five gradient styles.

You now choose a gradient style by clicking an icon on the Options bar. The old shortcut for cycling through the styles, Shift+G, now toggles the gradient and paint bucket tools, which occupy the same flyout menu in the Version 6 toolbox. If you turn off the Use Shift Key for Tool Switch check box in the Preferences dialog box (Ctrl+K), you need only press G to toggle the tools.

✦ **Layer fills:** Photoshop 6 provides two additional ways to fill an entire layer. You can use the Dynamic Fill and Layer Style features to fill a layer with a solid color, gradient, or pattern.

The next sections explain the first four fill options. To find out more about dynamic fills and layer styles, trek off to Chapters 13 and 14.

The paint bucket tool

Unlike remedial paint bucket tools in other painting programs, which apply paint exclusively within outlined areas or areas of solid color, the Photoshop paint bucket tool offers several useful adjustment options.

In Version 6, you access the paint bucket controls in the Options bar, as with all tools. When you select the paint bucket, the Options bar automatically updates to show the available controls. If you don't see the Options bar, press Enter, double-click the paint bucket icon in the toolbox, or choose Window ➪ Show Options. Also note that the old keyboard shortcut for selecting the paint bucket — the K key — now selects the slice tool. The paint bucket and gradient tools share a flyout menu in the toolbox; press G to toggle between the two tools (or Shift+G, depending on your preferences setting for tool toggles).

Here's a look at the paint bucket options:

✦ **Fill:** In this pop-up menu, choose whether you want to apply the foreground color or a repeating pattern created using Edit ➪ Define Pattern. The Define Pattern command is covered in the "Applying Repeating Patterns" section of Chapter 7.

✦ **Pattern:** If you select Pattern from the Fill pop-up, click the Pattern icon (or the adjacent triangle) to display the Pattern drop-down palette, as shown in Figure 6-1. The palette contains icons representing the icons in the current pattern *preset* — Photoshop 6 lingo for a collection of patterns. Click the pattern you want to use.

You load, replace, edit, and create pattern presets just as you do brush presets, working either in the Preset Manager dialog box or the Pattern palette menu, which you display by clicking the triangle labeled in Figure 6-1. Photoshop 6 enables you to create multiple patterns; you're no longer limited to one custom pattern.

The Chapter 5 discussion of custom brushes details presets fully, so I won't waste space repeating everything here. Be sure to also check out Chapter 7, which explains ways of creating custom patterns.

Click to display palette menu

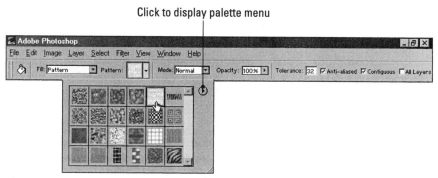

Figure 6-1: These options govern the performance of the paint bucket tool.

✦ **Tolerance:** Raise or lower the Tolerance value to increase or decrease the number of pixels affected by the paint bucket tool. The Tolerance value represents a range in brightness values, as measured from the pixel that you click with the paint bucket.

Immediately after you click a pixel, Photoshop reads the brightness value of that pixel from each color channel. Next, the program calculates a color range based on the Tolerance value — which can vary from 0 to 255. The program adds the Tolerance to the brightness value of the pixel you clicked to determine the top of the range and subtracts the Tolerance from the pixel's brightness value to determine the bottom of the range. For example, if the pixel's brightness value is 100 and the Tolerance value is 32, the top of the range is 132 and the bottom is 68.

Figure 6-2 shows the result of clicking on the same pixel three separate times, each time using a different Tolerance value. In Color Plate 6-1, I raised the Tolerance to 120. But even with this high setting, I had to click several times to recolor all the nooks and crannies of the oranges. The moral is, don't get too hung up on getting the Tolerance exactly right — no matter how you paint it, the bucket is not a precise tool.

✦ **Anti-aliased:** Select this option to soften the effect of the paint bucket tool. As demonstrated in the left example of Figure 6-3, Photoshop creates a border of translucent color between the filled pixels and their unaffected neighbors. If you don't want to soften the transition, turn off the Anti-aliased check box. Photoshop then fills only those pixels that fall inside the Tolerance range, as demonstrated in the right example of the figure.

✦ **Contiguous:** When you select this check box, Photoshop fills only contiguous pixels — that is, pixels that both fall inside the Tolerance range and touch another affected pixel. If you instead want to select all pixels that fall within the Tolerance Range, deselect the check box. I turned the option on when creating Figure 6-2 and Color Plate 6-1.

✦ **All Layers:** Select this option to make the paint bucket see beyond the current layer. When the option is selected, the tool takes all visible layers into account when calculating the area to fill. Mind you, it only fills the active layer, but the way it fills an area is dictated by all layers.

✦ **Mode:** This menu offers a selection of blend modes, which determine how and when color is applied. For example, if you select Darken (Shift+Alt+K), the paint bucket tool affects a pixel in the image only if the foreground color is darker than that pixel. If you select Color (Shift+Alt+C), the paint bucket colorizes the image without changing the brightness value of the pixels.

In Color Plate 6-1, for example, I used the Color mode to change a few oranges to blue and the background to green, all by clicking at five different spots with the paint bucket tool. I then touched up the stray pixels the paint bucket didn't catch with the paintbrush and airbrush tools.

Paint bucket cursor

Figure 6-2: The results of applying the paint bucket tool to the exact pixel after setting the Tolerance value to 16 (top), 32 (middle), and 64 (bottom). In each case, the foreground color is light gray.

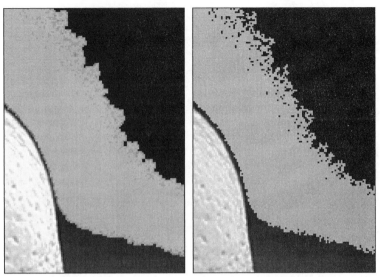

Figure 6-3: The results of turning on (left) and off (right) the Anti-aliased check box before using the paint bucket tool. It all depends on whether you want cottage cheese or little spiky coral edges.

For a thorough rundown of blend modes, see Chapter 13.

✦ **Opacity:** This option works just like when you paint with the paintbrush. Enter a new value or press a number key to change the translucency of a color applied with the paint bucket. (Press 0 for full opacity, 9 for 90 percent opacity, and so on.)

I feel the need at this point to expound a bit more on the All Layers option. For an example of how this feature works, look no further than Figure 6-4. The dog sits on one layer, and the fire hydrant rests on another layer directly below it. If I were to click the fire hydrant when the dog layer is active and the All Layers check box is turned off, I'd fill everything around the dog. The paint bucket can't see the hydrant; all the paint bucket can see is the transparent area of the dog layer, so it would try to fill that area. To avoid this, I selected All Layers and then clicked on the hydrant. With All Layers on, the paint bucket can see all layers, so it contains its fill within the hydrant, as in the middle example of the figure.

Figure 6-4: Although dog and hydrant are on separate layers (top), I can mix them together with Use All Layers. This option enables me to fill an area of the hydrant (middle), even though the dog layer is active. Then I paint in front of and behind the fill without harming the hydrant (bottom).

Because the fill and hydrant are on separate layers, I could edit the two independently. I used the airbrush to paint inside and behind the fill (using the Behind brush mode, discussed in the previous chapter). I painted the teeth and eyes with the paintbrush and used the smudge tool to mix colors around the white fill. (Naturally, I had to turn on the All Layers check box on the Options bar when working with the smudge tool as well.) As a result, all the bizarre alterations you see in the bottom example of Figure 6-4 were applied to the dog layer. I didn't change a single pixel in the hydrant layer (which is a good thing—in light of my changes, I might like to get that hydrant back).

To limit the area affected by the paint bucket, select a portion of the image before using the tool. As when using a paint or edit tool, the region outside the selection outline is protected from the paint bucket. To see an interesting application of this, skip ahead to the "Using the paint bucket inside a selection" section later in this chapter.

When working on a layer, you can protect pixels by locking the layer's transparency in the Layers palette. Like all layering issues, I cover the locking options in Chapter 12.

Tip

Here's one more paint bucket tip for good measure: You can use the paint bucket to color the empty window area around your image. First, make your image window larger than your image, so you can see some gray canvas area around the image. Now Shift-click with the paint bucket to fill the canvas area with the foreground color. This technique can come in handy if you're creating a presentation or you simply don't care for the default shade of gray.

The Fill command

The one problem with the paint bucket tool is its lack of precision. Although the tool is undeniably convenient, the effects of the Tolerance value are so difficult to predict that you typically have to click with the tool, choose Edit ⇨ Undo when you don't like the result, adjust the Tolerance value, and reclick several times more before you fill the image as desired. For my part, I rarely use the paint bucket for any purpose other than filling same-colored areas. On my machine, the Tolerance option is nearly always set to 0 and Anti-alias is generally off, which puts me right back in the all-the-subtlety-of-dumping-paint-out-of-a-bucket camp.

A better option is to choose Edit ⇨ Fill or press Shift+Backspace. (If you prefer function keys, try Shift+F5.) In this way, you can define the exact area of the image you want to color using the entire range of Photoshop's selection tools. For example, instead of putting your faith in the paint bucket tool's Anti-aliased option, you can draw a selection outline that features hard edges in one area, antialiased edges elsewhere, and downright blurry edges in between.

If you want to fill an entire layer, you don't need to create a selection outline before choosing Fill as you did in past versions of Photoshop. The program assumes that you want to fill the whole layer if it doesn't see a selection outline. (The Dynamic Fill and Layer Style commands provide additional ways to fill a layer; see Chapter 12 for details on how these fills differ from those you create with the Fill command.)

Selection outline or no, choosing the Fill command displays the dialog box shown in Figure 6-5. In this dialog box, you can apply a translucent color or pattern by entering a value in the Opacity option box. You can also choose a brush mode from the Mode pop-up menu. In addition to its inherent precision, the Fill command provides all the functionality of the paint bucket tool — and then some.

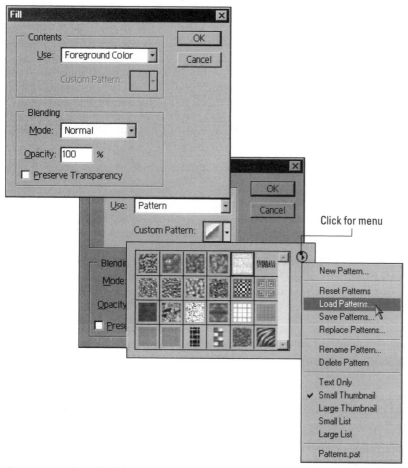

Figure 6-5: The Fill dialog box combines the opacity and brush mode options available for the paint bucket with an expanded collection of fill content options.

If you display the Use pop-up menu, you see a collection of fills that you can apply. Foreground Color and Pattern behave the same as they do for the paint bucket tool. When you select Pattern, the Custom Pattern option becomes available, as shown in the bottom dialog box in Figure 6-5. Click the icon to display the Pattern drop-down palette, which also works just as described in the preceding section. Click an icon to select a pattern; click the right-pointing arrow to display the palette menu and load a different pattern preset.

To find out how to load, save, edit, and create custom pattern presets, see the section in Chapter 5 that discusses the Brushes panel of the Preset Manager dialog box. You use the same techniques for brush presets and pattern presets.

You can also fill a selection with the background color and such monochrome options as Black, White, and 50% Gray. Black and White are useful if the foreground and background colors have been changed from their defaults; 50% Gray fills the selection with the absolute medium color without having to mess around with the Color palette. History enables you to revert the selected area to a previous appearance, as I discuss at length in Chapter 7.

The Preserve Transparency option gives you the same result as locking the active layer's transparency in the Layers palette, which you can read about in Chapter 12. If you select Preserve Transparency, you can't fill transparent pixels in the active layer. Turn Preserve Transparency off, and you can fill the selection outline uniformly. (The option is dimmed when you're working on the background layer or if you already locked the layer's transparency in the Layers palette.)

Backspace-key techniques

Of all the fill techniques, the Backspace key is by far the most convenient and, in most respects, every bit as capable as the others. The key's only failing is that it can neither fill a selection with a repeating pattern nor revert a selection to a previous state. But with the exception of those two items, you can rely on the Backspace key for the overwhelming majority of your fill needs.

Here's how to get a ton of functionality out of Backspace:

✦ **Background color, method 1:** To fill a selection on the background layer with solid background color, press Backspace. The selection outline remains intact.

✦ **Background color, method 2:** The problem with pressing Backspace is that it's unreliable. If the selection is floating, as I explain in Chapter 8, the Backspace key deletes it. The Backspace key also erases pixels on a layer. So there's no time like the present to get into a new habit — press Ctrl+Backspace instead. Ctrl+Backspace fills the selection with the background color, no matter where it is.

✦ **Foreground color:** To fill a selection or a layer with solid foreground color, press Alt+Backspace. This works when filling floating and nonfloating selections alike.

✦ **Black or white:** To fill an area with black, press D to get the default foreground and background colors and then press Alt+Backspace. To fill an area with white, press D for the defaults and then Ctrl+Backspace.

✦ **Preserve transparency:** Add the Shift key and you get two more key tricks that make more sense when you read Chapter 12. (Don't worry, I'll repeat the tricks then.) You can fill only the opaque pixels in a layer — regardless of whether you locked the layer's transparency in the Layers palette — by pressing Shift. Press Shift+Alt+Backspace to fill a selection with the foreground color while preserving transparency. Press Ctrl+Shift+Backspace to fill the opaque pixels with the background color.

Using the paint bucket inside a selection

So far, I've come up with two astounding generalizations: The paint bucket tool is mostly useless, and you can fill anything with the Backspace key. Well, just to prove you shouldn't believe everything I say — some might even suggest you dismiss everything I say — the following steps explain an effect you can create only with the paint bucket tool. Doubtless, it's the only such example you'll ever discover using Photoshop — after all, the paint bucket is mostly useless and you can fill anything with the Backspace key — but I'm man enough to eat my rules this once.

The following steps explain how to create an antique photographic frame effect, such as the one shown in Figure 6-6.

STEPS: Creating an Antique Framing Effect

1. **Use the rectangular marquee tool to select the portion of the image you want to frame.** Make certain the image extends at least 20 pixels outside the boundaries of the selection outline; and be sure to use a photo — this effect won't look right against a plain white background.

2. **Choose Select ➪ Feather (Ctrl+Alt+D).** Then specify a Radius value somewhere in the neighborhood of 6 to 12 pixels. I've found these values work for nearly any resolution of image. (If you enter too high a value, the color you'll add in a moment with the paint bucket will run out into the image.)

3. **Choose Select ➪ Inverse (Ctrl+Shift+I).** This exchanges the selected and deselected portions of the image.

4. **Press D to make certain the background color is white.** Then press Ctrl+Backspace to fill the selected area with the background color.

5. **Select the paint bucket tool.** If the Options bar isn't visible, press Enter to display it. Then enter 20 or 30 in the Tolerance option box and turn on the Anti-aliased check box. (You can also experiment with turning off this last option.)

6. **Click inside the feathered selection to fill it with black.** The result is an image fading into white and then into black, like the edges of a worn slide or photograph, as shown in Figure 6-6.

Figure 6-6: I created this antique frame effect by filling
a feathered selection with the paint bucket tool.

Figure 6-7 shows a variation on this effect that you can produce using the Dissolve
brush mode. Rather than setting the Tolerance value to 20, raise it to around 60. Then
select the Dissolve option from the Mode pop-up menu on the Options bar. When you
click inside the feathered selection with the paint bucket tool, you create a frame of
random pixels, as illustrated in the figure.

Figure 6-7: Select Dissolve from the Mode pop-up menu
on the Options bar to achieve a speckled frame effect.

Applying Gradient Fills

The two previous versions of Photoshop made great strides in the gradation department. Version 4 introduced the Edit button into the Gradient Options palette. This one button made it possible to create a gradient with as many as 32 colors, name gradients and save them to disk, and adjust the transparency of colors so that they fade in and out over the course of the fill. Version 5 widened the range of gradient styles, removed the limit on colors per gradient, and enabled you to reverse the foreground and background colors from within the Gradient Options palette, a nice convenience when applying radial and diamond fills.

Version 6 adds even more gradient features. You can create and save collections of your favorite gradients as presets, just as you can patterns and brushes. In addition, you can create noise gradients, use the new Dynamic Fill feature to create a gradient as an adjustment layer, and use the Layer Style command to add a gradient overlay to a layer. (I explain the first layer option along with the other adjustment layer options in Chapter 17; you can read about layer styles in Chapter 12.)

Note

If you're accustomed to using gradients in a drawing program — such as Illustrator or FreeHand — you'll find that Photoshop is better. Because Photoshop is a pixel editor, it lets you blur and mix colors in a gradation if they start *banding* — that is, if you can see a hard edge between one color and the next when you print the image; and Photoshop's gradations never choke the printer or slow it down, no matter how many colors you add. While each band of color in an object-oriented gradation is expressed as a separate shape — so that one gradation can contain hundreds, or even thousands, of objects — gradations in Photoshop are plain old colored pixels, the kind we've been editing for five and a half chapters.

Using the gradient tool

First, the basics. A *gradation* (also called a *gradient fill*) is a progression of colors that fade gradually into one another, as demonstrated in Figure 6-8. You specify a few key colors in the gradation, and Photoshop automatically generates the hundred or so colors in between to create a smooth transition.

In Version 6, the gradient tool and paint bucket share a toolbox slot and keyboard shortcut – press G to toggle between the two tools (or Shift+G, depending on whether you selected the Use Shift Key for Tool Switch check box in the Preferences dialog box, as discussed in Chapter 2). But unlike the paint bucket, which fills areas of similar color according to the Tolerance setting, the gradient tool affects all colors within a selection. If you don't select a portion of your image, Photoshop applies the gradation to the entire layer.

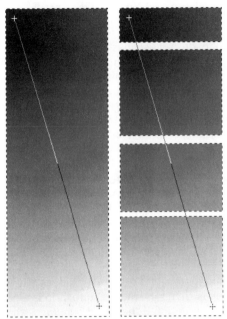

Figure 6-8: Dragging with the gradient tool within a single selection (left) and across multiple selections (right).

To use the tool, drag inside the selection, as shown in the left example of Figure 6-8. The point at which you begin dragging (the upper-left corner in the figure) defines the location of the first color in the gradation. The point at which you release (the lower-right corner) defines the location of the last color. If multiple portions of the image are selected, the gradation fills all selections continuously, as demonstrated by the right example of Figure 6-8.

Gradient options

As with other tools in Photoshop 6, the Options bar contains the gradient tool controls, which you can examine in Figure 6-9. If you don't see the Options bar, press Enter when a gradient tool is active or double-click the tool icon in the toolbox.

The following list explains how Options bar controls work. In all cases, you must adjust the options before using the gradient tool. They do not affect existing gradations.

✦ **Gradient preview:** The selected gradient appears in the gradient preview, labeled in Figure 6-9. Click the preview to open the Gradient Editor dialog box, discussed in the upcoming section "Creating custom gradations."

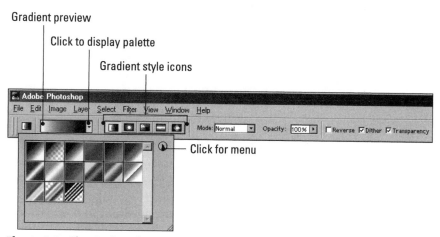

Figure 6-9: The Options bar gives you quick access to all the gradient tool options.

✦ **Gradient drop-down palette:** Click the triangle adjacent to the preview to display the Gradient palette, which contains icons representing gradients in the current gradient presets. Click the icon for the gradient you want.

In the default gradient preset, the first two gradations are dependent on the current foreground and background colors. The others contain specific colors bearing no relationship to the colors in the toolbox.

You load gradient presets using the same techniques that I describe in detail in the brush preset discussion in Chapter 5. Here's a brief recap:

• Click the triangle near the top of the drop-down palette to display the palette menu. The Photoshop collection of presets and any presets that you define appear at the bottom of the palette menu. Click a preset name to use the preset instead of the current preset or append the new preset to the current one.

• To append a preset from disk — such as when a coworker gives you a preset file — choose Load Gradients from the palette menu or click Load in the Preset Manager dialog box. If you want to replace the current preset instead, choose Replace Gradients from the palette menu or click Replace in the dialog box. To return to the default gradients, choose Reset Gradients from the palette menu, either from the Options bar palette or the one in the Preset Manager dialog box.

Tip You can edit a gradient and perform the aforementioned preset juggling acts from within the Gradient Editor dialog box, too. The upcoming section "Creating custom gradations" covers this dialog box.

✦ **Gradient style:** Click an icon to select the gradient style — a function that you formerly accomplished by choosing a specific gradient tool. The next section explains these five styles.

✦ **Mode and Opacity:** These options work as they do for the paint and edit tools, the Fill command, and every other tool or command that offers them as options. Select a different brush mode to change how colors are applied; lower the Opacity value to make a gradation translucent. Remember that you can change the Opacity value by pressing number keys as well as by using the Opacity control on the Options bar. Press 0 for 100 percent opacity, 9 for 90 percent, and so on.

✦ **Reverse:** When active, this simple check box begins the gradation with the background color and ends it with the foreground color. Use this option when you want to start a radial or other style of gradation with white, but you want to keep the foreground and background colors set to their defaults.

✦ **Dither:** In the old days, Photoshop drew its gradients one band at a time. Each band was filled with an incrementally different shade of color. The potential result was banding, in which you could clearly distinguish the transition between two or more bands of color. The Dither check box helps to eliminate this problem by mixing up the pixels between bands (much as Photoshop dithers pixels when converting a grayscale image to black and white). You should leave this option turned on unless you want to use banding to create a special effect.

✦ **Transparency:** You can specify different levels of opacity throughout a gradation. For example, the Transparent Stripes effect (available from the Gradient palette when the Default Gradients preset is loaded) lays down a series of alternately black and transparent stripes. But you needn't use this transparency information. If you prefer to apply a series of black and white stripes instead, you can make all portions of the gradation equally opaque by turning off the Transparency check box.

For example, in Figure 6-10, I applied Transparent Stripes as a radial gradation in two separate swipes, at top and bottom. Both times, I changed the Opacity setting to 50 percent, so the dog and the hydrant would never be obscured. (The Opacity setting works independently of the gradation's built-in transparency, providing you with additional flexibility.) In the top gradation, the Transparency check box is on, so the white stripes are completely transparent. In the bottom gradation, Transparency is turned off, so the white stripes become 50 percent opaque (as prescribed by the Opacity setting).

Transparency on

Transparency off

Figure 6-10: With the Opacity value set to 50 percent, I applied the Transparent Stripes gradation with Transparency on (top) and off (bottom). When Transparency is off, the white stripes obscure the view of the underlying image.

Gradient styles

In Photoshop 5, you selected different gradient tools to create specific styles of gradations. Now the toolbox contains just one gradient tool, and you select the gradient style by clicking the gradient style icons on the Options bar (refer back to Figure 6-9). Note that you can't use the old Shift+G shortcut for switching styles. Nor can you switch styles by Alt-clicking on the gradient tool icon in the toolbox.

Illustrated in Figure 6-11, the five styles are as follows:

✦ **Linear:** A linear gradation progresses in bands of color in a straight line between the beginning and end of your drag. The top two examples in Figure 6-11 show linear gradations created from black to white, and from white to black. The point labeled B marks the beginning of the drag; E marks the end.

✦ **Radial:** A radial gradation progresses outward from a central point in concentric circles, as in the second row of examples in Figure 6-11. The point at which you begin dragging defines the center of the gradation, and the point at which you release defines the outermost circle. This means the first color in the gradation appears in the center of the fill. So to create the gradation on the right side of Figure 6-11, you must set the foreground color to white and the background color to black (or select the Reverse check box on the Options bar).

✦ **Angle:** The angle gradient tool creates a fountain of colors flowing in a counterclockwise direction with respect to your drag, as demonstrated by the middle two examples of Figure 6-11. This type of gradient is known more commonly as a *conical gradation,* because it looks like the bird's eye view of the top of a cone.

Of course, a real cone doesn't have the sharp edge between black and white that you see in Photoshop's angle gradient. To eliminate this edge, create a custom gradation from black to white to black again, as I explain in the "Adjusting colors in a solid gradation" section later in this chapter. (Take a peek at Figure 6-16 later in this chapter if you're not sure what I'm talking about.)

✦ **Reflected:** Drag with the fourth gradient tool to create a linear gradation that reflects back on itself. Photoshop positions the foreground color at the beginning of your drag and the background color at the end, as when using the linear gradient tool. But it also repeats the gradient in the opposite direction of your drag, as demonstrated in Figure 6-10. It's great for creating natural shadows or highlights that fade in two directions.

✦ **Diamond:** The last gradient tool creates a series of concentric diamonds (if you drag at a 90-degree angle) or squares (if you drag at a 45-degree angle, as in Figure 6-11). Otherwise, it works exactly like the radial gradient tool.

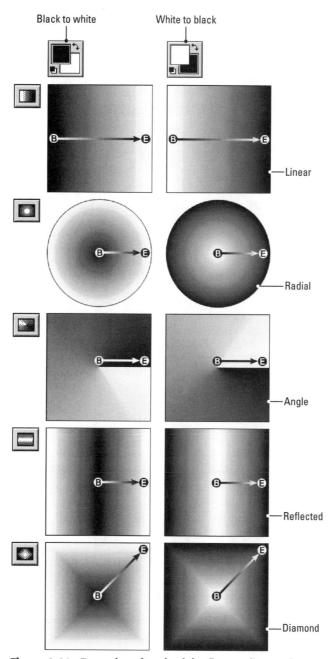

Figure 6-11: Examples of each of the five gradient styles created using the default foreground and background colors (left column) and with the foreground and background colors reversed (right column). B marks the beginning of the drag; E marks the end.

Creating custom gradations

If you're accustomed to editing gradients in earlier versions of Photoshop, you probably searched high and low for the key to opening the Gradient Editor dialog box, shown in Figure 6-12. Where's the Edit button that you clicked to open the dialog box in Version 5? In the Gradient palette menu? On the Options bar? Nope, and nope. The secret passageway to the dialog box — as you already know if you read the "Gradient options" section earlier in this chapter — is the color preview that appears at the left end of the Options bar. If you click the preview, you display the Gradient Editor dialog box; if you click the neighboring triangle, you display the Gradient palette, as shown earlier, in Figure 6-9.

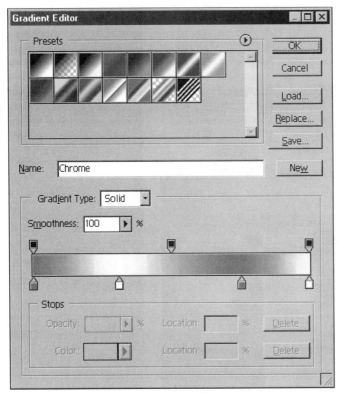

Figure 6-12: Click the gradient preview on the Options bar to display the Gradient Editor dialog box, which enables you to design custom gradations.

The Gradient Editor offers a new look as well as some new functions in Version 6. Upcoming sections cover these functions in detail, but I want to highlight the following changes:

✦ The scrolling list at the top of the dialog box mirrors the Option bar's Gradient palette and the Gradients panel of the Preset Manager dialog box; if you click the triangle at the top of the scrolling list, you display a virtual duplicate of the palette menu.

If you want to see gradient names instead of icons in the list, choose Text Only from the dialog box menu. Or choose Small List or Large List to see both icon and gradient name.

✦ To create a new gradient, find an existing gradient that's close to what you have in mind. Then type a name for the gradient in the Name option box and click the New button. The new gradient appears in the scrolling list, and you can edit the gradient as you see fit.

Even though the gradient appears in the dialog box (as well as in the Gradient palette and Preset Manager dialog box), it's vulnerable until you save it as part of a preset. If you make further edits to the gradient or replace the current gradient preset, the original gradient is a goner. Deleting your main Photoshop preferences file also wipes out an unsaved gradient. See the upcoming section "Saving and managing gradients" for more details.

✦ You now can create *noise gradients* as well as solid-color gradations. If you select Noise from the Gradient Type pop-up menu, Photoshop introduces random color information into the gradient, the result of which is a sort of special-effect gradient that would be difficult to create manually.

✦ The options at the bottom of the dialog box change depending on whether you select Solid or Noise from the Gradient Type pop-up. For solid gradients, Photoshop now provides a Smoothness slider, which you can use to adjust how abrupt you want to make the color transitions in the gradient.

✦ You can resize the dialog box by dragging the size box in the lower-right corner.

Editing solid gradients

If you select Solid from the Gradient Type pop-up menu, you use the options shown in Figure 6-13 to adjust the gradient. (Note that this is a doctored screen shot—I made all the options visible in the figure, but normally, only some of these options are available at a time.)

The *fade bar* (labeled in Figure 6-13) shows the active gradient. The starting color appears as a house-shaped *color stop* on the left; the ending color appears on the far right. The upside-down houses on the top of the fade bar are *opacity stops*. These stops determine where colors are opaque and where they fade into translucency or even transparency.

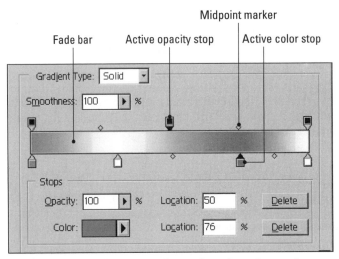

Figure 6-13: Use these controls to adjust the colors and transparency in a solid gradient.

To select either type of stop, click it. The triangle portion of the stop appears black to show you which stop is active. After you select a stop, diamond-shaped *midpoint markers* appear between the stop and its immediate neighbors. On the color-stop side of the fade bar, the midpoint marker represents the spot where the two colors mix in exactly equal amounts. On the transparency side, a marker indicates the point where the opacity value is midway between the values that you set for the stops on either side of the marker.

You can change the location of any stop or marker by dragging it. Or you can click a stop or marker to select it and then enter a value in the Location option box below the fade bar:

✦ When numerically positioning a stop, a value of 0 percent indicates the left end of the fade bar; 100 percent indicates the right end. Even if you add more stops to the gradation, the values represent absolute positions along the fade bar.

✦ When repositioning a midpoint marker, the initial setting of 50 percent is smack dab between two stops; 0 percent is all the way over to the left stop, and 100 percent is all the way over to the right. Midpoint values are, therefore, measured relative to stop positions. In fact, when you move a stop, Photoshop moves the midpoint marker along with it to maintain the same relative positioning.

Figure 6-14 shows four black-to-white radial gradations that I created by setting the midpoint between the black and white color stops to four different positions. The midpoint settings range from the minimum to maximum allowable Location values. If you enter a value below 13 percent or over 87, Photoshop politely ignores you. In all cases, I set the opacity to 100 percent along the entire gradient.

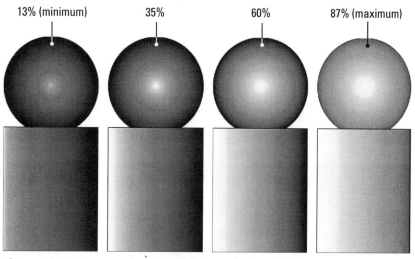

13% (minimum)   35%   60%   87% (maximum)

Figure 6-14: Four sets of white-to-black gradations—radial on top and linear at bottom—subject to different midpoint settings.

Tip

Pressing Enter after you enter a value into the Location option box is tempting, but don't do it. If you do, Photoshop dumps you out of the Gradient Editor dialog box.

Adjusting colors in a solid gradation

When editing a solid gradation, you can add colors, delete colors, change the positioning of the colors within the gradient, and control how two colors blend together. After clicking a color stop to select it, you can change its color in several ways:

To change the color to the current foreground color, open the Color pop-up menu, as shown in Figure 6-15, and select Foreground. Select Background to use the background color instead.

✦ When you select Foreground or Background, the color stop becomes filled with a grayscale pattern instead of a solid color. If you squint real hard and put your nose to the screen, you can see that the pattern is actually a representation of the Foreground and Background color controls in the toolbox.

The little black square appears in the upper-left corner when the foreground color is active, as shown in the first stop on the fade bar in Figure 6-15; the black square moves to the bottom-right corner when the background color is active, as shown in the end stop in the figure.

✦ If you change the foreground or background color after closing the Gradient Editor, the gradient changes to reflect the new color. When you next open the Gradient Editor, you can revert the stop to the original foreground or background color by selecting User Color from the pop-up menu.

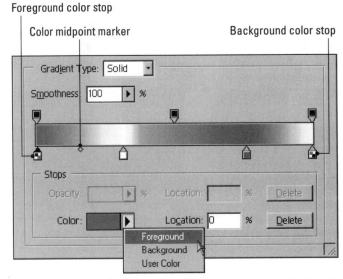

Figure 6-15: A look at the new color stop options in Version 6

✦ To set the color stop to some other color, click the Color swatch or double-click the color stop to open the Color Picker and define the new color. Select your color and press Enter.

✦ You may have noticed that when you opened the Gradient Editor dialog box, Photoshop automatically selected the eyedropper tool for you and displayed that tool's controls on the Options bar. Here's why: You can click with the eyedropper in an open image window to lift a color from the image and assign the color to the selected color stop. You can also click the Color palette's color bar or a swatch in the Swatches palette. Or, if you see the color you want in the fade bar in the dialog box, click it there.

To change the point at which two colors meet, drag the midpoint marker between the two stops. Or click the midpoint marker and enter a new value into the Location box. As I mentioned earlier, a value of 0 puts the midpoint marker smack up against the left color stop; a value of 100 scoots the stop all the way over to the right stop.

You add or delete stops as follows:

✦ To add a color stop, click anywhere along the bottom of the fade bar. A new stop appears where you click. Photoshop also adds a midpoint marker between the new color stop and its neighbors. You can add as many color stops as your heart desires. (But if your goal is a gradient featuring tons of random colors, you may be able to create the effect you want more easily by using the new Noise gradient option, discussed shortly.)

✦ To duplicate a color stop, Alt-drag it to a new location along the fade bar. One great use for this to create a reflecting gradation.

For example, select Foreground to Background from the scrolling list of gradients and click New to duplicate the gradient. After naming your new gradient — something like Fore to Back to Fore — click the background color stop and change the Location value to 50. Then Alt-drag the foreground color stop all the way to the right. This new gradient is perfect for making true conical gradations with the angle gradient tool, as demonstrated in Figure 6-16.

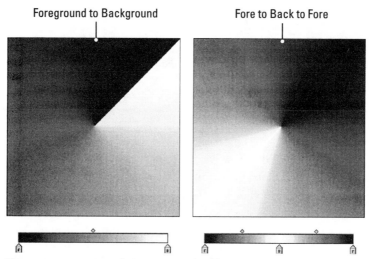

Figure 6-16: Two gradations created with the angle gradient tool, one using the standard Foreground to Background gradient (left) and the other with my reflected Fore to Back to Fore style (right). Which looks better to you?

✦ To remove a color stop, drag the stop away from the fade bar. Or click the stop and click the Delete button. The stop icon vanishes and the fade bar automatically adjusts as defined by the remaining color stops.

Adjusting the transparency mask

If you like, you can include a *transparency mask* with each gradation. The mask determines the opacity of different colors along the gradation. You create and edit this mask independently of the colors in the gradation.

To create a transparency mask in Version 6, you play with the opacity stops across the top of the fade bar. You don't have to toggle between editing the opacity and color stops as you did in earlier versions of Photoshop; both attributes are always within reach. When you click a transparency stop, the transparency options become available beneath the fade bar and the color options dim, as shown in Figure 6-17.

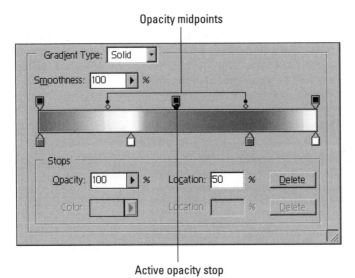

Figure 6-17: Click a stop along the top of the fade bar to adjust the opacity of the gradient at that location.

To add an opacity stop, click above the fade bar. By default, each new stop is 100 percent opaque. You can modify the transparency by selecting a stop and changing the Opacity value. The fade bar updates to reflect your changes. To reposition a stop, drag it or enter a value in the Location option box.

Midpoint markers represent the spot where the opacity value is half the difference between the opacity values of a pair of opacity stops. In other words, if you set one opacity stop to 30 percent and another to 90 percent, the midpoint marker shows you where the gradient reaches 60 percent opacity. You can relocate the midpoint marker, and thus change the spot where the gradient reaches that mid-range opacity value, by dragging the marker or entering a new value in the Location box.

Color Plate 6-2 demonstrates the effect of applying a three-color gradation to a photograph. The gradation fades from red to transparency to green to transparency and, finally, to blue. In the first example in the color plate, I dragged over a standard checkerboard pattern with the gradient tool, from the lower-left corner to the upper-right corner. The second example shows the photograph before applying the gradation. In the last example, I applied the gradient — again from lower left to upper right — using the Overlay brush mode.

Creating noise gradients

Adobe describes a noise gradient as a gradient that "contains random components along with the deterministic ones that create the gradient." Allow me to translate: Photoshop adds random colors between the defined colors of the selected gradient. Did that help? No? Then take a look at Figure 6-18, which shows examples of three noise gradients based on a simple black-to-white gradient. You could create these same gradients using the regular Solid gradient controls, of course, but it would take you forever to add all the color and midpoint stops required to produce the same effect.

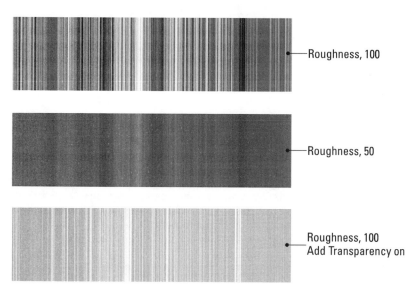

Roughness, 100

Roughness, 50

Roughness, 100
Add Transparency on

Figure 6-18: Here you see three gradients created using the new Noise option in the Gradient Editor dialog box. I created the first two using two different Roughness values; for the bottom example, I used the same Roughness value as in the middle example but selected the Add Transparency option.

To create a noise gradient, select Noise from the Gradient Type menu in the Gradient Editor dialog box, as shown in Figure 6-19. You can adjust the gradient as follows:

✦ Raise the Roughness value to create more distinct bands of color, as in the top example in Figure 6-18. Lowering the Roughness value results in softer color transitions, as you can see from the middle example, which I set at one half the Roughness value of the top example.

✦ Use the color sliders at the bottom of the dialog box to define the range of allowable colors in the gradient. You can work in one of three color modes: RGB, HSB, or Lab. Select the mode you want from the pop-up menu above the sliders.

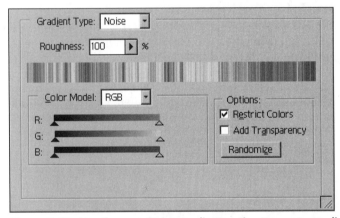

Figure 6-19: Use the new Noise gradient option to create gradients like the ones you see in Figure 6-18.

✦ The Restrict Colors option, when selected, adjusts the gradient so that you don't wind up with any oversaturated colors. Deselect the option for more vibrant hues.

✦ If you select Add Transparency, Photoshop adds random transparency information to the gradient, as if you had added scads of opacity stops to a regular gradient. In the bottom example of Figure 6-17, I started with the gradient from the top example, selected the Add Transparency check box, and left the Roughness value at 100.

✦ Click the Randomize button, and Photoshop shuffles all the gradient colors and transparency values to create another gradient. If you don't like what you see, just keep clicking Randomize until you're satisfied.

Tip

For some really cool effects, try applying special effects filters to a noise gradient. Figure 6-20 shows the results of applying the Crystallize, Twirl, and Ripple filters on the original noise gradient shown in the upper-left example.

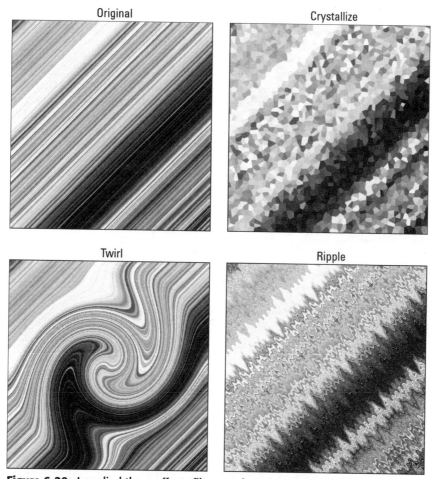

Figure 6-20: I applied three effects filters to the original noise gradient to create some interesting random patterns.

Saving and managing gradients

When you define a new gradient, its icon appears in the palette, the Preset Manger dialog box, and the Gradient Editor dialog box. But if you replace the current gradient set or edit the gradient, the original gradient gets trashed. You also lose the gradient if you delete your Photoshop 6 preferences file because that's where the temporary gradient information is stored.

If you want to preserve a gradient, you must save it as part of a preset—which is nothing more than a collection of gradients. As I mentioned earlier, Photoshop ships with several gradient presets that are stored in the Gradients folder, which lives inside the Presets folder in the main Photoshop program folder. You also can create as many custom presets as you like. Gradient presets have the file extension .grd.

You can save all the gradients in the active preset–including any custom gradients that you define–by clicking Save in the Gradient Editor dialog box or by choosing Save Gradients from the Gradient palette pop-up menu. But if you want to save only some of the current gradients as a preset, choose Edit ⇨ Preset Manager and display the Gradients panel, shown in Figure 6-21, by pressing Ctrl+3 or by choosing Gradients from the Preset Type pop-up menu. Shift-click the gradients you want to save and then click Save Set. If you want to dump the selected gradients into an existing preset, select the preset file and press Enter. Alternatively, you can enter a new preset name to create a brand new preset that contains only the selected gradients.

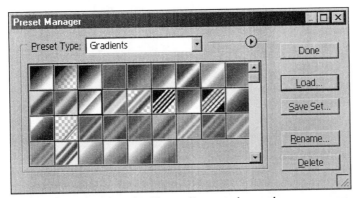

Figure 6-21: To select specific gradients and save them as a new preset, use the Preset Manager.

To delete a gradient, Alt-click its icon in the palette, the Preset Manager, or the Gradient Editor dialog box. To delete multiple gradients, Shift-click the gradients in the Preset Manager and then click the Delete button. Save the preset immediately if you want the deleted gradients gone for good; otherwise, it remains an official part of the preset and reappears the next time you load the preset.

All the standard brush modes are available when you apply gradations, and they make a tremendous impression on the performance of the gradient tool. This section examines yet another way to apply a brush mode in conjunction with the tool. Naturally, it barely scrapes the surface of what's possible, but it may inspire you to experiment and discover additional effects on your own.

The following steps tell you how to use the Dissolve mode with a radial gradation to create a supernova explosion. (At least, it looks like a supernova to me—not that I've ever seen one up close, mind you.) Figures 6-22 through 6-24 show the nova in progress. The steps offer you the opportunity to experiment with a brush mode setting and some general insight into creating radial gradations.

These steps involve the use of the elliptical marquee tool. Generally speaking, it's an easy tool to use. But if you find you have problems making it work according to my instructions, you may want to read the "Geometric selection outlines" section of Chapter 8. It's only a few pages long.

STEPS: Creating a Gradient Supernova

1. **Create a new image window.** Make it 500×500 pixels. A grayscale image is fine for this exercise.

2. **Click with the pencil tool at the apparent center of the image.** Don't worry if it's not the exact center. This point is merely intended to serve as a guide. If a single point is not large enough for you to identify easily, draw a small cross.

3. **Alt-drag from the point with the elliptical marquee tool to draw the marquee outward from the center.** While dragging with the tool, press and hold Shift to constrain the marquee to a circle. Release Shift after you release the mouse button. Draw a marquee that fills about 3/4 of the window.

4. **Choose Image ⇨ Adjust ⇨ Invert (Ctrl+I).** This fills the marquee with black and makes the center point white.

5. **Choose Select ⇨ Deselect (Ctrl+D).** As the command name suggests, this deselects the circle.

6. **Again, Alt-drag from the center point with the elliptical marquee tool.** And, again, press Shift to constrain the shape to a circle. Create a marquee roughly 20 pixels larger than the black circle.

7. **Alt-drag from the center point with the elliptical marquee tool.** This subtracts a hole from the selection. After you begin dragging, release Alt (but keep that mouse button down). Then press and hold both Shift and Alt together and keep them down. Draw a marquee roughly 20 pixels smaller than the black circle. Release the mouse button and finally release the keys. The result is a doughnut-shaped selection—a large circle with a smaller circular hole—as shown in Figure 6-22.

8. **Choose Select ⇨ Feather (Ctrl+Alt+D) and enter 10 for the Radius value.** Then press Enter to feather the section outline.

9. **Press D and then press X.** This makes the foreground color white and the background color black.

10. **Select the gradient tool and click the radial gradient icon on the Options bar.** That's the icon that has the white circle at its center. (Flip back to Figure 6-11 if you still don't know what I mean.) If the Options bar is hidden, press Enter to display it.

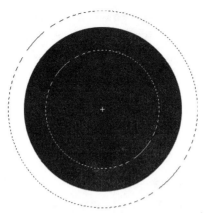

Figure 6-22: The result of creating a black circle and two circular marquees, all centered about a single point

11. **Open the Gradient palette and select the Foreground to Background gradient.** Assuming that you have the default gradients preset loaded and haven't altered the preset, the icon is the first one in the palette.

12. **Select Dissolve from the Mode menu on the Options bar.**

13. **Drag from the center point in the image window to anywhere along the outer rim of the largest marquee.** The result is the fuzzy gradation shown in Figure 6-23.

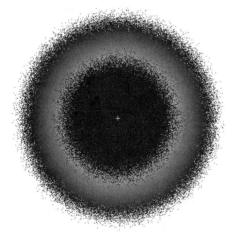

Figure 6-23: The Dissolve brush mode option randomizes the pixels around the feathered edges of the selection outlines.

14. **Choose Select ➪ Deselect (Ctrl+D) to deselect the image.**

15. **Choose Image ➪ Adjust ➪ Invert (Ctrl+I) to invert the entire image.**

16. **Press D to restore black and white as foreground and background colors, respectively.** Then use the eraser tool to erase the center point. The finished supernova appears in Figure 6-24.

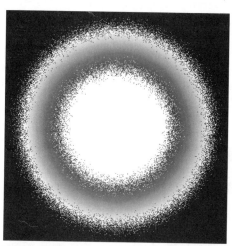

Figure 6-24: By inverting the image from the previous figure and erasing the center point, you create an expanding series of progressively lighter rings dissolving into the black void of space, an effect better known to its friends as a supernova.

Applying Strokes and Arrowheads

Photoshop is nearly as adept at drawing lines and outlines as it is at filling selections. The following sections discuss how to apply a border around a selection outline — which is practical, if not terribly exciting — and how to create arrowheads — which can yield more interesting results than you might think.

This chapter concentrates on *raster* lines — that is, lines made of pixels that you create with the line tool set to the Fill Region mode. To find out how to use the tool to produce vector lines and work paths, see Chapters 14 and 8, respectively. Some, but not all, line tool techniques discussed here apply to the line tool also when it's set to vector or work path mode.

Stroking a selection outline

Stroking is useful for creating frames and outlines. Generally speaking, you can stroke an image in Photoshop in four ways:

✦ **The Stroke command:** Select the portion of the image you want to stroke and choose Edit ⇨ Stroke to display the Stroke dialog box shown in Figure 6-25. Or, if you're working on a multilayered image, you can choose the Stroke command without making a selection; Photoshop then applies the stroke to the entire layer.

In the Stroke dialog box, enter the thickness of the stroke in the Width option box. The default unit of measurement here is pixels, but you can now use inches and centimeters as well. Just type the value and then the unit abbreviation (*px* for pixels, *in* for inches, or *cm* for centimeters).

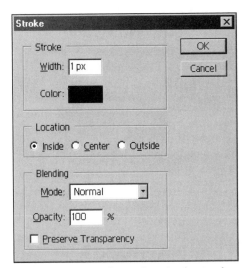

Figure 6-25: Use the options in the Stroke dialog box to specify the thickness of a stroke and its location with respect to the selection outline.

In its former life, the Stroke command always applied the foreground color, which meant that you had to remember to set the color before choosing the command. In Version 6, you can set the stroke color from within the dialog box. Click the color swatch to select a color from the Color Picker — don't forget that you can click inside an image window while the Color Picker is open to pick up a color in the image. Press Enter to close the Color Picker and return to the Stroke dialog box.

Tip

Select a Location radio button to specify the position of the stroke with respect to the selection outline. When in doubt, select Inside from the Location radio buttons. This setting ensures that the stroke is entirely inside the selection outline in case you decide to move the selection. If you select Center or Outside, Photoshop applies part or all of the stroke to the deselected area around the selection outline — unless, of course, your selection extends to the edge of the canvas, in which case you wind up with no stroke at all for Outside and half a stroke inside the selection outline for Center.

The Stroke dialog box also includes Opacity, Mode, and Preserve Transparency options that work like those in the Fill dialog box.

✦ **The Border command:** Select a portion of the image and choose Select ⇨ Modify ⇨ Border to retain only the outline of the selection. Specify the size of the border by entering a value in pixels in the Width option box and press Enter. To fill the border with the background color, press Ctrl+Backspace. To fill the border with the foreground color, press Alt+Backspace. To apply a repeating pattern to the border, choose Edit ⇨ Fill and select the Pattern option from the Use pop-up menu. You can even apply a command under the Filter menu or some other special effect.

✦ **Layer Style effects:** If you want to stroke an entire layer, also check out the options provided by the new Layer Styles feature. Choose Layer ⇨ Layer Style ⇨ Stroke to display the dialog box shown in Figure 6-26. At first glance, the options here appear to mirror those you find in the regular Stroke dialog box; and they do, as long as you select Color from the Fill pop-up menu. But if you crack open that pop-up menu, you discover two goodies. First, you can fill the stroke with a gradient or a pattern. Second, you can adjust the pattern and gradient on the fly and preview the results inside the dialog box. For example, you can scale the gradient and change its angle — two things you can't do inside the regular Gradient Editor dialog box, I might add. By using the settings shown in the figure, I adapted a plain old black-to-white gradient to produce the shadowed frame effect you see in the preview.

Cross-Reference

I cover Layers Styles in detail in Chapter 12, so if you have trouble figuring out the stroke options, look there for help.

✦ **The Canvas Size trick:** Okay, so this one is a throwaway, but I use it all the time. To create an outline around the entire image, change the background color (yes, the background color) to the color you want to apply to the outline. Then choose Image ⇨ Canvas Size and add twice the desired border thickness to the Width and Height options in pixels.

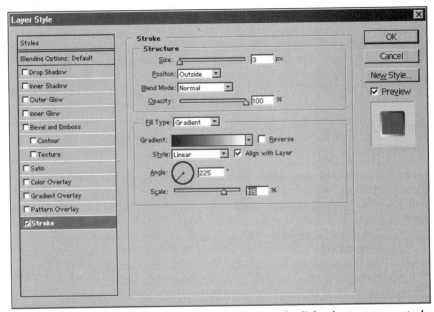

Figure 6-26: With the Stroke options in the Layer Style dialog box, you can stroke a layer with a solid color, gradient, or pattern. You also can adjust the angle and scale of gradients, as I did to create the effect shown in the preview.

For example, to create a 1-pixel border all the way around, add 2 pixels to the Width value (1 for the left side and 1 for the right) and 2 pixels to the Height value (1 for the top and 1 for the bottom). Leave the Anchor option set to the center tile. When you press Enter, Photoshop enlarges the canvas size according to your specifications and fills the new pixels around the perimeter of the image with the background color. Simplicity at its best.

Applying arrowheads

The one function missing from all the operations in the preceding list is applying arrowheads. The fact is, in Photoshop, you can apply arrowheads only to straight lines drawn with the line tool.

The line tool no longer shares a toolbox flyout with the pencil tool; in Version 6, the line tool is grouped with the drawing tools. You can cycle between the tools by pressing U (or Shift+U, depending on whether you select the Use Shift for Tool Switch check box in the Preferences dialog box). As I mentioned previously, the line tool can now create three different kinds of shapes. You can paint raster lines — that is, lines made up of pixels — as with the line tool of old. Or you can draw vector-based lines on a new shape layer, as explained in Chapter 14. Finally, you can create a work path using the line tool, as I discuss in Chapter 8.

You specify which type of line you want to create by clicking one of the three icons near the left end of the Options bar, which I labeled in Figure 6-27. (If you don't see the Options bar on screen, press Enter or double-click the line tool icon in the toolbox.)

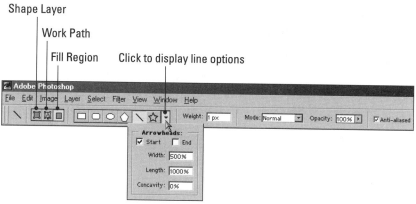

Figure 6-27: In Version 6, all the arrowhead options appear on this drop-down palette.

Regardless of which type of line you're creating, you set the width of the line by entering a value into the Weight box on the Options bar. Then you add arrowheads via the drop-down options palette in the figure. To display the options, click the triangle at the end of the strip of shape icons (again, see the figure). Use the Arrowheads options as follows:

✦ **Start:** Select this check box to append an arrowhead to the beginning of a line drawn with the line tool.

✦ **End:** Select this check box to append an arrowhead to the end of a line. (Like you needed me to tell you this.)

✦ **Width:** Enter the width of the arrowhead in this option box. The width is measured as a percentage of the line weight, so if the Weight is set to 6 pixels and the Width value is 500 percent, the width of the arrowhead will be 30 pixels. Math in action.

✦ **Length:** Enter the length of the arrowhead, measured from the base of the arrowhead to its tip, again as a percentage of the line weight.

✦ **Concavity:** You can specify the shape of the arrowhead by entering a value between negative and positive 50 percent in the Concavity option box. Figure 6-28 shows examples of a few Concavity settings applied to an arrowhead 50 pixels wide and 100 pixels long.

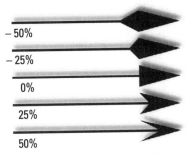

- 50%
- 25%
0%
25%
50%

Figure 6-28: Examples of a 50 × 100-pixel
arrowhead subject to five different
Concavity values.

Appending arrowheads to curved lines

Applying arrowheads to straight lines is a simple matter. Applying an arrowhead to
a stroked selection outline is a little trickier, but still possible. The following steps
explain the process.

Note

For the effect shown in this example, you need raster arrowheads, so click the Fill
Region icon on the Options bar (see Figure 6-28). Now your line tool creates raster
lines rather than vector lines or work paths.

STEPS: Adding an Arrowhead to a Free-form Stroke

1. **Create a new layer.** Display the Layers palette by pressing the F7 key. Then
   click the little page icon at the bottom of the palette to create a new layer.

2. **Draw and stroke a selection.** Draw any selection outline you like. Stroke it
   by choosing Edit ⇨ Stroke and applying whatever settings strike your fancy.
   Remember the value you enter in the Width option. In Figure 6-29, I drew
   a wiggly line with the lasso tool and applied a 4-pixel black stroke set to
   30 percent Opacity.

3. **Press Ctrl+D.** This deselects all portions of the image.

4. **Erase the portions of the stroke you don't need.** Select the eraser tool by
   pressing E. Then drag to erase through the stroke layer without harming the
   layer below. Erase the areas of the stroke where you want to add arrowheads.
   I wanted to add an arrowhead behind the fly, so I erased around the fly.

5. **Select the line tool and click the Fill Region icon on the Options bar.**

6. **Specify the line weight and arrowhead settings.** Enter the line weight you
   used when stroking the selection outline into the Weight option box (in my
   case, 4 pixels). Next, display the line options palette. Just click the triangle at
   the end of the strip of shape icons, as shown previously in Figure 6-27. Select
   the End check box and deselect the Start check box. Then specify the width,
   length, and concavity of the arrowhead as desired.

Figure 6-29: Here I created a new layer, drew a free-form shape with the lasso tool, and stroked it with a 4-pixel black outline at 30 percent Opacity.

7. **Set the foreground color as needed.** I applied a black stroke at 30 percent Opacity, so I set the foreground color to 30 percent gray. (Click the stroke with the eyedropper to change the foreground color to the stroke color.)

8. **Zoom in to the point in the image where you want to add the arrowhead.** You have to get in close enough to see what you're doing, as in Figure 6-30.

9. **At the tip of the stroke, draw a very short line exactly the length of the arrowhead.** Figure 6-30 illustrates what I mean. This may take some practice to accomplish. Start the line a few pixels in from the end of the stroke to make sure the base of the arrowhead fits snugly. If you mess up the first time, choose Edit ➪ Undo (Ctrl+Z) and try again.

That's all there is to it. From then on, you can continue to edit the stroke as you see fit. In Figure 6-31, for example, I erased a series of scratches across the stroke to create a dashed-line effect, all the rage for representing cartoon fly trails. I then set the eraser brush size to the largest, fuzziest setting and erased the end of the stroke (above the dog's head) to create a gradual trailing off. That crazy fly is now officially distracting our hero from his appointed rounds.

Figure 6-30: Use the line tool to draw a line no longer than the arrowhead. This appends the arrow to the end of the stroke. The view size of this image is magnified to 300 percent.

Figure 6-31: I finished by erasing dashes into the line and softening the end of the trail with a large, fuzzy eraser.

✦   ✦   ✦

Retouching, Repeating, and Restoring

Three of the Best

So far in Part II, we've looked at a host of editing disciplines —
smearing and sponging, filling and stroking, and plain old
painting. Although most of these tools perform as well as can
be expected, they don't add up to a hill of beans compared
with Photoshop's foremost retouchers — the rubber stamp,
eraser, and history brush. These remarkable three permit you
to repair damaged images, create and apply repeating patterns, erase away mistakes, and restore operations from your
recent past. And with the art history brush, magic eraser, and
background eraser, all added in Version 5.5, you get even more
ways to restore and erase.

Together, these tools permit you to perform the sorts of miracles that simply weren't possible in the days before computer
imaging, all without the slightest fear of damaging your image.
Very briefly, here's how each tool works:

✦ **Rubber stamp and pattern stamp:** Use the rubber stamp
to replicate pixels from one area in an image to another.
This one feature makes the rubber stamp the perfect tool
for removing dust and scratches, repairing defects, and
eliminating distracting background elements. Alt-click
the rubber stamp icon in the toolbox or press S to switch
to the pattern stamp tool, which paints with a repeating
image fragment defined using Edit ⇨ Define Pattern. (If
you selected Use Shift for Key for Tool Switch in the
Preferences dialog box, press Shift+S.)

✦ **Erasers:** When used in a single-layer image or on the background layer, the eraser paints in the background color. When applied to a layer, it erases pixels to reveal the layers below. The background eraser, as its name implies, erases the background from an image and leaves the foreground intact — or at least, that's what happens if you use the tool correctly. Otherwise, it just erases everything.

The final tool in the eraser triad, the magic eraser, works like the fill tool but in reverse. When you click the magic eraser, you delete a range of similarly colored pixels. Don't confuse this tool with the eraser you get when you Alt-drag with the standard eraser tool. Formerly known as the magic eraser, that tool now takes the name history eraser.

You can cycle through the erasers by Alt-clicking the eraser icon in the tool-box or by pressing E (or Shift+E).

✦ **History brush and art history brush:** The history brush selectively reverts to any of several previous states listed in the History palette. With the art history brush, you can recreate a past state using various artistic brushes.

To select the "source state" that you want to paint with, click in the first column of the History palette. A brush icon identifies the source state, as illustrated by the Diffuse Glow item in Figure 7-1. If Photoshop displays a little "not-allowed" cursor when you try to use the history brush, it means you can't paint from the selected state. Click another state in the History palette and try again.

Obviously, these are but the skimpiest of introductions, every bit as stingy with information as a 19th-century headmaster might have been with his Christmas gruel and treacle. But fear not, my hungry one. This chapter doles out so many courses of meaty facts, fibrous techniques, and sweet, buttery insights that you'll need a whole box of toothpicks to dislodge the excess tips from your incisors.

Cloning Image Elements

One of the most useful tools in all of Photoshop is the rubber stamp. Personally, I've always found the name "rubber stamp" misleading. First, no tree sap is involved — let's get that sticky issue resolved right off the bat. Second, you don't use the tool to stamp an image. When I think of rubber stamps, I think of those things you see in stationery stores that plunk down smiley faces and Pooh bears. Elementary school teachers and little girls use rubber stamps. I've never seen a professional image editor walking around with a rubber stamp in my life.

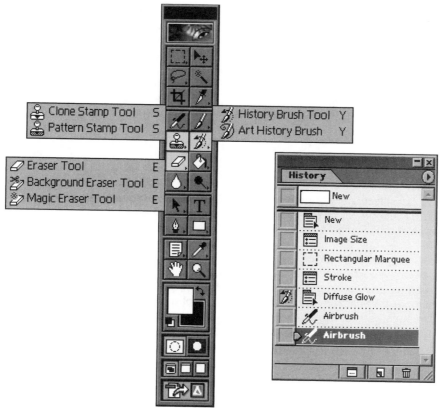

Figure 7-1: By using these tools and the History palette, you can erase pixels and restore an image to an earlier state.

A better name for the rubber stamp is the clone tool, because that's precisely what it does — duplicates portions of an image. After selecting the tool, Alt-click in the image window to specify the portion of the image you want to clone. Then paint with the tool to clone from the area that you Alt-clicked.

If this is your first experience with a clone tool, it might sound peculiar. Sheep, cows, dinosaurs, these are things you might want to clone. Pixels, never. But as any dyed-in-the-wool Photoshop user will tell you, the rubber stamp is nothing short of invaluable for touching up images. You can remove dust fragments, hairs, and other impurities; rebuild creased or torn photographs, and even eliminate elements that wandered into your picture when you weren't looking. So get set for what is undoubtedly the best retouching tool of them all.

You also can use the rubber stamp to duplicate specific elements in an image, such as petals in a flower or umbrellas on a beach (actual suggestions from previous editions of Photoshop's manual). But this is rarely an efficient use of the tool. If you want to duplicate an element, you'll have better luck if you select it and clone it, as explained in Chapter 8. Selection tools let you specify the exact boundaries of the element, the softness of the edges, and the precise location of the clone. Because of its reliance on a brush metaphor — that is, you drag across the image window to paint with it — the rubber stamp is better suited to buffing away defeats and filling in missing details.

The cloning process

You can select the rubber stamp by pressing S — or, if the pattern stamp tool is visible in the toolbox, by pressing S twice (or Shift+S, depending on your tool-switch setting in the Preferences dialog box).

To clone part of an image, Alt-click in the image window to specify a point of reference in the portion of the image you want to clone. Then click or drag with the tool in some other region of the image to paint a cloned spot or line. In Figure 7-2, for example, I Alt-clicked above and to the right of the bird's head, as demonstrated by the appearance of the stamp pickup cursor. I then painted the line shown inside the white rectangle. The rubber stamp cursor shows the end of my drag; the clone reference crosshair shows the corresponding point in the original image.

The rubber stamp clones the image as it existed before you began using the tool. Even when you drag over an area containing a clone, the tool references the original appearance of the image. This prevents you from creating more than one clone during a single drag and produces the entirely predictable effect pictured in Figure 7-3.

Photoshop lets you clone not only from within the image you're working on but also from a separate image window. This technique makes it possible to merge two different images, as demonstrated in Figure 7-4. To achieve this effect, Alt-click in one image, bring a second image to the foreground, and then drag with the rubber stamp tool to clone from the first image. You can also clone between layers. Alt-click one layer and then switch to a different layer and drag.

Clone reference crosshair
Stamp pickup cursor

Rubber stamp cursor

Figure 7-2: After Alt-clicking at the point indicated by the stamp pickup cursor, I dragged with the rubber stamp tool to paint with the image. (The only reason I painted inside the white rectangle was to set off the line so you can see it better.)

Figure 7-3: As the result of my cloning, this memorialized hero suffers twice the indignation of being used as a lofty perch for loitering birds.

Figure 7-4: I merged the area around the horse and rider with a water image from another open window (see the upcoming Figure 7-6). The translucent effects were created by periodically adjusting the Opacity value to settings ranging from 50 to 80 percent.

When the rubber stamp is active, the Options bar gives you access to the Brush palette as well as the standard Mode, Opacity, and Use All Layers options that I cover in Chapter 5. The only unique item is the Aligned check box. To understand how this option works, think of the locations where you Alt-click and begin dragging with the rubber stamp as opposite ends of an imaginary straight line, as illustrated in the top half of Figure 7-5. When Aligned is turned on, the length and angle of this imaginary line remains fixed until the next time you Alt-click. As you drag, Photoshop moves the line, cloning pixels from one end of the line and laying them down at the other. The upshot is that regardless of how many times you start and stop dragging with the stamp tool, all brushstrokes match up as seamlessly as pieces in a puzzle.

If you want to clone from a single portion of an image repeatedly, turn off the Aligned check box. The second example in Figure 7-5 shows how Photoshop clones from the same point every time you paint a new line with the rubber stamp tool. As a result, each of the four brushstrokes features part of the bird and none line up with each other.

Aligned

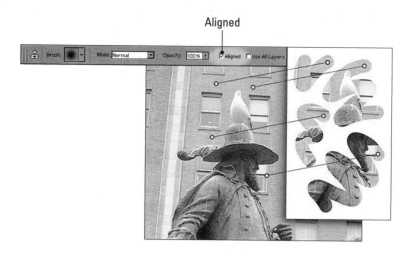

Not aligned

Figure 7-5: Turn on the Aligned check box to instruct Photoshop to clone an image continuously, no matter how many lines you paint (top). If you turn off the option, Photoshop clones each new line from the point at which you Alt-click.

Touching up blemishes

One great use of the rubber stamp tool is to touch up a scanned photo. Figure 7-6 shows a Photo CD image desperately in need of the stamp tool's attention. Normally, Kodak's Photo CD process delivers some of the best consumer-quality scans money can buy. But this particular medium-resolution image looks like the folks at the lab got together and blew their respective noses on it. It's too late to return to the service bureau and demand they rescan the photo, so my only choice is to touch it up myself.

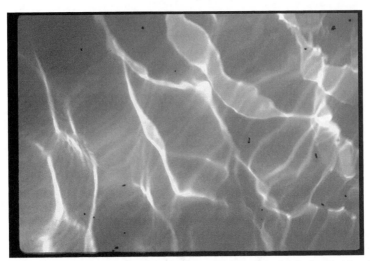

Figure 7-6: This appallingly bad Photo CD image is riddled with blotches and big hulky wads of dust that didn't exist on the original 35mm slide.

The best way to fix this image — or any image like it — is to use the rubber stamp over and over again, repeatedly Alt-clicking at one location and then clicking at another. Begin by selecting a brush shape slightly larger than the largest blotch. Of the default brushes, the hard-edged varieties with diameters of 5 and 9 pixels generally work best. (The soft-edged brush shapes have a tendency to only partially hide the blemishes and leave ghosted versions behind.)

Alt-click with the stamp tool at a location that features similarly colored pixels to the blemished area. Be sure to Alt-click far enough away from the blemish that you don't run the risk of duplicating the blemish as you clone. Then click — do not drag — directly on the blemish to clone over it. The idea is to change as few pixels as possible.

If the retouched area doesn't look quite right, press Ctrl+Z to undo it, Alt-click at a different location, and try again. If your touchup appears seamless — *absolutely* seamless, there's no reason to settle for less — move on to the next blemish. Repeat the Alt-click and click routine for every dust mark on the photo.

This process isn't necessarily time-consuming, but it does require patience. For example, although it took more than 40 Alt-click and click combinations (not counting 10 or so undos) to arrive at the image shown in Figure 7-7, the process itself took less than 15 minutes. Boring, but fast.

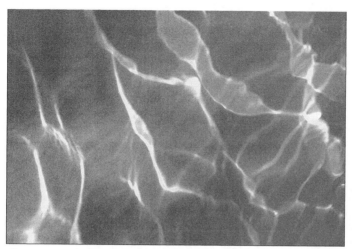

Figure 7-7: The result of Alt-clicking and clicking more than 40 times on the photo shown in Figure 7-6. I also cropped the image and added a border.

Retouching hairs is a little trickier than dust and other blobs because a hair, although very thin, can be surprisingly long. The retouching process is the same, though. Rather than dragging over the entire length of the hair, Alt-click and click your way through it, bit by little bit. The one difference is brush shape. Because you'll be clicking so many times in succession, and because the hair is so thin, you'll probably achieve the least-conspicuous effects if you use a soft brush shape, such as the default 9-pixel model in the second row of the Brush drop-down palette.

At this point you might wonder, "Why go to all this work to remove dust and scratches when Photoshop provides the automated feature Filter ➪ Noise ➪ Dust & Scratches?" The reason is — and I'm going to be painfully blunt here — the Dust & Scratches filter stinks. No offense to the designers of this filter: They're wonderful people, every one of them, but the filter simply doesn't produce the effect it advertises. It mucks up the detail in your image by averaging neighboring pixels, and this simply isn't an acceptable solution. Do your photograph a favor — fix its flaws manually (not to mention lovingly) with the rubber stamp tool.

Restoring an old photograph

Dust, hairs, gloops, and other blemishes are introduced during the scanning process. But what about more severe problems that trace back to the original image? Figure 7-8 is a prime example. This photograph was shot sometime before 1910. It's a wonderful photo, but 90 years is a long time for something as fragile and transient as a scrap of paper. It's torn, faded, stained, creased, and flaking. The normally simple act of extracting it from its photo album took every bit as long as scanning it.

Figure 7-8: This photo's seen better days. Then again,
I hope to look as good when I'm 90 years old.

But despite the photo's rough condition, I was able to restore it in Photoshop, as evidenced by Figure 7-9. (For a full-color view of the before and after images, see Color Plate 7-1.) As in the case of the pool image (Figure 7-7), I used the rubber stamp to do most of the work. And as before, the process was tedious but straightforward. After about an hour and a few hundred brushstrokes, I had the image well in hand.

Note   If an hour sounds like a long time to fix a few rips and scrapes, wake up and smell the coffee. This is not one-button editing. Photographic restoration is a labor-intensive activity that relies heavily on your talents and your mastery of Photoshop. The rubber stamp tool goes a long way toward making your edits believable, but it does little to automate the process. Retouching calls for a human touch, and that's where you come in.

Figure 7-9: The same image after about an hour of work with the rubber stamp tool.

I considered documenting every single one of my brushstrokes, but I value your time (yes, and my own) too highly. Suffice it to say that the general approach was the same as it was for the pool image. Alt-click in an area that looks like it'd do a good job of covering up the blemish and then drag over the blemish. And repeat about 250 times.

That said, I do have some advice that specifically addresses the art of photo restoration:

✦ Most images in this kind of condition are black-and-white. Scan them in color and then peruse the color channels to see which grayscale version of the image looks best. As you can see in Color Plate 7-1, the original image had lots of yellow stains around the tears.

So when I viewed the individual color channels (Figure 7-10), I was hardly surprised to see dark blotches in the blue channel. (Blue is the opposite of yellow, so where yellow is prominent, the blue channel was dark.) In my case, the red channel was in the best shape, so I switched to the red channel and disposed of the other two by choosing Image ⇨ Mode ⇨ Grayscale. The simple act of trashing the green and blue channels went a long way toward getting rid of the splotches.

Red   Green   Blue

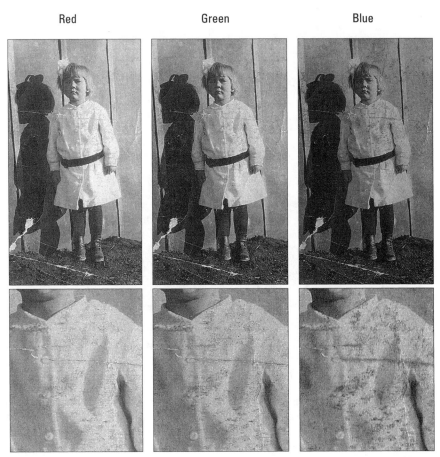

Figure 7-10: A quick peek through the color channels shows the red channel to be my best choice. The blotches are most evident in the girl's blouse, enlarged along the bottom.

✦ Work at 100 percent view size (Ctrl+Alt+0) or larger. It's impossible to judge scratches and other defects accurately at smaller zoom ratios.

✦ Keep the original photo next to you as you work. What looks like a scratch on screen may actually be a photographic element, and what looks like an element may be a scratch. Only by referring to the original image can you be sure.

Don't crop until you're finished retouching the image. You'd be surprised how useful that extra garbage around the perimeter is when it comes to covering up really big tears.

✦ Use hard brush shapes against sharp edges. But when working in general areas such as the shadow, the ground, and the wall, mix it up between hard and soft brushes. Staying random is the best way to avoid harsh transitions, repeating patterns, and other digital giveaways.

✦ Paint in short strokes. This helps keep things random, but it also means you don't have to redraw a big long brushstroke if you make a mistake.

When you *do* make a mistake, don't press Ctrl+Z. Instead, use the history brush to paint back the image as it appeared before the last rubber stamp operation. (I explain more about the history brush later in this chapter.)

✦ Another way to stay random is to change the source of your clone frequently. That means Alt-clicking after every second or third brushstroke. And keep the Aligned check box turned off. An aligned clone is not a random one.

✦ Feel free to experiment with the brush modes and the Opacity setting. For example, as shown magnified in Figure 7-11, the girl has a scratch on the left eye (her right). I corrected this by cloning the right eye, but the cloned eye was so much lighter that it gave the girl a possessed look. To fix this, I set the brush mode to Multiply and changed the Opacity to 30 percent. Then I cloned a bit of the shadowed flesh over the eye to get the finished effect.

You also can try applying Edit ⇨ Fade to change the opacity and brush mode of pixels you just cloned. Adobe expanded the Fade filter in Photoshop 5.5 so that you can use the filter to fade tool effects as well as filters.

✦ Don't attempt to smooth out the general appearance of grain in the image. Grain is integral to an old photo and hiding it usually makes the image look faked. If your image gets too smooth, or if your cloning results in irregular patterns, select the problem area and apply Filter ⇨ Noise ⇨ Add Noise. Enter very small Amount values (4 to 8); if necessary, press Ctrl+F to reapply the filter one or more times. Remember, grain is good.

Figure 7-11: The left eye in the original image is scratched (top). I clone the right eye (middle), but it's too bright. So I set the brush mode to Multiply, lower the Opacity to 30 percent, and clone a little flesh over the eye (bottom).

With Photoshop's history brush at your side, there's really no way to permanently harm an image. You can even let four or five little mistakes go and then correct them *en masse* with the history brush. Just click to the left of the state in the History palette that directly precedes your first screw-up and then drag with the history brush. It's easy, satisfying, and incredibly freeing. To paint back to the original scanned image, click in front of the very top item in the History palette. For more information, check out "Stepping Back through Time" later in this chapter.

Eliminating distracting background elements

The stamp tool's cloning capabilities also come in handy for eliminating background action that competes with the central elements in an image. For example, Figure 7-12 shows a nifty news photo shot by Michael Probst for the Reuters image library. Although the image is well-photographed and historic and all that good stuff, that rear workman doesn't contribute anything to the scene; in fact, he draws your attention away from the foreground drama. I mean, hail to the worker and everything, but the image would be better off without him. The following steps explain how I eradicated the offending workman from the scene.

Figure 7-12: You have to love that old Soviet state-endorsed art. So bold, so angular, so politically intolerant. But you also have to lose that rear workman.

Note

Remember as you read the following steps that deleting an image element with the rubber stamp tool is something of an inexact science; it requires considerable patience and a dash of trial and error. So regard the following steps as an example of how to approach the process of editing your image rather than as a specific procedure that works for all images. You may need to adapt the process slightly depending on your image.

On the other hand, any approach that eliminates an element as big as the workman can also correct the most egregious of photographic flaws, including mold, holes, and fire damage. You can even restore photos that have been ripped into pieces, a particular problem for pictures of ex-boyfriends and the like. These steps qualify as major reconstructive surgery.

STEPS: Eliminating Distracting Elements from an Image

1. **My first step was to clone the area around the neck of the statue with a soft brush shape.** Abandoning the controlled clicks I recommended in the last section, I allowed myself to drag with the tool because I needed to cover relatively large portions of the image. The apartment building (or whatever that structure is) behind the floating head is magnificently out of focus, just the thing for hiding any incongruous transitions I might create with the rubber stamp. So I warmed up to the image by retouching this area first. Figure 7-13 shows my progress.

   I covered the workman's body by cloning pixels from both his left and right sides. I also added a vertical bar where the workman's right arm used to be to maintain the rhythm of the building. Remember, variety is the key to using the rubber stamp tool: If you consistently clone from one portion of the image, you create an obvious repetition the viewer can't help but notice.

Figure 7-13: Cloning over the background worker's upper torso was fairly easy because the background building is so regular and out of focus, it provides a wealth of material from which to clone.

2. **The next step was to eliminate the workman's head.** This was a little tricky because it involved rubbing up against the focused perimeter of Lenin's neck. I had to clone some of the more intricate areas using a hard-edged brush. I also ended up duplicating some of the neck edges to maintain continuity. In addition, I touched up the left side of the neck (your left, not Lenin's) and removed a few of the white spots from his face. You see my progress in Figure 7-14.

Figure 7-14: I eliminated the workman's head and touched up details around the perimeter of his neck.

3. **Now for the hard part: eliminating the worker's legs and lower torso.** See that fragment of metal that the foreground worker is holding? What a pain. Its edges were so irregular, there was no way I could restore it with the rubber stamp tool on the off chance that I messed up while trying to eradicate the background worker's limbs. So I lassoed around the fragment to select it and chose Select ⇨ Inverse (Ctrl+Shift+I) to protect it. I also chose Select ⇨ Feather (Ctrl+Alt+D) and gave it a Radius value of 1 to soften its edges slightly. This prevented me from messing up the metal no matter what edits I made to the background worker's remaining body parts.

4. **From here on, it was just more cloning.** Unfortunately, I barely had anything from which to clone. See the little bit of black edging between the two "legs" of the metal fragment? That's it. This was all I had to draw the strip of edging to the right of the fragment that eventually appears in Figure 7-15. To pull off this feat, I made sure that the Aligned check box was turned off in Options bar. Then I Alt-clicked on the tiny bit of edging and click, click, clicked my way down the street.

Figure 7-15: After about 45 minutes of monkeying around with the rubber stamp tool — a practice declared illegal during Stalin's reign — the rear workman is gone, leaving us with an unfettered view of the dubious V. I. Lenin himself.

5. **Unfortunately, the strip I laid down in Step 4 appeared noticeably blobular — it looked for all the world like I clicked a bunch of times.** Darn. To fix this problem, I clicked and Shift-clicked with the smudge tool set to about 30 per-cent pressure. This smeared the blobs into a continuous strip but, again, the effect was noticeable. It looked as if I had smeared the strip. So I went back and cloned some more, this time with the Opacity value set to 50 percent.

6. **To polish the image off, I chose Select ⇨ Deselect (Ctrl+D) and ran the sharpen tool along the edges of the metal fragment.** This helped to hide my retouching around it and further distinguished the fragment from the unfocused background. I also cropped away 20 or so pixels from the right side of the image to correct the balance of the image.

What I hope I demonstrated in these steps is this: Cloning with the rubber stamp tool requires you to alternate between patching and whittling away. There are no rights and wrongs, no hard and fast rules. Anything you can find to clone is fair game. As long as you avoid mucking up the foreground image, you can't go wrong (so I guess there is *one* hard and fast rule). If you're careful and diligent, no one but you will notice your alterations.

Any time you edit the contents of a photograph, you tread on sensitive ground. Although some have convincingly argued that electronically retouching an image is, theoretically, no different than cropping a photograph — a technique available and in use since the first daguerreotype — photographers have certain rights under copyright law that cannot be ignored. A photographer may have a reason for including an element you want to eliminate. So, before you edit any photograph, be sure to get permission either from the original photographer or from the copyright holder (as I did for this photo).

Applying Repeating Patterns

The rubber stamp's cousin, the pattern stamp tool, paints with a rectangular pattern tile. You can use the pattern stamp to create frames, paint wallpaper-type patterns, or retouch textured patches of grass, dirt, or sky. To switch from the rubber stamp to the pattern stamp tool, Alt-click the stamp tool icon in the toolbox or press S (or Shift+S, depending on your preferences setting for tool switches).

The pattern stamp, unlike the rubber stamp, doesn't require you to Alt-click to set a source. Instead, you select a pattern from the Pattern drop-down palette, shown in Figure 7-16. The palette displays icons representing the available patterns in the current pattern preset, just as when you apply patterns using the paint bucket. (To find out how to change, load, and save presets, refer to Chapter 5.) If you pause your cursor over an icon and have tool tips turned on, Photoshop displays the pattern name.

Here's another pattern upgrade in Version 6: You now can define and save as many custom patterns as you like. To create a pattern, select a portion of the image with the rectangular marquee tool and choose Edit ⇨ Define Pattern. Or, if you want to use the entire image as a pattern, you can skip the selecting step (also a new option). Note that if you do draw a selection, you must use the rectangular marquee tool — no other selection tool will do. Also, the selection cannot be feathered, smoothed, expanded, or in any other way altered. After you choose the command, you can change the name that Photoshop assigns to the pattern — Pattern 1, Pattern 2, and so on — to a name that will better help you identify the pattern later.

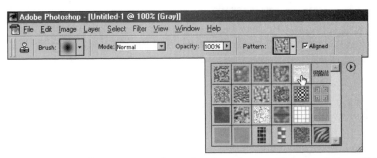

Figure 7-16: Select a pattern from the drop-down palette and then click or drag with the pattern stamp tool.

Figure 7-17 shows an example of how you can apply repeating patterns. I selected the single apartment window (labeled in the figure) and chose Edit ➪ Define Pattern. I then painted with the pattern stamp tool at 80 percent opacity over the horse and rider statue.

Aligning patterns (or not)

As is the case with the rubber stamp, the Options bar for the pattern stamp tool provides an Aligned check box. If you select the check box, Photoshop aligns all patterns you apply with the stamp tool, regardless of how many times you start and stop dragging. The two left examples in Figure 7-18 show the effects of selecting this option. The elements in the pattern remain exactly aligned throughout all the brushstrokes. I painted the top-left image with the Opacity value set to 50 percent, which is why the strokes darken when they meet.

To allow patterns in different brushstrokes to start and end at different locations, turn the Aligned option off. The point at which you begin dragging determines the position of the pattern within each stroke. I dragged from right to left to paint the horizontal strokes and from top to bottom to paint the vertical strokes. The two right examples in Figure 7-18 show how nonaligned patterns overlap.

Note

As discussed in Chapter 6, you can also apply a pattern to a selected portion of an image by choosing Edit ➪ Fill and selecting the Pattern option from the Use pop-up menu. If you have an old grayscale image saved in the Photoshop 2 format sitting around, you can alternatively choose Filter ➪ Render ➪ Texture Fill to open the image and repeat it as many times as it takes to fill the selection. (Texture Fill is intended primarily for preparing textures and bump maps for a three-dimensional drawing program, so most folks never touch this filter.)

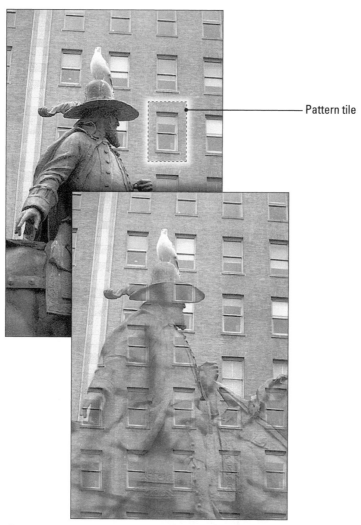

Pattern tile

Figure 7-17: After marqueeing a single window (top) and choosing Edit ⇨ Define Pattern, I painted a translucent coat of the pattern over the statue with the pattern stamp tool (bottom).

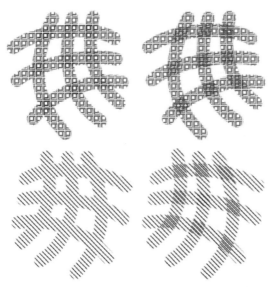

Figure 7-18: Select the Aligned check box to align the patterns in all brushstrokes so that they match up perfectly (left). If you turn the option off, Photoshop starts each pattern with the beginning of the brushstroke (right).

Also investigate the new Fill Layers and Layer Style options for filling layers with patterns. You can explore both in Chapter 14.

Creating patterns and textures

Photoshop 6 provides a few sample patterns inside the Patterns folder, which lives inside the Presets folder. But if none of those patterns float your boat, you can create your own patterns. Ideally, your pattern should repeat continuously, without vertical and horizontal seams. Here are some ways to create repeating, continuous patterns:

✦ **Load a displacement map:** Photoshop offers a Displacement Maps folder inside the Plug-Ins folder. This folder contains several images, each of which represents a different repeating pattern, as illustrated in Figure 7-19. To use one of these patterns, open the image, choose Select ➪ All (Ctrl+A), and choose Edit ➪ Define Pattern. (For more information on displacement maps, see Chapter A on the CD-ROM accompanying this book.)

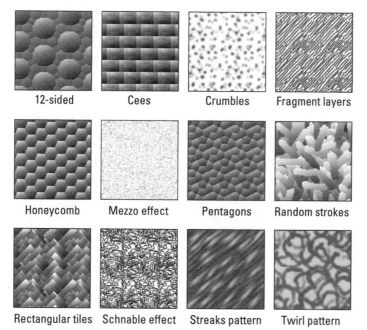

Figure 7-19: These 12 patterns are in the Displacement Maps folder included with Photoshop.

✦ **Illustrator patterns:** If you open the Presets folder, then the Patterns folder, and then the PostScript Patterns folder, you can find Illustrator EPS files that contain repeating object patterns. The patterns, some of which appear in Figure 7-20, are all seamless repeaters. You can open them and rasterize them to any size you like. Then press Ctrl+A, choose Edit ➪ Define Pattern, and you have your pattern.

✦ **Using filters:** As luck would have it, you can create your own custom textures without painting a single line. In fact, you can create a nearly infinite variety of textures by applying several filters to a blank document. To create the texture shown in the top row of Figure 7-21, for example, I created a new 200 × 200-pixel image. I then chose Filter ➪ Noise ➪ Add Noise, entered a value of 64, and selected the Gaussian radio button. I pressed Ctrl+F twice to apply the noise filter two more times. Finally, I chose Filter ➪ Stylize ➪ Emboss and entered 45 in the Angle option box, 2 in the Height option box, and 100 in the Amount option box. The result is a bumpy surface that looks like stucco.

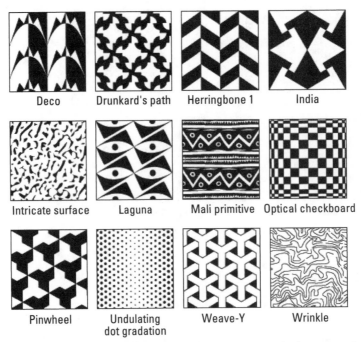

Deco   Drunkard's path   Herringbone 1   India

Intricate surface   Laguna   Mali primitive   Optical checkboard

Pinwheel   Undulating dot gradation   Weave-Y   Wrinkle

Figure 7-20: A random sampling of the illustrations in the PostScript Patterns folder, found inside the Presets/Patterns folder.

To get the second row effects in Figure 7-21, I started with the noise pattern and applied Filter ➪ Pixelate ➪ Crystallize with a Cell Size of 10 pixels. Then I again applied the Emboss filter with the same settings as before. To create the third row of textures, I started with a blank image and chose Filter ➪ Render ➪ Clouds. Then I applied the Emboss filter with an Amount value of 500. To punch up the contrast, I choose Image ➪ Adjust ➪ Auto Levels (Ctrl+Shift+L).

Cross-Reference

I could go on like this for days. To learn more about filters so you can make up your own textures, read Chapters 10 and 11. Chapter 10 covers Add Noise; Chapter 11 explains Emboss, Crystallize, and Clouds.

✦ **Marquee and clone:** You can use the rectangular marquee and pattern stamp tools to transform an image into a custom pattern. Because this technique is more complicated as well as more rewarding than the others, I explain it in the following section.

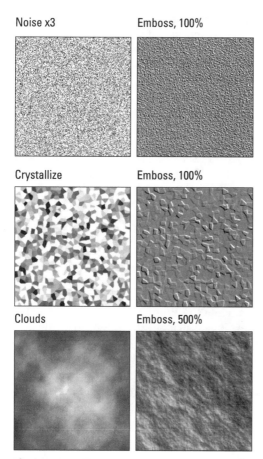

Noise x3   Emboss, 100%

Crystallize   Emboss, 100%

Clouds   Emboss, 500%

Figure 7-21: To create a stucco texture, apply Filter ➪ Noise ➪ Add Noise three times in a row (upper left, upper right, lower left). Then choose Filter ➪ Stylize ➪ Emboss and enter a Height value of 1 (lower right).

Building your own seamless pattern

The following steps describe how to change a scanned image into a seamless, repeating pattern. To illustrate how this process works, Figures 7-22 through 7-25 show various stages in a project I completed. You need only two tools to carry out these steps: the rectangular marquee tool and the rubber stamp tool.

Cross-Reference Those of you reading sequentially may notice that these steps involve a few selection and layering techniques I haven't yet discussed. If you become confused, you can find out more about selecting, moving, and cloning images in Chapter 8.

STEPS: Building a Repeating Pattern from an Image

1. **Open the image that you want to convert into a pattern.** I started with an image from the PhotoDisc image library.

2. **Select the rectangular marquee tool and then press Enter to display the Options bar, if it's not already visible.** Select Fixed Size from the Style pop-up menu and enter specific values in the Width and Height option boxes. This way, you can easily reselect a portion of the pattern in the steps that follow, as well as use the fixed-size marquee to define the pattern when you finish. To create the patterns shown in the figures, I set the marquee to 128 × 128 pixels.

3. **Select the portion of the image you want to feature in the pattern.** Because you've specified an exact marquee size, Photoshop selects a fixed area whenever you click. You can drag to move the marquee around in the window.

4. **Press Ctrl+C.** This copies the selection to the Clipboard.

5. **Choose File ➪ New (Ctrl+N) and triple the Width and Height values.** In my case, Photoshop suggested a new image size of 128 × 128 pixels, which matches the size of the selection I copied to the Clipboard. By tripling these values, I arrived at a new image size of 384 × 384 pixels.

6. **Press Ctrl+V.** Photoshop pastes the copied selection smack dab in the center of the window, which is exactly where you want it. This image will serve as the central tile of your repeating pattern.

7. **Ctrl-click the item labeled Layer 1 in the Layers palette.** Photoshop pasted the image on a new layer. But to duplicate the image and convert it into a pattern, you need to flatten it, which you do in the next step. Before you flatten, you want to **Ctrl**-click the layer name to select the pasted pixels.

8. **Press Ctrl+E.** This merges the layer with the background, thereby flattening it. Or you can choose Layer ➪ Flatten Image. Either way, the selection outline remains intact.

9. **Choose Edit ➪ Define Pattern.** This establishes the selected image as a pattern tile. Give the pattern a name when Photoshop prompts you.

10. **Press Ctrl+D to deselect the image.** You neither need nor want the selection outline any more. You'll need to be able to fill and clone freely without a selection outline getting in the way.

11. **Press Shift+Backspace or choose Edit ➪ Fill.** Then select Pattern from the Use pop-up menu, select the pattern from the Custom Pattern palette, and press Enter. This fills the window with a 3 × 3-tile grid, as shown in Figure 7-22.

Figure 7-22: To build the repeating pattern shown in Figure 7-25, I started by creating a grid of nine image tiles. As you can see, the seams between the tiles in this grid are harsh and unacceptable.

12. **Drag the title bar of the new image window to position it so you can see the portion of the image you copied in the original image window.** If necessary, drag the title bar of the original image window to reposition it, as well. After you have your windows arranged, click the title bar of the new image to make it the active window.

13. **Select the rubber stamp.** Press S. (Press S twice if the pattern stamp tool is active; press Shift+S if you turned on the Use Shift Key for Tool Switch option in the Preferences dialog box.)

14. **Turn off the Aligned check box in the Options bar.** Ironic as it may sound, it's easier to get the alignment between clone-from and clone-to points established with Aligned turned off.

15. **Specify the image you want to clone by Alt-clicking in the original image window.** No need to switch out of the new window. Alt-click an easily identifiable pixel that belongs to the portion of the image you copied. The exact pixel you click is very important. If you press Caps Lock, you get the crosshair cursor, which makes it easier to narrow in on a pixel. In my case, I clicked the corner of the Buddha's mouth. (At least, I assume that's Buddha. Then again, I'm a Western-bred ignoramus, so what do I know?)

16. **Now click with the stamp tool on the matching pixel in the central tile of the new window.** If you clicked the correct pixel, the tile should not change one iota. If it shifts at all, press Ctrl+Z and try again. Because Aligned is turned off, you can keep undoing and clicking over and over again without resetting the clone-from point in the original image.

17. **Turn on the Aligned check box.** Once you click in the image without seeing any shift, select the Aligned option to lock in the alignment between the clone-from and clone-to points.

18. **Use the stamp tool to fill in portions of the central tile.** For example, in Figure 7-23, I extended the Buddha's cheek and neck down into the lower row of tiles. I also extended the central forehead to meet the Buddha on the left.

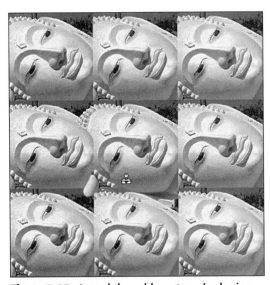

Figure 7-23: I used the rubber stamp's cloning capability to extend the features in the central face toward the left and downward.

19. **Select a portion of the modified image.** After you establish one continuous transition between two tiles in any direction — up, down, left, or right — click with the rectangular marquee tool to select an area that includes the transition. In my case, I managed to create a smooth transition between the central and bottom tiles. Therefore, I selected a region that includes half the central tile and half the tile below it.

20. **Repeat Steps 9 through 11.** That is, choose Edit ➪ Define Pattern, press Ctrl+D, choose Edit ➪ Fill, select the pattern you just defined, and press Enter. This fills the image with your new transition. Don't worry if the tiles shift around a bit — that's to be expected.

If you plan on creating a lot of patterns, you may want to record Steps 9 through 11 as a script in the Actions palette. Then you can replay the script after each time you clone away a seam.

21. **If you started by creating a horizontal transition, use the rubber stamp tool to create a vertical transition.** Likewise, if you started vertically, now go horizontally. You may need to turn off the Aligned check box again to establish the proper alignment between clone-from and clone-to points. In my case, I shifted the clone-to point several times — alternatively building on the central Buddha, the right-hand one, and the middle one in the bottom row. Each time you get the clone-to point properly positioned, turn the Aligned check box back on to lock in the alignment. Then clone away.

As long as you get the clone-from and clone-to points properly aligned, you can't make a mistake. If you change your mind, realign the clone points and try again. In my case, I cloned the long droopy earlobe down into the face of the Buddha below. (I guess our young Buddha didn't stop to think that once the droopy-ear fad passed, he would be stuck with it for the rest of his life.) I also cloned the god's chin onto the forehead of the one to the right, ultimately achieving the effect shown in Figure 7-24.

22. **After you build up one set of both horizontal and vertical transitions, click with the rectangular marquee tool to select the transitions.** Figure 10-24 shows where I positioned my 128 × 128-pixel selection boundary. This includes parts of each of four neighboring heads, including the all-important droopy ear. Don't worry if the image doesn't appear centered inside the selection outline. What counts is that the image flows seamlessly inside the selection outline.

23. **Repeat Steps 9 through 11 again.** Or play that script I suggested in Step 20 if you bothered to record it. If the tiles blend together seamlessly, as in Figure 7-25, you're finished. If not, clone some more with the rubber stamp tool and try again.

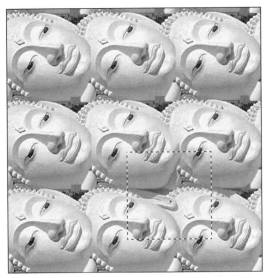

Figure 7-24: After completing a smooth transition between the central tile and the tiles below and to the right of it, I selected a portion of the image and chose Edit ➡ Define Pattern.

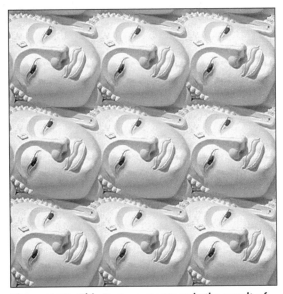

Figure 7-25: This Eastern montage is the result of applying the Buddha pattern. Buddha sure looks serene and comfortable, especially considering he's resting on his own head.

Stepping Back through Time

Since roughly the dawn of recorded time, folks begged, pleaded, and screamed at the top of their lungs for multiple undos in Photoshop. But it wasn't until Photoshop 5 that Adobe delivered what the masses craved. The payoff for the long wait was huge: Version 5 offered up the History palette, which provides the best implementation of multiple undos I've ever seen.

Moving beyond simple backstepping, the History palette takes the whole reversion metaphor into *Slaughterhouse Five* territory. If you've never read the novel (or you've somehow forgotten), Kurt Vonnegut, Jr. suggested that humans live from one moment to the next like a person strapped to a boxcar, unable to change the speed or direction of the train as it hurtles through time. In most programs that offer multiple undos, you can make the train stop and back up, but you're still strapped to it. The History palette is the first tool that lets you get off the train and transport to any point on the track— instantaneously. In short, we now have a digital version of time travel.

Here are just a few of the marvelous innovations of the History palette:

✦ **Undo-independent stepping:** Step backward by pressing Ctrl+Alt+Z; step forward by pressing Ctrl+Shift+Z. Every program with multiple undos does this, but Photoshop's default keyboard equivalents are different. Why? Because you can backstep independently of the Undo command, so that even backstepping is undoable.

Just to sweeten the pot, Photoshop 6 enables you to change the keys assigned to the step forward, step backward, and Undo/Redo actions. Open the Preferences dialog box (Ctrl+K) and look for the Redo Key pop-up menu. Select Ctrl+Y from the menu, and step forward becomes Ctrl+Y, step backward becomes Ctrl+Z, and the Undo/Redo key toggle becomes Ctrl+Alt+Z. To instead use Ctrl+Shift+Z as forward and Ctrl+Z as backward, select Ctrl+Shift+Z from the menu.

Note

The shortcuts that I mention in this book assume that you leave the Redo Key option set to the default, which makes Ctrl+Z the shortcut to toggle between the Undo and Redo commands. If you think you might have changed this setting, choose Edit ➪ Preferences ➪ General and inspect the condition of the Redo Key pop-up menu.

✦ **Before and after:** Revert to a point in history to see a "before" view of your image, and then fly forward to see the "after" view. From then on, Ctrl+Z becomes a super-undo, toggling between the before and after views. The opportunities for comparing states and changing your mind are truly colossal.

✦ **Dynamic time travel:** If before and after aren't enough, how about animated history? You can drag a control to slide dynamically forward and backward through operations. It's as if you recorded the operations to videotape, and now you're rewinding and fast-forwarding through them.

✦ **Sweeping away the mistakes:** Select a point in the history of your image and paint back to it using the history brush. You can let the mistakes pile up and then brush them away. This brush isn't a paintbrush; it's a hand broom. Want even more variety? Use the art history brush to paint back to the image using various artistic styles.

✦ **Take a picture, it'll last longer:** You can save any point in the History palette as a snapshot. That way, even several hundred operations after that point in history are long gone, you can revisit the snapshot.

✦ **This is your life, Image A:** Each and every image has its own history. So after performing a few hundred operations on Image A, you can still go back to Image B and backstep through operations you performed hours ago. The caveat is that the history remains available only as long as an image is open. Close the image, and its history goes away.

✦ **Undo the Revert command:** Before Photoshop 5.5, you couldn't undo the Revert command. Now, the History palette tracks Revert. So if you don't like the image that was last saved to disk, you can undo the reversion and get back to where you were. Also notice that when you choose File ⇨ Revert, Photoshop no longer asks you to confirm the reversion. There's no reason for that warning dialog box any more because Revert is fully undoable.

In Photoshop 5.5, Photoshop asked whether you wanted to save the file if you chose Revert and then closed the file. Previously, Photoshop knew the reverted image and the saved image were identical — in Version 5.5, it got a bit mixed up. This weirdness has been corrected in Version 6.

The only thing you can't do through the History palette is travel forward into the future — say, to about three days from now when you've finished your grueling project, submitted it to your client, and received your big fat paycheck. Believe it or not, that's actually good news. The day Adobe can figure out how to do your work for you, your clients will hire Photoshop and stop hiring you.

So I ask you — Photoshop, *Slaughterhouse Five*, just a coincidence? Well, yes, I suppose it is. But the fact remains, you have the option of getting off the boxcar. How you make use of your freedom is up to you.

Using the traditional undo functions

Before I dive into the History palette, I should take a moment to summarize Photoshop's more traditional reversion functions. (If you already know about this stuff, skip to the next section.)

Again, remember that all the shortcuts I mention here assume that you choose Ctrl+Z (Toggles Undo/Redo) from the Redo Key pop-up menu in the Preferences dialog box (the default setting):

✦ **Undo:** To restore an image to the way it looked before the last operation, choose Edit ⇨ Undo (Ctrl+Z). You can undo the effect of a paint or edit tool, a change made to a selection outline, or a special-effect or color-correction command. You can't undo disk operations, such as opening or saving. Photoshop does enable you to undo an edit after printing an image, though. You can test an effect, print the image, and then undo the effect if you think it looks awful.

✦ **Revert:** Choose File ⇨ Revert (or press the F12 key) to reload an image from disk. This is generally the last-resort function, the command you choose after everything else has failed.

To restore the image to the way it looked when you originally opened it — which may precede the last-saved state — scroll to the top of the History palette and click the topmost item. (This assumes that you haven't turned off the Automatically Create First Snapshot check box in the History Options dialog box.)

✦ **Selective reversion:** To revert a selected area to the way it appeared when it was first opened — or some other source state identified in the History palette — choose Edit ⇨ Fill (Shift+Backspace). Then select History from the Use pop-up menu and press Enter.

Better yet, just press Ctrl+Alt+Backspace. This one keystroke fills the selection with the source state in a jiffy. (You set the source state by clicking in the left column of the History palette, as I explain in the very next section.)

✦ **The erasers:** Drag in the background layer with the eraser tool to paint in the background color. You're essentially erasing the image back to bare canvas. Or apply the eraser to a layer to delete pixels and expose underlying layers. For additional erasing flexibility, the magic eraser and background eraser (introduced in Photoshop 5.5) rub away similarly colored pixels and background pixels, respectively.

You can also Alt-drag with the eraser to revert to the targeted state in the History palette. Or select Erase to History in the Options bar and just drag. But you're better off using the history brush for this purpose. The history brush offers more capabilities — notably, brush modes.

Where warranted, I explain these functions in greater detail in the following sections. But first, the next few paragraphs look at the central headquarters for reversion in Photoshop, the History palette.

The History palette

Choose Window ⇨ Show History to view the History palette, annotated with the palette menu in full view in Figure 7-26. The History palette records each significant operation — everything other than settings and preferences (for example, selecting a new foreground color) — and adds it to a list. The oldest operations appear at the top of the list with the most recent operations at the bottom.

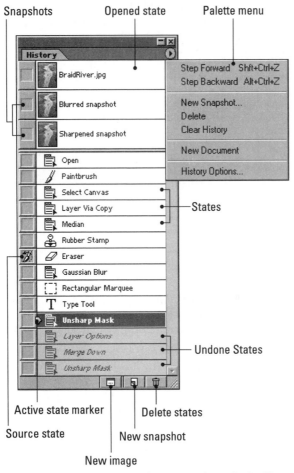

Figure 7-26: The History palette records each significant event as an independent state. To return to a state, just click on it.

Each item in the list is called a *state*. That's not my word, it's Adobe's, and several have voiced the opinion that the term is too stiff and formal. But I think it's dead on. Each item in the palette represents a stepping stone in the progression of the image, a condition at a moment in time — in other words, a state.

Photoshop automatically names each item according to the tool, command, or operation used to arrive at the state. The icon next to the name helps to identify the state further. But the best way to find out what a state is like is to click it. Photoshop instantaneously undoes all operations performed after that state and returns you to the state so that you can inspect it in detail. To redo all the operations you just did in one fell swoop, press Ctrl+Z or choose Edit ➪ Undo State Change.

That one action—clicking on a state—is the gist of what you need to know to travel forward and backward through time in Photoshop. If that's all you ever learn, you'll find yourself working with greater speed, freedom, and security than is possible in virtually any other graphics application. But this represents only the first in a long list of the History palette's capabilities. Here's the rest of what you might want to know:

✦ **Changing the number of undos:** By default, Photoshop records the last 20 operations in the History palette. When you perform the 21st operation, the first state is shoved off the list.

In Photoshop 6, you set the number of operations that the History palette tracks in the Preferences dialog box. Choose Edit ⇨ Preferences ⇨ General or press Ctrl+K to open the dialog box and enter the value you want to use in the History States box. If your computer is equipped with 32MB or less of RAM, you might want to lower the value to 5 or 10 to maintain greater efficiency. On the other hand, if you become a time-traveling freak (like me) and have plenty of RAM, turn it up, baby, all the way up!

✦ **Undone states:** When you revert to a state by clicking on it, every subsequent state turns gray to show that it's been undone. You can redo a grayed state simply by clicking on it. But if you perform a new operation, all grayed states disappear. You have one opportunity to bring them back by pressing Ctrl+Z; if you perform another new operation, the once-grayed states are gone for good.

✦ **Working with non-sequential states:** If you don't like the idea of losing your undone states—every state is sacred, after all—choose the History Options command and select the Allow Non-Linear History check box (see Figure 7-27). Undone states no longer drop off the list when you perform a new operation. They remain available on the off chance that you might want to revisit them. It's like having multiple possible time trails.

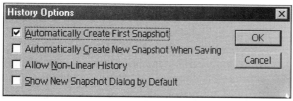

Figure 7-27: Choose the History Options command to permit Photoshop to record states out of order.

The Allow Non-Linear History check box does not permit you to undo a single state without affecting the subsequent states. For example, let's say you paint with the airbrush, smear with the smudge tool, and then clone with the rubber stamp. You can revert back to the airbrush state and then apply other operations without losing the option of restoring the smudge and clone. But you can't undo the smudge and leave the clone intact. Operations can only occur in the sequence they were applied.

If you revert back to a state and then apply an edit, the reverted state and all actions that fall between that state and the new edit are set off by horizontal lines running across the palette. The lines show you which operations you'll lose if you undo the first state in the group.

✦ **Stepping through states:** As I mentioned earlier, you can press -Ctrl+Alt+Z to undo the active step or Ctrl+Shift+Z to redo the next step in the list. Backstepping goes up the list of states in the History palette; forward stepping goes down. Keep in mind that if the Allow Non-Linear History check box is active, backstepping may take you to a state that was previously inactive.

✦ **Flying through states:** Drag the right-pointing active state marker (labeled in Figure 7-26) up and down the list to rewind and fast-forward, respectively, through time. If the screen image doesn't appear to change as you fly by certain states, it most likely means those states involve small brushstrokes or changes to selection outlines. Otherwise, the changes are quite apparent.

✦ **Taking a snapshot:** Every once in a while, a state comes along that's so great, you don't want it to fall by the wayside 20 operations from now. To set a state aside, choose New Snapshot or click the little page icon at the bottom of the History palette.

By default, Photoshop no longer displays the New Snapshot dialog box asking you to name the snapshot. If you want to name a snapshot, Alt-click the New Snapshot icon. Or choose History Options from the palette menu and select the Show New Snapshot Dialog by Default option. Photoshop then presents the dialog box. In the dialog box, you also can specify whether you want to save all layers (as by default), flatten the image, or retain just the active layer. The new *snapshot*—as it's called—then appears in the top portion of the palette.

If you turn on the Show New Snapshot Dialog by Default check box, you can circumvent the dialog box by Alt-clicking the New Snapshot icon. (The state has to be active to convert it to a snapshot, so you can't drag a state and drop it onto the page icon, as you can drag-and-drop elements in other palettes.)

Photoshop lets you store as many snapshots as your computer's RAM permits. Also worth noting, the program automatically creates a snapshot of the image as it appears when it's first opened. If you don't like this opening snapshot, you can turn it off inside the History Options dialog box.

✦ **Creating a snapshot upon saving the image:** Select the Automatically Create New Snapshot When Saving box in the History Options dialog box to create a new snapshot every time you save your image.

✦ **Saving the state permanently:** The problem with snapshots is that they last only as long as the current session. If you quit Photoshop or the program crashes, you lose the entire history list, snapshots included. To save a state so you can refer to it several days from now, choose the New Document command or click the leftmost icon at the bottom of the History palette. You can also drag and drop a state onto the icon. Either way, Photoshop duplicates the state to a new image window. Then you can save the state to the format of your choice.

✦ **Setting the source:** Click to the left of a state to identify it as the *source state*. The history brush icon appears where you click. The source state affects the performance of the history brush, art history brush, Fill command, and eraser, if you select Erase to History. The keystroke Ctrl+Alt+Backspace fills the selection with the source state.

✦ **Trashing states:** To delete any state and those that follow, drag the state to the trash icon at the bottom of the palette. Your image updates accordingly. If the Allow Non-Linear History check box is on, clicking the trash can deletes just the active state.

If your machine is equipped with little RAM or you're working on a particularly large image, Photoshop may slow down as the states accumulate. If it gets too slow, you may want to purge the History palette. You can clear every state from the active state forward without affecting the image by Alt-clicking Clear History in the palette menu. You can also choose Edit ➪ Purge ➪ Histories to purge the list of states for all open documents.

You can't undo either purge command. So if you want to clear the states from the palette but have the option of choosing Undo to bring them back, choose Clear History *without* Alt-clicking.

Painting away the past

The History palette represents the regimental way to revert images inside Photoshop. You can retreat, march forward, proceed in linear or non-linear formation, capture states, and retire them. Every state plays backward in the same way it played forward. It's precise, predictable, and positively by the book.

But what if you want to get free-form? What if you want to brush away the present and paint in the past? In that case, a palette isn't going to do you any good. What you need is a pliable, emancipated, free-wheeling tool.

As luck would have it, Photoshop offers five candidates — the eraser, magic eraser, background eraser, history brush, and art history brush. The eraser washes away pixels to reveal underlying pixels or exposed canvas. The magic eraser and background eraser, both added in Version 5.5, erase a range of similarly colored pixels and background pixels, respectively. The history brush takes you back to a kinder, simpler state; the art history brush does the same but enables you to paint using special artistic effects. Although the functions of these tools overlap slightly, they each have a very specific purpose, as becomes clear in the following sections.

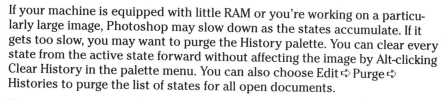

As you work with any of these tools, remember that you can use the Edit ➪ Fade command (formerly on the Filter menu) to blend the altered pixels with the originals, just as you can when applying a filter. You can adjust both the opacity and blend mode of the erased or painted pixels. Chapter 10 explores the Fade command in detail.

The eraser tool

When you work with the eraser, you can select from four eraser styles: Paintbrush, Airbrush, Pencil, and Block. Block is the old 16 × 16-pixel square eraser that's great for hard-edged touch-ups. The other options work exactly like the tools for which they're named.

In earlier versions of Photoshop, pressing E cycled you through the eraser styles. That shortcut now cycles through the eraser, magic eraser, and background eraser, all of which share a flyout menu and keyboard shortcut (E) in Version 6. You now must select the eraser style from the Mode pop-up menu on the Options bar, as shown in Figure 7-28 (press Enter with the eraser selected in the toolbox to display the bar).

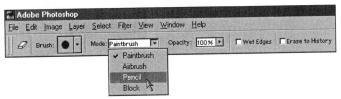

Figure 7-28: When the eraser is selected, the Mode pop-up menu offers a choice of eraser styles rather than the brush modes available for the painting tools.

In addition to four styles, the Options bar provides the Brush palette, the Opacity control, and the Brush Dynamics palette, all of which work as described in Chapter 5. When the Paintbrush option is active, you even have access to the Wet Edges check box, also covered in Chapter 5. The only thing you can't do is choose a brush mode (Normal, Overlay, Darken, Lighten, and so on) — although, as I mentioned a little while ago, you can apply the Fade command after the fact to fade and blend your eraser strokes.

Although the eraser is pretty straightforward, there's no sense in leaving any stone unturned. So here's everything you ever wanted to know about the art of erasing:

✦ **Erasing on a layer:** When you're working on the Background layer, the eraser merely paints in the background color. Big whoop. What distinguishes the eraser tool from the other brushes is layers. If you drag on a layer and deselect the Lock check boxes for transparency and image pixels in the Layers palette, the eraser tool removes paint and exposes portions of the underlying image. The eraser tool suddenly performs like a real eraser.

If you select the transparency Lock check box in the Layers palette, Photoshop won't let the eraser bore holes in the layer or alter areas that are already transparent. Instead, the eraser can paint opaque pixels with the background color. If you select the check box for locking image pixels, you can't erase or paint any part of the layer. For more information on the check boxes in the Layers palette, read Chapter 12.

✦ **Erasing lightly:** Change the Opacity setting on the Options bar to make portions of a layer translucent in inverse proportion to the Opacity value. For example, if you set the Opacity to 90 percent, you remove 90 percent of the opacity from the layer and, therefore, leave 10 percent of the opacity behind. The result is a nearly transparent stroke through the layer.

✦ **Erasing versus using layer masks:** As described in the "Creating layer-specific masks" section of Chapter 12, you can also erase holes in a layer using a layer mask. But unlike the eraser — which eliminates pixels for good — a layer mask doesn't do any permanent damage. On the other hand, using the eraser tool doesn't increase the size of your image as much as a layer mask does. (You can argue that *any* operation — even a deletion — increases the size of the image in RAM because the History palette has to track it. But the eraser is still more memory-efficient than a layer mask.) So it's a trade-off.

✦ **Erasing with the pencil:** When you work with the pencil tool and select the Auto Erase check box on the Options bar, you draw in the background color any time you click or drag a pixel colored in the foreground color. This technique can be useful when you're drawing a line against a plain background. Set the foreground color to the color of the line; set the background color to the color of the background. Then use the pencil tool to draw and erase the line until you get it just right. I use this feature all the time when preparing screen shots. Adobe engineers call the Auto Erase check box their "ode to Fatbits," from the ancient MacPaint zoom function.

Like the eraser, the pencil tool is affected by the Lock check boxes in the Layers palette. Unlike the eraser, the pencil always draws either in the foreground or background color, even when used on a layer.

✦ **Erasing to history:** Press Alt as you drag with the eraser to paint with the source state identified by the history brush icon in the History palette. (By default, Photoshop sets the source state to the image as it appeared when first opened.) It's like scraping away the paint laid down by the operations following the source state, as demonstrated quite graphically in Figure 7-29.

Figure 7-29: After making a dreadful mistake (left), I Alt-dragged with the eraser tool to restore the image to the way it looked in the source state (right).

Alternatively, you can select the Erase to History check box on the Options bar. In this case, dragging with the eraser reverts and Alt-dragging paints in the background color.

Many people use the term "magic eraser" to refer to the eraser set in revert mode. But Photoshop 5.5 introduced an official magic eraser, which erases background pixels instead of erasing to history. So be careful not to get the two confused.

The magic eraser

As I just mentioned, the magic eraser, found on the same flyout as the regular eraser, erases background pixels. Or, at least, that's the idea. When used incorrectly, the magic eraser wipes out any pixels that it touches.

If you're familiar with the magic wand, which I cover in Chapter 8, using the magic eraser is a cinch. The two tools operate virtually identically, except that the wand selects and the magic eraser erases.

When you click a pixel with the magic eraser, Photoshop identifies a range of similarly colored pixels, just as it does with the magic wand. But instead of selecting the pixels, the magic eraser makes them transparent, as demonstrated in Figure 7-30. Bear in mind that in Photoshop, transparency requires a separate layer. So if the image is flat (without layers), Photoshop automatically floats the image to a separate layer with nothing underneath. Hence the checkerboard pattern shown in the second example in the figure—transparency with nothing underneath.

Figure 7-30: To delete a homogeneously colored background, such as the sky in this picture, click inside it with the magic eraser (bottom).

The Lock check boxes in the Layers palette affect the magic eraser. When you have no check boxes selected, the magic eraser works as I just described it. But if you lock transparent pixels, the magic eraser paints opaque pixels in the background color and leaves transparent areas untouched. You can't use the magic eraser at all on a layer for which you've locked image pixels.

You can further alter the performance of the magic eraser through the controls on the Options bar, as described in the following list. Except for the Opacity value, these options work the same way for both the magic eraser and magic wand:

✦ **Opacity:** Lower this value to make the erased pixels translucent instead of transparent. Low values result in more subtle effects than high ones.

✦ **Use All Layers:** When turned on, this check box tells Photoshop to factor in all visible layers when erasing pixels. The tool continues to erase pixels on the active layer only, but it erases them according to colors found across all layers.

✦ **Anti-aliased:** To create a soft fringe around the outline of your transparent area, leave this option turned on. If you'd prefer a hard edge—as when using a very low Tolerance value, for example—turn this check box off.

✦ **Contiguous:** Select this final check box, and the magic eraser deletes *contiguous* colors only—that is, similar colors that touch each other. If you prefer to delete all pixels of a certain color—such as the blue pixels in Figure 7-30 that are divided from the rest of the sky by the lion—turn the Contiguous check box off.

The more magical background eraser

The magic eraser is as simple to use as a hammer, and every bit as indelicate. It pounds away pixels, but it leaves lots of color fringes and shredded edges in its wake. You might as well select an area with the magic wand and press Backspace. The effect is the same.

The more capable, more scrupulous tool is the background eraser. As demonstrated in Figure 7-31, the background eraser deletes background pixels as you drag over them. (Again, if the image is flat, Photoshop floats the image to a new layer to accommodate the transparency.) The tool is intelligent enough to erase background pixels and retain foreground pixels provided that—and here's the clincher—you keep the cross in the center of the eraser cursor squarely centered on a background-color pixel. Move the cross over a foreground pixel, and the background eraser deletes foreground pixels as well. As Figure 7-32 demonstrates, it's the position of the cross that counts.

As is the case when you work with the magic eraser, the Lock check boxes in the Layers palette affect the background eraser. In this case, locking image pixels prevents you from using the background eraser. Be aware that if you drag over a selection that's already partially transparent, locking transparent pixels does not protect the selection from the background eraser.

Figure 7-31: Drag around the edge of an image with the background eraser to erase the background but leave the foreground intact.

You can select a brush for the background eraser in the Brush drop-down palette on the Options bar. In Photoshop 6, you can press the arrow keys to move from one brush icon to another in the palette. Pressing the bracket keys, [and], lowers and raises the brush size — by 10 pixels for brushes smaller than 100 pixels in diameter, by 25 pixels for brushes from 100 pixels to 199 pixels in diameter, and by 50 pixels for brushes 200 pixels and larger. If you simply want to switch from a hard brush to a soft one, press Shift-left bracket; press Shift-right bracket to go from a soft brush to a hard one.

You can also modify the performance of the background eraser using the Options bar controls, pictured in Figure 7-33. These options are a bit intimidating at first, but they're actually pretty easy to use:

✦ **Limits:** Choose Contiguous from this pop-up menu, and the background eraser deletes colors inside the cursor as long as they are contiguous with the color immediately under the cross. To erase all similarly colored pixels, whether contiguous or not, select Discontiguous. One additional option, Find Edges, searches for edges as you brush and emphasizes them. Although interesting, Find Edges has a habit of producing halos and is rarely useful.

✦ **Tolerance:** Raise the Tolerance value to erase more colors at a time; lower the value to erase fewer colors. Low Tolerance values are useful for erasing around tight and delicate details, such as hair.

Figure 7-32: Keep the cross of the background eraser cursor over the background you want to erase (top). If you inadvertently move the cross over the foreground, the foreground gets erased (bottom).

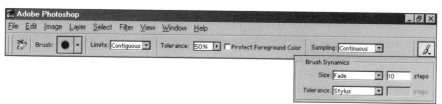

Figure 7-33: The seemingly intimidating background eraser options are actually pretty intuitive.

> ✦ **Protect Foreground Color:** Select this check box to prevent the current foreground color (by default, black) from ever being erased. Stupid, really, but there it is.

> ✦ **Sampling:** This pop-up menu determines how the background eraser determines what it should and should not erase. The default setting, Continuous, tells the erasers to continuously reappraise which colors should be erased as you drag. If the background is pretty homogenous, you might prefer to use the Once option, which samples the background color when you first click and erases only that color throughout the drag. Select Background Swatch to erase only the current background color (by default, white).

Like other brush-oriented tools, the background eraser responds to the settings in the Brush Dynamics palette, also shown in Figure 7-33. Select Fade from the pop-up menus to taper your eraser strokes as you drag. If you set the Tolerance pop-up to Fade, the tool becomes more and more sensitive as you drag. The values that you enter in the adjacent options boxes control how quickly the Size or Tolerance values fade. If you own a pressure-sensitive tablet, such as the Pen Partner or Intuos from Wacom, select Stylus to adjust the size or tolerance according to pen pressure.

Chapter 5 covers the Brush Dynamics palette, as well as all things brush-oriented, including creating and managing brush presets.

The history brush

Painting with the history brush tool gives you results similar to Option-dragging with the eraser (or selecting the eraser's Erase to History option). Just drag with the history brush to paint down to the source state targeted in the History palette. You also can vary the opacity of your strokes with the Opacity setting on the Options bar. But the history brush offers two advantages over the eraser.

First, you can take advantage of brush modes. By choosing a different brush mode from the Mode pop-up menu on the Options bar, you can mix pixels from the changed and saved images to achieve interesting, and sometimes surprising, effects. Second, you don't have to cycle through brush styles as with the eraser tool. Just select the history brush and start painting.

If you fell in love with the history brush in Version 5, you may be wondering what happened to the Impressionist mode, which enabled you to retrieve the source state and smear it around to create a gooey, unfocused effect. As of Version 5.5, that function, as well as some other effects, come to you by way of the art history brush, discussed next. The two brushes share a flyout menu in the toolbox, as well as a keyboard shortcut, the Y key. If you selected the Use Shift Key for Tool Switch option in the Preferences dialog box, you toggle between the two tools by pressing Shift+Y. Otherwise, pressing Y alone toggles the tools.

I advise you to get in the habit of using the history brush instead of using the eraser's Erase to History function. Granted, the eraser offers you four brush styles (paintbrush, pencil, airbrush, and block). But when weighed against brush modes, the brush styles aren't much of an advantage. All things considered, the history brush is superior, and it doesn't require you to press Alt or select a check box to switch to history mode. The history brush is also more intuitive because its icon matches the source state icon in the History palette.

As you play with the history brush, keep in mind that you don't have to limit yourself to painting into the past. Just as the History palette lets you skip back and forth along the train track of time, the history brush lets you paint to any point in time. The following steps provide an example of how you can use the History palette to establish an alternative reality and then follow up with the history brush to merge that reality with the present. It's trippy stuff, I realize, but I'm confident that with a little effort, you can give that post-modern brain of yours a half twist and wrap it around these steps like a big, mushy Möbius strip.

STEPS: Brushing to a Parallel Time Line

1. **Open the image you want to warp into the fourth dimension.** I begin with a map of Japan (Figure 7-34). Japan is a wacky combination of 17th-century cultural uniformity, 1950's innocence, and 21st-century corporate imperialism, so it strikes me as a perfect subject for my compound-time experiment.

2. **Apply a couple of filters.** I choose Filter ⇨ Pixelate ⇨ Mosaic and set the Cell Size value to 20 pixels. Then I apply Filter ⇨ Stylize ⇨ Emboss with a Height of 5 pixels and an Amount of 200 percent. Figure 7-35 shows the results.

3. **Choose the History Options command from the History palette menu.** Then turn on the Allow Non-Linear History check box and press Enter.

4. **Click the Open item in the History palette.** This reverts the image to the state at which it existed when you first opened it. But thanks to non-linear history, Photoshop retains the alternate filtered versions of the image just in case you'd like to revisit this timeline in the future.

5. **Click in front of the first filter effect in the History palette to make it the source state.** In my case, I click in front of the Mosaic item.

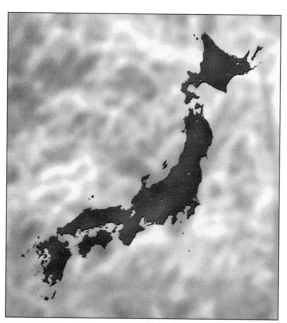

Figure 7-34: This map of Japan comes from the Digital Stock image library.

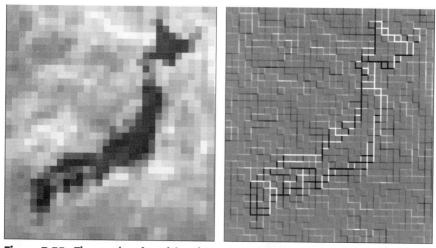

Figure 7-35: The results of applying the Mosaic (left) and Emboss (right) filters. Both effects are overstated, so I'll undo them and then paint them back in with the history brush.

6. **Select the history brush and start painting.** As you do, you'll paint with the filtered version of the image. For my part, I set the blend mode to Darken and painted around the island country to give it a digital edge, as in the first example of Figure 7-36.

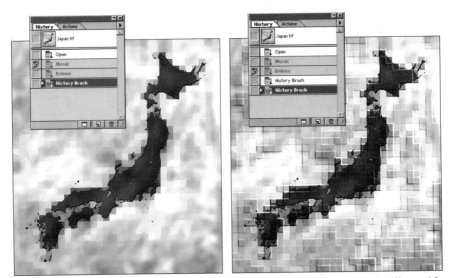

Figure 7-36: I set the brush mode to Darken and painted in the Mosaic effect with the history brush (left). Then I changed the brush mode to Overlay and brushed in the Emboss effect (right).

7. **Switch the source state by clicking in front of the second filter effect.** Naturally, I clicked in front of the Emboss item.

8. **Paint again with the history brush.** This time, I changed the brush mode to Overlay and painted randomly over Japan and the surrounding ocean. The result appears in the second example of Figure 7-36.

After you finish, you can toss the filtered states. This alternate timeline has served its purpose. Or keep it around as a snapshot to come back to later.

The art history brush

With the art history brush, you can create impressionistic effects with the aid of the History palette. Try this. Open any old file. Then press D to get the default foreground and background colors and press Alt+Backspace to fill the entire image with black. Then select the art history brush, which shares a flyout menu and keyboard shortcut (Y) with the history brush. Now paint inside your black image. Each stroke reveals a bit of your image in painterly detail, as illustrated in Color Plate 7-2.

The performance of the art history brush depends both on the tool options that you select from the Options bar and the source state specified in the History palette. For information on setting the source state, read "The History palette" section, earlier in this chapter. From the Options bar, shown in Figure 7-37, you can select a brush, a brush mode, and the opacity just as you do when using the paintbrush, covered in Chapter 5. You can also use the Brush Dynamics options to create tapering and fading strokes using either a mouse or a pressure-sensitive palette. Read about these options in Chapter 5 as well.

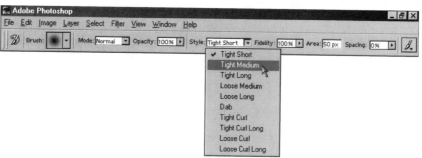

Figure 7-37: Select an option from the Style menu to change the type of strokes applied by the art history brush.

The remaining options work as follows:

✦ **Style:** The art history brush paints with randomly generated corkscrews of color. You can decide the basic shapes of the corkscrews by selecting an option from the Style pop-up menu. Combine these options with different brush sizes to vary the detail conveyed by the impressionistic image. Tight and small shapes give you better detail; loose and big shapes produce less detail.

✦ **Fidelity:** The brush colors each corkscrew according to a color lifted by the cursor from the original source state. Lowering the Fidelity value lets the corkscrew color drift away from the source color. This results in random coloring (true to the impressionist tradition) but slows down the brush's response.

✦ **Area:** This value defines the area covered by a single dollop of paint. Larger values generally mean more strokes are laid down at a time; reduce the value for a more sparse look.

Spacing: This option, formerly known as the Tolerance value, limits where the art history brush can paint. A value of 0 lets the brush paint anywhere; higher values let the brush paint only in areas where the current state and source state differ in color.

If impressionism interests you, I encourage you to experiment. If not, give this brush the slip. I happen to think it's pretty nifty (and surprisingly well implemented), but it definitely falls under the heading of Whimsical Creative Tools to Play with When You're Not under Deadline.

Tip   For even more creative variety, you can follow the steps outlined in the preceding section to paint from several different History states.

Source state limitations

Photoshop displays the cancel cursor and won't let you paint with the history brush or art history brush if the source state is a different width or height than the current image. One pixel difference, and the source state is a moot point. This same restriction applies when you set the eraser to the Erase to History mode as well as when you select the History fill option in the Fill dialog box (Edit ➪ Fill) or press Ctrl+Alt+Backspace.

As I mentioned earlier, you may see the cancel cursor if you lock transparency or image pixels in the Layers palette (using the Lock check boxes). To find out whether that's the problem or you're dealing with a source state issue, click the image to display an explanatory box. If the problem relates to the source state, move the source state icon in the History palette to a point after you modified the width or the height of the image. The crop tool and the Image ➪ Image Size, Canvas Size, Rotate Canvas, and Crop commands can mix up the history brush. If you applied one of these operations in the very last state, you either have to backstep before that operation or find some alternative to the history brush.

It's not a big deal, though. Give it some time and you'll learn to anticipate this problem. In the case of my experiment with Japan, I made sure to resample and crop the image before I began my experiment. Get the dimensions ironed out, and then start laying down your time trails.

✦   ✦   ✦

Selections, Masks, and Filters

Selections and Paths

C H A P T E R

8

Selection Fundamentals

Selections direct and protect. If it weren't for Photoshop's selection capabilities, you and I would be flinging paint on the canvas for all we're worth, like so many Jackson Pollock and Vasily Kandinsky wannabes, without any means to constrain, discriminate, or otherwise regulate the effects of our actions. Without selections, there'd be no filters, no color corrections, and no layers. In fact, we'd all be dangerously close to real life, that dreaded environment we've spent so much time and money to avoid.

No other program gives you as much control over the size and shape of selections as Photoshop. You can finesse selection outlines with unparalleled flexibility, alternatively adding to and subtracting from selected areas and moving and rotating selections independently of the pixels inside them. You can even mix masks and selection outlines together, as covered in Chapter 9.

That's why this chapter and the one that follows are the most important chapters in this book.

Pretty cool, huh? You put a provocative sentence like that on a line by itself and it resonates with authority. Granted, it's a little overstated, but can you blame me? I mean, I can't have a sentence like, "If you want my opinion, I think these are some pretty doggone important chapters — at least, that's the way it seems to me; certainly, you might have a different opinion," on a line by itself. The other paragraphs would laugh at it.

At any rate, I invite you to pay close attention to the fundamental concepts and approaches documented throughout this chapter. Although I wouldn't characterize each and every technique as essential — lots of artists get by without paying much attention to paths, for example, while other artists swear by them — a working knowledge of selection outlines is key to using Photoshop successfully.

How selections work

Before you can edit a portion of an image, you must first *select* it, which is computerese for indicating the boundaries of the area you want to edit. To select part of an image in a painting program, you surround it with a selection outline or a marquee, which tells Photoshop where to apply your editing instructions. The selection outline appears as a moving pattern of dash marks, lovingly termed *marching ants* by doughheads who've been using computers too long. (See Figure 8-1 for the inside story.)

Figure 8-1: A magnified view of a dash mark in a selection outline reveals a startling discovery.

Visible selection outlines can be helpful sometimes, but they can as readily impede your view of an image. When they annoy you, you can press Ctrl+H to shoo them away, as in earlier versions of Photoshop. However, in Version 6, Ctrl+H invokes the new View ⇨ Hide Extras command, which hides and displays *all* on-screen aids, not just those pesky ants. So you also lose guides, the grid, note icons, slices, and target paths. If you want to hide just the ants, choose View ⇨ Hide ⇨ Selection Edges. Choose the command again to toggle the ants back on. You also can control which items disappear when you press Ctrl+H by choosing View ⇨ Show ⇨ Show Options. In the resulting dialog box, check the items that you want Photoshop to display at all times.

As for creating selections, you have at your disposal a plethora of tools, all shown in Figure 8-2 and described briefly in the following list. You can access most of the tools by using keyboard shortcuts, which appear in parentheses.

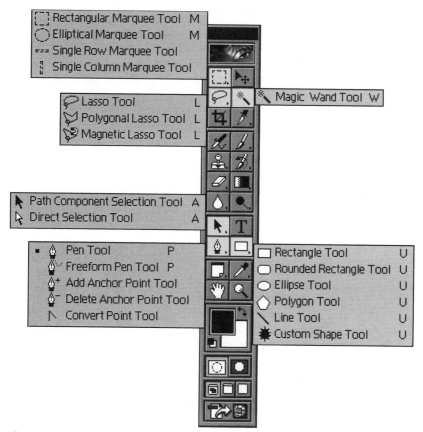

Figure 8-2: Photoshop 6 offers a bounty of selection tools.

When multiple tools share the same shortcut, you press the key once to activate the tool that's visible in the toolbox and press the key repeatedly to cycle through the other tools. This assumes that you turn off the Use Shift Key for Tool Switch check box in the Preferences dialog box (Ctrl+K). Otherwise, press Shift and the shortcut key to cycle through the following tools:

✦ **Rectangular marquee (M):** Long a staple of painting programs, this tool enables you to select rectangular or square portions of an image.

✦ **Elliptical marquee (M):** The elliptical marquee tool works like the rectangular marquee except it selects elliptical or circular portions of an image.

✦ **Single-row and single-column:** The single-row and single-column tools enable you to select a single row or column of pixels that stretches the entire width or height of the image. These are the only tools in Photoshop that you can't access from the keyboard.

✦ **Lasso (L):** Drag with the lasso tool to select a free-form portion of an image. Unlike the lasso tools in most painting programs, which shrink selection outlines to disqualify pixels in the background color, Photoshop's lasso tool selects the exact portion of the image you enclose in your drag.

✦ **Polygonal lasso (L):** Click different points in your image to set corners in a straight-sided selection outline. This is a great way to select free-form areas if you're not good at wielding the mouse or your wrists are a tad sore. (You can achieve this same effect by Alt-clicking with the lasso tool; I explain this more in the "Free-form outlines" section in this chapter.)

✦ **Magnetic lasso (L):** Click with the magnetic lasso along the edge of an image element that you want to select independently from its background. Then move (you don't have to drag) the magnetic lasso around the edge of the element. It's a tricky tool to use, so you can be sure I describe it in excruciating detail in the coming pages.

✦ **Magic wand (W):** First introduced by Photoshop, this tool lets you select a contiguous region of similarly colored pixels by clicking inside the region. For example, you might click inside the boundaries of a face to isolate it from the hair and background elements. Novices tend to gravitate toward the magic wand because it seems like such a miracle tool, but, in fact, it's the least predictable and ultimately the least useful of the bunch.

✦ **Pen (P):** The pen tool is difficult to master, but it's the most accurate and versatile of the selection tools. You use the pen tool to create a *path,* which is an object-oriented breed of selection outline. You click and drag to create individual points in the path. You can edit the path after the fact by moving, adding, and deleting points. You can even transfer a path by dragging and dropping between Photoshop, Illustrator, and FreeHand. For a discussion of the pen tool, read the "How to Draw and Edit Paths" section later in this chapter.

✦ **Freeform pen and magnetic pen (P):** If you hate setting points but you need to create a clipping path, the freeform pen is the tool for you. You just drag with the tool as if you were selecting with the lasso tool and let Photoshop define the points automatically. Obviously, you can expect the same level of accuracy that you get from the standard pen tool, but it's child's play to use.

In Photoshop 6, selecting the Magnetic check box on the Options bar transforms the freeform pen into the magnetic pen, which used to be a tool in its own right. The magnetic pen is basically an object-oriented version of the magnetic lasso tool. Click to set the first point and then move your mouse and watch Photoshop create the other points automatically. It's not a great tool, but it can prove handy when selecting image elements that stand out very clearly from their backgrounds.

✦ **Shape tools (U):** To draw paths in simple geometric shapes — rectangles, polygons, and so on — give the shape tools a whirl. First, put the tools into path mode by clicking the Work Path icon at the left end of the Options bar. Then simply drag to create the path. To find out more about working with these tools, visit Chapter 14.

✦ **Path and shape selection tools:** Use the path component selection tool (the black arrow) and the direct selection tool (the white arrow) to select and edit paths and vector shapes. You can read more about these tools later in this chapter, in the section "How to Draw and Edit Paths."

Photoshop's type tool, when set to the type mask mode, is also technically a selection tool because Photoshop converts each character of type to a selection outline. But type involves other issues that would merely confuse the contents of this chapter, so I've awarded type its own chapter (Chapter 15). Also, if your purpose for selecting an area is to separate it from its background, you should investigate the Extract command (Chapter 9) and the magic eraser and background eraser (Chapter 7). If this were all you needed to know to use the selection tools in Photoshop, the application would be on par with the average paint program. Part of what makes Photoshop exceptional, however, is that it provides literally hundreds of little tricks to increase the functionality of every selection tool.

Furthermore, all of Photoshop's selection tools work together in perfect harmony. You can exploit the specialized capabilities of the selection tools to create a single selection boundary. After you understand which tool best serves which purpose, you can isolate any element in an image, no matter how complex or how delicate its outline.

Geometric selection outlines

Tools for creating simple geometric selection outlines occupy the very first slot in the Photoshop toolbox. By default, the rectangular marquee tool has the stage. You select the elliptical, single-row, and single-column marquee tools from the flyout menu that appears when you drag from the marquee tool icon.

Press M to select the tool that's currently visible in the toolbox. Press M again to toggle between the rectangular and elliptical marquee tools. Alternatively, Alt-click the tool icon to toggle between the rectangular and elliptical marquee tools.

The marquee tools are more versatile than they may appear at first glance. You can adjust the performance of each tool as follows:

✦ **Constraining to a square or circle:** Press and hold Shift *after* beginning your drag to draw a perfect square with the rectangular marquee tool or a perfect circle with the elliptical marquee tool. (Pressing Shift *before* dragging also works if no other selection is active; otherwise, this adds to a selection, as I explain later in the "Ways to Change Selection Outlines" section.)

✦ **Drawing a circular marquee:** When I was perusing an online forum a while back, someone asked how to create a perfect circular marquee. Despite more than a month of helpful suggestions — some highly imaginative — no one offered the easiest suggestion of all (well, I ultimately did, but I'm a know-it-all). So remember to press Shift after you begin to drag and you'll be one step ahead of the game.

✦ **Drawing out from the center:** Press and hold Alt after you begin dragging to draw the marquee from the center outward instead of from corner to corner. (Again, pressing Alt before dragging works if no selection outline is active; otherwise, this subtracts from the selection.) This technique is especially useful when you draw an elliptical marquee. Locating the center of the area you want to select is frequently easier than locating one of its corners — particularly because ellipses don't have corners.

Tip

✦ **Moving the marquee on the fly:** While drawing a marquee, press and hold the spacebar to move the marquee rather than resize it. When you get the marquee in place, release the spacebar and keep dragging to modify the size. The spacebar is most helpful when drawing elliptical selections or when drawing a marquee out from the center — this eliminates the guesswork, so you can position your marquees exactly on target.

✦ **Selecting a single-pixel line:** Use the single-row or single-column tools to select a single row or column (respectively) of pixels. I use these tools to fix screw-ups such as a missing line of pixels in a screen shot, to delete random pixels around the perimeter of an image, or to create perpendicular lines in a fixed space.

✦ **Constraining the aspect ratio:** If you want to create an image that conforms to a certain aspect ratio, you can constrain either a rectangular or an elliptical marquee so that the ratio between height and width remains fixed, no matter how large or small a marquee you create. To accomplish this, select Constrained Aspect Ratio from the Style pop-up menu on the Options bar, as shown in Figure 8-3. Enter the desired ratio values into the Width and Height option boxes. (Press Enter to display the Options bar.)

Figure 8-3: Select Constrained Aspect Ratio from the Style pop-up menu on the Options bar to constrain the width and height of a rectangular selection outline.

Tip

If you work with a digital camera, you may find this feature especially helpful. Digital cameras typically produce images that fit the 4 × 3 aspect ratio used by computer screens and televisions. If you want to crop an image to a standard photo size — say, 4 × 6 inches — enter 4 and 6, respectively, in the Width and Height option boxes and press Enter to confirm your changes. Then drag the marquee around to select the portion of the picture you want to retain, as shown in the figure, and choose Image ⇨ Crop.

Remember that you're just establishing the image aspect ratio here, not setting the output width and height. So you could just as easily enter 2 and 3 in the Width and Height option boxes. The size of the final, cropped image depends on how large you draw the marquee and the Resolution value you set in the Image Size dialog box.

✦ **Sizing the marquee numerically:** If you're editing a screen shot or some other form of regular or schematic image, you may find it helpful to specify the size of the marquee numerically. To do so, select Fixed Size from the Style pop-up menu and enter size values in the Width and Height option boxes. To match the selection to a 640 × 480-pixel screen, for example, change the Width and Height values to 640 and 480, respectively. Then click in the image to create the marquee.

You can now set the marquee size in any unit of measurement you like. Just type the number followed by one of these units: px (pixels), in, mm, cm, pt (points), pica, or %.

✦ **Drawing feathered selections:** A Feather option box is available when you use either marquee tool. To *feather* a selection is to blur its edges beyond the automatic antialiasing afforded by most tools. For more information on feathering, refer to the "Softening selection outlines" section later in this chapter.

✦ **Creating jagged ellipses:** By default, elliptical selection outlines are antialiased. If you don't want antialiasing — you might prefer harsh edges when editing screen shots or designing screen interfaces — deselect the Anti-aliased check box. (This option is dimmed when you use the rectangular marquee because antialiasing is always on for this tool.)

Photoshop novices often misunderstand the rectangular and elliptical marquee tools and expect them to create filled and stroked shapes. In the past, the program offered no tools for creating such shapes — you had to draw a geometric marquee and then fill or stroke the selection. Now Photoshop provides the shape tools, which can create filled vector and raster shapes. You can apply strokes and other effects to these shapes if you like. Chapter 14 takes you on a guided tour of the shape tools.

Free-form outlines

In comparison to the rectangular and elliptical marquee tools, the lasso tool provides a rather limited range of options. Generally speaking, you drag in a free-form path around the image you want to select. The few special considerations are as follows:

✦ **Feathering and antialiasing:** Just as you can feather rectangular and elliptical marquees, you can feather selections drawn with the lasso tool by selecting the Feather check box on the Options bar. To soften the edges of a lasso outline, select the Anti-aliased check box.

Although you can adjust the feathering of any selection after you draw it by choosing Select ➪ Feather, you must specify antialiasing before you draw a selection. Unless you have a specific reason for doing otherwise, leave the Anti-aliased check box turned on (as it is by default).

✦ **Drawing polygons:** If you press and hold Alt, the lasso tool works like a free-form polygon tool. (*Polygon,* incidentally, means a shape with multiple straight sides.) With the Alt key down, click to specify corners in a free-form polygon, as shown in Figure 8-4. If you want to add curves to the selection outline, drag with the tool while still pressing Alt. Photoshop closes the selection outline the moment you release both the Alt key and the mouse button.

You can extend a polygon selection outline to the absolute top, right, or bottom edges of an image. If the image window is larger than the image, you can Alt-click with the lasso tool on the background canvas surrounding the image. You can even click on the scroll bars. Figure 8-4 illustrates the idea.

✦ **The polygonal lasso tool:** If you don't want to bother with pressing Alt, select the polygonal lasso. When the lasso is active, you can switch to the polygonal lasso by pressing L. Or drag from the lasso tool icon to display the lasso flyout menu and select the polygonal lasso that way. Then click inside the image to set corners in the selection. Click the first point in the selection or double-click with the tool to complete the selection outline.

If you make a mistake while creating a selection outline with the polygonal lasso, press Backspace to eliminate the last segment you drew. Keep pressing Backspace to eliminate more segments in the selection outline. This technique works until you close the selection outline and it turns into marching ants.

To create free-form curves with the polygonal lasso tool, press Alt and drag.

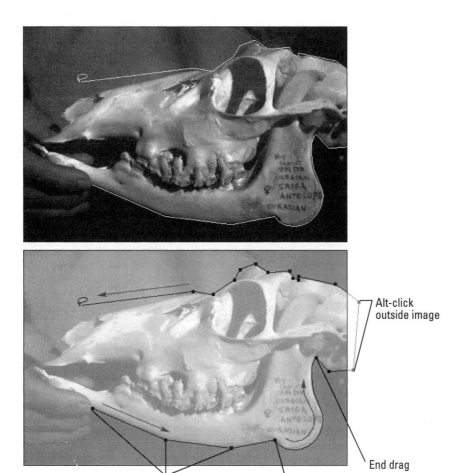

Figure 8-4: Alt-click with the lasso tool to create corners in a selection outline, shown as black squares in the bottom image. Drag to create free-form curves. Surprisingly, you can Alt-click anywhere within the image window, even on the scroll bars, to add corners outside the boundaries of the image.

Adobe added the polygonal lasso for those times when Alt-clicking isn't convenient. If no portion of the image is selected, it's no trick to Alt-click with the standard lasso to draw a straight-sided selection. But if some area in the image is selected, pressing Alt tells Photoshop that you want to subtract from the selection outline. For this reason, it's often easier to use the polygonal lasso (although you still can make it work by pressing Alt *after* you click with the lasso tool, as I explain in the "Using Shift and Alt like a pro" section later in this chapter).

Magnetic selections

In the old days of black-and-white painting programs — most notably MacPaint on the Mac — black pixels were considered foreground elements and white pixels were the background. To select a black element, you had only to vaguely drag around it with the lasso tool and the program would automatically omit the white pixels and "shrink" the selection around the black ones.

The magnetic lasso tool is Adobe's attempt to transfer shrinking into the world of color. Under ideal conditions — very ideal conditions, I might add — a selection drawn with the magnetic lasso automatically shrinks around the foreground element and omits the background. Naturally, it rarely works this miraculously, but it does produce halfway decent selection outlines with very little effort — provided that you know what you're doing.

Using the magnetic lasso tool

Typically, when people have a problem using the magnetic lasso tool, it's because they're trying to make the process too complex. Work less, and the tool works better. Here are the basic steps for using this unusual tool:

STEPS: Making Sense of the Magnetic Lasso Tool

1. **Select an image with very definite contrast between the foreground image and its background.** The skull in Figure 8-5 is a good example: a light gray skull against a dark gray background. Here's something that Photoshop can really sink its teeth into.

2. **Select the magnetic lasso.** If any tool but a lasso tool is active, press L to grab the lasso that's showing in the toolbox. Then press L as necessary to cycle to the magnetic lasso.

3. **Click anywhere along the edge of the foreground element.** I clicked at the top of the skull, as labeled in Figure 8-5.

4. **Move the cursor around the edge of the foreground element.** Just *move* the mouse, don't drag — that is, there's no need to press the mouse button. As your cursor passes over the image, Photoshop lays down a line along the edge of the element, as Figure 8-5 shows. If you don't like the placement of the line, back up the cursor and try moving along the edge again. The magnetic lasso also lays down anchor points at significant locations around the image. If you don't like where the program puts a point, press Backspace. Each time you press Backspace, Photoshop gets rid of the most recent point along the line. To set your own anchor points, just click.

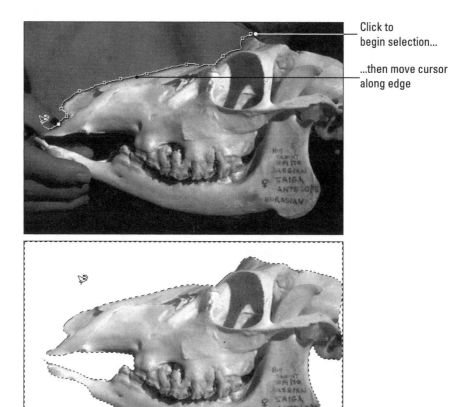

Click to
begin selection...

...then move cursor
along edge

Figure 8-5: After clicking to set the start point (top), I moved the magnetic lasso
cursor along the edge of the skull. Then I reversed the completed selection
(Ctrl+Shift+I) and pressed Backspace to fill it with white (bottom).

5. **When you make it all the way around to the beginning of the shape, click
the first point in the outline to close the selection.** Or just double-click to
close with a straight edge.

As I mentioned before, the magnetic lasso does not perform miracles. It almost
never selects an image exactly the way you would like it to. After moving the cursor
around the skull, I reversed the selection by choosing Select ➪ Inverse (Ctrl+Shift+I)
and then I pressed Backspace to fill the background with white. The result appears
in the second example in Figure 8-5. As you can see, the magnetic lasso did a very
nice job of isolating the skull—much better than I could have done with the lasso
alone—but the selection isn't perfect. Notice the gap on the right side of the skull

and the clumsy treatment of the tip of the pointy lower jaw on left. Okay, no automated selection tool is perfect, but the magnetic lasso makes as few mistakes as any I've seen.

Tip

To create a straight segment while working with the magnetic lasso tool, press Alt, click to set the start of the segment, and click again at the end point. The next time you click without holding down Alt, the tool reverts to its normal magnetic self.

Modifying the magnetic lasso options

You modify the performance of the magnetic lasso tool by adjusting the values on the Options bar. (If you don't see the Options bar, press Enter to display it.) The first two options — Feather and Anti-aliased — define the softness of the final selection outline, just as they do for the standard lasso tool. The others control how the magnetic lasso positions lines and lays down points:

✦ **Width:** I might have named this option Sloppiness Factor. It determines how close to an edge you have to move the cursor for Photoshop to accurately see the image element. Large values are great for smooth elements that stand out clearly from their backgrounds. If I raise the Width to 20 when selecting the top of the skull, for example, I can move the cursor 20 pixels away from the skull and Photoshop still shrinks the selection tight around the skull's edge. That's a lot of wiggle room and makes my life easier. But when you're selecting narrow passageways, you need a low value to keep Photoshop from veering off to the wrong edge. The spot where the pointy jaw meets with the snout is a good example of a place where I need to set a small Width and move very carefully around the edge.

Tip

The great advantage to the Width value is that you can change it on the fly by pressing a bracket key. Press the [key to lower the Width value; press the] key to raise the value. Shift+[lowers the value to its minimum, 1, and Shift+] raises it to the maximum, 40.

If you have a pressure-sensitive tablet and select the Stylus Pressure check box, you can control the sloppiness factor dynamically according to how hard you press on the pen. Bear down to be careful; let up to be sloppy. Because this is the way you probably work naturally, you'll be able to adjust the width as needed without even thinking much about it.

✦ **Frequency:** This option tells the magnetic lasso when to lay down points. As you drag with the tool, the line around the image changes to keep up with your movements. When some point in the line stays still for a few moments, Photoshop decides it must be on target and anchors it down with a point. If you want Photoshop to anchor points more frequently, raise the value. For less frequent anchoring, lower the option. High values tend to be better for rough edges; lower values are better for smooth edges.

✦ **Edge Contrast:** This is the simplest of the options. It tells Photoshop how much contrast there has to be between the element you're trying to select and its background to even be recognized. If the foreground element stands out clearly, you may want to raise the Edge Contrast value to avoid selecting random flack around the edges. If the contrast between foreground and background is subtle, lower the value.

Most of the time, you can rely on the bracket keys to adjust the Lasso Width and leave the Frequency and Edge Contrast values set to their defaults. When dealing with a low-contrast image, lower the Edge Contrast value to 5 percent or so. And when selecting unusually rough edges, raise the Frequency to 70 or more. But careful movements with the magnetic lasso tool go farther than adjusting any of these settings.

The world of the wand

Using the magic wand tool is a no-brainer, right? You just click with the tool and it selects all neighboring colors that fall within a selected range. The problem is getting the wand to recognize the same range of colors that you see on screen. For example, if you're editing a photo of a red plate against a pink tablecloth, how do you tell the magic wand to select the plate and leave the tablecloth alone?

Sadly, adjusting the wand is pretty tricky and frequently unsatisfying. If you press Enter when the magic wand is active, you'll see four controls on the Options bar:

✦ **Anti-aliased** softens the selection, just as it does for the lasso tool.

✦ **Contiguous,** when selected, tells Photoshop to select a contiguous region of pixels emanating from the pixel on which you click. If you're trying to select landmasses on a globe, for example, clicking on St. Louis selects everything from Juneau to Mexico City. It doesn't select London, though, because an ocean of water that doesn't fall within the tolerance range separates the cities. To select all similarly colored pixels throughout the picture, deselect the option.

✦ **Tolerance** determines the range of colors the tool selects when you click with it in the image window.

✦ **Use All Layers** allows you to take all visible layers into account when defining a selection.

You now know what you need to know about the Anti-aliased and Contiguous options; the next two sections explain Tolerance and Use All Layers.

Adjusting the tolerance

You may have heard the standard explanation for adjusting the Tolerance value: You can enter any number from 0 to 255 in the Tolerance option box. Enter a low number to select a small range of colors; increase the value to select a wider range of colors.

Nothing is wrong with this explanation—it's accurate, in its own small way—but it doesn't provide one iota of information you couldn't glean on your own. If you really want to understand this option, you have to dig a little deeper.

When you click a pixel with the magic wand tool, Photoshop first reads the brightness value that each color channel assigned to that pixel. If you're working with a grayscale image, Photoshop reads a single brightness value from the one channel only; if you're working with an RGB image, it reads three brightness values, one each from the red, green, and blue channels; and so on. Because each color channel permits 8 bits of data, brightness values range from 0 to 255.

Next, Photoshop applies the Tolerance value, or simply *tolerance,* to the pixel. The tolerance describes a range that extends in both directions—lighter and darker—from each brightness value.

Suppose you're editing a standard RGB image. The tolerance is set to 32 (as it is by default); you click with the magic wand on a turquoise pixel, whose brightness values are 40 red, 210 green, and 170 blue. Photoshop subtracts and adds 32 from each brightness value to calculate the magic wand range that, in this case, is 8 to 72 red, 178 to 242 green, and 138 to 202 blue. Photoshop selects any pixel that both falls inside this range and can be traced back to the original pixel through an uninterrupted line of other pixels, which also fall within the range.

From this information, you can draw the following basic conclusions about the magic wand tool:

✦ **Clicking on midtones maintains a higher range:** Because the tolerance range extends in two directions, you cut off the range when you click a light or dark pixel, as demonstrated in Figure 8-6. Consider the two middle gradations: In both cases, I selected the Contiguous check box and set the Tolerance value to 60. In the top gradation, I clicked on a pixel with a brightness of 140, so Photoshop calculated a range from 80 to 200. But when I clicked on a pixel with a brightness value of 10, as in the bottom gradation, the range shrank to 0 to 70. Clicking on a medium-brightness pixel, therefore, permits the most generous range.

✦ **Selecting brightness ranges:** Many people have the impression that the magic wand selects color ranges. The magic wand, in fact, selects brightness ranges within color channels. So if you want to select a flesh-colored region—regardless of shade—set against an orange or a red background that is roughly equivalent in terms of brightness values, you probably should use a different tool.

✦ **Selecting from a single channel:** If the magic wand repeatedly fails to select a region of color that appears unique from its background, try isolating that region inside a single-color channel. You'll probably have the most luck isolating a color on the channel that least resembles it. For example, to select the yellow Sasquatch Xing sign shown in Color Plate 8-1, I switched to the blue channel (Ctrl+3). Because yellow contains no blue and the brambly background contains quite a bit of blue—as demonstrated in the last example of Figure 8-7—the magic wand can distinguish the two relatively easily. Experiment with this technique and it will prove even more useful over time.

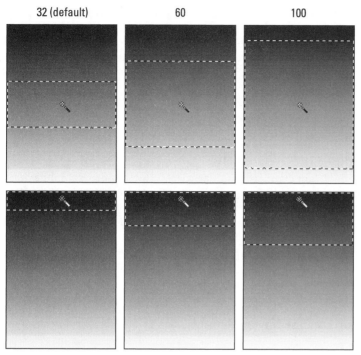

Figure 8-6: Note the results of clicking on a pixel with a brightness value of 140 (top row) and a brightness value of 10 (bottom row) with the tolerance set to three different values.

Figure 8-7: Because the yellow Sasquatch sign contains almost no blue, it appears most clearly distinguished from its background in the blue channel. So the blue channel is the easiest channel in which to select the sign with the magic wand.

Here's one more twist to the Tolerance story: The magic wand is affected by the Sample Size option that you select for the eyedropper tool. If you select Point Sample, the wand bases its selection solely on the single pixel that you click. But if you select 3 by 3 Average or 5 by 5 Average, the wand takes into account 15 or 25 pixels, respectively. As you can imagine, this option can have a noticeable impact on the extent of the selection that you get from the wand. Try clicking the same spot in your image using each of these Sample Size settings, using the same Tolerance value throughout, to see what I mean.

Making the wand see beyond a single layer

The Use All Layers option enables you to create a selection based on pixels from different layers (see Chapter 12 for more about layers). Returning to my previous landmass example, suppose you set Europe on one layer and North America on the layer behind it so the two continents overlap. Normally, if you clicked inside Europe with the magic wand, it would select an area inside Europe without extending out into the area occupied by North America on the other layer. Because the wand doesn't even see the contents of other layers, anything outside Europe is an empty void. We're talking pre-Columbus Europe here.

If you select Use All Layers, though, the situation changes. Suddenly, the wand can see all the layers you can see. If you click on Europe, and if North America and Europe contain similar colors, the wand selects across both shapes.

Mind you, while the Use All Layers option enables the wand to consider pixels on different layers when creating a selection, it does not permit the wand to actually select images on two separate layers. Strange as this may sound, no selection tool can pull off this feat. Every one of the techniques explained in this chapter is applicable to only a single layer at a time. Use All Layers merely allows the wand to draw selection outlines that appear to encompass colors on many layers.

What good is this? Well, suppose you want to apply an effect to both Europe and North America. With the help of Use All Layers, you can draw a selection outline that encompasses both continents. After you apply the effect to Europe, you can switch to the North America layer — the selection outline remains intact — and then reapply the effect.

Ways to Change Selection Outlines

If you don't draw a selection outline correctly the first time, you have two options. You can either draw it again from scratch, which is a real bore, or you can change your botched selection outline, which is likely to be the more efficient solution.

You can deselect a selection, add to a selection, subtract from a selection, and even select the stuff that's not selected and deselect the stuff that is. (If this sounds like a load of nonsense, keep reading.)

Quick changes

Some methods of adjusting a selection outline are automatic: You choose a command and you're finished. The following list explains how a few commands — all members of the Select menu — work:

✦ **Deselect (Ctrl+D):** You can deselect the selected portion of an image in three ways. You can select a different portion of the image; click anywhere in the image window with the rectangular marquee tool, the elliptical marquee tool, or the lasso tool; or choose Select ➪ Deselect. Remember, though, when no part of an image is selected, the entire image is susceptible to your changes. If you apply a filter, choose a color-correction command, or use a paint tool, you affect every pixel of the foreground image.

✦ **Reselect (Ctrl+Shift+D):** If you accidentally deselect an image, you can retrieve the most recent selection outline by choosing Select ➪ Reselect. It's a great function that operates entirely independently of the Undo command and History palette, and it works even after performing a long string of selection-unrelated operations. (You can restore older selections from the History palette, but that usually means undoing operations along the way.)

✦ **Inverse (Ctrl+Shift+I):** Choose Select ➪ Inverse to reverse the selection. Photoshop deselects the portion of the image that was previously selected and selects the portion of the image that was not selected. This way, you can begin a selection by outlining the portion of the image you want to protect, rather than the portion you want to affect.

Tip You can also access the Inverse and Deselect commands from a context-sensitive pop-up menu in the image window. Right-click to make the menu appear underneath your cursor.

Manually adding and subtracting

Ready for some riddles? When editing a portrait, how do you select both eyes without affecting any other portion of the face? Answer: By drawing one selection and then tacking on a second selection. How do you select a doughnut and leave the hole behind? Answer: Encircle the doughnut with the elliptical marquee tool, and then use the same tool to subtract the center.

Photoshop enables you to whittle away at a selection, add pieces on again, whittle away some more, ad infinitum, until you get it exactly right. Short of sheer laziness or frustration, no reason exists why you can't eventually create the selection outline of your dreams:

✦ **Adding to a selection outline:** To increase the area enclosed in an existing selection outline, Shift-drag with one of the marquee or lasso tools. You also can Shift-click with the magic wand tool or Shift-click with one of the marquee tools when the Fixed Size option is active (as described in the "Geometric selection outlines" section earlier in this chapter).

✦ **Subtracting from a selection outline:** To take a bite from an existing selection outline, press Alt while using one of the selection tools.

✦ **Intersecting one selection outline with another:** Another way to subtract from an existing selection outline is to Shift+Alt-drag around the selection with the rectangular marquee, elliptical marquee, or lasso tool. You also can Shift+Alt-click with the magic wand tool. Shift+Alt-dragging instructs Photoshop to retain only the portion of an existing selection that also falls inside the new selection outline. I frequently use this technique to confine a selection within a rectangular or elliptical border.

If the key-press techniques seem bothersome, use the selection state buttons at the left end of the Options bar to set your selection tool to add, subtract, or intersect mode. (Figure 8-8 labels the icons.) After clicking a button, simply drag to alter the selection outline. To toggle the tool back to normal operating mode, click the first button in the bunch. Note that the keyboard techniques described in the preceding list work no matter what button you select in the Options bar. For example, if you click the Intersect icon, Alt-dragging still subtracts from the selection outline.

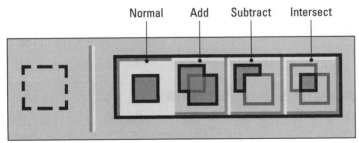

Figure 8-8: You can use the selection state buttons as well as the Shift and Alt keys when modifying a selection outline.

Tip

When you're working with the magic wand, you can right-click to display a context-sensitive menu that contains the add, subtract, and intersect mode options. Click the mode you want to use.

Tip

Photoshop displays special cursors to help you keep track of a tool's selection state. Suppose that you select part of an image and the lasso tool is active. When you press Shift or click the Add button on the Options bar, Photoshop appends a little plus sign to the lasso cursor to show you're about to add. A minus sign indicates that you're set to subtract from the selection outline; a multiply sign appears when you work in intersect mode. If you're pressing keys to switch tool modes, Photoshop temporarily selects the corresponding selection state button on the Options bar as well.

Using Shift and Alt like a pro

The roles of the Shift and Alt keys in adding, subtracting, and intersecting selection outlines can interfere with your ability to take advantage of other functions of the selection tools. For example, when no portion of an image is selected, you can Shift-drag with the rectangular marquee tool to draw a square. But after a selection is active, Shift-dragging adds a rectangle — not a square — to the selection outline.

This is one reason why Adobe added the selection state buttons to the Options bar. After you click a button, the tool adds, subtracts, or intersects, with no additional key presses on your part, depending on which button you click. But if you want to hide the Options bar or you just prefer pressing keys to clicking buttons, you can control the selection tools from the keyboard without giving up any selection flexibility.

The trick is to learn when to press Shift and Alt. Sometimes you have to press the key before you begin your drag; other times you must press the key after you begin the drag but before you release. For example, to add a square to a selection outline, Shift-drag, release Shift while keeping the mouse button pressed, and press Shift again to snap the rectangle to a square. The same goes for adding a circle with the elliptical marquee tool.

The following list introduces you to a few other techniques. They sound pretty elaborate, I admit, but with a little practice, they become second nature (so does tightrope walking, but don't let that worry you). Before you try any of them, be sure to select Normal from the Style pop-up menu on the Options bar.

✦ To subtract a square or a circle from a selection, Alt-drag, release Alt, press Shift, drag until you get it right, release the mouse button, and then release Shift.

✦ To add a rectangle or an ellipse by drawing from the center outward, Shift-drag, release Shift, press Alt, and hold Alt until after you release the mouse button. You can even press the spacebar during the drag to move the marquee around, if you like.

✦ To subtract a marquee drawn from the center outward, Alt-drag, release Alt, press Alt again, and hold the key down until after you release.

✦ What about drawing a straight-sided selection with the lasso tool? To add a straight-sided area to an existing selection, Shift-drag with the tool for a short distance. With the mouse button still down, release Shift and press Alt. Then click around as you normally would, while keeping the Alt key down.

✦ To subtract a straight-sided area, Alt-drag with the lasso, release Alt, press Alt again, and click around with the tool.

If you can't manage the last two lasso-tool techniques, switch to the polygonal lasso instead. In fact, the reason Adobe provided the polygonal lasso tool was to accommodate folks who don't want to deal with pressing Alt seven times during a single drag (which I strangely quite enjoy).

Adding and subtracting by command

Photoshop provides several commands under the Select menu that automatically increase or decrease the number of selected pixels in an image according to numerical specifications. The commands in the Select ➪ Modify submenu work as follows:

✦ **Border:** This command selects an area of a specified thickness around the perimeter of the current selection outline and deselects the rest of the selection. For example, to select a 6-point-thick border around the current selection, choose Select ➪ Modify ➪ Border, enter 6 in the Width option box, and press Enter. But what's the point? After all, if you want to create an outline around a selection, you can accomplish this in fewer steps by choosing Edit ➪ Stroke. The Border command, however, broadens your range of options. You can apply a special effect to the border, move the border to a new location, or even create a double-outline effect by first applying Select ➪ Modify ➪ Border and then applying Edit ➪ Stroke.

✦ **Smooth:** This command rounds off the sharp corners and weird anomalies in the outline of a selection. When you choose Select ➪ Modify ➪ Smooth, the program asks you to enter a Sample Radius value. Photoshop smoothes out corners by drawing little circles around them; the Sample Radius value determines the radius of these circles. Larger values result in smoother corners.

The Smooth command is especially useful in combination with the magic wand. After you draw one of those weird, scraggly selection outlines with the wand tool, use Select ➪ Modify ➪ Smooth to smooth out the rough edges.

✦ **Expand and Contract:** Both of these commands do exactly what they say, either expanding or contracting the selected area by a specified amount. For example, if you want an elliptical selection to grow by 8 pixels, choose Select ➪ Modify ➪ Expand, enter 8, and call it a day. These are extremely useful commands; I refer to them several times throughout the book.

Photoshop 6 enables you to expand and contract selections by as many as 100 pixels, up from the previous limit of 16. The upper limits of the Border and Smooth commands were raised also (to 200 and 100 pixels, respectively), but my guess is that you'll have less reason to take advantage of those changes than you will the new ranges for Expand and Contract.

Both Expand and Contract have a flattening effect on a selection. To round things off, apply the Smooth command with a Sample Radius value equal to the number you just entered into the Expand Selection or Contract Selection dialog box. You end up with a pretty vague selection outline, but what do you expect from automated commands?

In addition to the Expand command, Photoshop provides two other commands — Grow and Similar — that increase the area covered by a selection outline. Both commands resemble the magic wand tool because they measure the range of eligible pixels by way of a Tolerance value. In fact, the commands rely on the same Tolerance value (on the Options bar) that you set for the magic wand. So if you want to adjust the impact of either command, you must first select the magic wand and then apply the commands:

✦ **Grow:** Choose Select ⇨ Grow to select all pixels that both neighbor an existing selection and resemble the colors included in the selection, in accordance with the Tolerance value. In other words, Select ⇨ Grow is the command equivalent of the magic wand tool. If you feel constrained because you can only click one pixel at a time with the magic wand tool, you may prefer to select a small group of representative pixels with a marquee tool and then choose Select ⇨ Grow to initiate the wand's magic.

✦ **Similar:** Another member of the Select menu, Similar works like Grow, except the pixels needn't be adjacent. When you choose Select ⇨ Similar, Photoshop selects any pixel that falls within the tolerance range, regardless of the location of the pixel in the foreground image.

Although both Grow and Similar respect the magic wand's Tolerance value, they pay no attention to the other wand options — Contiguous, Use All Layers, and Anti-aliased. Grow always selects contiguous regions only; Similar selects noncontiguous areas. Neither can see beyond the active layer or produce antialiased selection outlines.

One of the best applications for the Similar command is to isolate a complicated image set against a consistent background whose colors are significantly lighter or darker than the image. Consider Figure 8-9, which features a dark and ridiculously complex foreground image set against a continuous background of medium-to-light brightness values. The following steps explain how to separate this image using the Similar command in combination with a few other techniques I've described thus far.

STEPS: Isolating a Complex Image Set Against a Plain Background

1. **Use the rectangular marquee tool to select some representative portions of the background.** In Figure 8-9, I selected the lightest and darkest portions of the background along with some representative shades in between. Remember, you make multiple selections by Shift-dragging with the tool.

Figure 8-9: Before choosing Select ⇨ Similar, select a few sample portions of the background for Photoshop to base its selection range.

2. **Double-click the magic wand tool icon to display the Tolerance option box on the Options bar.** For my image, I entered a Tolerance value of 16, a relatively low value, in keeping with the consistency of the background. If your background is less homogenous, you may want to enter a higher value. Make certain you turn on the Anti-aliased check box.

3. **Choose Select ⇨ Similar.** Photoshop should select the entire background. If Photoshop fails to select all the background, choose Edit ⇨ Undo (Ctrl+Z) and use the rectangular marquee tool to select more portions of the background. You may also want to increase the magic wand's Tolerance value. If Photoshop's selection bleeds into the foreground image, try reducing the Tolerance value.

4. **Choose Select ⇨ Inverse.** Or press Ctrl+Shift+I. Photoshop selects the foreground image and deselects the background.

5. **Modify the selection as desired.** If the detail you want to select represents only a fraction of the entire image, Shift+Alt-drag around the portion of the image you want to retain using the lasso tool. In Figure 8-10, I Shift+Alt-dragged with the polygonal lasso tool to draw a straight-sided outline around the selection.

6. **Congratulations, you've isolated your complex image.** Now you can filter your image, colorize it, or perform whatever operation inspired you to select this image in the first place. I wanted to superimpose the image onto a different background, so I copied the image to the Clipboard (Ctrl+C), opened the desired background image, and then pasted the first image into place (Ctrl+V). The result, shown in Figure 8-11, still needs some touching up with the paint and edit tools, but it's not half bad for an automated selection process.

Figure 8-10: Shift+Alt-drag with the polygonal lasso tool to intersect the area you want to select with a straight-sided outline.

Figure 8-11: The completed selection superimposed onto a new background.

Note   Whenever you introduce a selection into another image — by copying and pasting or by dragging the selection and dropping it into another image window — Photoshop automatically assigns the selection to a new layer. This is a great safety mechanism because it prevents you from permanently affixing the selection to its new background. But it also limits your file format options when saving an image; you can't save in a format other than the native Photoshop format, PDF, or TIFF (the last two now offer layer support) without first flattening the image. For the big story on layers, read Chapter 12.

Softening selection outlines

You can soften a selection in two ways. The first method is antialiasing, introduced in Chapter 5. Antialiasing is an intelligent and automatic softening algorithm that mimics the appearance of edges you'd expect to see in a sharply focused photograph.

Note   Where did the term *antialias* originate? Anytime you try to fit the digital equivalent of a square peg into a round hole — say, by printing a high-resolution image to a low-resolution printer — the data gets revised during the process. This revised data, called an *alias,* is frequently inaccurate and undesirable. Antialiasing is the act of revising the data ahead of time, essentially rounding off the square peg so it looks nice as it goes into the hole. According to a reader who spent time at MIT's Architecture Machine Group, "We did the first work with displaying smooth lines. We called the harsh transitions *jaggies* and the display process *dejaggying.* Somehow, this easy-to-understand term slid sideways into 'alias' (which it isn't, really, but it's too late to change)." Now you know.

When you draw an antialiased selection outline in Photoshop, the program calculates the hard-edged selection at twice its actual size. The program then shrinks the selection in half using bicubic interpolation (described in Chapter 2). The result is a crisp image with no visible jagged edges.

The second softening method, feathering, is more dramatic. Feathering gradually dissipates the selection outline, giving it a blurry edge. Photoshop accommodates partially selected pixels; feathering fades the selection both inward and outward from the original edge.

You can specify the number of pixels affected either before or after drawing a selection. To feather a selection before you draw it with a marquee or lasso tool, enter a value in the Feather option box, found on the Options bar in Photoshop 6. To feather a selection after drawing it, choose Select ⇨ Feather or press Ctrl+Alt+D. You also can right-click in the image window and then choose Feather from the pop-up menu that appears next to your cursor.

The Feather Radius value determines the approximate distance over which Photoshop fades a selection, measured in pixels in both directions from the original selection outline. Figure 8-12 shows three selections lifted from the image at the bottom of the figure.

The first selection is antialiased only. I feathered the second and third selections, assigning Feather Radius values of 4 and 12, respectively. As you can see, a small feather radius makes a selection appear fuzzy; a larger radius makes it fade into view.

Figure 8-12: Three clones selected with the elliptical marquee tool. The top image is antialiased and not feathered, the next is feathered with a radius of 4 pixels, and the third is feathered with a radius of 12 pixels.

The math behind the feather

A few eagle-eyed readers have written to ask me why feathering blurs a selection outline more than the number of pixels stated in the Feather Radius value. A radius of 4 pixels actually affects a total of 20 pixels: 10 inward and 10 outward. The reason revolves around Photoshop's use of a mathematical routine called the *Gaussian bell curve*, which exaggerates the distance over which the selection outline is blurred.

Figure 8-13 demonstrates the math visually. The top-left image shows a hard-edged elliptical selection filled with white against a black background. To its right is a side view of the ellipse, in which black pixels are short and white pixels are tall. (Okay, so it's really a graph, but I didn't want to scare you.) Because no gray pixels are in the ellipse, the side view has sharp vertical walls.

The bottom-left image shows what happens if I first feather the selection with a radius of 4 pixels and then fill it with white. The side view now graphs a range of gray values, which taper gradually from black to white. See those gray areas on the sides (each labeled *Diameter*)? Those are the pixels that fall into the 8-pixel diameter, measured 4 pixels in and out from the original selection outline. These gray areas slope in straight lines.

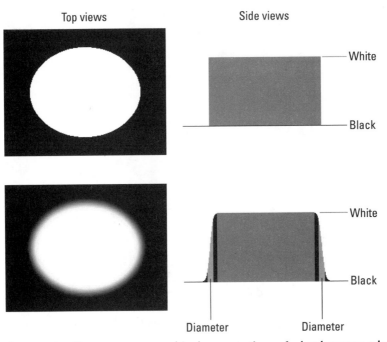

Figure 8-13: Here are some graphic demonstrations of what happens when you feather a selection. Photoshop tapers the ends of the feathered selections (shown by the black areas, bottom right) to prevent your eye from easily detecting where the feathering starts and stops.

The rounded areas of the side view — painted black — are the Gaussian bell curves. These are appended to the radius of the feather to ensure smooth transitions between the blurry edges and the selected and deselected pixels. Programs that do not include these extra Gaussian curves end up producing ugly feathered selections that appear to have sharp, incongruous edges.

Tip

If exact space is an issue, you can count on the Feather command affecting about 2.7 times as many pixels as you enter into the Feather Radius option box, both in and out from the selection. That's a total of 5.4 times as many pixels as the radius in all.

If this was more than you wanted to know, cast it from your mind. Feathering makes the edges of a selection fuzzy — 'nuff said.

Putting feathering to use

You can use feathering to remove an element from an image while leaving the background intact, a process described in the following steps. The image described in these steps, shown in Figure 8-14, is a NASA photo of a satellite with the Earth in the background. I wanted to use this background with another image, but to do so I first had to eliminate that satellite. By feathering and cloning a selection outline, I covered the satellite with a patch so seamless you'd swear the satellite was never there.

STEPS: Removing an Element from an Image

1. **Draw a selection around the element using the lasso tool.** The selection needn't be an exact fit; in fact, you want it rather loose, so allow a buffer zone of at least 6 pixels between the edges of the image and the selection outline.

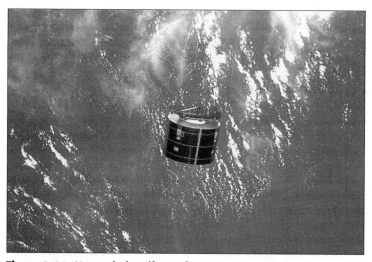

Figure 8-14: Your mission, if you choose to accept it, is to remove the satellite by covering it with selections cloned from the background.

2. **Drag the selection outline over a patch in the image.** Now that you've specified the element you want to remove, you must find a patch, that is, some portion of the image to cover the element in a manner that matches the surrounding background. In Figure 8-15, the best match seemed an area just below and to the right of the satellite. To select this area, move the selection outline independently of the image merely by dragging it with the lasso tool. (Dragging a selection with a selection tool moves the outline without affecting the pixels.) Make certain you allow some space between the selection outline and the element you're trying to cover.

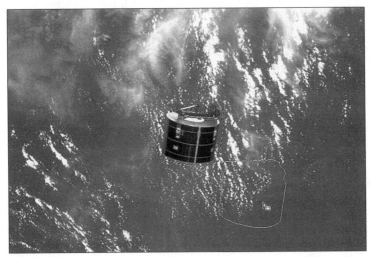

Figure 8-15: After drawing a loose outline around the satellite with the lasso tool, I dragged the outline to select a portion of the background.

3. **Choose Select ➪ Feather.** Or press Ctrl+Alt+D. Enter a small value (8 or less) in the Feather Radius option box — just enough to make the edges fuzzy. (I entered 3.) Then press Enter to initiate the operation.

4. **Clone the patch onto the area you want to cover.** Select the move tool by pressing V. Then Alt-drag the feathered selection to clone the patch and position it over the element you want to cover, as shown in Figure 8-16. To align the patch correctly, choose Select ➪ Hide Extras (Ctrl+H) to hide the marching ants and then nudge the patch into position with the arrow keys.

5. **Repeat as desired.** My patch was only partially successful. The upper-left corner of the selection matches clouds in the background, but the lower-right corner is dark and cloudless, an obvious rift in the visual continuity of the image. The solution: Try again. With the lasso tool, I drew a loose outline around the dark portion of the image and dragged it up and to the left as shown in Figure 8-17.

Figure 8-16: Next, I used the move tool to Alt-drag the feathered selection over the satellite. Sadly, the patch was imperfect and required further adjustments.

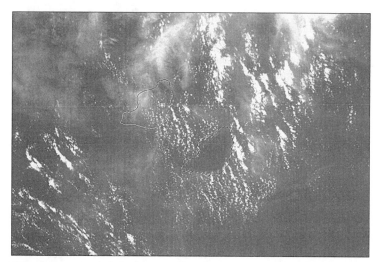

Figure 8-17: I used the lasso tool to draw a new outline around the dark, cloudless portion of the patch. Then I dragged the outline to a different spot in the background.

6. **It's all déjà vu from here.** I chose Select ➪ Feather, entered 6 in the Feather Radius option box — thus allowing the clouds a sufficient range to taper off — and pressed Enter. I then selected the move tool and Alt-dragged the feathered patch over the dark, cloudless rift. Finally, I nudged, nudged, nudged with the arrow keys, and voilà, no more satellite. Figure 8-18 shows $200 million worth of hardware vaporized in less than five minutes.

Figure 8-18: I selected a new bit of cloudy sky and placed it over the formerly cloudless portion of the patch. Satellite? What satellite?

Moving and Duplicating Selections

In the preceding steps, I mentioned that you can move either the selected pixels or the empty selection outline to a new location. Now it's time to examine these techniques in greater depth.

The role of the move tool

To move selected pixels, you have to use the move tool. No longer is it acceptable merely to drag inside the selection with the marquee, lasso, or wand tool, as it was in Photoshop 3 and earlier. If you haven't gotten used to it yet, now is as good a time as any. The move tool is here to stay.

You can select the move tool at any time by pressing V (for *mooV*). The advantage of using the move tool is that there's no chance of deselecting an image or harming the selection outline. Drag inside the selected area to move the selection; drag outside the selection to move the entire layer, selection included. I explain layers in more detail in Chapter 12.

Tip

To access the move tool on a temporary basis, press and hold Ctrl. The move tool remains active as long as you hold Ctrl. This shortcut works when any tool except the hand, pen, or any shape or slice tool is active. Assign this shortcut to memory at your earliest convenience. Believe me, you spend a lot of time Ctrl-dragging in Photoshop.

Making precise movements

Photoshop provides three methods for moving selections in prescribed increments. In each case, the move tool is active, unless otherwise indicated:

✦ First, you can nudge a selection in 1-pixel increments by pressing an arrow key on the keyboard or nudge in 10-pixel increments by pressing Shift with an arrow key. This technique is useful for making precise adjustments to the position of an image.

Tip

To nudge a selected area when the move tool is not active, press Ctrl with an arrow key. Press Ctrl+Shift with an arrow key to move in 10-pixel increments. After the selection is floating — that is, after your first nudge — you can let up on the Ctrl key and use only the arrows (assuming a selection tool is active).

✦ Second, you can press Shift during a drag to constrain a move to a 45-degree direction — that is, horizontally, vertically, or diagonally.

✦ And third, you can use the Info palette to track your movements and to help locate a precise position in the image.

To display the Info palette, shown in Figure 8-19, choose Window ➪ Show Info or press F8. The first section of the Info palette displays the color values of the image area beneath your cursor. When you move a selection, the other eight items in the palette monitor movement, as follows:

✦ **X, Y:** These values show the coordinate position of your cursor. The distance is measured from the upper-left corner of the image in the current unit of measure. The unit of measure in Figure 8-19 is pixels.

✦ **ΔX, ΔY:** These values indicate the distance of your move as measured horizontally and vertically.

✦ **A, D:** The A and D values reflect the angle and direct distance of your drag.

✦ **W, H:** These values reflect the width and height of your selection.

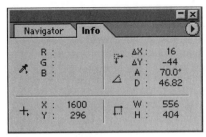

Figure 8-19: The Info palette provides a world of numerical feedback when you move a selection.

Cloning a selection

When you move a selection, you leave a hole in your image in the background color, as shown in the top half of Figure 8-20. If you prefer to leave the original in place during a move, you have to *clone* the selection — that is, create a copy of the selection without upsetting the contents of the Clipboard. Photoshop offers several ways to clone a selection:

✦ **Alt-dragging:** When the move tool is active, press Alt and drag a selection to clone it. The bottom half of Figure 8-20 shows a selection I Alt-dragged three times. (Between clonings, I changed the gray level of each selection to set them apart a little more clearly.)

✦ **Ctrl+Alt-dragging:** If some tool other than the move tool is active, Ctrl+Alt-drag the selection to clone it. This is probably the technique you'll end up using most often.

✦ **Alt+arrowing:** When the move tool is active, press Alt in combination with one of the arrow keys to clone the selection and nudge it one pixel away from the original. If you want to move the image multiple pixels, press Alt+arrow the first time only. Then nudge the clone using the arrow key alone. Otherwise, you'll create a bunch of clones, which can be a pain in the neck to undo.

✦ **Ctrl+Alt+arrowing:** If some other tool is active, press Ctrl and Alt with an arrow key. Again, press only Alt the first time, unless you want to create a string of clones.

✦ **Drag-and-drop:** Like about every other program on the planet, Photoshop lets you clone a selection between documents by dragging it with the move tool from one open window and dropping it in another, as demonstrated in Figure 8-21. As long as you manage to drop into the second window, the original image remains intact and selected in the first window. My advice: Don't worry about exact positioning during a drag-and-drop; first get it into the second window and then worry about placement.

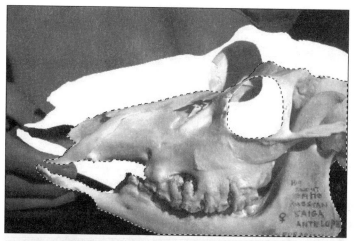

Figure 8-20: When you move a selection, you leave a gaping hole in the selection's wake (top). When you clone an image, you leave a copy of the selection behind. To illustrate this point, I cloned the selection in the bottom image three times.

 Cross-Reference

You can drag-and-drop multiple layers if you link the layers first. For more information on this subject, see Chapter 12.

✦ **Shift-drop:** If the two images are exactly the same size — pixel for pixel — press Shift when dropping the selection to position it in the same spot it occupied in the original image. This is called *registering* the selection.

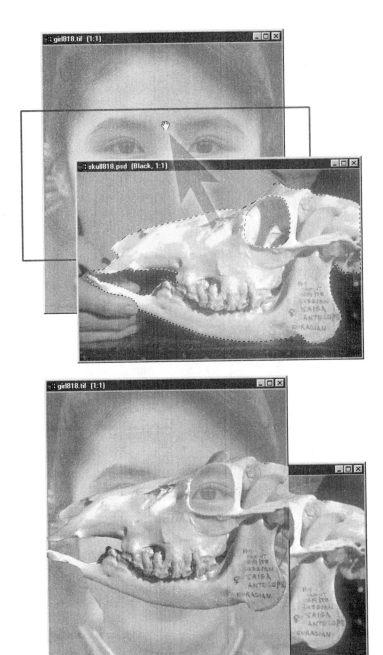

Figure 8-21: Use the move tool to drag a selection from one open window and drop it into another (top). This creates a clone of the selection in the receiving window (bottom).

If an area is selected in the destination image, Shift-dropping positions the selection you're moving in the center of the selection in the destination image. This tip works regardless of whether the two images are the same size.

✦ **Ctrl-drag-and-drop:** Again, if some other tool than the move tool is selected, you must press Ctrl when you drag to move the selected pixels from one window to the other.

Moving a selection outline independently of its contents

After all this talk about the move tool and the Ctrl key, you may be wondering what happens if you drag a selection with the marquee, lasso, or wand. The answer is, you move the selection outline independently of the image. This technique, which I used earlier in this chapter in the steps "Removing an Element from an Image," serves as yet another means to manipulate inaccurate selection outlines. It also enables you to mimic one portion of an image inside another portion of the image or inside a completely different image window.

In the top image in Figure 8-22, I used the marquee tool to drag the skull outline down and to the right, so that it only partially overlapped the skull. I then lightened the new selection, applied a few strokes to set it off from its background, and gave it stripes, as shown in the bottom image. For all I know, this is exactly what a female Russian Saiga antelope looks like.

You can nudge a selection outline independently of its contents by pressing an arrow key when a selection tool is active. Press Shift with an arrow key to move the outline in 10-pixel increments.

For even more selection fun, you can drag-and-drop empty selection outlines between images. Just drag the outline from one image and drop it into another, as demonstrated in the first example of Figure 8-21. The only difference is that only the selection outline gets cloned; the pixels remain behind. This is a great way to copy pixels back and forth between images. You can set up an exact selection outline in Image A, drag it into Image B with the marquee tool, move it over the pixels you want to clone, and Ctrl-drag-and-drop the selection back into Image A. This is slick as hair grease, I'm telling you.

So remember: The selection tools affect the selection outline only. The selection tools never affect the pixels themselves; that's the move tool's job.

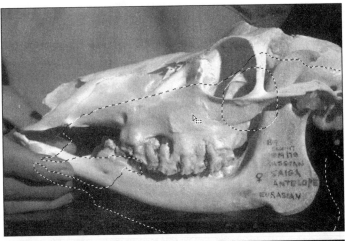

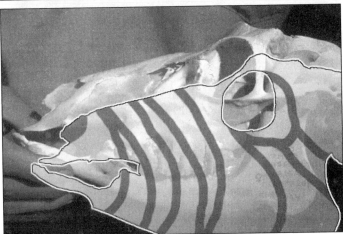

Figure 8-22: Drag a selection with a selection tool to move the outline independently of its image (top). Wherever you drag the selection outline becomes the new selection (bottom).

Scaling or rotating a selection outline

In case you fell asleep during the last two sentences, let me repeat the important part: Selection outlines stay independent — and entirely changeable — as long as a selection tool is active. In addition to moving a selection outline, you can transform it by choosing Select ➪ Transform Selection.

When you select this command, Photoshop displays a transformation boundary framed by eight handles, as shown in Figure 8-23. You can drag the handles to adjust the outline as described in the upcoming list. If you display the Options bar (press Enter), you get access to a slew of mysterious option boxes, as shown at the bottom of the figure. These options take the place of those formerly accessed through the Numeric Transform dialog box. You can enter specific values to relocate, size, rotate, and skew the selection outline precisely.

The handles and Options bar controls work just as they do for the Edit ➪ Free Transform command, which I cover in gripping detail in Chapter 12. To save you the backbreaking chore of flipping ahead four chapters, though, here's the short course:

✦ **Scale:** Drag any of the handles to scale the selection, as shown in Figure 8-23. Shift-drag to scale proportionally, Alt-drag to scale with respect to the origin (labeled in the figure). You can move the origin just by dragging it.

Alternatively, enter a scale percentage in the W (width) and H (height) boxes on the Options bar. By default, Photoshop maintains the original proportions of the outline. If that doesn't suit you, click the Constrain Proportions button between the two boxes.

See that little replica of the transformation boundary near the left end of the Options bar? The black square represents the current origin. You can click the boxes to relocate the origin to one of the handles. Use the X and Y values to change the position of the origin numerically. Click the triangular delta symbol, labeled in Figure 8-23, to measure positioning relative to the transformation origin.

✦ **Rotate:** Enter a value in the Rotate box or drag outside the transformation boundary to rotate the selection, as in the second example in Figure 8-23. The rotation always occurs with respect to the origin.

To rotate the outline by 90 or 180 degrees, right-click the image window and choose the rotation amount you want from the resulting pop-up menu.

✦ **Flip:** You can flip a selection outline by dragging one handle past its opposite handle, but this is a lot of work. The easier way is to right-click inside the image window and choose Flip Horizontal or Flip Vertical from the pop-up menu.

✦ **Skew and distort:** To skew the selection outline, Ctrl-drag a side, top, or bottom handle. Or enter values in the H (horizontal) and V (vertical) skew boxes on the Options bar. To distort the selection, Ctrl-drag a corner handle.

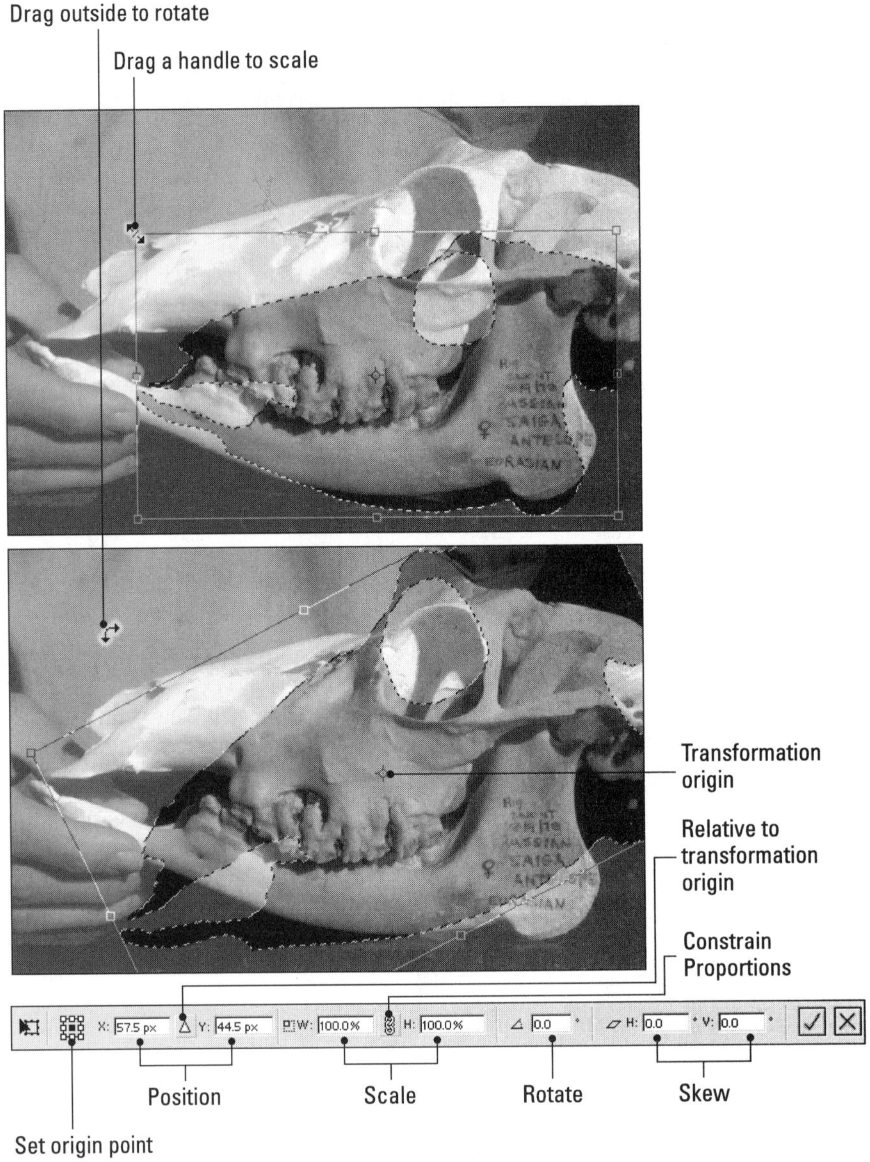
Drag outside to rotate
Drag a handle to scale
Transformation origin
Relative to transformation origin
Constrain Proportions
Position
Scale
Rotate
Skew
Set origin point

Figure 8-23: After choosing Select ➪ Transform Selection, you can scale the selection outline (top) and rotate it (bottom), all without harming the image in the slightest.

When you get the selection outline the way you want it, press Enter or double-click inside the boundary. To cancel the transformation, press Escape.

Alternatively, click the check mark button near the right end of the Options bar to apply the transformation or click the X button to cancel out of the operation.

The untimely demise of floating selections

As you may (or may not) recall, Photoshop 4 bludgeoned floating selections into a state of unconsciousness. While Version 5 didn't entirely kill them, it moved them to the critical list.

In case you're unsure what I'm talking about, a *floating selection* is an element that hovers above the surface of the image. Any time you move a selection or clone it, Photoshop floats the selection onto a temporary layer. This way, you can move the selection or nudge it into position without harming the underlying image. And if you press Backspace, Photoshop deletes the floater rather than filling the selection with the background color.

But that's all there is to floating selections now. The Floating Selection item that used to appear in the Layers palette is a thing of the past, so you don't even know when a selection is floating or not. And the only way to defloat a floater is to deselect it.

Quite unexpectedly, Photoshop still lets you mix a floater with the image behind it by modifying the opacity and blend mode settings. After dragging a selection to float it, choose Edit ⇨ Fade (Ctrl+Shift+F). Then modify the settings inside the Fade dialog box to mix the floater with the background. The process is incredibly nonintuitive, but it works.

How to Draw and Edit Paths

Photoshop's path tools provide the most flexible and precise ways to define a selection short of masking. However, while a godsend to the experienced user, the path tools represent something of a chore to novices and intermediates. Most people take some time to grow comfortable with the pen tool, for example, because it requires you to draw a selection outline one point at a time.

If you're familiar with Illustrator's pen tool and other path-editing functions, you'll find Photoshop's tools nearly identical. Photoshop doesn't provide the breadth of options available in Illustrator, but the basic techniques are the same.

Photoshop 6 includes a new set of path-drawing tools to help smooth out the learning curve for inexperienced users. You can use any of the shape tools — rectangle, rounded rectangle, line, ellipse, polygon, and custom shape — to draw a simple geometric path.

The following pages get you up and running with all the path features. I explain how to draw a path, edit it, convert it to a selection outline, and stroke it with a paint or edit tool. All in all, you learn more about paths than you ever wanted to know.

Paths overview

You create and edit paths by using the various pen tools or shape tools. (Figure 8-2, earlier in this chapter, shows all the path-related tools along with their selection tool counterparts.) Path management options — which enable you to convert paths to selections, fill and stroke paths, and save and delete them — reside in the Paths palette, shown in Figure 8-24.

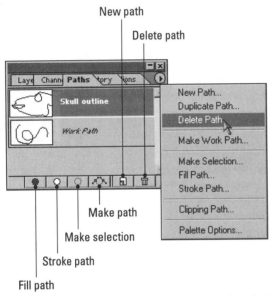

Figure 8-24: To save and organize your paths, display the Paths palette by choosing Window ⇨ Show Paths.

How paths work

Paths differ from normal selections because they exist on the equivalent of a distinct, object-oriented layer that sits in front of the bitmapped image. This setup enables you to edit a path with point-by-point precision with no fear that you'll accidentally mess up the image, as you can when you edit ordinary selection outlines. After you get a path just so, you convert it into a standard selection outline, which you can then use to edit the contents of the image. (I detail this part of the process in the section "Converting and saving paths" later in this chapter.)

The following steps explain the basic process of drawing a selection outline with the path tools. I explain each step in more detail throughout the remainder of this chapter.

STEPS: Creating a Selection with the Path Tools

1. **Draw the path.** Use a pen tool or a shape tool to draw the outline of your prospective selection.

   If your goal is to select multiple areas of the image, draw outlines around all of them. A path can include as many separate segments as you like. Technically, the individual segments in a path are called *subpaths*.

2. **Edit the path.** If the path requires some adjustment, reshape it using the other path tools.

3. **Save the path.** When you get the path exactly as you want it, save the path by choosing the Save Path command from the Paths palette menu. Or double-click the *Work Path* item in the scrolling list.

4. **Convert the path to a selection.** You can make the path a selection outline by choosing the Make Selection command or by pressing Enter on the numeric keypad when a path or selection tool is active.

That's it. After you convert the path to a selection, it works like any of the selection outlines described earlier. You can feather a selection, move it, copy it, clone it, or apply one of the special effects described in future chapters. The path remains intact in case you want to do further editing or use it again.

Sorting through the path tools

Before I get into my long-winded description of how you draw and edit paths, here's a quick introduction to the path tools. First up, the tools on the pen tool flyout:

Pen: Use the pen tool to draw paths in Photoshop one point at a time. Click to create a corner in a path; drag to make a smooth point that results in a continuous arc. (Never fear, I explain this tool *ad nauseam* in the "Drawing paths with the pen tool" section later in this chapter.) You can select the pen tool by pressing P; press P again to toggle to the freeform pen, described next. (As always, the shortcuts assume that you turned off the Use Shift Key for Tool Switch option in the Preferences dialog box.)

Freeform pen: Drag with this tool to create a path that automatically follows the twists and turns of your drag. Simplicity at its best; control at its lowest. Luckily, you can turn around and edit the path after you initially draw it.

The magnetic pen, which debuted in Photoshop 5, evidently wasn't a huge hit on the path tool circuit. In Version 6, the magnetic pen no longer appears in the toolbox. But if you select the freeform pen and then select the Magnetic check box on the Options bar, the freeform pen does a dandy impression of the magnetic pen. Click the edge of the foreground element you want to select and then move the cursor along the edge of the shape. Photoshop automatically assigns points as it deems appropriate.

Add anchor point: Click an existing path to add a point to it.

Delete anchor point: Click an existing point in a path to delete the point without creating a break in the path's outline.

Convert point: Click or drag a point to convert it to a corner or smooth point. You also can drag a handle to convert the point. To access the convert point tool, press Alt when the pen is active. Press Ctrl+Alt when an arrow tool (explained in the next section) is active. (The terms *anchor point, smooth point,* and others associated with drawing paths are explained in the upcoming section.)

You can use a pen tool to add, delete, and convert points, too, providing that you turn on the Auto Add/Delete check box on the Options bar. Pass the cursor over a segment in a selected path to toggle to the add anchor point tool; move the cursor over a point to get the delete anchor point tool. Press Alt over a point to get the convert point tool.

If all you need is a simple, geometric path, you can save time by creating the path with the new shape tools. I cover these tools in detail in Chapter 14, so I won't repeat everything here. Just know that after you select a shape tool, you shift it into path-drawing mode by clicking the Work Path button on the Options bar, labeled in Figure 8-25. (The pen that appears on the button face serves as a reminder that you're in path country.) If you don't see the buttons, you're already in path mode. Photoshop sets the shape tools to that mode automatically if you select them while working on an existing path.

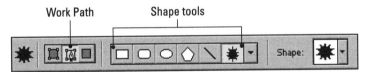

Figure 8-25: Click the Work Path icon to draw paths with the new shape tools.

As you draw, Photoshop automatically adds whatever points are needed. You only need to worry about selecting a path overlap button, which determines how the program regards overlapping areas when you turn the path into a selection. See the next section to find out which button to choose when.

After you create a path, you can select it or edit it by using the two tools on the flyout directly above the pen tools flyout:

> **Path component selection tool (black arrow):** This tool, new to Photoshop 6, selects an entire path. Just click inside the path to select it. If you created subpaths, the tool selects only the one underneath your cursor. You also use this tool to select vector objects, as explained in Chapter 14.

> **Direct selection tool (white arrow):** This tool permits you to drag points and handles to reshape a path. You can access the tool when any other path tool is active by pressing and holding Ctrl. And you can Alt-click inside a path to select the entire path without switching to the path component selection (black arrow) tool.

Note

From this point on, I refer to these two tools as the black arrow and white arrow. First off, because we Photoshop users are a visually oriented lot, I'm guessing that you can find the right tool more quickly if I say "click with the black arrow" or "drag with the white arrow" than if I use the technical tool names. Second, the nicknames save some page space, enabling me to fill your head with even more jaw-dropping insights than would otherwise be possible.

You can access the arrows from the keyboard by pressing A. You know the drill: Press A to switch to the tool that's currently active; press A again to toggle to the other tool. (Add Shift if you turned on the Use Shift Key for Tool Switch option in the Preferences dialog box.)

Drawing paths with the pen tool

When drawing with the regular pen tool, you build a path by creating individual points. Photoshop automatically connects the points with segments, which are simply straight or curved lines.

Note

Adobe prefers the term *anchor points* rather than *points* because the points anchor the path into place. But most folks just call 'em points. I mean, *all* points associated with paths are anchor points, so it's not like there's some potential for confusion.

All paths in Photoshop are *Bézier* (pronounced bay-zee-ay) paths, meaning they rely on the same mathematical curve definitions that make up the core of the PostScript printer language. The Bézier curve model allows for zero, one, or two levers to be associated with each point in a path. These levers, labeled in Figure 8-26, are called *Bézier control handles* or simply *handles*. You can move each handle in relation to a point, enabling you to bend and tug at a curved segment like it's a piece of soft wire.

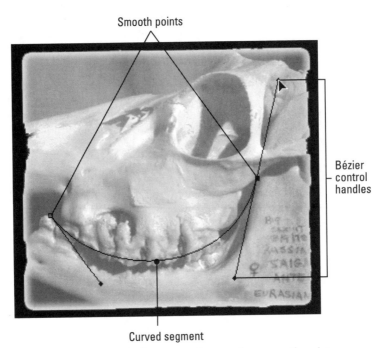

Figure 8-26: Drag with the pen tool to create a smooth point flanked by two Bézier control handles.

The following list summarizes how you can use the pen tool to build paths in Photoshop:

✦ **Adding segments:** To build a path, create one point after another until the path is the desired length and shape. Photoshop automatically draws a segment between each new point and its predecessor. (The next section gets specific about how you use the tool to create points.)

✦ **Closing the path:** If you plan to convert the path to a selection outline, you need to complete the outline by clicking again on the first point in the path. Every point will then have one segment entering it and another segment exiting it. Such a path is called a *closed path* because it forms one continuous outline.

✦ **Leaving the path open:** If you plan to apply the Stroke Path command (explained later), you may not want to close a path. To leave the path open, so it has a specific beginning and ending, deactivate the path by saving it (choose the Save Paths command from the Paths palette menu).

✦ **Extending an open path:** To reactivate an open path, click or drag one of its endpoints. Photoshop draws a segment between the endpoint and the next point you create.

✦ **Joining two open subpaths:** To join one open subpath with another, click or drag an endpoint in the first subpath and then click or drag an endpoint in the second.

✦ **Specifying path overlap:** You can set the path tools to one of four settings, which control how Photoshop treats overlapping areas in a path when you convert the path to a selection.

To make your will known, click one of the buttons near the left end of the Options bar. The buttons, which are labeled in Figure 8-27, become available only after you make your first click or drag with a pen tool. And the button you click remains in effect until you choose another button.

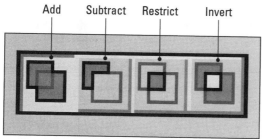

Figure 8-27: Click one of these buttons on the Options bar to control how Photoshop treats overlapping areas when you convert a path to a selection.

Note

These buttons also appear when you draw paths with the shape tools. With either set of tools, your choices are as follows:

• **Add:** Select this button if you want all areas, overlapping or not, to be selected.

• **Subtract:** Select this button to draw a subpath that eats a hole in an existing path. Any areas that you enclose with the subpath are not selected. Note that if you select a path and the Make Selection command is dimmed in the Paths palette, it's probably because you drew the path with the subtract option in force.

• **Restrict path area:** The opposite of Invert, this option selects *only* overlapping areas.

• **Invert:** Any overlapping regions are not included in the selection.

You can change the overlap setting for a subpath after you draw it if necessary. Click inside the path with the black arrow tool and then click the overlap button for the setting you want to use.

✦ **Deactivating paths:** At any time, you can click the check-mark button at the right end of the Options bar or press Enter to *dismiss* — deactivate — the path. When you do, Photoshop hides the path from view. To retrieve the path, click its name in the Paths palette. Be careful with this one, though: If you dismiss an unsaved path and then start drawing a new path, you can lose the dismissed one. For more details, see "Converting and saving paths," later in this chapter.

✦ **Hiding paths:** If you merely want to hide paths from view, press Ctrl+H, which hides selections, guides, and other screen elements as well. Or choose View ⇨ Show ⇨ Target Paths to toggle the path display on and off. To select which items you want to hide with Ctrl+H, choose View ⇨ Show ⇨ Show Options.

Tip

To get a better sense of how the pen tool works, turn on the Rubber Band check box on the Options bar. (Press Enter to display the bar and the check box.) This tells Photoshop to draw an animated segment between the last point drawn and the cursor. Unless you're an old pro and the connecting segment gets in your face, there's no reason not to select Rubber Band. (Besides, what with the '70s being so hot with the teenies, the Rubber Band check box makes the pen tool seem, well, kind of funky. Consider it another chance to bond with today's youth.)

The anatomy of points and segments

Points in a Bézier path act as little road signs. Each point steers the path by specifying how a segment enters it and how another segment exits it. You specify the identity of each little road sign by clicking, dragging, or Alt-dragging with the pen tool. The following items explain the specific kinds of points and segments you can create in Photoshop. See Figure 8-28 for examples.

✦ **Corner point:** Click with the pen tool to create a *corner point*, which represents the corner between two straight segments in a path.

✦ **Straight segment:** Click at two different locations to create a straight segment between two corner points. Shift-click to draw a 45-degree-angle segment between the new corner point and its predecessor.

✦ **Smooth point:** Drag to create a smooth point with two symmetrical Bézier control handles. A *smooth point* ensures that one segment meets with another in a continuous arc.

✦ **Curved segment:** Drag at two different locations to create a curved segment between two smooth points.

✦ **Curved segment followed by straight:** After drawing a curved segment, Alt-click the smooth point you just created to delete the forward Bézier control handle. This converts the smooth point to a corner point with one handle. Then click at a different location to append a straight segment to the end of the curved segment.

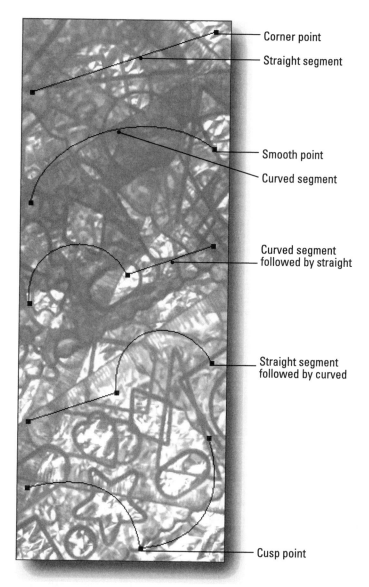

Corner point

Straight segment

Smooth point

Curved segment

Curved segment
followed by straight

Straight segment
followed by curved

Cusp point

Figure 8-28: The different kinds of points and
segments you can draw with the pen tool

✦ **Straight segment followed by curved:** After drawing a straight segment, drag
from the corner point you just created to add a Bézier control handle. Then
drag again at a different location to append a curved segment to the end of
the straight segment.

    ✦ **Cusp point:** After drawing a curved segment, Alt-drag from the smooth point you just created to redirect the forward Bézier control handle, converting the smooth point to a corner point with two independent handles, sometimes known as a *cusp point.* Then drag again at a new location to append a curved segment that proceeds in a different direction than the previous curved segment.

Going freeform

If the pen tool is too much work, try the freeform pen tool, which is just a press of the P key away from the standard pen. As you drag, Photoshop tracks the motion of the cursor with a continuous line. After you release the mouse button, the program automatically assigns and positions the points and segments needed to create the Bézier path.

Tip

You can draw straight segments with the freeform pen: As you're dragging, press and hold Alt. Then click around to create points. When you're finished drawing straight segments, drag again and release Alt. (If you release Alt when the mouse button is not pressed, Photoshop completes the path.)

Alas, automation is rarely perfect. (If it were, what need would these machines have for us?) When the program finishes its calculations, a path may appear riddled with far too many points or equipped with too few.

Fortunately, you can adjust the performance of the freeform pen to accommodate your personal drawing style using the Curve Fit control on the Options bar. When the freeform pen is active, press Enter to highlight the Curve Fit value. You can enter any value between 0.5 and 10, which Photoshop interprets in screen pixels. The default value of 2, for example, instructs the program to ignore any jags in your mouse movements that do not exceed 2 pixels in length or width. Setting the value to 0.5 makes the freeform pen extremely sensitive; setting the value to 10 smoothes the roughest of gestures.

A Curve Fit from 2 to 4 is generally adequate for most folks, but you should experiment to determine the best setting. Like the magic wand's Tolerance setting, you can't alter the Curve Fit value for a path after you've drawn it. Photoshop calculates the points for a path only once, after your release the mouse button.

Going magnetic

As I mentioned earlier, the official magnetic pen is gone from the Photoshop 6 toolbox but lives on. To use it, select the freeform pen tool and then select the Magnetic check box on the Options bar.

The magnetic pen works like a combination of the magnetic lasso and the freeform pen. As with the magnetic lasso, you begin by clicking anywhere along the edge of the image element you want to select. (For a pertinent blast from the past, see Figure 8-5.) Then move the cursor — no need to drag — around the perimeter of the element and watch Photoshop do its work. To set an anchor point, click. When you come full circle, click the point where you started to complete the path.

Photoshop

6

You can create straight segments by Alt-clicking, just as you can when using the freeform pen without Magnetic turned on. And the Curve Fit option (on the Options bar) controls the smoothness of the path. Lower values trace the edges more carefully; higher values result in fewer points and smoother edges.

To uncover the remaining options for the magnetic pen, click the tool's icon on the Options bar, as shown in Figure 8-29. A drop-down palette gives you access to the Width, Contrast, Frequency, and Stylus Pressure options, all of which are lifted right out of the magnetic lasso playbook. Read "Modifying the magnetic lasso options" near the beginning of this chapter for complete information.

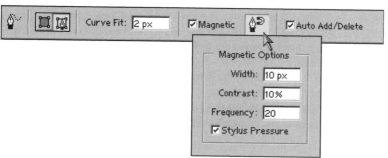

Figure 8-29: While the freeform pen is active, select the Magnetic check box to access the magnetic pen. Click the adjacent icon to display additional options.

Editing paths

If you take time to master the default pen tool, you'll find yourself drawing accurate paths more and more frequently. But you'll never get it right 100 percent of the time — or even 50 percent of the time. And when you rely on the freeform or magnetic pen tools, the results are never dead on. From your first timid steps until you develop into a seasoned pro, you'll rely heavily on Photoshop's capability to *reshape* paths by moving points and handles, adding and deleting points, and converting points to change the curvature of segments. So don't worry too much if your path looks like an erratic stitch on the forehead of Frankenstein's monster. The path-edit tools provide all the second chances you'll ever need.

Reshaping paths

The white arrow tool — known in official Adobe circles as the direct selection tool — represents the foremost path-reshaping function in Photoshop. To select this tool from the keyboard, first press A to select the new black arrow tool and then press A again to toggle to the white arrow. Or just Alt-click the black arrow tool in the toolbox. (You use the black arrow to select, relocate, and duplicate entire paths or subpaths, as explained in the upcoming section "Moving and cloning paths.")

Tip

Press and hold Ctrl to access the white arrow tool temporarily when one of the pen or path-edit tools are selected. When you release Ctrl, the cursor returns to the selected tool. This is a great way to edit a path while you're drawing it.

However you put your hands on the white arrow, you can perform any of the following functions with it:

✦ **Selecting points:** Click a point to select it independently of other points in a path. Shift-click to select an additional point, even if the point belongs to a different subpath than other selected points. Alt-click a path to select all its points in one fell swoop. You can even marquee points by dragging in a rectangle around them. You cannot, however, apply commands from the Select menu, such as All or None, to the selection of paths.

✦ **Drag selected points:** To move one or more points, select them and then drag one of the selected points. All selected points move the same distance and direction. When you move a point while a neighboring point remains stationary, the segment between the two points shrinks, stretches, and bends to accommodate the change in distance. Segments located between two selected or deselected points remain unchanged during a move.

Tip

You can move selected points in 1-pixel increments by pressing arrow keys. If both a portion of the image and points in a path are selected, the arrow keys move the points only. Because paths reside on a higher layer, they take precedence in all functions that might concern them.

✦ **Drag a straight segment:** You also can reshape a path by dragging its segments. When you drag a straight segment, the two corner points on either side of the segment move as well. As illustrated in Figure 8-30, the neighboring segments stretch, shrink, or bend to accommodate the drag.

Caution

This technique works best with straight segments drawn with the default pen tool. Segments created by Alt-clicking with the freeform or magnetic pen may include trace control handles that make Photoshop think the segment is actually curved.

✦ **Drag a curved segment:** When you drag a curved segment, you stretch, shrink, or bend that segment, as demonstrated in Figure 8-31.

Tip

When you drag a curved segment, drag from the middle of the segment, approximately equidistant from both its points. This method provides the best leverage and ensures that the segment doesn't go flying off in some weird direction you hadn't anticipated.

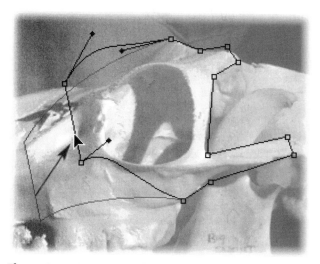

Figure 8-30: Drag a straight segment to move the segment and change the length, direction, and curvature of the neighboring segments.

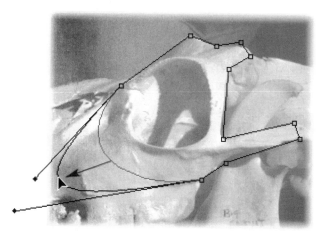

Figure 8-31: Drag a curved segment to change the curvature of that segment only and leave the neighboring segments unchanged.

✦ **Drag a Bézier control handle:** Select a point and drag either of its Bézier control handles to change the curvature of the corresponding segment without moving any of the points in the path. If the point is a smooth point, moving one handle moves both handles in the path. If you want to move a smooth handle independently of its partner, you must use the convert point tool, as discussed in the "Converting points" section later in this chapter.

Adding and deleting points and segments

The quantity of points and segments in a path is forever subject to change. Whether a path is closed or open, you can reshape it by adding and deleting points, which, in turn, forces the addition or deletion of a segment:

✦ **Appending a point to the end of an open path:** If a path is open, you can activate one of its endpoints by clicking or dragging it with the pen tool, depending on the identity of the endpoint and whether you want the next segment to be straight or curved. Photoshop is then prepared to draw a segment between the endpoint and the next point you create.

✦ **Closing an open path:** You also can use the technique I just described to close an open path. Select one endpoint, click or drag it with the pen tool to activate it, and then click or drag the opposite endpoint. Photoshop draws a segment between the two endpoints, closing the path and eliminating both endpoints by converting them to *interior points,* which simply means the points are bound on both sides by segments.

✦ **Joining two open subpaths:** You can join two open subpaths to create one longer open path. To do so, activate an endpoint of the first subpath and then, using the pen tool, click or drag an endpoint of the second subpath.

✦ **Inserting a point in a segment:** Using the add point tool, click anywhere along an open or closed path to insert a point and divide the segment into two segments. Photoshop automatically inserts a corner or smooth point, depending on its reading of the path. If the point does not exactly meet your needs, use the convert point tool to change it.

In Photoshop 6, you can no longer pick up the add point tool pressing the plus key as in versions past. Instead, Version 6 gives you this alternative option: When a pen tool is active, select the Auto Add/Delete check box on the Options bar. Now, whenever you pass the pen tool cursor over a segment, you see the little plus sign next to your cursor, indicating that the add point tool is temporarily in the house. This trick works only if the path is selected, however.

✦ **Deleting a point and breaking the path:** The simplest way to delete a point is to select it with the white arrow and press Delete or Clear. (You also can choose Edit ➪ Clear, though why you would want to expend so much effort is beyond me.) When you delete an interior point, you delete both segments associated with that point, resulting in a break in the path. If you delete an endpoint from an open path, you delete the single segment associated with the point.

✦ **Removing a point without breaking the path:** Select the remove point tool and click a point in an open or closed path to delete the point and draw a new segment between the two points that neighbor it. The remove point tool ensures that no break occurs in a path.

Photoshop
6

Tip

To access the remove point tool when using one of the pen tools, select the Auto Add/Delete check box on the Options bar and then hover your cursor over a selected interior point in an existing path. You see the minus sign next to the cursor, indicating that the remove point tool is active. Click the point and it goes away. Alternately, you can remove a point when the add point tool is active by Alt-clicking, and vice versa.

✦ **Deleting a segment:** You can delete a single interior segment from a path without affecting any point. To do so, first click outside the path with the white arrow tool to deselect the path. Then click the segment you want to delete and press Delete. When you delete an interior segment, you create a break in your path.

Converting points

Photoshop lets you change the identity of an interior point. You can convert a corner point to a smooth point and vice versa. You perform all point conversions using the convert point tool as follows:

✦ **Smooth to corner:** Click an existing smooth point to convert it to a corner point with no Bézier control handle.

✦ **Smooth to cusp:** Drag one of the handles of a smooth point to move it independently of the other, thus converting the smooth point to a cusp.

✦ **Corner to smooth:** Drag from a corner point to convert it to a smooth point with two symmetrical Bézier control handles.

✦ **Cusp to smooth:** Drag one of the handles of a cusp point to lock both handles back into alignment, thus converting the cusp to a smooth point.

Tip

Press Alt to access the convert point tool temporarily when one of the three pen tools is active and positioned over a selected point. To do the same when an arrow tool is active, press Ctrl+Alt.

Transforming paths

In addition to all the aforementioned path-altering techniques, you can scale, rotate, skew, and otherwise transform paths using the following techniques:

✦ To transform all subpaths in a group — such as both the eye and skull outline in the first example of Figure 8-32 — select either arrow tool and click off a path to make sure all paths are deselected. Then choose Edit ➪ Free Transform Path.

✦ To transform a single subpath independently of others in a group, click it with the black arrow and then select the Show Bounding Box check box on the Options bar. Or click the path with the white arrow and choose Edit ➪ Free Transform Path.

Photoshop 6

✦ Photoshop even lets you transform some points independently of others inside a single path, as demonstrated in the second example of Figure 8-32. Just use the white arrow to select the points you want to modify and then choose Edit ⇨ Free Transform Points.

Tip

The keyboard shortcut for all of these operations is Ctrl+T. If you select an independent path — or specific points inside a path — press Ctrl+Alt+T to transform a duplicate of the path and leave the original unaffected.

Rotate cursor   Transformation origin

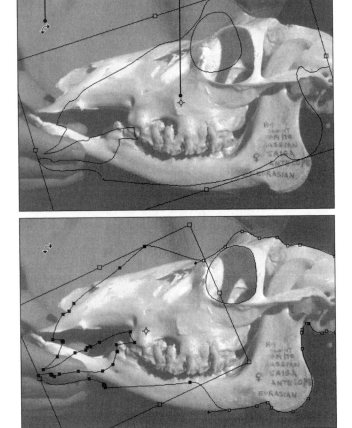

Figure 8-32: To transform multiple paths at once (top), deselect all paths and press Ctrl+T. You can alternatively transform independent paths or points by selecting them and pressing Ctrl+T (bottom).

In an attempt to conserve tree matter — which is being wasted liberally enough in this tome — I explain the larger topic of transformation in one central location, the "Applying Transformations" section of Chapter 12. Even so, here's a brief rundown of your transformation options after you press Ctrl+T:

✦ **Scale:** To scale a path, drag one of the eight square handles that adorn the transformation boundary. Alt-drag a handle to scale with respect to the origin point. You can move the origin by dragging it or by clicking one of the boxes in the little bounding box icon at the left end of the Options bar.

✦ **Rotate:** Drag outside the boundary to rotate the paths or points, as demonstrated in Figure 8-32.

✦ **Flip:** Right-click to access a pop-up menu of transformation options. Choose Flip Horizontal or Flip Vertical to create a mirror image of the path.

✦ **Skew:** Ctrl-drag one of the side handles to slant the paths. Press Shift along with Ctrl to constrain the slant along a consistent axis.

✦ **Distort:** Ctrl-drag one of the corner handles to distort the paths.

✦ **Perspective:** Ctrl+Shift+Alt-drag a corner handle to achieve a perspective effect.

You can't take advantage of the distortion or perspective features when individual points are selected. These techniques apply to whole paths only.

✦ **Numerical transformations:** If you need to transform a path by a very specific amount, use the controls on the Options bar, which are the same ones you get when transforming a regular selection. Modify the values as desired and press Enter. (Figure 8-23 earlier in this chapter labels the options.)

When you finishing stretching and distorting your paths, press Enter or double-click inside the boundary to apply the transformation. You also can click the checkmark button at the right end of the Options bar. To undo the last transformation inside the transform mode, press Ctrl+Z. Or bag the whole thing by pressing Escape.

To repeat the last transformation on another path, press Ctrl+Shift+T.

Moving and cloning paths

You can relocate and duplicate paths as follows:

✦ **Clone a path:** Click inside the path with the black arrow tool to select it. To select multiple subpaths, Shift-click them. Then Alt-drag to clone all selected paths.

✦ **Move a path:** After selecting the path with the black arrow, drag the path to its new home.

✦ **Align and distribute paths:** You can align two or more paths by selecting them with the black arrow and then clicking an alignment button on the Options bar. To space the paths evenly across the image, click one of the distribution buttons, which are shown in Figure 8-33. Press Enter or click the check-mark button on the Options bar to apply the transformation.

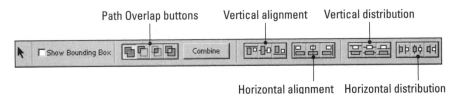

Figure 8-33: You can now align and distribute multiple selected paths, just as you can layers and vector objects.

Merging and deleting paths

When the black arrow is selected, the Options bar contains a Combine buttons (see Figure 8-33). Clicking this button merges all selected subpaths into one. When Photoshop combines the subpaths, it does so according to which path overlap options were active when you drew the subpaths. Remember, you can select a subpath with the black arrow to change its overlap setting if necessary. Just click inside the subpath and then click the appropriate overlap button on the Options bar (see Figure 8-33). Refer to the earlier section, "Drawing paths with the pen tool," for more information about overlap options.

To get rid of a path, click inside it with the black arrow or drag around it with the white arrow. Then press Delete. That path is outta here.

Filling paths

After you finish drawing a path, you can convert it to a selection outline — as described in the upcoming "Converting paths to selections" section — or you can paint it. You can paint the interior of the path by choosing the Fill Path command from the Paths palette menu, or you can paint the outline of the path by choosing Stroke Path. In either case, Photoshop applies the fill on the active image layer.

The Fill Path command works much like Edit ⇨ Fill. After drawing a path, choose the Fill Path command or Alt-click the fill path icon in the lower-left corner of the palette (the one that looks like a filled circle). Photoshop displays a slight variation of the Fill dialog box discussed in Chapter 6; the only difference is the inclusion of two

Rendering options. Enter a value in the Feather Radius option box to blur the edges of the fill, as if the path were a selection with a feathered outline. Select the Anti-aliased check box to slightly soften the outline of the filled area.

If you select one or more subpaths, the Fill Path command changes to Fill Subpaths, enabling you to fill the selected subpaths only. The fill path icon also affects only the selected subpaths.

When applying the fill, Photoshop adheres to the overlap option you used when creating the path. Suppose that you draw two round paths, one fully inside the other. If you drew both circles with the Add overlap option active, both circles get filled. If you drew the interior circle with the Invert option active, Photoshop fills only the area between the two paths, resulting in the letter *O*.

If the Fill Path command fills only part or none of the path, the path probably falls outside the selection outline. Choose Select ➪ Deselect (Ctrl+D) to deselect the image and then choose the Fill Path command again.

Painting along a path

Unlike the Fill Path command, which bears a strong resemblance to Edit ➪ Fill, the Stroke Path command is altogether different from Edit ➪ Stroke. Edit ➪ Stroke creates outlines and arrowheads, whereas the Stroke Path command enables you to paint a brush stroke along the contours of a path. This may not sound like a big deal at first, but this feature enables you to combine the spontaneity of the paint and edit tools with the structure and precision of a path.

To paint a path, choose the Stroke Path command from the Paths palette menu to display the Stroke Path dialog box shown in Figure 8-34. In this dialog box, you can choose the paint or edit tool with which you want to stroke the path (which only means to paint a brush stroke along a path). Photoshop drags the chosen tool along the exact route of the path, retaining any tool or brush shape settings that were in force when you chose the tool.

You can also display the Stroke Path dialog box by Alt-clicking on the stroke path icon, the second icon at the bottom of the Paths palette (labeled back in Figure 8-24). If you prefer to bypass the dialog box, select a paint or edit tool and then either click the stroke path icon or simply press Enter. Instead of displaying the dialog box, Photoshop assumes that you want to use the selected tool and strokes away. If any tool but a paint or edit tool is active, Photoshop strokes the path using the tool you previously selected in the Stroke Path dialog box.

If you select one or more subpaths, the Stroke Path command becomes a Stroke Subpath command. Photoshop then strokes only the selected path, rather than all paths saved under the current name.

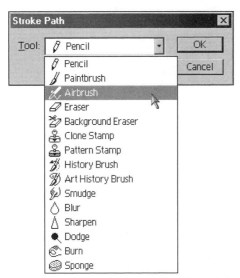

Figure 8-34: Select the paint or edit tool that you want Photoshop to use to stroke the path.

The following steps walk you through a little project I created by stroking paths with the paintbrush and smudge tools. Figures 8-35 through 8-37 show the progression and eventual outcome of the image.

STEPS: Stroking Paths with Paint and Edit Tools

1. **After opening a low-resolution version of a hurricane image, I drew the zigzag path shown in Figure 8-35.** As you can see, the path extends from the eye of the hurricane. I drew the path starting at the eye and working upward, which is important because Photoshop strokes a path in the same direction as you draw the path.

2. **I saved the path.** I double-clicked the *Work Path* item in the Paths palette, entered a name for my path, and pressed Enter.

3. **I used the Brush drop-down palette to create three custom brush shapes.** Each one had a Roundness value of 40. The largest brush had a diameter of 16, the next largest had a diameter of 10, and the smallest had a diameter of 4.

4. **I selected the paintbrush and pressed Enter to display the Options bar.** Then I opened the Brush Dynamics palette (by clicking the brush icon on the right end of the Options bar) and set the Color option to Fade, entering a Fade value of 400. This option fades the brush stroke from the foreground color to the background color over the course of your drag, as explained in Chapter 5.

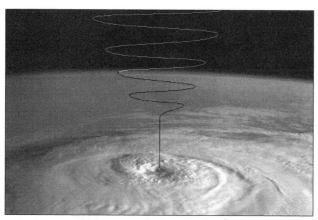

Figure 8-35: I drew this path starting at the eye of the hurricane and working my way upward.

5. **I stroked the path with the paintbrush three times using the Stroke Path command.** I changed the foreground and background colors for each stroke. The first time, I used the largest brush shape and stroked the path from gray to white; the second time, I changed to the middle brush shape and stroked the path from black to white; and the final time, I used the smallest brush shape and stroked the path from white to black. The result of all this stroking is shown in Figure 8-36.

6. **Next, I created two clones of the zigzag path by Alt-dragging the path with the black arrow tool.** I pressed Shift while dragging to ensure the paths aligned horizontally. I then clicked in an empty portion of the image window to deselect all paths, so they appeared as shown in Figure 8-36. This enabled me to stroke them all simultaneously in Step 9.

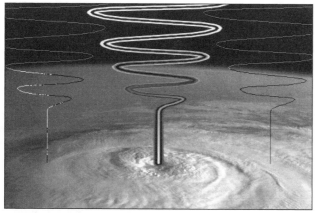

Figure 8-36: After stroking the path three times with the paintbrush tool, I cloned the path twice.

7. **I created a 60-pixel version of my brush shape and reduced its Hardness value to 0 percent.** I then painted a single white spot at the bottom of each of the new paths. I painted a black spot at the bottom of the original path.

8. **I selected the smudge tool, set the Pressure value to 98 percent, and selected a brush with a radius of 16 pixels.** At this setting, the tool has a tremendous range, but it eventually fades out.

9. **I pressed Enter on the numeric keypad to apply the smudge tool to all three paths at once.** The finished image appears in Figure 8-37.

Figure 8-37: I stroked all three paths with the smudge tool set to 98 percent pressure to achieve this unusual extraterrestrial-departure effect. At least, I guess that's what it is. It could also be giant space Slinkys probing the planet's surface. Hard to say.

Tip

If you're feeling really precise — I think they have a clinical term for that — you can specify the location of every single blob of paint laid down in an image. When you deselect the Spacing value in the Brush Options dialog box, Photoshop applies a single blob of paint for each point in a path. If this isn't sufficient control, I'm a monkey's uncle. (What a terrible thing to say about one's nephew!)

Converting and saving paths

Photoshop provides two commands to switch between paths and selections, both of which are located in the Paths palette menu. The Make Selection command converts a path to a selection outline; the Make Path command converts a selection to a path. Regardless of how you create a path, you can save it with the current image, which enables you not only to reuse the path, but also to hide and display it at will.

Converting paths to selections

When you choose the Make Selection command or Alt-click the make selection icon (which looks like a dotted circle, as shown back in Figure 8-24), Photoshop displays the dialog box shown in Figure 8-38. You can specify whether to antialias or feather the selection and to what degree. You can also instruct Photoshop to combine the prospective selection outline with any existing selection in the image. The Operation options correspond to the keyboard functions discussed in the "Manually adding and subtracting" section earlier in this chapter.

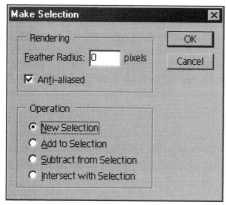

Figure 8-38: When you choose the Make Selection command, you have the option of combining the path with an existing selection.

Photoshop offers several alternative ways to convert a path to a selection outline, all of which are more convenient than the Make Selection command:

✦ **Press Ctrl+Enter:** As long as a path, shape, or selection tool is active, this keyboard shortcut converts the path to a selection. Note that this is a change from earlier versions of Photoshop, when pressing Enter on the numeric keypad did the trick. In this version, you have to press Ctrl, but the regular old Enter key works as well as Enter on the numeric keypad.

✦ **Ctrl-click the path name:** If a tool other than a path, shape, or selection tool is active, you can Ctrl-click the name of a path in the Paths palette. The path needn't be active.

✦ **Ctrl+Shift+Enter or Ctrl+Shift-click:** To add the path to an existing selection, press Shift with one of the previous techniques.

✦ **Alt-Enter or Ctrl+Alt-click:** Naturally, if you can add, you can subtract.

✦ **Shift+Alt+Enter or Ctrl+Shift+Alt-click:** Now we're starting to get into some obscure stuff, but what's possible is possible. You select the intersection of a path and a selection outline by pressing a whole mess of keys.

All these techniques offer the advantage of hiding the path when converting the path to a selection, giving you full, unobstructed access to your selection outline.

Caution

By contrast, the Make Selection command leaves the path on screen in front of the converted selection. If you try to copy, cut, delete, or nudge the selection, you perform the operation on the path instead.

Converting selections to paths

You turn a selection into a path by choosing the Make Work Path command from the Paths palette. When you choose the command, Photoshop produces a dialog box containing a single option, Tolerance. Unlike the Tolerance options you've encountered so far, this one is accurate to ¹⁄₁₀ pixel and has nothing to do with colors or brightness values. Rather, it works like the Curve Fit option for the freeform pen and magnetic pen. That is, it permits you to specify Photoshop's sensitivity to twists and turns in a selection outline. The value you enter determines how far the path can vary from the original selection. The lowest possible value, 0.5, not only ensures that Photoshop retains every nuance of the selection, but also can result in overly complicated paths with an abundance of points. If you enter the highest value, 10, Photoshop rounds the path and uses few points. If you plan on editing the path, you probably won't want to venture any lower than 2.0, the default setting.

To bypass the Make Work Path dialog box and turn your selection into a path using the current Tolerance settings, click the make path icon at the bottom of the Paths palette. (It's labeled back in Figure 8-24.)

Saving paths with an image

As I mentioned at the beginning of the paths discussion, saving a path is an integral step in the path-creation process. You can store every path you draw and keep it handy in case you decide later to reselect an area. Because Photoshop defines paths as compact mathematical equations, they take up virtually no room when you save an image to disk.

You save one or more paths by choosing the Save Path command from the Paths palette menu or by simply double-clicking the italicized *Work Path* item in the scrolling list. After you perform the save operation, during which you name the path, the path name appears in upright characters in the palette. A path listed in the palette can include any number of separate paths. In fact, if you save a path and then set about drawing another one, Photoshop automatically adds the new path in with the saved path. To start a new path under a new name, you first must hide the existing path. Or click the new path icon—the little page at the bottom of the Paths palette—to establish an independent path.

To hide paths in Photoshop 6, you have two options. You can click the empty portion of the scrolling list below the last saved path name or click the check-mark button at the far right end of the Options bar. You can even hide unsaved paths in this way. If you hide an unsaved path and then begin drawing a new one, however, the unsaved path is deleted, never to return again.

Importing and Exporting Paths

Paths come in handy not only for working inside Photoshop, but also for importing images into drawing programs, such as Illustrator and FreeHand, and into page-layout programs, such as InDesign. By saving a path as a clipping path, you can mask regions of an image so that it appears transparent when placed in other programs that support clipping paths.

In addition, you can swap paths directly with the most recent versions of Illustrator and FreeHand. That way, you can take advantage of the more advanced path-creation features found in those programs.

The last few sections of this chapter explain these added uses for your Photoshop paths.

Swapping paths with Illustrator

You can exchange paths between Photoshop and Illustrator or FreeHand by using the Clipboard. This special cross-application compatibility feature expands and simplifies a variety of path-editing functions.

For example, suppose that you want to scale and rotate a path. Select the path in Photoshop with the black arrow tool and copy it to the Clipboard (Ctrl+C). Then switch to Illustrator, paste the path, and edit as desired. About 95 percent of Illustrator's capabilities are devoted to the task of editing paths, so you have many more options at your disposal in Illustrator than in Photoshop. When you finish modifying the path, copy it again, switch to Photoshop, and paste.

When you paste an Illustrator path into Photoshop, you have the option of rendering the path to pixels (just as you can render an Illustrator EPS document using File ⇨ Open), keeping the path information intact, or creating a new shape layer. Select the Paths radio button to add the copied paths to the selected item in the Paths palette. (If no item is selected, Photoshop creates a new *Work Path* item.) You can then use the path to create a selection outline or whatever you want.

Incidentally, to avoid having problems transferring data between Photoshop and Illustrator, go into Illustrator, choose Edit ⇨ Preferences ⇨ Files & Clipboards, and turn on the AICB check box. I also recommend that you turn on the Preserve Paths radio button when using Illustrator to alter Photoshop paths.

Tip

Things can get pretty muddled in the Clipboard, especially when you're switching applications. If you copy something from Illustrator, but the Paste command is dimmed inside Photoshop, you may be able to force the issue a little. You may simply need to wake up the Clipboard by opening the Windows Clipbook Viewer (Start ➪ Programs ➪ Accessories ➪ System Tools ➪ Clipbook Viewer). Don't worry if you see a message about an unsupported format, or if the image looks a complete mess. Just minimize the viewer window and try to paste again. (Computers are kind of slow sometimes. Every once in a while you must give them a kick in the pants.)

Note

You can copy paths from Photoshop and paste them into Illustrator or some other drawing program regardless of the setting of the Export Clipboard check box in the Preferences dialog box. That option affects pixels only. Paths are so tiny, Photoshop always exports them.

Exporting to Illustrator

If you don't have enough memory to run both Illustrator and Photoshop at the same time, you can export Photoshop paths to disk and then open them in Illustrator. To export all paths in the current image, choose File ➪ Export ➪ Paths to Illustrator. Photoshop saves the paths as a fully editable Illustrator document. This scheme enables you to trace images exactly with paths in Photoshop and then combine those paths as objects with the exported EPS version of the image inside Illustrator. Whereas tracing an image in Illustrator can prove a little tricky because of resolution differences and other previewing limitations, you can trace images in Photoshop as accurately as you like.

Note

Unfortunately, Illustrator provides no equivalent function to export paths for use in Photoshop, nor can Photoshop open Illustrator documents from disk and interpret them as paths. This means the Clipboard is the only way to take a path created or edited in Illustrator and use it in Photoshop.

Cross-Reference

Only about half of Photoshop users own Illustrator. Meanwhile, close to 90 percent of Illustrator users own Photoshop. This is why I cover the special relationship between Illustrator and Photoshop in depth in my Illustrator book, *Real World Illustrator 9* (Berkeley, CA: Peachpit Press, 2000).

Retaining transparent areas in an image

When you import an image into Illustrator, FreeHand, CorelDraw, QuarkXPress, PageMaker, InDesign, or some other object-oriented program, the image comes in as a rectangle with opaque pixels. Even if the image appeared partially transparent in Photoshop—on a layer, for example—the pixels are filled with white or some other color in the receiving application. These same object-oriented applications, however, enable you to establish a *clipping path* to mask portions of an image that you want to appear transparent. Elements that lie inside the clipping path are opaque;

elements outside the clipping path are transparent. Photoshop enables you to export an image in the EPS format with an object-oriented clipping path intact. When you import the image into the object-oriented program, it appears premasked with a perfectly smooth perimeter, as illustrated by the clipped image in Figure 8-39.

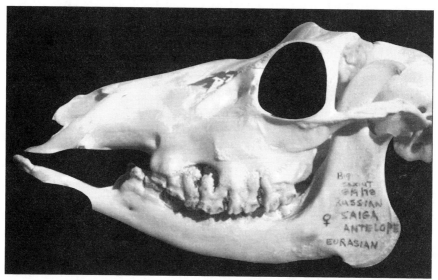

Figure 8-39: I drew one path around the perimeter of the skull and another around the eye socket. After defining the paths as clipping paths, I exported the image in the EPS format, imported it into Illustrator, and set it against a black background for contrast.

The following steps explain how to assign a set of saved paths as clipping paths.

STEPS: Saving an Image with Clipping Paths

1. **Draw one or more paths around the portions of the image that you want to appear opaque.** Areas outside the paths will be transparent.

2. **Save the paths.** Double-click the *Work Path* item in the Paths palette, enter a path name, and press Enter. (Try to use a name that will make sense three years from now when you have to revisit this document and determine what the heck you did.)

3. **Choose the Clipping Path command from the Paths palette menu, as shown in Figure 8-40.** Photoshop displays the dialog box shown at the top of the figure, asking you to select the saved paths you want to assign as the clipping path. Remember, you can't make the *Work Path* a clipping path; you must save it as a named path first.

Note

If you like, enter a value in the Flatness option box. This option enables you to simplify the clipping paths by printing otherwise fluid curves as polygons. The Flatness value represents the distance — between 0.2 and 100, in printer pixels — that the polygon may vary from the true mathematical curve. A higher value leads to a polygon with fewer sides. This means it looks chunkier, but it also prints more quickly. I recommend a value of 3. Many experts say you can go as high as 7 when printing to an imagesetter without seeing the straight edges. But I strongly suspect it depends on how much of a perfectionist you are. Me? I like 3.

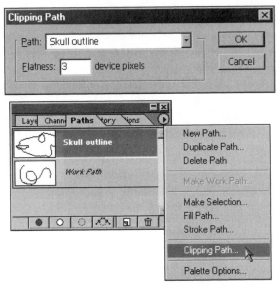

Figure 8-40: Choose the Clipping Path command from the Paths palette menu (bottom) and then select the path that you want to use from the Clipping Path dialog box (top).

4. **Choose File ➪ Save As and select Photoshop EPS from the Format pop-up menu.** Select the desired Preview and Encoding settings and then press Enter. Photoshop saves the EPS image with masked transparencies to disk.

Note

PageMaker and InDesign support clipping paths saved in the TIFF format. So if you plan on placing the image in PageMaker, you can save the image in TIFF instead of EPS in Step 4.

Figure 8-41 shows an enhanced version of the clipped skull from Figure 8-39. In addition to exporting the image with clipping paths in the EPS format, I saved the paths to disk by choosing File ➪ Export ➪ Paths to Illustrator. Inside Illustrator, I used the exported paths to create the outline around the clipped image. I also used them to create the shadow behind the image. The white of the eyeball is a reduced version of the eye socket, as are the iris and pupil. The background features a bunch of flipped and reduced versions of the paths. This may look like a lot of work, but the only drawing required was the creation of the two initial Photoshop paths.

Figure 8-41: It's amazing what you can accomplish by combining scans edited in a painting program with smooth lines created in a drawing program.

Be prepared for your images to grow by leaps and bounds when imported into Illustrator. The EPS illustration shown in Figure 8-41 consumes six times as much space on disk as the original Photoshop image saved in the TIFF format.

When used in excess, clipping paths will present problems for the most sophisticated printing devices. You should use a clipping path only when it's absolutely necessary and can't be avoided. If you want to place an image against a bitmapped background, for example, do it in Photoshop, not in Illustrator, QuarkXPress, or any other application. This invariably speeds printing and may mean the difference between whether or not a file prints successfully.

✦   ✦   ✦

Masks and Extractions

Selecting Via Masks

Most Photoshop users don't use masks. If my personal experience is any indication, it's not only because masks seem complicated but also because they strike most folks as being more trouble than they're worth. Like nearly everyone, when I first started using Photoshop, I couldn't even imagine a possible application for a mask. I have my lasso tool and my magic wand. If I'm really in a rut, I can pull out my pen tool. What more could I possibly want?

Quite a bit, as it turns out. Every one of the tools I just mentioned is only moderately suited to the task of selecting images. The lasso tools let you create free-form selections, but none of the tools — not even the magnetic lasso — can account for differences in focus levels. The magic wand selects areas of color, but it usually leaves important colors behind, and the edges of its selection outlines often appear ragged and ugly. The pen tool is extremely precise, but it results in mechanical outlines that may appear incongruous with the natural imagery they contain.

Masks offer all the benefits of the other tools. With masks, you can create free-form selections, select areas of color, and generate amazingly precise selections. Masks also address all the deficiencies associated with the selection tools. They can account for different levels of focus, they give you absolute control over the look of the edges, and they create selections every bit as natural as the image itself.

In fact, a mask *is* the image itself. Masks use pixels to select pixels. Masks are your way to make Photoshop see what you see using the data inherent in the photograph. Masks enable you to devote every one of Photoshop's powerful capabilities to the task of creating a selection outline. Masks are, without a doubt, the most accurate selection mechanism available in Photoshop.

Masking defined

If you're not entirely clear about what I mean by the term *mask*, I'll tell you: A mask is a selection outline expressed as a grayscale image.

✦ Selected areas appear white.

✦ Deselected areas appear black.

✦ Partially selected parts of the image appear in gray. Feathered edges are also expressed in shades of gray, from light gray near the selected area to dark gray near the deselected area.

Figure 9-1 shows two selection outlines and their equivalent masks. The top-left example shows a rectangular selection that I inverted by choosing Image ➪ Adjust ➪ Invert (Ctrl+I). Below this example is the same selection expressed as a mask. Because the selection is hard-edged with no antialiasing or feathering, the mask appears hard-edged, as well. The selected area is white and is said to be *unmasked;* the deselected area is black, or *masked.*

The top-right example in Figure 9-1 shows a feathered selection outline. Again, I've inverted the selection so that you can better see the extent of the selection outline. (Marching ants can't accurately express softened edges, so the inversion helps show things off more.) The bottom-right image is the equivalent mask. Here, the feathering effect is completely visible.

When you look at the masks along the bottom of Figure 9-1, you may wonder where the heck the image went. One of the wonderful things about masks is that you can view them independently of an image, as in Figure 9-1, or with an image, as in Figure 9-2. In the second figure, the mask is expressed as a color overlay. By default, the color of the overlay is a translucent red, like a conventional rubylith. (To see the overlay in its full, natural color, see Color Plate 9-1.) Areas covered with the rubylith are masked (deselected); areas that appear normal — without any red tint — are unmasked (selected). When you return to the standard marching ants mode, any changes you make to your image affect only the unmasked areas.

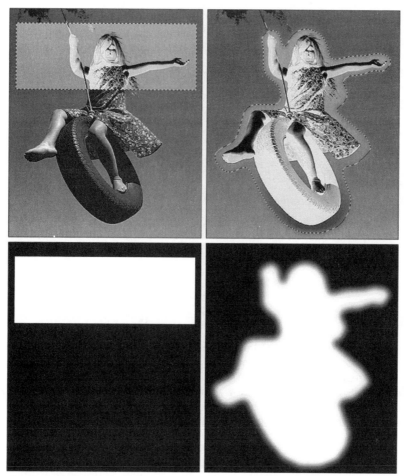

Figure 9-1: Two selection outlines with inverted interiors (top) and their equivalent masks (bottom).

Now that you know roughly what masks are (the definition becomes progressively clearer throughout this chapter), the question remains what good are they? Because a mask is essentially an independent grayscale image, you can edit the mask using paint and edit tools, filters, color correction options, and almost every other Photoshop function. You can even use the selection tools, as discussed in the previous chapter. With all these features at your disposal, you can't help but create a more accurate selection outline in a shorter amount of time.

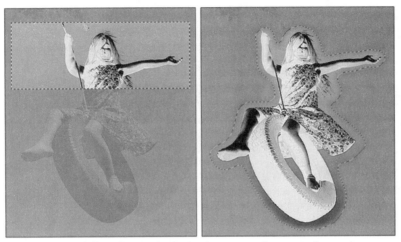

Figure 9-2: Here are the masks from Figure 9-1, shown as they appear when viewed along with an image.

Painting and Editing Inside Selections

Before we immerse ourselves in masking techniques, let's start with a warm-up topic: *selection masking*. When you were in grade school, you may have had a teacher who nagged you to color within the lines. (I didn't. My teachers were more concerned about preventing me from writing on the walls and coloring on the other kids, or so I'm told.) If so, your teacher would have loved this incredibly straightforward feature. In Photoshop, all selection outlines act as masks — hence the term *selection masking*. (And you thought this chapter was going to be hard.) Regardless of which tool you use to create the selection — marquee, lasso, magic wand, or pen — Photoshop permits you to paint or edit only the selected area. The paint can't enter the deselected (or protected) portions of the image, so you can't help but paint inside the lines. If you dread painting inside an image because you're afraid you'll screw it up, selection masking is the answer.

Figures 9-3 through 9-6 show the familiar skull image subject to some pretty free-and-easy use of the paint and edit tools. (You think I ought to lay off the heavy metal or what?) The following steps describe how I created these images using a selection mask.

STEPS: Painting and Editing inside a Selection Mask

1. **I selected the slightly rotting skull of the enchanting Russian Saiga antelope.** You can see the selection outline in the top example in Figure 9-3. For the record, I drew this selection outline using the pen tool, explained in Chapter 8.

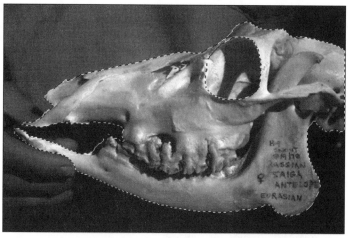

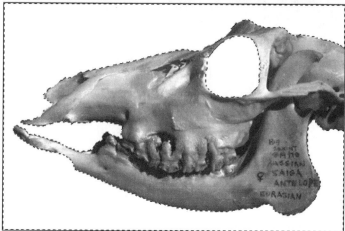

Figure 9-3: After drawing a selection outline around the antelope skull (top), I inversed the selection and deleted the background (bottom).

2. **I reversed the selection with the Inverse command.** I wanted to edit the area surrounding the skull, so I chose Select ⇨ Inverse (Ctrl+Shift+I) to reverse which areas were selected and which were not.

3. **I pressed Ctrl+Backspace to fill the selected area with the background color.** In this case, the background color was white—as shown in the bottom half of Figure 9-3.

4. **I painted inside the selection mask.** But before I began, I chose View ➪ Hide Extras (Ctrl+H). This enabled me to paint without being distracted by those infernal marching ants. (In fact, this is one of the most essential uses for the Hide Extras command.)

5. **I selected the paintbrush tool and expressed myself.** I chose the 21-pixel soft brush shape in the Brush drop-down palette. With the foreground color set to black, I dragged around the perimeter of the skull to set it apart from its white background, as shown in Figure 9-4. No matter how sloppily I painted, the skull remained unscathed.

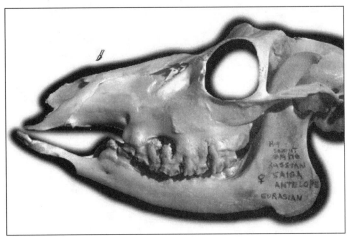

Figure 9-4: I painted inside the selection mask with a 21-pixel soft brush shape.

6. **I selected and used the smudge tool.** I set the tool's Pressure value to 80 percent by pressing the 8 key. I dragged from inside the skull outward 20 or so times to create a series of curlicues. I also dragged from outside the skull inward to create white gaps between the curlicues. As shown in Figure 9-5, the smudge tool can smear colors from inside the protected area, but it does not apply these colors until you go inside the selection. This is an important point to remember, because it demonstrates that although the protected area is safe from all changes, the selected area may be influenced by colors from protected pixels.

7. **I added some additional embellishments with the airbrush.** After selecting the airbrush, I opened the Brush Dynamics palette on the Options bar and set the Opacity pop-up menu to Fade so that my paint strokes would fade gradually from full opacity to transparency. I entered a Fade value of 20, selected a

60-pixel soft brush shape, and dragged outward from various points along the perimeter of the skull. As demonstrated in Figure 9-6, combining airbrush and mask is as useful in Photoshop as it is in the real world.

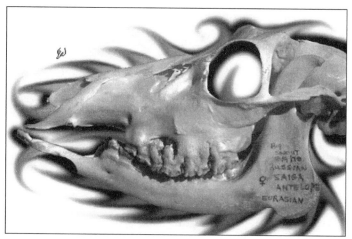

Figure 9-5: Dragging with the smudge tool smeared colors from pixels outside the selection mask without changing the appearance of those pixels.

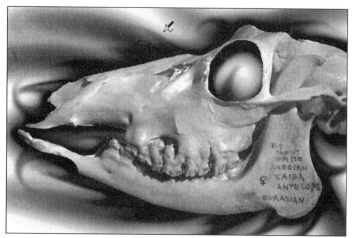

Figure 9-6: I dragged around the skull with the airbrush to distinguish it further from its background. Pretty cool effect, huh? Well, if this is not your cup of tea, maybe you can track down a teenager who will appreciate it.

Working in Quick Mask Mode

Selection masks give you an idea of what masks are all about, but they only scrape the surface. The rest of this chapter revolves around using masks to define complex selection outlines.

The most straightforward environment for creating a mask is the *quick mask mode*. In the quick mask mode, a selection is expressed as a rubylith overlay. All dese-lected areas appear coated with red, and selected areas appear without red coating, as shown in the top examples of Color Plate 9-1. You can then edit the mask as desired and exit quick mask mode to return to the standard selection outline. The quick mask mode is — as its name implies — expeditious and convenient, with none of the trappings or permanence of more conventional masks. It's kind of like a fast food restaurant — you use it when you aren't overly concerned about quality and you want to get in and out in a hurry.

How the quick mask mode works

Typically, you'll at least want to rough out a selection with the standard selection tools before entering the quick mask mode. Then you can concentrate on refining and modifying your selection inside the quick mask, rather than having to create the selection from scratch. (Naturally, this is only a rule of thumb. I violate the rule several times throughout this chapter, but only because the quick mask mode and I are such tight friends.)

To enter the quick mask mode, click the quick mask mode icon in the toolbox, as I've done in Figure 9-7. Or press Q. When I pressed Q after wreaking my most recent havoc on the extinct antelope skull, I got the image shown in Figure 9-7. The skull receives the mask because it is not selected. (In Figure 9-7, the mask appears as a light gray coating; on your color screen, the mask appears in red.) The area outside the skull looks the same as it always did because it's selected and, therefore, not masked.

Notice that the selection outline disappears when you enter the quick mask mode. This happens because the outline temporarily ceases to exist. Any operations you apply affect the mask itself and leave the underlying image untouched. When you click the marching ants mode icon (to the left of the quick mask mode icon) or press Q, Photoshop converts the mask back into a selection outline and again enables you to edit the image.

Note If you click the quick mask mode icon and nothing changes on screen, your com-puter isn't broken; you simply didn't select anything before you entered quick mask mode. When nothing is selected, Photoshop makes the whole image open for edit-ing. In other words, everything's selected. (Only a smattering of commands under the Edit, Layer, and Select menus require something to be selected before they work.) If everything is selected, the mask is white; therefore, the quick mask overlay is transparent and you don't see any difference on screen. This **is** another reason why it's better to select something before you enter the quick mask mode — you get an immediate sense you're accomplishing something.

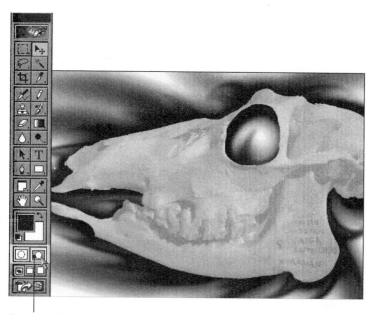

Quick mask icon

Figure 9-7: Click the quick mask mode icon (highlighted in the toolbox) to instruct Photoshop to express the selection temporarily as a grayscale image.

Also, Photoshop enables you to specify whether you want the red mask coating to cover selected areas or deselected areas. For information on how to change this setting, see "Changing the red coating," later in this chapter.

In quick mask mode, you can edit the mask in the following ways:

✦ **Subtracting from a selection:** Paint with black to add red coating **and, thus,** deselect areas of the image, as demonstrated in the top half of Figure 9-8. This means you can selectively protect portions of your image by merely **painting** over them.

✦ **Adding to a selection:** Paint with white to remove red coating and, **thus,** add to the selection outline. You can use the eraser tool to whittle away **at the** masked area (assuming the background color is set to white). Or **you can** swap the foreground and background colors so you can paint in **white with** one of the painting tools.

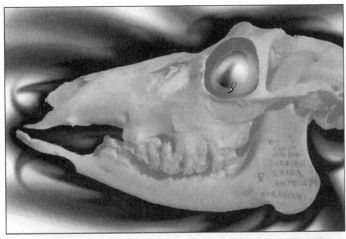

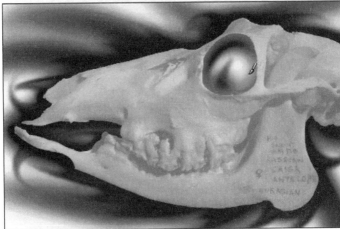

Figure 9-8: After subtracting some of the selected area inside the eye socket by painting in black with the paintbrush tool (top), I feathered the outline by painting with white, using a soft 45-pixel brush shape (bottom).

✦ **Adding feathered selections:** If you paint with a shade of gray, you add feathered selections. You also can feather an outline by painting with black or white with a soft brush shape, as shown in the bottom image in Figure 9-8.

✦ **Clone selection outlines:** If you have a selection outline that you want to repeat in several locations throughout the image, the quick mask is your friend. Select the transparent area with one of the standard selection tools and Ctrl+Alt-drag it to a new location in the image, as shown in Figure 9-9. Although I use the lasso tool in the figure, the magic wand tool also works well for this purpose. To select an antialiased selection outline with the wand tool, set the Tolerance value to about 10 and be sure the Anti-aliased check box is active. Then click inside the selection. It's that easy.

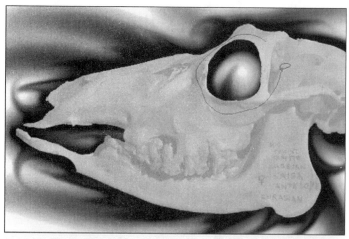

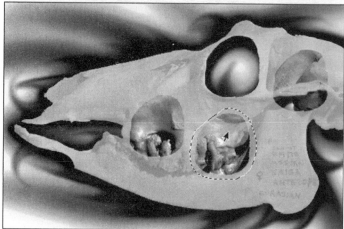

Figure 9-9: To clone the eye socket selection, I lassoed around it (top) and Ctrl+Alt-dragged it (bottom).

✦ **Transform selection outlines:** You can scale or rotate a selection independently of the image, just as you can with the Transform Selection command (covered in Chapter 8). Enter the quick mask mode, select the mask using one of the standard selection tools, and choose Edit ➪ Free Transform or press Ctrl+T. (See Chapter 12 for more information on Free Transform and related commands.)

These are only a few of the unique effects you can achieve by editing a selection in the quick mask mode. Others involve tools and capabilities I haven't yet discussed, such as filters and color corrections.

When you finish editing your selection outlines, click the marching ants mode icon (to the left of the quick mask mode icon) or press Q again to return to the marching ants mode. Your selection outlines again appear flanked by marching ants, and all tools and commands return to their normal image-editing functions. Figure 9-10 shows the results of switching to the marching ants mode and deleting the contents of the selection outlines created in the last examples of the previous two figures.

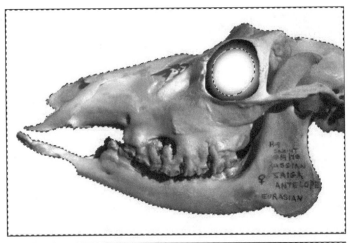

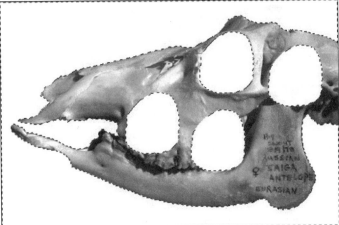

Figure 9-10: The results of deleting the regions selected in the bottom examples of Figures 9-8 (top) and 9-9 (bottom). Kind of makes me want to rent *It's the Great Pumpkin, Charlie Brown.* I mean, who wouldn't give this antelope a rock?

Tip

As demonstrated in the top example of Figure 9-10, the quick mask mode offers a splendid environment for feathering one selection outline, while leaving another hard-edged or antialiased. Granted, because most selection tools offer built-in feathering options, you can accomplish this task without resorting to the quick mask mode. But the quick mask mode enables you to change feathering selectively after drawing selection outlines, something you can't accomplish with Select ➪ Feather. The quick mask mode also enables you to see exactly what you're doing. Kind of makes those marching ants look piddly and insignificant, huh?

Changing the red coating

By default, the protected region of an image appears in translucent red in the quick mask mode, but if your image contains a lot of red, the mask can be difficult to see. Luckily, you can change it to any color and any degree of opacity that you like. To do so, double-click the quick mask icon in the toolbox (or double-click the *Quick Mask* item in the Channels palette) to display the dialog box shown in Figure 9-11.

✦ **Color Indicates:** Choose Selected Areas to reverse the color coating so that the translucent red coating covers selected areas, and deselected areas appear normally. Choose Masked Areas (the default setting) to cover deselected areas in color.

Tip

You can reverse the color coating without ever entering the Quick Mask Options dialog box. Simply Alt-click the quick mask icon in the toolbox to toggle between coating the masked or selected portions of the image. The icon itself changes to reflect your choice.

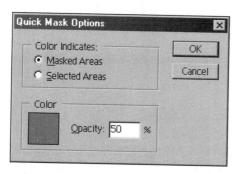

Figure 9-11: Double-click the quick mask mode icon to access the Quick Mask Options dialog box. You then can change the color and opacity of the protected or selected areas when viewed in the quick mask mode.

✦ **Color:** Click the Color icon to display the Color Picker dialog box and select a different color coating. (If you don't know how to use this dialog box, see the "Using the Color Picker" section of Chapter 4.) You can lift a color from the image with the eyedropper after the Color Picker dialog box comes up, but you probably want to use a color that isn't in the image so that you can better see the mask.

✦ **Opacity:** Enter a value to change the opacity of the translucent color that coats the image. A value of 100 percent makes the coating absolutely opaque.

Change the color coating to achieve the most acceptable balance between being able to view and edit your selection and being able to view your image. For example, the default red coating shows up poorly on my grayscale screen shots, so I changed the color of the coating to light blue and the Opacity value to 65 percent before shooting the screens featured in Figures 9-7 through 9-9.

Gradations as masks

If you think that the Feather command is a hot tool for creating softened selection outlines, wait until you get a load of gradations in the quick mask mode. There's no better way to create fading effects than selecting an image with the one of the gradient tools.

Fading an image

Consider the U.S. Capitol building shown in Figure 9-12. Whether or not you care for the folks who reside inside — personally, I'm sick of all this cynicism about the government, but I'm happy to exploit it for a few cheap laughs — you must admit, this is one beautiful building. Still, you may reckon the structure would be even more impressive if it were to fade into view out of a river of hot Hawaiian lava, like the one to the Capitol's immediate right. Well, you're in luck, because this is one of the easiest effects to pull off in Photoshop.

Figure 9-12: You can create a linear gradient in the quick mask mode to make the Capitol (left) fade out of the lava (right).

Switch to the quick mask mode by pressing Q. Then use the gradient tool to draw a linear gradation from black to white. (Chapter 6 explains exactly how to do so.) The white portion of the gradation represents the area you want to select. I decided to select the top portion of the Capitol, so I drew the gradation from the top of the second tier to the top of the flag, as shown in the first example of Figure 9-13. Because the gradient line is a little hard to see, I've added a little arrow to show the direction of the drag. (To see the mask in full color, check out the first image in Color Plate 9-2.)

Figure 9-13: After drawing a linear gradation in the quick mask mode near the center of the image (left), I hid the image and applied the Add Noise filter with an Amount of 24 (right).

Banding can be a problem when you use a gradation as a mask. To eliminate the banding effect, therefore, apply the Add Noise filter at a low setting several times. To create the right example in Figure 9-13, I applied Add Noise using an Amount value of 24 and the Uniform distribution option.

Tip

In the right example of Figure 9-13, I hid the image so that only the mask is visible. As the figure shows, the Channels palette lists the *Quick Mask* item in italics. This is because Photoshop regards the quick mask as a temporary channel. You can hide the image and view the mask in black and white by clicking the eyeball in front of the color composite view, in this case RGB. Or just press the tilde key (~) to hide the image. Press tilde again to view mask and image together.

To apply the gradation as a selection, I returned to the marching ants mode by again pressing Q. I then Ctrl-dragged the selected portion of the Capitol and dropped it into the lava image to achieve the effect shown in Figure 9-14. I could say something about Congress rising up from the ashes, but I have no idea what I'd mean by this. For the color version of this splendid image, see Color Plate 9-2.

Figure 9-14: The result of selecting the top portion of the Capitol using a gradient mask and then Ctrl-dragging and dropping the selection into the lava image.

Applying special effects gradually

You also can use gradations in the quick mask mode to fade the outcomes of filters and other automated special effects. For example, I wanted to apply a filter around the edges of the Lincoln colossus that appears in Figure 9-15. I began by deselecting everything in the image (Ctrl+D) and switching to the quick mask mode. Then I selected the Gradient tool, selected the linear gradient style icon on the Options bar, and selected the Foreground to Transparent gradient from the Gradient drop-down palette. I also selected the Transparency check box on the Options bar.

Figure 9-15: This time around, my intention is to surround Lincoln with a gradual filtering effect.

I pressed D to make the foreground color black and the background color white. Then I dragged with the linear gradient tool from each of the four edges of the image inward to create a series of short gradations that trace around the boundaries of the image, as shown in Figure 9-16. (As you can see, I've hidden the image so that you see the mask in black and white.) Because I've selected the Foreground to Transparent option, Photoshop adds each gradation to the previous gradation.

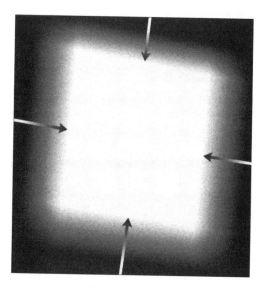

Figure 9-16: Inside the quick mask mode, I dragged from each of the four edges with the gradient tool (as indicated by the arrows).

To jumble the pixels in the mask, I applied Filter ➪ Noise ➪ Add Noise with an Amount value of 24. You see the effect in Figure 9-16.

The only problem is that I want to select the outside of the image, not the inside. So I need the edges to appear black and the inside to appear white, the opposite of what you see in Figure 9-16. No problem. All I do is press Ctrl+I (Image ➪ Adjust ➪ Invert) to invert the image. Inverting inside the quick mask mode produces the same effect as applying Select ➪ Inverse to a selection.

Finally, I switched back to the marching ants mode by again pressing Q. Then I applied Filter ➪ Render ➪ Clouds to get the atmospheric effect you see in Figure 9-17. Yes, he's Abe the Illusionist — Lincoln as you've never seen him before! Once he gets to Vegas, he'll wipe the floor with David Copperfield.

Figure 9-17: After switching back to the marching ants mode, I chose Filter ➪ Render ➪ Clouds to create the foggy effect shown here.

Notice the corners in the mask in Figure 9-16? These corners are rounded, but you can achieve all kinds of corner effects with the linear gradient tool. For harsher corners, select the Foreground to Background gradient and select Lighten from the Mode pop-up menu on the Options bar. For some *really* unusual corner treatments, try out the Difference and Exclusion brush modes. Wild stuff.

Creating gradient arrows

A few sections ago, Figure 9-13 featured an upward-pointing arrow that faded into view with a dark halo around it. I could have created this arrowhead in a drawing program to get nice sharp points and smooth outlines. But I chose to create it in Photoshop, so I could take advantage of two options drawing programs don't offer: gradient lines and halos. Naturally, you can create both in the quick mask mode.

The following steps explain how to add cool fading arrows to any image, as demonstrated in Figures 9-18 and 9-19. The steps involve the quick mask mode, the gradient tool, the Fill command, and good old Backspace.

STEPS: Creating Fading Arrows with Halos

1. **Choose the New Snapshot command from the History palette menu.** Photoshop adds a new snapshot thumbnail at the top of the palette. Click in front of it to make it the source state. Now you're ready to revert to this state if need be, as called for in Step 15.

2. **Deselect everything (Ctrl+D) and switch to the quick mask mode (Q).** The image should appear absolutely normal.

3. **Select the line tool (press U as necessary to get the tool).** Also press Enter to display the Options bar, if it's not already visible. First, click the Fill Region button to set the line tool into raster mode—that is, so that it creates a pixel-based line. (The Fill Region button is the third mode button and looks like a solid square.) Enter the line width in the Weight option box to suit your needs. Then click the down-pointing arrow at the end of the strip of shape icons to display the Arrowheads palette and enter the arrowhead values that you want to use. To create my first arrows (the ones that come inward from the corners in Figure 9-19), I set the Size value to 20 and the Width, Length, and Concavity values in the Arrowheads palette to 400, 600, and 20, respectively. I selected the End option box to append the arrowheads at the end of my lines. (See Chapter 6 if you want more information about working with the line tool options in Photoshop 6.)

4. **Press D to switch to the default colors.**

5. **Draw your line, which shows up in red.** If you don't get it right the first time—as is often the case with this tool—press Ctrl+Z and try again. The beauty of drawing a line in the quick mask mode is you can edit the line after the fact without damaging the image. (You could also do the same on a separate layer, but the quick mask mode affords you a little more flexibility in this specific exercise.)

6. **Select the gradient tool (G) and select the Foreground to Background gradient from the Gradients drop-down palette on the Options bar.** Also set the Opacity value to 100 percent and choose Lighten from the Mode pop-up menu.

7. **Use the gradient tool to fade the base of the line.** Drag from the point at which you want the line to begin to fade, down to the base of the line. Try to make the direction of your drag parallel to the line itself, thus ensuring a smooth fade. The first example in Figure 9-18 shows me in the process of dragging along one of my arrows with the gradient tool. The small white arrow shows the direction of my drag. (The black line shows the actual cursor you see on screen.) The second image shows the result of the drag.

Figure 9-18: Drag from the point at which you want the arrow to begin fading to the base of the line (left). Keep the drag parallel to the line itself (indicated here by the white arrow) to fade the line out smoothly (right).

8. **Choose Image ➪ Adjust ➪ Invert (Ctrl+I).** This inverts the quick mask, thus making the arrow the selected area.

9. **Copy the quick mask to a separate channel.** Drag the *Quick Mask* item in the Channels palette onto the little page icon at the bottom of the palette to copy the quick mask to a permanent mask channel. You'll need it again.

10. **Press Q to switch back to the marching ants mode.** Your arrow appears as a selection outline.

11. **Expand the selection to create the halo.** Choose Select ➪ Modify ➪ Expand and enter the desired value, based on the size and resolution of your image. I entered 6 to expand the selection outline 6 pixels.

12. **Choose Select ➪ Feather (Ctrl+Alt+D).** Enter the same value and press Enter.

13. **Fill the selection with white for a light halo, or black for a dark one.** I wanted a white halo, so I pressed D to restore the default foreground and background colors. Then I pressed Ctrl+Backspace to fill the selection with white.

14. **Ctrl-click the Quick Mask Copy item in the Channels palette.** This regains your original arrow-shaped selection outline. (I explain channel masks in detail later in this chapter, but for now, just Ctrl-click.)

15. **Press Ctrl+Alt+Backspace.** If you set the source state properly in Step 1, this shortcut reverts the portion of the image inside the arrows to its original appearance.

16. **Copy the selection to an independent layer.** Press Ctrl+J or choose Layer ⇨ New ⇨ Layer via Copy.

17. **Fill the layered arrow with a color.** Change the foreground color to anything you like and press Shift+Alt+Backspace to fill the arrow (and only the arrow).

18. **Choose Multiply from the pop-up menu in the Layers palette.** This burns the colored arrow into the image. Then set the Opacity value to the desired level. I set the Opacity to 40 percent.

After that, I simply kept adding more and more arrows by repeating the process to create the effect shown in Figure 9-19. I saved occasional snapshot states so that I could create arrows on top of arrows. Most notably, I made a snapshot of the image before adding the last, big arrow that shoots up from the bottom. Then I filled the arrow with the snapshot to bring back bits and pieces of a few of the other arrows. (Had I not filled back in time via the History palette, the arrow fragments behind the big arrow would have disappeared.)

Figure 9-19: I don't know whether this guy's in store for a cold front or what, but if you ever need to annotate an image with arrows, this gradient-arrowhead trick is certainly the way to do it.

Generating Masks Automatically

In addition to the quick mask mode and selection masking, Photoshop offers a few tools that automate the masking process — well, automate *some* parts of the process. You still need to provide some input to tell the program exactly what you're trying to mask.

Photoshop 5.5 added a trio of tools designed to select the foreground of an image while cutting away the background: the background eraser, magic eraser, and Extract command. I cover the two erasers along with the plain old eraser tool in Chapter 7 because all three erasers share some common characteristics. The next section in this chapter explores the Extract command, which Adobe upgraded significantly in Photoshop 6. Following that, I explain how to generate a mask based on a range of colors in your image.

Extracting a subject from its surroundings

Like the background eraser and magic eraser, the Extract command aims to separate — extract, if you will — an image element from its surroundings. After you draw a rough highlight around the subject you want to retain, Photoshop analyzes the situation and automatically deletes everything but the subject. In my estimation, though, Extract is only slightly more powerful than the background eraser and several times more complex. Some images respond very well to the command, others do not.

That said, Extract can produce reasonably good results if you get the steps right. And in Photoshop 6, Extract offers some added features — most notably, an Undo function — that improve on the first incarnation of the command. So take Extract for a test drive, as follows:

1. **Choose Extract from the Image menu.** Or use the keyboard shortcut, Ctrl+Alt+X. Either way, Photoshop displays the large Extract window shown in Figure 9-20.

2. **Select the edge highlighter tool.** Most likely, this tool is already active, but if not, press B to select it.

3. **Outline the subject that you want to retain.** In my case, I want to delete the background, so I traced around the lion, as shown in Figure 9-20. Be sure to either completely encircle the subject or, if the subject is partially cropped, trace all the way up against the outer boundaries of the photograph.

Tip

Often, it's easier to Shift-click around the perimeter of an image than drag manually. Shift-clicking creates a straight highlight from one click point to the next. As long as you do a reasonably careful job, the performance of the Extract command won't be impaired.

Edge highlighter

Fill Eraser

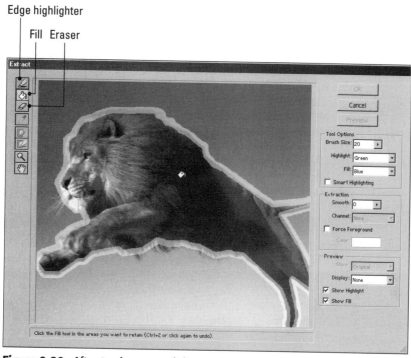

Figure 9-20: After tracing around the portion of the image you want to retain, click inside the outline with the fill tool.

Turn on the Smart Highlighting check box, in the Tool Options section of the Extract dialog box, to get some assistance in drawing your outline. Smart Highlighting seeks out edges in the image and places the highlight along them. When you turn on Smart Highlighting, your cursor becomes a circle with four inward-pointing lines. Keep the center of the circle over the edge between the subject and the background as you drag. This feature works best when your subject has well-defined edges, of course. Note that you can't Shift-click with the tool to draw straight segments when Smart Highlighting is active.

Tip

Ctrl-drag to temporarily turn off Smart Highlighting without deselecting the check box. Or go the opposite direction: Deselect the check box and then Ctrl-drag to temporarily take advantage of Smart Highlighting.

4. **As you trace, use the bracket keys, [and], to make the brush larger or smaller.** When you work with brushes from 1 to 9 pixels in diameter, each press of [or] changes the brush size by 1 pixel. The increment of change gets larger as you increase the brush size.

Small brush sizes result in sharper edges. Larger brush sizes are better for fragile, intricate detailing, such as hair, foliage, wispy fabric, bits of steel wool, thin pasta—you get the idea.

5. **If you make a mistake, press Ctrl+Z.** As I mentioned before, the Extract window now has a much needed Undo function. But you get only one Undo level here—you can only undo and redo your last stroke with the highlighter tool.

   If you want to erase more of the highlight, drag over the botched region with the eraser tool (press E to access it from the keyboard) or use Alt-drag with the edge highlighter tool. To delete the entire highlight and start over, press Alt+Backspace.

6. **Navigate as needed.** If you can't see all of your image, you can access the hand tool by pressing the spacebar or clicking the hand tool icon. You can also zoom by pressing Ctrl+plus or Ctrl+minus, or by using the zoom tool.

7. **Select the fill tool.** It's the one that looks like a paint bucket. To select the fill tool from the keyboard, press G, same as you do to select the paint bucket in the regular Photoshop toolbox. (Formerly, the shortcut for both the fill tool and paint bucket was K.)

8. **Click inside the subject of the image.** The highlighted outline should fill with color. If the fill color spills outside the outline, then there's probably a break in your outline someplace. Press Ctrl+Z to undo the fill and then scroll the image with the hand tool to find the break. Patch it with the edge highlighter and then click with the fill tool again.

   You also can click inside a filled area with the fill tool or eraser to remove the fill.

9. **Click the Preview button.** Before you can apply your prospective mask, you need to preview it so you can gauge the finished effect, as in Figure 9-21.

   If you Shift-click with the fill tool in Step 8, Photoshop fills the outline and processes the preview automatically, saving you the trouble of clicking the Preview button.

10. **Edit the mask as needed.** You have several tools at your disposal in Photoshop 6. The tools are labeled in Figure 9-21; you can read about them in the list following these steps.

11. **Click the OK button to delete the masked portion of the image.** If the image was flat, Photoshop floats it to a separate layer. You can then use the move tool to drag the masked image against a different background. In Figure 9-22, I set my lion against an Italian landscape. The composite isn't perfect, but it's not half bad for five to ten minutes of work.

Eyedropper

Cleanup ┌Edge touchup

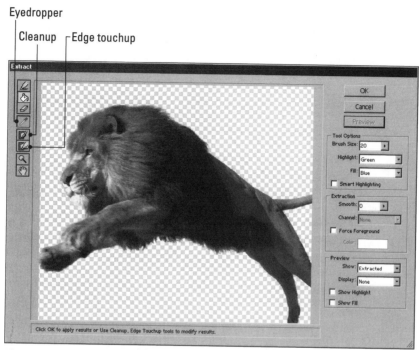

Figure 9-21: Click the Preview button to gauge the appearance of the final masked image.

Figure 9-22: I believe this particular lion is stuffed, but even a dead creature may enjoy a change in its diorama.

12. After you exit the Extract window, fix any problems using the background eraser and history brush. Use the background eraser (explained in Chapter 7) to erase stray pixels that you wish the Extract command had deleted. Use the history brush to restore details that you wish the Extract command hadn't deleted.

Back in Step 10, I alluded to ways that you can refine the mask within the Extract dialog box. In Photoshop 6, you can use the following techniques to touch up the mask before clicking OK to create it:

✦ **Drag with the cleanup tool (C) to change mask opacity:** Press the number keys to adjust the pressure of the tool and thus alter the amount of opacity that the tool subtracts. To erase to full transparency, press 0, as you do when working with the eraser on a layer. Press 9 for 90 percent transparency, 8 for 80 percent, and so on. Alt-drag to add opacity.

✦ **Drag along the boundaries of the mask with the edge touchup tool (T) to sharpen the mask edges.** If the boundary between mask and subject isn't well defined, dragging with this tool adds opacity to the subject and removes it from the mask. In other words, it turns soft, feathery edges into crisp, clearly defined edges. Again, you can press the number keys to adjust the impact of the tool.

✦ **Raise the Smooth value to remove stray pixels from the mask:** A high value smoothes out the edges around the image and fills in holes. Basically, if your edges are a big mess, give this option a try.

✦ **Drag with the edge highlighter or eraser tools to edit the mask boundary.** When you select either tool, the original mask highlight reappears, and the tools work as they do when you initially draw the highlight. After you adjust the highlight, Shift-click inside it to redraw and preview the adjusted mask.

✦ **Choose an option from the Show pop-up menu to toggle between the original highlight and the extracted image preview.** Figure 9-23 spotlights this option. You can press X to toggle between the two views without bothering with the pop-up menu.

Figure 9-23: To toggle between the extraction preview and the original highlight, choose the view you want from the Show pop-up menu or just press X.

That's 99 percent of what you need to know about the Extract command. For those of you who care to learn the other 1 percent, here's a quick rundown of the remaining options that appear along the right side of the Extract window.

Note that some of the option names have changed in Version 6, but all the functions remain the same as in Version 5.5. You do, however, have access to some new keyboard shortcuts for these options:

✦ **Highlight, Fill:** Use these pop-up menus to change the highlighter and fill colors. It doesn't matter what colors you use, so long as they show up well against the image.

✦ **Channel:** Advanced users may prefer to prepare the highlighter work by tracing around the image inside an independent mask channel, which you can create in the Channels palette prior to choosing the Extract command. Then load the mask by selecting it from the Channel pop-up menu. You can further modify the highlight using the edge highlight and eraser tools. One weirdness: When loading a mask, black in the mask channel represents the highlighted area, white represents the nonhighlighted area. Strikes me as upside-down, but that's how it goes.

✦ **Force Foreground:** If the subject of your image is predominantly a single color, select Force Foreground and use the eyedropper to sample the color in the image that you want to preserve. (Alternatively, you can define the color using the Color swatch, but it's much more work.) Then use the edge highlighter tool to paint over all occurrences of the foreground color. (Note that this check box is an alternative to the fill tool. When Force Foreground is selected, the fill tool is dimmed.)

✦ **Display:** You don't have to preview the image against the transparent checkerboard background. You can also view it against white (White Matte) or some other color. Or you can view it as a mask, where white represents the opaque area and black the transparent area. (Ironically, you can't export the extraction as a mask — go figure.)

Press F to select the next display mode in the menu; press Shift+F to switch to the previous mode in the menu.

✦ **Show Highlight, Show Fill:** Use these check boxes to hide and show the highlight and fill colors.

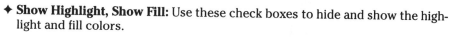

One final tip: Before using the Extract command — or the magic eraser or background eraser, for that matter — you may want to copy the image to a separate layer or take a snapshot of the image in the History palette. Either way, you have a backup in case things don't go exactly according to plan.

Using the Color Range command

Another convenient method for creating a mask is the Color Range command under the Select menu. This command enables you to generate selections based on color ranges. Use the familiar eyedropper cursor to specify colors that should be considered for selection and colors that you want to rule out. The Color Range command is a lot like the magic wand tool, except that it enables you to select colors with more precision and to change the tolerance of the selection on the fly.

When you choose Select ⇨ Color Range, Photoshop displays the Color Range dialog box shown in Figure 9-24. Like the magic wand with the Contiguous option enabled, Color Range selects areas of related color all across the image, whether or not the colors are immediate neighbors. Click in the image window to select and deselect colors, as you do with the wand. But rather than adjusting a Tolerance value before you use the tool, you adjust a Fuzziness option any old time you like. Photoshop dynamically updates the selection according to the new value. Think of Color Range as the magic wand on steroids.

Note

So why didn't the folks at Adobe merely enhance the functionality of the magic wand instead of adding this strange command? The Color Range dialog box offers a preview of the mask—something a tool can't do—which is pretty essential for gauging the accuracy of your selection. And the magic wand is convenient, if nothing else. If Adobe were to combine the two functions, you would lose functionality.

Preview

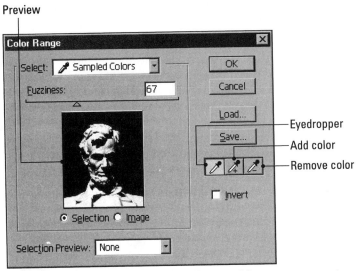

Figure 9-24: The Color Range dialog box enables you to generate a mask by dragging with the eyedropper tool and adjusting the Fuzziness option.

When you move your cursor outside the Color Range dialog box, it changes to an eyedropper. Click to specify the color on which you want to base the selection—I call this the base color—as if you were using the magic wand. Or click inside the preview, labeled in Figure 9-24. In either case, the preview updates to show the resulting mask.

You can also do the following:

✦ **Add colors to the selection:** To add base colors to the selection, select the add color tool inside the Color Range dialog box and click inside the image window or preview. You can access the tool while the standard eyedropper is selected by Shift-clicking (just as you Shift-click with the magic wand to add colors to a selection). You can even Shift-drag with the eyedropper to add multiple colors in a single pass, something you can't do with the magic wand.

✦ **Remove colors from the selection:** To remove base colors from the selection, click with the remove color tool or Alt-click with the eyedropper. You can also drag or Alt-drag to remove many colors at a time.

Tip

If adding or removing a color sends your selection careening in the wrong direction, press Ctrl+Z. Yes, the Undo command works inside the Color Range dialog box as well as out of it.

✦ **Adjust the Fuzziness value:** This option resembles the magic wand's Tolerance value because it determines the range of colors to be selected beyond the ones on which you click. Raise the Fuzziness value to expand the selected area; lower the value to contract the selection. A value of 0 selects the clicked color only. Unlike changes to Tolerance, however, changing the Fuzziness value adjusts the selection on the fly; no repeat clicking is required, as it is with the wand tool.

Fuzziness and Tolerance also differ in the kind of selection outlines they generate. Tolerance entirely selects all colors within the specified range and adds antialiased edges. If the selection were a mask, most of it would be white with a few gray pixels around the perimeter. By contrast, Fuzziness entirely selects only the colors on which you click and Shift-click, and it partially selects the other colors in the range. That's why most of the mask is expressed in shades of gray. The light grays in the mask represent the most similar colors; the dark grays represent the least similar pixels that still fall within the Fuzziness range. The result is a tapering, gradual selection, much more likely to produce natural results.

✦ **Reverse the selection:** Select the Invert check box to reverse the selection, changing black to white and white to black. As when using the magic wand, it may be easier to isolate the area you don't want to select than the area you do want to select. When you encounter such a situation, select Invert.

✦ **Toggle the preview area:** Use the two radio buttons below the preview area to control the preview's contents. If you select the first option, Selection, you see the mask that will be generated when you press Enter. If you select Image, the preview shows a reduced version of the image.

Tip

Press and hold Ctrl to toggle between the two previews. My advice is to leave the option set to Selection and press Ctrl when you want to view the image.

✦ **Control the contents of the image window:** The Selection Preview pop-up menu at the bottom of the dialog box enables you to change what you see in the image window. Leave the option set to None — the default setting — to view the image normally in the image window. Select Grayscale to see the mask on its own. Select Quick Mask to see the mask and image together. Select Black Matte or White Matte to see what the selection would look like against a black or white background.

Although they may sound weird, the Matte options enable you to get an accurate picture of how the selected image will mesh with a different background. Figure 9-25 shows Lincoln's head at the top with the grayscale mask on the right. The mask calls for the shadows in Lincoln's face to be selected, with the highlights deselected. The two Matte views help you see how this particular selection looks against two backgrounds as different as night and day. Use the Fuzziness option in combination with Black Matte or White Matte to come up with a softness setting that will ensure a smooth transition.

None   Grayscale

Black Matte   White Matte

Figure 9-25: The options in the Selection Preview pop-up menu change the way the Color Range command previews the selection in the image window.

✦ **Select by predefined colors:** Choose an option from the Select pop-up menu at the top of the dialog box to specify the means of selecting a base color. If you choose any option besides Sampled Colors, the Fuzziness option and eyedropper tools become dimmed to show they are no longer operable. Instead, Photoshop selects colors based on their relationship to a predefined color. For example, if you select Red, the program entirely selects red and partially selects other colors based on the amount of red they contain. Colors composed exclusively of blue and green are not selected.

The most useful option in this pop-up menu is Out of Gamut, which selects all the colors in an RGB or Lab image that fall outside the CMYK color space. You can use this option to select and modify the out-of-gamut colors before converting an image to CMYK.

✦ **Load and save settings:** Click the Save button to save the current settings to disk. Click Load to open a saved settings file.

After you define the mask to your satisfaction, click OK or press Enter to generate the selection outline. Although the Color Range command is more flexible than the magic wand, you can no more expect it to generate perfect selections than any other automated tool. After Photoshop draws the selection outline, therefore, you'll probably want to switch to quick mask mode and paint and edit the mask to taste.

If you learn nothing else about the Color Range dialog box, at least learn to use the Fuzziness option and the eyedropper tools. Basically, you can approach these options in two ways. If you want to create a diffused selection with gradual edges, set the Fuzziness option to a high value — 60 or more — and click and Shift-click two or three times with the eyedropper. To create a more precise selection, enter a Fuzziness of 40 or lower and Shift-drag and Alt-drag with the eyedropper until you get the exact colors you want.

Figure 9-26 shows some sample results. To create the left images, I clicked with the eyedropper tool once in Lincoln's face and set the Fuzziness value to 160. To create the right images, I lowered the Fuzziness value to 20; then I clicked, Shift-clicked, and Alt-clicked with the eyedropper to lift exactly the colors I wanted. The top examples show the effects of stroking the selections, first with 6-pixel white strokes and then with 2-pixel black strokes. In the two bottom examples, I copied the selections and pasted them against an identical background of — what else? — the Lincoln Memorial. In all four cases, the higher Fuzziness value yields more generalized and softer results; the lower value produces a more exact but harsher selection.

Figure 9-26: After creating two selections with the Color Range command—one with a high Fuzziness value (left) and one with a low one (right)—I alternately stroked the selections (top) and pasted them against a different background (bottom).

A few helpful Color Range hints

You can limit the portion of an image that Select ➪ Color Range affects by selecting part of the image before choosing the command. When a selection exists, the Color Range command masks only those pixels that fall inside it. Even the preview area reflects your selection.

You also can add or subtract from an existing selection using the Color Range command. Press Shift when choosing Select ➪ Color Range to add to a selection. Press Alt when choosing Color Range to subtract from a selection.

If you get hopelessly lost when creating your selection and you can't figure out what to select and what to deselect, click with the eyedropper tool to start over. This clears all the colors from the selection except the one you click. Or you can press Alt to change the Cancel button to a Reset button. Alt-click the button to return the settings inside the dialog box to those in force when you first chose Select ➪ Color Range.

Creating an Independent Mask Channel

The problem with masks generated via the quick mask mode and Color Range command is that they're here one day and gone the next. Photoshop is no more prepared to remember them than it is a lasso or wand selection.

Most of the time, that's okay. You'll only use the selection once, so there's no reason to sweat it. But what if the selection takes you a long time to create? What if, after a quarter hour of Shift-clicking here and Alt-dragging there, adding a few strokes in the quick mask mode, and getting the selection outline exactly right, your boss calls a sudden meeting or the dinner bell rings? You can't just drop everything; you're in the middle of a selection. But nor can you convey your predicament to non-Photoshop users because they'll have no idea what you're talking about and no sympathy for your plight.

The simplest solution is to back up your selection, save your file, and move on to the next phase of your life. In fact, anytime that you spend 15 minutes or more on a selection, save it. After all, you never know when all heck is going to break loose, and 15 minutes is just too big a chunk of your life to repeat. (The average person racks up a mere 2.5 million quarter hours, so use them wisely!) You wouldn't let 15 minutes of image-editing go by without saving, and the rules don't change just because you're working on a selection.

Saving a selection outline to a mask channel

The following steps describe how to back up a selection to an independent mask channel, which is any channel above and beyond those required to represent a grayscale or color image. Mask channels are saved along with the image itself, making them a safe and sturdy solution.

STEPS: Transferring a Selection to an Independent Channel

1. **Convert the selection to a mask channel.** One way to do this is to choose
   Select ➪ Save Selection (or right-click in the image window and choose Save
   Selection from the pop-up menu), which saves the selection as a mask. The
   dialog box shown in Figure 9-27 appears, asking you where you want to put
   the mask. In most cases, you'll want to save the mask to a separate channel
   inside the current image. To do so, make sure that the name of the current
   image appears in the Document pop-up menu. Then select New from the
   Channel pop-up menu, enter any name for the channel that you like, and
   press Enter.

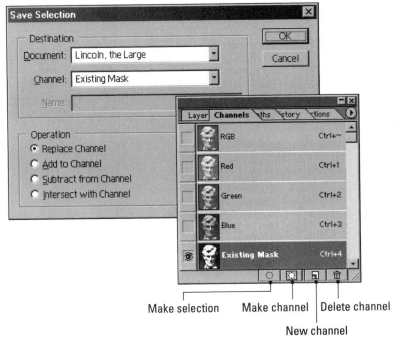

Figure 9-27: The Save Selection dialog box enables you to convert your
selection outline to a mask and save it to a new or existing channel.

If you have an old channel you want to replace, select the channel's name
from the Channel pop-up menu. The radio buttons at the bottom of the dialog
box become available, permitting you to add the mask to the channel, subtract it, or intersect it. These radio buttons work like the equivalent options
that appear when you make a path into a selection outline (as discussed in
the previous chapter), but they blend the masks together, instead. The result
is the same as if you were adding, subtracting, or intersecting selection outlines, except it's expressed as a mask.

Alternatively, you can save the mask to a new multichannel document all its own. To do this, choose New from the Document pop-up menu and press Enter.

Tip

Man, what a lot of options! If you only want to save the selection to a new channel and be done with it, you needn't bother with the Save Selection command or dialog box. Just click the make channel icon at the bottom of the Channels palette (labeled in Figure 9-27). Photoshop automatically creates a new channel, converts the selection to a mask, and places the mask in the channel.

Regardless of which of these many methods you choose, your selection outline remains intact.

2. **View the mask in the Channels palette.** To do so, click the appropriate channel name in the Channels palette — automatically named *Alpha 1* unless you assigned a name of your own. In Figure 9-27, I replaced the contents of a channel called Existing Mask, so this is where my mask now resides.

This step isn't the least bit mandatory. It just lets you see your mask and generally familiarize yourself with how masks look. Remember, white represents selection, black is deselected, and gray is partial selection.

Tip

If you didn't name your mask in Step 1 and you want to name it now, double-click the Alpha 1 item in the Channels palette and enter a name in the resulting dialog box.

3. **Return to the standard image-editing mode by clicking on the first channel name in the Channels palette.** Better yet, press Ctrl+1 if you're editing a grayscale image or Ctrl+tilde (~) if the image is in color.

4. **Save the image to disk to store the selection permanently as part of the file.** A handful of formats — PICT, Pixar, PNG, TIFF, Targa, and native Photoshop — accommodate RGB images with an extra mask channel. But only the TIFF and native Photoshop format can handle more than four channels, both saving up to 24 channels in all. I generally use the TIFF format with LZW compression when saving images with masks. Because TIFF supports layers in Photoshop 6, you aren't restricted to the Photoshop format for multilayered images with masks. (See Chapter 3 for more on that exciting news.)

Both the native Photoshop format and TIFF can compress masks so that they take up substantially less room on disk. The Photoshop format does this automatically. When saving a TIFF image, be sure to turn on the LZW Compression check box. In both cases, this run-line compression is entirely safe. It does not change a single pixel in the image; it merely writes the code in a more efficient manner.

Tip

If you performed the steps in the "Creating gradient arrows" section earlier in this chapter, you know that you can also save a quick mask to its own channel for later use. But in case you missed those steps, or you're saving them for a special occasion, here's how it works. When you enter the quick mask mode, the Channels palette displays an item called *Quick Mask*. The italic letters show the channel is temporary and will not be saved with the image. (To clone it to a permanent channel, drag the *Quick Mask* item onto the page icon at the bottom of the Channels palette). Now save the image to the TIFF or Photoshop format, and you're backed up.

Converting a mask to a selection

To retrieve your selection later, choose Select ➪ Load Selection. A dialog box nearly identical to the one shown in Figure 9-27 appears except for the addition of an Invert check box. Select the document and channel that contain the mask you want to use. You can add it to a current selection, subtract it, or intersect it. Select the Invert option if you want to reverse the selected and deselected portions of the mask.

Want to avoid the Load Selection command? Ctrl-click the channel name in the Channels palette that contains the mask you want to use. For example, if I Ctrl-clicked the Existing Mask item in Figure 9-27, Photoshop would load the equivalent selection outline into the image window.

Tip

But wait, there's more:

✦ You can press Ctrl+Alt plus the channel number to convert the channel to a selection. For example, Ctrl+Alt+4 would convert the Existing Mask channel shown in Figure 9-27.

✦ You can also select the channel and click the far-left mask selection icon at the bottom of the Channels palette. But for my money, this takes too much effort.

✦ To add a mask to the current selection outline, Ctrl+Shift-click the channel name in the Channels palette.

✦ Ctrl+Alt-click a channel name to subtract the mask from the selection.

✦ And Ctrl+Shift+Alt-click to find the intersection.

You can convert color channels to selections, as well as mask channels. For example, if you want to select the black pixels in a piece of scanned line art in grayscale mode, Ctrl-click the first item in the Channels palette. This selects the white pixels; press Ctrl+Shift+I (or choose Select ➪ Inverse) to reverse the selection to the black pixels.

Viewing mask and image

Photoshop lets you view any mask channel along with an image, just as you can view mask and image together in the quick mask mode. To do this, click in the first column of the Channels palette to toggle the display of the eyeball icon. An eyeball in front of a channel name indicates you can see that channel. If you are currently viewing the image, for example, click in front of the mask channel name to view the mask as a translucent color coating, again as in the quick mask mode. Or if the contents of the mask channel appear by themselves on screen, click in front of the image name to display it as well.

When the mask is active, you can likewise toggle the display of the image by pressing the tilde (~) key. Few folks know about this shortcut, but it's a good one to assign to memory. It works whether the Channels palette is open or not, and it permits you to focus on the mask without moving your mouse all over the screen.

Using a mask channel is different from using the quick mask mode in that you can edit either the image or the mask channel when viewing the two together. You can even edit two or more masks at once. To specify which channel you want to edit, click the channel name in the palette. To edit two channels at once, click one and Shift-click another. All active channel names appear highlighted.

You can change the color and opacity of each mask independently of other mask channels and the quick mask mode. Double-click the mask channel name or choose the Channel Options command from the Channels palette menu. (This command is dimmed when editing a standard color channel, such as Red, Green, Blue, Cyan, Magenta, Yellow, or Black.) A dialog box similar to the one shown back in Figure 9-11 appears, but this one contains a Name option box so you can change the name of the mask channel. You can then edit the color overlay as described in the "Changing the red coating" section earlier in this chapter.

If you ever need to edit a selection outline inside the mask channel using paint and edit tools, click the quick mask mode icon in the toolbox. It may sound a little like a play within a play, but you can access the quick mask mode even when working within a mask channel. Make sure the mask channel color is different from the quick mask color so you can tell what's happening.

Building a Mask from an Image

So far, everything I've discussed in this chapter has been pretty straightforward. Now it's time to see how the professionals do things. This final section in this chapter explains every step required to create a mask for a complex image. Here's how to select the image you never thought you could select, complete with wispy little details such as hair.

Take a gander at Figure 9-28 and see what I mean. I chose this subject not for her good looks or her generous supply of freckles, but for that hair. I mean, look at all that hair. Have you ever seen such a frightening image-editing subject in your life? Not only is this particular girl blessed with roughly 15 googol strands of hair, but every one of them is leaping out of her head in a different direction and at a different level of focus. Can you imagine selecting any one of them with the magnetic lasso or magic wand? No way. As demonstrated by the second example of Figure 9-28, these tools lack sufficient accuracy to do any good. Furthermore, you'd be fit for an asylum by the time you finished selecting the hairs with the pen tools, and the edges aren't definite enough for Select ⇨ Color Range to latch onto.

Figure 9-28: Have you ever wanted to select wispy details, such as the hair shown on left? You certainly aren't going to make it with the magnetic lasso (right) or other selection tools. But with masks, it's a piece of cake.

So, what's the solution? Manual masking. Although masking styles vary as widely as artistic style, a few tried-and-true formulas work for everyone. First, you peruse the channels in an image to find the channel that lends itself best to a mask. You're looking for high degrees of contrast, especially around the edges. Next, you copy the channel and boost the level of contrast using Image ➪ Adjust ➪ Levels. (Some folks prefer Image ➪ Adjust ➪ Curves, but Levels is more straightforward.) Then you paint inside the lines until you get the mask the way you want it.

The only way to get a feel for masking is to try it out for yourself. The following steps explain exactly how I masked this girl and pasted her against a different background. The final result is so realistic, you'd think she was born there.

STEPS: Selecting a Monstrously Complicated Image Using a Mask

1. **Browse the color channels.** Press Ctrl+1 to see the red channel, Ctrl+2 for green, and Ctrl+3 for blue. (This assumes you're working inside an RGB image. You can also peruse CMYK and Lab images. If you're editing a grayscale image, you have only one channel from which to choose — Black.)

Figure 9-29 shows the three channels in my RGB image. Of the three, the red channel offers the most contrast between the hair, which appears very light, and the background, which appears quite dark.

Red

Blue

Green

Figure 9-29: Of the three color channels, the red channel offers the best contrast between hair and background.

2. **Copy the channel.** Drag the channel onto the little page icon at the bottom of the Channels palette. (I naturally copy the red channel.) Now you can work on the channel to your heart's content without harming the image itself.

3. **Choose Filter ➪ Other ➪ High Pass.** The next thing you want to do is to force Photoshop to bring out the edges in the image so you don't have to hunt for them manually. And when you think edges, you should think filters. All of Photoshop's edge-detection prowess is packed into the Filter menu. Several edge-detection filters are available to you — Unsharp Mask, Find Edges, and many others that I discuss in Chapter 10. But the best filter for finding edges inside a mask is Filter ➪ Other ➪ High Pass.

High Pass selectively turns an image gray. High Pass may sound strange, but it's quite useful. The filter turns the non-edges completely gray while leaving the edges mostly intact, thus dividing edges and non-edges into different brightness camps, based on the Radius value in the High Pass dialog box. Unlike in most filters, a low Radius value produces a more pronounced effect than a high one, in effect locating more edges.

Figure 9-30 shows the original red channel on left with the result of the High Pass filter on right. I used a Radius of 10, which is a nice, moderate value. The lower you go, the more edges you find and the more work you make for yourself. A Radius of 3 is accurate, but it'll take you an hour to fill in the mask. Granted, 10 is less accurate, but if you value your time, it's more sensible.

Figure 9-30: After copying the red channel (left), I apply the High Pass filter with a Radius value of 10 to highlight the edges in the image (right).

4. **Choose Image ➪ Adjust ➪ Levels (Ctrl+L).** After adding all that gray to the image, follow it up by increasing the contrast. And the best command for enhancing contrast is Levels. Although I discuss this command in-depth in Chapter 17, here's the short version: Inside the Levels dialog box, raise the first Input Levels value to make the dark colors darker, and lower the third Input Levels value to make the light colors lighter. (For now you can ignore the middle value.)

Figure 9-31 shows the result of raising the first Input Levels value to 110 and lowering the third value to 155. As you can see in the left-hand image, this gives me some excellent contrast between the white hairs and black background.

To demonstrate the importance of the High Pass command in these steps, I've shown what would happen if I had skipped Step 3 in the right-hand image in Figure 9-31. I applied the same Levels values as in the left image, and yet the image is washed out and quite lacking in edges. Look at that wimpy hair. It simply is unacceptable.

Figure 9-31: Here are the results of applying the Levels command to the mask after the High Pass step (left) and without High Pass (right). As you can see, High Pass has a pronounced effect on the edge detail.

5. **Use the lasso tool to remove the big stuff you don't need.** By way of High Pass and Levels, Photoshop has presented you with a complex coloring book. From here on, it's a matter of coloring inside the lines. To simplify things, get rid of the stuff you know you don't need. All you care about is the area where the girl meets her background—mostly hair and arms. Everything else goes to white or black.

For example, in Figure 9-32, I selected a general area inside the girl by Alt-clicking with the lasso tool. Then I filled it with white by pressing Ctrl+Delete. I also selected around the outside of the hair and filled it with black. At all times, I was careful to stay about 10 to 20 pixels away from the hair and other edges; these I need to brush in carefully with the eraser. (Be sure to press Ctrl+D to eliminate the selection before continuing to the next step.)

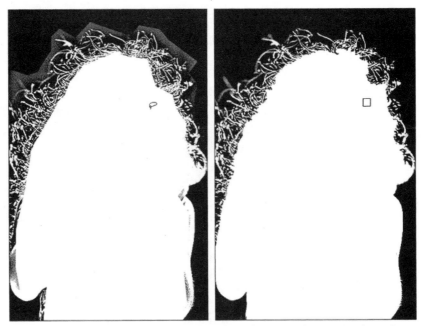

Figure 9-32: To tidy things up a bit, I selected the general areas inside and outside the girl with the lasso tool and filled them with white or black (left). Then I painted inside the lines with the block eraser (right).

6. **Erase inside the lines with the block eraser.** This is the most time-consuming part. You now have to paint inside the lines to make the edge pixels white (selected) or black (not). I like to use the block eraser because it's a hard-edged block. See, Photoshop has already presented me with these lovely and accurate edges. I don't want to gum things up by introducing new edges with a soft paintbrush or airbrush. The block eraser is hard, you can easily see its exact boundaries, and it automatically adjusts as you zoom in and out — affecting fewer pixels at higher levels of magnification, which is what you need. When working in a mask, the eraser always paints in the background color. So, use the X key to toggle the background color between white and black.

   The second example in Figure 9-32 shows the fruits of my erasing. As you can see, I make a few judgment calls and decide — sometimes arbitrarily — where the hair gets so thick that background imagery won't show through. You may even disagree with some of my eraser strokes. But you know what? It doesn't matter. Despite whatever flaws I may have introduced, my mask is more than accurate enough to select the girl and her unruly hair, as I soon demonstrate.

7. **Switch to the color composite view.** Press Ctrl+tilde (~). Or if you're working in a grayscale image, press Ctrl+1. By the way, now is a good time to save the image if you haven't already done so.

8. **Ctrl-click the mask channel to convert it to a selection.** This mask is ready to go prime time.

9. **Ctrl-drag the selection and drop it into a different image.** Figure 9-33 shows the result of dropping the girl into a background of rolling California hills. Thanks to my mask, she looks as natural in her new environment as she did in her previous one. In fact, an uninitiated viewer might have difficulty believing this isn't how she was originally photographed. But if you take a peek at Figure 9-29, you can confirm that Figure 9-33 is indeed an artificial composite. I lost a few strands of hair in the transition, but she can afford it.

Figure 9-33: Thanks to masking, our girl has found a new life in Southern California. Now she's ready to finally put on those sunglasses.

The grayscale Figure 9-33 looks great but, in all honesty, your compositions may not fare quite so well in color, as illustrated by the first girl in Color Plate 9-3. Her hair is fringed with blue, an unavoidable holdover from her original blue background.

The solution is to brush in the color from her new background. Using the paintbrush tool set to the Color brush mode, you can Alt-click in the Background layer to lift colors from the new background and then paint them into the hair. I also took the liberty of erasing a few of the more disorderly hairs, especially the dark ones above her head. (I used a soft paintbrush-style eraser, incidentally, not the block.) After a minute or two of painting and erasing, I arrived at the second girl in the color plate. Now if that isn't compositing perfection, I don't know what is.

✦　　✦　　✦

Corrective Filtering

CHAPTER 10

Filter Basics

In Photoshop, *filters* enable you to apply automated effects to an image. Though named after photographers' filters, which typically correct lighting and perspective fluctuations, Photoshop's filters can accomplish a great deal more. You can slightly increase the focus of an image, introduce random pixels, add depth to an image, or completely rip it apart and reassemble it into a hurky pile of goo. Any number of special effects are made available via filters.

At this point, a little bell should be ringing in your head, telling you to beware of standardized special effects. Why? Because everyone has access to the same filters that you do. If you rely on filters to edit your images for you, your audience will quickly recognize your work as poor or at least unremarkable art.

Imagine this scenario: You're wasting away in front of your TV, flipping aimlessly through the channels. Just as your brain is about to shrivel and implode, you stumble across the classic "Steamroller" video. Outrageous effects, right? Peter Gabriel rides an imaginary roller coaster, bumper cars crash playfully into his face, fish leap over his head. You couldn't be more amused or impressed.

As the video fades, you're so busy basking in the glow that you neglect for a split second to whack the channel-changer. Before you know it, you're midway through an advertisement for a monster truck rally. Like the video, the ad is riddled with special effects — spinning letters, a reverberating voice-over slowed down to an octave below the narrator's normal pitch, and lots of big machines filled with little men filled with single brain cells working overtime.

In and of themselves, these special effects aren't bad. There was probably even a time when you thought that spinning letters and reverberating voice-overs were hot stuff. But sometime after you passed beyond preadolescence, you managed to grow tired of these particular effects. You've come to associate them with raunchy, local car-oriented commercials. Certainly these effects are devoid of substance, but, more importantly, they're devoid of creativity.

This chapter and the next, therefore, are about the creative application of special effects, as is Chapter A on the CD at the back of this book. Rather than trying to show an image subject to every single filter — a service already performed quite adequately by the manual included with your software — these chapters explain exactly how the most important filters work and offer some concrete ways to use them.

You also learn how to apply several filters in tandem and how to use filters to edit images and selection outlines. My goal is not so much to teach you what filters are available — you can find that out by tugging on the Filter menu — but how and when to use filters.

A first look at filters

You access Photoshop's special effects filters by choosing commands from the Filter menu. These commands fall into two general camps — *corrective* and *destructive*.

Corrective filters

Corrective filters are workaday tools that you use to modify scanned images and prepare an image for printing or screen display. In many cases, the effects are subtle enough that the viewer won't even notice that you applied a corrective filter. As demonstrated in Figure 10-1 and Color Plate 10-1, these filters include those that change the focus of an image, enhance color transitions, and average the colors of neighboring pixels. Find these filters in the Filter ➪ Blur, Noise, Sharpen, and Other submenus.

Many corrective filters have direct opposites. Blur is the opposite of Sharpen, Add Noise is the opposite of Median, and so on. This is not to say that one filter entirely removes the effect of the other; only reversion functions such as the History palette provide that capability. Instead, two opposite filters produce contrasting effects.

Corrective filters are the subject of this chapter. Although they number fewer than their destructive counterparts, I spend more time on them because they represent the functions you're most likely to use on a day-to-day basis.

Unsharp Mask

Gaussian Blur

Median

High Pass

Figure 10-1: The gigantic head of 4th-century Roman emperor Constantine subject to four corrective filters, including one each from the Sharpen, Blur, Other, and Noise submenus (reading clockwise from upper left).

Destructive filters

The destructive filters produce effects so dramatic that they can, if used improperly, completely overwhelm your artwork, making the filter more important than the image itself. For the most part, destructive filters reside in the Filter ➪ Distort, Pixelate, Render, and Stylize submenus. A few examples of overwhelmed images appear in Figure 10-2 and Color Plate 10-2.

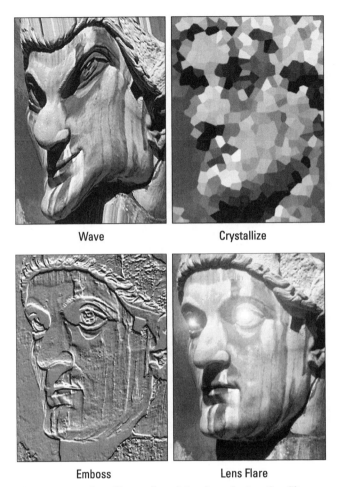

Wave   Crystallize

Emboss   Lens Flare

Figure 10-2: The effects of applying four destructive filters, one each from the Distort, Pixelate, Render, and Stylize submenus (clockwise from upper left). Note that Lens Flare is applicable to color images only, so I had to convert Constantine to the RGB mode before applying the filter.

Destructive filters produce way-cool effects, and many people gravitate toward them when first experimenting with Photoshop. But the filters invariably destroy the original clarity and composition of the image. Granted, every Photoshop function is destructive to a certain extent, but destructive filters change your image so extensively that you can't easily disguise the changes later by applying other filters or editing techniques.

Destructive filters are the subject of Chapter 11. Rather than explaining every one of these filters in detail, I try to provide a general overview.

Effects filters

Photoshop also provides a subset of 47 destructive filters called the *effects* filters. These filters originally sire from the Gallery Effects collection, developed by Silicon Beach, which got gobbled up by Aldus (of PageMaker fame), and finally acquired by Adobe Systems. Not knowing what exactly to do with this grab bag of plug-ins, Adobe integrated them into Photoshop.

Little about these filters has changed since Gallery Effects 1.5 came out in 1993. A couple of filters have been renamed — the old GE Ripple filter is now Ocean Ripple to avoid confusion with Photoshop's own Ripple filter. And one filter, GE Emboss, is gone, presumably because it detracted from the popular Filter ⇨ Stylize ⇨ Emboss. But Adobe hasn't bothered with any meaningful retooling. You can't preview the effect in the image window and a few filters are dreadfully slow.

As a result, I devote only passing attention to the effects filters, explaining those very few that fulfill a real need. Of course, I encourage you to experiment and derive your own conclusions. After all, as Figure 10-3 illustrates, these filters do produce intriguing special effects. I mean, that Plaster effect is just plain cool. For the record, most of the effects filters reside in the Filter ⇨ Artistic, Brush Strokes, Sketch, and Texture submenus. A few have trickled out into other submenus, including Filter ⇨ Distort ⇨ Diffuse Glow, Glass, and Ocean Ripple; and Filter ⇨ Stylize ⇨ Glowing Edges.

Tip

If your experimentation leads you to the same conclusion as it did me — that you can live through most days without the effects filters — you can turn them off. All the effects filters are stored in the Effects folder inside the Plug-Ins folder on your hard drive. Rename the Effects folder ~Effects, and all 47 filters will be turned off.

How filters work

When you choose a command from the Filter menu, Photoshop applies the filter to the selected portion of the image on the current layer. If no portion of the image is selected, Photoshop applies the filter to the entire image. Therefore, if you want to filter every nook and cranny of the current layer, press Ctrl+D to cancel any existing selection outline and then choose the desired command.

External plug-ins

Some filters are built into the Photoshop application. Others are external modules that reside in the Plug-Ins folder. This enables you to add functionality to Photoshop by purchasing additional filters from third-party collections. Gallery Effects used to be such a collection. Eye Candy, from Alien Skin, is another popular collection.

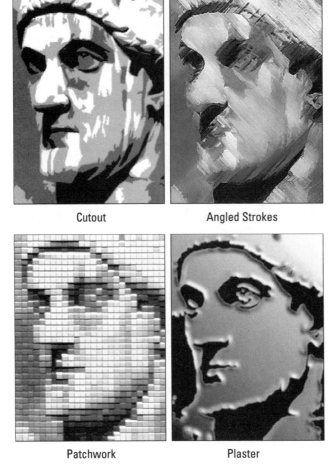

Cutout   Angled Strokes

Patchwork   Plaster

Figure 10-3: The *effects* filters come from Gallery Effects, a little toy surprise that Adobe accidentally acquired when it purchased Aldus Corporation. Here we see the impact of one filter each from the Filter ⇨ Artistic, Brush Strokes, Sketch, and Texture submenus (clockwise from upper left).

If you open the Plug-Ins folder inside the Photoshop folder, you see that it contains several subfolders. By default, Photoshop places the filters in the Filters and Effects subfolders, but you can place additional filters anywhere inside the Plug-Ins folder. Even if you create a new folder inside the Plug-Ins folder and call it *No Filters Here,* create another folder inside that called *Honest, Fresh Out of Filters,* toss in one more folder called *Carpet Beetles Only,* and put every plug-in you own inside this latest folder, Photoshop sees through your clever ruse and displays the exact same filters you always see under their same submenus in the Filter menu. The only purpose of the subfolders is to keep things tidy, so that you don't have to look through a list of 6,000 files.

Previewing filters

For years, the biggest problem with Photoshop's filters was that none offered previews to help you predict the outcome of an effect. You just had to tweak your 15,000 meaningless settings and hope for the best. But today, life is much better. Photoshop 3 introduced previews, Version 4 made them commonly available to all but the most gnarly filters, and Versions 5 and 6 had the good sense to leave well enough alone.

Photoshop offers two previewing capabilities:

✦ **Dialog box previews:** Labeled in Figure 10-4, the 100 × 100-pixel preview box is now a common feature to all filter dialog boxes. Drag inside the preview box to scroll the portion of the image you want to preview. Move the cursor outside the dialog box to get the square preview cursor (labeled in the figure). Click with the cursor to center the contents of the preview box at the clicked position in the image.

Click the zoom buttons (+ and −) to reduce the image inside the preview box. You can even take advantage of the standard zoom tool by pressing Ctrl+ spacebar or Alt+spacebar, depending on whether you want to zoom in or out.

✦ **Image window previews:** Most corrective filters — as well as a couple of destructives such as Mosaic and Emboss — also preview effects in the full image window. Just select the Preview check box to activate this function. While the effect is previewing, a blinking progress line appears under the zoom value in the dialog box. In Figure 10-4, for example, you can see that the bottom of the image still hasn't finished previewing, so the progress line strobes away. If you're working on a relatively poky computer, you'll probably want to turn the Preview check box off to speed up the pace at which the filter functions.

Incidentally, the Preview check box has no affect on the contents of the preview box. The latter continually monitors the effects of your settings, whether you like it or not.

Use the Preview check box to compare the before and after effects of a corrective filter in the image window. Turn it on to see the effect; turn it off to see the original image. You can also compare the image in the preview box by clicking in the box. Mouse down to see the old image; release to see the filtered image. It's like an electronic, high-priced, adult version of peek-a-boo. But not nearly as likely to induce giggles.

Even though a dialog box is on screen and active, you can zoom and scroll the contents of the image window. Press Ctrl+plus or Ctrl+spacebar-click to zoom in; press Ctrl+minus or Alt+spacebar-click to zoom out. Spacebar-drag to scroll. You can also choose commands from the View and Window menus.

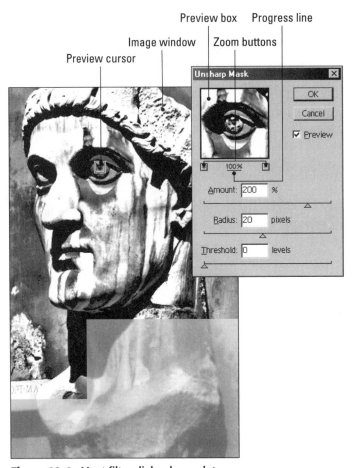

Figure 10-4: Most filter dialog boxes let you preview the effects of the filter both inside the dialog box and in the image window.

Tip

One more tip: When you press Alt, the Cancel button changes to a Reset button. Alt-click this button to restore the settings that appeared when you first opened the dialog box. (These are not necessarily the factory default settings; they are the settings you last applied to an image.)

Most destructive filters make no attempt to preview effects in the image window. And seven filters continue to offer no previews whatsoever: Radial Blur, Displace, Color Halftone, Extrude, Tiles, De-Interlace, and Offset. Of course, single-shot filters — the ones that don't bring up dialog boxes — don't need previews because there aren't any settings to adjust.

Reapplying the last filter

To reapply the last filter used in the current Photoshop session, choose the first command from the Filter menu or simply press Ctrl+F. If you want to reapply the filter subject to different settings, Alt+choose the first Filter command or press Ctrl+Alt+F to redisplay that filter's dialog box.

Both techniques work even if you undo the last application of a filter. However, if you cancel a filter while in progress, pressing Ctrl+F or Ctrl+Alt+F applies the last uncanceled filter.

Nudging numerical values

In addition to entering specific numerical values inside filter dialog boxes, you can nudge the values using the up and down arrow keys. When working with percentage values, press an arrow key to raise or lower the value by 1. Press Shift-up or -down arrow to change the value in increments of 10. Note that with some of the destructive filters, most notably those associated with the old Gallery Effects filters, you must use the arrow keys on the numeric keypad; the regular navigation arrow keys don't work.

If the value accommodates decimal values, it's probably more sensitive to the arrow key. Press an arrow for a 0.1 change; press Shift+arrow for 1.0.

Fading a filter

In many cases, you apply filters to a selection or image at full intensity — meaning that you marquee an area using a selection tool, choose a filter command, enter whatever settings you deem appropriate if a dialog box appears, and sit back and watch the fireworks.

What's so full intensity about that? Sounds normal, right? Well, the fact is, you can reduce the intensity of the last filter applied by choosing the Fade command. This command permits you to mix the filtered image with the original, unfiltered one.

In Photoshop 6, the Fade command appears on the Edit menu instead of the Filter menu; the new placement makes sense because Adobe expanded the Fade feature in Version 5.5 to enable you to apply it to brush strokes and other edits in addition to filter applications. But the result of the command — as well as its keyboard shortcut (Ctrl+Shift+F) — remains the same as in versions past.

As shown in Figure 10-5, the Fade dialog box provides you with the basic tools of image mixing — an Opacity value and a blend mode pop-up menu. To demonstrate the wonders of Filter ➪ Fade, I've applied two particularly destructive Gallery Effects filters to the colossal marble head — Filter ➪ Stylize ➪ Glowing Edges and Filter ➪ Sketch ➪ Note Paper. In the second column of heads, I pressed Ctrl+Shift+F and lowered the Opacity of the two effects to 30 percent. The right-hand images show the effects of two blend modes, Lighten and Overlay, with the Opacity value restored to 100 percent.

Glowing Edges   Lighten

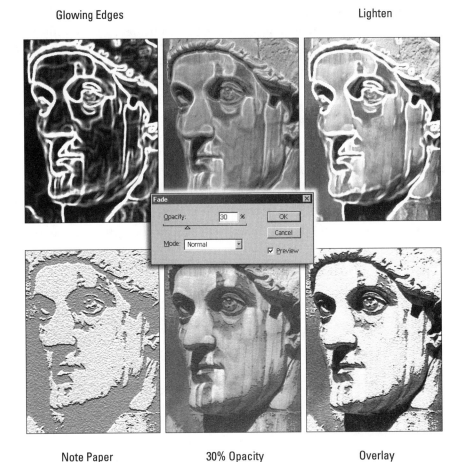

Note Paper   30% Opacity   Overlay

Figure 10-5: Press Ctrl+Shift+F to mix the filtered image with the unfiltered original. Now, is it me, or is Constantine on Note Paper the spitting image of Rambo? That's got to be keeping some art historian awake at night.

Creating layered effects

The drawback of the Fade command is that it's only available immediately after you apply a filter (or other applicable edit). If you so much as modify a selection outline after applying the filter, the Fade command dims, only to return when you apply the next filter.

Therefore, you may find it more helpful to copy a selection to a separate layer (Ctrl+J) before applying a filter. This way, you can perform other operations, and even apply many filters in a row, before mixing the filtered image with the underlying original.

Filtering inside a border

And here's another reason to layer before you filter: If your image has a border around it — like the ones shown in Figure 10-6 — you don't want Photoshop to factor the border into the filtering operation. To avoid this, select the image inside the border and press Ctrl+J to layer it prior to applying the filter. The reason is that most filters take neighboring pixels into consideration even if they are not selected. By contrast, when a selection floats, it has no neighboring pixels, and therefore the filter affects the selected pixels only.

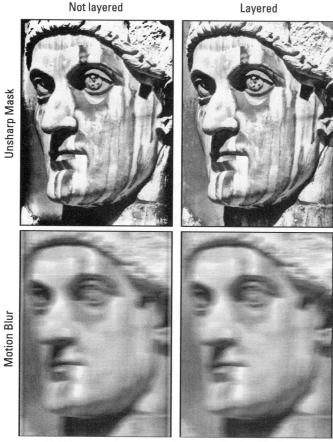

Figure 10-6: The results of applying two sample filters to images surrounded by borders. In each case, only the image was selected; the border was not. Layering the right examples prevented the borders from affecting the performance of the filters.

Figure 10-6 shows the results of applying two filters discussed in this chapter — Unsharp Mask and Motion Blur — when the image is anchored in place and when it's layered. In all cases, the 2-pixel border was not selected. In the left examples, the Unsharp Mask filter leaves a high-contrast residue around the edge of the image, while Motion Blur duplicates the left and right edges of the border. Both problems vanish when the filters are applied to layered images, as seen on the right.

Even if the area outside the selection is not a border per se — perhaps it's just a comparatively dark or light area that serves as a visual frame — layering comes in handy. You should always layer the selection unless you specifically want edge pixels to be calculated by the filter.

Undoing a sequence of filters

Okay, here's one last reason to layer before you filter. Copying an image to a layer protects the underlying image. If you just want to experiment a little, pressing Ctrl+J is often more convenient than restoring a state in the History palette. After applying four or five effects to a layer, you can undo all that automated abuse by Alt-clicking the trash icon at the bottom of the Layers palette, which deletes the layer. The underlying original remains unharmed.

Heightening Focus and Contrast

If you've experimented at all with Photoshop, you've no doubt had your way with many of the commands in the Filter ➪ Sharpen submenu. By increasing the contrast between neighboring pixels, the sharpening filters enable you to compensate for image elements that were photographed or scanned slightly out of focus.

The Sharpen, Sharpen More, and Sharpen Edges commands are easy to use and immediate in their effect. However, you can achieve better results and widen your range of sharpening options if you learn how to use the Unsharp Mask and High Pass commands, which I discuss at length in the following pages.

Using the Unsharp Mask filter

The first thing you need to know about the Unsharp Mask filter is that it has a weird name. The filter has nothing to do with unsharpening — whatever that is — nor is it tied into Photoshop's masking capabilities. Unsharp Mask is named after a traditional film compositing technique (which is also oddly named) that highlights the edges in an image by combining a blurred film negative with the original film positive.

That's all very well and good, but the fact is most Photoshop artists have never touched a stat camera (an expensive piece of machinery, roughly twice the size of a washing machine, used by image editors of the late Jurassic, pre-Photoshop epoch).

Even folks like me who used to operate stat cameras professionally never had the time to delve into the world of unsharp masking. In addition—and much to the filter's credit—Unsharp Mask goes beyond traditional camera techniques.

To understand Unsharp Mask—or Photoshop's other sharpening filters, for that matter—you first need to understand some basic terminology. When you apply one of the sharpening filters, Photoshop increases the contrast between neighboring pixels. The effect is similar to what you see when you adjust a camera to bring a scene into sharper focus.

Two of Photoshop's sharpening filters, Sharpen and Sharpen More, affect whatever area of your image is selected. The Sharpen Edges filter, however, performs its sharpening operations only on the *edges* in the image—those areas that feature the highest amount of contrast.

Unsharp Mask gives you both sharpening options. It can sharpen only the edges in an image or it can sharpen any portion of an image according to your exact specifications, whether it finds an edge or not. It fulfills the exact same purposes as the Sharpen, Sharpen Edges, and Sharpen More commands, but it's much more versatile. Simply put, the Unsharp Mask tool is the only sharpening filter you'll ever need.

When you choose Filter ➪ Sharpen ➪ Unsharp Mask, Photoshop displays the Unsharp Mask dialog box, shown in Figure 10-7, which offers the following options:

✦ **Amount:** Enter a value between 1 and 500 percent to specify the degree to which you want to sharpen the selected image. Higher values produce more pronounced effects.

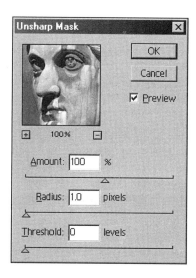

Figure 10-7: Despite any conclusions you may glean from its bizarre name, the Unsharp Mask filter sharpens images according to your specifications in this dialog box.

✦ **Radius:** This option determines the thickness of the sharpened edge. Low values produce crisp edges. High values produce thicker edges with more contrast throughout the image.

✦ **Threshold:** Enter a value between 0 and 255 to control how Photoshop recognizes edges in an image. The value indicates the numerical difference between the brightness values of two neighboring pixels that must occur if Photoshop is to sharpen those pixels. A low value sharpens lots of pixels; a high value excludes most pixels from the running.

The preview options offered by the Unsharp Mask dialog box are absolutely essential visual aids that you're likely to find tremendously useful throughout your Photoshop career. Just the same, you'll be better prepared to experiment with the Amount, Radius, and Threshold options and less surprised by the results if you read the following sections, which explain these options in detail and demonstrate the effects of each.

Specifying the amount of sharpening

If Amount were the only Unsharp Mask option, no one would have any problems understanding this filter. If you want to sharpen an image ever so slightly, enter a low percentage value. Values between 25 and 50 percent are ideal for producing subtle effects. If you want to sharpen an image beyond the point of good taste, enter a value somewhere in the 300 to 500 percent range. And if you're looking for moderate sharpening, try out some value between 50 and 300 percent. Figure 10-8 shows the results of applying different Amount values while leaving the Radius and Threshold values at their default settings of 1.0 and 0, respectively.

If you're not sure how much you want to sharpen an image, try out a small value in the 25 to 50 percent range. Then reapply that setting repeatedly by pressing Ctrl+F. As you can see in Figure 10-9, repeatedly applying the filter at a low setting produces a nearly identical result to applying the filter once at a higher setting. For example, you can achieve the effect shown in the middle image in the figure by applying the Unsharp Mask filter three times at 50 percent or once at 250 percent. I created the top-row results in Figure 10-9 using a constant Radius value of 1.0. In the second row, I lowered the Radius progressively from 1.0 (left) to 0.8 (middle) to 0.6 (right).

The benefit of using small values is that they enable you to experiment with sharpening incrementally. As the figure demonstrates, you can add sharpening bit by bit to increase the focus of an image. You can't, however, reduce sharpening incrementally if you apply too high a value; you must press Ctrl+Z and start again.

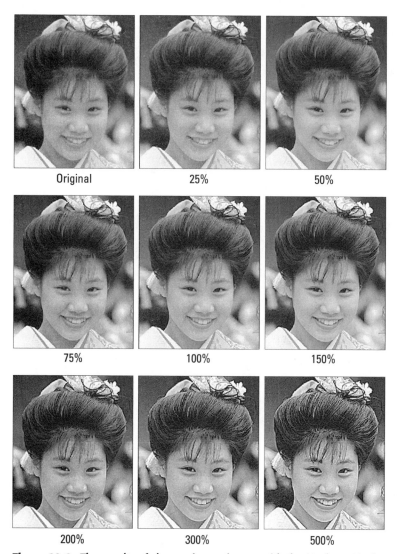

Figure 10-8: The results of sharpening an image with the Unsharp Mask filter using eight different Amount values. The Radius and Threshold values used for all images were 1.0 and 0, respectively (the default settings).

50% twice   50% times three   50% times four

100%   250%   500%

Figure 10-9: Repeatedly applying the Unsharp Mask filter at 50 percent (top row) is nearly equivalent on a pixel-by-pixel basis to applying the filter once at higher settings (bottom row).

Just for fun, Color Plate 10-3 shows the results of applying the Unsharp Mask filter to each of the color channels in an RGB image independently. In each case, I maxed out the Amount value to 500 percent and set the Radius and Threshold to 4.0 and 0 respectively. The top row shows the results of applying the filter to a single channel; in the second row, I applied the filter to two of the three channels (leaving only one channel unfiltered). You can see how the filter creates a crisp halo of color around the chess pieces. Sharpening the red channel creates a red halo on the inside of the pieces and a blue-green halo on the outside; sharpening the red and green channels together creates a yellow halo on the inside and a bluish halo on the outside; and so on. Applying the filter to the red and green channels produced the most noticeable effects because these channels contain the lion's share of the image detail. The blue channel contained the least detail — as is typical — so sharpening this channel produced the least dramatic results.

Cross-Reference

If you're a little foggy on how to access individual color channels, read Chapter 4. Incidentally, you can achieve similar effects by sharpening the individual channels in a Lab or CMYK image.

Tip

As I mentioned in Chapter 4, Photoshop is ultimately a grayscale editor, so when you apply the Unsharp Mask command to a full-color image, Photoshop actually applies the command in a separate pass to each of the color channels. Therefore, the command always results in the color halos shown in Color Plate 10-3 — it's just that the halos get mixed together, minimizing the effect. To avoid any haloing whatsoever, convert the image to the Lab mode (Image ⇨ Mode ⇨ Lab Color) and apply Unsharp Mask to only the Lightness channel in the Channels palette. (Do not filter the *a* and *b* channels.) This sharpens the brightness values in the image and leaves the colors 100 percent untouched.

Setting the thickness of the edges

The Unsharp Mask filter works by identifying edges and increasing the contrast around those edges. The Radius value tells Photoshop how thick you want your edges. Large values produce thicker edges than small values.

The ideal Radius value depends on the resolution of your image and the quality of its edges:

✦ When creating screen images — such as Web graphics — use a very low Radius value such as 0.5. This results in terrific hairline edges that look so crisp, you'll think you washed your bifocals.

✦ If a low Radius value brings out weird little imperfections — such as grain, scan lines, or JPEG compression artifacts — raise the value to 1.0 or higher. If that doesn't help, don't fret. I include two different sure-fire image-fixing techniques later in this chapter, one designed to sharpen grainy old photos, and another that accommodates compressed images.

✦ When printing an image at a moderate resolution — anywhere from 120 to 180 ppi — use a Radius value of 1.0. The edges will look a little thick on-screen, but they'll print fine.

✦ For high-resolution images — around 300 ppi — try a Radius of 2.0. Because Photoshop prints more pixels per inch, the edges have to be thicker to remain nice and visible.

Tip

If you're looking for a simple formula, I recommend 0.1 of Radius for every 15 ppi of final image resolution. That means 75 ppi warrants a Radius of 0.5, 120 ppi warrants 0.8, 180 ppi warrants 1.2, and so on. If you have a calculator, just divide the intended resolution by 150 to get the ideal Radius value.

You can of course enter higher Radius values — as high as 250, in fact. Higher values produce heightened contrast effects, almost as if the image had been photocopied too many times, generally useful for producing special effects.

But don't take my word for it; you be the judge. Figure 10-10 demonstrates the results of specific Radius values. In each case, the Amount and Threshold values remain constant at 100 percent and 0, respectively.

Original	0.5	1.0
1.5	2.5	5.0
10.0	50.0	100.0

Figure 10-10: The results of applying eight different Radius values, ranging from precise edges to very gooey.

Figure 10-11 shows the results of combining different Amount and Radius values. You can see that a large Amount value helps to offset the softening of a high Radius value. For example, when the Amount is set to 200 percent, as in the first row, the Radius value appears to mainly enhance contrast when raised from 0.5 to 2.0. However, when the Amount value is lowered to 50 percent, the higher Radius value does more to distribute the effect than boost contrast.

200%, 0.5   200%, 2.0   200%, 10.0

100%, 0.5   100%, 2.0   100%, 10.0

50%, 0.5   50%, 2.0   50%, 10.0

Figure 10-11: The effects of combining different Amount and Radius settings. The Threshold value for each image was set to 0, the default setting.

For those few folks who are thinking, "By gum, I wonder what would happen if you applied an unusually high Radius value to each color channel independently," you have only to consult Color Plate 10-4. In this figure, I again applied the Unsharp Mask filter to each channel and each pair of channels in the RGB chess image independently. But I changed the Amount value to 250 percent, raised the Radius value to a whopping 20.0 pixels, and left the Threshold at 0. To make the splash more apparent, I applied the filter twice to each image. The colors now bound out from the king, queen, and knight, bleeding into the gray background by as much as 20 pixels, the Radius value. Notice how the color fades away from the pieces, almost as if I had selected and feathered them? A high Radius value spreads the sharpening effect and, in doing so, allows colors to bleed. Because you normally apply the filter to all channels simultaneously, the colors bleed uniformly to create thick edges and high-contrast effects.

Recognizing edges

By default, the Unsharp Mask filter sharpens every pixel in a selection. However, you can instruct the filter to sharpen only the edges in an image by raising the Threshold value from zero to some other number. The Threshold value represents the difference between two neighboring pixels — as measured in brightness levels — that must occur for Photoshop to recognize them as an edge.

Suppose that the brightness values of neighboring pixels are 10 and 20. If you set the Threshold value to 5, Photoshop reads both pixels, notes that the difference between their brightness values is more than 5, and treats them as an edge. If you set the Threshold value to 20, however, Photoshop passes them by. A low Threshold value, therefore, causes the Unsharp Mask Filter to affect a high number of pixels, and vice versa.

In the top row of images in Figure 10-12, the high Threshold values result in tiny slivers of sharpness that outline only the most substantial edges in the woman's face. As I lower the Threshold value incrementally in the second and third rows, the sharpening effect takes over more and more of the face, ultimately sharpening all details uniformly in the lower-right example.

Using the preset sharpening filters

So how do the Sharpen, Sharpen Edges, and Sharpen More commands compare with the Unsharp Mask filter? First of all, none of the preset commands permit you to vary the thickness of your edges, a function provided by Unsharp Mask's Radius option. Second, only the Sharpen Edges command can recognize high-contrast areas in an image. And third, all three commands are set in stone — you can't adjust their effects in any way (except, of course, to fade the filter after the fact). Figure 10-13 shows the effect of each preset command and the nearly equivalent effect created with the Unsharp Mask filter.

Sharpening grainy photographs

Having completed my neutral discussion of Unsharp Mask, king of the Sharpen filters, I hasten to interject a little bit of commentary, along with a helpful solution to a common sharpening problem.

Figure 10-12: The results of applying nine different Threshold values. To best show off the differences between each image, I set the Amount and Radius values to 500 percent and 2.0 respectively.

First, the commentary: While Amount and Radius are the kinds of superior options that will serve you well throughout the foreseeable future, I urge young and old to observe Threshold with the utmost scorn and rancor. The idea is fine — we can all agree that you need some way to draw a dividing line between those pixels that you want to sharpen and those that you want to leave unchanged. But the Threshold setting is nothing more than a glorified on/off switch that results in harsh transitions between sharpened and unsharpened pixels.

| Sharpen | Sharpen Edges | Sharpen More |

| 100%, 0.5, 0 | 100%, 0.5, 5 | 300%, 0.5, 0 |

Figure 10-13: The effects of the three preset sharpening filters (top row) compared with the Unsharp Mask equivalents (bottom row). Unsharp Mask values are listed in the following order: Amount, Radius, Threshold.

Consider the picture of pre-presidential Eisenhower in Figure 10-14. Like so many vintage photographs, this particular image of Ike is a little softer than we're used to seeing these days. But if I apply a heaping helping of Unsharp Mask — as in the second example in the figure — I bring out as much film grain as image detail. The official Photoshop solution is to raise the Threshold value, but the option's intrinsic harshness results in a pockmarked effect, as shown on the right. Photoshop has simply replaced one kind of grain with another.

These abrupt transitions are quite out of keeping with Photoshop's normal approach. Paintbrushes have antialiased edges, selections can be feathered, the Color Range command offers Fuzziness — in short, everything mimics the softness found in real life. Yet right here, inside what is indisputably Photoshop's most essential filter, we find no mechanism for softness whatsoever.

Soft

Sharpened, Threshold: 0

Sharpened, Threshold: 20

Figure 10-14: The original Ike is a bit soft (left), a condition I can remedy with Unsharp Mask. Leaving the Threshold value set to 0 brings out the film grain (middle), but raising the value results in equally unattractive artifacts (right).

While we wait for Photoshop to give us a better Threshold—one with a Fuzziness slider or similar control—you can create a better Threshold using a very simple masking technique. Using a few filters that I explore at greater length throughout this chapter and the next, you can devise a selection outline that traces the essential edges in the image—complete with fuzzy transitions—and leaves the non-edges unmolested. So get out your favorite old vintage photograph and follow along with these steps.

STEPS: Creating and Using an Edge Mask

1. **Duplicate one of the color channels.** Bring up the Channels palette and drag one of the color channels onto the little page icon. Ike is a grayscale image, so I duplicate the one and only channel.

2. **Choose Filter ⇨ Stylize ⇨ Find Edges.** As I explain in Chapter 11, the Find Edges filter automatically traces the edges of your image with thick, gooey outlines that are ideal for creating edge masks.

3. **Press Ctrl+I.** Or choose Image ⇨ Adjust ⇨ Invert. Find Edges produces black lines against a white background, but in order to select your edges, you need white lines against a black background. The Invert command reverses the lights and darks in the mask, as in the first example in Figure 10-15.

Find Edges, Invert

Sharpened edges

Find edge mask

Figure 10-15: I copy a channel, find the edges, and invert (left). I then apply a string of filters to expand and soften the edges (middle). After converting the mask to a selection outline, I reapply Unsharp Mask with winning results (right).

4. **Choose Filter ➪ Noise ➪ Median.** You need fat, gooey edges, and the current ones are a bit tenuous. To firm up the edges, choose the Median filter, enter a value of 2 (or thereabouts), and press Enter.

5. **Choose Filter ➪ Other ➪ Maximum.** The next step is to thicken up the edges. The Maximum filter expands the white areas in the image, serving much the same function in a mask as Select ➪ Modify ➪ Expand serves when editing a selection outline. Enter 4 for the Radius value and press Enter.

6. **Choose Filter ➪ Blur ➪ Gaussian Blur.** Unfortunately, the Maximum filter results in a bunch of little squares that don't do much for our cause. You can merge the squares into a seamless line by choosing the Gaussian Blur command and entering 4, the same radius you entered for Maximum. Then press Enter.

The completed mask is pictured in the second example of Figure 10-15. Though hardly an impressive sight to the uninitiated eye, you're looking at the perfect edge mask—soft, natural, and extremely accurate.

7. **Return to the standard composite view.** Press Ctrl+tilde (~) in a color image. In a grayscale image, press Ctrl+1.

8. **Convert the mask to a selection outline.** Ctrl-click the mask name in the Channels palette. Photoshop selects the most essential edges in the image without selecting the grain.

9. **Choose Filter ➪ Sharpen ➪ Unsharp Mask.** In the last example in Figure 10-15, I applied the highest permitted Amount value, 500 percent, and a Radius of 2.0.

10. **Whatever values you use, make sure the Threshold is set to 0.** And always leave it at 0 from this day forward.

In case Figures 10-14 and 10-15 are a little too subtle, I include enlarged views of the great general's eyes in Figure 10-16. The top eyes show the result of using the Threshold value, the bottom eyes were created using the edge mask. Which ones appear sharper and less grainy to you?

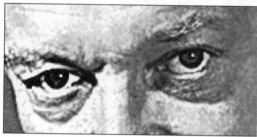

Figure 10-16: Enlarged views of the last examples from Figures 10-14 (top) and 10-15 (bottom). A good edge mask beats the Threshold value every time.

Using the High Pass filter

The High Pass filter falls more or less in the same camp as the sharpening filters but is not located under the Filter ➪ Sharpen submenu. This frequently overlooked gem enables you to isolate high-contrast image areas from their low-contrast counterparts.

When you choose Filter ➪ Other ➪ High Pass, Photoshop offers a single option: the familiar Radius value, which can vary from 0.1 to 250.0. As demonstrated in Figure 10-17, high Radius values distinguish areas of high and low contrast only slightly. Low values change all high-contrast areas to dark gray and low-contrast areas to a slightly lighter gray. A value of 0.1 (not shown) changes all pixels in an image to a single gray value and is therefore useless.

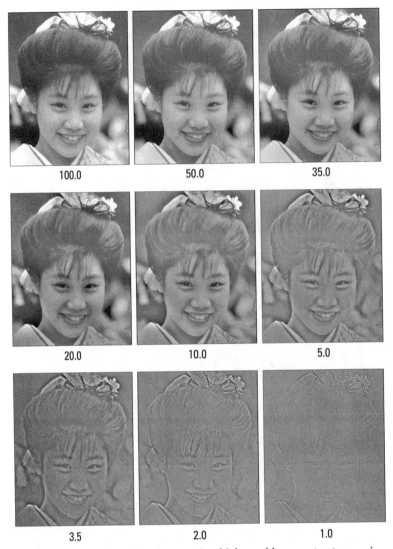

Figure 10-17: The results of separating high- and low-contrast areas in an image with the High Pass filter set at eight different Radius values.

Applying High Pass to individual color channels

In my continuing series of color plates devoted to adding a bit of digital color to the ages-old game of chess, Color Plate 10-5 shows the results of applying the High Pass filter set to a Radius value of 5.0 to the various color channels. This application is a pretty interesting use for this filter. When applied to all channels at once, High Pass has an irritating habit of robbing the image of color in the low-contrast areas, just where the color is needed most. But when you apply it to a single channel, there's no color to steal. In fact, the filter adds color. For example, because there is almost no contrast in the dark shadows, High Pass elevates the black to gray in each of the affected color channels. The gray in the red channel appears red, the gray in the red channel mixed with the gray in the green channel appears yellow, and so on. As a result, the filter imbues each image with a chalky glow.

Note

I enhanced the High Pass effect slightly in Color Plate 10-5 by increasing the contrast of each affected color channel using the Levels command. Using the Input option boxes at the top of the Levels dialog box, I changed the first value to 65 and the third value to 190, thereby compressing the color space equally on both the black and white sides. Had I not done this, the images would appear a little more washed out. (Not a lot, but I figure that you deserve the best color I can deliver.) For detailed information on the Levels command, read Chapter 17.

Converting an image into a line drawing

The High Pass filter is especially useful as a precursor to Image ⇨ Adjust ⇨ Threshold, which converts all pixels in an image to black and white (again, covered in Chapter 17). As illustrated in Figure 10-18, the Threshold command produces entirely different effects on images before and after you alter them with the High Pass filter. In fact, applying the High Pass filter with a low Radius value and then issuing the Threshold command converts your image into a line drawing.

In the second row of examples in the figure, I followed Threshold with Filter ⇨ Blur ⇨ Gaussian Blur (the subject of the next section). I set the Gaussian Blur Radius value to 1.0. Like the Threshold option in the Unsharp Mask dialog box, the Threshold command results in harsh transitions; Gaussian Blur softens them to produce a more natural effect.

Why change your image to a bunch of slightly different gray values and then apply a command such as Threshold? One reason is to create a mask, as discussed at length in the "Building a Mask from an Image" section of Chapter 9. (In Chapter 9, I used Levels instead of Threshold, but both are variations on the same theme.)

You might also want to bolster the edges in an image. For example, to achieve the last row of examples in Figure 10-18, I layered the images prior to applying High Pass, Threshold, and Gaussian Blur. Then I monkeyed around with the Opacity setting and the blend mode to achieve an edge-tracing effect.

Note

I should mention that Photoshop provides several automated edge-tracing filters — including Find Edges, Trace Contour, and the Gallery Effects acquisition, Glowing Edges. But High Pass affords more control than any of these commands and permits you to explore a wider range of alternatives. Also worth noting, several Gallery Effects filters — most obviously Filter ⇨ Sketch ⇨ Photocopy — lift much of their code directly from High Pass. Although it may seem at first glance a strange effect, High Pass is one of the seminal filters in Photoshop.

Figure 10-18: Several applications of the High Pass filter with low Radius values (top row), followed by the same images subject to Image ➪ Adjust ➪ Threshold and Filter ➪ Blur ➪ Gaussian Blur (middle). I then layered the second row onto the first and modified the Opacity and blend mode settings to create the third row.

Blurring an Image

The commands under the Filter ⇨ Blur submenu produce the opposite effects of their counterparts under the Filter ⇨ Sharpen submenu. Rather than enhancing the amount of contrast between neighboring pixels, the Blur filters diminish contrast to create softening effects.

Applying the Gaussian Blur filter

The preeminent Blur filter, Gaussian Blur, blends a specified number of pixels incrementally, following the bell-shaped Gaussian distribution curve I touched on earlier. When you choose Filter ⇨ Blur ⇨ Gaussian Blur, Photoshop produces a single Radius option box, in which you can enter any value from 0.1 to 250.0. (Beginning to sound familiar?) As demonstrated in Figure 10-19, Radius values of 1.0 and smaller blur an image slightly; moderate values, between 1.0 and 5.0, turn an image into a rude approximation of life without my glasses on; and higher values blur the image beyond recognition.

Moderate to high Radius values can be especially useful for creating that hugely amusing *Star Trek* Iridescent Female effect. This is the old *Star Trek*, of course. Captain Kirk meets some bewitching ambassador or scientist who has just beamed on board. He takes her hand in sincere welcome as he gives out with a lecherous grin and explains how truly honored he is to have such a renowned guest in his transporter room, and so charming to boot. Then we see it — the close-up of the fetching actress shrouded in a kind of gleaming halo that prevents us from discerning if her lips are chapped or perhaps she's hiding an old acne scar, because some cockeyed cinematographer smeared Vaseline all over the camera lens. I mean, what *wouldn't* you give to be able to recreate this effect in Photoshop?

Unfortunately, I don't have any images of actresses adorned in futuristic go-go boots, so Constantine cum Rambo will have to do in a pinch. The following steps explain how to make the colossal head glow as demonstrated in Figure 10-20.

STEPS: The Captain Kirk Myopia Effect

1. **Press Ctrl+A to select the entire image.** If you only want to apply the effect to a portion of the image, feather the selection with a radius in the neighborhood of 5 to 8 pixels.

2. **Choose Filter ⇨ Blur ⇨ Gaussian Blur.** Enter some unusually large value into the Radius option box — say, 8.0 — and press Enter.

3. **Press Ctrl+Shift+F to bring up the Fade dialog box.** To achieve the effects shown in Figure 10-20, I reduced the Opacity value to 70 percent, making the blurred image slightly translucent. This way, you can see the hard edges of the original image through the filtered one.

4. You can achieve additional effects by selecting options from the Mode pop-up menu. For example, I created the upper-right example in the figure by selecting the Screen option, which uses the colors in the filtered image to lighten the original. I created the two bottom examples in the figure by applying the Darken and Lighten options.

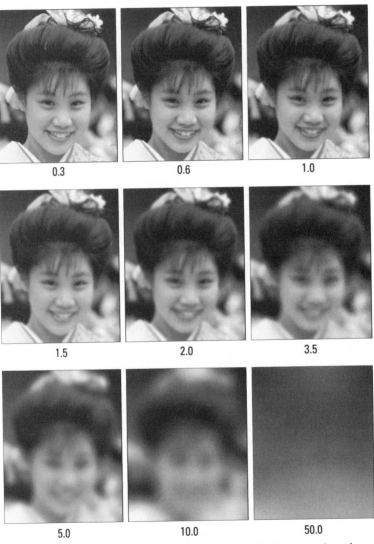

0.3   0.6   1.0

1.5   2.0   3.5

5.0   10.0   50.0

Figure 10-19: The results of blurring an image with the Gaussian Blur filter using eight different Radius values, ranging from slightly out of focus to Bad Day at the Ophthalmologist's Office.

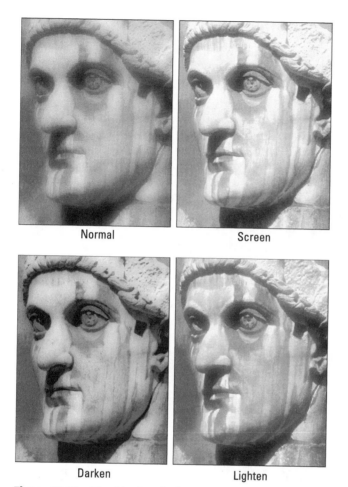

Normal   Screen

Darken   Lighten

Figure 10-20: After blurring the image, I chose Edit ⇨ Fade Gaussian Blur and changed the Opacity value to 70 percent. Then I applied the labeled blend modes to alter the image further.

Color Plate 10-6 shows an image that's more likely to interest Captain Kirk. It shows a young agrarian woman subject to most of the same settings I applied earlier to Constantine. Again, I applied the Gaussian Blur filter with a Radius of 8.0. Then I used Edit ⇨ Fade Gaussian Blur to adjust the Opacity value and blend mode. The upper-left image shows the Normal mode, but the upper-right image shows the Luminosity mode. In this case, the Screen mode resulted in a washed-out effect, whereas Luminosity yielded an image with crisp color detail and fuzzy brightness values. As a result, there are some interesting places where the colors leap off her checkered dress. As in Figure 10-20, the bottom two images show the effects of the Darken and Lighten modes.

You know, though, as I look at this woman, I'm beginning to have my doubts about her and Captain Kirk. I mean, she has Scotty written all over her.

The preset blurring filters

Neither of the two preset commands in the Filter ⇨ Blur submenu, Blur and Blur More, can distribute its blurring effect over a bell-shaped Gaussian curve. For that reason, these two commands are less functional than the Gaussian Blur filter. However, just so you know where they stand in the grand Photoshop focusing scheme, Figure 10-21 shows the effect of each preset command and the nearly equivalent effect created with the Gaussian Blur filter.

Blur   Blur More

0.3   0.7

Figure 10-21: The effects of the two preset blurring filters (top row) compared with their Gaussian Blur equivalents (bottom row), which are labeled according to Radius values.

Antialiasing an image

If you have a particularly jagged image, such as a 256-color GIF file, there's a better way to soften the rough edges than applying the Gaussian Blur filter. The best solution is to antialias the image. How? After all, Photoshop doesn't offer an Antialias filter. Well, think about it. Back in the "Softening selection outlines" section of Chapter 8, I described how Photoshop antialiases a brushstroke or selection outline at twice its normal size and then reduces it by 50 percent and applies bicubic interpolation. You can do the same thing with an image.

Choose Image ⇨ Image Size and enlarge the image to 200 percent of its present size. Make sure that the Resample Image check box is turned on and set to Bicubic. (You can also experiment with Bilinear for a slightly different effect, but don't use Nearest

Neighbor.) Next, turn right around and choose Image ➪ Image Size again, but this time shrink the image by 50 percent.

The top-left example in Figure 10-22 shows a jagged image subject to this effect. I used Image ➪ Adjust ➪ Posterize to reduce Moses to four colors. It's ugly, but it's not unlike the kind of images you may encounter, particularly if you have access to an aging image library. To the right is the same image subject to Gaussian Blur with a very low Radius value of 0.5. Rather than appearing softened, the result is just plain fuzzy.

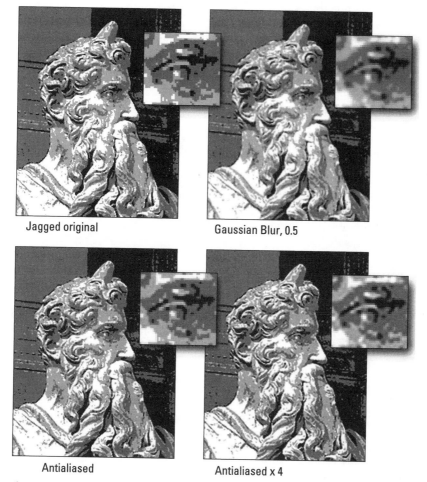

Jagged original   Gaussian Blur, 0.5

Antialiased   Antialiased x 4

Figure 10-22: A particularly jagged image (top left) followed by the image blurred using a filter (top right). By enlarging and reducing the image one or more times (bottom left and right), I soften the pixels without making them appear blurry. The enlarged details show each operation's effect on the individual pixels.

However, if I instead enlarge and reduce the image with the Image Size command, I achieve a true softening effect, as shown in the lower-left example in the figure, commensurate with Photoshop's antialiasing options. Even after enlarging and reducing the image four times in a row — as in the bottom-right example — I don't make the image blurry, I simply make it softer.

Directional blurring

In addition to its everyday blurring functions, Photoshop provides two *directional blurring* filters, Motion Blur and Radial Blur. Instead of blurring pixels in feathered clusters like the Gaussian Blur filter, the Motion Blur filter blurs pixels in straight lines over a specified distance. The Radial Blur filter blurs pixels in varying degrees depending on their distance from the center of the blur. The following pages explain both of these filters in detail.

Motion blurring

The Motion Blur filter makes an image appear as if either the image or camera was moving when you shot the photo. When you choose Filter ➪ Blur ➪ Motion Blur, Photoshop displays the dialog box shown in Figure 10-23. You enter the angle of movement into the Angle option box. Alternatively, you can indicate the angle by dragging the straight line inside the circle on the right side of the dialog box, as shown in the figure. (Notice that the arrow cursor actually appears outside the circle. Once you begin dragging on the line, you can move the cursor anywhere you want and still affect the angle.)

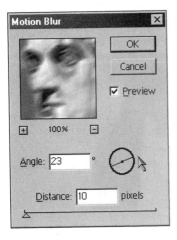

Figure 10-23: Drag the line inside the circle to change the angle of the blur.

You then enter the distance of the movement in the Distance option box. Photoshop permits any value between 1 and 999 pixels. The filter distributes the effect of the blur over the course of the Distance value, as illustrated by the examples in Figure 10-24.

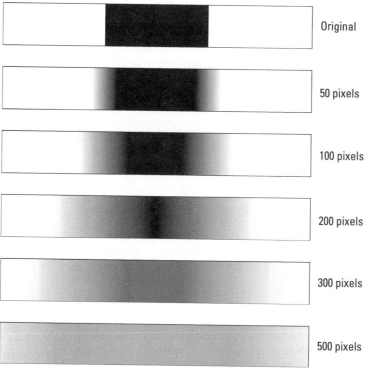

Original

50 pixels

100 pixels

200 pixels

300 pixels

500 pixels

Figure 10-24: A single black rectangle followed by five different applications of the Motion Blur filter. Only the Distance value varied, as labeled. A 0-degree Angle value was used in all five examples.

Note

Mathematically speaking, Motion Blur is one of Photoshop's simpler filters. Rather than distributing the effect over a Gaussian curve — which one might argue would produce a more believable effect — Photoshop creates a simple linear distribution, peaking in the center and fading at either end. It's as if the program took the value you specified in the Distance option, created that many clones of the image, offset half the clones in one direction and half the clones in the other — all spaced 1 pixel apart — and then varied the opacity of each.

Using the Wind filter

The problem with the Motion Blur filter is that it blurs pixels in two directions. If you want to distribute pixels in one absolute direction or the other, try the Wind filter, which you can use either on its own or in tandem with Motion Blur.

When you choose Filter ➪ Stylize ➪ Wind, Photoshop displays the Wind dialog box shown in Figure 10-25. You can select from three methods and two directions to distribute the selected pixels. Figure 10-26 compares the effect of the Motion Blur filter to each of the three methods offered by the Wind filter. Notice that the Wind filter does not blur pixels. Rather, it evaluates a selection in 1-pixel-tall horizontal strips and offsets the strips randomly inside the image.

Figure 10-25: Use the Wind filter to randomly distribute a selection in 1-pixel horizontal strips in one of two directions.

To get the best results, try combining the Motion Blur and Wind filters with a translucent selection. For example, to create Figure 10-27, I cloned the entire image to a new layer and applied the Wind command twice, first selecting the Stagger option and then selecting Blast. Next, I applied the Motion Blur command with a 0-degree angle and a Distance value of 30. I then set the Opacity option in the Layers palette to 80 percent and selected Lighten from the blend mode pop-up menu.

The result is a perfect blend between two worlds. The motion effect in Figure 10-27 doesn't obliterate the image detail, as the Wind filter does in Figure 10-26. And the motion appears to run in a single direction — to the right — something you can't accomplish using Motion Blur on its own.

Motion Blur   Wind

Blast   Stagger

Figure 10-26: The difference between the effects of the Motion Blur filter (upper left) and the Wind filter (other three). In each case, I selected From the Right from the Direction radio buttons.

Radial blurring

Choosing Filter ➪ Blur ➪ Radial Blur displays the Radial Blur dialog box shown in Figure 10-28. The dialog box offers two Blur Method options: Spin and Zoom.

Figure 10-27: The result of combining the Wind and Motion Blur filters with a translucent selection.

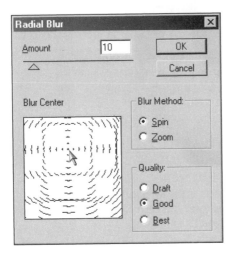

Figure 10-28: Drag inside the Blur Center grid to change the point about which the Radial Blur filter spins or zooms the image.

If you select Spin, the image appears to be rotating about a central point. You specify that point by dragging in the grid inside the Blur Center box (as demonstrated in the figure). If you select Zoom, the image appears to rush away from you, as if you were zooming the camera while shooting the photograph. Again, you specify the central point of the Zoom by dragging in the Blur Center box. Figure 10-29 features examples of both settings.

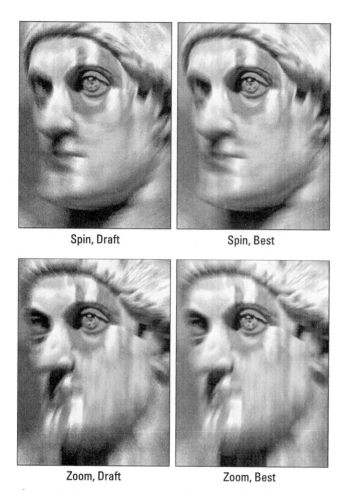

Spin, Draft   Spin, Best

Zoom, Draft   Zoom, Best

Figure 10-29: Four examples of the Radial Blur filter set to both Spin and Zoom, subject to different Quality settings (left and right). I specified Amount values of 10 pixels for the Spin examples and 30 for the Zooms. Each effect is centered about the right eye (your right, that is).

After selecting a Blur Method option, you can enter any value between 1 and 100 in the Amount option box to specify the maximum distance over which the filter blurs pixels. (You can enter a value of 0, but doing so merely causes the filter to waste time without producing an effect.) Pixels farthest away from the center point move the most; pixels close to the center point barely move at all. Keep in mind that large values take more time to apply than small values. The Radial Blur filter, incidentally, qualifies as one of Photoshop's most time-consuming operations.

Select a Quality option to specify your favorite time/quality compromise. The Good and Best Quality options ensure smooth results by respectively applying bilinear and bicubic interpolation (as explained in the "General preferences" section of Chapter 2). However, they also prolong the amount of time the filter spends calculating pixels in your image.

The Draft option *diffuses* an image, which leaves a trail of loose and randomized pixels but takes less time to complete. I used the Draft setting to create the left-hand images in Figure 10-29; I selected the Best option to create the images on the right.

Blurring with a threshold

The purpose of the Filter ➪ Blur ➪ Smart Blur is to blur the low-contrast portions of an image while retaining the edges. This way, you can downplay photo grain, blemishes, and artifacts without harming the real edges in the image. (If you're familiar with Filter ➪ Pixelate ➪ Facet, it may help to know Smart Blur is essentially a customizable version of that filter.)

The two key options inside the Smart Blur dialog box (see Figure 10-30) are the Radius and Threshold slider bars. As with all Radius options, this one expands the number of pixels calculated at a time as you increase the value. Meanwhile, the Threshold value works just like the one in the Unsharp Mask dialog box, specifying how different two neighboring pixels must be to be considered an edge.

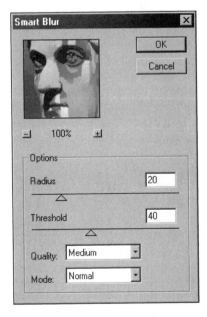

Figure 10-30: The Smart Blur filter lets you blur the low-contrast areas of an image without harming the edges.

But the Threshold value has a peculiar and unexpected effect on the Radius. The Radius value actually produces more subtle effects if you raise the value beyond the Threshold. For example, take a look at Figure 10-31. Here we have a grid of images subject to different Radius and Threshold values. (The first value below each image is the radius.) In the top row of the figure, the 5.0 radius actually produces a more pronounced effect than its 20.0 and 60.0 cousins. This is because 5.0 is less than the 10.0 threshold, while 20.0 and 60.0 are more.

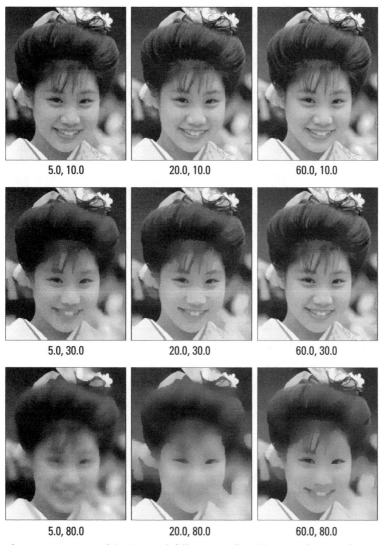

Figure 10-31: Combinations of different Radius (first number) and Threshold (second) values. Notice that the most dramatic effects occur when the radius is equal to about half the threshold.

The Quality settings control the smoothness of the edges. The High setting takes more time than Medium and Low, but it looks smoother as well. (I set the value to High to create all the effects in Figure 10-31.) The two additional Mode options enable you to trace the edges defined by the Threshold value with white lines. Overlay Edge shows image and lines, while Edge Only shows just the traced lines. About the only practical purpose for these options is to monitor the precise effect of the Threshold setting in the preview box. Otherwise, the Edge options are clearly relegated to special effects.

Frankly, I'm not convinced that Smart Blur is quite ready for prime time. You already know what I think of the Threshold option, and it hasn't gotten any better here. Without control over the transitions between focused and unfocused areas, things are going to look pretty strange.

Tip   The better way to blur low-contrast areas is to create an edge mask, as I explained back in the "Sharpening grainy photographs" section. Just reverse the selection by choosing Select ➪ Inverse and apply the Gaussian Blur filter.

Figure 10-32 shows how the masking technique compares with Smart Blur. In the first image, I applied Unsharp Mask with a Threshold of 20. Then I turned around and applied Smart Blur with a Radius of 2.0 and a Threshold of 20.0, matching the Unsharp Mask value. The result makes Ike look like he has dandruff coming out of every pore in his face.

Figure 10-32: The difference between relying on Photoshop's automated Threshold capabilities (left) and sharpening and blurring with the aid of an edge mask (right). Despite the advent of computers, a little manual labor still wins out over automation.

In the second image, I created an edge mask—as explained in the "Creating and Using an Edge Mask" steps—and applied Unsharp Mask with a Threshold of 0. Then I pressed Ctrl+Shift+I to reverse the selection and applied Gaussian Blur with a Radius of 2.0. The result is a smooth image with sharp edges that any president would be proud to hang in the Oval Office.

Softening a selection outline

Gaussian Blur and other Blur filters are equally as useful for editing masks as they are for editing image pixels. As I mentioned earlier, applying Gaussian Blur to a mask has the same effect as applying Select ⇨ Feather to a selection outline. But Gaussian Blur affords more control. Where the Feather command affects all portions of a selection outline uniformly, you can apply Gaussian Blur selectively to a mask, permitting you to easily mix soft and hard edges within a single selection outline.

Another advantage to blurring a mask is that you can see the results of your adjustments on-screen, instead of relying on the seldom-helpful marching ants. For example, suppose that you want to establish a buffer zone between a fore-ground image and its background. You've managed to accurately select the foreground image—how do you now feather the selection exclusively outward, so that no portion of the foreground image becomes selected? Although you can pull off this feat using selection commands such as Expand and Feather, it's much easier to apply filters such as Maximum and Gaussian Blur inside a mask. But before I go any farther, I need to back up and explain how Maximum and its pal Minimum work.

Maximum and Minimum

Filter ⇨ Other ⇨ Maximum expands the light portions of an image, spreading them outward into other pixels. Its opposite, Filter ⇨ Other ⇨ Minimum, expands the dark portions of an image. In traditional stat photography, these techniques are known as *spreading* and *choking*.

When you are working in the quick mask mode or an independent mask channel, applying the Maximum filter has the effect of incrementally expanding the selected area, adding pixels uniformly around the edges of the selection outline. The Maximum dialog box presents you with a single Radius value, which tells Photoshop how many edge pixels to expand. Just the opposite, the Minimum filter incrementally decreases the size of white areas, which subtracts pixels uniformly around the edges of a selection.

Feathering outward from a selection outline

The following steps describe how to use the Maximum and Gaussian Blur filters to feather an existing selection outline outward so that it doesn't encroach on the foreground image.

STEPS: Adding a Soft Edge in the Quick Mask Mode

1. **Select the foreground image.** As shown in Figure 10-33, my foreground image is the layered television that figured so heavily into Chapter 12. I convert the layer's transparency mask to a selection outline by Ctrl-clicking on the layer's name in the Layers palette.

2. **If you're working on a layer, switch to the background image.** The quickest route is Shift+Alt+[.

3. **Press Q to enter the quick mask mode.** You can create a new mask channel if you prefer, but the quick mask mode is more convenient.

4. **Choose Filter ⇨ Other ⇨ Maximum.** Enter a Radius value to expand the transparent area into the rubylith. In Figure 10-33, I entered a Radius value of 10 pixels. After pressing Enter, I decided this wasn't enough, so I pressed Ctrl+Alt+F to bring up the filter again, and further expanded the selection by 4 pixels.

The range of acceptable values for both the Maximum and Minimum filters now stretches to an impressive 100 pixels, giving you 90 pixels more to play with than in previous versions of Photoshop.

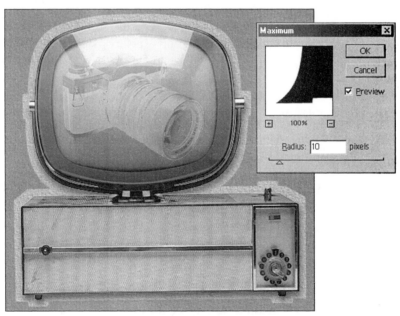

Figure 10-33: The Maximum filter increases the size of the transparent area inside the quick mask mode, thereby expanding the selection outline.

5. **Choose Filter ➪ Blur ➪ Gaussian Blur.** To ensure that you don't blur into the foreground image, enter a Radius value that's no more than half the value you entered into the Maximum dialog box. Altogether, I expanded the selection by 14 pixels, so I entered 7 into the Gaussian Blur dialog box. Photoshop blurs the transparent area, as shown in Figure 10-34.

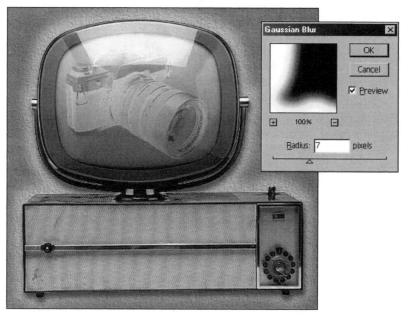

Figure 10-34: Use the Gaussian Blur filter to soften the transparent area, thus feathering the selection outline.

6. **Invert the mask by pressing Ctrl+I.** So far, I selected the TV, but I really want to edit the background. So I pressed Ctrl+I to invert the mask and inverse the prospective selection.

7. **Press Q to exit the quick mask mode.** Ah, back in the workaday world of marching ants.

8. **Apply the desired effect.** I copied a zebra-skin pattern from another image. Then I chose Edit ➪ Paste Into (Ctrl+Shift+V) to paste the pattern inside the selection. Photoshop created a new layer with layer mask. After Ctrl-dragging the pattern into position, I applied the Overlay blend mode to achieve the effect shown in Figure 10-35.

Thanks to my expanded and softened selection outline, the stripes fade toward the television without ever quite touching it. As I said, you can achieve this effect using Select ➪ Modify ➪ Expand and Feather, but unless you have a special aversion to the quick mask mode, it's easier to be sure of your results when you can see exactly what you're doing.

Figure 10-35: I copied some zebra skin from one image window and pressed Ctrl+Shift+V to paste it into my new selection.

Noise Factors

Photoshop offers four loosely associated filters in its Filter ➪ Noise submenu. One filter adds random pixels — known as *noise* — to an image. The other three, Despeckle, Dust and Scratches, and Median, average the colors of neighboring pixels in ways that theoretically remove noise from poorly scanned images. But in fact, they function nearly as well at removing essential detail as they do at removing extraneous noise. In the following sections, I show you how the Noise filters work, demonstrate a few of my favorite applications, and leave you to draw your own conclusions.

Adding noise

Noise adds grit and texture to an image. Noise makes an image look like you shot it in New York on the Lower East Side and were lucky to get the photo at all because someone was throwing sand in your face as you sped away in your chauffeur-driven, jet-black Maserati Bora, hammering away at the shutter release. In reality, of course, a guy over at Sears shot the photo while you toodled around in your minivan trying to find a store that sold day-old bread. But that's the beauty of Noise. It makes you look cool, even when you aren't.

You add noise by choosing Filter ⇨ Noise ⇨ Add Noise. Shown in Figure 10-36, the Add Noise dialog box features the following options:

✦ **Amount:** This value determines how far pixels in the image can stray from their current colors. The value represents a color range rather than a brightness range.

In previous versions of Photoshop, the Amount value was measured in brightness values. Now, you enter a percentage value for Amount. You can enter a value as high as 400 percent. The percentage is based on 256 brightness values per channel if you're working with a 24-bit image and 32,768 brightness values for 16-bit images. So with a 24-bit image (8-bit channels), the default value of 12.5 percent is equivalent to the Photoshop 5.5 default of 32 brightness levels, which is 12.5 percent of 256.

For example, if you enter a value of 12.5 percent for a 24-bit image, Photoshop can apply any color that is 32 shades more or less red, more or less green, *and* more or less blue than the current color. If you enter 400 percent, Photoshop theoretically can go 1024 brightness values lighter or darker. But that results in colors that are out of range; therefore, they get clipped to black or white. The result is higher contrast inside the noise pixels.

Figure 10-36: The Add Noise dialog box asks you to specify the amount and variety of noise you want to add to the selection.

✦ **Uniform:** Select this option to apply colors absolutely randomly within the specified range. Photoshop is no more likely to apply one color within the range than another, thus resulting in an even color distribution.

✦ **Gaussian:** When you select this option, you instruct Photoshop to prioritize colors along the Gaussian distribution curve. The effect is that most colors added by the filter either closely resemble the original colors or push the boundaries of the specified range. In other words, this option results in more light and dark pixels, thus producing a more pronounced effect.

✦ **Monochromatic:** When working on a full-color image, the Add Noise filter distributes pixels randomly throughout the different color channels. However, when you select the Monochrome check box, Photoshop distributes the noise in the same manner in all channels. The result is grayscale noise. (This option does not affect grayscale images; the noise can't get any more grayscale than it already is.)

Figure 10-37 compares three applications of Gaussian noise to identical amounts of Uniform noise. Figure 10-38 features magnified views of the noise so that you can compare the colors of individual pixels.

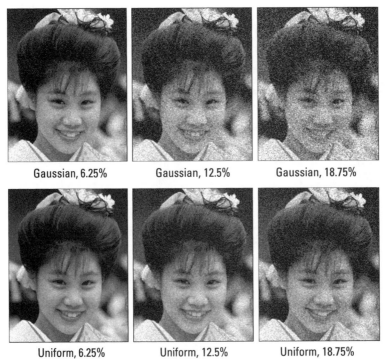

Gaussian, 6.25%   Gaussian, 12.5%   Gaussian, 18.75%

Uniform, 6.25%   Uniform, 12.5%   Uniform, 18.75%

Figure 10-37: The Gaussian option produces more pronounced effects than the Uniform option at identical Amount values.

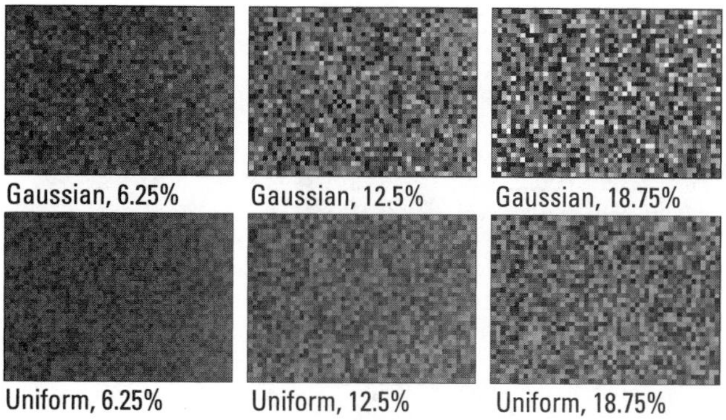

| Gaussian, 6.25% | Gaussian, 12.5% | Gaussian, 18.75% |
| Uniform, 6.25% | Uniform, 12.5% | Uniform, 18.75% |

Figure 10-38: The upper-left corners of the examples from Figure 10-37 enlarged to four times their original size.

Noise variations

Normally, the Add Noise filter adds both lighter and darker pixels to an image. If you prefer, however, you can limit the effect of the filter to strictly lighter or darker pixels. To do so, apply the Add Noise filter, and then apply the Fade command (Ctrl+Shift+F) and select the Lighten or Darken blend mode. Or you can copy the image to a new layer, apply the filter, and merge the filtered image with the underlying original.

Remember, the Fade command now resides on the Edit menu, not the Filter menu. But everything else about Fade is the same as it was in the past.

Figure 10-39 shows sample applications of lighter and darker noise. After copying the image to a separate layer, I applied the Add Noise filter with an Amount value of 40 percent, and selected Gaussian. To create the upper-left example in the figure, I selected Lighten from the blend mode pop-up menu. To create the right example, I selected the Darken mode. In each case, I added a layer of strictly lighter or darker noise while at the same time retaining the clarity of the original image.

To achieve the streaked noise effects in the bottom example of Figure 10-39, I applied Motion Blur and Unsharp Mask to the layered images. Inside the Motion Blur dialog box, I set the Angle value to –30 degrees and the Distance to 30 pixels. Then I applied Unsharp Mask with an Amount value of 200 percent and a Radius of 1. Naturally, the Threshold value was 0.

Lighten   Darken

Motion Blur, Lighten   Motion Blur, Darken

Figure 10-39: You can limit the Add Noise filter to strictly lighter (left) or darker (right) noise by applying the filter to a layered clone. To create the rainy and scraped effects (bottom examples), I applied Motion Blur and Unsharp Mask to the noise layers.

Chunky noise

My biggest frustration with the Add Noise filter is that you can't specify the size of individual specks of noise. No matter how you cut it, noise only comes in 1-pixel squares. It may occur to you that you can enlarge the noise dots in a layer by applying the Maximum or Minimum filter. But in practice, doing so simply fills in the image, because there isn't sufficient space between the noise pixels to accommodate the larger dot sizes.

Luckily, Photoshop provides several alternatives. One is the Pointillize filter, which adds variable-sized dots and then colors those dots in keeping with the original colors in the image. Though Pointillize lacks the random quality of the Add Noise filter, you can use it to add texture to an image.

To create the top-left image in Figure 10-40, I chose Filter ⇨ Pixelate ⇨ Pointillize and entered 5 into the Cell Size option box. After pressing Enter to apply the filter, I pressed Ctrl+Shift+F to fade the filter, changing the Opacity value to 50 percent. The effect is rather like applying chunky bits of noise.

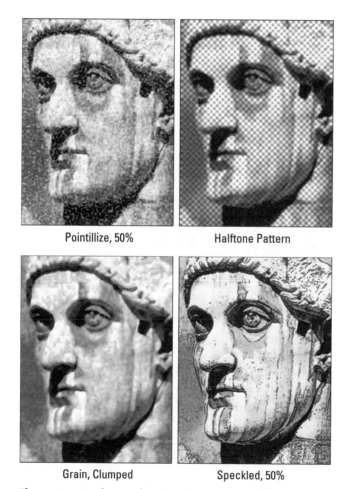

Pointillize, 50%   Halftone Pattern

Grain, Clumped   Speckled, 50%

Figure 10-40: The results of applying several different Add Noise-like filters, including Pointillize, Halftone Pattern, and Grain. A percentage value indicates that I modified the Opacity setting in the Fade dialog box.

The Gallery Effects filters provide a few noise alternatives. Filter ➪ Sketch ➪ Halftone Pattern adds your choice of dot patterns, as shown in the upper-right example in Figure 10-40. But like all filters in the Sketch submenu, it replaces the colors in your image with the foreground and background colors. Filter ➪ Texture ➪ Grain is a regular noise smorgasbord, permitting you to select from 10 different Grain Type options, each of which produces a different kind of noise. The bottom examples in Figure 10-40 show off two of the Grain options, Clumped and Speckled. I used Edit ➪ Fade Grain to reduce the Opacity value for the Speckled effect to 50 percent.

Removing noise with Despeckle

Now for the noise removal filters. Strictly speaking, the Despeckle command probably belongs in the Filter ➪ Blur submenu. It blurs a selection while at the same time preserving its edges — the idea being that unwanted noise is most noticeable in the continuous regions of an image. In practice, this filter is nearly the exact opposite of the Sharpen Edges filter.

The Despeckle command searches an image for edges using the equivalent of an Unsharp Mask Threshold value of 5. It then ignores the edges in the image and blurs everything else with the force of the Blur More filter, as shown in the upper-left image in Figure 10-41.

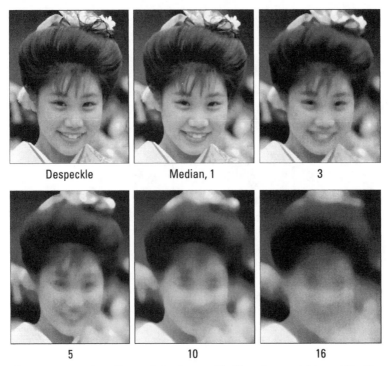

Figure 10-41: The effects of the Despeckle filter (upper left) and Median filter. The numbers indicate Median filter Radius values.

Averaging pixels with Median

Another command in the Filter ⇨ Noise submenu, Median removes noise by averaging the colors in an image, one pixel at a time. When you choose Filter ⇨ Noise ⇨ Median, Photoshop produces a Radius option box. For every pixel in a selection, the filter averages the colors of the neighboring pixels that fall inside the specified radius — ignoring any pixels that are so different that they might skew the average — and applies the average color to the central pixel.

You can now enter any value between 1 and 100. However, even at the old limit, 16, significant blurring occurs, as you can see from the bottom-right example in Figure 10-41 (in the preceding section). At the maximum Radius value, you wind up with a sort of soft, blurry gradient, with all image detail obliterated.

As with Gaussian Blur, you can achieve some very interesting and useful effects by backing off the Median filter with the Fade command. But rather than creating a *Star Trek* glow, Median clumps up details, giving an image a plastic, molded quality, as demonstrated by the examples in Figure 10-42. To create every one of these images, I applied the Median Filter with a Radius of 5 pixels. Then I pressed Ctrl+Shift+F to display the Fade dialog box and lowered the Opacity value to 70 percent. The only difference between one image and the next is the blend mode.

Another difference between Gaussian Blur and Median is that Gaussian Blur destroys edges and Median invents new ones. This means you can follow up the Median filter with Unsharp Mask to achieve even more pronounced sculptural effects. I sharpened every one of the examples in Figure 10-42 using an Amount value of 150 percent and a Radius of 1.5.

Sharpening a compressed image

Digital cameras are the hottest thing in electronic imaging. You can take as many images as you like, download them to your computer immediately, and place them into a printed document literally minutes after snapping the picture. In the next five years, I have little doubt that you — yes, *you* — will purchase a digital camera (if you haven't already).

Unfortunately, the technology is still very young. And if you're using one of the mid- or low-priced cameras — read that, under $500 — even the slightest application of the Unsharp Mask filter sometimes results in jagged edges and unsightly artifacts. These blemishes stem from a stingy supply of pixels, heavy-handed compression schemes (all based on JPEG), or both. The situation is improving; cameras at the high end of the consumer price range ($700 and up) can produce 3-megapixel images and often enable you to store uncompressed images in the TIFF format. But as with all good things in life, it will take a while for those options to be available in moderately priced equipment.

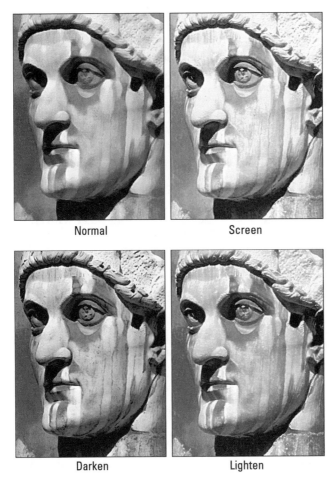

Normal   Screen

Darken   Lighten

Figure 10-42: After applying the Median filter, I reversed the effect slightly using Edit ⇨ Fade Median. Although I varied the blend mode—as labeled beneath the images—the Opacity value remained a constant 70 percent.

In the meantime, firm up the detail and smooth out the color transitions in your digital photos by applying a combination of filters—Median, Gaussian Blur, and Unsharp Mask—to a layered version of the image. The following steps tell all.

Note

If you own a digital camera, I encourage you to record these steps with the Actions palette, as explained in Chapter B on the CD accompanying this book. This way, you can set Photoshop to open squads of images, batch-process them, and save them in a separate folder, leaving you free to do something fun, like read more of this book.

STEPS: Adjusting the Focus of Digital Photos

1. **Select the entire image and copy it to a new layer.** That's Ctrl+A,
   Ctrl+J. Figure 10-43 shows the image that I intend to sharpen, a picture
   of a friend's child.

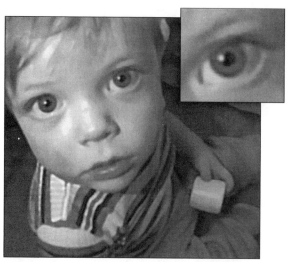

Figure 10-43: I captured this youthful fellow
with a low-end digital camera equipped with a
removable fish-eye lens. How innocent and happy
he looks — obviously not a computer user.

2. **Choose Filter ➪ Noise ➪ Median.** After processing several thousand of
   these images, I've found that a Radius value of 2 is almost always the
   optimal choice. But if the image is particularly bad, 3 may be warranted.

3. **Choose Filter ➪ Blur ➪ Gaussian Blur.** Now that you've gummed up the detail
   a bit and rubbed out most of the compression, use the Gaussian Blur filter
   with a Radius of 1.0 to blur the gummy detail slightly. This softens the edges
   that the Median filter creates. (You don't want any fake edges, after all.)

4. **Choose Filter ➪ Sharpen ➪ Unsharp Mask.** All this blurring demands some
   intense sharpening. So apply Unsharp Mask with a maximum Amount value
   of 500 percent and a Radius of 1.0 (to match the Gaussian Blur radius). This
   restores most of the definition to the edges, as shown in Figure 10-44.

5. **Lower the layer's Opacity value.** By itself, the filtered layer is a bit too smooth.
   So mix the filtered floater with the underlying original with an Opacity value
   between 30 and 50 percent. I found that I could go pretty high — 45 percent —
   with Cooper. Kids have clearly defined details that survive filtering quite nicely.

Figure 10-44: Thanks to Median, Gaussian Blur, and Unsharp Mask, Cooper is a much smoother customer. In fact, he's beyond smooth — he's a gummy kid.

6. **Merge the image.** Press Ctrl+E to send the layer down.

7. **Continue to correct the image as you normally would.** The examples in Figure 10-45 show the difference between applying the Unsharp Mask filter to the original image (top) and the filtered mixture (bottom). In both cases, I applied an Amount value of 200 percent and a Radius of 1.0. The top photo displays an unfortunate wealth of artifacts — particularly visible in the magnified eye — while the bottom one appears smooth and crisp.

These steps work well for sharpening other kinds of compressed imagery, including old photographs that you over-compressed without creating backups, and images that you've downloaded from the Internet. If applying the Unsharp Mask filter brings out the goobers, try these steps instead.

Cleaning up scanned halftones

Photoshop offers one additional filter in the Filter ➪ Noise submenu called Dust & Scratches. The purpose of this filter is to remove dust particles, hairs, scratches, and other imperfections that may accompany a scan. The filter offers two options, Radius and Threshold. As long as the offending imperfection is smaller or thinner than the Radius value and different enough from its neighbors to satisfy the Threshold value, the filter deletes the spot or line and interpolates between the pixels around the perimeter.

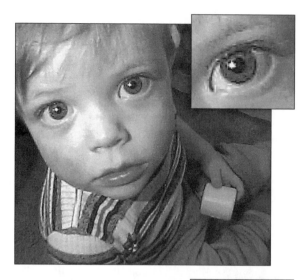

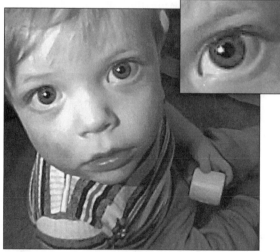

Figure 10-45: Here you can see the difference between sharpening a digital photograph right off the bat (top) and waiting to sharpen until after you've prepared the image with Median, Gaussian Blur, and Unsharp Mask (bottom).

But like so many automated tools, this one works only when conditions are favorable. I'm not saying that you shouldn't ever use it — in fact, you may always want to give this filter the first crack at a dusty image. But if it doesn't work (as it probably won't), don't get your nose out of joint. Just hunker down and eliminate the imperfections manually using the rubber stamp tool, as explained in the "Touching up blemishes" section of Chapter 7.

Now, as I say, Dust & Scratches was designed to get rid of gunk on a dirty scanner. But another problem that the filter may be able to eliminate is moiré patterns. These patterns appear when scanning halftoned images from books and magazines. See, any time you scan a printed image, you're actually scanning a collection of halftone dots rather than a continuous-tone photograph. In most cases, the halftone pattern clashes with the resolution of the scanned image to produce rhythmic and distracting moirés.

Caution   When scanning published photographs or artwork, take a moment to find out if what you're doing is legal. It's up to you to make sure that the image you scan is no longer protected by copyright — most, but not all, works over 75 years old are considered free game — or that your noncommercial application of the image falls under the fair-use umbrella of commentary or criticism.

The Dust & Scratches filter can be pretty useful for eliminating moirés, particularly if you reduce the Threshold value below 40. But this also goes a long way toward eliminating the actual image detail, as shown in Color Plate 10-7. This figure features an image scanned from a previous issue of *Macworld* magazine. (Because I created the original image, *Macworld* probably won't sue me, but you shouldn't try it.)

The left half of Color Plate 10-7 shows the individual color channels in the image; the right half shows the full-color image. I've blown up a detail in each image so that you can better see the pixels in the moiré pattern.

The top example in the color plate shows the original scanned image with its awful moirés. (Actually, I've slightly exaggerated the moirés to account for any printing anomalies; but believe me, with or without enhancement, the image is a mess on screen.) The middle example shows the same image subject to the Dust & Scratches filter with a Radius of 2 and a Threshold value of 20. The moirés are gone, but the edges have all but disappeared as well. I'm tempted to describe this artwork using adjectives such as "soft" and "doughy," and them are fightin' words in the world of image editing.

But what about that bottom example? How did I manage to eliminate the moirés *and* preserve the detail that is shown here? Why, by applying the Gaussian Blur, Median, and Unsharp Mask filters to individual color channels.

The first step is to examine the channels independently (by pressing Ctrl+1, Ctrl+2, and Ctrl+3). You'll likely find that each one is affected by the moiré pattern to a different extent. In the case of this scan, all three channels need work, but the blue channel — the usual culprit — is the worst. The trick, therefore, is to eliminate the patterns in the blue channel and draw detail from the red and green channels.

To fix the blue channel, I applied both the Gaussian Blur and Median commands in fairly hefty doses. I chose Filter ➪ Blur ➪ Gaussian Blur and specified a Radius value of 1.5 pixels, rather high considering that the image measures only about 300 pixels tall. Then I chose Filter ➪ Noise ➪ Median and specified a Radius of 2.

The result was a thickly modeled image with no moirés but little detail. To firm things up a bit, I chose Filter ⇨ Sharpen ⇨ Unsharp Mask and entered 200 percent for the Amount option and 1.5 for the Radius. I opted for this Radius value because it matches the Radius that I used to blur the image. When correcting moirés, a Threshold value of 0 is almost always the best choice. A higher Threshold value not only prevents the sharpening of moiré pattern edges but also ignores real edges, which are already fragile enough as it is.

The green and red channels required incrementally less attention. After switching to the green channel, I applied the Gaussian Blur filter with a Radius of 1.0. Then I sharpened the image with the Unsharp Mask filter set to 200 percent and a Radius value of 0.5. In the red channel (Ctrl+1), I applied Gaussian Blur with a Radius value of 0.5. The gradual effect wasn't enough to warrant sharpening.

When you're finished, switch back to the RGB view (Ctrl+0) to see the combined result of your labors. (Or keep an RGB view of the image up on screen by choosing Window ⇨ New Window.) The focus of the image will undoubtedly be softer than it was when you started. You can cure this to a limited extent by applying very discreet passes of the Unsharp Mask filter, say, with an Amount value of 100 percent and a low Radius value. Keep in mind that oversharpening may bring the patterns back to life or even uncover new ones.

Tip

One last tip: Always scan halftoned images at the highest resolution available to your scanner. Then resample the scan down to the desired resolution using Image ⇨ Image Size, as covered in Chapter 3. This step by itself goes a long way toward eliminating moirés.

✦   ✦   ✦

Full-Court Filtering

Destructive Filters

Corrective filters enable you to eliminate image flaws and apply special effects. *Destructive filters,* on the other hand, are devoted solely to special effects. Even though Photoshop offers nearly twice as many destructive filters as corrective counterparts, destructive filters are less frequently used and ultimately less useful.

Don't get me wrong — these filters are a superb bunch. But because of their more limited appeal, I don't explain each and every one of them. Rather, I concentrate on the ones that I think you'll use most often, breeze over a handful of others, and let you discover on your own the ones that I ignore.

In addition to explaining the commands found on the Filter menu, this chapter also explains the new Liquify command, which probably ought to be on the Filter menu but isn't. Liquify enables you to shove pixels around your image by dragging them, providing a means for freeform, interactive distortion.

A million wacky effects

Oh heck, I guess I can't just go and ignore half of the commands on the Filter menu — they're not completely useless, after all. It's just that you aren't likely to use them more than once every lunar eclipse. So here are the briefest of all possible descriptions of these filters:

> ✦ **Color Halftone:** Located under the Filter ➪ Pixelate sub-menu, this command turns an image into a piece of Roy Lichtenstein artwork, with big, comic-book halftone dots. Although scads of fun, the filter is ultimately a novelty that takes about a year and a half to apply.

✦ **Fragment:** Ooh, it's an earthquake! This lame filter repeats an image four times in a square formation and lowers the opacity of each to create a sort of jiggly effect. You don't even have any options to control it. It's quite possible I'm missing the genius behind Filter ⇨ Pixelate ⇨ Fragment. Then again, maybe not.

✦ **Lens Flare:** Found in the Render submenu, this filter adds sparkles and halos to an image to suggest light bouncing off the camera lens. Even though photographers work their behinds off trying to make sure that these sorts of reflections don't occur, you can add them after the fact. You can select from one of three Lens Type options, adjust the Brightness slider between 10 and 300 percent (though somewhere around 100 is bound to deliver the best results), and move the center of the reflection by dragging a point around inside the Flare Center box.

In addition, you now can Alt-click inside the preview to position the center point numerically.

If you want to add a flare to a grayscale image, first convert it to the RGB mode. Then apply the filter and convert the image back to grayscale. The Lens Flare filter is applicable to RGB images only.

Here's another great tip for using Lens Flare. Before choosing the filter, create a new layer, fill it with black, and apply the Screen blend mode (Shift+Alt+S with a non-painting tool selected). Now apply Lens Flare. You get the same effect as you would otherwise, but the effect floats above the background image, protecting your original image from harm. You can even move the lens flare around and vary the Opacity value, giving you more control over the final effect.

✦ **Diffuse:** Located in the Stylize submenu — as are the three filters that follow — Diffuse dithers the edges of color, much like the Dissolve brush mode dithers the edges of a soft brush. Diffuse is moderately useful but not likely to gain a place among your treasured few.

✦ **Solarize:** This single-shot command is easily Photoshop's worst filter. It's really just a color-correction effect that changes all medium grays in the image to 50 percent gray, all blacks and whites to black, and remaps the other colors to shades in between. (If you're familiar with the Curves command, the map for Solarize looks like a pyramid.) It really belongs in the Image ⇨ Adjust submenu or, better yet, on the cutting room floor.

✦ **Tiles:** This filter breaks an image up into a bunch of regularly sized but randomly spaced rectangular tiles. You specify how many tiles fit across the width and height of the image — a value of 10, for example, creates 100 tiles — and the maximum distance each tile can shift. You can fill the gaps between tiles with foreground color, background color, or an inverted or normal version of the original image. A highly intrusive and not particularly stimulating effect.

✦ **Extrude:** The more capable cousin of the Tiles filter, Extrude breaks an image into tiles and forces them toward the viewer in three-dimensional space. The Pyramid option is a lot of fun, devolving an image into a collection of spikes.

When using the Blocks option, you can select a Solid Front Faces option that renders the image as a true 3D mosaic. The Mask Incomplete Blocks option simply leaves the image untouched around the perimeter of the selection where the filter can't draw complete tiles.

Actually, I kind of like Extrude. For the sheer heck of it, Color Plate 11-1 shows an example of Extrude applied to what was once a red rose. I set the Type to Blocks, the Size to 10, the Depth to 30 and Random, with both the Solid Front Faces and Mask Incomplete Blocks radio buttons selected. Pretty great, huh? I only wish that the filter would generate a selection outline around the masked areas of the image so that I could get rid of anything that hadn't been extruded. It's a wonderful effect, but it's not one that lends itself to many occasions.

✦ **Diffuse Glow:** The first of the Gallery Effects that I mostly ignore, Filter ⇨ Distort ⇨ Diffuse Glow sprays a coat of dithered, background-colored pixels onto your image. Yowsa, let me at it.

✦ **The Artistic filters:** As a rule, the effects under the Filter ⇨ Artistic submenu add a painterly quality to your image. Colored Pencil, Rough Pastels, and Watercolor are examples of filters that successfully emulate traditional mediums. Other filters — Fresco, Smudge Stick, and Palette Knife — couldn't pass for their intended mediums in a dim room filled with dry ice.

✦ **The Brush Strokes filters:** I could argue that the Brush Strokes submenu contains filters that create strokes of color. This is true of some of the filters — including Angled Strokes, Crosshatch, and Sprayed Strokes. Others — Dark Strokes and Ink Outlines — generally smear colors, while still others — Accented Edges and Sumi-e — belong in the Artistic submenu. Whatever.

✦ **The Sketch filters:** In Gallery Effects parlance, Sketch means color sucker. Beware, every one of these filters replaces the colors in your image with the current foreground and background colors. If the foreground and background colors are black and white, the Sketch filter results in a grayscale image. Charcoal and Conté Crayon create artistic effects, Bas Relief and Note Paper add texture, and Photocopy and Stamp are stupid effects that you can produce better and with more flexibility using High Pass.

To retrieve some of the original colors from your image after applying a Sketch filter, press Ctrl+Shift+F to display the Fade dialog box and try out a few different Mode settings. Overlay and Luminosity are particularly good choices. In Color Plate 11-2, I applied the Charcoal filter with the foreground and background colors set to light blue and dark green. Then I used the Fade command to select the Overlay mode.

✦ **The Texture filters:** As a group, the commands in the Filter ⇨ Texture submenu are my favorite effects filters. Craquelure, Mosaic Tiles, and Patchwork apply interesting depth textures to the image. Texturizer provides access to several scalable textures and permits you to load your own (as long as the pattern is saved in the Photoshop format), as demonstrated in Figure 11-1. The one dud is Stained Glass, which creates polygon tiles like Photoshop's own Crystallize filter, only with black lines around the tiles.

Burlap

Canvas

Sandstone

Random Strokes

Figure 11-1: Filter ➪ Texture ➪ Texturizer lets you select from four built-in patterns — including the first three shown here — and load your own. In the last example, I loaded the Random Strokes pattern included with Photoshop.

Certainly, there is room for disagreement about which filters are good and which are awful. After I wrote a two-star *Macworld* review about the first Gallery Effects collection back in 1992 — I must admit, I've never been a big fan — a gentleman showed me page after page of excellent artwork he created with them. Recently, a woman showed me her collection of amazing Lens Flare imagery. I mean, here's a filter that just creates a bunch of bright spots, and yet this talented person was able to go absolutely nuts with it.

The moral is that just because I consider a filter or other piece of software to be a squalid pile of unspeakably bad code doesn't mean that a creative artist can't come along and put it to remarkable use. But that's because *you* are good, not the filter. So if you're feeling particularly creative today, give the preceding filters a try. Otherwise, skip them with a clear conscience.

Color Plate 3-1
My personal 256-Color, 1024 × 768-pixel wallpaper image saved as a BMP file and applied to the desktop using the Display control panel.

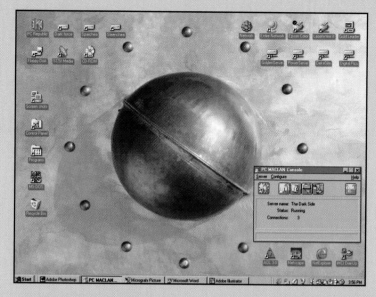

Color Plate 3-2
This little warlock shows off the differences between the four different JPEG compression settings, from maximum quality, minimum compression (upper left) to minimum quality, maximum compression (lower right). Inspect the enlarged eye and sharpened staff for subtle erosions in detail.

Maximum 116K

High 66K

Medium 50K

Low 46K

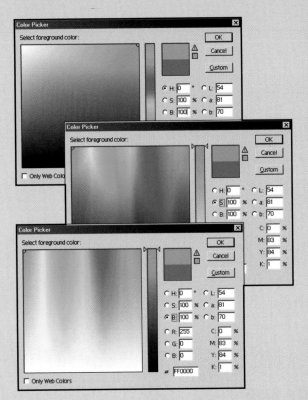

Color Plate 4-1
The colors inside the field and slider in the Color Picker dialog box change to reflect the selection of the H (Hue), S (Saturation), and B (Brightness) radio buttons.

Color Plate 4-2
This colorful image is the basis for an awful lot of channel discussions in Chapter 4. Right about now, I'm wishing I was in that inner tube instead of editing it.

Color Plate 4-3
One of the wonderful things about the Lab mode is that it allows you to edit the colors in an image independently of the brightness values. Here I've inverted and boosted the contrast of the a and b color channels to produce some startling effects, all without harming a smidgen of detail.

Invert a

Auto Levels b

Invert and Auto Levels a and b

Replace red with blue

Replace green with red

Replace blue with red

Color Plate 4-4
You can wreak some pretty interesting havoc on the colors in an image by replacing one color channel with another or by swapping the contents of two color channels using the Channel Mixer command.

Swap red and blue

Swap red and green

Swap green and blue

Color Plate 5-1
Starting with an image of typical saturation (upper left), I applied the sponge tool set to Desaturate to the inside of the pepper and the corn in the background (upper right). I then repeated the effect twice more to make the areas almost gray (lower right). Returning to the original image, I then selected Saturate and again scrubbed inside the pepper and in the corn to boost the colors (lower left).

Behind

Dissolve

Normal

Color Plate 5-2
Here I've gone and desecrated a pivotal work of European iconography by scribbling the name of America's patron saint of graffiti. Reading up from the bottom, the Normal brush mode applies paint normally. The Dissolve mode scatters pixels along the fuzzy edge of the brushstroke. And the Behind mode paints behind the current layer, in this case, a layer containing the Madonna's head.

Multiply

Screen

Overlay

Soft Light

Hard Light

Color Dodge

Color Burn

Color Plate 5-3
Here I've painted green lines using the seven brush modes in the middle of the Mode pop-up menu on the Options bar. Multiply darkens uniformly and Screen lightens uniformly. (In fact, Multiply and Screen are direct opposites.) Overlay, Soft Light, and Hard Light all multiply the darkest pixels and screen the lightest ones to produce different contrast-enhancing effects. Color Dodge and Color Burn work like dodge and burn tools that also add color to an image.

Color Plate 5-4
Here are the effects of the final eight entries in Photoshop's enormous arsenal of brush modes. Darken and Lighten are opposites, Difference and Exclusion are very closely related, and the last four apply different bits and pieces of the HSL color model. Because many of these modes produce slight effects — particularly the Saturation and Luminosity modes — I have added dark halos around the brushstrokes to offset them slightly from the background. Naturally, the halos feel right at home.

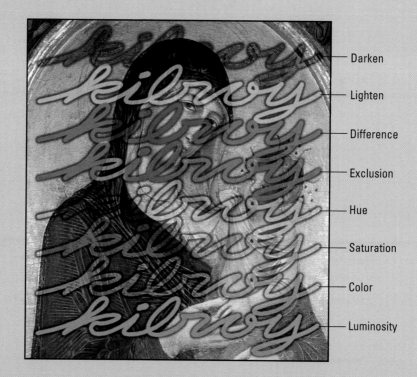

Darken

Lighten

Difference

Exclusion

Hue

Saturation

Color

Luminosity

Color Plate 6-1

Here I've used the paint bucket to colorize two oranges (top) with bright blue. First, I set the Tolerance value on the Options bar to 120, selected the Contiguous check box, and selected Color from the Mode pop-up menu. Then I clicked at each of the four points marked with blue arrows (middle). After that, I changed the foreground color to green and clicked just once in the lower right corner of the image (marked with the green arrow). Unfortunately, the paint bucket isn't very precise, so I had to touch up the dimples and edges with the paintbrush, also set to the Color mode. Finally, I used the airbrush — set to the Color Burn mode — to deepen some of the blue shadows inside the fruit.

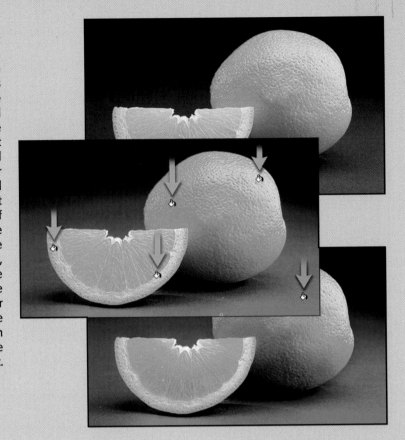

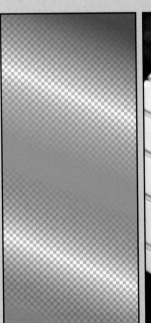

Color Plate 6-2

I started by designing a three-color gradient that fades twice into transparency, as demonstrated by the checkerboard background (left). Such a gradation is meant to be blended with an image, such as the piano keys (middle). So I selected Overlay from the Mode menu on the Options bar and tickled my gradation across the ivories (right).

Color Plate 7-1
To see how I scanned this 90-year-old photograph (left) and cloned away its considerable supply of tears, creases, stains, and flaking (right), read the "Restoring an old photograph" section of Chapter 7.

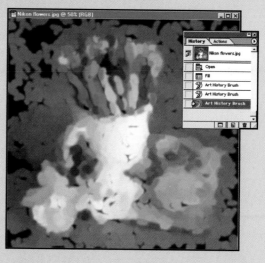

Color Plate 7-2
An original image (top) and the same image filled with black and then brought back to life with the art history brush (bottom).

Color Plate 8-1

If you attempt to select this whimsical sign with the magic wand tool, you end up selecting little fragments of the yellow areas at a time. However, by switching to the blue channel — in which both sign and Sasquatch appear black against a relatively light background — you can easily select both portions of the sign in two easy clicks. I then inverted the sign (right) by pressing Ctrl+I. The effect isn't perfect, but it's as good as it gets with the magic wand.

Color Plate 9-1

At top, we see two selection outlines (both from Figure 9-1) expressed as masks. The masks appear as transparent red overlays, permitting you to see mask and image at the same time. Red-tinted areas are masked, representing deselected areas in the image; untinted areas are unmasked, and represent selected areas. In the bottom examples, I inverted the selected areas to demonstrate the full extent of the selection outlines.

Color Plate 9-2
In the left example, I drew a black-to-white gradation in the quick mask mode, extending from the base of the top row of pillars to the top of the flagpole. Then I applied the Add Noise filter to jumble up the pixels a little. Finally, I exited the quick mask mode to convert the mask to a selection, and Ctrl-dragged the Capitol into the lava image (right).

Color Plate 9-3
Which twin has the Toni? With the help of a very precise mask, I dragged this girl from her old environment into this new one. But despite the mask's accuracy, I managed to bring in some blue from her prior background (left). To fix this problem, I brushed in some color from the new background, and erased a few of the overly dark hairs (right).

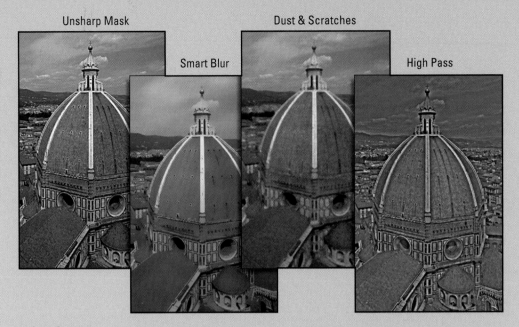

Color Plate 10-1
Shown here are the results of four corrective filters, including representatives from the Filter ➪ Sharpen, Blur, Noise, and Other submenus. Normally, the High Pass filter takes the saturation out of an image, leaving many areas gray, like an old, sun-bleached slide. To restore the colors, I chose Edit ➪ Fade High Pass (Ctrl+Shift+F) and selected Luminosity from the Mode pop-up menu in the Fade dialog box.

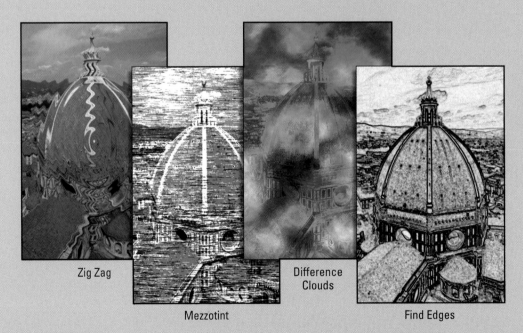

Color Plate 10-2
Here are the effects of four destructive filters from the Filter ➪ Distort, Pixelate, Render, and Stylize submenus. Every one of these filters has a dramatic impact on the color and detail of an image. From a pixel's perspective, destructive filters are dynamite, so use with care and moderation

Color Plate 10-3
The results of applying the Unsharp Mask filter to independent color channels in an RGB image. In each case, the Amount value was 500, the Radius value was 4.0, and the Threshold was 0.

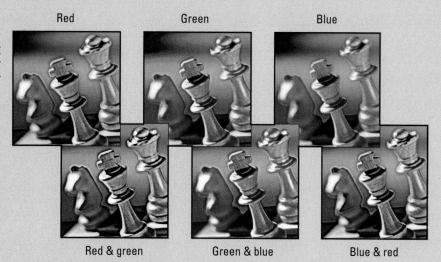

Red   Green   Blue

Red & green   Green & blue   Blue & red

Color Plate 10-4
Again, I applied Unsharp Mask to the independent color channels, but this time with an exaggerated Radius value, 20.0, a more moderate Amount value, 250, and the default Threshold, 0. Rather than pinpointing the sharpening effect, as in Color Plate 10-3, the high Radius value allows the colors to bleed as they are strengthened by the Amount value.

Red   Green   Blue

Red & green   Green & blue   Blue & red

Color Plate 10-5
The results of applying Filter ➪ Other ➪ High Pass with a Radius value of 5.0 to each channel and pair of channels in an RGB image. To boost the color values in the images slightly, I applied the Auto Levels command (Ctrl+Shift+L) after each application of High Pass.

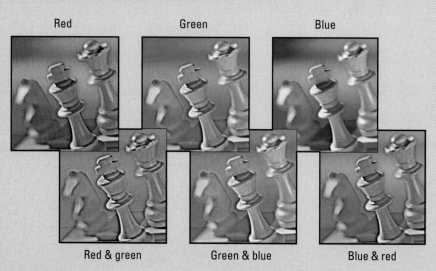

Red   Green   Blue

Red & green   Green & blue   Blue & red

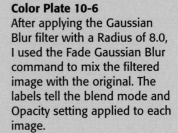

Color Plate 10-6
After applying the Gaussian Blur filter with a Radius of 8.0, I used the Fade Gaussian Blur command to mix the filtered image with the original. The labels tell the blend mode and Opacity setting applied to each image.

Normal, 60%

Luminosity, 50%

Darken, 80%

Lighten, 80%

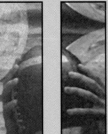

Color Plate 10-7
An image scanned from an ancient issue of Macworld magazine shown as it appears in the normal RGB mode (top right) and when each channel is viewed separately (top left). The middle images show the affects of the Dust & Scratches filter set to a Radius of 2 and a Threshold of 20. The bottom images show how the channels look after suppressing the moiré patterns with the Gaussian Blur, Median, and Unsharp Mask filters.

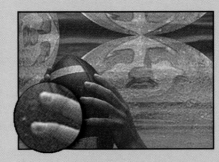

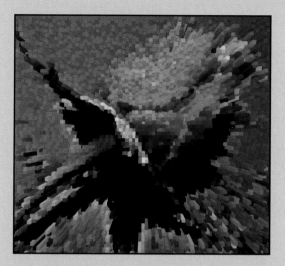

Color Plate 11-1
The result of applying the Extrude filter to a red rose. If you select the Blocks and Solid Front Faces options, the filter transforms the image into mosaic tiles and shoves the tiles out at you in 3D space.

Color Plate 11-2
Here I applied Filter ⇨ Sketch ⇨ Charcoal with the foreground color set to dark green and the background color set to light blue (as demonstrated in the upper left inset). Then I used the Fade Charcoal command to change the blend mode to Overlay.

Color Plate 11-3
I applied the Mezzotint filter set to the Long Strokes effect in each of the RGB, Lab, and CMYK color modes (top row). After each application of the filter, I pressed Ctrl+Shift+F and faded the filtered image into the original using the Overlay mode and an Opacity setting of 40 percent (bottom row).

RGB   Lab   CMYK

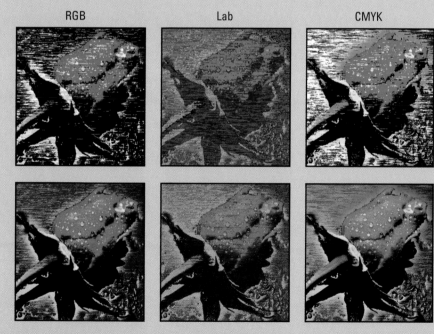

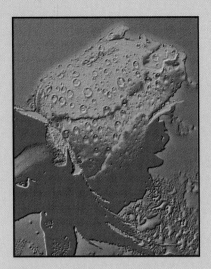

Color Plate 11-4
In both examples, I applied the Emboss filter armed with an Angle of 135 degrees, a Height value of 2, and an Amount of 300 percent. To create the left image, I used the Fade command to mix embossed and original images together using the Luminosity blend mode and an Opacity setting of 80 percent. To get the psychedelic effect on right, I selected the Difference mode and reduced the Opacity value to 40 percent.

Original

Blur and Find Edges

Overlay, 80%

Color Plate 11-5
After selecting an image from the PhotoDisc library (top left), I layered the image, blurred it, applied the Find Edges filter, and darkened it with the Levels command (top middle). I then composited the image using the Overlay mode and an Opacity setting of 80 percent (top right). The bottom row shows the results of applying three effects filters set to the Luminosity mode and 80 percent Opacity settings.

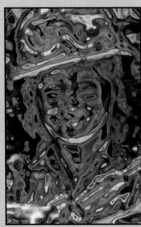

Bas Relief

Plastic Wrap

Chrome

Color Plate 11-6
These two rows of images show a step-by-step experiment in abstract imagery. Starting with a two-color gradation, I convert it to a spiral with Filter ⇨ Distort ⇨ Twirl. Then I copy the spiral to a layer, flip it, rotate it (top right), and apply the Difference mode to achieve the orange image (bottom left). I clone the layer again and rotate it, then I clone a third time and rotate and flip the layer. The final image is the result of tweaking each layer with another distortion filter, including Twirl, Spherize, and ZigZag.

Gradation

Twirl x3

Flip Horizontal

Rotate 90° CW

Difference

Rotate 90° CW

Rotate and Flip

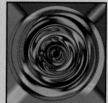
and more . . .

Color Plate 11-7
In this piece, titled Knowing Risk, distortion expert Mark Collen combines a variety of distortion filtering effects to create a surrealistic landscape. The cat, the book, the mongoose, and the twigs are the only scanned images.

Color Plate 11-8
You can force 3D Transform to generate a 3D shape on an independent layer, as I did when creating this goblet. But 3D Transform provides no control over lighting. The easiest workaround is to apply layer effects. In my case, I used the Drop Shadow and Inner Bevel options. The result is hardly true three-dimensional rendering, but the goblet definitely leaps off the page.

Color Plate 11-9
This time, I took my 3D goblet and set it against a different background. To achieve the more realistic lighting, I applied manual shadow and highlight techniques in combination with a few swipes of the airbrush tool. It took more than 90 minutes to put this image together, but the finished effect is well worth the effort.

Color Plate 11-10
The top row shows the results of Shift-choosing the Clouds filter (left), Shift-choosing Difference Clouds (middle), and pressing Ctrl+F ten times in a row (right). I then took each of the images from the top row and mixed it with the rose using one of three blend modes (labeled below bottom row). You can create clouds, haze, and imaginative fill patterns with the Clouds filters.

Clouds   Difference Clouds   x10

Overlay   Screen   Hue

Color Plate 11-11
Here I used the Lighting Effects filter to assign a total of five white spotlights, two pointing down from above and three pointing up from below. The bumpy surfaces of the second and third images are the results of texture maps. To create the right image, I used the green channel as the texture. In the bottom image, I used a pattern created with the Pointillize filter.

Color Plate 12-1

Here I've used a clipping group to fill some characters of type with a water pattern. I started by adding a couple of pool images that I shot with a digital camera to a layer above my text — which is itself on an independent layer — as demonstrated on the left. Then I just Alt-clicked on the horizontal line between the two layers in the Layers palette. Photoshop automatically assigned the type layer's transparency mask to the pool layer, filling the letters.

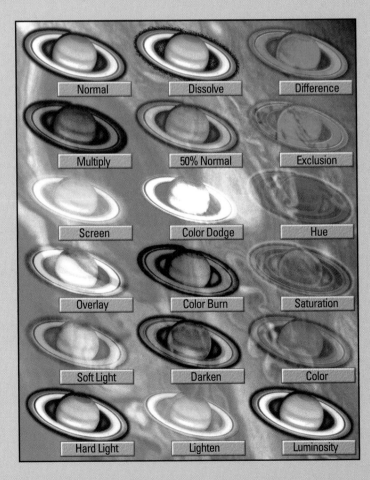

Normal	Dissolve	Difference
Multiply	50% Normal	Exclusion
Screen	Color Dodge	Hue
Overlay	Color Burn	Saturation
Soft Light	Darken	Color
Hard Light	Lighten	Luminosity

Color Plate 13-1

Examples of the 17 blend mode options applied to a bright blue Saturn set against the fiery backdrop of Jupiter. I also inserted an 18th Saturn set to the Normal mode and 50 percent Opacity (second down, middle column) just for the sake of comparison. That, and to take up space.

Color Plate 13-2
Blend modes change their meaning depending on which layer is in front and which is in back. Here I've taken images of a woman and a leaf and placed them on separate layers. In the top row, the leaf layer is in front, and in the bottom row, the woman is in front. The irony is that every one of these blend modes favors the layer on bottom. Only a few — Normal, Hard Light, and Luminosity — favor the image on top.

Overlay   Soft Light   Color Dodge   Hue

Leaf in front

Woman in front

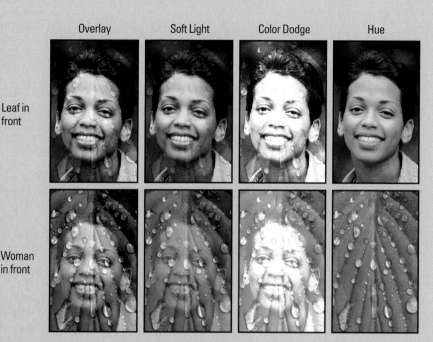

Charcoal

Hard Light

Color

Difference

Original

Soft Light

Color Dodge

Luminosity

Color Plate 13-3
Each column of images shows a progression in which I sandwiched an image filtered with the Charcoal effect (top left) between two originals (bottom left). Each image in the top row shows the filtered image interacting with the original background layered according to the labeled blend mode. The bottom images show the results of adding the top layer of the sandwich and applying another blend mode. For example, applying Difference to the filtered layer and Luminosity to the top layer creates the bottom right effect.

Unsharp Mask   Motion Blur   Lens Flare   Find Edges

Difference Sandwich

Color Plate 13-4
The top row shows the results of a series of corrective and destructive filters, each of which goes a long way toward destroying the detail in my image. But when I insert the filter effect in between two copies of the original image, and then apply the Difference blend mode to the middle and top layers, I bring back much of the detail, as shown in the bottom row. No other technique restores detail quite like a tasty Difference sandwich.

Color Plate 13-5
The upper left image shows a man layered with an Outer Glow layered against a sunset. Lowering the Fill Opacity in the right example makes the man translucent without affecting the Outer Glow style. The bottom examples show the effects of restoring the Fill Opacity to 100 percent and turning off the Channels check boxes — first I turned off the blue channel, then I turned off the red.

Thinker and sunset

Fill Opacity: 25%

Channels: Red and Green

Channels: Green only

Color Plate 13-6
For the sake of comparison, the first image shows the result of compositing an RGB image onto itself using the Hard Light mode. Other examples show the different effects you can achieve by duplicating the image, converting it to the Lab mode, and then mixing the RGB and Lab images together using the Apply Image command, again set to Hard Light.

RGB on RGB

Lightness on RGB

Inverted *b* on RGB

Blue on Lab

Color Plate 13-7
After creating a separate mask channel using the Color Range command (shown as a rubylith, top left), I used the mask to protect the background from my Apply Image manipulations. Although I applied some heavy duty blend modes, the blue gray background remained altogether unharmed.

Mask

Color Dodge *b* on RGB

Color Burn

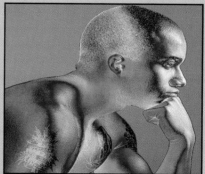

Difference inverted RGB on RGB

Color Plate 14-1

Photoshop lets you copy layer styles from one layer and paste them onto another. After applying the Outer Glow effect to some bananas and Pillow Emboss to a pineapple (left), I decided the pillow emboss is all wrong. So I copied the pillow emboss effect from the pineapple and applied it to the new thought-balloon layer. Then I copied the outer glow from the bananas and pasted it onto the pineapple (right).

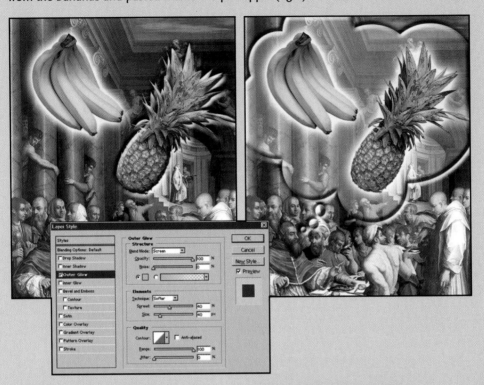

Color Plate 16-1

An image created on the Mac in the Adobe RGB space (left) and then opened on the PC and converted to sRGB (right). If you look closely in the medium blue areas, you'll see a slight shift toward green on the right. Even so, Photoshop has done a terrific job of converting the colors.

RGB Lab CMYK

Color Plate 17-1
The results of applying the Invert command to a single image in each of the three color modes. I inverted all channels in the RGB and Lab images and all but the black channel in the CMYK image.

RGB Lab CMYK

Color Plate 17-2
Here I administered the High Pass filter with a Radius of 3.0, and then applied Threshold separately to each color channel within the three color modes. To smooth the jagged edges, I resampled each image up to 200 percent and then back down to 50 percent using the Image Size command. Then I repeated the process.

Luminosity Hard Light Hue

Color Plate 17-3
After cloning the image to a new layer, I applied the High Pass filter and the Posterize command. Then I mixed the layer and the underlying original by choosing each of three overlay modes from the Layers palette. All effects were created with Opacity settings of 100 percent. To make things more colorful, I gave the saturation a healthy boost using the Hue/Saturation command.

Color Plate 17-4
You can downplay the colors in selected portions of an image by applying Desaturate to convert the pixels to gray values (top left). You can then use Filter ⇨ Fade to reduce the Opacity setting and bring back some colors (top right). Alternatively, you can Invert the selection, choose Filter ⇨ Fade, select the Color blend mode, and lower the Opacity value to 50 percent (bottom left). Raising the Opacity increases the presence of inverted colors (bottom right).

Desaturate

Fade to 50%

Invert and fade to 50%

Invert and fade to 70%

Color Plate 17-5
Starting with the uncorrected pumpkin image (top left), I applied Image ⇨ Adjust ⇨ Auto Levels to it in each of the three color modes. The command is really designed for RGB images and tends to mess up CMYK images (lower right). As you folks who live outside Love Canal are probably aware, few pumpkins are fire-engine red.

Uncorrected

RGB

Lab

CMYK

Color Plate 17-6
The results of correcting a
washed out image (top)
with Auto Levels (middle)
and Auto Contrast
(bottom).

Master, -40°

Master, +20°

Master, +60°

Cyan only, -40°

Cyan only, +20°

Cyan only, +60°

Color Plate 17-7
The results of choosing Image ⇨ Adjust ⇨ Hue/Saturation and applying various Hue values to an entire image (top row) and to only the cyan portions of the image (bottom row).

Master, -50°

Master, +50°

All but cyan and blue, -100

Cyan and blue, -100
All others, +50

Color Plate 17-8
The results of applying various Saturation values to an entire image (top row) and to certain colors — namely cyan and blue — independently of others (bottom row). Without creating a selection or mask, you can isolate colored areas using the Hue/Saturation command.

Master, -90°

Master, +90°

Blue areas, 120°
Other, -50°

Blue areas, -60°
Other, 110°

Color Plate 17-9
The results of applying various Hue values to an image when the Colorize option is turned off (top row) and on (bottom row). In the bottom images, I selected the blue areas of the horse with the Color Range command and then colorized the blue and non-blue areas as indicated by the labels. Notice that while the top two images continue to possess a variety of differently colored pixels, the bottom images contain only two apiece – pink and green.

Color Plate 17-10
These images show the results of correcting images with two of Photoshop's more specialized color commands, Replace Color (top row) and Selective Color (bottom row). The Replace Color command lets you adjust colors while at the same time modifying which pixels are affected and which are not with the help of a Fuzziness option. The Selective Color command adjusts the amount of CMYK ink assigned to predefined color ranges.

Fuzziness, 40

Fuzziness, 200

Red to violet, Relative

Red to violet and
black to white, Absolute

Color Plate 17-11
The effects of applying each of the thumbnails offered in the Variations dialog box to the familiar pumpkin. In each case, the slider bar was set to its default setting of midway between Fine and Coarse with the Midtones radio button selected.

More Green

Lighter

More Yellow

More Cyan

Original

More Red

More Blue

Darker

More Magenta

Original digital photo

Increase saturation to +80

Median, Gaussian Blur,
and Color mode

Final sharpened image

Color Plate 17-12
Starting with a rather typically washed out image that I shot with a Kodak DC50 (top), I copied the
image to a new layer and boosted the saturation with Hue/Saturation command (second). Then I
applied the Median and Gaussian Blur commands and mixed the layer with the underlying original
using the Color blend mode and an Opacity value of 70 percent (third). Finally, I used Median,
Gaussian Blur, and Unsharp Mask to sharpen the image (bottom).

Color Plate 17-13
The celebrated Virginia statesman before (left) and after (right) I corrected him with the Levels command. The white histograms superimposed on Jefferson's chest show the original and corrected distribution of brightness values. The colored histograms illustrate the corrections made to the individual red, green, and blue channels.

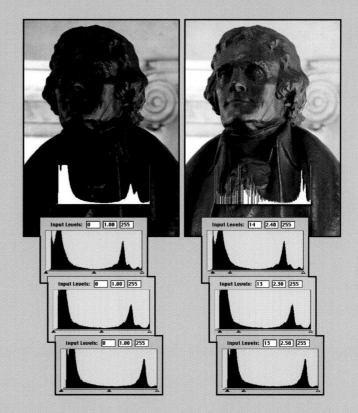

Color Plate 17-14
You can use the Curves dialog box to apply gradations as color maps. In the top row, I copied the famous Roman to a new layer, blurred him silly, and applied each of three gradients (saved to disk by Ctrl-clicking on the Save button in the Gradient Editor dialog box). Then I mixed the images with their underlying originals using the Color blend mode (Shift+Alt+C).

Chrome   Blue, Red, Yellow   Spectrum

Color blend mode

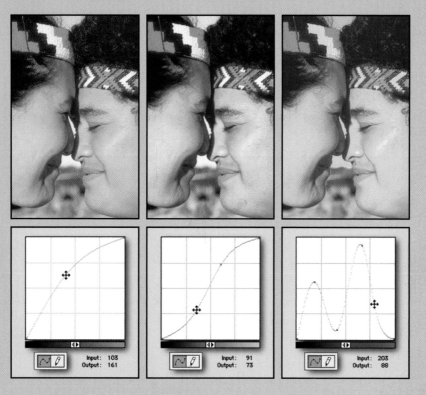

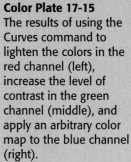

Color Plate 17-15
The results of using the Curves command to lighten the colors in the red channel (left), increase the level of contrast in the green channel (middle), and apply an arbitrary color map to the blue channel (right).

Color Plate 17-16
These images illustrate one way to use adjustment layers to correct the colors in a flat image. After observing that my original image was way too dark (left), I created a new adjustment layer and used the Curves command to lighten the image (middle). I then added two additional layers to increase the saturation levels with Hue/Saturation and correct the brightness levels of the topiary animal with Levels (right).

Color Plate 18-1
I converted this grayscale piece by Seattle-based artist Mark Collen to a quadtone using the colors navy blue, rose, teal, and dull orange. All colors were defined and printed using CMYK pigments.

Color Plate 18-2
After converting Mark's quadtone to a multichannel image, I experimented with hiding different channels. In the top row, I hid one spot color and left the other three visible. In the bottom row, I hid two channels per image.

Navy, Orange, Teal

Orange, Teal, Rose

Navy, Orange, Rose

Navy, Orange

Teal, Rose

Orange, Rose

Original

System (Macintosh)

System (Windows)

Color Plate 19-1
Examples of a 24-bit image (top left) downgraded using the Indexed Color command. I applied the fixed palettes from the Macintosh and Windows operating systems in the upper middle and right examples. I used the Adaptive option to create the bottom row of images. As you can see, the Adaptive option produces reasonably good results, even at low-color settings.

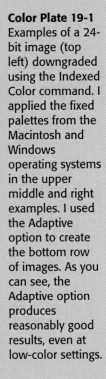

Adapative, 256 colors

Adaptive, 64 colors

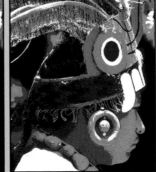
Adaptive, 16 colors

None, 94K

Pattern, 105K

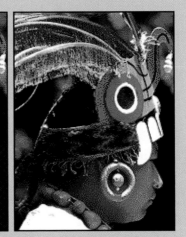
Diffusion, 118K

Color Plate 19-2
I reduced the image from Color Plate 19-1 using three different Dither options — None, Pattern, and Diffusion. Beside each option name is the size of the file when saved in the GIF format. As you can see, GIF is better suited to compressing an image when no dithering is involved.

What about the others?

Some filters don't really belong in either the corrective or destructive camp. Take Filter ⇨ Video ⇨ NTSC Colors, for example, and Filter ⇨ Other ⇨ Offset. Both are examples of commands that have no business being under the Filter menu, and both could have been handled much better.

The NTSC Colors filter modifies the colors in your RGB or Lab image for transfer to videotape. Vivid reds and blues that might otherwise prove very unstable and bleed into their neighbors are curtailed. The problem with this function is that it's not an independent color space; it's a single-shot filter that changes your colors and is done with them. If you edit the colors after choosing the command, you may very well reintroduce colors that are incompatible with NTSC devices and therefore warrant a second application of the filter. Conversion to NTSC — another light-based system — isn't as fraught with potential disaster as conversion to CMYK pigments, but it still deserves better treatment than this.

The Offset command moves an image a specified number of pixels. Why didn't I cover it in Chapter 8 with the other movement options? Because the command actually moves the image inside the selection outline while keeping the selection outline itself stationary. It's as if you had pasted the entire image into the selection outline and were now moving it around. The command is a favorite among fans of channel operations, a topic I cover in Chapter 13. You can duplicate an image, offset the entire duplicate by a few pixels, and then mix the duplicate and original to create highlight or shadow effects. But I much prefer the more interactive control of layering and nudging with the arrow keys. I imagine the Offset filter might find favor with folks who want to automate movements from the Actions palette, but now that Photoshop records movements made with the move tool, I'm not even sure about that. Okay, I admit it; the Offset command is a primitive feature with no purpose in our high-tech modern world.

Cross-Reference

Among the filters I've omitted from this chapter is Filter ⇨ Stylize ⇨ Wind, which is technically a destructive filter but is covered along with the blur and noise filters in Chapter 10. I discussed Filter ⇨ Render ⇨ Texture Fill in Chapter 7. And finally, for complete information on the Custom and Displace filters, crack open Chapter A on the CD-ROM at the back of this book.

As for the other filters in the Filter ⇨ Distort, Pixelate, Render, and Stylize submenus, stay tuned to this chapter to discover all the latest and greatest details.

Third-party filters

In addition to using the filters provided by Photoshop, you can purchase all sorts of plug-in filters from other companies. In fact, Photoshop supports its own flourishing cottage industry of third-party solutions from wonderful companies such as Extensis, Alien Skin, Andromeda, and others.

The CD-ROM at the back of this book includes sample versions of some of my favorite filters. For complete information on the specific filters and the companies that provide them, read the appendix. Many of the filters are demo versions of the shipping products, which means that you can see what they do but you can't actually apply the effects or they work for only a limited period of time. I know, it's a drag, but these folks claim that they like to make money every once in a while, and I can't say that I blame them.

One final note about RAM

Memory — that is, real RAM — is a precious commodity when applying destructive filters. As I mentioned in Chapter 2, the scratch disk space typically enables you to edit larger images than your computer's RAM might permit. But all the filters in the Distort submenu and most of the commands in the Render submenu operate exclusively in memory. If they run out of physical RAM, they choke.

Fortunately, there is one potential workaround: When editing a color image, try applying the filter to each of the color channels independently. One color channel requires just a third to a fourth as much RAM as the full-color composite. Sadly, this technique does not help either Lighting Effects or Lens Flare. These delicate flowers of the filter world are compatible only with full-color images; when editing a single channel, they appear dimmed.

The Pixelate Filters

The Filter ➪ Pixelate submenu features a handful of commands that rearrange your image into clumps of solid color:

✦ **Crystallize:** This filter organizes an image into irregularly shaped nuggets. You specify the size of the nuggets by entering a value from 3 to 300 pixels in the Cell Size option.

✦ **Facet:** Facet fuses areas of similarly colored pixels to create a sort of hand-painted effect.

✦ **Mosaic:** The Mosaic filter blends pixels together into larger squares. You specify the height and width of the squares by entering a value in the Cell Size option box.

✦ **Pointillize:** This filter is similar to Crystallize, except it separates an image into disconnected nuggets set against the background color. As usual, you specify the size of the nuggets by changing the Cell Size value.

The Crystal Halo effect

By applying one of the Pixelate filters to a feathered selection, you can create what I call a Crystal Halo effect, named after the Crystallize filter, which tends to deliver the most successful results. (For a preview of these effects, sneak a peek at Figure 11-2.) The following steps explain how to create a Crystal Halo, using the images in Figures 11-2 and 11-3 as an example.

STEPS: Creating the Crystal Halo Effect

1. **Select the foreground element around which you want to create the halo.** Then choose Select ⇨ Inverse to deselect the foreground element and select the background.

2. **Press Q to switch to the quick mask mode.**

3. **Choose Filter ⇨ Other ⇨ Minimum.** As I explained in Chapter 10, this filter enables you to increase the size of the deselected area around the foreground element. The size of the Radius value depends on the size of the halo you want to create. I entered 15 because I wanted a 15-pixel halo. (Photoshop 6 no longer limits the Radius value to a measly 10 pixels; you can now enter values as high as 100.)

4. **Choose Filter ⇨ Blur ⇨ Gaussian Blur.** Then enter a Radius value 0.1 less than the amount by which you increased the size of the deselected area. In my case, I entered 14.9. This cuts into the image slightly, but hardly enough to be visible, as you can see in the image on the left in Figure 11-2.

Figure 11-2: Create a heavily feathered selection outline (left) and then apply the Crystallize filter to refract the feathered edges (right).

5. **Choose Filter ⇨ Pixelate ⇨ Crystallize.** Enter a moderate value in the Cell Size option box. I opted for the value 12, just slightly larger than the default value. After pressing Enter, you get something along the lines of the selection outline shown in the right image in Figure 11-2. The filter refracts the softened edges, as if you were viewing them through textured glass.

6. **Switch back to the marching ants mode.** Then use the selection as desired. I merely pressed Ctrl+Backspace to fill the selection with white, as shown in the top-left image in Figure 11-3.

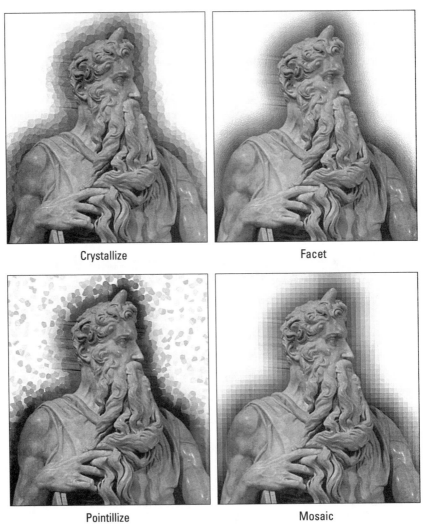

Crystallize   Facet

Pointillize   Mosaic

Figure 11-3: Which aura will Moses don today? The images illustrate the effects of applying each of four filters to a heavily feathered selection in the quick mask mode and pressing Ctrl+Backspace.

You may find this technique particularly useful for combining images. You can copy the selection and paste it against a different background or copy a background from a different image and choose Edit ⇨ Paste Into to paste it inside the crystal halo's selection outline.

Figure 11-3 shows several variations on the Crystal Halo effect. To create the upper-right image, I substituted Filter ⇨ Pixelate ⇨ Facet for Filter ⇨ Pixelate ⇨ Crystallize in Step 5. I also sharpened the result to increase the effect of the filter (which nevertheless remains subtle). To create the lower-right image, I applied the Mosaic filter in place of Crystallize, using a Cell Size value of 8. Finally, to create the lower-left image, I applied the Pointillize filter. Because Pointillize creates gaps in a selection, I had to paint inside Moses to fill in the gaps and isolate the halo effect to the background before returning to the marching ants mode.

Creating a mezzotint

A *mezzotint* is a special halftone pattern that replaces dots with a random pattern of swirling lines and wormholes. Photoshop's Mezzotint filter is an attempt to emulate this effect. Although not entirely successful — true mezzotinting options can be properly implemented only as PostScript printing functions, not as filtering functions — they do lend themselves to some pretty interesting interpretations.

The filter itself is straightforward. You choose Filter ⇨ Pixelate ⇨ Mezzotint, select an effect from the Type submenu, and press Enter. A preview box enables you to see what each of the ten Type options looks like. Figure 11-4 shows off four of the effects at 230 ppi.

To create Figure 11-5, I applied the Mezzotint filter set to the Long Lines effect. Then I used the Edit ⇨ Fade Mezzotint command to mix filtered and original images. I selected Overlay from the Mode pop-up menu and set the Opacity value to 40 percent. The result is a scraped image. (I've decreased the resolution of the image to 180 ppi so that you can see the effect a little more clearly.)

When applied to grayscale artwork, the Mezzotint filter always results in a black-and-white image. When applied to a color image, the filter automatically applies the selected effect independently to each of the color channels. Although all pixels in each channel are changed to either black or white, you can see a total of eight colors — black, red, green, blue, yellow, cyan, magenta, and white — in the RGB composite view. The upper-left example of Color Plate 11-3 shows an image subject to the Mezzotint filter in the RGB mode.

If the Mezzotint filter affects each channel independently, it follows that the color mode in which you work dramatically affects the performance of the filter. For example, if you apply Mezzotint in the Lab mode, you again whittle the colors down to eight, but a very different eight — black, cyan, magenta, green, red, two muddy blues, and a muddy rose — as shown in the top-middle example of Color Plate 11-3. If you're looking for bright happy colors, don't apply Mezzotint in the Lab mode.

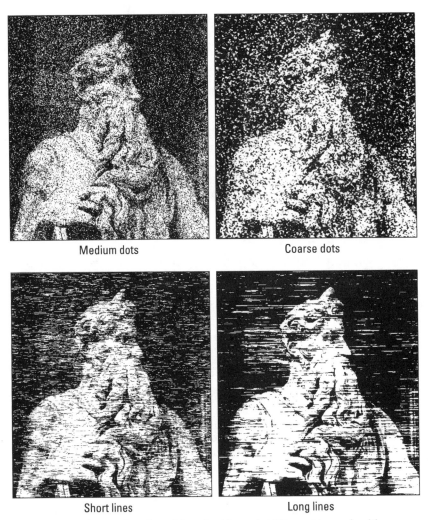

Medium dots

Coarse dots

Short lines

Long lines

Figure 11-4: The results of applying the Mezzotint filter set to each of four representative effects. These line patterns are on par with the halftoning options offered when you select Mode ⇨ Bitmap, as discussed back in Chapter 4.

Figure 11-5: To get this effect, I applied the Mezzotint filter and then chose the Fade command (on the Edit menu in Photoshop 6). In the Fade dialog box, I selected the Overlay mode and set the Opacity value to 40 percent.

In CMYK, the filter produces roughly the same eight colors that you get in RGB — white, cyan, magenta, yellow, violet-blue, red, deep green, and black. However, as shown in the top-right example of the color plate, the distribution of the colors is much different. The image appears much lighter and more colorful than its RGB counterpart. This happens because the filter has a lot of black to work with in the RGB mode but very little — just that in the black channel — in the CMYK mode.

The bottom row of Color Plate 11-3 shows the effects of the Mezzotint filter after using the Fade command to mix it with the original image. As in Figure 11-4, I chose Overlay from the Mode pop-up menu and set the Opacity value to 40 percent. These three very different images were all created using the same filter set to the same effect. The only difference is color mode.

Edge-Enhancement Filters

The Filter ⇨ Stylize submenu offers access to a triad of filters that enhance the edges in an image. The most popular of these is undoubtedly Emboss, which adds dimension to an image by making it look as if it were carved in relief. The other two, Find Edges and Trace Contour, are less commonly applied but every bit as capable and deserving of your attention.

Embossing an image

The Emboss filter works by searching for high-contrast edges (just like the Sharpen Edge and High Pass filters), highlighting the edges with black or white pixels, and then coloring the low-contrast portions with medium gray. When you choose Filter ⇨ Stylize ⇨ Emboss, Photoshop displays the Emboss dialog box shown in Figure 11-6. The dialog box offers three options:

✦ **Angle:** The value in this option box determines the angle at which Photoshop lights the image in relief. For example, if you enter a value of 90 degrees, you light the relief from the bottom straight upward. The white pixels therefore appear on the bottom sides of the edges, and the black pixels appear on the top sides. Figure 11-7 shows eight reliefs lit from different angles. I positioned the images so that they appear lit from a single source.

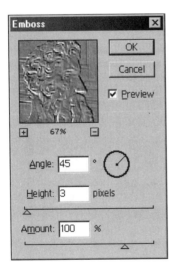

Figure 11-6: The Emboss dialog box lets you control the depth of the filtered image and the angle from which it is lit.

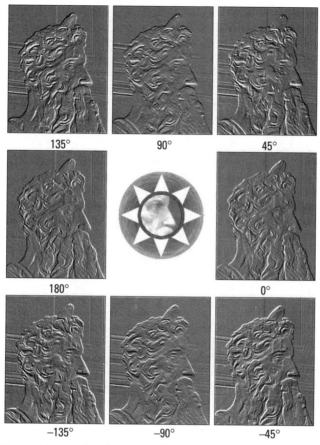

Figure 11-7: Reliefs lit from eight different angles, in 45-degree increments. In all cases, the central sun image indicates the location of the light source. Height and Amount values of 1 pixel and 250 percent were used for all images.

✦ **Height:** The Emboss filter accomplishes its highlighting effect by displacing one copy of an image relative to another. Using the Height option, you specify the distance between the copies, which can vary from 1 to 10 pixels. Lower values produce crisp effects, as demonstrated in Figure 11-8. Values above 3 goop up things pretty good unless you also enter a high Amount value. Together, the Height and Amount values determine the depth of the image in relief.

Tip

The Height value is analogous to the Radius value in the Unsharp Mask dialog box. You should therefore set the value according to the resolution of your image — 1 for 150 ppi, 2 for 300 ppi, and so on.

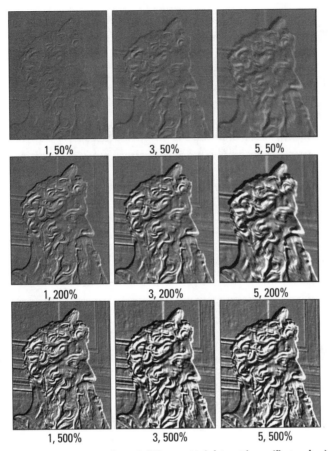

Figure 11-8: Examples of different Height settings (first value)
and Amount settings (second value). The Angle value used
for each image was 135 degrees.

✦ **Amount:** Enter a value between 1 and 500 percent to determine the amount of
black and white assigned to pixels along the edges. Values of 50 percent and
lower produce almost entirely gray images, as you can see in the top row of
Figure 11-8. Higher values produce sharper edges, as if the relief were carved
more deeply.

As a stand-alone effect, Emboss is only so-so. It's one of those filters that makes you
gasp with delight the first time you see it but never quite lends itself to any practical application after you become acquainted with Photoshop. But if you think of
Emboss as an extension of the High Pass filter, it takes on new meaning. You can use

it to edit selection outlines in the quick mask mode, just as you might use the High Pass filter. You also can use it to draw out detail in an image.

Figure 11-9 shows the result of using the Fade command immediately after applying the Emboss filter. (Remember, Fade now resides on the Edit menu, not the Filter menu.) First, I applied the Emboss filter at an Angle of 135 degrees, a Height of 2 pixels, and an Amount of 250 percent. Then I pressed Ctrl+Shift+F to display the Fade dialog box. To create the left example, I selected Darken from the Mode pop-up menu. This added shadows to the edges of the image, thus boosting the texture without unduly upsetting the original brightness values. I selected the Lighten blend mode to create the right example. In both cases, I set the Opacity value to 70 percent.

Figure 11-9: After applying the Emboss filter, I used my old friend the Fade command to darken (left) and lighten (right) the image.

To create a color relief effect, apply the Emboss filter and then select the Luminosity option in the Fade dialog box. This retains the colors from the original image while applying the lightness and darkness of the pixels from the filtered selection. The effect looks something like an inked lithographic plate, with steel grays and vivid colors mixing together. An example of this effect at 80 percent Opacity appears in the first example of Color Plate 11-4.

The second example in that same color plate shows a more impressive — if less practical — technique. Rather than applying Luminosity, I chose the Difference mode inside the Fade dialog box. With its hard edges and vivid colors, this image looks like some impossible frame from an educational film on genetic engineering. I can just hear the narrator commenting, "Prom dates have changed dramatically since scientists discovered how to splice the red rose with the poppy."

Tracing around edges

Photoshop provides three filters that trace around pixels in your image and accentuate the edges. All three filters live on the Filter ⇨ Stylize submenu:

✦ **Find Edges:** This filter detects edges similarly to High Pass. Low-contrast areas become white, medium-contrast edges become gray, and high-contrast edges become black, as in the labeled image in Figure 11-10. Hard edges become thin lines; soft edges become fat ones. The result is a thick, organic outline that you can overlay onto an image to give it a waxy appearance. To achieve the bottom-left effect in the figure, I chose Edit ⇨ Fade Find Edges and applied the Overlay mode and an 80 percent Opacity setting. She'll never get her hand off that canning jar as long as she lives.

✦ **Glowing Edges:** This Gallery Effects filter is a variation on Find Edges, with two important differences: Glowing Edges produces an inverted effect, changing low-contrast areas to black and edges to white, as in the middle image in Figure 11-10. This filter also enables you to adjust the width, brightness, and smoothness of the traced edges. Glowing Edges is a great backup command. If you aren't satisfied with the effect produced by the Find Edges filter, choose Glowing Edges instead and adjust the options as desired. If you want black lines against a white background, press Ctrl+I to invert the effect.

✦ **Trace Contour:** Illustrated on the right side of Figure 11-10, Trace Contour is a little more involved than the others and slightly less interesting. The filter traces a series of single-pixel lines along the border between light and dark pixels. Choosing the filter displays a dialog box containing three options: Level, Upper, and Lower. The Level value indicates the lightness value above which pixels are considered to be light and below which they are dark. For example, if you enter 128 — medium gray, the default setting — Trace Contour draws a line at every spot where an area of color lighter than medium gray meets an area of color darker than medium gray. The Upper and Lower options tell the filter where to position the line — inside the lighter color's territory (Upper) or inside the space occupied by the darker color (Lower).

Like Mezzotint, Trace Contour applies itself to each color channel independently and renders each channel as a 1-bit image. A collection of black lines surrounds the areas of color in each channel; the RGB, Lab, or CMYK composite view shows these lines in the colors associated with the channels. When you work in RGB, a cyan line indicates a black line in the red channel (no red plus full-intensity green and blue becomes cyan). A yellow line indicates a black line in the blue channel, and so on. You get a single black line when working in the grayscale mode.

Find Edges   Glowing Edges   Trace Contour

Overlay, 80%   Overlay, 60%   Multiply, 100%

Figure 11-10: The top row of images demonstrates the effect of the three edge-tracing commands available from the Filter ⇨ Stylize submenu. After applying each command, I used the Fade command to apply the blend modes and Opacity values demonstrated in the bottom row.

Creating a metallic coating

The edge-tracing filters are especially fun to use in combination with Edit ⇨ Fade. I became interested in playing with these filters after trying out the Chrome filter included with the first Gallery Effects collection. Now included with Photoshop as Filter ⇨ Sketch ⇨ Chrome, this filter turns an image into a melted pile of metallic goo. No matter how you apply Chrome, it completely wipes out your image and leaves a ton of jagged color transitions in its wake. It's really only useful with color images, and then only if you follow up with the Fade command and the Luminosity mode. Even then, I've never been particularly satisfied with the results.

But all that experimenting got me thinking: How can you create a metallic coating, with gleaming highlights and crisp shadows, without resorting to Chrome? Find Edges offers a way. First, copy your image to a separate layer (Ctrl+J). Then apply the Gaussian Blur filter. A Radius value between 1.0 and 4.0 produces the best results, depending on how gooey you want the edges to be. Next, apply the Find Edges filter. Because the edges are blurry, the resulting image is light, so I recommend you darken it using Image ⇨ Adjust ⇨ Levels (raise the first Input Levels value to 100 or so, as explained in Chapter 17). The blurry edges appear in the top-left example in Figure 11-11.

To produce the bottom-left image, I mixed the layer with the underlying original using the Overlay blend mode (Shift+Alt+O with a non-painting tool selected) and an Opacity of 80 percent. The result is a shiny effect that produces a metallic finish without altogether destroying the detail in the image.

If you decide you like this effect, there's more where it came from. The second and third columns of Figure 11-11 show the results of applying Filter ⇨ Sketch ⇨ Bas Relief and Filter ⇨ Artistic ⇨ Plastic Wrap, respectively. After applying each filter, I chose Edit ⇨ Fade, selected the Overlay mode, and set the Opacity value to 80 percent, repeating the effect I applied to the Gaussian Blur and Find Edges layer.

Color Plate 11-5 shows the same effects in color. Starting with an unedited construction worker, I went through the usual calisthenics of selecting and layering the image. Next, I applied Gaussian Blur (3.0 Radius) and Find Edges. The effect was too light so I chose Image ⇨ Adjust ⇨ Levels and entered 128 in the first option box. Everything darker than medium gray went to black, uniformly strengthening the effect. The result is the full-color metallic coating shown in the second example in the top row of the color plate. To get the top-right image, I merely selected Overlay from the pop-up menu in the Layers palette (Shift+Alt+O) and changed the Opacity value to 80 percent.

In the bottom row of Color Plate 11-5, I really went nuts. In each case, I applied one of three effects filters — Bas Relief, Plastic Wrap, and the infamous Filter ⇨ Sketch ⇨ Chrome. And each time, I chose Edit ⇨ Fade, selected the Luminosity mode, and reduced the Opacity value to 80 percent.

Okay, okay, so Chrome still looks more metallic than the other effects, but it also plays havoc with the detail. I'm willing to settle for a more subtle effect if it means I can still recognize my subject when I'm finished.

Blur & Find Edges   Bas Relief   Plastic Wrap

Overlay, 80%

Figure 11-11: After applying Gaussian Blur and Find Edges to a layered version of the image (top left), I composited the filtered image with the original using the Overlay mode (bottom left). The second and third columns show similar effects achieved using the effects filters Bas Relief and Plastic Wrap.

Distortion Filters

For the most part, commands in the Distort submenu are related by the fact that they move colors in an image to achieve unusual stretching, swirling, and vibrating effects. They're rather like the transformation commands from the Layer menu in that they perform their magic by relocating and interpolating colors rather than by altering brightness and color values.

The distinction, of course, is that whereas the transformation commands let you scale and distort images by manipulating four control points, the Distort filters provide the equivalent of hundreds of control points, all of which you can use to affect different portions of an image. In some cases, you're projecting an image into a funhouse mirror; other times, it's a reflective pool. You can fan images, wiggle them, and change them in ways that have no correlation to real life, as illustrated in Figure 11-12.

Figure 11-12: This is your image (left); this is your image on distortion filters (right). Three filters, in fact: Spherize, Ripple, and Polar Coordinates.

Distortion filters are powerful tools. Although they are easy to apply, they are extremely difficult to use well. Here are some rules to keep in mind:

✦ **Practice makes practical:** Distortion filters are like complex vocabulary words. You don't want to use them without practicing a little first. Experiment with a distortion filter several times before trying to use it in a real project. You may even want to write down the steps you take so that you can remember how you created an effect.

✦ **Use caution during tight deadlines:** Distortion filters are enormous time-wasters. Unless you know exactly how you want to proceed, you may want to avoid using them when time is short. The last thing you need when you're working under the gun is to get trapped trying to pull off a weird effect.

✦ **Apply selectively:** The effects of distortion filters are too severe to inflict all at once. You can achieve marvelous, subtle effects, however, by distorting feathered and layered selections. Although I wouldn't call the image in Figure 11-12 subtle, no single effect was applied to the entire image. I applied the Spherize filter to a feathered elliptical marquee that included most of the image. I then reapplied Spherize to the eye. I selected the hair and beard and applied the

Ripple filter twice. Finally, after establishing two heavily feathered vertical columns on either side of the image in the quick mask mode, I applied the Polar Coordinates filter, which reflected the front and back of the head. Turn the book upside down and you'll see a second face.

✦ **Combine creatively:** Don't expect a single distortion to achieve the desired effect. If one application isn't enough, apply the filter again. Experiment with combining different distortions.

Distortion filters interpolate between pixels to create their fantastic effects. This means the quality of your filtered images depends on the setting of the Interpolation option in the General Preferences dialog box. If a filter produces jagged effects, the Nearest Neighbor option is probably selected. Try selecting the Bicubic or Bilinear option instead.

If none of the distortion filters does the trick, investigate the new Liquify command, found on the Image menu. With this one command, you can warp, twirl, shift, and otherwise distort your image by dragging on the image in a preview window. The section "Distorting with the Liquify command" explains how to use this tool.

Reflecting an image in a spoon

Most folks take their first venture into distortion filters by using Pinch and Spherize. Pinch maps an image on the inside of a sphere or similarly curved surface; Spherize maps it on the outside of a sphere. It's sort of like looking at your reflection on the inside and outside of a spoon.

You can apply Pinch to a scanned face to squish the features toward the center or apply Spherize to accentuate the girth of the nose. Figure 11-13 illustrates both effects. It's a laugh, and you pretty much feel as though you're onto something that no one else ever thought of before. (At least that's how I felt — but I'm easily amazed.)

You can pinch or spherize an image using either the Pinch or Spherize command. Figure 11-14 shows the dialog boxes for both filters. Note that a positive Amount value in the Pinch dialog box produces a similar effect to a negative value in the Spherize dialog box. There is a slight difference between the spatial curvature of the 3D calculations: Pinch pokes the image inward or outward using a rounded cone — we're talking bell-shaped, much like a Gaussian model. Spherize wraps the image on the outside or inside of a true sphere. As a result, the two filters yield subtly different results. Pinch produces a soft transition around the perimeter of a selection; Spherize produces an abrupt transition. If this doesn't quite make sense to you, just play with one, try out the same effect with the other, and see which you like better.

Another difference between the two filters is that Spherize provides the additional options of enabling you to wrap an image on the inside or outside of a horizontal or vertical cylinder. To try out these effects, select the Horizontal Only or Vertical Only options from the Mode pop-up menu at the bottom of the Spherize dialog box.

Figure 11-13: Constantine does the popular throbbing facial dance — well, it was popular back in A.D. 300 — thanks to the Pinch (left) and Spherize (right) filters.

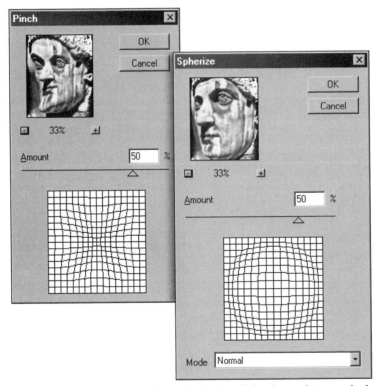

Figure 11-14: Both the Pinch and Spherize dialog boxes let you pinch and spherize images. Pinch wraps an image on a rounded cone; Spherize wraps onto a sphere.

Tip

Both filters can affect elliptical regions only. If a selection outline is not elliptical, Photoshop applies the filter to the largest ellipse that fits inside the selection. As a result, the filter may leave behind a noticeable elliptical boundary between the affected and unaffected portions of the selection. To avoid this effect, select the region you want to edit with the elliptical marquee tool and then feather the selection before filtering it. This softens the effect of the filter and provides a more gradual transition (even more so than Pinch already affords).

One of the more remarkable properties of the Pinch filter is that it lets you turn any image into a conical gradation. Figure 11-15 illustrates how the process works. First, blur the image to eliminate any harsh edges between color transitions. Then apply the Pinch filter at full strength (100 percent). Reapply the filter several more times. Each time you press Ctrl+F, the center portion of the image recedes farther and farther into the distance, as shown in Figure 11-15. After 10 repetitions, the face in the example all but disappeared.

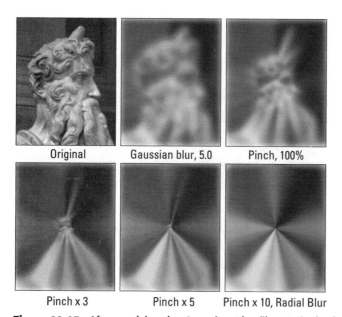

Original   Gaussian blur, 5.0   Pinch, 100%

Pinch x 3   Pinch x 5   Pinch x 10, Radial Blur

Figure 11-15: After applying the Gaussian Blur filter, I pinched the image 10 times and applied the Radial Blur filter to create a conical gradation.

Next, apply the Radial Blur filter set to Spin 10 pixels or so to mix the color boundaries a bit. The result is a type of gradation that you can't create using Photoshop's gradient tool.

Twirling spirals

The Twirl filter rotates the center of a selection while leaving the sides fixed in place. The result is a spiral of colors that looks for all the world as if you poured the image into a blender set to a very slow speed.

When you choose Filter ➪ Distort ➪ Twirl, Photoshop displays the Twirl dialog box, shown in Figure 11-16. Enter a positive value from 1 to 999 degrees to spiral the image in a clockwise direction. Enter a negative value to spiral the image in a counterclockwise direction. As you are probably already aware, 360 degrees make a full circle, so the maximum 999-degree value equates to a spiral that circles around almost three times, as shown in the bottom-right example in Figure 11-17.

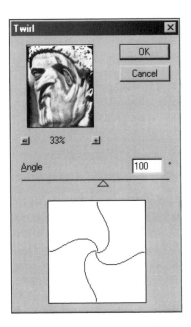

Figure 11-16: The Twirl dialog box enables you to create spiraling images.

Tip

The Twirl filter produces smoother effects when you use lower Angle values. Therefore, you're better off applying a 100-degree spiral 10 times rather than applying a 999-degree spiral once, as you can see in Figure 11-17.

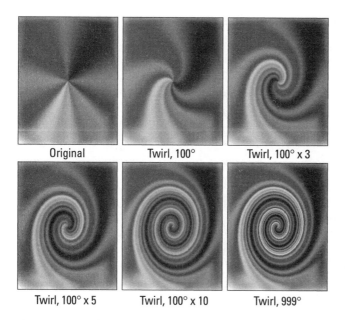

| Original | Twirl, 100° | Twirl, 100° x 3 |
| Twirl, 100° x 5 | Twirl, 100° x 10 | Twirl, 999° |

Figure 11-17: The effects of applying the Twirl filter. Repeatedly applying the Twirl filter at a moderate value (bottom middle) produces a smoother effect than applying the filter once at a high value (bottom right).

In addition to creating ice-cream swirls like those shown in Figure 11-17, you can use the Twirl filter to create organic images virtually from scratch, as witnessed by Figures 11-18 and 11-19.

To create the images shown in Figure 11-18, I used the Spherize filter to flex the conical gradation vertically by entering 100 percent in the Amount option box and selecting Vertical Only from the Mode pop-up menu. After repeating this filter several times, I eventually achieved a stalactite-stalagmite effect, as shown in the center example of the figure. I then repeatedly applied the Twirl filter to curl the flexed gradations like two symmetrical hairs. The result merges the simplicity of pure math with the beauty of bitmapped imagery.

Figure 11-19 illustrates a droplet technique designed by Mark Collen. I took the liberty of breaking down the technique into the following steps.

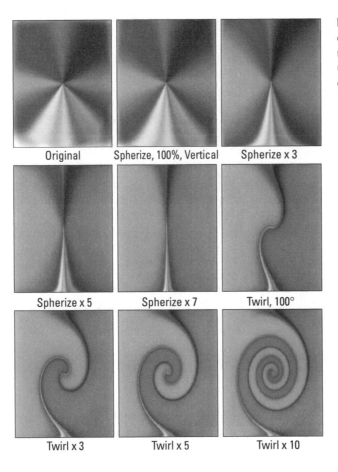

Original · Spherize, 100%, Vertical · Spherize x 3

Spherize x 5 · Spherize x 7 · Twirl, 100°

Twirl x 3 · Twirl x 5 · Twirl x 10

Figure 11-18: You can create surprisingly naturalistic effects using distortion filters exclusively.

Figure 11-19: Although they appear as if they might be the result of the ZigZag filter, these images were created entirely by using the gradient tool, the Twirl filter, and a couple of transformations.

STEPS: Creating a Thick-Liquid Droplet

1. **Press D to restore the default foreground and background colors.**

2. **Shift-drag with the rectangular marquee tool to select a square portion of an image.**

3. **Create a linear gradation by dragging inside the selection outline with the gradient tool.** Before you drag, select the linear gradient style on the Options bar and select the foreground to background gradient from the Gradients drop-down palette, also on the Options bar. Drag a short distance near the center of the selection from upper left to lower right, creating the gradation shown in the top-left box in Figure 11-19.

4. **Choose the Twirl filter and apply it at –360 degrees so that the spiral moves counterclockwise.** To create the top-right image in the figure, I applied the Twirl filter three times. Each repetition of the filter adds another ring of ripples.

5. **Press Ctrl+J to copy the selection to a layer.**

6. **Choose Edit ⇨ Transform ⇨ Flip Horizontal.**

7. **Lower the Opacity value to 50 percent.** You can do this from the keyboard by selecting the rectangular marquee tool and pressing 5. The result appears in the lower-left example in Figure 11-19.

8. **Choose Edit ⇨ Transform ⇨ Rotate 90° CW.** This rotates the layer a quarter turn, thus creating the last image in the figure. You can achieve other interesting effects by choosing Lighten, Darken, and others from the brush modes pop-up menu.

Now, if a few twirls and transformations can produce an effect this entertaining in black and white, just imagine what you can do in color. On second thought, don't imagine; check out Color Plate 11-6 instead. The first row in this eight-part color plate is nothing more than a color version of Figure 11-19, intended merely to set the scene. As you can see, I've created a gradation using two complementary colors, blue and yellow. In the fifth example (lower left), I apply the Difference blend mode to the layer (Shift+Alt+E with a non-painting tool selected) and return the Opacity setting to 100 percent. Next, I clone that layer and rotate it another 90 degrees clockwise to produce the sixth example. The Difference blend mode remains in effect for this cloned layer as well. Not satisfied, I clone that layer, rotate it another 90 degrees, and flip it horizontally. The result, also subject to Difference, is the seventh example. Then for the *coup de grâce,* I randomly apply the Twirl, Spherize, and ZigZag filters to the layers to mutate the concentric rings into something a little more interesting.

If that went a little fast for you, not to worry. More important than the specific effects is this general category of distortion drawings. A filter such as Pinch or Twirl permits you to create wild imagery without ever drawing a brushstroke or scanning a photograph. If you can do this much with a simple two-color gradation, just think of what you can do if you throw in a few more colors. Pixels are little more than fodder for these very powerful functions.

Creating concentric pond ripples

I don't know about you, but when I think of zigzags, I think of cartoon lightning bolts, wriggling snakes, scribbles — anything that alternately changes directions along an axis, like the letter *Z*. The ZigZag filter does arrange colors into zigzag patterns, but it does so in a radial fashion, meaning that the zigzags emanate from the center of the image like spokes in a wheel. The result is a series of concentric ripples. If you want parallel zigzags, check out the Ripple and Wave filters, described in the next section. (The ZigZag filter creates ripples and the Ripple filter creates zigzags. Go figure.)

When you choose Filter ➪ Distort ➪ ZigZag, Photoshop displays the ZigZag dialog box, shown in Figure 11-20. The dialog box offers the following options:

✦ **Amount:** Enter an amount between negative and positive 100 in whole-number increments to specify the depth of the ripples. If you enter a negative value, the ripples descend below the surface. If you enter a positive value, the ripples protrude upward. Examples of three representative Amount values appear in Figure 11-21.

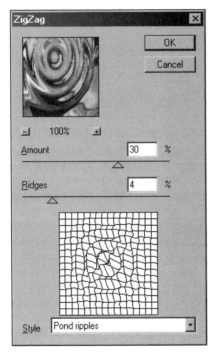

Figure 11-20: The ZigZag dialog box lets you add concentric ripples to an image, as if the image were reflected in a pond into which you dropped a pebble.

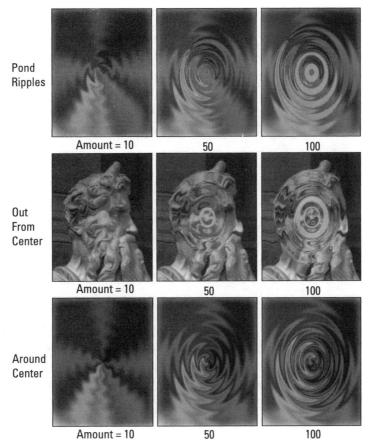

Figure 11-21: The effects of the ZigZag filter subject to three Amount values and the Pond Ripples, Out From Center, and Around Center settings. In all cases, the Ridges value was 5.

✦ **Ridges:** This option box controls the number of ripples in the selected area and accepts any value from 1 to 20. Figure 11-22 demonstrates the effect of three Ridges values.

✦ **Pond Ripples:** This option is really a cross between the two that follow. It moves pixels outward and rotates them around the center of the selection to create circular patterns. As demonstrated in the top rows of Figures 11-21 and 11-22, this option truly results in a pond ripple effect.

Pond
Ripples

Out
From
Center

Around
Center

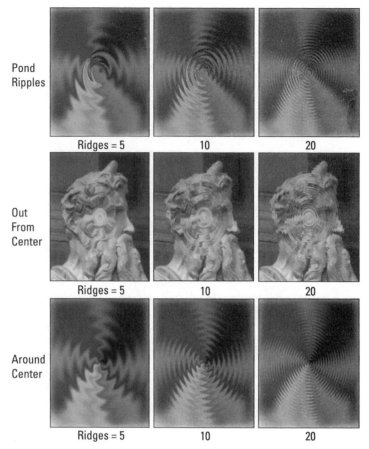

Figure 11-22: The effects of the ZigZag filter using three Ridges values and each of the three Style pop-up menu settings. In all cases, the Amount value was 20.

✦ **Out From Center:** When you select this option, Photoshop moves pixels outward in rhythmic bursts according to the value in the Ridges option box. Because the gradation image I created in Figure 11-15 was already arranged in a radial pattern, I brought in Moses to demonstrate the effect of the Out From Center option, as shown in the second rows of Figures 11-21 and 11-22.

✦ **Around Center:** Select this option to rotate pixels in alternating directions around the circle without moving them outward. This is the only option that produces what I would term a zigzag effect. The last rows of Figures 11-21 and 11-22 show the effects of the Around Center option.

Creating parallel ripples and waves

Photoshop provides four means to distort an image in parallel waves, as if the image were lying on the bottom of a shimmering or undulating pool. Of the four, the ripple filters — which include Ripple, Ocean Ripple, and Glass — are only moderately sophisticated, but they're also relatively easy to apply. The fourth filter, Wave, affords you greater control, but its options are among the most complex Photoshop has to offer.

The Ripple filter

To use the Ripple filter, choose Filter ➪ Distort ➪ Ripple. Photoshop displays the Ripple dialog box shown in Figure 11-23. You have the following options:

✦ **Amount:** Enter an amount between negative and positive 999 in whole-number increments to specify the width of the ripples from side to side. Negative and positive values change the direction of the ripples, but visually speaking, they produce identical effects. The ripples are measured as a ratio of the Size value and the dimensions of the selection — all of which translates to, "Experiment and see what happens." You can count on getting ragged effects from any value over 300, as illustrated in Figure 11-24.

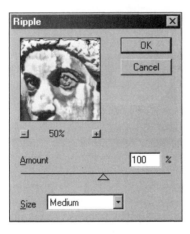

Figure 11-23: The Ripple filter makes an image appear as if it were refracted through flowing water.

✦ **Size:** Select one of the three options in the Size drop-down menu to change the length of the ripples. The Small option results in the shortest ripples and therefore the most ripples. As shown in the upper-right corner of Figure 11-24, combining the Small option with a high Amount value results in a textured-glass effect. The Large option results in the longest and fewest ripples.

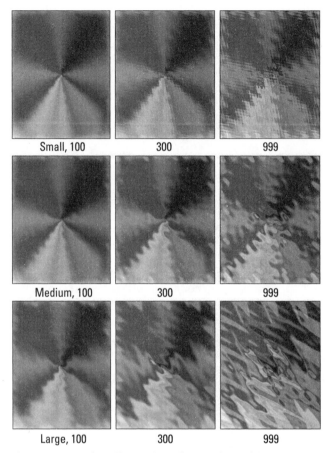

Figure 11-24: The effects of combining three different
Ripple filter Amount values with three different Size settings.

You can create a blistered effect by overlaying a negative ripple onto a positive ripple. Try this: First, copy the selection. Then apply the Ripple filter with
a positive Amount value — say, 300. Next, paste the copied selection and
apply the Ripple filter at the exact opposite Amount value, in this case, –300.
Press 5 to change the Opacity value to 50 percent. The result is a series of dia-
metrically opposed ripples that cross each other to create teardrop blisters.

Ocean Ripple and Glass

The Ocean Ripple and Glass filters are gifts from Gallery Effects. Both filters emulate the effect of looking at an image through textured glass. These two distorters so closely resemble each other that they would be better merged into one. But where the effects filters are concerned, interface design is as fickle and transitory as the face on the cover of *Tiger Beat Magazine*.

The Ocean Ripple and Glass dialog boxes appear joined at the hip in Figure 11-25. While the names and effects of the specific slider bars vary, the only real difference between the two filters is that Ocean Ripple subscribes to a fixed ripple texture, and Glass lets you switch out the texture by selecting from a pop-up menu.

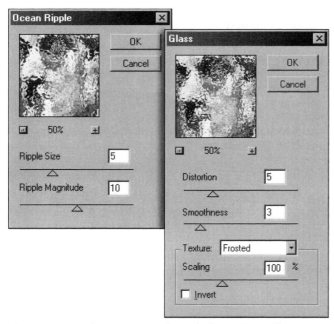

Figure 11-25: The Ocean Ripple and Glass effects filters are two birds of a feather, ultimately born from the same egg.

To guide you in your experimentations, Figure 11-26 shows the Pinch gradation subject to several Ocean Ripple settings. The first number represents the Ripple Size value (listed first in the dialog box); the second number in the figure represents the Ripple Magnitude value. As you can see, you can vary the Size value with impunity. But raise the Magnitude value, and you're looking through sculpted glass.

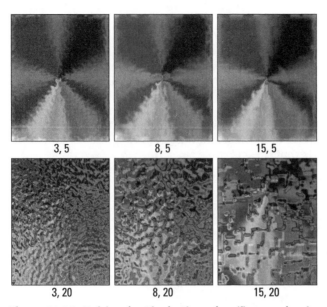

Figure 11-26: Raising the Ripple Size value (first number in each pair) spreads out the effect; raising the Ripple Magnitude (second number) adds more depth and contrast to the ripples.

The Wave filter

Now that you've met the ripple family, it's time to ride the Wave. I've come to love this filter — I use it all the time — but it's complex enough to warrant its own book. It wouldn't be a very big book and no one would buy it, but you never know what a freelancer like me will do next. Keep an eye out for *Wave Filter Bible* at your local bookstore.

In the meantime, choose Filter ➪ Distort ➪ Wave (that's the easy part) to display the Wave dialog box shown in Figure 11-27. Photoshop presents you with the following options, which make applying a distortion every bit as easy as operating an oscilloscope:

✦ **Number of Generators:** Right off the bat, the Wave dialog box boggles the brain. A friend of mine likened this option to the number of rocks you throw in the water to start it rippling. One generator means that you throw in one rock to create one set of waves, as demonstrated in Figure 11-28. You can throw in two rocks to create two sets of waves (see Figure 11-29), three rocks to create three sets of waves, and all the way up to a quarryful of 999 rocks to create, well, you get the idea. If you enter a high value, however, be prepared to wait a few years for the preview to update. If you can't wait, press Escape, which turns off the preview until the next time you enter a value in the dialog box.

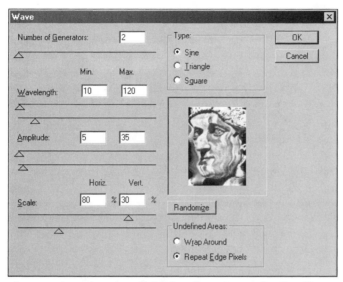

Figure 11-27: The Wave dialog box lets you wreak scientific havoc on an image. Put on your pocket protector, take out your slide rule, and give it a whirl.

✦ **Wavelength and Amplitude:** Beginning to feel like you're playing with a ham radio? The Wave filter produces random results by varying the number and length of waves (Wavelength) as well as the height of the waves (Amplitude) between minimum and maximum values, which can range from 1 to 999. (The Wavelength and Amplitude options, therefore, correspond in theory to the Size and Amount options in the Ripple dialog box.) Figures 11-28 and 11-29 show examples of representative Wavelength and Amplitude values.

✦ **Scale:** You can scale the effects of the Wave filter between 1 and 100 percent horizontally and vertically. All the effects featured in Figures 11-28 and 11-29 were created by setting both Scale options to 15 percent.

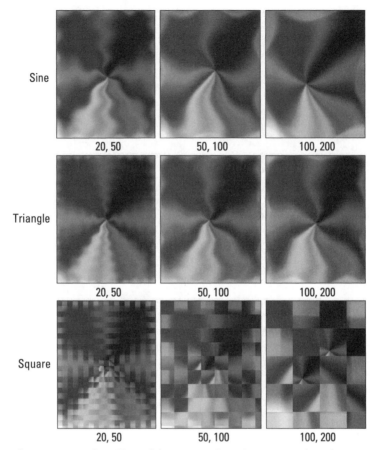

Figure 11-28: The effect of three sets of Maximum Wavelength (first value) and Amplitude (second value) settings when combined with each of the three Type settings. The Number of Generators value was 1 in all cases.

✦ **Type:** You can select from three kinds of waves. The Sine option produces standard sine waves that rise and fall smoothly in bell-shaped curves, just like real waves. The Triangle option creates zigzags that rise and fall in straight lines, like the edge of a piece of fabric cut with pinking shears. The Square option has nothing to do with waves at all, but rather organizes an image into a series of rectangular groupings, reminiscent of Cubism. You might think of this option as an extension of the Mosaic filter. Figures 11-28 and 11-29 demonstrate all three options.

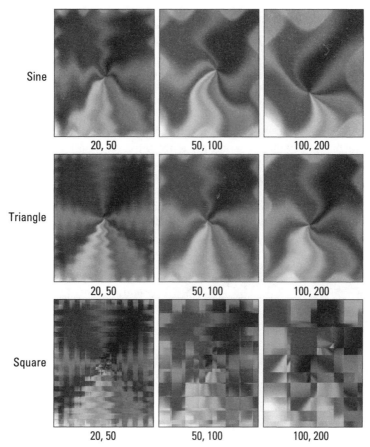

Figure 11-29: The only difference between these images and their counterparts in Figure 11-28 is that the Number of Generators value used for all images was 2.

✦ **Randomize:** The Wave filter is random by nature. If you don't like the effect you see in the preview box, click the Randomize button to stir things up a bit. You can keep clicking the button until you get an effect you like.

✦ **Undefined Areas:** The Wave filter distorts a selection to the extent that gaps may appear around the edges. You can fill those gaps either by repeating pixels along the edge of the selection, as in the figures, or by wrapping pixels from the left side of the selection onto the right side and pixels from the top edge of the selection onto the bottom.

Distorting an image along a curve

The Distort command, which isn't discussed elsewhere in this book, creates four corner handles around an image. You drag each corner handle to distort the selected image in that direction. Unfortunately, you can't add other points around the edges to create additional distortions, which can be frustrating if you're trying to achieve a specific effect. If you can't achieve a certain kind of distortion using Edit ➪ Free Transform, the Shear filter may be your answer.

Shear distorts an image along a path. When you choose Filter ➪ Distort ➪ Shear, you get the dialog box shown in Figure 11-30. Initially, a single line that has two points at either end appears in the grid at the top of the box. When you drag the points, you slant the image in the preview. This, plus the fact that the filter is named Shear — Adobe's strange term for skewing (it appears in Illustrator as well) — leads many users to dismiss the filter as nothing more than a slanting tool. But in truth, it's more versatile than that.

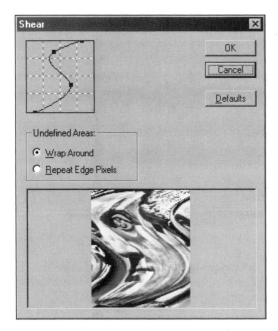

Figure 11-30: Click the grid line in the left corner of the Shear dialog box to add points to the line. Drag these points to distort the image along the curve.

You can add points to the grid line simply by clicking on it. A point springs up every time you click an empty space in the line. Drag the point to change the curvature of the line and distort the image along the new curve. To delete a point, drag it off the left or right side of the grid. To delete all points and return the line to its original vertical orientation, click the Defaults button.

The Undefined Areas options work just as they do in the Wave dialog box (described in the preceding section). You can either fill the gaps on one side of the image with pixels shoved off the opposite side by selecting Wrap Around or repeat pixels along the edge of the selection by selecting Repeat Edge Pixels.

Changing to polar coordinates

The Polar Coordinates filter is another one of those gems that a lot of folks shy away from because it doesn't make much sense at first glance. When you choose Filter ➪ Distort ➪ Polar Coordinates, Photoshop presents two radio buttons, as shown in Figure 11-31. You can either map an image from rectangular to polar coordinates or from polar to rectangular coordinates.

Figure 11-31: In effect, the Polar Coordinates dialog box enables you to map an image onto a globe and view the globe from above.

All right, time for some global theory. The first image in Figure 11-32 shows a stretched detail of the world map from the Digital Stock library. This map falls under the heading of a *Mercator projection,* meaning that Greenland is all stretched out of proportion, looking as big as the United States and Mexico combined.

The reason for this has to do with the way different mapping systems handle longitude and latitude lines. On a spherical globe, lines of latitude converge at the poles. On a Mercator map, they run absolutely parallel. Because the Mercator map exaggerates the distance between longitude lines as you progress away from the equator, it likewise exaggerates the distance between lines of latitude. The result is a map that becomes infinitely enormous at each of the poles.

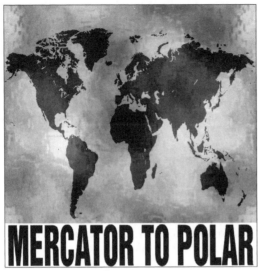

Figure 11-32: The world from the equator up expressed in rectangular (top) and polar (bottom) coordinates.

When you convert the map to polar coordinates (by selecting the Rectangular to Polar radio button in the Polar Coordinates dialog box), you look down on it from the extreme North or South Pole. This means that the entire length of the top edge of the Mercator map becomes a single dot in the exact center of the polar projection. The length of the bottom edge of the map wraps around the entire perimeter of the circle. The second example in Figure 11-32 shows the result. As you can see, the Rectangular to Polar option is just the tool for wrapping text around a circle.

If you select the Polar to Rectangular option, the Polar Coordinates filter produces the opposite effect. Imagine for a moment that the conical gradation shown in the upper-left corner of Figure 11-33 is a fan spread out into a full circle. Now imagine closing the fan, breaking the hinge at the top, and spreading out the rectangular fabric of the fan. The center of the fan unfolds to form the top edge of the fabric, and what was once the perimeter of the circle is now the bottom edge of the fabric. Figure 11-33 shows two examples of what happens when you convert circular images from polar to rectangular coordinates.

Figure 11-33: Two familiar circular images (left) converted from polar to rectangular coordinates (right). The top example is simple enough that you can probably predict the results of the conversion in your head. The lower example looks cool, but you'd need a brain extension to predict the outcome.

Tip

The Polar Coordinates filter is a great way to edit gradations. After drawing a linear gradation with the gradient tool (as discussed in Chapter 6), try applying Filter ⇨ Distort ⇨ Polar Coordinates with the Polar to Rectangular option selected. (Rectangular to Polar just turns it into a radial gradation, sometimes with undesirable results.) You get a redrawn gradation with highlights at the bottom of the selection. Press Ctrl+F to reapply the filter to achieve another effect. You can keep repeating this technique until jagged edges start to appear. Then press Ctrl+Z to go back to the last smooth effect.

Distorting an image inside out

The following exercise describes how to achieve a sizzling Parting of the Red Sea effect. Although it incorporates several distortion filters, the star of the effect is the Polar Coordinates filter, which is used to turn the image inside out and then convert it back to polar coordinates after flipping it upside down. No scanned image or artistic talent is required. Rumor has it that Moses puts in a guest appearance in the final image.

This effect is the brainchild of Mark Collen, easily the most imaginative distortion expert I've had the pleasure of knowing. I already mentioned his name in this chapter, in connection with the steps for "Creating a Thick-Liquid Droplet." To be perfectly honest, I probably should have mentioned him more than that because many of the ideas in this chapter were based on long, expensive telephone conversations with the guy.

At any rate, Figures 11-34 through 11-39 show the progression of the image through the following steps, starting with a simplistic throwback to Dada (the art movement, not the family member) and continuing to the fabled sea rising in billowing streams. Color Plate 11-7 shows one of Mark's most vivid images, which was created in part using many of the techniques from the following steps. Obviously, Mark used a couple of other filtering and nonfiltering techniques to create his image, but gee whiz folks, you can't expect the guy to share everything he knows in one fell swoop. He has to make a living, after all.

STEPS: The Parting of the Red Sea Effect

1. **Draw some random shapes in whatever colors you like.** My shapes appear against a black background in Figure 11-34, but you can use any shapes and colors you like. To create each shape, I used the lasso tool to draw the outline of the shape and pressed Alt+Backspace to fill the lassoed selection with the foreground color. The effect works best if your colors have a lot of contrast.

Figure 11-34: Draw several meaningless shapes with the lasso tool and fill each with a different color.

2. **Choose Image ⇨ Rotate Canvas ⇨ 90° CCW.** In Step 3, you apply the Wind Filter to add streaks to the shapes you just created, as shown in Figure 11-35. Because the Wind filter creates horizontal streaks only and your goal is to add vertical streaks, you must temporarily reorient your image before applying the filter.

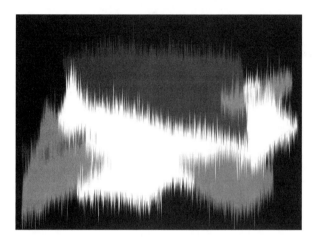

Figure 11-35: The result of rotating the image a quarter turn, blasting it in both directions with the Wind filter, rotating it back into place, and applying the Motion Blur filter vertically

3. **Choose Filter ⇨ Stylize ⇨ Wind.** Select Blast and From the Left and press Enter. To randomize the image in both directions, choose the Wind filter again and select Blast and From the Right.

4. **Choose Image ⇨ Rotate ⇨ 90° CW.** This returns the image to its original orientation.

5. **Choose Filter ⇨ Blur ⇨ Motion Blur.** Enter 90 degrees in the Angle option and use 20 pixels for the Distance option. This blurs the image vertically to soften the blast lines, as in Figure 11-35.

6. **Choose Filter ⇨ Distort ⇨ Wave.** Then enter the values shown in Figure 11-36 in the Wave dialog box. Most of these values are approximate; experiment with other settings if you like. The only essential value is 1 percent in the Vert. option box, which ensures that the filter waves the image in a horizontal direction only.

7. **Choose Filter ⇨ Distort ⇨ Ocean Ripple.** I entered 15 for the Ripple Size and 5 for the Ripple Magnitude to get the effect shown in Figure 11-37.

8. **Expand the canvas size.** To perform the next step, the Polar Coordinates filter needs lots of empty room in which to maneuver. If you filled up your canvas like I did, choose Image ⇨ Canvas Size and add 200 pixels both vertically and horizontally. The new canvas size, with generous borders, appears in Figure 11-37.

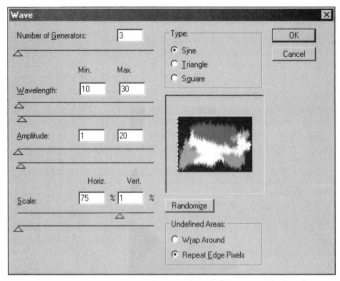

Figure 11-36: Apply these settings from the Wave dialog box to wave the image in a vertical direction only.

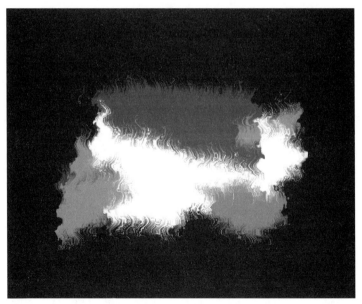

Figure 11-37: After applying the Ripple filter, use the Canvas Size command to add a generous amount of empty space around the image.

9. **Choose Filter ⇨ Distort ⇨ Polar Coordinates.** So far, you've probably been a little disappointed by your image. I mean, it's just this disgusting little hairy thing that looks like a bad rug or something. Well, now's your chance to turn it into something special. After you choose Filter ⇨ Distort ⇨ Polar Coordinates, select the Polar to Rectangular radio button. Photoshop in effect turns the image inside out, sending all the hairy edges to the bottom of the screen. Finally, an image worth waiting for.

10. **Choose Image ⇨ Rotate Canvas ⇨ Flip Vertical.** This turns the image upside down. As I believe Hemingway said, the hair also rises, as shown in Figure 11-38. This step prepares the image for the next major polar conversion, due in the year 2096.

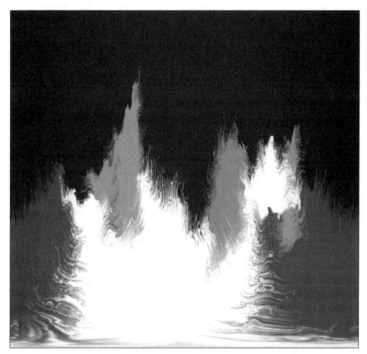

Figure 11-38: Convert the image from polar to rectangular coordinates to turn it inside out. Then flip it vertically to prepare it for the next polar conversion.

11. **Use the rectangular marquee tool to select the central portion of the image.** Leave about 50 pixels along the top and bottom of the image deselected, as well as 100 pixels along both sides. Then feather the selection with a 15-pixel radius.

12. **Press Ctrl+F to reapply the Polar Coordinates filter using the same settings as before.** Okay, so it happened before 2096. How could I have known? The pixels inside the selection now billow into a fountain.

13. **Add Moses to taste.** The finished image appears in Figure 11-39.

Figure 11-39: Marquee the central portion of the image with a heavily feathered selection outline, convert the selection from rectangular to polar coordinates, and put Moses into the scene. My, doesn't he look natural in his new environment?

Distorting with the Liquify command

Photoshop 6 introduces the Liquify command, which offers boundless opportunities for image distortion. With Liquify, you can drag in your image to warp, shift, twirl, expand, contract, and even copy pixels. Unlike filters, which apply a uniform distortion across a selection, Liquify enables you to distort pixels by pushing them around with a brush.

You might expect to find Liquify on the Filter menu, but those expectations are wrong. This command instead appears on the Image menu. When you choose the command, Photoshop displays the immense Liquify image window shown in Figure 11-40, which tops even the Extract window (explored in Chapter 9) in terms of icons and options. You also can display the Liquify window by pressing Ctrl+Shift+X.

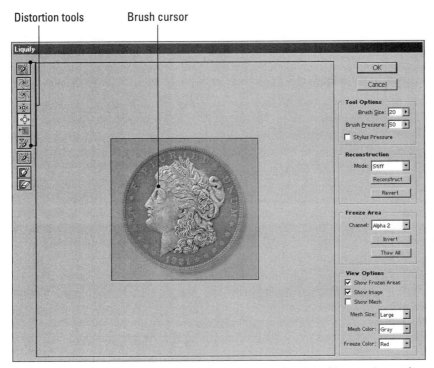

Figure 11-40: Choose Image ⇨ Liquify to shove pixels around in your image by dragging them with a brush.

The miniature toolbox on the left side of the window contains seven tools for distorting the image. You drag or click with the tools as explained in the upcoming list. (You can select the tools from the keyboard by pressing the keys indicated in parentheses). But before you begin, take in the following Liquify facts:

✦ All tools respond to the Brush Size setting on the right side of the window. Press the right and left bracket keys to raise and lower the brush size from the keyboard by one pixel. Your cursor reflects the approximate brush size, as shown in Figure 11-40. Note, however, that most distortions affect the pixels at the center of the cursor more quickly than those on the perimeter.

✦ The Brush Pressure option controls the impact of the tools; higher values produce more pronounced effects. If you work with a pressure-sensitive tablet, select the Stylus Pressure check box to make Photoshop adjust the tool pressure based on the amount of pressure you put on the pen stylus.

✦ To speed up the performance of the Liquify filter, Photoshop distorts the image in the dialog box using screen-resolution data. When you click OK or press Enter, the program applies the warp to the full resolution image. Unfortunately, this design means that you can't zoom in or out on your image in the Liquify window. So if you need to get a closer look at your image, exit the dialog box and select the area you want to alter. Photoshop then displays only the selected area at a larger size inside the Liquify window.

✦ Any deselected areas are considered *frozen,* which just means that they're unaffected by the distortion tools. You can freeze and then *thaw* — make available for editing — portions of the image as explained in the next section. You can even create partially frozen or thawed areas, which further limits the impact of the distortion tools.

✦ By default, frozen regions are covered with a red translucent coating, just like masked areas in the quick mask mode. (The coating appears around the coin in Figure 11-40.) You can change the appearance of the overlay by selecting a new color from the Freeze Color pop-up menu at the bottom of the Liquify window. If you don't want to see the coating at all, deselect the Show Frozen Areas check box.

✦ Select the Show Mesh check box to display gridlines on top of the image. You can use the gridlines as a guide if you want to apply very precise distortions. If you want, you can even apply your distortions while viewing only the grid by deselecting the Show Image check box. Set the grid size and color by selecting options from the Mesh Size and Mesh Color pop-up menus.

The next section goes into more detail about freezing and thawing image areas as well as how to reconstruct the original image or a distortion. But because I can see that you're itching to start mucking around in your pixels, the following list shows you how the distortion tools work:

Warp tool (W): Drag to shove the pixels under your cursor around the image. In the top-right example in Figure 11-41, I used a small brush at 100 percent pressure and dragged slightly upward on the corner of Miss Liberty's mouth, giving the icon a slight smile — or is that a smirk?

Twirl clockwise (R): Click or drag to spin pixels under your cursor in a clockwise direction or, if you prefer, to the right. In the lower-left example of Figure 11-41, I centered my brush on Miss Liberty's eye and moused down for a few seconds until I got the result you see in the figure.

Original   Warp

Twirl clockwise   Pucker, Bloat

Figure 11-41: Here, you see the distortions I achieved by using the warp, twirl clockwise, pucker, and bloat tools inside the Liquify window.

Twirl counterclockwise (L): The opposite of twirl clockwise, this tool spins pixels counterclockwise (left).

Pucker (P): Drag with this tool to send pixels scurrying toward the center of the tool cursor. The effect is similar to applying the Pinch filter with a positive Amount value. If you mouse down instead of dragging, Photoshop steadily increases the extent of the distortion until you release the mouse button.

Bloat (B): When you drag or mouse down with this tool, pixels underneath the brush cursor move outward, like a stomach after too many trips to the buffet line. As is the case with Pucker, the longer you hold down the mouse button, the more bloating you get.

To create the lower-right example in Figure 11-41, I moused down with the pucker tool over the mouth area and then moused down again on the eye area, this time with the bloat tool.

Shift pixels (S): As you drag with this tool, pixels underneath the cursor move in a direction perpendicular to your drag. For example, if you drag down, pixels flow to the right. Drag straight up, and pixels move to the left.

Reflection (M): The M, it appears, stands for *mirror;* dragging with this tool creates a reflection, albeit one you might see in a funhouse mirror. As you drag, Photoshop copies pixels from the area perpendicular to the direction you move the cursor. So if you drag down, you clone pixels to the left of the cursor onto the area underneath the cursor.

Tip

Theoretically, you can create a mirror image of an object by using this tool. But unless you're really going for a *distorted* mirror image, duplicate and flip it using the ordinary Duplicate and Flip commands. Dragging with the Reflection tool is too unpredictable for this purpose (remember, this is a tool intended to distort, not duplicate). You can, however, limit the distortion by freezing the area that you're going to copy, as explained in the next section. Then Alt-drag from the edge of the frozen area into the unfrozen region.

After you drag with any of these tools, you can undo the effect by pressing Ctrl+Z. If you want to go further back in time or explore some additional reversion options, read the next section.

Freezing and thawing pixels

As I mentioned a few paragraphs ago, Photoshop automatically freezes selected pixels when you enter the Liquify dialog box, which means that any distortions you apply don't affect them. You can freeze additional areas at any time. You also can thaw pixels so that they once again become slaves to the distortion tools.

To freeze a portion of your image from the Liquify window, you have two options:

✦ Press F to select the freeze tool, shown along with the Freeze options in Figure 11-42, and then drag over areas that you want to protect. You can adjust the brush size and pressure as you can when working with the distortion tools. But in this case, the pressure setting determines how deeply frozen the pixels become. At anything less than 100 percent, the pixels become partially distorted when you drag over them with a distortion tool. If you set the pressure to 50 percent, the distortion is applied with half the pressure as in unfrozen areas.

✦ If you created a mask channel before choosing the Liquify command, you can freeze the masked area by selecting the channel from the Channel pop-up menu.

Thaw

Freeze

Reconstruct

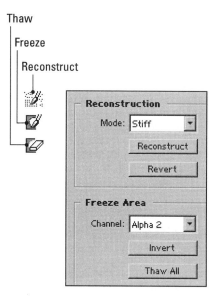

Figure 11-42: Use the freeze, thaw, and reconstruction tools and options to mask off areas from distortions and to revert distorted pixels to their original appearance.

To thaw frozen areas, thereby making them editable again, paint over them with the thaw tool (T). The Brush Pressure setting affects this tool just as it does the freeze tool. To thaw the entire image, click the Thaw All button.

Tip

Just as you can inverse a selection outline or invert a mask in the quick mask mode, you can click the Invert button to quickly freeze any unfrozen pixels and thaw any frozen ones.

Reconstructing and reverting

In the Reconstruction section of the Liquify window, you see a Mode pop-up menu plus two buttons, Reconstruct and Revert. You can use these options not only to revert an image to the way it looked before you applied a distortion, but also to redo a distortion so that it affects the image differently.

The following list outlines reversion possibilities:

✦ To undo your last drag, just press Ctrl+Z, as always. Press again to undo the undo.

✦ To return everything back to the way it was when you first opened the Liquify window, Alt-click the Cancel button, which turns into the Reset button, and then Alt-click the button. Again, everything works as usual.

✦ To revert unfrozen areas to their original appearance, choose Revert from the Mode menu and then click Revert. Alternatively, drag over the areas you want to revert with the reconstruct tool, labeled in Figure 11-42. As is the case when you work with the freeze and thaw tools, the Brush Pressure setting determines the impact of the tool.

Tip

If you press Escape while a reversion is in progress, Photoshop stops in its tracks. This technique enables you to use the Revert button to reverse some, but not all, distortions that you applied to unfrozen areas.

Now for reconstruction techniques, which are considerably more complex than the reversion techniques. By selecting one of the following options from the Mode menu and then clicking the Reconstruct button or dragging with the reconstruct tool, you can reconstruct a distortion so that it extends from a frozen area into neighboring unfrozen pixels. The Reconstruct button affects all unfrozen areas, but dragging with the tool alters only pixels under your cursor, subject to the limits of the Brush Pressure setting.

Tip

All the reconstruction modes calculate the change to the image based on the warp mesh (grid). To get a better feel for how each mode works, deselect the Show Image check box, turn on Show Mesh, and then apply a simple distortion across a portion of the grid. Freeze part of the distorted region and then keep an eye on the grid lines at the intersections between frozen and unfrozen regions as you try out each of the modes:

✦ Rigid extends the distortion only as needed to maintain right angles in the mesh where frozen and unfrozen areas collide. Any unaffected unfrozen areas revert to their original appearance. The result is unfrozen areas that look almost but not exactly as they did originally.

✦ Stiff interpolates the distortion so that the effect lessens as you move farther from the boundary between the frozen and unfrozen areas.

✦ Smooth and Loose both extend the distortion from the frozen areas fully into the unfrozen areas. With Loose, you get a little more continuity in the distortion between the frozen and unfrozen regions.

✦ Displace, Amplitwist, and Affine work only with the reconstruct tool. Using these modes, you can apply one or more distortions that are in force at a specific reference point in the image. Click to set the reference point and then drag through unfrozen areas to distort them. Use the Displace mode to move pixels to match the displacement of the reference point; select Amplitwist to match the displacement, rotation, and scaling at the reference point; and choose Affine to match all distortions at the reference point.

Although Liquify certainly gives you plenty of ways to reconstruct distortions, predicting the outcome of your drags with the reconstruct tool can be difficult. So if you don't get the results you want after your first few tries, you may find it just as easy to revert the whole image and start from scratch.

Wrapping an Image around a 3D Shape

I've long maintained that three-dimensional drawing programs would catch on better if they were sold as plug-in utilities for Photoshop. Imagine being able to import DXF objects, add a line or two of text, move the objects around in 3D space, apply surface textures, and then render the piece directly to independent Photoshop layers. After that, you could change the stacking order of the layers, edit the pixels right there on the spot, or maybe even double-click a layer to edit it in 3D space. Virtually every digital artist working in 3D visits Photoshop somewhere during the process, so why not do the whole process in Photoshop and save everyone a few steps? Experienced artists would love it and novices would take to 3D in droves.

Frankly, my little fantasy isn't likely to take form any time soon. Photoshop would have to modify its plug-in specifications, and some brave programming team would have to spend a lot of time and money producing an aggressive suite of plug-ins. Even so, Adobe seems to share my dream. Filter ➪ Render ➪ 3D Transform lets you wrap an image around a three-dimensional shape. Although the drawing tools are rudimentary, the spatial controls are barely adequate, and the filter lacks any kind of lighting controls, 3D Transform is a first tentative step in the right direction.

Figure 11-43 shows exactly what 3D Transform can do. In each case, I started with the brick image shown in the upper-left corner of the figure. Then I wrapped the image around the three basic kinds of *primitives* permitted by the 3D Transform filter — a cube, a sphere, and a cylinder. 3D Transform lets you add points to the side of a cylinder, as I did to get the hourglass shape. You can also mix and match primitives, as the final example in Figure 11-43 illustrates.

Notice that in each case, 3D Transform merely distorts the image. It has no affect on the brightness values of the pixels, nor does it make any attempt to light the shapes (which is why I'd prefer to see it under the Distort submenu as opposed to Render). I added the shadows using Layer ➪ Layer Style ➪ Drop Shadow.

Note

To be perfectly fair, 3D Transform is not the first three-dimensional plug-in for Photoshop. That honor went out years ago to the Series 2: Three-D Filter from Andromeda (*www.andromeda.com*). Even now, Series 2 offers features that Photoshop's 3D Transform plug-in lacks, including a wider range of numerical controls and lighting functions — but 3D Transform is easier to use.

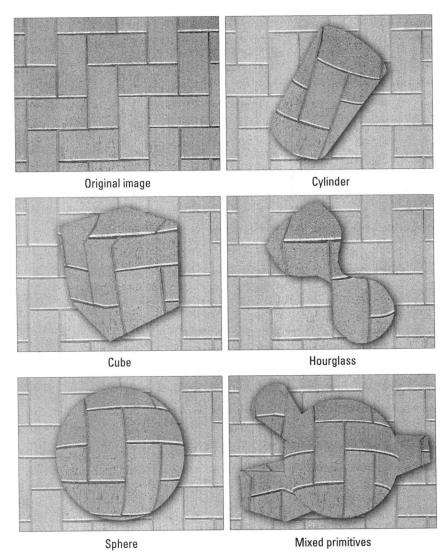

Original image   Cylinder

Cube   Hourglass

Sphere   Mixed primitives

Figure 11-43: The 3D Transform filter lets you wrap an image (upper left) around each of three basic primitives (cube, sphere, and cylinder), a modified cylinder (hourglass), or several shapes mixed together.

Using the 3D Transform filter

Choose Filter ➪ Render ➪ 3D Transform to bring up the window shown in Figure 11-44. Less a dialog box than a separate editing environment, the 3D Transform window contains a wealth of tools and a preview area in which you can draw and evaluate the effect. There are a dozen tools in all, but they make a bit more sense if you regard them as members of five basic categories, itemized in the following sections. Like Photoshop's standard tools, you can select the 3D Transform tools from the keyboard (assuming that you have any headroom left to memorize the shortcuts). Shortcut keys are listed in parentheses.

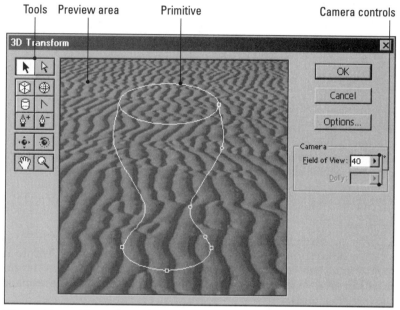

Figure 11-44: The 3D Transform dialog box contains a dozen tools that permit you to draw and edit three-dimensional shapes.

Primitive shape tools

Use one of the primitive shape tools to draw a basic 3D shape in the preview area. This is the shape around which 3D Transform will wrap the selected image.

Cube (M): Use this tool to draw a six-sided box. Adobe selected *M* as the shortcut to match Illustrator, which uses *M* for its rectangle tool. And that *M* is based in turn on Photoshop's marquee tool.

Sphere (N): This tool creates a perfect sphere. Again, the shortcut comes from Illustrator, this time from the ellipse tool. Just remember, *N* follows *M*. (Ironically, *S* goes unused. Ain't cross-application consistency a pain in the neck?)

Cylinder (C): This cylinder tool draws your basic, everyday, dowel-like cylinders. But you can edit them to make lots of other shapes, as I explain in the upcoming "Cylinder editors." Thankfully, Illustrator offers no equivalent for the cylinder tool, so we get a sensible shortcut, *C*.

Basic edit tools

The two arrow tools — the black select tool and the white direct select tool — enable you to change a shape by dragging it around or moving the points. Both tools work just like their counterparts in Illustrator:

Select (V): Drag a shape with the black arrow tool to move the whole shape. If you know Illustrator, you already know about the weird V-key shortcut. If not, think of Photoshop's own move tool.

Direct select (A): Use the white arrow to move individual points. Dragging a point in a sphere resizes it. Dragging a point in a cube or a cylinder stretches or rotates the shape. Experiment and you'll quickly see how it works. (Unlike paths, dragged points have no control handles. All you have to work with are anchor points.)

Tip   You can switch between the black and white arrow tools by pressing Ctrl+Tab. But really, there's no point. The white arrow does everything the black arrow does — just drag a segment to move the entire shape. In fact, there's just one keyboard trick you need to remember: press Ctrl to temporarily get the white arrow tool when any other tool is active. If you know that, the other keys are redundant.

Cylinder editors

The three path-edit tools are applicable exclusively to cylinders. Why? Because cylinders can be modified to create a whole family of tubular shapes. Throw the cylinder on the lathe and you can make an hourglass, a goblet, a cone — in short, any shape with radial symmetry and a flat top or bottom. To make these shapes, you use the following tools:

Insert point (+): Click the right side of the cylinder — unless you turn it upside-down, in which case you click the left side — to add a point. Then drag the point with the white arrow tool to move both sides symmetrically. It's a virtual potter's wheel.

Remove point (–): Click a point you've added with the insert point tool to remove it. Don't click any of the square points that Photoshop put in there or the program will whine at you.

Convert point: The insert point tool adds circular smooth points that create continuous arcs in the side of the cylinder. To change the point to a sharp corner, click it with the convert point tool. Click again to change the point back to a smooth point.

Moving in 3D space

The next two tools are the most powerful and the hardest to use. They permit you to move the object in 3D space. When you switch to one of these tools, Photoshop renders the preview so you can see the image wrapped around the shape, as in Figure 11-45.

> **Pan camera (E):** Drag the image to move it up, down, left, or right. How is this different than moving the primitive with the arrow tool? This time, you're moving the image in 3D space across your field of vision. (To be more precise, you're moving the camera — which is your window into the image — while the object remains still.) As you move the image to the left, you see more of its right side. Move it up, and you see its bottom.

> **Trackball (R):** The trackball rotates the image in 3D space. Meanwhile, it's ultimately a 2D control — you can't move your cursor into or out of the screen; just up, down, and side to side — making it difficult to predict the outcome of a drag.

Tip

Inevitably, you'll end up exposing the back, empty side of a shape. When this happens, spin the shape by dragging against the grain. To spin the shape head over heels, for example, drag directly up or down. To spin the shape sideways, drag horizontally. Don't fret too much about moving through the 3D world; just watch how the program behaves when you move your mouse from one location to another. In time, you'll see some very simple patterns that you can exploit to your advantage.

Rendered preview

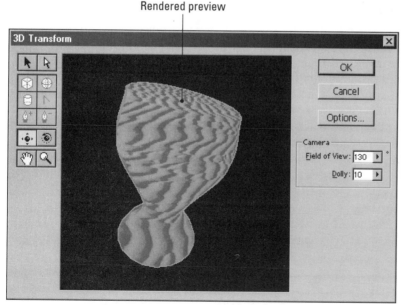

Figure 11-45: When you select either the pan camera or the trackball tool, Photoshop renders the image inside the preview area.

The camera controls

When you select the pan camera or trackball tool, Photoshop offers two Camera options on the right side of the dialog box. At first, the two options seem to do the same thing. A low value moves you in; a high value takes you out. But, in truth, they produce subtly different effects. Think of the Field of View option as a wide-angle lens and the Dolly option as a zoom lens, with both operating at the same time. A low Field of View with a high Dolly results in shallow shapes. A high Field of View with a low Dolly shrinks you to the size of a bug so that the depth is really coming at you.

Basic navigation

The last two tools in the 3D Transform dialog box are the standard hand and magnifying glass. They work just like their counterparts outside the 3D Transform dialog box:

Hand (H): Drag the image to move it around inside the preview area. You can press either *H* or the spacebar to get this tool.

Zoom (Z): Click with this tool to zoom in, Alt-click to zoom out. When any other tool is selected, Ctrl+spacebar-click and Alt+spacebar-click to zoom in and out.

Layer before you apply

When you press Enter, Photoshop merges your new 3D shape with the original image. Because the 3D Transform filter provides no lighting controls, the shape may be virtually indistinguishable from its background, as Figure 11-46 makes abundantly clear. And that, dear friends, is a giant drag.

Figure 11-46: By default, the 3D Transform filter merges the 3D image into the original image, making for an extraordinarily subtle effect.

Tip

Luckily, you can force Photoshop to deliver the 3D shape on a separate layer. Here's what you do. First copy the image to a separate layer by dragging it onto the page icon at the bottom of the Layers palette. Then choose Filter ⇨ Render ⇨ 3D Transform and click the Options button inside the dialog box. Turn off the Display Background check box, spotlighted in Figure 11-47, and press Enter.

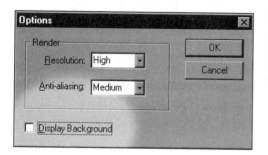

Figure 11-47: Copy the image to a separate layer and turn off the Display Background check box to make the area outside the 3D shape transparent.

Not only will the 3D Transform filter restrict its efforts to the active layer, it will also make the area outside the 3D shape transparent, as in the first example of Figure 11-48. Then you can apply layer effects or other lighting techniques to distinguish the 3D shape from its background, as in the second example.

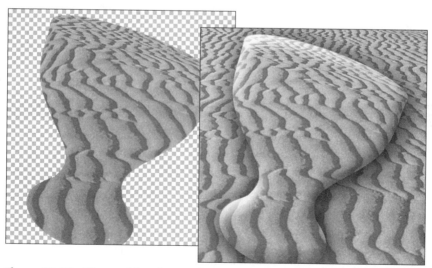

Figure 11-48: After applying the 3D shape to a separate layer (shown by itself at left), I used the Drop Shadow and Inner Bevel effects to add some fake volumetric lighting to my goblet (right).

Color Plates 11-8 and 11-9 demonstrate some of the fun you can have with 3D Transform. In Color Plate 11-8, I relied entirely on the Drop Shadow and Inner Bevel layer styles to light the layered 3D goblet. I also added a bit of red to the goblet using Image ➪ Adjust ➪ Hue/Saturation to distinguish the layer from its sandy background.

Color Plate 11-9 illustrates the merits of manual lighting techniques. After setting the goblet against a different background, I applied the drop shadow and haloing techniques that I discuss in the section "Selecting the Contents of Layers" in Chapter 12. I also applied the airbrush tool set alternatively to the Multiply and Screen brush modes to hand-brush some natural tinting. Finally, I darkened the top of the goblet with the help of the elliptical marquee tool. After drawing my initial marquee, I chose Select ➪ Transform to rotate and scale it into position, pressed Ctrl+J to send the selection to a separate layer, and applied the Multiply blend mode set to a low opacity. Admittedly, the finished effect involved a lot of effort, but it looks significantly more realistic than anything Photoshop can approximate automatically.

Adding Clouds and Spotlights

The remaining five filters in the Render submenu produce lighting effects. You can use Clouds and Difference Clouds to create a layer of haze over an image. Lens Flare creates light flashes and reflections (as I mentioned earlier). Lighting Effects lights an image as if it were hanging on a gallery wall. You can even use the unremarkable Texture Fill to add an embossed texture to a piece embellished with the Lighting Effects filter.

Creating clouds

The Clouds filter creates an abstract and random haze between the foreground and background colors. Difference Clouds works exactly like layering the image, applying the Clouds filter, and selecting the Difference blend mode in the Layers palette.

Why on earth should Difference Clouds make special provisions for a single blend mode? Because you can create cumulative effects. Try this: Select blue as the foreground color and then choose Filter ➪ Render ➪ Clouds. Ah, just like a real sky, huh? Now choose Filter ➪ Render ➪ Difference Clouds. It's like some kind of weird Halloween motif, all blacks and oranges. Press Ctrl+F to repeat the filter. Back to the blue sky. Keep pressing Ctrl+F over and over and notice the results. A pink cancer starts invading the blue sky; a green cancer invades the orange one. Multiple applications of the Difference Clouds filter generate organic oil-on-water effects.

 Tip

To strengthen the colors created by the Clouds filter, press Shift when choosing the command. This same technique works when using the Difference Clouds filter as well. In fact, I don't know of any reason *not* to press Shift while choosing one of these commands, unless you have some specific need for washed-out effects.

Color Plate 11-10 shows some entertaining applications of the Clouds filters. With the foreground and background colors set to blue and orange, respectively, I applied the Clouds filter to a layered copy of the rose image. For maximum effect, I pressed Shift and chose the filter to create the top-left image in the color plate. I then pressed Shift and chose the Difference Clouds filter to create the purple montage in the figure, and pressed Ctrl+F ten times to achieve the top-right image. Looks to me like I definitely have something growing in my petri dish.

Yeah, so really groovy stuff, right? Shades of "Purple Haze" and all that. But now that I've created this murky mess, what the heck do I do with it? Composite it, of course. The bottom row of Color Plate 11-10 shows examples of mixing each of the images from the top row with the original rose. In the example on the left, I chose the Overlay option from the Layers palette. In the example in the middle, I chose the Screen mode. And in the last example, I chose Hue. This last one is particularly exciting, completely transforming the colors in the rose while leaving the gray (and therefore unsaturated) background untouched. Without a mask, without anything but a rectangular marquee, I've managed to precisely color the interior of the rose.

Lighting an image

Photoshop ventures further into 3D drawing territory with the Lighting Effects filter. This very complex function enables you to shine lights on an image, color the lights, position them, focus them, specify the reflectivity of the surface, and even create a surface map. In many ways, it's a direct lift from MetaCreations' Painter. But whereas Painter provides predefined paper textures and light refraction effects that bolster the capabilities of its excellent tool, Photoshop offers better controls and more lighting options.

The Lighting Effects filter is applicable exclusively to RGB images. Also, don't expect to be able to apply 3D lighting to shapes created with the 3D Transform filter. Sadly, the two filters share no common elements that would permit them to work directly with each other.

When you choose Filter ⇨ Render ⇨ Lighting Effects, Photoshop displays what is easily its most complex dialog box, as shown in Figure 11-49. The dialog box has two halves: one in which you actually position light with respect to a thumbnail of the selected image, and one that contains about a billion intimidating options.

No bones about it, this dialog box is a bear. The easiest way to apply the filter is to choose one of the predefined lighting effects from the Style pop-up menu at the top of the right side of the dialog box, see how it looks in the preview area, and — if you like it — press Enter to apply the effect.

But if you want to create your own effects, you have to work a little harder. Here are the basic steps involved in creating a custom effect.

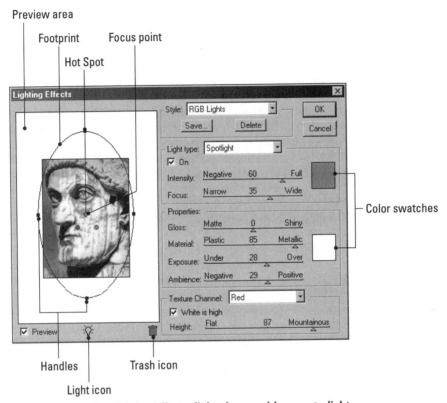

Figure 11-49: The Lighting Effects dialog box enables you to light an image as if it were hanging in a gallery, lying on a floor, or perhaps resting too near a hot flame.

STEPS: Lighting an Image

1. **Drag from the light icon at the bottom of the dialog box into the preview area to create a new light source.** I call this area the *stage* because it's as if the image is painted on the floor of a stage and the lights are hanging above it.

2. **Select the kind of light you want from the Light Type pop-up menu.** It's just below the Style pop-up menu. You can select from Directional, Omni, and Spotlight:

   • Directional works like the sun, producing a general, unfocused light that hits a target from an angle.

   • Omni is a bare light bulb hanging in the middle of the room, shining in all directions from a center point.

   • Spotlight is a focused beam that is brightest at the source and tapers off gradually.

3. **Specify the color of the light by clicking the top color swatch.** You can also muck about with the Intensity slider bar to control the brightness of the light. If Spotlight is selected, the Focus slider becomes available. Drag the slider toward Narrow to create a bright laser of light; drag toward Wide to diffuse the light and spread it over a larger area.

4. **Move the light source by dragging at the *focus point* (the colored circle in the preview area).** When Directional or Spotlight is selected, the focus point represents the spot at which the light is pointing. When Omni is active, the focus point is the actual bulb. (Don't burn yourself.)

5. **If Directional or Spotlight is active, you can change the angle of the light by dragging the hot spot.** The *hot spot* represents the location in the image that's liable to receive the most light. When you use a Directional light, the hot spot appears as a black square at the end of a line joined to the focus point. The same holds true when you edit a Spotlight; the confusing thing is that there are four black squares altogether. The light source is joined to the focus point by a line; the three *handles* are not.

To make the light brighter, drag the hot spot closer to the focus point. Dragging the hot spot away from the focus point dims the light by increasing the distance that it has to travel. It's like having a flashlight in the living room when you're in the garage—the light gets dimmer as you move away from it.

6. **With Omni or Spotlight in force, you can edit the elliptical footprint of the light.** When Omni is in force, a circle surrounds the focus point. When editing a Spotlight, you see an ellipse. Either way, this shape represents the *footprint* of the light, which is the approximate area of the image affected by the light. You can change the size of the light by dragging the handles around the footprint. Enlarging the shape is like raising the light source. When the footprint is small, the light is close to the image so it's concentrated and very bright. When the footprint is large, the light is high above the image, so it's more generalized.

When editing the footprint of a Spotlight, Shift-drag a handle to adjust the width or height of the ellipse without affecting the angle. To change the angle without affecting the size, Ctrl-drag a handle.

7. **Introduce more lights as you see fit.**

You can use a bunch of different techniques to add and subtract lights on the stage. Press Tab to switch from one light to the next. Duplicate a light in the stage by Alt-dragging its focus point. To delete the active light, just press Backspace. Or if you prefer, you can drag the focus point onto the trash can icon at the bottom of the dialog box.

8. **Change the Properties and Texture Channel options as you see fit.** I explain these in detail after the steps.

9. **If you want to save your settings for future use, click the Save button.**
   Photoshop invites you to name the setup, which then appears as an option
   in the Style pop-up menu. If you want to get rid of one of the presets, select
   it from the pop-up menu and click the Delete button.

10. **Press Enter to apply your settings to the image.**

That's almost everything. The only parts I left out are the Properties and Texture
Channel options. The Properties slider bars control how light reflects off the surface of your image:

✦ **Gloss:** Is the surface dull or shiny? Drag the slider toward Matte to make the
  surface flat and nonreflective, like dull enamel paint. Drag the slider toward
  Shiny to make it glossy, as if you had slapped on a coat of lacquer.

✦ **Material:** This option determines the color of the light that reflects off the
  image. According to the logic employed by this option, Plastic reflects back
  the color of the light; Metallic reflects the color of the object itself. If only I
  had a bright, shiny plastic thing and a bright, shiny metal thing, I could check
  to see whether this logic holds true in real life (like maybe that matters).

✦ **Exposure:** I'd like this option better if you could vary it between Sun Block 65
  and Melanoma. Unfortunately, the more prosaic titles are Under and Over—
  exposed, that is. This option controls the brightness of all lights like a big dimmer switch. You can control a single selected light using the Intensity slider,
  but the Exposure slider offers the added control of changing all lights in the
  stage (preview) area and the ambient light (described next) together.

✦ **Ambience:** The last slider enables you to add *ambient light,* which is a general, diffused light that hits all surfaces evenly. First, select the color of the
  light by clicking the color swatch to the right. Then drag the slider to cast
  a subtle hue over the stage. Drag toward Positive to tint the image with the
  color in the swatch; drag toward Negative to tint the stage with the swatch's
  opposite. Keep the slider set to 0—dead in the center—to cast no hue.

The Texture Channel options enable you to treat one channel in the image as a
texture map, which is a grayscale surface in which white indicates peaks and black
indicates valleys. (As long as the White is high check box is selected, that is. If you
deselect that option, everything flips, and black becomes the peak.) It's as if one
channel has a surface to it. By selecting a channel from the pop-up menu, you create an emboss effect, much like that created with the Emboss filter except much
better because you can light the surface from many angles at once and it's in color
to boot.

Choose a channel to serve as the embossed surface from the pop-up menu. Then
change the Height slider to indicate more or less Flat terrain or huge Mountainous
cliffs of surface texture.

Color Plate 11-11 shows an image lit with a total of five spotlights, two from above and three from below. In the first example, I left the Texture Channel option set to None. In the second example, I selected the green channel as the surface map. And in the third example, I filled a separate mask channel with a bunch of white and black dollops using Filter ➪ Pixelate ➪ Pointillize and then I selected the mask from the Texture Channel pop-up menu in the Lighting Effects dialog box. The result is a wonderfully rough paper texture.

✦   ✦   ✦

Layers, Objects, and Text

Working with Layers

Layers, Layers Everywhere

Layers started out as little more than their name implies —
sheets of pixels that you could edit and transform independently of each other. But over time, layers have become
increasingly more sophisticated. Since the feature was introduced in Version 3, every major release of Photoshop has
witnessed some kind of fantastic, and occasionally frustrating,
layer enhancement. Photoshop 4 forced you to embrace
the feature by creating a new layer every time you imported
an image; but it also rewarded you with floating *adjustment
layers* that let you correct colors without permanently
affecting a single pixel (see Chapter 17). Photoshop 5
witnessed the birth of layer effects, which included editable
drop shadows, glows, and edge bevels (see Chapter 14).
Now comes Photoshop 6, which permits you to bundle and
color-code layers into logical clusters (this chapter), blend
color channels independently of each other (Chapter 13), and
even add vector-based lines and shapes (Chapter 14), not to
mention object-oriented text (Chapter 15).

In fact, in a long line of layer-boosting champions, Photoshop
6 bears the standard with more gusto than any release since
Version 3. Mind you, there's still room for improvement. For
example, one day I hope to see Photoshop integrate paramet-
ric effects, in which filters such as Unsharp Mask and Motion
Blur are fully editable, interactive, and interchangeable, on
the order of Adobe's full-motion editor, After Effects. But
in the meantime, Photoshop 6's layers provide us with more
freedom and flexibility than we've ever had before.

For those of your who are wondering what I'm talking about,
permit me to back up for a moment. The first and foremost
benefit of layers is that they add versatility. Because each
layer in a composition is altogether independent of other
layers, you can change your mind on a moment's notice.
Consider Figure 12-1. Here I've compiled the ingredients

for a very bad day at the doctor's office. Each of the bits and pieces of hardware are located on a separate layer, all of which float above the surface of the background X-ray. Although the pixels from the hardware blend with the X-ray and with each other, I can easily reposition and modify them as the mood strikes me. Photoshop automatically reblends the pixels on the fly.

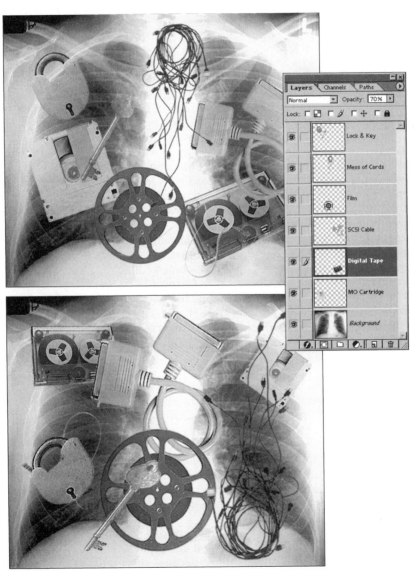

Figure 12-1: So that's what I did with my old SCSI cable! Thanks to the flexibility of layers, you can arrange a bunch of images one way one moment (top) and quite differently the next (bottom). Layers let you modify a composition without sacrificing quality.

To show what I mean, I've repositioned and transformed every single layer in the second example in Figure 12-1. The MO cartridge is smaller and rotated, the mess of chords hangs up instead of down, and the lock and key are just plain skewed. I can also exchange the order of the layers, merge layers, and adjust their translucency until I keel over from sheer alternative overload.

Layers make it harder to make mistakes, they make it easier to make changes, and they expand your range of options. More than anything else, they permit you to restructure a composition and examine how it was put together after you assemble it. Layers can be very challenging to use or relatively simple. But whatever you do, don't shy away. If a layer might help, there's no reason not to add one.

Sending a Selection to a Layer

To its credit, Photoshop lets you establish a new layer in roughly a billion ways. If you want to add a selected portion of one image to another image, the easiest method is to Ctrl-drag the selection and drop it into its new home, as demonstrated in Figure 12-2. Photoshop makes you a new layer, lickety-split.

Dropped selection becomes new layer

Figure 12-2: Ctrl-drag a selection and drop it into a different image window to introduce the selection as a new layer. As you can see in the Layers palette, the camera becomes a new layer in front of the television.

Caution

Be sure to Ctrl-drag or use the move tool. If you merely drag the selection with the marquee, lasso, or wand, you drop an empty selection outline into the new image window. Also, be aware that pressing Ctrl delivers the move tool. But if the pen, arrow, or shape tool is active, you get the arrow tool instead, which won't work for you. Press M to get the good old marquee tool, and then try Ctrl-dragging again.

When you drop the selection, your selection outline disappears. Not to worry, though. Now that the image resides on an independent layer, the selection outline is no longer needed. You can move the layer using the move tool, as you would move a selection. You can even paint inside what was once the selection by selecting the first of the Lock check boxes in the Layers palette. I explain both the move tool and the Lock check boxes in greater detail throughout this chapter.

If you want to clone a selection to a new layer inside the same image window — useful when performing complex filter routines and color corrections — choose Layer ➪ New ➪ Layer Via Copy. Or press Ctrl+J, as in Jump.

Other ways to make a layer

Those are only two of many ways to create a new layer in Photoshop. Here are a few others:

✦ Copy a selection (Ctrl+C) and paste it into another image (Ctrl+V). Photoshop pastes the selection as a new layer.

✦ If you want to relegate a selection exclusively to a new layer, choose Layer ➪ New ➪ Layer Via Cut or press Ctrl+Shift+J. Rather than cloning the selection, Layer Via Cut removes the selection from the background image and places it on its own layer.

✦ To convert a floating selection — one which you've moved or cloned — to a new layer, press Ctrl+Shift+J. The Shift key is very important. If you press Ctrl+J without Shift, Photoshop clones the selection and leaves an imprint of the image on the layer below.

✦ To create an empty layer — as when you want to paint a few brushstrokes without harming the original image — choose Layer ➪ New ➪ Layer or press Ctrl+Shift+N. Or click the new layer icon at the bottom of the Layers palette (labeled in Figure 12-3).

✦ When you create a new layer, Photoshop positions it in front of the active layer. To create a new layer behind the active layer, Ctrl-click the new layer icon.

Incidentally, you can also create a new layer by choosing New Layer from the Layers palette menu. But as you can see in Figure 12-3, nearly all the palette commands are duplicated in the Layer menu. The only unique palette command is

Palette Options, which lets you change the size of the thumbnails in front of the layer names. And you can do that more easily by right-clicking in the empty space below the layer names and choosing an option.

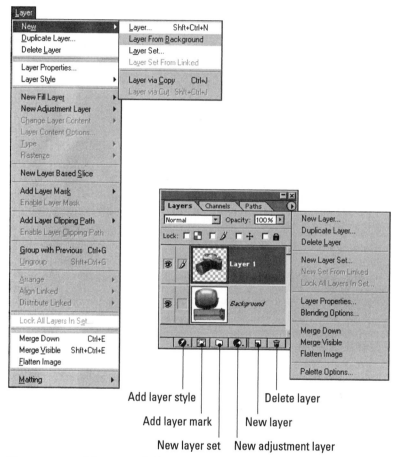

Add layer style

Add layer mark

New layer set   New adjustment layer

Delete layer

New layer

Figure 12-3: All but one of the commands in the Layers palette menu are duplicated in the Layer menu.

Tip

When you choose the Layer Via Copy or Layer Via Cut command or click the new layer icon, Photoshop automatically names the new layer for you. Unfortunately, the automatic names — Layer 1, Layer 2, and so on — are fairly meaningless and don't help to convey the contents of the layer. I mean, really, what kind of program doesn't know a camera when it sees one?

If you want to specify a more meaningful name, add the Alt key. Press Ctrl+Alt+J to clone the selection to a layer, press Ctrl+Shift+Alt+J to cut the selection, or Alt-click the new layer icon to create a blank layer. In any case, you see the dialog box shown in Figure 12-4. Enter a name for the layer. If you like, you can also assign a color to a layer, which is helpful for identifying a layer name at a glance. Then press Enter. (For now, you can ignore the other options in this dialog box.)

When creating a new layer from the keyboard, press Ctrl+Shift+Alt+N to bypass the dialog box. Alt works both ways, forcing the dialog box some times and suppressing it others. The only time it produces no effect is when pasting or dropping an image. Too bad—I for one would get a lot of use out of it.

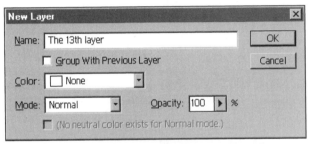

Figure 12-4: Press Alt to force the display of the New Layer dialog box, which lets you name the new layer. When renaming a layer, only the Name and Color options appear.

Renaming a layer used to be as simple as double-clicking on its name in the Layers palette. Now that brings up the large and complex Layer Styles dialog box, so extensive that I cover it in two chapters, 13 and 14. The simple act of renaming a layer is a bit harder to get to but at least you have lots of options. You can choose Layer Options, either from the Layer or Layers palette menu. Better yet, right-click a layer name and choose Layer Properties. Best of all, press Alt and double-click a layer name. Then enter a new name, assign a color if you like, and press Enter.

Duplicating a layer

To clone the active layer, you can choose Layer ➪ Duplicate Layer. But that's the sucker's way. The more convenient way is to drag the layer name you want to clone onto the new layer icon at the bottom of the Layers palette.

To specify a name for the cloned layer or to copy the layer into another image, Alt-drag the layer onto the new layer icon. Always the thoughtful program, Photoshop displays the dialog box shown in Figure 12-5. You can name the cloned layer by entering something in the As option box. To jettison the layer to some other open image, choose the image name from the Document pop-up menu. Or choose New and enter the name for an entirely different image in the Name option box, as the figure shows.

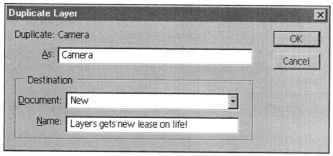

Figure 12-5: You can duplicate the layer into an entirely different image by Alt-dragging the layer onto the new layer icon in the Layers palette.

You can clone a layer by simply Ctrl-Alt-dragging it inside the image window. This way, you clone the layer and reposition it in one operation. Just be sure not to begin your drag inside a selection outline; if you do, you create a floating selection.

Working with Layers

Regardless of how you create a new layer, Photoshop lists the layer along with a little thumbnail of its contents in the Layers palette. The new layer's name appears highlighted to show that it's active. The little paintbrush icon in front of the layer name also indicates an active layer.

To the left of the paintbrush icon is a column of eyeballs, which invite you to hide and display layers temporarily. Click on an eyeball to hide the layer. Click where the eyeball previously was to bring it back and redisplay the layer. Whether hidden or displayed, all layers remain intact and ready for action.

To view a single layer by itself, Alt-click the eyeball icon before the layer name to hide all other layers. Alt-click in front of the layer again to bring all the layers back into view.

Switching between layers

You can select a different layer by clicking on its name in the Layers palette. This layer becomes active, enabling you to edit it. Note that only one layer may be active in Photoshop — you can't Shift-click to select and edit multiple layers, I'm sorry to say. So although you *can* link multiple layers and combine them into sets — as I explain in the section "Moving, Linking, and Aligning Layers" — you cannot select, paint, filter, or otherwise change the pixels on more than a single layer at a time.

Tip

If your image contains several layers — like the one back in Figure 12-1 — it might prove inconvenient, or even confusing, to switch from one layer to another in the Layers palette. Luckily, Photoshop offers a better way. With any tool, Ctrl+Alt+right-click an element in your composition to go directly to the layer containing the element. For example, Ctrl+Alt+right-clicking on the SCSI cable in Figure 12-1 would take me to the SCSI Cable layer.

Why Ctrl+Alt+right-clicking? Here's how it breaks down:

✦ Ctrl gets you the move tool. (If the move tool is already selected, you don't have to press Ctrl; Alt+right-clicking works just fine.)

✦ Right-clicking alone brings up a context-sensitive pop-up menu. When you right-click with the move tool — or Ctrl+right-click with any other tool — Photoshop displays a pop-up menu that lists the layer that the image is on and any other layers in the image, as in Figure 12-6. (If a layer is completely transparent at the spot where you right-click, that layer name doesn't appear in the pop-up menu.) Select the desired layer to go there.

✦ The Alt key bypasses the pop-up menu and goes straight to the clicked layer.

Add them all together, and you get Ctrl+Alt+right-click. It's a lot to remember, but believe me, it's a great trick once you get the hang of it.

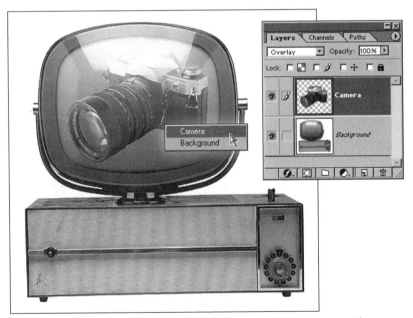

Figure 12-6: Ctrl+Alt+right-click an image to view a pop-up menu. The menu lists the location of the image on which you've clicked and the background layer.

Tip

If you'd prefer Photoshop to *always* go directly to the layer on which you click and avoid all these messy keyboard tricks, press V to select the move tool. The first check box in the Options bar is called Auto Select Layer. Turn it on. Now whenever you click a layer with the move tool—or Ctrl-click with some other tool—Photoshop goes right to that layer.

Switching layers from the keyboard

You can also ascend and descend the layer stack from the keyboard:

✦ **Alt+]:** Press Alt+right bracket to go to the next layer up in the stack. If you're already at the top layer, Photoshop takes you back around to the lowest one.

✦ **Alt+[:** Press Alt+left bracket to go down a layer. If the background layer is active, Alt+[takes you to the top layer.

✦ **Shift+Alt+]:** This takes you to the top layer in the image.

✦ **Shift+Alt+[:** This activates the background layer (or the lowest layer if no background exists).

You have to pardon me for alluding to a feature out of order, but I thought you should note that Photoshop treats a closed folder in the Layers palette (better known as a *layer set*) as if it was a layer. So every one of these tricks skips to or over the set in a single bound. For the complete lowdown on layer sets, see the "Uniting layers into sets" section later in this same chapter.

Understanding transparency

Although the selection outline disappears when you convert a selection to a layer, no information is lost. Photoshop retains every little nuance of the original selection outline—whether it's a jagged border, a little bit of antialiasing, or a feathered edge. Anything that wasn't selected is now transparent. The data that defines the opacity and transparency of a layer is called the *transparency mask*.

To see this transparency in action, click the eyeball icon in front of the Background item in the Layers palette. This hides the background layer and enables you to view the new layer by itself. In Figure 12-7, I hid the background TV from Figure 12-6 to view the camera on its own. The transparent areas are filled with a checkerboard pattern. Opaque areas look like the standard image, and translucent areas—where they exist—appear as a mix of image and checkerboard.

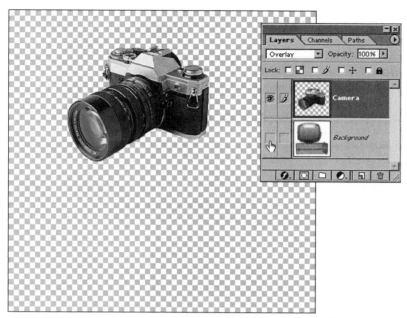

Figure 12-7: When you hide the background layer, you see a checkerboard pattern that represents the transparent portions of the layer.

Tip

If the checkerboard pattern is hard to distinguish from the image, you can change the appearance of the pattern. Press Ctrl+K and then Ctrl+4 to go to the Transparency & Gamut panel of the Preferences dialog box. Then edit the colors as you see fit (as explained back in Chapter 2).

If you apply an effect to the layer while no portion of the layer is selected, Photoshop changes the opaque and translucent portions of the image but leaves the transparent region intact. For example, if you press Ctrl+I (or choose Image ➪ Adjust ➪ Invert), Photoshop inverts the image but doesn't change a single pixel in the checkerboard area. If you click in the left column in front of the Background item to bring back the eyeball icon, you may notice a slight halo around the inverted image, but the edge pixels blend with the background image as well as they ever did. In fact, it's exactly as if you applied the effect to a selection, as demonstrated in Figure 12-8. The only difference is that this selection is independent of its background. You can do anything you want to it without running the risk of harming the underlying background.

Only a few operations affect the transparent areas of a layer, and most of these are limited to tools. You can paint on transparent pixels to make them opaque. You can clone with the rubber stamp or smear pixels with the edit tools. To send pixels back to transparency, paint with the eraser. All these operations change both the contents of the layer and the composition of the transparency mask.

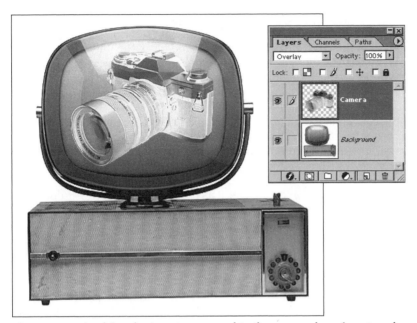

Figure 12-8: Applying the Invert command to the camera layer inverts only the camera without affecting any of the transparent pixels. The TV remains every bit as visible as ever.

Tip

You can fill all pixels also by pressing Alt+Backspace for the foreground color and Ctrl+Backspace for the background color. To fill the pixels in a layer without altering the transparency mask, toss in the Shift key. Shift+Alt+Backspace fills the opaque pixels with the foreground color; Ctrl+Shift+Backspace fills them with the background color. In both cases, the transparent pixels remain every bit as transparent as they ever were.

When a portion of the layer is selected, pressing plain old Backspace eliminates the selected pixels and makes them transparent, revealing the layers below.

Note

Transparent pixels take up next to no space in memory, but opaque and translucent pixels do. Thus, a layer containing 25 percent as many pixels as the background layer takes up roughly 25 percent as much space. Mind you, I wouldn't let this influence how you work in Photoshop, but it is something to keep in mind.

Modifying the background layer

At the bottom of the layer stack is the *background layer,* the fully opaque layer that represents the base image. The background image is as low as you go. Nothing can be slipped under the background layer, and pixels in the background layer cannot be made transparent, unless you first convert the background to a floating layer.

To make the conversion, double-click the item labeled Background in the Layers palette. A dialog box appears. Enter a name for the new layer — Photoshop suggests Layer 0 — and press Enter. You can now change the order of the layer or erase down to transparency.

Tip   To skip the dialog box and accept Layer 0 as the new layer name, Alt-double-click the Background item in the Layers palette.

In Figure 12-9, I converted the background television to a layer. This particular image (from the PhotoDisc Object Series) included a predrawn path that encircled the TV. I Ctrl-clicked on the path to convert it to a selection outline and then I pressed Ctrl+Shift+I to reverse the selection. Finally, I pressed Backspace to erase the pixels outside the TV, as the figure demonstrates. From this point on, I can reorder the camera and television layers or add layers in back of the TV. I can also introduce a new background layer.

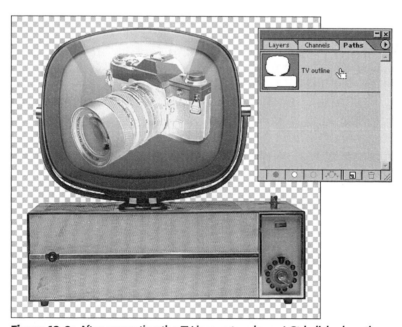

Figure 12-9: After converting the TV image to a layer, I Ctrl-clicked on the path, inversed the selection, and pressed Backspace to reveal the transparent void below.

A program such as QuarkXPress or PageMaker doesn't recognize Photoshop's transparency, so there's no point in leaving the background transparent. As I mention in Chapter 8, if you want to export transparency, you must use a clipping path.

To convert the active layer to a background layer, choose Layer ➪ New ➪ Background From Layer. It doesn't matter whether the active layer is at the top of the stack, the bottom, or someplace in between—Photoshop takes the layer and makes a new background out of it.

To establish a blank background, create an empty layer by pressing Ctrl+Shift+N and then choose Layer ➪ New ➪ Background From Layer. In Figure 12-10, I did just that. Next I used the Add Noise and Emboss filters to create a paper texture pattern (as I explain in Chapter 7). Finally, I chose Layer ➪ Layer Style ➪ Drop Shadow to add a drop shadow that matched the contours of the TV. (I explain all there is to know about the Layer Styles commands in Chapter 14.)

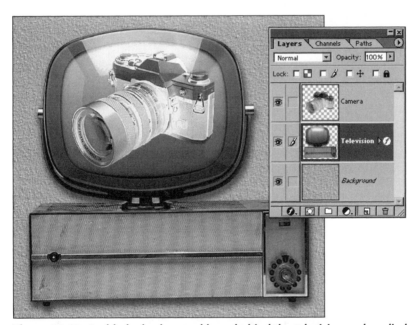

Figure 12-10: I added a background layer behind the television and applied a paper texture and drop shadow to give my composition a little false depth.

Photoshop permits only one background layer per image. If an image already contains a background layer, the command Layer ➪ New ➪ Background From Layer changes to Layer From Background, which converts the background layer to a floating layer, as when you double-click the Background item in the Layers palette.

Reordering layers

What good are layers if you can't periodically change what's on the top and what's on the bottom? You can reorder layers in two ways. First, you can drag a layer name up or down in the scrolling list to move it forward or backward in layering order. The only trick is to make sure that the black bar appears at the point where you want to move the layer before you release the mouse button, as illustrated in Figure 12-11.

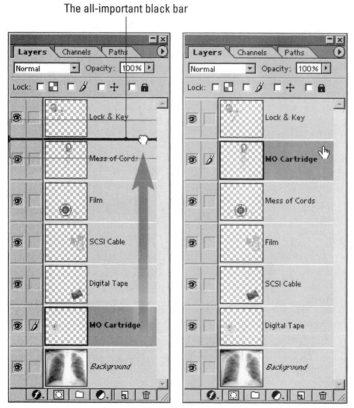

Figure 12-11: Drag a layer between two other layers to make the all-important black bar appear (left). Then release the mouse button to change the hierarchy of the layer (right).

The second way to reorder layers is to choose a command from the Layer ⇨ Arrange submenu. For example, choose Layer ⇨ Arrange ⇨ Bring Forward to move the active layer up one level; choose Layer ⇨ Arrange ⇨ Send to Back to move the layer to above the background layer.

You can move faster if you remember the following keyboard shortcuts:

✦ **Ctrl+Shift+]:** Press Ctrl+right bracket to move the active layer to the top of the stack.

✦ **Ctrl+Shift+[:** This shortcut moves the active layer to the bottom of the stack, just above the background layer.

✦ **Ctrl+]:** This nudges the layer up one level.

✦ **Ctrl+[:** This nudges the layer down.

Note   You can neither reorder the background layer nor move any other layer below the background until you first convert the background to a floating layer, as explained in the previous section.

Automated matting techniques

When you convert an antialiased selection to a layer, you sometimes take with you a few pixels from the selection's previous background. These *fringe pixels* can result in an unrealistic outline around your layer that cries out, "This image was edited by a hack." For example, Figure 12-12 shows a magnified detail from one of my original attempts to add a drop shadow to the TV. Although the selection outline was accurate, I managed to retain a few white pixels around the edges, as you can see around the outline of the picture tube and the arm that holds the tube.

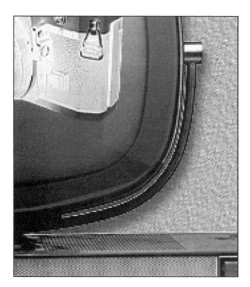

Figure 12-12: This enlarged detail of the TV layer against the textured background shows the fringe pixels left over from the TV's original white background.

You can instruct Photoshop to replace the fringe pixels with colors from neighboring pixels by choosing Layer ➪ Matting ➪ Defringe. Enter the thickness of the perceived fringe in the Width option box to tell Photoshop which pixels you want to replace. To create the image shown in Figure 12-13, I entered a Width value of 1. But even at this low value, the effect is pretty significant, leaving gummy edges in its wake.

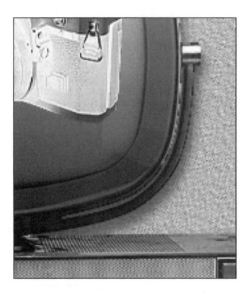

Figure 12-13: Here I used the Defringe command set to a Width value of 1 to replace the pixels around the perimeter of the layer with colors borrowed from neighboring pixels.

Photoshop provides two additional commands under the Layer ➪ Matting submenu: Remove Black Matte and Remove White Matte. Frankly, it's unlikely you'll have much call to use them, but here's the scoop:

✦ **Remove Black Matte:** This command removes the residue around the perimeter of a layer that was lifted from a black background.

✦ **Remove White Matte:** This command removes a white ring around a layer.

Adobe tells me that these commands were designed for compositing a scene rendered in a 3D drawing program against a black or white background. But for other purposes, they almost never work. For example, my television is a prime candidate for Remove White Matte—it originated from a white background—and yet it leaves behind more white pixels than the Defringe command set to its lowest setting.

Tip

If you encounter unrealistic edge pixels and the automatic matting commands don't solve your problem, you may be able to achieve better results by fixing the edges manually. First, switch to the layer that's giving you fits and Ctrl-click its name in the Layers palette. This creates a tight selection around the contents of the layer. Then choose Select ➪ Modify ➪ Contract and enter the width of the fringe in the Contract By option box. Next, choose Select ➪ Feather (Ctrl+Shift+D) and enter this same value in the Feather Radius option box. Finally, press Ctrl+Shift+I to inverse the selection and press Backspace to eliminate the edge pixels.

Figure 12-14 shows the results of applying this technique to my television. By setting the Contract and Feather commands to 1 pixel, I managed to remove the edges without harming the layer itself. And the effect looks better than that produced by the Defringe command (as you can compare for yourself with Figure 12-13).

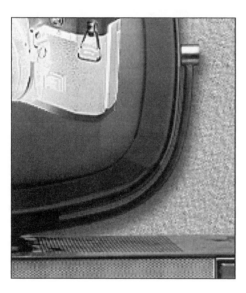

Figure 12-14: Here I removed the edges manually using the Contract, Feather, and Inverse commands. This looks way better than anything Photoshop can do automatically.

Blending layers

Photoshop lets you blend layers like no other program in the business. In fact, Photoshop does such a great job that it takes me an entire chapter — Chapter 13 — to explain these options in detail. I offer this section by way of introduction so that you're at least aware of the basics. If you have bigger questions, Chapter 13 is waiting to tell all.

The Layers palette provides three basic ways to blend pixels between layers (see Figure 12-15). None of these techniques changes as much as a pixel in any layer, so you can always return and reblend the layers at a later date.

✦ **The Opacity value:** Enter a value in the Opacity option box near the top of the Layers palette to change the opacity of the active layer or floating selection. If you reduce the Opacity value to 50 percent, for example, Photoshop makes the pixels on the active layer translucent, so the colors in the active layer mix evenly with the colors in the layers below.

If any tool other than a paint or edit tool is active—including the selection and navigation tools—you can press a number key to change the Opacity value. Press 1 for 10 percent, 2 for 20 percent, up to 0 for 100 percent. Or you can enter a specific Opacity value by pressing two number keys in a row. For example, press 3 and then 7 for 37 percent.

✦ **The blend mode pop-up menu:** Choose an option from the blend mode pop-up menu—open in Figure 12-15—to mix every pixel in the active layer with the pixels below it, according to one of several mathematical equations. For example, when you choose Multiply, Photoshop really does multiply the brightness values of the pixels and then divides the result by 255, the maximum brightness value. Blend modes use the same math as the brush modes covered in Chapter 5. But you can accomplish a lot more with blend modes, which is why I spend so much time examining them in Chapter 13.

As with Opacity, you can select a blend mode from the keyboard when a selection or navigation tool is active. Press Shift+plus to advance incrementally down the list; press Shift+minus to inch back up. You can also press Shift+Alt and a letter key to select a specific mode. For example, Shift+Alt+M selects the Multiply mode. Shift+Alt+N restores the mode to Normal.

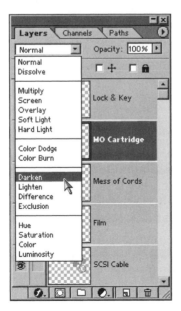

Figure 12-15: The blend mode pop-up menu and the Opacity option box enable you to mix layers without making any permanent changes to the pixels.

✦ **Layer Options:** Choose Layer ➪ Blending Options or double-click a layer name to display the Layer Style dialog box. The General Blending area of this dialog box provides access to a Blend Mode pop-up menu and an Opacity value, but it also offers a world of unique functions. As discussed in Chapter 13, you can hide one or more color channels, specify which colors are visible in the active layer, and force other colors to show through from the layers behind it. Select an item from the left-hand list to apply a layer style, as discussed in Chapter 14.

Although far short of the whole story, that should be enough to prepare you for anything I throw at you throughout the remainder of this chapter.

Fusing several layers

Although layers are wonderful and marvelous creatures, they have their price. Layers expand the size of an image in RAM and ultimately lead to slower performance. And as I noted in Chapter 3, only three formats — PDF, TIFF, and the native PSD format — permit you to save layered compositions.

In the interest of slimming the size of your image, Photoshop provides the following methods for merging layers together:

✦ **Merge Down (Ctrl+E):** Choose Layer ➪ Merge Down to merge a layer with the layer immediately below it. When generating screen shots, I use this command 50 or 60 times a day. I paste the screen shot into the image window, edit the layer as desired, and then press Ctrl+E to set it down. Then I can save the screen shot to the smallest possible file on disk, essential when e-mailing the screens to my editor.

If the active layer is part of a clipping group or is linked to other layers — two conditions I discuss later in this chapter — the Merge Down command changes to Merge Linked or Merge Group, respectively. Again, these commands use Ctrl+E as a shortcut. Merge Down is forever changing to suit the situation.

✦ **Merge Visible (Ctrl+Shift+E):** Choose the Merge Visible command to merge all visible layers into a single layer. If the layer is not visible — that is, if no eyeball icon appears in front of the layer name — Photoshop doesn't eliminate it; the layer simply remains independent.

To create a merged clone, press Alt when applying either Layer ➪ Merge Down or Layer ➪ Merge Visible. Pressing Alt and choosing Merge Down (or pressing Ctrl+Alt+E) clones the contents of the active layer into the layer below it. Pressing Alt and choosing Merge Visible (or pressing Ctrl+Shift+Alt+E) copies the contents of all visible layers to the active layer.

More useful, I think, is the ability to copy the merged contents of a selected area. To do so, choose Edit ➪ Copy Merged or press Ctrl+Shift+C. You can then paste the selection into a layer or make it part of a different image.

✦ **Flatten Image:** This command merges all visible layers and throws away the invisible ones. The result is a single, opaque background layer. Photoshop does not give this command a keyboard shortcut because it's so dangerous. More often than not, you'll want to flatten an image incrementally using the two Merge commands.

Note that Photoshop suggests that you flatten an image when converting from one color mode to another by choosing a command from the Image ➪ Mode submenu. You can choose not to flatten the image (by pressing D) but this may come at the expense of some of the brighter colors in your image. As discussed in Chapter 13, many of the blend modes perform differently in RGB than they do in CMYK.

Dumping layers

You can also merely throw a layer away: Drag the layer name onto the trash can icon at the bottom of the Layers palette. Or click the trash can icon to delete the active layer.

When you click the trash can icon, Photoshop displays a message asking whether you really want to toss the layer. To give this message the slip in the future, Alt-click the trash can icon.

Saving a flattened version of an image

As I mentioned, only three file formats — PDF, TIFF, and the native Photoshop format — save images with layers. If you want to save a flattened version of your image — that is, with all layers fused into a single image — in some other file format, choose File ➪ Save As (Ctrl+Shift+S) and select the desired format from the Format pop-up menu. If you select a format that doesn't support layers — such as JPEG, GIF, or EPS — the program dims the Layers check box.

The Save As command does not affect the image in memory. All layers remain intact. And if you select the As a Copy check box — which I recommend you do — Photoshop doesn't even change the name of the image in the title bar. It merely creates a flattened version of the image on disk. Nevertheless, be sure to save a layered version of the composition as well, just in case you want to edit it in the future.

Selecting the Contents of Layers

A few sections back, I mentioned that every layer (except the background) includes a *transparency mask*. This mask tells Photoshop which pixels are opaque, which are translucent, and which are transparent. Like any mask, Photoshop lets you convert the transparency mask for any layer — active or not — to a selection outline. In fact, you use the same keyboard techniques you use to convert paths to selections (as explained in Chapter 8) and channels to selections (Chapter 9):

✦ Ctrl-click an item in the Layers palette to convert the transparency mask for that layer to a selection outline.

✦ To add the transparency mask to an existing selection outline, Ctrl+Shift-click the layer name. The little selection cursor includes a plus sign to show you that you're about to add.

✦ To subtract the transparency mask, Ctrl+Alt-click the layer name.

✦ And to find the intersection of the transparency mask and the current selection outline, Ctrl+Shift+Alt-click the layer name.

If you're uncertain that you'll remember all these keyboard shortcuts, you can use Select ⇨ Load Selection instead. After choosing the command, select the Transparency item from the Channel pop-up menu. (You can even load a transparency mask from another open image if the image is exactly the same size as the one you're working on.) Then use the Operation radio buttons to merge the mask with an existing selection.

Selection outlines exist independently of layers, so you can use the transparency mask from one layer to select part of another layer. For example, to select the part of the background layer that exactly matches the contents of another layer, press Shift+Alt+[to descend to the background layer and then Ctrl-click the name of the layer you want to match.

The most common reason to borrow a selection from one layer and apply it to another is to create manual shadow and lighting effects. After Ctrl-clicking on a layer, you can use this selection to create a drop shadow that precisely matches the contours of the layer itself. No messing with the airbrush or the lasso tool — Photoshop does the tough work for you.

Now, you might think with Photoshop 6's extensive range of layer styles, manual drop shadows and the like would be a thing of the past. After all, you have only to choose Layer ⇨ Layer Style ⇨ Drop Shadow and, bang, the program adds a drop shadow. But the old, manual methods still have their advantages. You don't have to visit a complicated dialog box to edit a manual drop shadow. You can reposition a manual shadow from the keyboard, and you can expand and contract a manual shadow with more precision than you can an automatic one.

On the other hand, this is not to say the old ways are always better. A shadow created with the Drop Shadow command takes up less room in memory, it moves and rotates with a layer, and you can edit the softness of the shadow long after creating it.

What we have is two equally powerful solutions, each with its own characteristic pros and cons. Therefore, the wise electronic artist develops a working knowledge of both. This way, you're ready and able to apply the technique that makes the most sense for the job at hand.

Cross-Reference

The following sections explore the manual drop shadows, highlights, and spotlights. For everything you ever wanted to know about the Layer Styles commands, read Chapter 14.

Drop shadows

In these first steps, I take the dolphin from Figure 12-16 and insert a drop shadow behind it. This might not be the exact subject you'll apply drop shadows to — sea critters so rarely cast such shadows onto the water's surface — but it accurately demonstrates how the effect works.

Figure 12-16: A dolphin in dire need of a drop shadow.

STEPS: Creating a Drop Shadow

1. **Select the subject that you want casting the shadow.** In my case, I selected the dolphin by painting the mask shown in Figure 12-17 inside a separate mask channel. These days, I add a mask to nearly every image I create to distinguish the foreground image from its background. I converted the mask to a selection outline by Ctrl-clicking on the mask name in the Channels palette and then pressing Ctrl+tilde (~) to switch back to the composite view.

2. **Send the image to a separate layer by pressing Ctrl+J.** Now that the selection is elevated, you can slip in the drop shadow beneath it.

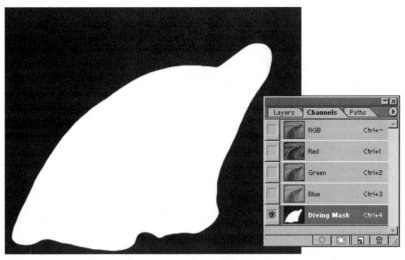

Figure 12-17: This mask separates the dolphin from its watery home.

3. **Retrieve the selection outline for your new layer and apply it to the background layer.** To do this, Ctrl-click the new layer name (presumably Layer 1) and then press Shift+Alt+[to switch to the background layer. (Because I saved the mask to a separate channel, I could have instead Ctrl-clicked on the Mask item in the Channels panel to retrieve the selection. Or I could have pressed Ctrl+Alt+4.)

4. **To create a softened drop shadow — indicative of a diffused light source — choose Select ➪ Feather (Ctrl+Alt+D).** The Radius value you enter depends on the resolution of your image. I recommend dividing the resolution of your image by 20. When working on a 200-ppi image, for example, enter a Radius value of 10. My image is a mere 140 ppi, so I entered 7. Then press Enter to soften the selection.

5. **Press Ctrl+J to send the feathered selection to a new layer.**

6. **Fill the feathered area with black.** If necessary, press D to make the foreground color black. Then press Shift+Alt+Backspace to fill only the area inside the transparency mask. A slight halo of dark pixels forms around the edges of the image.

7. **Press Ctrl with the arrow keys to nudge the shadow to the desired location.** In Figure 12-18, I nudged the shadow 12 pixels to the right. (Press Ctrl+Shift+arrow key to nudge the shadow in 10-pixel increments.)

8. **Lower the Opacity setting.** If the shadow is too dark — black lacks a little subtlety — change the Opacity value in the Layers palette to change the opacity of the shadow. Or press M to make sure a selection tool is active and then press a number key to change the opacity. I typically press 7 (for 70 percent), but I'm probably in a rut.

Figure 12-18: I nudged this drop shadow 12 pixels due right from the dolphin head, which is situated on the layer above it.

Tip

If you don't like a black drop shadow, you can make a colored one with only slightly more effort. Instead of filling the shadow with black in Step 6, select a different foreground color and press Shift+Alt+Backspace. For the best result, select a color that is the complementary opposite of your background color. Next, choose Multiply from the blend mode pop-up menu in the Layers palette (or press Shift+Alt+M). This burns the colors in the shadow into those in the lower layers to create a darkened mix. Finally, press a number key to specify the opacity.

Halos

Creating a halo is similar to creating a drop shadow. The only differences are that you must expand the selection outline and fill the halo with white (or some other light color) instead of black. The following steps tell all.

STEPS: Creating a Downright Angelic Halo

1. **Follow Steps 1 through 3 of the preceding instructions.** You end up with a version of the selected image on an independent layer and a matching selection outline applied to the background image. (See, I told you this was like creating a drop shadow.)

2. **Expand the selection outline.** Unlike a drop shadow, which is offset slightly from an image, a halo fringes the perimeter of an image pretty evenly. You need to expand the selection outline beyond the edges of the image so you can see the halo clearly. To do this, choose Select ➪ Modify ➪ Expand. An "Expand By" option box greets you. Generally speaking, you want the expansion to match the size of your feathering so that the softening occurs outward.

Therefore, I entered 7. (The maximum permissible value is 16; if you want to expand more than 16 pixels, you must apply the command twice.)

3. **Choose Select ➪ Feather and enter the same value you entered in the Expand By option box.** Again, you decide this value by dividing the resolution of your image by 20 (or thereabouts).

4. **Send the selection to a new layer.** Press Ctrl+J.

5. **Fill the halo with white.** Assuming the background color is white, press Ctrl+Shift+Backspace.

That's it. Figure 12-19 shows an enlightened looking dolphin set against a halo effect. I also drew a conventional halo above its head, added some sparklies, and even changed my finned friend's eye using the eyeball brush shape included in the Assorted Brushes document. I mean, if this aquatic mammal isn't bound for glory, I don't know who is.

Figure 12-19: Few dolphins reach this level of spiritual awareness, even if you do set them apart from their backgrounds using the halo effect.

Tip

Incidentally, you needn't create a white halo any more than you must create a black drop shadow. In Step 5, set the background color to something other than white. Then select the Screen option from the blend mode pop-up menu in the Layers palette (Shift+Alt+S), thus mixing the colors and lightening them at the same time. If you don't like the effect, select a different background color and press Ctrl+Shift+Backspace again. With the halo on a separate layer, you can do just about anything to it without running the risk of harming the underlying original.

Spotlights

Now, finally, for the spotlight effect. I use spotlights about a billion times in this book to highlight some special option I want you to look at in a palette or dialog box. I've received so many questions (from fellow authors mostly) on how to perform this effect, I've decided to write the information in this book and be done with it. So here goes.

STEPS: Shining a Spotlight on Something Inside an Image

1. **Draw an oval selection inside your image.** The best tool for this purpose is the elliptical marquee tool. The selection represents the area where the spotlight will shine. If you don't like where the oval is located, but you basically like its size and shape, drag the outline to a more satisfactory location.

2. **Choose Select ⇨ Feather and enter whatever Radius value you please.** Again, you may want to follow the divide-the-resolution-by-20 rule. (Although there's no such thing as a wrong Radius value.) To create Figure 12-20, I doubled my Radius value to 14 pixels to create a soft effect.

3. **Press Ctrl+Shift+I.** Most likely, you really want to darken the area outside the spotlight, not lighten the spotlight itself. So choose Select ⇨ Inverse (Ctrl+Shift+I) to swap what's selected and what's not.

4. **Send the selection to a new layer.** That's Ctrl+J, of course.

5. **Fill the transparency mask with black.** With the foreground color set to black, press Shift+Alt+Backspace.

6. **Lower the Opacity setting by pressing a number key.** To get the effect in Figure 12-20, I pressed 6 for 60 percent.

Actually, the image in Figure 12-20 isn't all that convincing. Although the preceding steps are fine for spotlighting flat images such as screen shots, they tend to rob photographs of some of their depth. After all, in real life, the spotlight wouldn't hit the water in the same way it hits the dolphin.

Tip

There is a way around this. You can combine the oval selection outline with the mask used to select the foreground image, thereby eliminating the background from the equation entirely. First establish the selection and feather it (Steps 1 and 2). Assuming your image has a mask saved in a separate channel, Ctrl+Shift+Alt-click the mask name in the Channels palette. This retains just the intersection of the mask and the spotlight selection. Then perform the preceding Steps 3 through 6 — that is, inverse the selection (Ctrl+Shift+I), send it to a layer (Ctrl+J), fill the transparency mask with black (Shift+Alt+Backspace), and change the opacity. For my part, I first rotated the oval selection using Select ⇨ Transform Selection. I found the intersection of the mask and rotated oval to achieve the more natural spotlight shown in Figure 12-21.

Figure 12-20: Create an elliptical selection, feather it, inverse it, layer it, fill it with black, and lower the opacity to create a spotlight effect like this one.

Figure 12-21: You can mix the feathered selection with the contents of a mask channel to limit the spotlighting effect to the foreground character only.

Sometimes, the darkness of the area around the spotlight appears sufficiently dark that it starts bringing the spotlighted area down with it. To brighten the spotlight, inverse the selection (Ctrl+Shift+I) so the spotlight is selected again. Then apply the Levels command (Ctrl+L) to brighten the spotlighted area. The Levels command is explained at length in Chapter 17.

Moving, Linking, and Aligning Layers

You can move an entire layer or the selected portion of a layer by dragging in the image window with the move tool. If you have a selection going, drag inside the marching-ants outline to move only the selection; drag outside the selection to move the entire layer.

As I mentioned in Chapter 8, you can temporarily access the move tool when some other tool is active by pressing Ctrl. To nudge a layer, press Ctrl with an arrow key. Press Ctrl+Shift to nudge in 10-pixel increments.

If part of the layer disappears beyond the edge of the window, no problem. As long as you don't move your cursor outside the image window, Photoshop saves even the hidden pixels in the layer, enabling you to drag the rest of the layer into view later.

Note that this works only when moving all of a layer. If you move a selection beyond the edge of the image window using the move tool, Photoshop clips the selection at the window's edge the moment you deselect it. Also be aware: If you move your cursor outside the image window, Photoshop thinks you are trying to drag-and-drop pixels from one image to another and responds accordingly.

If you Ctrl-drag the background image — either when no portion of the image is selected or by dragging outside the selection outline — Photoshop automatically converts the background to a new layer (called Layer 0). The area revealed by the move becomes a hole, as indicated by the checkerboard transparency. Photoshop saves the hidden portions of the background image in case you ever decide to move the background back into its original position.

If you regularly work on huge images or your machine is old and kind of slow, Photoshop lets you speed the display of whole layers on the move. Press Ctrl+K and then Ctrl+3 to display the Display & Cursors panel of the Preferences dialog box. Then select the Pixel Doubling check box. From now on, Photoshop will show you a low-resolution proxy of a selection or a layer as you drag (or Ctrl-drag) it across the screen.

Linking layers

Photoshop lets you move multiple layers at a time. To do so, you have to establish a *link* between the layers you want to move and the active layer. Begin by selecting the first layer in the Layers palette you want to link. Then click in the second column to the left of the other layer you want to link. A chain-link icon appears in front of each linked layer, as in Figure 12-22. This icon shows that the linked layers move in unison when you Ctrl-drag the active layer. To break the link, click a link icon, which hides the icon.

Note   Dragging inside a selection outline moves the selection independently of any linked layers. Dragging outside the selection moves all linked layers at once.

Link icons

Link column

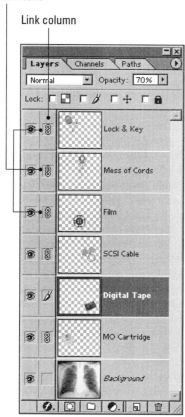

Figure 12-22: Click in the second column in the Layers palette to display or hide link icons. Here I've linked all layers except the background, so I can Ctrl-drag them in unison.

Tip   To link many layers at a time, drag up and down the link column. To unlink the active layer from all others, Alt-click the paintbrush icon in the link column.

You can also link layers with the context-sensitive pop-up menu. As you may recall from the "Switching between layers" section earlier in this chapter, you can bring up a pop-up menu listing the layers in an image by Ctrl+right-clicking on an image element with any tool. Add Shift while selecting a layer from the pop-up menu to link or unlink the layer rather than switch to it.

But that's not all. If you're plum crazy for shortcuts, you can change the link state without visiting the pop-up menu by—drum roll please—Ctrl+Shift+Alt+right-clicking on an element in the image window. Okay, I love shortcuts, but even *I* have to admit that this one is gratuitous!

When you drag-and-drop linked layers into another document, all linked layers move together and the layers retain their original order—provided that you Ctrl-drag the layers from one image window into another. If you want to move just one layer without its linked buddies, drag the layer name from the Layers palette and drop it into another open image window.

If you hold down Shift when dropping, Photoshop centers the layers in the document. If the document is exactly the same size as the one from which you dragged the layers, Shift-dropping lands the image elements in the same position they held in the original document. And finally, if something is selected in the document, the Shift-dropped layers are centered inside that selection.

Uniting layers into sets

Linking isn't the only way to keep layers together. In Photoshop 6, you can toss multiple layers into a folders called a *set*. To create a new set, click the little folder button along the bottom of the Layers palette. Or better yet, Alt-click the button to display the dialog box shown in Figure 12-23. Here you can name the set, assign a color, and set the blend mode and opacity.

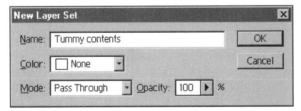

Figure 12-23: Choose the New Layer Set command or Alt-click the folder button at the bottom of the Layers palette to create and name a new set.

Notice in Figure 12-23 that a unique Mode option—Pass Through—appears when working with sets. This tells Photoshop to observe the blend modes assigned to the individual layers inside the set. By contrast, if you apply a different blend mode such as Multiply to the set, Photoshop overrides the blend modes of the layers inside the set and applies Multiply to them all.

The set appears as a folder icon in the Layers palette scrolling list. To add a layer to the set, drag the layer name in the scrolling list and drop it on the folder icon. Layers that are part of a set appear indented, as in Figure 12-24. The triangle to the left of the folder icon permits you to expand and collapse the layers inside the set, a tremendous help when working inside images with a dozen or more layers. Figure 12-25 shows the layers associated with a typical page design I put together for my Web site. When all sets are expanded, the layers don't even begin to fit on screen. But with sets collapsed, you can assess the construction of the image at a glance.

Expand/collapse

Layer set

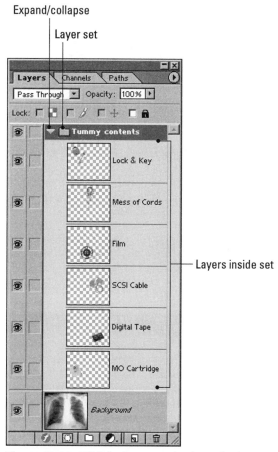

Layers inside set

Figure 12-24: Click in the second column in the Layers palette to display or hide link icons. Here I've linked all layers except the background, so I can Ctrl-drag them in unison.

Figure 12-25: Sets are a terrific help when working with complex, multilayer compositions, such as this sketch for a Web page. Witness the difference between all sets expanded (first palette) and all sets collapsed (second).

Here are some other ways to create and modify sets:

✦ Double-click a set name to rename it.

✦ Drag a set name up or down the palette to move it.

✦ When a set is expanded, you can drag a layer within the set, move a layer out of the set, or drop a layer into the set at a specific position.

✦ Drag a set name and drop it onto another set to empty all layers from the former into the latter.

✦ To duplicate a set, drag it onto the folder icon at the bottom of the Layers palette.

✦ Hate dragging all those layers into a set? Wish you could move more than one at a time? Well, you can't, but you can do the next best thing. Link the layers that you want to make part of a set. Then choose "New Set From Linked" from the Layers palette menu. All linked layers go into the new set.

✦ In case you're wondering, *Can I link layers in different sets?,* yes, you can. If you're wondering, *Can I create sets within sets?,* no, you cannot. But don't be disillusioned, because the moment you ask, *Can I link sets together?*, I'll be happy to tell you that it's possible not only to link sets, but also to link individual layers to whole sets. You have to admit, it's pretty hot stuff.

✦ As you know, Ctrl+right-clicking in the image window displays a shortcut menu of layers under the cursor. If one of the layers belongs to a set, Photoshop lists the set name along with the individual layer names in the shortcut menu. Select the set name to make it active.

Anytime a set name is active in the Layers palette, you can move or transform all layers in the set as a unit, much as if they were linked. To move or transform a single layer inside the set, just select that layer and go about your business as you normally would.

Locking layers

Photoshop 6 lets you protect a layer by locking it. But unlike other programs that lock or unlock layers in their entirety, Photoshop lets you lock some attributes of a layer and leave other attributes unlocked. Figure 12-26 labels the four Lock check boxes available in the Layers palette. Here's how they work:

✦ **Lock transparency.** This check box protects the transparency of a layer. When selected, you can paint inside a layer without harming the transparent pixels. It's so useful, I devote an entire section to the topic (see "Preserving transparency" later in this chapter).

✦ **Lock pixels.** Select this check box to prohibit the pixels in the active layer from further editing. Paint and edit tools will no longer function, nor will filters or other pixel-level commands. However, you'll still be able to move and transform the layer as you like. Note that selecting this check box dims and selects the Lock Transparency check box as well. After all, if you can't edit pixels, you can't edit pixels — whether they're opaque or transparent.

✦ **Lock position.** Select this check box to prevent the layer from being moved or transformed. You can, however, edit the pixels.

✦ **Lock all.** To lock everything about a layer, select this check box. You can't paint, edit, filter, move, transform, delete, or otherwise change a hair on the layer's head. About all you can do is duplicate the layer, move it up and down the stack, add it to a set, and merge it with one or more other layers. This check box is applicable to layers and sets alike.

Photoshop shows you which layers are locked by displaying two kinds of lock icons in the Layers palette. As labeled in Figure 12-26, the hollow lock means one attribute or other is locked; the filled lock means all attributes are locked.

Lock transparency

Lock pixels

Lock position

Lock all

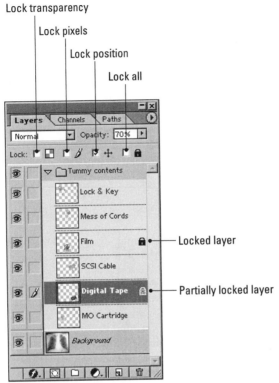

Locked layer

Partially locked layer

Figure 12-26: Click in the second column in the
Layers palette to display or hide link icons. Here I've
linked all layers except the background, so I can
Ctrl-drag them in unison.

Using guides

Photoshop's grids and guides allow you to move selections and layers into alignment.
When combined with the move tool, they also enable you to create rows and columns
of image elements and even align layers by their centers.

To create a guide, press Ctrl+R (View ➪ Show Rulers) to display the horizontal and
vertical rulers. Then drag a guideline from the ruler. At the top of Figure 12-27, you
can see me dragging a horizontal guide down from the top ruler. Then Ctrl-drag layers and selections in alignment with the guide. In the bottom portion of the figure,
I've dragged the MO disk, film reel, and tape — each on different layers — so they
snap into alignment at their centers. (The reel has some film hanging from it, which
Photoshop considers in calculating the center.) You'll know when the layer snaps
into alignment because the move cursor becomes hollow, like the labeled cursor
in Figure 12-27.

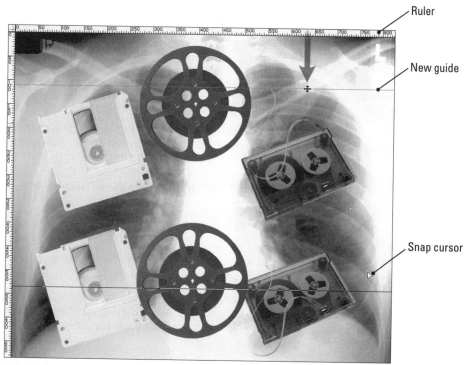

Ruler

New guide

Snap cursor

Figure 12-27: Drag from one of the rulers to create a guide (top) and then Ctrl-drag each layer or selection into alignment (bottom).

Note

Text layers snap to guides a little differently than other kinds of layers. Rather than snapping by the top or bottom edge of the layer, Photoshop snaps a text guide by its baseline. It's just what you need when aligning type.

Guides are straightforward creatures. I mean, you don't have to study them rigorously for years to understand them — a few minutes are all you need to master them. But there are a few hidden treats:

✦ If you know the exact position where you want to put a guideline, choose View ➪ New Guide. After selecting from a horizontal or vertical guide, enter the location of the guide as measured from the ruler origin, by default in the upper-left corner of the image. For example, enter "1 in" for 1 inch, "2.5 cm" for 2.5 centimeters, or "200 px" for 200 pixels.

✦ You can show and hide all guides by choosing View ➪ Show ➪ Guides. When the guides are hidden, layers and selections do not snap into alignment.

✦ In Photoshop 6, you can hide or show guides by pressing Ctrl+H. But be aware that this turns on or off the visibility of other elements, including the grid, selection outlines, paths, and notes. To hide and show just the guides, press Ctrl+quote (').

✦ You can turn a guide's snappiness on and off by choosing View ➪ Snap To ➪ Guides. You can also press Ctrl+Shift+semicolon (;). Again, this shortcut affects the snappiness of *everything,* including the grid, the perimeter of the image, and Web slices.

✦ To turn off the snappiness in the middle of a brushstroke or layer movement, press Ctrl in mid drag. Release Ctrl to return to snappy land.

✦ As with all image elements in Photoshop, you can move a guide with the move tool. If some other tool is active, Ctrl-dragging also works.

✦ To lock all guides so you can't accidentally move them while you're trying to Ctrl-drag something else, press Ctrl+Alt+semicolon or choose View ➪ Lock Guides. Press Ctrl+Alt+semicolon again to unlock all guides.

✦ When moving a guide, press Shift to snap the guide to the nearest ruler tick mark.

✦ To convert a horizontal guide to a vertical guide or vice versa, press Alt while moving the guide.

✦ If you rotate your document in exact multiples of 90 degrees or flip the image horizontally or vertically, your guides also rotate unless they are locked.

✦ You can position a guide outside the image if you want. To do so, make the image window larger than the image. Now you can drag a guide into the empty canvas surrounding the image. You can then snap a layer or selection into alignment with the guide.

✦ To edit the color of the guides, Ctrl-double-click a guide to display the Guides & Grid panel of the Preferences dialog box. You can also change the guides from solid lines to dashed. (This is only for screen purposes, by the way. Guides don't print.)

✦ Although Photoshop lets you add guides to any kind of file, you can't always save them. The only formats that let you save guides are Photoshop (PSD), JPEG, TIFF, PDF, and EPS.

✦ If you don't need your guides anymore, choose View ➪ Clear Guides to delete them all in one housekeeping operation. I wish I had a command like this built into my office — I'd choose Maid ➪ Clear Dust and be done with it.

Automatic alignment and distribution

Photoshop lets you align and distribute layers by choosing commands from the Layer ➪ Align or Distribute Linked submenu. The commands are straightforward — and familiar if you've ever used a drawing or page-layout program — but applying them is a little unusual. The following steps show you how to align two or more layers.

STEPS: Aligning Layers

1. **Select the layer that will serve as the anchor.** Whenever you align layers, one layer remains still and the others align to it. The active layer is the one that remains still.

2. **Link the layers you want to align.** Click in front of the layers you want to align to display the link icon. (And be sure to unlink any layers you *don't* want to align.) You have to link at least two layers — after all, there's no point in aligning a layer to itself.

3. **Choose a command from the Layer ⇨ Align Linked submenu.** If you don't like the result, press Ctrl+Z and try a different command.

Tip

You can likewise align linked layers to a selection outline. Just select an area inside any layer, and choose a command from the Layer ⇨ Align To Selection submenu. The selection remains stationary, and the layers move into alignment.

The Distribute Linked commands space linked layers evenly. So it doesn't matter which of the linked layers is selected — the command distributes all linked layers with respect to the two horizontal or vertical extremes. Naturally, it's meaningless to space one or two layers, so the Distribute Linked commands require three or more layers to be linked. And there is no such thing as Distribute To Selection.

Photoshop 6 provides easy access to the align and distribute functions in the Options bar. Just select the move tool (by pressing V) and there they are. You can also align and distribute paths by selecting two or more paths with the black arrow tool and clicking buttons in the Options bar.

Setting up the grid

Photoshop offers a grid, which is a regular series of snapping increments. You view the grid — and turn it on — by choosing View ⇨ Show ⇨ Grid. Turn the snapping forces of the grid on and off by choosing View ⇨ Snap To ⇨ Grid.

You edit the grid in the Guides & Grid panel of the Preferences dialog box (which you can get to by pressing Ctrl+K and then Ctrl+6 or by Ctrl-double-clicking on a guide). I explain how to use these options in the "Guides & Grid" section of Chapter 2. But for the record, you enter the major grid increments in the Gridline Every option box and enter the minor increments in the Subdivisions option box. For example, in Figure 12-28, I set the Gridline Every value to 50 pixels and the Subdivisions value to 5. This means a moved layer will snap in 10-pixel (50 pixels divide by 5) increments. Figure 12-28 also demonstrates each of the three Style settings.

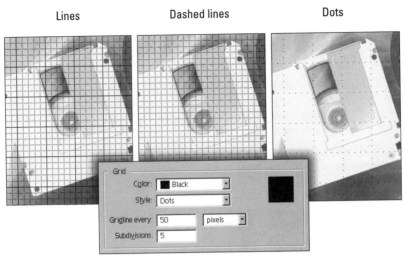

Figure 12-28: Here are the three styles of grid with the Grid Preferences options shown at the bottom.

Using the measure tool

The final method for controlling movements in Photoshop is the measure tool. Alt-click the eyedropper tool a couple of times or press Shift+I to select the measure tool. Then drag from one point to another point in the image window. Photoshop itemizes the distance and angle between the two points in the Info palette. The measure tool is even smart enough to automatically display the Info palette if it's hidden.

From that point on, any time you select the measure tool, Photoshop displays the original measurement line. This way, you can measure a distance, edit the image, and press I (or Shift+I) to refer back to the measurement.

To measure the distance and angle between two other points, you can draw a new line with the measure tool. Or drag the endpoints of the existing measurement line.

Photoshop accommodates only one measurement line per document. But you can break the line in two using what Adobe calls the "protractor" feature. Alt-drag on one of the endpoints to draw forth a second segment. The Info palette then measures the angle between the two segments. As demonstrated in Figure 12-29, the D1 item in the Info palette lists the length of the first segment, D2 lists the length of the second segment, and A tells the angle between the segments.

Measure cursor

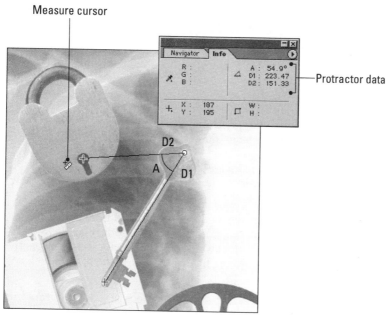

Protractor data

Figure 12-29: Here I measured the angle of the key, and then Alt-dragged from the top endpoint to measure the angle between the key and lock.

Tip

The measure tool is great for straightening crooked layers. After drawing a line with the measure tool, choose Image ⇨ Rotate Canvas ⇨ Arbitrary. The Angle value automatically conforms to the A (angle) value listed in the Info palette. If you look closely, the two values may not exactly match. That's because Photoshop intelligently translates the value to between –45 and +45 degrees, which happens to be the simplest way to express any rotation. If you're unclear what I'm talking about, just trust in Photoshop. It does the math so you don't have to.

Applying Transformations

Photoshop treats some kinds of edits differently than others. Edits that affect the geometry of a selection or a layer are known collectively as *transformations*. These transformations include scaling, rotating, flipping, slanting, and distorting. (Technically, moving is a transformation as well.) Transformations are a special breed of edits inside Photoshop because they can affect a selection, a layer, multiple layers, or an entire image at a time.

Transforming the entire image

Photoshop has two varieties of transformations. Transformation commands that affect the entire image — including all layers, paths, channels, and so on — are listed in the Image menu. Those that affect layers and selected portions of layers are in the Edit menu.

The following list explains how to apply transformations to every pixel in an image, regardless of whether the image is selected or not:

✦ **Scale:** To resize the image, use Image ➪ Image Size. Because this command is one of the most essential low-level functions in the program, I covered it way back in Chapter 3.

✦ **Rotate:** To rotate the entire image, choose a command from the Image ➪ Rotate Canvas submenu. To rotate an image scanned on its side, choose the 90° CW or 90° CCW command. (That's clockwise and counterclockwise, respectively.) Choose 180° to spin the image on its head. To enter some other specific value, choose Image ➪ Rotate Canvas ➪ Arbitrary.

To fix a crooked scanned image, for example, select the measure tool from the eyedropper flyout in the toolbox (press I, and then press Shift+I twice). Drag along what should be a vertical or horizontal edge in the image. If you like, note the A value in the Info palette. Then choose Image ➪ Rotate Canvas ➪ Arbitrary. Look, the Angle value is preset to the angle you just measured. That Photoshop, it's one sharp cookie. Press Enter and the job's done.

Whenever you apply the Arbitrary command, Photoshop has to expand the canvas size to avoid clipping any of your image. This results in background-colored wedges at each of the four corners of the image. You need to either clone with the rubber stamp tool to fill in the wedges or clip them away with the crop tool.

✦ **Flip:** Choose Image ➪ Rotate Canvas ➪ Flip Horizontal to flip the image so left is right and right is left. To flip the image upside down, choose Image ➪ Rotate Canvas ➪ Flip Vertical.

No command is specifically designed to slant or distort the entire image. In the unlikely event you're keen to do this, you'll have to link all layers and apply one of the commands under the Edit ➪ Transform submenu, as explained in the next section.

Transforming layers and selected pixels

To transform a layer or selection, you can apply one of the commands in the Edit ➪ Transform submenu. Nearly a dozen commands are here, all of which you can explore on your own. I'm not copping out; it's just that it's unlikely you'll use any of these commands on a regular basis. They aren't bad, but one command — Free Transform — is infinitely better.

With Free Transform, you can scale, flip, rotate, slant, distort, and move a selection or layer in one continuous operation. This one command lets you get all your transformations exactly right before pressing Enter to apply the final changes.

To initiate the command, press Ctrl+T or choose Edit ➪ Free Transform. Photoshop surrounds the layer or selection with an eight-handle marquee. You are now in the Free Transform mode, which prevents you from doing anything except transforming the image or canceling the operation.

Here's how to work in the Free Transform mode:

✦ **Scale:** Drag one of the eight square handles to scale the image inside the marquee. To scale proportionally, Shift-drag a corner handle. To scale about the central *transformation origin* (labeled in Figure 12-30), Alt-drag a corner handle.

By default, the origin is located in the center of the layer or selection. But you can move it to any place inside the image by dragging it. The origin snaps to the grid and guides, as well as to the center or any corner of the layer.

✦ **Flip:** You can flip the image by dragging one handle past its opposite handle. For example, dragging the left side handle past the right side handle flips the image horizontally.

If you want to perform a simple flip, it's generally easier to choose Edit ➪ Transform ➪ Flip Horizontal or Flip Vertical. Better yet, right-click in the image window and choose one of the Flip commands from the shortcut menu. Quite surprisingly, you can choose any of the shortcut menu commands while working in the Free Transform mode.

✦ **Rotate:** To rotate the image, drag outside the marquee, as demonstrated in the first example in Figure 12-30. Shift-drag to rotate in 15-degree increments.

✦ **Skew:** Ctrl-drag a side handle (including the top or bottom handle) to slant the image. To constrain the slant, which is useful for producing perspective effects, Ctrl+Shift-drag a side handle.

✦ **Distort:** You can distort the image by Ctrl-dragging a corner handle. You can tug the image to stretch it in any of four directions.

To tug two opposite corner handles in symmetrical directions, Ctrl+Alt-drag either of the handles. I show this technique in the second example in Figure 12-30.

✦ **Perspective:** For a one-point perspective effect, Ctrl+Shift-drag a corner handle. To move two points in unison, Ctrl+Shift+Alt-drag a corner handle.

Rotate cursor

Skew cursor

Transformation
origin

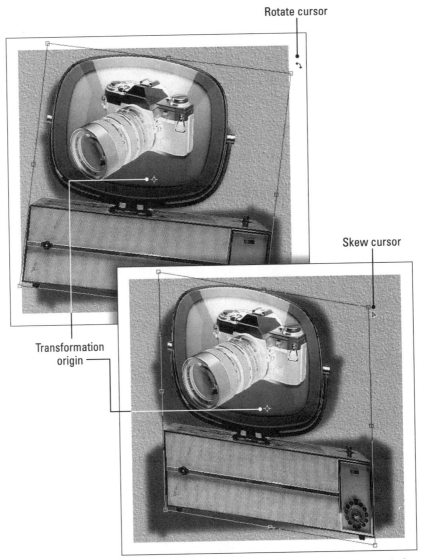

Figure 12-30: After pressing Ctrl+T to initiate the Free Transform command, drag outside the marquee to rotate the layer (top). You can also Ctrl+Alt-drag a corner handle to move the opposite corner handle symmetrically and skew the layer.

✦ **Move:** Drag inside the marquee to move the image. This is useful when you're trying to align the selection or layer with a background image and you want to make sure the transformations match up properly.

✦ **Undo:** To undo the last modification without leaving the Free Transform mode altogether, press Ctrl+Z.

✦ **Zoom:** You can change the view size by choosing one of the commands in the View menu. You can also use the keyboard zoom shortcuts (Ctrl+spacebar-click, Alt+spacebar-click, Ctrl+plus, or Ctrl+minus).

✦ **Apply:** Press Enter to apply the final transformation and interpolate the new pixels. You can also double-click inside the marquee.

If the finished effect looks jagged, it's probably because you selected Nearest Neighbor from the Interpolation pop-up menu in the Preferences dialog box. To correct this problem, press Ctrl+Z to undo the transformation and then press Ctrl+K and select the Bicubic option from the General panel of the Preferences dialog box. Then press Ctrl+Shift+T to reapply the transformation.

✦ **Cancel:** To cancel the Free Transform operation, press Escape.

To transform a clone of a selected area, press Alt when choosing the Free Transform command, or press Ctrl+Alt+T. This only works with selected areas — you can't clone an entire layer any more than you can by Alt-dragging with the move tool.

If no part of the image is selected, you can transform multiple layers at a time by first linking them, as described in the "Linking layers" section earlier in this chapter. For example, I could have linked the TV and camera layers to transform the two in unison back in Figure 12-30.

To replay the last transformation on any layer or selection, choose Edit ➪ Transform ➪ Again or press Ctrl+Shift+T. This is a great technique to use if you forgot to link all the layers that you wanted to transform. You can even transform a path or selection outline to match a transformed layer. It's a handy feature.

Neither Free Transform nor any of the commands in the Edit ➪ Transform submenu are available when a layer is locked, either with the Lock Position or Lock All check box. If a transformation command appears dimmed, therefore, the Lock check boxes are very likely your culprits.

Numerical transformations

To track your transformations numerically, display the Info palette (F8) before you apply the Free Transform command. Even after you initiate Free Transform, you can access the Info palette by choosing Window ➪ Show Info.

You can also track the numerical equivalents of your transformations in the Options bar. Shown in Figure 12-31, the Options bar contains a series of numerical transformation controls anytime you enter the Free Transform mode. These values not only reflect the changes you've made so far, but also permit you to further transform the selection or layer numerically.

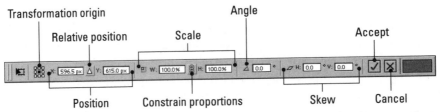

Figure 12-31: Normally, the options in the Options bar change only when you select a different tool, but choosing Free Transform adds a series of controls that permit you to transform a selection or layer numerically.

For the most part, the controls in the Options bar are straightforward. Click in the grid of nine squares to reposition the transformation origin. Use the X and Y values to change the location of the origin numerically. Click the triangular delta symbol to measure the movement relative to the transformation origin. Use the W and H values to scale the selection or layer. Click the link button to constrain the W and H values and resize the selection or layer proportionally. The angle value rotates; t he H and V values skew.

I imagine most folks use the Options bar strictly for scaling and rotating. You'd need the spatial awareness of a NASA navigation system to predict a numerical slant.

Masking and Layers

Layers offer special masking options unto themselves. You can paint inside the confines of a layer as if it were a selection mask; you can add a special mask for a single layer; or you can group multiple layers and have the bottom layer in the group serve as the mask. Quite honestly, these are the kinds of thoughtful and useful functions I've come to expect from Photoshop. Although they're fairly complicated to use — you must be on your toes once you start juggling layer masks — these functions provide new realms of opportunities.

Preserving transparency

As you may recall, I mentioned we'd be talking more about the Lock Transparency check box, first mentioned in the "Locking layers" section and highlighted in Figure 12-32. Well, sure enough, the time has come to do exactly that. When selected, this check box prevents you from painting inside the transparent portions of the layer. And although that may sound like a small thing, it is in fact the most useful Lock option of them all.

Figure 12-32: The Lock Transparency check box enables you to paint inside the layer's transparency mask without harming the transparent pixels.

Suppose I want to paint inside the girl shown in Figure 12-32. If this were a flat, non-layered image, I'd have to draw a selection outline carefully around her hair and arms, as I did back in Chapter 9. But there's no need to do this when using layers. Because the girl lies on a different layer than her background, a permanent selection outline tells Photoshop which pixels are transparent and which are opaque. This is the *transparency mask*.

The first example in Figure 12-33 shows the girl on her own with the background hidden. The transparent areas outside the mask appear in the checkerboard pattern. When the Lock Transparency check box is turned off, you can paint anywhere you want inside the layer. Selecting Lock Transparency activates the transparency mask and places the checkerboard area off limits.

Figure 12-33: The layered girl as she appears on her own (left) and when airbrushed with the Lock Transparency check box turned on (right).

The right image in Figure 12-33 shows what happens after I select Lock Transparency and paint around the girl with the airbrush. The foreground color is set to white. Notice that no matter how much paint I might apply, none of it leaks out onto the background.

Although this enlightening discussion pretty well covers it, I feel compelled to share a few additional words about Lock Transparency:

Tip

✦ You can turn Lock Transparency on and off from the keyboard by pressing the standard slash character, /, right there on the same key with the question mark.

✦ Remember, you can only fill the opaque pixels in a layer, whether Lock Transparency is on or off. Use Ctrl+Shift+Backspace to fill with the background color and Shift+Alt+Backspace to fill with the foreground color.

✦ The Lock Transparency check box is dimmed when the background layer is active because this layer is entirely opaque. There's no transparency to lock, eh? (That's my impression of a Canadian explaining layer theory. It needs a little work, but I think I'm getting close.)

And finally, here's a question for all you folks who think you may have Photoshop mastered. Which of the brush modes (explained in Chapter 5) is the exact opposite of Lock Transparency? The answer is Behind. To see what I mean, turn off Lock Transparency. Then select the paintbrush tool and choose the Behind brush mode in the Options bar. Now paint. Photoshop applies the foreground color exclusively *outside* the transparency mask, thus protecting the opaque pixels. So it follows, when Lock Transparency is turned on, the Behind brush mode is dimmed.

The moral? Behind is not a true brush mode and should not be grouped with the likes of Multiply and Screen in the Options bar. If you ask me, the better solution would be a Lock Opacity check box in the Layers palette. Alas, Adobe's engineers seem to have better things to do, such as add three *other* Lock check boxes, none of which have the slightest thing to do with locking opacity. But just because I've been complaining about the Behind "brush mode" for the last, oh gosh, *seven years* doesn't mean that I'm bitter or anything. Heavens no. I *like* to be ignored! It robs my life of meaning, which is precisely what I'm looking for. In fact, I think I'll go and end it all right now. And for what? A check box. That's all I want. A small and unobtrusive check box, possibly with a picture of my face next to it and a little caption reading, "Yes, Deke, you were right. Can you ever forgive us for being such knot-heads?" I mean, really, am I asking too much?

So, in conclusion, Lock Transparency is your friend; Behind is the tool of Satan. Too bad so few things in the world are this black and white.

Creating layer-specific masks

In addition to the transparency mask that accompanies every layer (except the background), you can add a mask to a layer to make certain pixels in the layer transparent. Now, you might ask, "Won't simply erasing portions of a layer make those portions transparent?" The answer, of course, is yes. And I hasten to add, that was a keen insight on your part. But when you erase, you delete pixels permanently. By creating a layer mask, you instead make pixels temporarily transparent. You can return several months later and bring those pixels back to life again simply by adjusting the mask. So layer masks add yet another level of flexibility to a program that's already a veritable image-editing contortionist.

To create a layer mask, select the layer you want to mask and choose Layer ➪ Add Layer Mask ➪ Reveal All. Or more simply, click the layer mask icon at the bottom of the Layers palette, as labeled in Figure 12-34. A second thumbnail preview appears to the left of the layer name, also labeled in the figure. A second outline around the preview shows the layer mask is active.

Tip   If the second outline is hard to see, keep your eye on the icon directly to the left of the layer name. If the icon is a paintbrush, the layer and not the mask is active. If the icon is a little dotted circle, the mask is active.

Indicates layer mask is active

Link icon

Layer mask thumbnail

Layer mask icon

Figure 12-34: The black area in the layer mask (which you can see in the thumbnail view, top right) translates to transparent pixels in the layer.

To edit the mask, simply paint in the image window. Paint with black to make pixels transparent. Because black represents deselected pixels in an image, it makes these pixels transparent in a layer. Paint with white to make pixels opaque.

Thankfully, Photoshop is smart enough to make the default foreground color in a layer mask white and the default background color black. This ensures that painting with the paintbrush or airbrush makes pixels opaque, whereas painting with the eraser makes them transparent, just as you would expect.

In Figure 12-34, I created a feathered oval, inversed it, and filled it with black by pressing Ctrl+Backspace. This results in a soft vignette around the layer. If I decide

I eliminated too much of the hair, not to worry. I merely paint with white to bring it back again.

Photoshop goes nuts in the layer mask department, adding lots of bells and whistles to make the function both convenient and powerful. Here's everything you need to know:

✦ **Reveal Selection:** If you select some portion of your layer, Photoshop automatically converts the selection to a layer mask when you click the layer mask icon at the bottom of the palette. The area outside the selection becomes transparent. (The corresponding command is Layer ➪ Add Layer Mask ➪ Reveal Selection.)

✦ **Hide Selection:** You can also choose to reverse the prospective mask, making the area inside the selection transparent and the area outside opaque. To do this, choose Layer ➪ Add Layer Mask ➪ Hide Selection. Or better yet, Alt-click the layer mask icon in the Layers palette.

✦ **Hide everything:** To begin with a black mask that hides everything, choose Layer ➪ Add Layer Mask ➪ Hide All. Or press Ctrl+D to deselect everything and then Alt-click the layer mask icon.

✦ **View the mask:** Photoshop regards a layer mask as a layer-specific channel. You can actually see it listed in italics in the Channels palette. To view the mask on its own — as a black-and-white image — Alt-click the layer mask thumbnail in the Layers palette. Alt-click again to view the image instead.

✦ **Layer mask rubylith:** To view the mask as a red overlay, Shift+Alt-click the layer mask icon. Or simply press the backslash key, \, which is above the Enter key.

After you have both layer and mask visible at once, you can hide the mask by pressing \, or you can hide the layer and view only the mask by pressing the tilde key (~). So many alternatives!

✦ **Change the overlay color:** Double-click the layer mask thumbnail to access the Layer Mask Display Options dialog box, which enables you to change the color and opacity of the rubylith.

✦ **Turn off the mask:** You can temporarily disable the mask by Shift-clicking on the mask thumbnail. A red *X* covers the thumbnail when it's disabled, and all masked pixels in the layer appear opaque. Shift-click again to put the mask back in working order.

✦ **Switch between layer and mask:** As you become more familiar with layer masks, you'll switch back and forth between layer and mask quite frequently, editing the layer one minute and editing the mask the next. You can switch between layer and mask by clicking on their respective thumbnails. As I mentioned, look to the icon to the left of the layer name to see whether the layer or the mask is active.

You can also switch between layer and mask from the keyboard. Press Ctrl+tilde (~) to make the layer active. Press Ctrl+\ to switch to the mask.

✦ **Link layer and mask:** A little link icon appears between the layer and mask thumbnails in the Layers palette. When the link icon is visible, you can move or transform the mask and layer as one. If you click the link icon to turn it off, the layer and mask move independently. (You can always move a selected region of the mask or layer independently of the other.)

✦ **Convert mask to selection:** As with all masks, you can convert a layer mask to a selection. To do so, Ctrl-click the layer mask icon. Throw in the Shift and Alt keys if you want to add or subtract the layer mask with an existing selection outline.

✦ In Photoshop 6, you can apply a mask to a set of layers. Just select the set and click the layer mask icon. The mask affects all layers in the set. If a layer in the set contains its own mask, no worries; Photoshop's smart enough to figure out how to mix them together. For another method of masking multiple layers, see the section "Masking groups of layers," coming up soon.

When and if you finish using the mask — you can leave it in force as long as you like — you can choose Layer ➪ Remove Layer Mask. Or just drag the layer mask thumbnail to the trash can icon. Either way, an alert box asks whether you want to discard the mask or permanently apply it to the layer. Click the button that corresponds to your innermost desires.

Pasting inside a selection outline

One command, Edit ➪ Paste Into (Ctrl+Shift+V), creates a layer mask automatically. Choose the Paste Into command to paste the contents of the Clipboard into the current selection, so that the selection acts as a mask. Because Photoshop pastes to a new layer, it converts the selection into a layer mask. But here's the interesting part: By default, Photoshop turns off the link between the layer and the mask. This way, you can Ctrl-drag the layer inside a fixed mask to position the pasted image.

Once upon a time in Photoshop, a command existed named Edit ➪ Paste Behind. (Or something like that. It might have been Paste in Back. My memory's a little hazy.) The command (whatever its name) pasted a copied image in back of a selection. Although the command is gone, its spirit still lives. Now you press Alt when choosing Edit ➪ Paste Into. Or just press Ctrl+Shift+Alt+V. Photoshop creates a new layer with an inverted layer mask, masking away the selected area.

Masking groups of layers

About now, you may be growing fatigued with the topic of layering masking. But one more option requires your immediate attention. You can group multiple layers into something called a *clipping group,* in which the lowest layer in the group masks the others. Where the lowest layer is transparent, the other layers are hidden; where the lowest layer is opaque, the contents of the other layers are visible.

Note

Despite the similarities in name, a clipping group bears no relation to a clipping path. That is, a clipping group doesn't allow you to prepare transparent areas for import into QuarkXPress and the like.

There are two ways to create a clipping group:

✦ Alt-click the horizontal line between any two layers to group them into a single unit. Your cursor changes to the group cursor labeled in Figure 12-35 when you press Alt; the horizontal line becomes dotted after you click. To break the layers apart again, Alt-click the dotted line to make it solid.

Group cursor

Figure 12-35: Alt-click the horizontal line between two layers to group them.

✦ Select the higher of the two layers you want to combine into a clipping group. Then choose Layer ➪ Group with Previous or press Ctrl+G. To make the layers independent again, choose Layer ➪ Ungroup (Ctrl+Shift+G).

Figures 12-35 and 12-36 demonstrate two steps in a piece of artwork I created for *Macworld* magazine. I had already created some text on an independent layer using the type tool (the subject of the next chapter), and I wanted to fill the text with water. So I added some photographs I shot of a swimming pool to a layer above the text, as shown in Figure 12-35. Then I combined text and pool images into a clipping group. Because the text was beneath the water, Photoshop masked the pool images according to the transparency mask assigned to the text. The result is a water pattern that exactly fills the type, as in Figure 12-36. (For a full-color version of these figures, see Color Plate 12-1.)

Figure 12-36: After combining pool water and type layers into a single clipping group, Photoshop applies the type layer's transparency mask to the pool layer.

Note If you're familiar with Illustrator, you may recognize this clipping group metaphor as a relative to Illustrator's clipping mask. One object in the illustration acts as a mask for a collection of additional objects. In Illustrator, however, the topmost object in the group is the mask, not the bottom one. So much for consistency.

✦   ✦   ✦

The Wonders of Blend Modes

Mixing Images Together

There must be 50 ways to combine and compare differently colored pixels in Photoshop. So far, we've seen how you can smear and blur pixels into each other, select pixels using other pixels, layer pixels in front of pixels, compare a pixel to its neighbors using automated filters, and more. Any time that you edit, mask, composite, filter, or color correct an image, you're actually breeding the image with itself or with other images to create a new and unique offspring.

This chapter explores the final and ultimate experiment in Photoshop's great genetics laboratory. *Blend modes,* also called *calculations,* permit you to mix the color of a pixel with that of every pixel in a straight line beneath it. A single blend mode is as powerful as a mask, a filter, and a color map combined, and best of all, it's temporary. As long as one image remains layered in front of another, you can replace one calculation with another as easily as you change a letter of text in a word processor.

To appreciate the most rudimentary power of blend modes, consider Figure 13-1. The first image shows a terrestrial thrill seeker composited in front of the Apollo crew's old stomping grounds. Both layers are as opaque as if you had cut them out with scissors and glued them together. (Granted, you'd have to be very skilled with scissors.) The antialiased edges of the parachute mix slightly with the moon pixels below them. But beyond that, every pixel is a digital hermit, steadfastly avoiding interaction.

Figure 13-1: Layers permit you to combine images from different sources (left), but blend modes permit you to mix images together to create intriguing if sometimes unexpected interactions (right).

The second image in Figure 13-1 paints a different picture. Here I've created several clones of the parachute and moon and mixed them together using Photoshop's considerable array of calculation capabilities. Although I used just two images, I composited them onto ten layers, only one of which — the background layer — was fully opaque. I don't know if it's moon men invading earth or the other way around, but whatever it is, it wouldn't have been possible without blend modes and their ilk.

Photoshop gives you three ways to mix images:

✦ **The Layers palette:** You can combine the active layer with underlying pixels using the Opacity value and blend mode pop-up menu, both members of the Layers palette. Figure 13-2 shows these two illustrious items in the context of the layers list for Figure 13-1. To learn everything there is to know about the Opacity value and blend mode pop-up menu, read the next section.

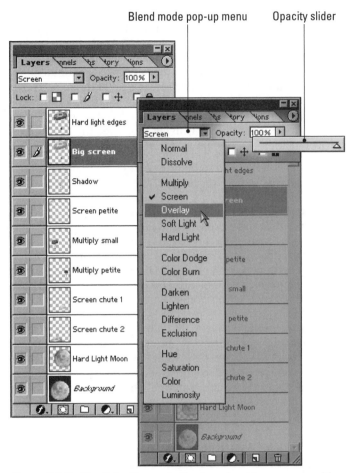

Blend mode pop-up menu   Opacity slider

Figure 13-2: The list of layers in the Invasion Moon composition, with the blend mode pop-up menu proudly displayed on the right.

✦ **Blending options:** Double-click a layer name in the Layers palette to display the new Layer Style dialog box, which contains controls formerly found in the Layer Options dialog box and more. Along with the standard Opacity slider and blend mode pop-up menu, you get an assortment of advanced blending options.

Using the Blend If sliders, you can drop colors out of the active layer and force colors to show through from layers below. This is one of Photoshop's oldest, finest, and least used features. Adding to this capability, Photoshop 6 provides a Knockout option, which enables you to blend a layer with one that's not immediately below. In addition, you can blend individual color channels independently and choose to blend a filled area with or without any interior layer effects (such as an inner glow).

✦ **Channel operations:** The so-called channel operations permit you to combine two open images of identical size, or one image with itself. Photoshop offers two commands for this purpose, Image ⇨ Apply Image and Image ⇨ Calculations. Unusually complex and completely lacking in sizing and placement functions, these commands provide access to two unique blend modes named Add and Subtract. Simply put, unless a technique involves the Add or Subtract mode, or you want to clone two images into a third image window, you can mix images with greater ease, flexibility, and feedback using the Layers palette. For more on this lively topic, see the "Using Channel Operation Commands" section later in this chapter.

Photoshop 6 also enables you to blend layers on a channel-by-channel basis, an option you can explore in the section "Blending individual color channels."

Blend modes are not Photoshop's most straightforward feature. There may even come a time when you utter the words, "Blend modes are stupid." They demand a generous supply of experimentation, and even then they'll fool you. I was a math major in college (with a double-major in art, for what it's worth), so I well understand the elementary arithmetic behind Photoshop's calculations. And yet, despite roughly a decade of experience with blend modes in Photoshop and other programs, I am frequently surprised by their outcome.

The key, therefore, is to combine a basic understanding of how blend modes and other compositing features work with your natural willingness to experiment. Sometime when you don't have a deadline looming over your head, take some multilayered composition you have lying around and hit it with a few calculations. Even if the result is a disaster that you wouldn't share with your mother, let alone a client, you can consider it time well spent.

Using Opacity and Blend Modes

This is not the first time in this book that I've touched on the Opacity value or the blend mode pop-up menu. And given that the Layers palette's blend modes mimic the brush modes (both in name and in function) as I discussed in "The 19 paint tool modes" section near the end of Chapter 5, we're covering some familiar territory. But you'll soon find that there's a significant difference between laying down a single color with a brush and merging the all the colors that inhabit a single layer. This difference is the stuff of the following pages.

Note

Incidentally, both the Opacity and blend mode options are dimmed when working on the background layer or in a single-layer image. There's nothing underneath, so there's nothing to mix. Naturally, this goes double when editing black-and-white and indexed images or when editing masks, because neither of these circumstances supports layers.

The Opacity setting

The Opacity value is the easiest of the layer mixers to understand. It permits you to mix the active layer with the layers beneath it in prescribed portions. It's sort of like mixing a drink. Suppose you pour one part vermouth and four parts gin into a martini glass. (Any martini enthusiast knows that's too much vermouth, but bear with me on this one.) The resulting beverage is ⅕ vermouth and ⅘ gin. If the vermouth were a layer, you could achieve the same effect by setting the Opacity to 20 percent. This implies that 20 percent of what you see is vermouth and the remaining 80 percent is underlying gin.

Tip

When any selection or navigation tool is active, you can change the Opacity setting for a layer from the keyboard. Press a single number key to change the Opacity in 10-percent increments. That's 1 for 10 percent, 2 for 20 percent, up to 0 for 100 percent — in order along the top of your keyboard. If you have the urge to be more precise, press two keys in a row quickly to specify an exact two-digit Opacity value.

You also can change the opacity by dragging the Opacity slider in the Layers palette (see Figure 13-2). Click the arrowhead to the right of the Opacity value to display the slider bar, and then drag the triangle to change the value. Or press the up and down arrows to nudge the triangle along. Press Shift with the arrow key to nudge in 10-percent increments. Press Enter to confirm the slider setting. Press Escape to cancel and restore the previous setting.

For yet another opacity maneuver, double-click the layer name to open the Layer Style dialog box. At the top of this gargantuan dialog box, you find a standard Opacity slider. In the Advanced Blending section of the dialog box, you find the Fill Opacity slider, which adjusts the opacity of filled areas only — that is, any pixels not devoted to creating layer effects. You can vary the opacity of interior layer effects, such as an inner glow, along with the filled areas or leave those effects untouched as well. For more about these intriguing possibilities, visit the section "Applying Advanced Blending Options," later in this chapter.

The blend modes

Photoshop offers a total of 17 blend modes. Thanks to the diminished role of floating selections, two former blend modes, Behind and Clear, are now officially ex-modes. Once upon a time, Behind and Clear were quite useful for slipping floaters behind layers and cutting movable holes. But they became significantly more cumbersome in Version 4. Let us take a moment of silence to mourn their passing.

Note   Although the Behind and Clear modes are no longer available for layers, they are still available for use with the line and paint bucket tools and the Edit ⇨ Fill and Edit ⇨ Stroke commands. You must be working on a layer with the Lock Transparency check box turned off to use these modes.

Okay, enough of that. The remaining 17 modes — Normal through Luminosity — are still alive and well, so I suppose we should count our blessings. As you read through my upcoming discussions, you can check out examples of the blend modes both in the accompanying grayscale figures and in Color Plate 13-1. The grayscale figures show the results of compositing the two images shown in Figure 13-3. The thinker is on top; the sunset is on bottom. The color plate features a series of Saturns layered against the stormy gaseous planet of Jupiter. Although the planets aren't to scale — I understand that both bodies are several times larger than this book, for example — they do a fair job of showing the effects of Photoshop's modes.

Figure 13-3: To demonstrate the effects of Photoshop's blend modes, I composit the thinker (top) against a sunset background (bottom). In each case, the blend mode is applied to the thinker.

Tip

You can access every one of the blend modes from the keyboard by pressing Shift+Alt plus a letter, as long as the selected tool doesn't offer blend mode options. (If the tool does support blend modes, the shortcuts set the mode for the tool and not the layer.) In addition, the dodge, burn, and sponge tools now respond to some Shift+Alt shortcuts: With dodge and burn, Shift+Alt plus the S, M, or H key sets the tool range pop-up menu to Shadow, Midtones, or Highlights, respectively. And with the sponge tool, S sets the tool to saturate mode, and D changes the tool to desaturate mode.

Got all that? Good. Back to layer blend mode shortcuts. Some letters in the short-cuts make perfect sense—Shift+Alt+N for Normal, for example. Others are a bit of a stretch—such as Shift+Alt+I for Dissolve. Whether predictable or not, I list the letter in parentheses with each blend mode description.

Note

One more note: Every so often, I allude to a little something called a *composite pixel*. By this I mean the pixel color that results from all the mixing that's going on beneath the active layer. For example, your document may contain hoards of layers with all sorts of blend modes in effect, but as long as you work on, say, Layer 23, Photoshop treats the image formed by Layers 1 through 22 as if it were one flat-tened image filled with a bunch of static composite pixels.

Cool? Keen. So without any further notes and clarifications, here they are, the 17 blend modes, in order of appearance:

✦ **Normal (N):** In combination with an Opacity setting of 100 percent, this option displays every pixel in the active layer normally, regardless of the colors of the underlying image. When you use an Opacity of less than 100 percent, the color of each pixel in the active layer is averaged with the composite pixel in the layers behind it according to the Opacity value.

✦ **Dissolve (I):** This option specifically affects feathered or softened edges. If the active layer is entirely opaque with hard edges, this option has no effect. But when the edges of the layer are feathered, the Dissolve option randomizes the pixels along the edges. The first two images in Figure 13-4 compare a feathered layer subjected to the Normal and Dissolve modes. Dissolve also randomizes pixels when the Opacity value is set below 100 percent, as demon-strated in the final example in the figure.

✦ **Multiply (M):** To understand the Multiply and Screen modes, you have to use a little imagination. So here goes: Imagine that the active layer and the under-lying image are both photos on transparent slides. The Multiply mode pro-duces the same effect as holding those slides up to the light, one slide in front of the other. Because the light has to travel through two slides, the outcome is invariably a darker image that contains elements from both images. An exam-ple of the Multiply blend mode appears in Figure 13-5.

Normal feather   Dissolve feather   70% Dissolve

Figure 13-4: Here I applied Normal (left) and Dissolve (middle) to a layer with heavily feathered edges. The final example shows the effect of Dissolve when I reduce the Opacity value to 70 percent. (The superimposed characters indicate the keyboard shortcuts Shift+Alt+N for Normal, Shift+Alt+I for Dissolve, and 7 for 70 percent opacity.)

Figure 13-5: The Multiply blend mode produces the same effect as holding two overlapping transparencies up to the light. It always results in a darker image.

✦ **Screen (S):** Still have those transparent slides from the Multiply analogy? Well, place them both in separate projectors and point them at the same screen and you get the same effect as Screen. Rather than creating a darker image, as you do with Multiply, you create a lighter image, as demonstrated in Figure 13-6 and Color Plate 13-1.

You can use the Screen blend mode to emulate film that has been exposed multiple times. Ever seen Thomas Eakin's pioneering *Jumping Figure,* which shows rapid-fire exposures of a naked man jumping from one location to another? Each shot is effectively screened onto the other, lightening the film with each and every exposure. The photographer was smart enough to limit the exposure time so as not to overexpose the film; likewise, you should only apply Screen when working with images that are sufficiently dark so that you avoid overlightening.

Figure 13-6: The Screen mode produces the same effect as shining two projectors at the same screen. It always results in a lighter image.

✦ **Overlay (O), Soft Light (F), and Hard Light (H):** You just can't separate these guys. All three multiply the dark colors in the active layer and screen the light colors into the composite pixels in the layers below. But they apply their effects to different degrees. Overlay favors the composite pixels; Hard Light favors the layered pixels. (In fact, the two are direct opposites.) Soft Light is a washed-out version of Hard Light that results in a low-contrast effect.

The left-hand examples in Figure 13-7 show a blend mode applied individually to the thinking fellow. I then duplicated the thinker layer with the blend mode still in force to get the effects on the right. As these examples demonstrate, the modes effectively tattoo one image onto the image behind it. Even after multiple applications of the thinker layer, the sunset image still shows through as if the thinker were appliquéd on.

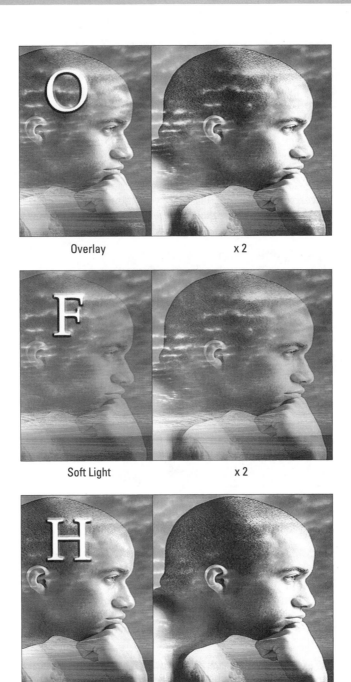

Figure 13-7: The results of the Overlay, Soft Light, and Hard Light blend modes as they appear when applied to a single version of the thinker layer (left) and a second thinker layer (right).

Tip

Start with the Overlay mode any time you want to mix both the active layer and the layers behind it to create a reciprocal blend. By a *reciprocal blend,* I mean a blend that mixes the colors evenly without eliminating any detail in either layer. After you apply Overlay, vary the Opacity to favor the composite pixels. I've said it before and I'll say it again: Overlay is Photoshop's most practical blend mode, the one you should always try first.

If you can't quite get the effect you want at lower Opacity settings, switch to the Soft Light mode and give that a try. On the other hand, if the Overlay mode at 100 percent seems too subtle, switch to Hard Light. You can even clone the layer to darn well emblazon the layer onto its background, as in the bottom-right image in Figure 13-7.

✦ **Color Dodge (D):** When you apply the Color Dodge mode, each color in the layer becomes a brightness-value multiplier. Light colors such as white produce the greatest effect, and black produces no effect. As a result, Color Dodge is Photoshop's most dramatic whitening agent, the equivalent of applying bleach to colored fabric. When applied to the thinker in Figure 13-8, Color Dodge exaggerates the sunset, resulting in a rougher effect than either Screen or the upcoming Lighten.

Figure 13-8: Color Dodge uses the active layer to bleach the pixels in the layer below. There is nothing subtle about this effect.

✦ **Color Burn (B):** If Color Dodge is bleach, then Color Burn is the charred surface of burnt toast. It uses the colors in the active layer to reduce brightness values, resulting in a radical darkening effect. Like Color Dodge, the Color Burn mode results in a radical, high-contrast effect, as shown in Figure 13-9. You may also want to sneak a peek at Color Plate 13-1, which illustrates how both Color Dodge and Color Burn sap the colors out of the active layer more surely than any other blend mode except Luminosity. If you want high-contrast stamping effects, these are the blend modes to use.

Figure 13-9: Color Burn sears an image charcoal black. No other darkening mode is this severe.

✦ **Darken (K):** When you select this option, Photoshop applies colors in the active layer only if they are darker than the corresponding pixels below. Keep in mind that Photoshop compares the brightness levels of pixels in a full-color image on a channel-by-channel basis. So although the red component of a pixel in the active layer may be darker than the red component of the underlying composite pixel, the green and blue components may be lighter. In this case, Photoshop would assign the red component but not the green or blue, thereby subtracting some red and making the pixel slightly more turquoise. Compare the predictable grayscale example in Figure 13-10 to its more challenging color counterpart in Color Plate 13-1.

✦ **Lighten (G):** If you select this option, Photoshop applies colors in the active layer only if they are lighter than the corresponding pixels in the underlying image. Again, Photoshop compares the brightness levels in all channels of a full-color image. Examples of the Lighten blend mode appear in Figure 13-11 and Color Plate 13-1.

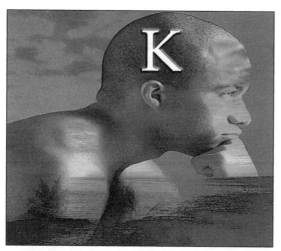

Figure 13-10: The same active layer subject to the Darken blend mode. Only those pixels in the thinker layer that are darker than the pixels in the underlying sunset remain visible.

Figure 13-11: Our friend the thinker subject to the Lighten blend mode. Only those pixels in the selection that are lighter than the pixels in the underlying sunset remain visible.

✦ **Difference (E) and Exclusion (X):** Difference inverts lower layers according to the brightness values in the active layer. White inverts the composite pixels absolutely, black inverts them not at all, and the other brightness values invert them to some degree in between. In the first example of Figure 13-12, the light sunset shows through the black pixels at the back of the thinker's head, while the light areas along the front of the man's face invert the sky and clouds.

Exclusion works just like Difference, except for one, er, difference. Shown in the second example of Figure 13-12, Exclusion sends medium-colored pixels to gray, creating a lower contrast effect, much as Soft Light is a low-contrast version of Hard Light.

Cross-Reference

One of my favorite uses for the Difference and Exclusion modes is to create a "Difference sandwich," in which you slide a filtered version of an image onto a layer between two originals. I explain this technique and others in the upcoming section "Sandwiching a filtered image."

✦ **Hue (U):** The Hue mode and the following three blend modes make use of the HSL color model to mix colors between the active layer and the underlying composite. When you select Hue, Photoshop retains the hue values from the active layer and mixes them with the saturation and luminosity values from the underlying image. An example of this mode appears in the right column of Color Plate 13-1.

Note

I don't include grayscale figures for the Hue, Saturation, Color, and Luminosity blend modes for the simple reason that these modes affect color images only. In fact, all four options are dimmed when you edit a grayscale document.

✦ **Saturation (T):** When you select this option, Photoshop retains the saturation values from the active layer and mixes them with the hue and luminosity values from the underlying image. This mode rarely results in anything but very subtle effects, as demonstrated by the bright orange Saturn in Color Plate 13-1. You'll usually want to apply it in combination with some other blend mode. For example, after applying a random blend mode to a layer, you might duplicate the layer and then apply the Saturation mode to either boost or downplay the colors, much like printing a gloss or matte coating over an image.

✦ **Color (C):** This option combines hue and saturation. Photoshop retains both the hue and saturation values from the active layer and mixes them with the luminosity values from the underlying image. Because the saturation portion of the Color mode has such a slight effect, Color frequently produces an almost identical effect to Hue. For example, the Hue and Color versions of Saturn in Color Plate 13-1 are very similar, with the former appearing only slightly less bright than the latter.

✦ **Luminosity (Y):** The Luminosity blend mode retains the lightness values from the active layer and mixes them with the hue and saturation values from the underlying image. An example of this mode appears in the lower-right corner in Color Plate 13-1. Here Saturn appears every bit as clearly defined as the Normal example in the upper-left corner, but it assumes the orange color of its Jupiterian background. So just as the Color mode uses the layer to colorize its background, the Luminosity mode uses the background to colorize the layer.

Difference

Exclusion

Figure 13-12: When you apply the Difference mode (top), white pixels invert the pixels beneath them; black pixels leave the background untouched. The Exclusion mode (bottom) performs a similar effect, but instead of inverting medium colors, it changes them to gray.

The best way to get a feel for blend modes is to give them a whirl. Just start whacking the Shift+Alt+key combos and see what you come up with. A handful of keys won't produce any effect. The beginning of the alphabet contains the mother lode of shortcuts. Of the first 15 letters (up through and including O), only A, J, and L go unused. That's B through O minus J and L, or BO – JL. The other good ones are S, T, U, X, and Y, which just happens to spell "Stuxy." Summing up, the magic formula is:

BO – JL + Stuxy

Remember that and you're golden.

Blend mode madness

Remember that scene in *Amadeus* where Mozart is telling the king about some obscure opera that he's writing — "Marriage of Franz Joseph Haydn" or something like that — and he's bragging about how many folks he has singing on stage at the same time? Remember that scene? Oh, you're not even trying. Anyway, you can do that same thing with Photoshop. Not with melody or recitative or anything like that, but with imagery. Just as Mozart might juggle several different melodies and harmonies at once, you can juggle layers upon layers of images, each filtered differently and mixed differently with the images below it.

Predicting the outcome of these monumental compositions takes a brain the magnitude of Mozart's. But screwing around with different settings takes no intelligence at all, which is where I come in.

The hierarchy of blend modes

The most direct method for juggling multiple images is "sandwiching." By this I mean placing a heavily filtered version of an image between two originals. This technique is based on the principal that most blend modes — all but Multiply, Screen, Difference, and Exclusion — change depending on which of two images is on top.

For example, Figure 13-13 shows two layers, A and B, and what happens when I blend them with the Overlay mode. When the leaf is on top, as in the third example, the Overlay mode favors the woman; but when the woman appears on the top layer, the Overlay mode favors the leaf.

| Layer A | Layer B | Overlay, B on A | Overlay, A on B |

Figure 13-13: After establishing two layers, woman and leaf, I placed the leaf on top and applied Overlay to get the third image. Then I switched the order of the layers and applied the Overlay mode to the woman to get the last image.

As I mentioned earlier, the Overlay mode always favors the lower layer. Its opposite, Hard Light, favors the active layer. Therefore, I could have achieved the exact effect shown in the third example of Figure 13-13 by placing the leaf underneath and setting the woman layer to Hard Light. Flip-flop the layers and apply Hard Light to the leaf to get the last example.

Other blend modes have opposites as well. Take the Normal mode, for example. When you apply Normal, whichever image is on top is the one that you see. However, if you change the Opacity, you reveal the underlying image. At 50 percent Opacity, it doesn't matter which image is on top. The color of every pair of pixels in both images is merely averaged. So an inverse relationship exists: If the filtered image is on top, an Opacity setting of 25 percent produces the same effect as if you reversed the order of the images and changed the Opacity to 75 percent.

The other obvious opposites are Color and Luminosity. If I were to position the green leaf in front of the woman and apply Color, the woman would turn green. The same thing would happen if I placed the woman in front and applied Luminosity.

The moral of this minutia is that the order in which you stack your layers is as important as the blend modes you apply. Even filters that have no stacking opposites — Soft Light, Color Dodge, Hue, and others — produce different effects depending on which layer is on top. Just for your general edification, Figure 13-14 and the possibly more enlightening Color Plate 13-2 show a few examples.

Sandwiching a filtered image

When you sandwich a filtered image between two originals — which, as you may recall, is what all this is leading up to — you can lessen the effect of the filter and achieve different effects than those I discussed in Chapter 11. Layers and blend modes give you the flexibility to experiment as much as you want and for as long as you please.

In Color Plate 13-3, I copied the woman's face to a new layer, and then I applied Filter ➪ Sketch ➪ Charcoal with the foreground color set to dark purple and the background color set to green. The top row of images in the color plate show what happened when I used three different blend modes — Hard Light, Color, and Difference — to mix the Charcoal image with the underlying original.

I next cloned the background layer and moved it above the Charcoal layer, so that the filtered image resided between two originals, creating a sandwich. The originals are the bread of the sandwich, and the Charcoal layer is the meat (or the eggplant, for you vegetarians). The bottom row demonstrates the effects of applying each of three blend modes to the top slice of bread, which interacts with the blend mode applied to the Charcoal meat shown above. For example, in the second column, I applied the Hard Light mode to the filtered image to achieve the top effect. Then I created the top layer and applied the Soft Light mode to get the bottom effect.

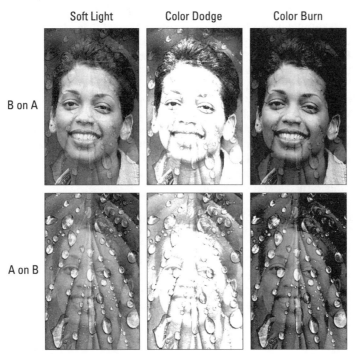

Figure 13-14: Examples of a few additional blend modes with the leaf on the front layer (top row) and the woman in front (bottom row).

Creating a Difference sandwich

Ask your local deli guy, and he'll tell you that everyone has a favorite sandwich. Where blend modes are concerned, my favorite is the Difference sandwich. By applying Difference to both the filtered layer and the cloned original on top, you effectively invert the filter into the original image, and then reinvert the image to create a more subtle and utterly unique effect.

Figure 13-15 and Color Plate 13-4 show a small sampling of the several thousand possible variations on the Difference sandwich theme. In the top rows of both figures, I've vigorously applied a series of standard filters — so vigorously, in fact, that I've pretty well ruined the image. But no fear. By stacking it on top of the original, cloning the original on top of it, and applying the Difference mode to both layers, you can restore much of the original image detail, as shown in the bottom examples of the two figures. (I corrected the colors of the images by adding an adjustment layer on top of the sandwich, but otherwise you see the effects in their raw form.)

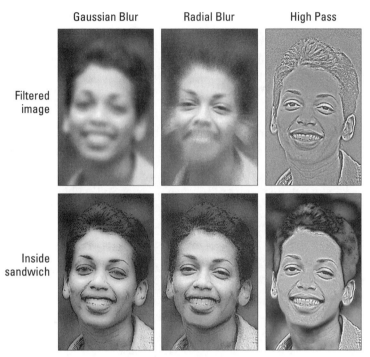

Gaussian Blur   Radial Blur   High Pass

Filtered
image

Inside
sandwich

Figure 13-15: Three different filtering effects as they appear on their own
(top row) and when inserted into a Difference sandwich (bottom row).

Note

A few notes about the Difference sandwich. First of all, the effect doesn't work
nearly so well if you start reducing the Opacity values. Second, try using the
Exclusion mode instead of Difference if you want to lower the contrast. And finally,
Difference is one of those few blend modes that produces the same effect regardless of how you order the layers. This means you can filter either the middle layer
or the bottom layer in the sandwich and get the same effect. But the top layer must
be the original image.

Applying Advanced Blending Options

Double-clicking a layer name in previous versions of Photoshop displayed the Layer
Properties dialog box, which included the same Opacity and blend mode pop-up
menu found in the Layers palette, plus options for changing the layer name and the
layer color displayed in the palette. Now, you must Alt-double-click to get the Layer
Properties dialog box, which contains only the name and layer color options.

A simple double-click on the background layer name in the Layers palette displays the New Layer dialog box, which you can use to turn the background layer into a regular layer, as discussed in Chapter 12. Double-clicking any other layer displays the Layer Style dialog box. This one dialog box holds controls for adding layer effects, changing the opacity and blend mode of a layer, and achieving some special blending tricks, such as blending the top layer in a multilayered image with the background layer instead of the layer immediately below.

By default, the Blending Options panel of the dialog box appears when you double-click the layer name, as shown in Figure 13-16. If you're working in some other area of the dialog box, click the Blending Options item at the top of the list on the left side of the dialog box. You can also display the blending options by choosing Blending Options from the Layers palette menu or the Layer ⇨ Layer Style submenu. If you're a fan of context-sensitive menus, right-click the layer name and choose Blending Options instead.

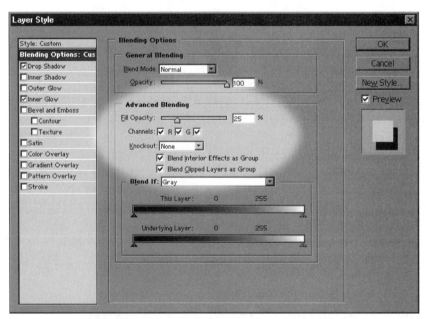

Figure 13-16: Using the Advanced Blending options, you can fade image pixels independent of layer effects, blend individual color channels, and more.

You already know how the two General Blending options, Blend Mode and Opacity, work; these are the same options found in the Layers palette (and discussed earlier in this chapter). The next few sections explain the Advanced Blending options, spotlighted in Figure 13-16. These features, like other aspects of blend modes, can be perplexing at first. But after you get the hang of them, they enable you to perform some pretty cool tricks that aren't possible with the standard Blend Mode and Opacity controls.

For details about all the layer styles listed on the left side of the dialog box, head for the next chapter.

Blending interior layer effects (or not)

You can choose to blend just the *filled area* of a layer — that is, everything but layer effects — or both the filled area and interior layer effects. By *interior effects,* I mean effects that appear within the boundaries of the filled areas, including the Inner Shadow, Inner Glow, Satin, and three Overlay effects. To blend these effects along with the filled areas, turn on the Blend Interior Effects as Group check box, as shown in Figure 13-16.

After you turn on the check box, Photoshop applies the selected blend mode to the interior layer effects as well as to the filled regions. Ditto for all the other blending options except the Opacity slider. That slider affects *all* pixels on the layer, regardless of the check box status or the position of effects with respect to the filled areas. If you want to alter the opacity of just the filled areas or filled areas and interior effects, use the Fill Opacity slider, spotlighted in Figure 3-16.

For an example of the different effects you can get using Fill Opacity, take a look at Figure 13-17. All four images contain two layers. The bottom layer consists of a pattern fill. On the second layer, I drew a medium gray rectangle. I added the solid, black drop shadow using the Drop Shadow option in the Layer Style dialog box; I created the white border using the Inner Glow option. I set the Opacity slider for the rectangle layer to 100 percent and blended it using the Normal mode.

The upper-right example shows the result of lowering the Opacity value to 25 percent. All pixels in the rectangle layer become equally translucent. In the lower-left example, I instead set the Opacity value at 100 percent and lowered the Fill Opacity value to 25 percent. I deselected the Blend Interior Effects as a Group check box, so neither the inner glow nor the drop shadow change. Only the filled pixels — in this case, the gray pixels in the rectangle — fade to 25 percent opacity.

For the lower-right example, I turned on the Blend Interior Effects as a Group check box. Now the glow fades by the same amount as the filled rectangle. But the drop shadow, because it lives outside the rectangle, remains at its original opacity.

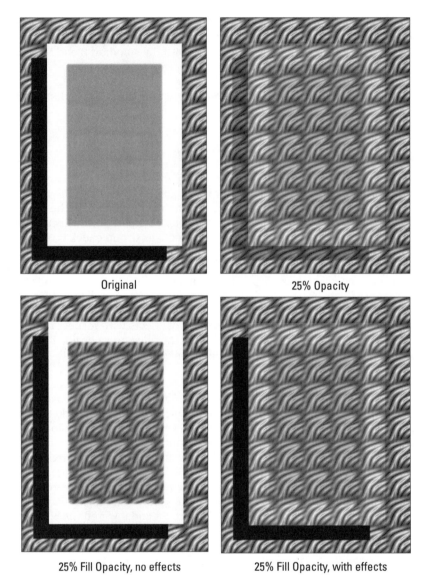

Original   25% Opacity

25% Fill Opacity, no effects   25% Fill Opacity, with effects

Figure 13-17: Here you see results achieved by blending the rectangle layer, which includes a white inner glow and black drop shadow, using different opacity controls.

Blending clipping groups

Just as you can control whether interior layer effects blend with filled areas of a layer, you can choose to blend the upper layers in a clipping group along with the base layer or leave them unchanged.

If you want all layers in the clipping group to blend as a unit, select the Blend Clipped Layers as Group check box (it's at the bottom of the spotlighted area in Figure 13-16). If you selected different blend modes for the individual layers in the clipping group, Photoshop uses the mode applied to the base layer for all layers.

To adjust blending of the base layer only, deselect the check box. Now all blending options except the Opacity slider have no impact on any layer in the clipping group except the base layer.

Blending individual color channels

Directly underneath the Fill Opacity slider, the Channels check boxes enable you to blend color channels independently of each other. (When you're working on a grayscale image, this option is unavailable because the image has only one channel.) For some examples of the creative possibilities afforded by the Channels feature, see Color Plate 13-5.

Knocking out layers

The Knockout pop-up menu is another of the blending options new to Photoshop 6. It turns the contents of the active layer into a floating hole that can bore through one or more layers. You specify how deep the hole goes using the Knockout option; use Opacity and blend mode options to define the translucency of the hole.

Select a Knockout option depending on what layers you want to blend together:

✦ **None** blends normally. The layer is treated as a standard layer, not a hole.

✦ **Shallow** cuts a hole through a layer set to expose the layer immediately below the layer set. In a clipping group, Shallow burrows down to the base layer of the group.

✦ **Deep** cuts all the way down to the Background layer. An exception arises when you're working with a layer in a clipping group. In that case, Deep blends the layer with the base of the clipping group, just like Shallow.

Figure 13-18 shows examples of each of these options. In all the examples, the top layer contains black text, to which I applied the Outer Glow and Bevel and Emboss layer effects. The next layer down holds an umbrella and a few associated layer effects. I grouped these two layers into a layer set, as shown in the Layers palette in the figure. The clouds occupy the layer immediately below the layer set. The background layer contains a gradient created with the new noise-gradient feature (see Chapter 6).

In the upper-left example, I set the Knockout option to None for all layers. I used the Normal blend mode and set the Opacity value and Fill Opacity value to 100 percent throughout. With this setup, each layer blends normally with the one below.

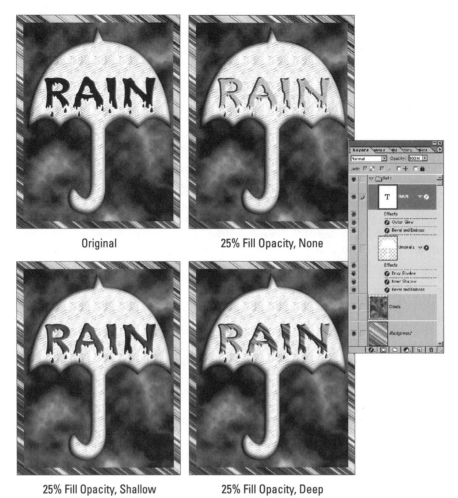

Original   25% Fill Opacity, None

25% Fill Opacity, Shallow   25% Fill Opacity, Deep

Figure 13-18: Here you see how the original image (top left) appears after I lowered the opacity of the text layer to 25 percent and then applied each of the three Knockout options.

To create the top-right image, I lowered the Fill Opacity value for the text layer to 25 percent and left the Knockout setting at None. You see the pattern of the umbrella through the faded text, as you would expect. The effects (Outer Glow and Bevel and Emboss) remain unchanged because they lie beyond the bounds of the filled portion of the layer and thus don't respond to the Fill Opacity slider.

For the bottom-left example, I left the Fill Opacity at 25 percent but set the Knockout option to Shallow. Now the text interior blends with the cloud layer, which is the layer immediately beneath the layer set that contains the text. For the final example, I selected Deep from the Knockout pop-up menu, blending the text interior with background layer and creating the nuclear rain environmentalists have worried about for years.

Knocking out by brightness value

The Blend If sliders, found at the bottom of the Blending Options panel of the Layer Style dialog box, enable you to drop out pixels in the active layer and force through pixels from lower layers according to their brightness values.

When you use the sliders, Photoshop applies your changes taking the Knockout option into account. For example, if you set the Knockout option to Deep, you force through pixels from the Background layer instead of from the layer immediately below the selected layer.

Select a color channel from the Blend If pop-up menu to apply the effects of the slider bars beneath the menu to one color channel independently of the others. Each time you select a different Blend If option, the slider triangles change to the positions at which you last set them for that color channel.

Select a color channel from the Blend If pop-up menu to apply the effects of the slider bars according to the contents of a single color channel. Choose Gray to base the changes on the grayscale composite. Each time you select a different Blend If option, the slider triangles change to the positions at which you last set them for that color channel. Regardless of how you set the sliders, Photoshop applies your changes evenly to all channels in the image; the selected channel is merely used for the calculation.

You can select any channel regardless of the settings of the Channels check boxes. For example, if you select Red from the pop-up menu, Photoshop applies the Blend If values according to the contents of the red channel even if you deselect the Red check box. In other words, the contents of the red channel are used to calculate how the green and blue channels in the layer merge with the rest of the image.

> ✦ **This Layer:** This slider bar lets you exclude ranges of colors according to brightness values in the active layer. When you exclude colors by dragging the black triangle to the right or the white triangle to the left, the colors disappear from view.
>
> ✦ **Underlying Layer:** This slider forces colors from the underlying layers to poke through the active layer. Any colors not included in the range set by the black and white triangles cannot be covered and are therefore visible regardless of the colors in the active layer.
>
> ✦ **Preview:** Select the Preview check box to continually update the image window every time you adjust a setting.

The slider bars are far too complicated to fully explain in a bulleted list. To find out more about these options, read the following sections.

Color exclusion sliders

The first slider bar, This Layer, hides pixels in the active layer according to their brightness values. You can abandon dark pixels by dragging the left slider triangle, and abandon light pixels by dragging the right slider triangle. Figure 13-19 shows examples of each.

✦ To create the first example, I first set the blend mode to Screen. Then I dragged the left slider bar until the value immediately to the right of the *This Layer* label read 170, thereby hiding all pixels whose brightness values were 170 or lower.

✦ To create the second example, I changed the blend mode to Multiply. I reset the left slider triangle to 0 and dragged the right slider triangle to 120, which hid those pixels with brightness values of 120 or higher.

Screen, This Layer: 170, 255

Multiply, This Layer: 0, 120

Figure 13-19: Two examples of modifying the blend mode and This Layer settings inside the Layer Style dialog box.

Drag the triangles along the Underlying Layer slider bar to force pixels in the underlying layers to show through, again according to their brightness values. To force dark pixels in the underlying image to show through, drag the left slider triangle; to force light pixels to show through, drag the right slider triangle.

Here's how I achieved the effects in Figure 13-20:

✦ To achieve the effect in the top example in Figure 13-20, I started off by applying the Hard Light mode. (Those blend modes, they're keepers.) Then I dragged the left slider triangle until the first Underlying Layer value read 140. This forced the pixels in the sunset that had brightness values of 140 or lower to show through.

✦ In the second example, I changed the blend mode to Overlay. Then I dragged the right Underlying Layer slider triangle to 150, uncovering pixels at the bright end of the spectrum.

Hard Light, Underlying Layer: 140, 255

Overlay, Underlying Layer: 0, 150

Figure 13-20: Here I changed the Underlying Layer slider bar settings to force through the darkest (top) and lightest (bottom) pixels in the sunset.

Bear in mind, every single adjustment made inside the Layer Style dialog box is temporary. The slider bars hide pixels; they don't delete them. As long as the layer remains intact, you can revisit the Layer Style dialog box and restore hidden pixels or hide new ones.

Fuzziness

The problem with hiding and forcing colors with the slider bars is that you achieve some pretty harsh color transitions. Both Figures 13-19 and 13-20 bear witness to this fact. Talk about your jagged edges! Luckily, you can soften the color transitions by abandoning and forcing pixels gradually over a fuzziness range, which works much like the Fuzziness value in the Color range dialog box, leaving some pixels opaque and tapering others off into transparency.

To taper the opacity of pixels in either the active layer or the underlying image, Alt-drag one of the triangles in the appropriate slider bar. The triangle splits into two halves, and the corresponding value above the slider bar splits into two values separated by a slash, as demonstrated in Figure 13-21.

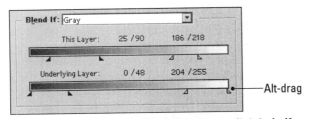

Figure 13-21: Alt-drag a slider triangle to split it in half. You can then specify a range across which brightness values fade into transparency.

The left triangle half represents the beginning of the fuzziness range — that is, the brightness values at which the pixels begin to fade into or away from view. The right half represents the end of the range — that is, the point at which the pixels are fully visible or invisible.

Figure 13-22 shows some fuzziness applied to the This Layer slider. Here are the specifics:

✦ In the top example, I set the blend mode to Multiply. I left the first This Layer triangle set to 0. I Alt-dragged the second triangle to split it. And I moved the left half of the split triangle to 55 and the right half to 128. The result is a gradual drop off. All pixels with brightness values of 0 to 55 are opaque, the pixels become gradually more translucent from 56 to 127, and pixels brighter than 128 are transparent.

✦ Next, I duplicated my layer and switched the blend mode to Screen. After splitting the first slider triangle with an Alt-drag, I set one half of the triangle to 128 and the other to 220. I dragged both halves of the second This Layer triangle back to 255. The darkest pixels are transparent, they fade into view from 129 to 219, and they become opaque from 220 on up. As shown in the bottom example in Figure 13-22, the result is a perfect blending of Multiply and Screen, with the sunset showing through in the gray areas.

Multiply, This Layer: 0, 55/128

Duplicate layer, Screen, This Layer: 128/220, 255

Figure 13-22: By Alt-dragging a This Layer slider triangle, you can create gradual transitions between the opaque and transparent portions of a layer.

Using the Underlying Layer slider is a bit trickier. It typically works best when you're trying to force through very bright or dark details, such as the highlights in the sunset sky and the shadows in the water. It also helps to work with a foreground layer that has lots of flat areas of color for the background to show through. Here's what I did to create Figure 13-23:

✦ For starters, I applied Filter ➪ Other ➪ High Pass to my thinker layer, as in the first example of Figure 13-23. This created lots of gray areas for the underlying pixels to shine through.

✦ I applied the radical Color Dodge mode to this layer. I left the first Underlying Layer triangle at 0. Then I split the second one and moved the left half to 80 and the right half to 200. This forced through the darkest pixels, fading them out as they got lighter.

✦ Next, I duplicated the layer, applied the Color Burn mode, and fiddled with the Underlying Layer triangles until the values read 100/150 and 180/255. The result is a vibrant composition that nicely sets off the thinker's tattoos.

Using Channel Operation Commands

Image ➪ Apply Image and Image ➪ Calculations provide access to Photoshop's *channel operations,* which composite one or more channels with others according to predefined mathematical calculations. Although once hailed as Photoshop's most powerful capabilities, channel operations have been eclipsed by the standard and more accessible functions available from the Layers and Channels palettes. One day, I suspect Adobe will scrap Apply Image and Calculations altogether. But until that day, I will dutifully document them both.

The Apply Image and Calculations commands allow you to merge one or two identically sized images using 12 of the 17 blend modes discussed earlier plus 2 additional modes, Add and Subtract. In a nutshell, the commands duplicate the process of dragging and dropping one image onto another (or cloning an image onto a new layer) and then using the blend mode and the Opacity settings in the Layers palette to mix the two images together.

Although Apply Image and Calculations are more similar than different, each command fulfills a specific — if not entirely unique — function:

✦ **Apply Image:** This command takes an open image and merges it with the foreground image (or takes the foreground image and composites it onto itself). You can apply the command to either the full-color image or one or more of the individual channels.

✦ **Calculations:** The Calculations command works on individual channels only. It takes a channel from one image, mixes it with a channel from another (or the same) image, and puts the result inside an open image or in a new image window.

High Pass filter

Color Dodge, Underlying Layer: 0, 80/200

Duplicate layer, Color Burn, Underlying Layer: 100/150, 180/255

Figure 13-23: After combining a High Pass effect with the radical Color Dodge and Color Burn blend modes, I used the Underlying Layer slider bar to force through pixels from the background so that the sunset and ocean didn't get lost.

The primary advantage of these commands over other, more straightforward compositing methods is that they allow you to access and composite the contents of individual color channels without a lot of selecting, copying and pasting, cloning, floating, and layering. You also get two extra blend modes, Add and Subtract, which may prove useful on a rainy day.

The Apply Image and Calculations commands provide previewing options, so you can see how an effect will look in the image window. But thanks to the sheer quantity of unfriendly options offered by the two commands, I suggest that you use them on only an occasional basis. The Calculations command can be a handy way to combine masks and layer transparencies to create precise selection outlines. Apply Image is good for compositing images in different color models, such as RGB and Lab (as I explain in the "Mixing images in different color modes" section later in this chapter).

But if your time is limited and you want to concentrate your efforts on learning Photoshop's most essential features, feel free to skip Apply Image and Calculations. I assure you, you won't be missing much.

The Apply Image command

Channel operations work by taking one or more channels from an image, called the *source,* and duplicating them to another image, called the *target.* When you use the Apply Image command, the foreground image is always the target, and you can select only one source image. Photoshop then takes the source and target, mixes them together, and puts the result in the target image. Therefore, the target image is the only image that the command actually changes. The source image remains unaffected.

When you choose Image ⇨ Apply Image, Photoshop displays the dialog box shown in Figure 13-24. Notice that you can select from a pop-up menu of images to specify the Source, but the Target item—listed just above the Blending box—is fixed. This is the active layer in the foreground image.

If this sounds a little dense, think of it this way: The source image is the floating selection and the target is the underlying original. Meanwhile, the Blending options are the blend modes pop-up menu and the Opacity value in the Layers palette.

Using the Apply Image command is a five-step process. You can always simply choose the command and hope for the best, but you'll get the most use out of it if you do the following.

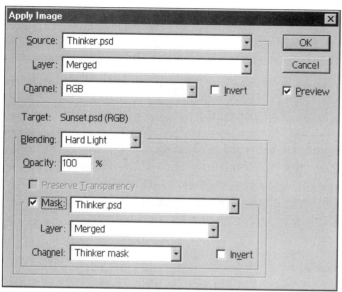

Figure 13-24: The Apply Image command lets you mix one source image with a target image and make the result the new target.

STEPS: Applying the Apply Image Command

1. **Open the two images that you want to mix.** If you want to mix the image with itself to create some effect, just open the one image.

2. **Make sure that the two images are exactly the same size, down to the last pixel.** Use the crop tool and Image Size command as necessary. (You don't have to worry about this step when mixing an image with itself.)

3. **Inside the target image, switch to the channel and layer that you want to edit.** If you want to edit all channels, press Ctrl+tilde (~) to remain in the composite view.

   Tip

   Even when you're editing a single channel, display all channels on-screen. For example, after pressing Ctrl+1 to switch to the red channel, click in front of the RGB item in the Channels palette to display the eyeball icon and show all channels. Only one channel is active, but all are visible. This way, you can see how your edits inside the Apply Image dialog box affect the entire image, not just the one channel.

4. **Select the portion of the target image that you want to edit.** If you want to affect the entire image, don't select anything.

5. **Choose Image ⇨ Apply Image and have at it.**

Obviously, that last step is a little more difficult than it sounds. That's why the following list explains how all those options in the Apply Image dialog box work:

✦ **Source:** The Source pop-up menu contains the name of the foreground image as well as any other images that are both open and exactly the same size as the foreground image. If the image you want to merge is not available, you must not have been paying much attention to Step 2. Press Escape to cancel, resize and crop as needed, choose Image ⇨ Apply Image, and try again.

✦ **Layer:** This pop-up menu lists all layers in the selected source image. If the image doesn't have any layers, Background is your only option. Otherwise, select the layer that contains the prospective source image. Select Merged to mix all visible layers in the source image with the target image.

✦ **Channel:** Select the channels that you want to mix from this pop-up menu. Both composite views and individual color and mask channels are included. Keep in mind that you'll be mixing these channels with the channels that you made available in the target image before choosing the command.

For example, if the target image is an RGB image shown in the full-color composite view, and you choose RGB from the Channel pop-up menu in the Apply Image dialog box, Photoshop mixes the red, green, and blue channels in the source image with the corresponding red, green, and blue channels in the target image. However, if you switched to the red channel before choosing Apply Image and then selected the RGB option, the program mixes a composite grayscale version of the RGB source image with the red channel in the target and leaves the other target channels unaffected.

✦ **Selection, Transparency, and Layer Mask:** If a portion of the source image is selected, the Channel pop-up menu offers a Selection option, which lets you apply the selection outline as if it were a grayscale image, just like a selection viewed in the quick mask mode. If you selected a specific layer from the Layer pop-up menu, you'll find a Transparency option that represents the transparency mask. If the layer includes its own layer mask, a Layer Mask option also appears.

None of the three options is particularly useful when you work in the composite view of the target image; you'll usually want to apply the Selection, Transparency, or Layer Mask option only to a single channel, as described in "The Calculations command" section toward the end of this chapter. (For an exception, see the upcoming tip.)

✦ **Invert:** Select this check box to invert the contents of the source image before compositing it with the target image. This option permits you to experiment with different effects. The lower-left example in Color Plate 13-6, for example, shows one use for the Invert check box. I inverted the *b* channel before compositing it with the RGB image to create an early dawn effect.

✦ **Target:** You can't change this item. It merely shows which image, which channels, and which layers are being affected by the command.

✦ **Blending:** This pop-up menu offers access to 12 of the blend modes I discussed in "The remaining 17 blend modes" section earlier in this chapter. The Dissolve, Hue, Saturation, Color, and Luminosity options are missing. Two additional options, Add and Subtract, are discussed in the "Add and Subtract" section later in this chapter.

✦ **Opacity:** I gather you're well aware of how this one works.

✦ **Preserve Transparency:** When you're editing a layer in the target image — that is, you activated a specific layer before choosing Image ⇨ Apply Image — the Preserve Transparency check box becomes available. Select it to protect transparent portions of the layer from any compositing, much as if the transparent portions were not selected and are therefore masked.

✦ **Mask:** Select this option to mask off a portion of the source image. I already mentioned that you can specify the exact portion of the target image you want to edit by selecting that portion before choosing the Apply Image command. But you can also control which portion of the source image is composited on top of the target through the use of a mask. When you select the Mask check box, three new pop-up menus and an Invert check box appear at the bottom of the Apply Image dialog box. For complete information on these options, see the upcoming "Compositing with a mask" section.

Mixing images in different color modes

Tip

Throughout my laborious explanations of all those options in the Apply Image dialog box, I've been eagerly waiting to share with you the command's one truly unique capability. Image ⇨ Apply Image is the only way to composite images in different color modes without setting the modes to match. For example, you could mix the lightness channel from a Lab image with each of the channels from an RGB image, or mix the green channel from an RGB image with each of the channels in a CMYK image. By contrast, if you were to simply drag and drop a Lab image into an RGB image, Photoshop would automatically convert the image to the RGB color space, which would result in a very different effect.

To help make things a little more clear, Color Plate 13-6 shows four examples of an image composited onto itself using the Hard Light blend mode. The first example shows the result of selecting the RGB image as both source and target. As always, this exaggerates the colors in the image and enhances contrast but retains the same basic color composition as before.

The other examples in the color plate show what happened when I duplicated the image by choosing Image ⇨ Duplicate, converted the duplicate to the Lab mode (Image ⇨ Mode ⇨ Lab Color), and then composited the Lab and RGB images together. To do this, I switched to the RGB image, chose Image ⇨ Apply Image, and selected the Lab image from the Source pop-up menu. In the top-right example, I chose Lightness from the Channel pop-up menu, which mixed the lightness channel with all three RGB channels. And in the bottom-left image, I chose *b* from the Channel pop-up menu and selected the Invert check box, which inverted the *b* channel before applying it. For the final, moderately psychedelic effect in Color Plate 13-6, I used the Lab image as the destination. I switched to the Lab image, chose the Apply Image command, selected the RGB image as the Source, and selected Blue from the Channel pop-up menu.

Compositing with a mask

The Mask option in the Apply Image dialog box provides a method for you to import only a selected portion of the source image into the target image. Select the Mask check box and choose the image that contains the mask from the pop-up menu on the immediate right. As with the Source pop-up menu, the Mask menu lists only those images that are open and happen to be the exact same size as the target image. If necessary, select the layer on which the mask appears from the Layer pop-up menu. Then select the specific mask channel from the final pop-up menu. This doesn't have to be a mask channel; you can use any color channel as a mask.

After you select all the necessary options, the mask works like so: Where the mask is white, the source image shows through and mixes in with the target image, just as if it were a selected portion of the floating image. Where the mask is black, the source image is absent. Gray values in the mask mix the source and target with progressive emphasis on the target as the grays darken.

If you prefer to swap the masked and unmasked areas of the source image, select the Invert check box at the bottom of the dialog box. Now, where the mask is black, you see the source image; where the mask is white, you don't.

The first example in Color Plate 13-7 shows a mask viewed as a rubylith overlay with the image. To make the mask, I selected the background with the Color Range command, inversed the selection, and saved the result as a separate channel. In the other examples in the color plate, I again composited the RGB and Lab versions of the image—as in the previous section—using Photoshop's most outrageous blend modes. No matter how dramatically the Apply Image command affected the thinker, his background remained unscathed, thanks to the mask. If the Mask option had not been turned on, the background would have changed with the mode, turning light blue for Color Dodge, black for Color Burn, and deep red for Difference.

Tip

You can even use a selection outline or layer as a mask. If you select some portion of the source image before switching to the target image and choosing Image ⇨ Apply Image, you can access the selection by choosing Selection from the Channel pop-up menu at the very bottom of the dialog box. Those pixels from the source image that fall inside the selection remain visible; those that do not are transparent. Use the Invert check box to inverse the selection outline. To use the boundaries of a layer selected from the Layer pop-up menu as a mask, choose the Transparency option from the Channel menu. Where the layer is opaque, the source image is opaque (assuming that the Opacity option is set to 100 percent, of course); where the layer is transparent, so too is the source image.

Add and Subtract

The Add and Subtract blend modes found in the Apply Image dialog box (and also in the Calculations dialog box) work a bit like the Custom filter that I discuss in Chapter A on the CD-ROM that accompanies this book. However, instead of multiplying brightness values by matrix numbers and calculating a sum, as the Custom filter does, these modes add and subtract the brightness values of pixels in different channels.

The Add option adds the brightness value of each pixel in the source image to that of its corresponding pixel in the target image. The Subtract option takes the brightness value of each pixel in the target image and subtracts the brightness value of its corresponding pixel in the source image. When you select either Add or Subtract, the Apply Image dialog box offers two additional option boxes, Scale and Offset. Photoshop divides the sum or difference of the Add or Subtract mode, respectively, by the Scale value (from 1.000 to 2.000), and then adds the Offset value (from negative to positive 255).

If equations help, here's the equation for the Add blend mode:

Resulting brightness value = (Target + Source) ÷ Scale + Offset

And here's the equation for the Subtract mode:

Resulting brightness value = (Target − Source) ÷ Scale + Offset

If equations only confuse you, just remember this: The Add option results in a destination image that is lighter than either source; the Subtract option results in a destination image that is darker than either source. If you want to darken the image further, raise the Scale value. To darken each pixel in the target image by a constant amount, which is useful when applying the Add option, enter a negative Offset value. If you want to lighten each pixel, as when applying the Subtract option, enter a positive Offset value.

Applying the Add command

The best way to demonstrate how these commands work is to offer an example. To create the effects shown in Figures 13-25 and 13-26, I began with the thinker and sunset shown way back in Figure 13-3.

After switching to the Sunset image and choosing Image ⇨ Apply Image, I selected the Thinker image from the Source pop-up menu. (I happened to be working with flat, grayscale images, so I didn't have to worry about the Layer and Channel options.) I selected the Add option from the Blending pop-up menu and accepted the default Scale and Offset values of 1 and 0, respectively, to achieve the first example in Figure 13-25. The thinker went blindingly white, much lighter than he would under any other blend mode, even Color Dodge. To improve the quality and detail of the image,

I changed the Scale value to 1.2 to slightly downplay the brightness values and entered an Offset value of –60 to darken the colors uniformly. The result of this operation is the more satisfactory image shown in the second example of the figure.

Add, Scale: 1, Offset: 0

Add, Scale: 1.2, Offset: -60

Figure 13-25: Two applications of the Add blend mode from the Apply Image command, each subject to different Scale and Offset values.

Applying the Subtract command

To create the first example in Figure 13-26, I selected the Subtract option from the Blending pop-up menu, once again accepting the default Scale and Offset values of 1 and 0, respectively. This time, the thinker turned pitch black because I subtracted the light values of his face from the light values in the sky, leaving no brightness value at all. Meanwhile, the thinker's hair had virtually no effect on the sunset because the hair pixels were very dark and in some cases black. Subtracting black from a color is like subtracting 0 from a number — it leaves the value unchanged.

Subtract, Scale: 1, Offset: 0

Subtract, Scale: 1.2, Offset: 180

Figure 13-26: Two applications of the Subtract command on the images from Figure 13-25, one subject to Scale and Offset values of 1 and 0 (top) and the other subject to values of 1.2 and 180 (bottom).

The result struck me as too dark, so I lightened it by raising the Scale and Offset values. To create the second image in Figure 13-26, I upped the Scale value to 1.2, just as in the second Add example, which actually darkened the image slightly. Then I raised the Offset value to 180, thus adding 180 points of brightness value to each pixel. This second image is more likely to survive reproduction with all detail intact.

The Calculations command

Although its options are nearly identical, the Calculations command performs a slightly different function than Apply Image. Rather than compositing a source image on top of the current target image, Image ⇨ Calculations combines two source channels and puts the result in a target channel. You can use a single image for both sources, a source and the target, or all three (both sources and the target). The target doesn't have to be the foreground image (although Photoshop previews the effect in the foreground image window). And the target can even be a new image. But the biggest difference is that instead of affecting entire full-color images, the Calculations command affects individual color channels only. Only one channel changes as a result of this command.

Choosing Image ➪ Calculations displays the dialog box shown in Figure 13-27. Rather than explaining this dialog box option by option—I'd just end up wasting 35 pages and repeating myself every other sentence—I attack the topic in a less structured but more expedient fashion.

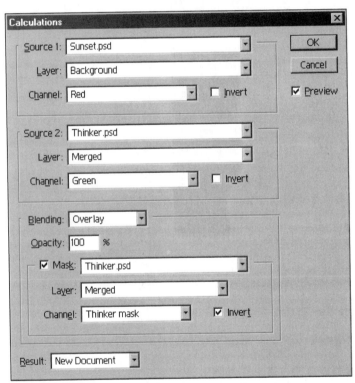

Figure 13-27: Use the Calculations command to mix two source channels and place them inside a new or an existing target channel.

When you arrive inside the dialog box, you select your source images from the Source 1 and Source 2 pop-up menus. As with Apply Image, the images have to be exactly the same size. You can composite individual layers using the Layer menus.

Select the channels you want to mix together from the Channel options. In place of the full-color options — RGB, Lab, CMYK — each Channel menu offers a Gray option, which represents the grayscale composite of all channels in an image.

The Blending pop-up menu offers the same 14 blend modes — including Add and Subtract — found in the Apply Image dialog box. However, it's important to keep in mind how the Calculations dialog box organizes the source images when working with blend modes. The Source 1 image is equivalent to the source when using the Apply Image command (or the floating selection when compositing conventionally); the Source 2 image is equivalent to the target (or the underlying original). Therefore, choosing the Normal blend mode displays the Source 1 image. The Subtract command subtracts the Source 1 image from the Source 2 image.

Half of the blend modes perform identically regardless of which of the two images is Source 1 and which is Source 2. The other half — including Normal, Overlay, Soft Light, and Hard Light — produce different results based on the image you assign to each spot. But as long as you keep in mind that Source 1 is the floater — hey, it's at the top of the dialog box, right? — you should be okay.

Tip

The only mode that throws me off is Subtract, because I see Source 1 at the top of the dialog box and naturally assume that Photoshop subtracts Source 2, which is underneath it. Unfortunately, this is exactly opposite to the way it really works. If you find yourself similarly confused and set up the equation backwards, you can reverse it by selecting both Invert options. Source 2 minus Source 1 results in the same effect as an inverted Source 1 minus an inverted Source 2. After all, the equation $(255 - Source 1) - (255 - Source 2)$, which represents an inverted Source 1 minus an inverted Source 2, simplifies down to *Source 2 – Source 1*. If math isn't your strong point, don't worry. I was just showing my work.

As you can in the Apply Image dialog box, you can specify a mask using the Mask options in the Calculations dialog box. The difference here is that the mask applies to the first source image and protects the second one. So where the mask is white, the two sources mix together normally. Where the mask is black, you see the second source image only.

The Result option determines the target for the composited channels. If you select New Document from the Result pop-up menu, as in Figure 13-27, Photoshop creates a new grayscale image. Alternatively, you can stick the result of the composited channels in any channel inside any image that is the same size as the source images.

Combining masks

As described for the Apply Image command, the Channel pop-up menus may offer Selection, Transparency, and Layer Mask as options. But here they have more purpose. You can composite layer masks to form selection outlines, selection outlines to form masks, and all sorts of other pragmatic combinations.

Figure 13-28 shows how the Calculations command sees selected areas. Whether you're working with masks, selection outlines, transparency masks, or layer masks, the Calculations command sees the area as a grayscale image. So in Figure 13-28, the white areas are selected or opaque, and the black areas are deselected or transparent.

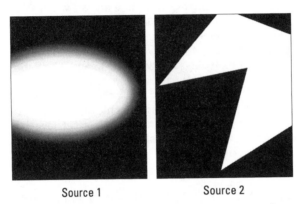

Source 1   Source 2

Figure 13-28: Two selections expressed as grayscale images (a.k.a. masks). The left image is the first source, and the right image is the second.

Assuming that I've chosen Image ⇨ Calculations and selected the images using the Source 1 and Source 2 options, the only remaining step is to select the proper blend mode from the Blending pop-up menu. Screen, Multiply, and Difference are the best solutions. The top row in Figure 13-29 shows the common methods for combining selection outlines. In the first example, I added the two together using the Screen mode, just as in the preceding steps. In fact, screening masks and adding selection outlines are equivalents. To subtract the Source 1 selection from Source 2, I inverted the former (by selecting the Invert check box in the Source 1 area) and applied the Multiply blend mode. To find the intersection of the two masks, I simply applied Multiply without inverting.

The Calculations command doesn't stop at the standard three — add, subtract, and intersect. The bottom row of Figure 13-29 shows three methods of combining selection outlines that are not possible using keyboard shortcuts. For example, if I invert the Source 1 mask and combine it with the Screen mode, I add the inverse of the elliptical selection and add it to the polygonal one. The Difference mode adds the portion of the elliptical selection that doesn't intersect the polygonal one and subtracts the intersection. And inverting Source 1 and then applying Difference retains the intersection, subtracts the portion of the polygonal selection that is not intersected, and inverts the elliptical selection where it does not intersect. These may not be options you use every day, but they are extremely powerful if you can manage to wrap your brain around them.

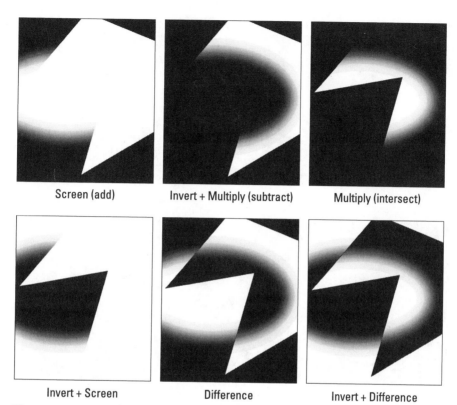

Screen (add)   Invert + Multiply (subtract)   Multiply (intersect)

Invert + Screen   Difference   Invert + Difference

Figure 13-29: I combined the masks shown in Figure 13-28 in traditional (top row) and nontraditional (bottom row) ways using the Calculations command.

Depending on how well you've been keeping up with this discussion, you may be asking yourself, "Why not apply Lighten or Add in place of Screen, or Darken or Subtract in place of Multiply?" The reason becomes evident when you combine two soft selections. Suppose that I blurred the Source 2 mask to give it a feathered edge. Figure 13-30 shows the results of combining the newly blurred polygonal mask with the elliptical mask using a series of blend modes. In the top row, I added the two selection outlines together using the Lighten, Add, and Screen modes. Lighten results in harsh corner transitions, and Add cuts off the interior edges. Only Screen does it just right. The bottom row of the figure shows the results of subtracting the elliptical mask from the polygonal one by applying Darken, Subtract, and Multiply, and occasionally inverting the elliptical mask. Again, Darken results in sharp corners. The Subtract mode eliminates the need to invert the elliptical marquee, but it brings the black area too far into the blurred edges, resulting in an overly abrupt interior cusp. Multiply ensures that all transitions remain smooth as silk.

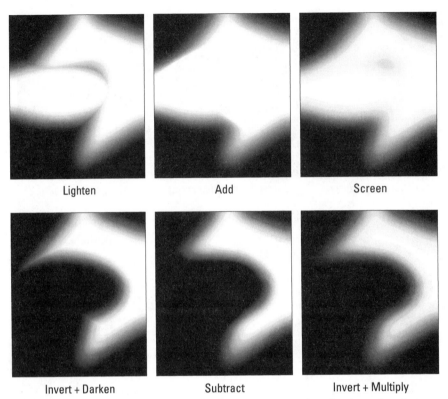

Lighten	Add	Screen
Invert + Darken	Subtract	Invert + Multiply

Figure 13-30: When adding softened selections (top row) and subtracting them (bottom row), the Screen and Multiply modes provide the most even and continuous transitions.

The reason for the success of the Screen and Multiply modes is that they mix colors together. Lighten and Darken simply settle on the color of one source image or the other — no mixing occurs — hence the harsh transitions. Add and Subtract rely on overly simplistic arithmetic equations — as I explained earlier, they really just add and subtract brightness values — which result in steep fall-off and build-up rates; in other words, there are cliffs of color transition where there ought to be rolling hills. Both Screen and Multiply soften the transitions using variations on color averaging that makes colors incrementally lighter or darker.

✦   ✦   ✦

Shapes and Styles

Some Stuff We Never Ordered

When a product manager touts her company's newest upgrade as "a direct response to user feedback," you know not to get your hopes up. Either the previous version was in such awful shape that users were jamming the technical support lines screaming for changes. Or the developers were running so behind their deadlines that they were forced to bag the exciting features and devote what little time remained to tweaking the existing stuff. For as every software developer knows, if you're looking for bold new initiatives, don't look to the users. We who use these programs day in and day out have an amazing knack for suggesting the obvious and the banal.

Don't believe me? For the past few years, the most commonly voiced request from Photoshop users has had nothing to do with layers, color matching, masking, dynamic effects, history, text warping, memory management, or any of the other hundred or so major capabilities that set Photoshop apart from its competitors. Instead, the number one request is — hold onto those hats — CMYK support for the old Gallery Effects filters. Covered in the "Effects filters" section of Chapter 10, the commands in the Filter ⇨ Artistic, Brush Strokes, Sketch, and Texture submenus function only when editing RGB images. Users, it seems, want that to change.

The problem is, it's an inane request. First, most of the Gallery Effects filters would do terrible things to the black channel and make a complete mess of a CMYK image. Second, these are special-effects filters, which means that they're more likely to draw out defects in the relatively small CMYK color space. Third, these filters work entirely in RAM, which means that they're more likely to choke when asked to process an additional color channel. Fourth, already notoriously slow, the filters would grow even slower in CMYK. And fifth, the Gallery

Effects filters are with few exceptions poorly designed, so if they don't work at times, I say count it as a blessing.

Naturally, it pleases me to report that rather than waste a lot of time and resources rewriting a bunch of filters that aren't all that good in the first place, Adobe has wisely decided to ignore its users and leave the Gallery Effects filters the same as they've ever been. Some hold this up as a sign of the Photoshop team's arrogance. But I see it as an indication of a well-informed group of programmers maintaining priorities, adhering to well-defined guidelines, and selectively empowering their users. After all, good software design is rarely a democratic process. It's not that users are too dumb to come up with good ideas. In fact, you and I as individuals often make brilliant suggestions, many of which have found their way into Photoshop's most beloved features. But when we raise our voices together, our most trite and tedious suggestions have a habit of finding almost unanimous agreement. The revolutionary stuff is born from a more thoughtful, deliberate process than conducting a simple popularity poll.

This is all by way of introducing a chapter full of features that I've never heard requested but turn out to be truly outstanding. (Mind you, I'm sure *someone* requested them, but I'll be danged if I know who.) All new or dramatically expanded in Photoshop 6, these are the kinds of options that might seem obscure, unnecessarily complicated, or just plain excessive at first glance. And yet, like layers, history, masking, and the other greats, they'll very likely have a huge impact on the way we work in the future.

First up are Photoshop's new shape tools. These permit you to draw object-oriented paths filled with anything from solid colors to gradients to photographic images. It's like using clipping paths directly inside Photoshop. Other image editors have done it before, but as is so often the case, none has done it better.

Next, we turn our attention to the expanded *layer styles*. In addition to permitting you greater control over drop shadows, glows, and bevels, you can coat layers with gradients, patterns, and contoured wave patterns, as well as trace outlines around layers. When combined with the advanced blending options introduced in Chapter 13, layer styles blossom into a powerful special-effects laboratory, one of the most far-reaching and flexible Adobe has ever delivered. Furthermore, you can save the effects and reapply them to future layers.

What we have, then, is a collection of features that takes time and patience to fully understand but will reward us with greater proficiency and versatility in the long run. It's the price we pay for an application that steadfastly refuses to listen to its users and instead anticipates their needs. Now if only the arrogant weenieheads would stop exporting the Clipboard by default, they'd really be on to something.

Drawing Shapes

Photoshop provides six new *shape tools* that allow you to draw geometric and predefined shapes. By default, the shapes are separated off into independent *shape layers*, which are a mix of objects and pixels. The vector-based outlines of the shapes print at the maximum resolution of your printer, while the interiors may consist of solid colors, gradients, or pixel-based patterns and images. It's as if some of Illustrator has been merged into Photoshop.

The pros and cons of shapes

What good are object-oriented shapes inside Photoshop? Well, I'll tell you:

✦ **Shapes are editable.** Unlike pixels, you can change a shape by moving points and control handles. Likewise, you can scale, rotate, skew, or distort shapes, or even transform specific points and segments inside shapes. Nothing is ever set in stone.

✦ **Shapes help to disguise low-resolution images.** Sharply defined edges can add clarity to a printed image. The first example in Figure 14-1 shows a standard image printed at 75 pixels per inch. The second example shows that same 75-ppi image, but this time using an object-oriented shape outline. The low resolution works fine for the blurry fill and shadow, but where clarity is needed, the mathematical outline is there to serve.

✦ **You can color a shape with a layer style.** As we see later in this same chapter, layer effects such as drop shadows and beveled edges are equally applicable to shape layers as they are to standard image layers. And it's amazing what wild effects you can achieve with a shape, a style, and no talent whatsoever. To create Figure 14-1, for example, I drew a cloverleaf shape and applied the Striped Cone style from the Styles palette.

✦ **Shapes result in smaller file sizes.** As a rule, an object takes up less space on disk than an image. Expressed in PostScript code, a typical path outline consumes 8 bytes per anchor point, as compared with 3 bytes for a single RGB pixel. But while a shape may contain as few as 4 points in the case of a rectangle or ellipse, an image routinely contains hundreds of thousands of pixels. For example, the grayscale image shown in Figure 14-1 consumes about 132K on disk when saved as an uncompressed TIFF file. If you created an image with comparable resolution using exclusively pixels, the file would balloon to 16 times the size, or nearly 2MB.

✦ **You can preview clipping paths directly inside Photoshop.** In previous versions of Photoshop, you were never quite sure if you traced an image properly with a clipping path until you imported it into QuarkXPress, InDesign, or some other application. Now you can preview exactly what your clipping path will look like directly inside Photoshop.

Figure 14-1: The difference between a 75-ppi graphic saved as a flat image (top) and as an object-oriented path outline (bottom). Although the blurry interiors appear identical, the shape outline becomes several times sharper when expressed as a path.

✦ **Shapes expand with an image.** In Chapter 3, I advise against using Image ⇨ Image Size to resample an image upward on the grounds that it adds pixels without adding meaningful detail (see the section "Resampling an image"). But with shapes, you can enlarge the image as much as you want. Because it's mathematically defined, the shape remains crystal clear no matter how big or small you make it. Layer styles likewise resize without problem. Suddenly, the old limitations of pixels are gone.

If vectors are so great, why not forsake pixels and start drawing entirely with shape layers instead? While a shape can clip a continuous-tone photograph, it can't replace one. Although there have been all kinds of experiments using objects and fractals, pixels are still the most viable medium for representing digital photographs. Because Photoshop's primary job is photo editing, pixels are (for the foreseeable future) the program's primary commodity.

An even larger downside to shape layers is compatibility. Photoshop 6 has stretched the TIFF and PDF formats to accommodate any kind of layer — shape layers included — but that doesn't mean other programs have any idea what Photoshop is doing. As I write this, the most recent version of Adobe's own page-layout program, InDesign 1.5, doesn't recognize objects inside TIFF files. But it does support PDF files with objects. Of all the formats, PDF is the most likely to work with other programs as well. Just be sure to proof the document on a laser printer before taking it to a commercial printer. After all, when you create objects in Photoshop, you're working on the bleeding edge, so be prepared for the consequences.

The shape tools

Now that I've painted my rosy picture, let's dig in and look at the tools. Or, if you're not feeling brave enough, take a break and come back later. Either way. Up to you. As you've probably discovered by now, I like to give my readers lots of autonomy. That way, you're responsible for your own actions and you can't sue me if you go and pour this piping hot book all over your lap.

Now as I was saying, click the rectangle tool to display a flyout menu of six shape tools, pictured in Figure 14-2. Or press U to select the rectangle tool. Then press Shift+U to switch from one shape tool to the next. Either way — remember, it's totally up to you, I make no recommendations, my lawyer told me to tell you — the six shape tools work as follows:

✦ **Rectangle tool:** It used to be a running gag that the hardest thing to do in Photoshop was to draw a simple rectangle. You had to draw a rectangular marquee and then fill it. Not hard, I guess, but what person outside the walls of a sanitarium would think to approach it that way? But the gag is dead — now drawing a rectangle is easy. Drag to draw a rectangle from one corner to the other, Shift-drag to draw a square, Alt-drag to draw the shape outward from the center.

While drawing a rectangle or any other shape, press the spacebar to reposition the shape. Then release the spacebar and continue dragging to resize the shape as you normally do.

✦ **Rounded rectangle tool:** When you select the rounded rectangle tool, a Radius value becomes available in the Options bar. If you think of each rounded corner as a quarter of a circle, the Radius value is the radius (half the diameter) of that circle. Bigger values result in more roundness.

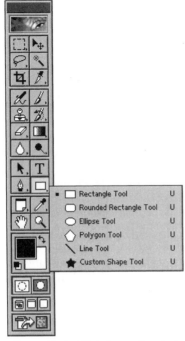

	Rectangle Tool	U
	Rounded Rectangle Tool	U
	Ellipse Tool	U
	Polygon Tool	U
	Line Tool	U
	Custom Shape Tool	U

Figure 14-2: Click the rectangle tool
to display the shape tools flyout menu.
Or press Shift+U to switch between tools.

✦ **Ellipse tool:** The ellipse tool draws ovals. Shift-drag for circles, Alt-drag to draw the oval outward from the center.

✦ **Polygon tool:** This tool draws regular polygons, which are straight-sided shapes with radial symmetry. Examples include isosceles triangles (3 sides), squares (4 sides), pentagons (5 sides), hexagons (6 sides), heptagons (7 sides), octagons (8 sides), decagons (10 sides), dodecagons (12 sides), and a bunch of other shapes with so many sides that they're virtually indistinguishable from circles. Enter a Sides value in the Options bar to set the number of sides in the next polygon you draw. Or better yet, press the bracket keys, [and], to decrease or increase the Sides value from keyboard. You can also draw stars and rounded shapes, as I explain in the next section.

✦ **Line tool:** Some of you are probably thinking to yourselves, "Deke, you blithering nincompoop, how can you call these 'shape tools' when one of them draws lines?" Well, despite your name-calling, I'll tell you. The truth is, even the line tool draws shapes. Enter a Weight value into the Options bar to define the thickness of the so-called "line," and then drag in the image window.

The result is an extremely long and skinny rectangle. As you see shortly, this makes editing a line exceedingly difficult. Honestly, it really breaks my heart that The Squirt Gun that Shoots Jelly has to live on the Island of Misfit Toys while The Line Tool that Draws Shapes gets to roam around free as a bird (one that doesn't swim).

✦ **Custom shape tool:** It saddens me to say this, but so far, the shape tools are a bunch of drips. You can't edit the roundness of an existing rectangle or add sides to a polygon while drawing it. And the line tool offends even the otherwise open-minded Cowboy on an Ostrich. Fortunately, the custom shape tool makes up for them all. Select a preset shape from the Shape option in the Options bar, and then draw it in the image window. It's a symbol library of instant clip art.

As a special bonus, Photoshop provides a seventh shape tool in the form of the pen tool. After selecting the pen, click the New Shape Layer button in the Options bar (see Figure 14-3) to draw your own custom shape layer. And in case you're thinking, "Wait, there's an eighth shape tool!" yes, the freeform pen tool can be a shape tool as well.

The shape drawing process

The act of drawing a shape can be as simple as dragging with a tool. When you're done, Photoshop creates a new shape layer. However, should you decide to invest more time, the program offers you a wealth of additional controls. Just for the record, here's the long way to approach the process of drawing a shape layer.

STEPS: Creating a New Shape Layer

1. **Specify the foreground color.** Select the color for the shape from the Color palette. If you want to fill the shape with a gradient, pattern, or image, you can do that after you finish drawing the shape, as I explain in the upcoming section "Editing the stuff inside the shape."

2. **Select the shape tool you want to use.** Remember, U is the keyboard shortcut for the shape tools.

3. **Specify how you want to draw the shape.** Pictured in Figure 14-3, the first three buttons in the Options bar determine what the shape tool draws. Selected by default, the first button tells Photoshop to draw an object-oriented shape layer. (This is likewise the button you select if you want to draw a shape layer with the pen tool.) Click the second button if you want to add a path to the Paths palette, great for drawing circular or geometric clipping paths that are a pain in the neck to create with the pen tool. Finally, click the third button to draw a pixel-based shape. Photoshop doesn't add a new layer; it merely recolors the pixels on the active layer.

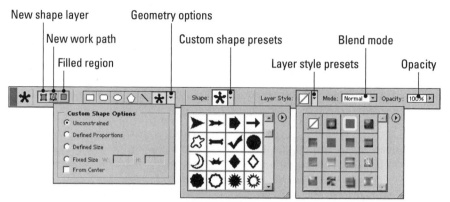

Figure 14-3: Use the options in the Options bar to specify the appearance of a shape before you draw it.

4. **Modify the geometry options.** Click the down-pointing arrowhead to the right of the tool buttons in the Options bar (labeled "Geometry options" in Figure 14-3) to see a pop-up palette of options geared to the selected shape tool. These permit you to constrain rectangles, ellipses, and custom shapes; indent the sides of a polygon to create a star; round off the corners of a polygon or star; and add arrowheads to a line.

   The one unusual option is Snap To Pixels, which is associated with the two rectangle tools. Object-oriented shapes don't have any resolution, so their sides and corners can land in the middle of pixels. To prevent potential anti-aliasing in rectangles, select the Snap To Pixels check box to precisely align them with the pixels in the image.

5. **Modify other tool-specific settings.** Depending on the tool, you may see options to the right of the geometry options arrowhead. The polygon tool offers a Sides option; the line tool offers a Weight option. When drawing a custom shape, click the shape button to display a pop-up palette of presets, as shown in Figure 14-3. You can load more shapes from the Photoshop CD-ROM by choosing the Load Shapes command or a predefined presets (.csh) file from the presets palette menu.

6. **Apply a layer style.** When drawing a shape layer, you can assign a layer style to your shape before drawing it. The Layer Style pop-up palette offers all presets available in the Styles palette, as discussed in the "Saving effects as styles" section at the end of this chapter.

7. **Blend mode and opacity.** Specify the blend mode and opacity of the new layer by selecting options or pressing the keyboard equivalents covered in the previous chapter.

8. **Draw the shape.** If you set the tool to draw a shape layer in Step 3, then Photoshop automatically creates a new layer. As shown in Figure 14-4, the Layers palette shows a colored fill (labeled "Layer contents" in the figure) with a clipping path to the right of it, masking the fill. If you assigned a layer style, a list of one or more effects appears under the layer name.

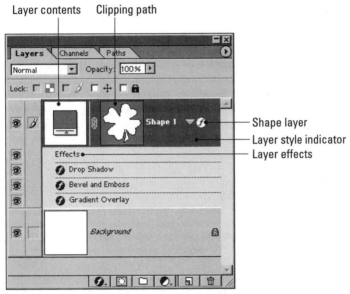

Figure 14-4: A shape layer is actually a clipping path that masks a color or other contents directly inside Photoshop.

9. **Switch tools and draw more shapes.** Photoshop adds each new shape that you draw to the existing shape layer. This means that they all get filled with the same contents. If you prefer to create a new shape layer with a different fill, click the clipping path thumbnail in the Layers palette to turn off the clipping path. Or click the check mark in the Options bar. Either way, you'll notice the clipping path turn off when the double outline around the thumbnail is replaced by a single outline. Then draw a new shape.

You can dismiss the clipping path from the keyboard by pressing Escape or Enter. To activate the clipping path, click its thumbnail or press Enter.

That's it. You now have a shape layer that you can use as you please. From this point on, it's a matter of editing the shape, as explained in the following sections.

Combining and editing shapes

A few years back, there was an image editor called Live Picture. Its creators heralded it as the first image editor to provide "infinite incremental undos." In fact, the program had a run-of-the-mill single-level Undo/Redo command. The infinite incremental undos were actually a result of an object metaphor that pervaded the program. After drawing an element, you had the option of changing it. It wasn't an automated undo, but rather a manual adjustment.

By this twisted marketing logic, Photoshop 6's shape layers permit infinite incremental undos. Although I'm being deliberately ironic, there is much to be said for a mask that is perpetually editable. Don't like a segment? Change it. Don't like a point? Move it. Hate the entire shape? Delete it. Here's how:

✦ **Compound path options:** As explained in Step 9 in the previous section, you can draw multiple shapes on a single layer. Because they all share a single fill, Photoshop thinks of the shapes as being bits and pieces of a single, complex path. In drawing parlance, such a path is called a *compound path*. This leads Photoshop to wonder, what do I do when the bits and pieces overlap? Because they share a fill, they could just merge together. Or perhaps you'd rather use one shape to cut a hole in the other. Or maybe you'd like the intersection to be transparent.

You specify your preference by selecting one of the four compound path buttons, shown in Figure 14-5. The buttons affect a single shape at a time. You can either apply the button to a shape before drawing it or after. Click the first button or press the plus key (+) to add the new shape to the others. Click the second button or press the minus key (–) to subtract the new shape from the others. The third button retains the intersection, the fourth makes the intersection transparent. Feel free to experiment.

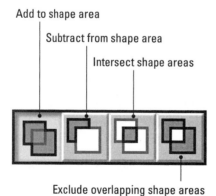

Add to shape area

Subtract from shape area

Intersect shape areas

Exclude overlapping shape areas

Figure 14-5: These four compound path buttons appear when editing or adding to an existing shape layer.

✦ **Selecting shapes:** You also see the buttons when selecting shapes with the arrow tool. Press A to get the black arrow tool—if you get the white arrow instead, press Shift+A—and then click a shape to select it. Or Ctrl-click a shape when using a shape tool.

✦ **Move and transform:** Drag a selected shape to move it. Select the Show Bounding Box check box in the Options bar to access the transformation controls. Or press Ctrl+T to enter the free transform mode. Then drag a handle to scale, drag outside the bounding box to rotate, and Ctrl+drag a handle to skew or distort. If you need a transformation refresher, check out the section "Applying Transformations" in Chapter 12.

✦ **Arranging and combining shapes:** After selecting a shape with the arrow tool, you can apply any of the four compound path buttons. As you do, bear in mind that the topmost shape takes precedence. So if Shape A is set to Add, Shape B is set to Intersect, and Shape B is in front, then Photoshop fills only the intersection. Meanwhile, the stacking order is entirely dependent on the order in which you draw the shapes, with more recent shapes in front. (The Layer ⇨ Arrange commands affect whole layers; they can't be used to reorder shapes.) Once you get the effect you're looking for, you can fix the relationship by selecting two or more paths and clicking the Combine button in the Options bar. Photoshop fuses the selected paths into one.

Technically, you can combine multiple shapes that don't overlap. But I advise against it. At first, the shapes behave as if they're grouped together. But try to combine other paths with them, and you may uncover some pretty strange relationships. Something about these paths reminds me of Jeff Goldblum in the last hour of *The Fly.* Some things on this planet just shouldn't be combined.

✦ **Selecting points and segments:** Press Shift+A to get the white arrow tool, which selects individual points and segments. Move individually selected points by dragging them; transform such points by pressing Ctrl+T. To select an entire shape, Alt-click on it.

✦ **Adding and deleting points:** The best tool for reshaping a shape is the pen tool. First select part of the shape with one of the arrow tools. Then click a segment to insert a point; drag on a segment to add a smooth point; click a point to remove it. You can likewise use the convert point tool, as well as any other technique that's applicable to paths.

✦ **Disabling a clipping path:** Shift-click the clipping path thumbnail in the Layers palette to turn it off and make visible the entire contents of the layer. Shift-click the thumbnail again to turn the clipping path on.

✦ **Duplicating a clipping path:** So far as Photoshop is concerned, shapes are just another kind of path. So it's not surprising that you can access the paths in an active shape layer from the Paths palette. Drag the *Clipping Path* item onto the tiny page icon at the bottom of the Paths palette to duplicate the shapes so you can use them elsewhere as standard paths (as discussed in Chapter 8).

✦ **Deleting a clipping path:** Click the clipping path thumbnail and then click the trash can icon at the bottom of the Layers palette to delete the shapes from the layer. To add a new shape to the layer, first choose Layer ⇨ Add Layer Clipping Path ⇨ Hide All. Then draw shapes in the layer to expose portions of the layer's contents.

✦ **Defining your own custom shape:** If you create a shape that you think you might want to repeat in the future, select the shape with either arrow tool and choose Edit ⇨ Define Custom Shape. Then name the shape and hit Enter. Photoshop adds the shape to the presets so you can draw it with the custom shape tool.

The moral of the story is, shapes work a lot like paths. If you find yourself strangely drawn to the Dark Art of Shape Editing and you're afraid I've forgotten to mention some amazing technique once known to the Oblique Brotherhood of Vector Druids — as I undoubtedly have — consult the "Reshaping paths" and "Transforming paths" scrolls, which I've sequestered inside the caliginous catacombs of Chapter 8.

Editing the stuff inside the shape

Here are a few ways to modify the color and general appearance of shape layers in Photoshop 6:

✦ **Changing the color:** To change the color of a shape layer, double-click the layer contents thumbnail in the Layers palette. Then select a new color from the Color Picker dialog box. Or better yet, change the foreground color and then press Alt+Backspace.

✦ **Changing the blending options:** You can change the blend mode and Opacity value for a shape layer using the standard controls in the Layers palette. Or double-click anywhere on the layer except the layer contents thumbnail to display the Blending Options section of the Layer Style dialog box. As discussed in Chapter 13, these options work the same for shape layers as they do for normal layers. You can also apply or modify layer effects, as I explain later in this chapter.

✦ **Changing the layer style:** Another way to apply or switch out layer effects is to apply a predefined style from the Styles palette. Just click on a preset in the Styles palette and Photoshop automatically applies it to the active layer. After that, you can edit an effect by double-clicking its name in the Layers palette.

✦ **Renaming the shape layer:** Press Alt and double-click a shape layer to rename it.

✦ **Fill with a gradient or repeating pattern:** Don't want to fill your shape with a solid color? Don't have to. To fill the active shape layer with a gradient, choose Layer ⇨ Change Layer Content ⇨ Gradient. Or choose Layer ⇨ Change Layer Content ⇨ Pattern to apply a repeating pattern.

Figure 14-6 shows the dialog box for each. Most of the options are familiar from the gradient tool (Chapter 6) and pattern stamp tool (Chapter 7) discussions. The only new options are in the Pattern Fill dialog box. Scale lets you resize the pattern inside the shape; Link With Layer makes sure the shape and pattern move together; and Snap To Origin snaps the pattern into alignment with the origin.

Tip   You can reposition a gradient or pattern inside its shape just by dragging inside the image window while the dialog box is up on screen.

After applying a gradient or pattern, you can edit it just by double-clicking the layer contents thumbnail in the Layers palette. Photoshop calls these kinds of editable contents *dynamic fills*.

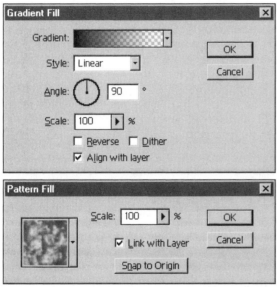

Figure 14-6: Gradients and patterns inside a shape layer are considered dynamic fills, which means you can edit them simply by double-clicking the layer contents thumbnail and editing the options above.

✦ **Making a color adjustment shape:** Where layer content is concerned, shape layers have unlimited potential. You can even fill a shape with a color adjustment. Just choose Levels, Curves, Hue/Saturation, or any of the other color correction classics from the Layer ➪ Change Layer Content submenu. Read the "Adjustment Layers" section of Chapter 17 for complete information.

✦ **Painting inside a shape layer:** Wish you could paint or edit the contents of a shape layer? Well now, thanks to subtle genetic alterations to Photoshop's core subroutines, you can. Assuming the shape is filled with a solid color, gradient, or pattern (this technique is not applicable to adjustment layers), choose Layer ⇨ Rasterize ⇨ Fill Content. From this point on, the fill is no longer dynamic. This means you can't double-click its thumbnail to edit it. However, you can edit it like any other layer full of pixels. Paint inside it, clone from another layer with the stamp tool, apply a filter, go nuts.

✦ **Filling a clipping path with an image:** Applying a clipping path to an image is a more delicate operation. Fortunately, there are several ways to do it, so you can select your favorite. Method number one: Draw a shape not as a new shape layer, but rather as a working path (see Step 3 of "The shape drawing process"). Then select the layer that you want to mask (it must be a floating layer, not the background) and choose Layer ⇨ Add Layer Clipping Path ⇨ Current Path.

Want to avoid that command? After establishing a work path, Ctrl-click the Add Mask icon at the bottom of the Layers palette to make the path clip the active image layer.

✦ **From clipping group to clipping path:** Okay, so that's one way. But what if you've already gone and made a shape layer, and you want to fill that shape with an image? Again, there are a few approaches, but the easiest is to paste the image onto a layer in front of the shape layer. Then press Ctrl+G to group it with the shape layer.

✦ **Fusing image and shape layer:** That's enough to create the same visual effect as a shape masking an image, but it involves two layers instead of one. If you want for any reason to fuse the two layers together, you have to once again take a special approach. First, select the shape layer and choose Layer ⇨ Rasterize ⇨ Fill Content to convert the dynamic fill to pixels. Then select the image layer and press Ctrl+E to merge it with the shape layer below.

If all this isn't enough, there is one more way to push the boundaries of shape layers and wring the last vestiges of cogent reasoning out of your by-now fragile mind. How? By adding a layer mask to a shape layer. That's right, Photoshop lets you combine pixel masking and vector masking on one layer, as shown in Figure 14-7. Why do it? Well, of course, there's always the chance it appeals to a latent strain of masochism on your part. But also, a layer mask permits you to soften some edges of a clipping path and leave others razor sharp. For example, in the figure, I added a black circle to the layer mask and blurred it to make the clover fade in a circular pattern toward its interior. Or you might want to feather an edge. Or add a motion blur. Or, again, just make yourself nuts. In any case, start with a shape layer. Then click the Add Mask icon at the bottom of the Layers palette and start painting away.

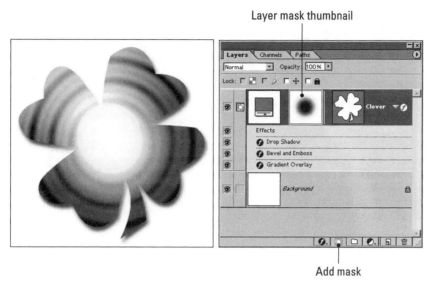

Layer mask thumbnail

Add mask

Figure 14-7: Add a layer mask to a shape layer to add pixel-based softening to the razor-sharp vector mask.

The Bold New Layer Styles

Photoshop 5 introduced a series of *layer effects* that automate the application of shadows, glows, and beveled edges. Now, Version 6 takes the metaphor several steps further. In addition to dramatically improving the quality of the existing effects — now you won't find yourself cursing at them half the time — the new Photoshop adds effects that overlay colors, stroke outlines, and create textures and contours. Plus, you can define exactly how effects are blended with background layers. And you can save them as preset *layer styles* for later use. Photoshop 6 elevates layer effects from nifty tools to some of the most powerful functions inside the program.

To apply a layer effect, start with an image on an independent layer. In Figure 14-8, I selected the dolphin's head and pressed Ctrl+J to copy it to an independent layer. But you can use any kind of layer, including text (Chapter 15) or a shape layer. Then click the Add Layer Style icon at the bottom of the Layers palette — the one that looks like a florin (cursive *f*) — and choose any of the commands following Blending Options. Or double-click the layer name to display the Layer Style dialog box, and then select an effect from the left-hand list. Use the check box to turn the effect on and off; highlight the effect name to edit its settings. You can select from one of the following 10 effects:

✦ **Drop Shadow:** The Drop Shadow command applies a common, everyday drop shadow. You specify the color, opacity, blend mode, position, size, and contour of the shadow; Photoshop does the rest.

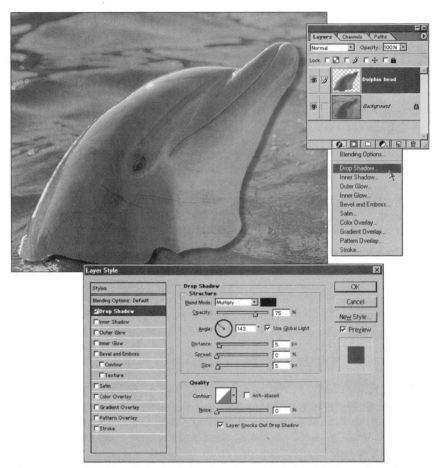

Figure 14-8: Starting with an independent layer, click the Add Layer Style icon at the bottom of the Layers palette and choose an effect (top). Then adjust the settings inside the sprawling Layer Style dialog box (bottom).

✦ **Inner Shadow:** This command applies a drop shadow inside the layer, as demonstrated by the second example in Figure 14-9. The command simulates the kind of shadow you'd get if the layer were punched out of the background — that is, the background looks like it's in front, casting a shadow onto the layer. Inner Shadow is especially effective with type, as I explain in the next chapter.

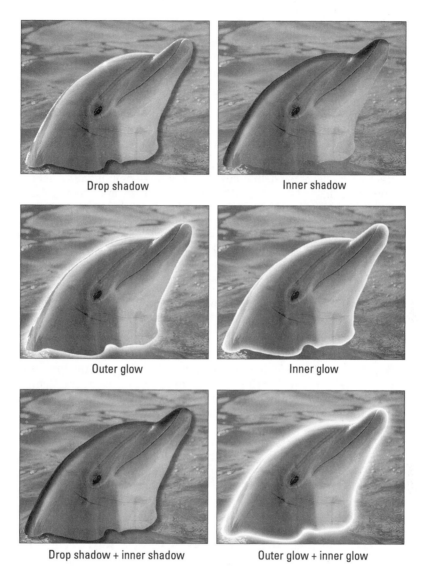

Drop shadow Inner shadow

Outer glow Inner glow

Drop shadow + inner shadow Outer glow + inner glow

Figure 14-9: The first four examples above illustrate the effects of the first four commands under the Layer ⇨ Layer Style submenu. You can also combine multiple effects on a single layer, as demonstrated by the two images at bottom.

✦ **Outer Glow:** The Outer Glow command creates a traditional halo, like the one I applied to our aquatic friend back in the "Halos" section of Chapter 12. However, you have lots of additional controls in case you want to get fancy.

✦ **Inner Glow:** This command applies the effect inside the layer rather than outside, as demonstrated in the second row of Figure 14-9.

To create a neon strip around the perimeter of a layer, apply both the Outer Glow and Inner glow commands. For an example of a neon edge, see the bottom-right example in Figure 14-9.

✦ **Bevel and Emboss:** The Bevel and Emboss option produces one of five distinct edge effects, as defined using the Style pop-up menu. The first four appear in Figure 14-10; the fifth one is exclusively applicable to stroked layers and requires the Stroke effect to be turned on. You can add a three-dimensional beveled edge around the outside of the layer, as in the first example in the figure. The Inner Bevel effect produces a beveled edge inside the layer. The Emboss effect combines inner and outer bevels. And the Pillow Emboss reverses the inner bevel so the image appears to sink in and then rise back up along the edge of the layer.

✦ **Contour and Texture:** The Contour and Texture options aren't actual effects, but rather modify the Bevel and Emboss effect. The Contour settings create waves in the surface of the layer that result in rippling lighting effects. Texture stamps a pattern into the surface of the layer, which creates a texture effect.

✦ **Satin:** This option creates regular waves of color, as in the first example of Figure 14-11. You define the behavior of the waves using the Contour options. One of the stranger effects, Satin can be difficult to predict. But so long as you keep the Preview check box turned on, you can experiment with a fair amount of success.

✦ **Color, Gradient, and Pattern Overlay:** These three options fill the layer with a coating of solid color, gradient, or repeating pattern, respectively. They work almost identically to the three dynamic fills available to shape layers, as discussed in the section "Editing the stuff inside the shape" earlier in this chapter. All three can be quite useful when defining your own style presets.

✦ **Stroke:** Use this option to trace a colored outline around a layer. The Stroke effect is often preferable to Edit ➪ Stroke because you can edit it long after creating it. By comparison, Edit ➪ Stroke is a permanent effect.

The Layer Style dialog box is a vast labyrinth of options. So it's handy to know a few additional ways to get around. To switch between effects without turning them on or off, press Ctrl plus a number key. Ctrl+1 highlights Drop Shadow, Ctrl+2 highlights Inner Shadow, Ctrl+3 highlights Outer Glow, and so on, all the way to Ctrl+0 for Stroke. You cannot get to Blending Options, Contour, or Texture from the keyboard.

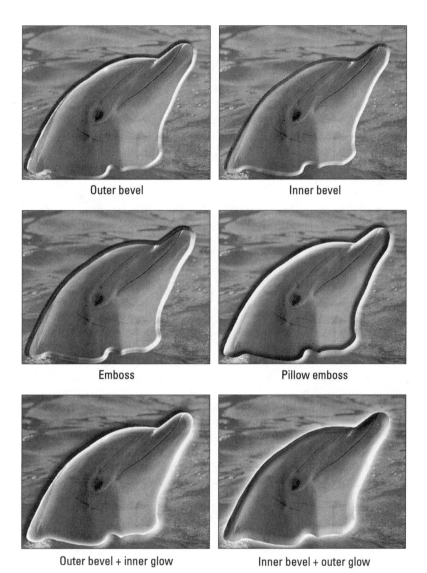

Outer bevel   Inner bevel

Emboss   Pillow emboss

Outer bevel + inner glow   Inner bevel + outer glow

Figure 14-10: Layer ⇨ Layer Style ⇨ Bevel and Emboss permits you to apply one of four effects, demonstrated in the first four examples above. The last row of images shows what happens when you combine beveled edges with glows.

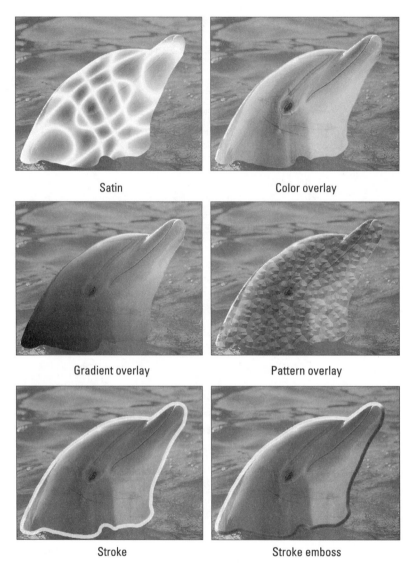

Figure 14-11: The five effects new to Photoshop 6 are Satin, the three overlays, and Stroke. Version 6 also adds an embossing option that works only with the Stroke effect.

The advantages of layer effects

Layer effects are a godsend to beginners and intermediate folks, but experienced users might be tempted to turn their noses up at them. After all, you can create many of these effects manually using layers, selection outlines, and blend modes. But there is much to like about automated layer effects:

✦ First, they stick to the layer. Move or transform the layer and the effect tags along with it.

✦ Second, the effect is temporary. So long as you save the image in one of the three layered formats — native Photoshop (PSD), TIFF, or PDF — you can edit the shadows, glows, bevels, overlays, and strokes long into the future.

✦ Third, layer effects are equally applicable to standard layers, shape layers, and editable text. This is unusual because both shape layers and editable text prohibit many kinds of changes.

✦ Fourth, thanks to the introduction of the Contour presets in Photoshop 6, layer effects now enable you to create effects that would prove otherwise exceedingly difficult or even impossible.

✦ Fifth, you can combine multiple effects on a single layer.

✦ Sixth, you can copy an effect from one layer and paste it onto another.

✦ Seventh, you can save groups of effects for later use in the Styles palette.

✦ Eighth, the effects show up as items in the Layers palette. You can expand and collapse a list of effects, as well as temporarily disable and enable effects by clicking on familiar eyeball icons.

✦ Ninth — why the heck do you need a ninth advantage? Didn't television teach us that *Eight Is Enough*? But what the heck. Ninth, strokes print as vector output, so they're guaranteed to be smooth. There, satisfied?

Now that you're champing at the bit — or as the dolphins say, "bonkin' at the beach ball" — to get your flippers on these effects, the following sections tell you how, why, and what for.

Inside the Layer Style dialog box

The Layer Style dialog box offers 13 panels containing more than 100 options. I discussed the first panel, Blending Options, in Chapter 13. The remaining 12 panels are devoted to layer effects. Select the desired effect from the list on the left; use the check box to turn the effect on and off.

Although there are gobs of options, many of them are self-explanatory. You select a blend mode from the Blend Mode pop-up menu. (For explanations of these, look to "The blend modes" section of Chapter 13.) You make the effect translucent by entering a value in the Opacity option box.

Other options appear multiple times throughout the course of the dialog box. All the options that appear in the Drop Shadow panel also appear in the Inner Shadow panel; the options from the Outer Glow panel appear in the Inner Glow panel; and so on. The modified dialog box in Figure 14-12 shows four representative effects panels — Inner Shadow, Inner Glow, Bevel and Emboss, and Texture — which together contain most of the options you'll encounter.

The following items explain the options in the order that they appear throughout the panels. I explain each option only once, so if an option appears multiple times (as so many do), look for its first appearance in a panel to locate the corresponding discussion in the following list:

✦ **Blend Mode:** This pop-up menu controls the blend mode. So much for the obvious. But did you know that you can use the Blend Mode menu to turn an effect upside-down? Select a light color and apply the Screen mode to change a drop shadow into a directional halo. Or use a dark color with Multiply to change an outer glow into a shadow that evenly traces the edge of the layer. Don't be constrained by pedestrian notions of shadows and glows. Layer effects can be anything.

✦ **Color Swatch:** To change the color of the shadow, glow, or beveled edge, click the color swatch. When the Color Picker is open, click in the image window to eyedrop a color from the layered composition. When editing a glow, you can apply a gradient in place of a solid color. Click the gradient preview to create a custom gradation, or select a preset from the pop-up palette.

✦ **Opacity:** Use this option to make the effect translucent. Remember, a little bit of effect goes a long way. When in doubt, reduce the Opacity value.

✦ **Angle:** Associated with shadows, bevels, the Satin effect, and gradients, this value controls the direction of the effect. In the case of shadows and bevels, the option controls the angle of the light source. With Satin, it controls the angle at which contour patterns overlap. And with a gradient, the Angle value represents the direction of the gradient.

Tip

You can avoid the numerical Angle option and simply drag an effect inside the image window. When the Drop Shadow or Inner Shadow panel is visible, drag inside the image window to move the shadow with respect to the layer. You can also drag the contour effect when working in the Satin panel. Other drag-gable effects include Gradient Overlay and Pattern Overlay, although dragging affects positioning, not angle.

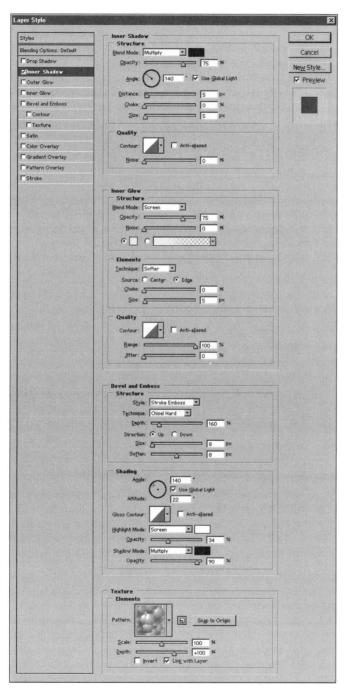

Figure 14-12: A modified picture of the Layer Style dialog box, featuring the Inner Shadow, Inner Glow, Bevel and Emboss, and Texture panels

✦ **Use Global Light:** In the real world, the sun casts all shadows in the same direction. Oh, sure, the shadows change minutely from one object to the next, but what with the sun being 90 million miles away and all, the changes are astronomically subtle. I doubt if a single-celled organism, upon admiring its shadow compared with that of its neighbor, could perceive the slightest difference. The fact that single-celled organisms lack eyes, brains, and other perceptual organs does not in any way lessen the truth of this powerful argument.

As I was saying, one sun means one lightness and one darkness. By turning on the Use Global Light check box, you tell Photoshop to cast *all* direction-dependent effects — drop shadows, inner shadows, and the five kinds of bevels — in the same direction. If you change the angle of a drop shadow applied to Layer 1, Photoshop rotates the sun in its heaven and so changes the angle of the pillow emboss applied to Layer 9, thus proving that even a computer program may subscribe to the immutable laws of nature.

Conversely, if you turn the check box off, you tell nature to take a hike. You can change an Angle value in any which way you like and none of the other layers will care.

Tip

If you have established a consistent universe, you can edit the angle of the sun by choosing Layer ⇨ Layer Style ⇨ Global Light. Change the Angle value and all shadows and bevels created with Use Global Light turned on will move in unison. You can also set the Altitude for bevels. "Sun rise, sun set," as the Yiddish fiddlers say. That doesn't shed any light on the topic, but when in doubt, I like to quote a great musical to class up the joint.

✦ **Distance:** The Drop Shadow, Inner Shadow, and Satin panels feature a Distance value that determines the distance between the farthest edge of the effect and the corresponding edge of the layer. Like Angle, this value is affected when you drag in the image window.

✦ **Spread/Choke:** Associated with the Drop Shadow and Outer Glow panels, the Spread option expands the point at which the effect begins outward from the perimeter of the layer. If you were creating the effect manually (as discussed in the section "Selecting the Contents of Layers" in Chapter 12), this would be similar to applying Select ⇨ Modify ⇨ Expand. Spread changes to Choke in the Inner Shadow and Inner Glow panels, in which case it contracts the point at which the effect begins. Note that both Spread and Choke are measured as percentages of the Size value, explained next.

✦ **Size:** One of the most ubiquitous settings, the Size value determines how far an effect expands or contracts from the perimeter of the layer. In the case of shadows and glows, the portion of the Size that is not devoted to Spread or Choke is given over to blurring. For example, if you set the Spread for Outer Glow to 100 percent and the Size to 10 pixels, then 0 percent is left for blurring. The glow expands 10 pixels out from the perimeter of the layer and has a sharp edge, as in the lower-left example in Figure 14-13. If you change the Spread to 0 percent, Photoshop blurs the glow across 100 percent of the Size.

As shown in the bottom-right example of the figure, this makes the effect seem smaller, but in fact, only the opaque portion of the effect has shrunk.

Size and Depth observe a similar relationship in the Bevel and Emboss panel, with Depth taking the place of Spread or Choke. When adjusting a Satin effect, Size affects the length of the contoured wave pattern. And in Stroke, Size controls the thickness of the outline.

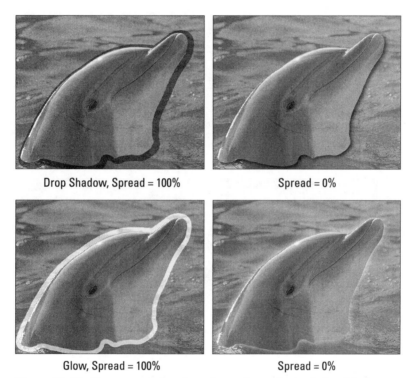

Figure 14-13: These examples show the codependent relationship between Spread (or Choke) and Size. Spread and Choke are actually subordinate to Size, though visually it often appears to be the other way around.

✦ **Contour:** Photoshop creates most effects — namely shadows, glows, bevel, and the Satin effect — by fading a color from a specified Opacity value to transparent. The rate at which the fade occurs is determined by the Contour option. Click the down-pointing arrowhead to select from a palette of preset contours; click the contour preview to design your own. If you think of the Contour preview as a graph, the top of the graph represents opacity and the bottom represents transparency. So a straight line from top to bottom shows a consistent fade. A spike in the graph shows the color hitting opacity and then fading away again. Figure 14-14 shows a few examples.

The most challenging contours are associated with Bevel and Emboss. The Gloss Contour option controls how colors fade in and out inside the beveled edge, as if the edge were reflecting other colors around it. The indented Contour effect — below Bevel and Emboss in the Layer Style list — wrinkles the edge of the layer so that it casts different highlights and shadows.

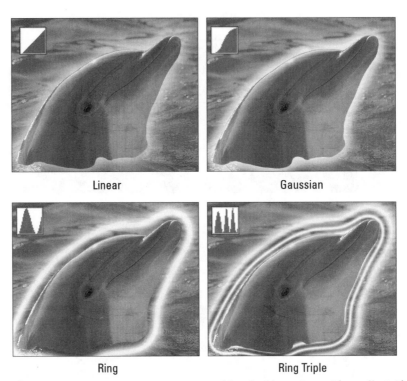

Linear   Gaussian

Ring   Ring Triple

Figure 14-14: Four Contour presets combined with an Outer Glow effect. The Contour setting controls how the halo drops from opacity to transparency, and sometimes back again.

✦ **Anti-aliased:** If a Contour setting consists of sharp corners, you can soften them by turning this check box on. Most presets have rounded corners, making antialiasing unnecessary.

✦ **Noise:** Associated strictly with shadows and glows, the Noise value randomizes the transparency of pixels. It's like using the Dissolve blend mode, except that you have control over how much randomization to apply. The Noise value does not change the color of pixels; that is the job of an option called Jitter.

✦ **Layer Knocks Out Drop Shadow:** In the real world, if an object was translucent, you could see through it to its own shadow. However, this turns out to be an unpopular law of nature with most image editors. So when creating a drop shadow, Photoshop gives us the Layer Knocks Out Drop Shadow check box, which when selected makes the drop shadow invisible directly behind the layer. Turn the option off for a more natural effect.

✦ **Technique:** Moving out of the Shadow panels and into Outer Glow, the first unique option is the Technique pop-up menu. Available when creating glow or bevel effects, Technique controls how the contours of the effect are calculated. When a glow is set to Softer, Photoshop applies a modified Gaussian Blur to ensure optimal transitions between the glow and background elements. Your other option is Precise, which calculates the effect without the Gaussian adjustment. Mind you, the effect may remain blurry, but strictly as a function of the Spread and Contour settings. Precise may work better in tight corners, common around type and shape layers. Otherwise, stick with Softer.

The Bevel and Emboss panel doesn't provide the same kind of blurring functions that you get with shadow and glow effects, so the Technique option works a bit differently. The default setting, Smooth, averages and blurs pixels to achieve soft, rounded edges. The two Chisel settings remove the averaging to create saw-tooth abrasions into the sides of the layer. Chisel Hard results in thick cut marks; Chisel Soft averages the perimeter of the layer to create finer cuts. Up the Soften value (described shortly) to blur the abrasions.

✦ **Source:** When working in the Inner Glow panel, Photoshop wants to know where the glow starts. Should it glow inward from the perimeter of the layer (Edge) or outward from the middle (Center)?

✦ **Range:** The two Glow panels and the Contour panel (subordinate to Bevel and Emboss) use Range values to modify the Contour settings. This value sets the midpoint of the contour with respect to the middle of the size. Values less than 50 percent move the midpoint away from the source, extending the effect. Values greater than 50 percent shrink the effect.

✦ **Jitter:** Where the Noise value randomizes the transparency of pixels, Jitter randomizes the colors. This option is operable only when creating gradient glows in which the gradation contains two or more colors (not a color and transparency).

✦ **Depth:** The first unique Bevel and Emboss setting is Depth, which makes the sides of a bevel steeper or shallower. In most cases, this translates to increased contrast between highlights and shadows as you raise the Depth value.

The Texture panel includes its own Depth setting. Here, Photoshop renders the pattern as a texture map, lighting the white areas of the pattern as high and the black areas as low. The Depth value determines the depth of the texture.

The difference is you can enter a negative value, which inverts the texture. Meanwhile, you also have an additional Invert check box, which you can use to reverse the lights and darks in the pattern. So a positive Depth value with Invert turned on produces the same effect as a negative Depth value with Invert turned off.

✦ **Direction:** When working in the Bevel and Emboss panel, you see two radio buttons: Up and Down. If the Angle value indicates the direction of the sun, then Up positions the highlight along the edge near the sun and the shadow along the opposite edge. Down reverses things, so the shadow is near the light source. Presumably, this means the layer sinks into its background rather than protrudes out from it. But, in practice, the layer usually appears merely as though it's lit differently.

✦ **Soften:** This value sets the amount of blur applied to the beveled highlights and shadows. Small changes make a big difference when Technique is set to one of the Chisel options.

✦ **Altitude:** The Bevel and Emboss panel includes two lighting controls, Angle and Altitude. The Angle value is just that: the angle of the sun with respect to the layer. The Altitude is measured on a half circle drawn across the sky. A maximum value of 90 degrees puts the sun directly overhead (noon); 0 degrees puts it on the horizon (sunrise). Values in the medium range — 30 to 60 degrees — generally produce the best results.

✦ **Scale:** The Texture and Pattern Overlay panels include Scale values, which scale the pattern tiles inside the layer. Values greater than 100 percent swell the pattern; values lower than 100 percent shrink it.

✦ **Link/Align with Layer:** When turned on, this check box centers a gradient inside a layer. If you want to draw a gradient across many layers, turn the option off to center the gradient inside the canvas. When editing a pattern, this option links the pattern to the layer so the two move together.

✦ **Position:** The final Layer Style option appears inside the Stroke panel. The Position pop-up menu defines how the width of the stroke aligns with the perimeter of the layer. Photoshop can draw the stroke outside the edge of the layer, inside the edge, or center the stroke exactly on the edge. It's up to you.

Modifying and Saving Effects

After you apply a layer effect, Photoshop stamps the layer with a florin symbol (*f*), as shown in Figure 14-15. A triangular toggle switch lets you collapse the effects to permit more room for layers inside the palette. From that point on, you can edit an effect by double-clicking its name in the Layers palette. Or double-click the florin symbol to display the Blending Options panel of the Layer Style dialog box.

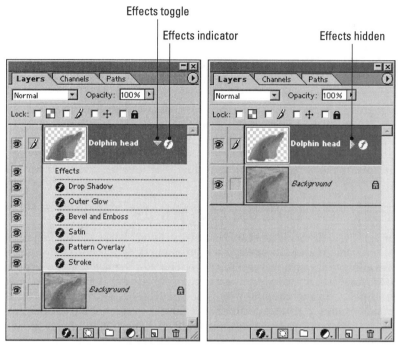

Figure 14-15: The florin symbol indicates that one or more layer effects have been applied to the layer. Use the toggle to hide and show effects.

Disabling effects

To temporarily disable all effects applied to a layer, choose Layer ⇨ Layer Style ⇨ Hide All Effects. Or better yet, just click the eyeball in front of the word "Effects" in the Layers palette. Click the eyeball spot again to show the effects. You can likewise hide and show individual effects — without permanently disabling them — by clicking eyeballs. Photoshop even goes so far as to save hidden effects. This makes it easy to bring an effect back to life later without re-entering settings.

To permanently disable an effect, drag it and drop it onto the trash icon at the bottom of the Layers palette. To delete all effects, drag the word "Effects" to the trash.

Duplicating effects

Once you apply an effect to a layer, the effect becomes an element that you can copy and apply to other layers. Select the layer with the effects you want to duplicate and choose Layer ⇨ Layer Style ⇨ Copy Layer Style. Or right-click the layer name in the Layers palette and choose Copy Layer Style from the context-sensitive menu. Then select another layer, right-click it, and choose Paste Layer Style. To paste a copied effect onto multiple layers at a time, link them together (as explained in the section "Linking layers" in Chapter 12) and choose the Paste Layer Style to Linked command.

The Copy and Paste Layer Style commands bypass the Clipboard. This means you can copy an image and then copy an effect without displacing the image.

Paste Layer Style duplicates all effects associated with one layer onto another. But what if you want to duplicate a single effect only? Just drag the effect name from one layer and drop it below another in the Layers palette. Be sure you see a bar below the layer name when dropping the effect — otherwise, it won't take.

Scattering effects to the four winds

When you apply an effect, Photoshop is actually doing all the manual layer work for you in the background. This means if Photoshop doesn't seem to be generating the precise effect you want, you can take over and edit the layers to your satisfaction. Choose Layer ⇨ Layer Style ⇨ Create Layers to resolve the automated effect into a series of layers and clipping groups. In some cases, a warning appears telling you that one or more attributes of an effect cannot be represented with layers. Go ahead and give it a try; you can always undo. If you like what you see, inspect it and edit at will.

After choosing Create Layers, you're on your own. From that point on, you lose the ability to edit the effects from the Layer Style dialog box (unless, of course, you decide to go back in time via the History palette).

Saving effects as styles

Photoshop 6 lets you save layer effects and blending options for later use by creating layer styles, which show up as items in the Styles palette. There are three ways to create a style:

✦ **Click the New Style icon.** When working in the Layer Style dialog box, click the New Style icon to display the options shown at the bottom of Figure 14-16. Name your style, and then use the check boxes to decide which settings in the Layer Style dialog box are preserved. The first check box saves the effects covered in this chapter, the second saves the blending options discussed in the previous chapter.

✦ **Click in the Styles palette.** Choose Window ⇨ Show Styles to view the Styles palette. Then move your cursor inside the palette and click with the paint bucket, as in the top example in Figure 14-16. Photoshop shows you the New Style dialog box. Set the options as described previously.

✦ **Drag and drop a layer.** Start with both the Layers and Styles palettes open. Now drag any layer, active or not, and drop it in the Styles palette. Again, Photoshop shows you the New Style dialog box.

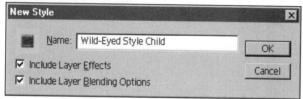

Figure 14-16: Click in the Styles palette (top) to display the New Style dialog box (bottom).

After you press Enter, Photoshop saves the style as a new preset. As with any preset, you can apply it to future images during future Photoshop sessions. Just click a style to apply it to the active layer, or drag the style and drop it on any layer name (active or not) in the Layers palette. And don't forget, Photoshop ships with scads of preset styles that you can explore at your leisure. Load a set of styles from the Styles palette menu, apply one to your favorite layer, and take a look at how it's put together in the Layer Style dialog box. It's a great way to get a feel for the amazing variety of effects that are possible in Photoshop 6.

Tip

A style may include blending options, layer effects, or both. Applying a new style to a layer replaces all blending options and/or effects associated with that style. If you would rather add the blending options and effects from a style to the existing blending options and effects associated with a layer, Shift-click an item in the Styles palette.

Note

Sadly, there is no way to update a style. And even if you could, the style and layer are not linked, so updating the style would have no effect on the layer. Photoshop lets you create new styles, rename existing styles, and delete old ones — that's about it.

✦   ✦   ✦

Fully Editable Text

The State of Type in Photoshop 6

Photoshop 5 gave us something you don't see often — editable bitmapped type. Long after you created a line or two of text, you had the option of changing the words, typeface, size, leading, kerning, and so on, just as you could in other graphics and electronic publishing programs. You could also mix and match formatting attributes inside a single text block, something you couldn't do in Version 4 and earlier. In only one upgrade cycle, Photoshop made a quantum leap from grim Stone Age letter wrangling to something that might actually pass for contemporary typesetting.

Photoshop 5.5 expanded your type possibilities further, adding options for underlining text, applying faux bold and italic effects, and adjusting how the program applied antialiasing and kerning to text. But all these advances pale in comparison to the bounty of text improvements in Photoshop 6.

The Photoshop 6 type tool creates vector text instead of bitmapped text. That means that you can scale text as large as you want without any repercussions, just as you can any vector object. (If you're unclear as to what I mean by bitmapped and vector objects, review Chapter 3.) In addition, you can do all the following:

✦ Create and edit text by typing directly on the image canvas — no more side trips to the Type Tool dialog box required.

✦ Create text inside a frame and then apply paragraph formatting to control hyphenation, justification, indents, alignment, and paragraph spacing. You can even create lists that use hanging punctuation and control word and character spacing in justified text, as you can in Adobe PageMaker and InDesign.

✦ Make per-character adjustments to color, width, height, spacing, and baseline shift.

✦ Bend, twist, and otherwise distort text using a simple Warp Text dialog box instead of wrestling with the Wave filter or other distortion filters.

✦ Convert characters to shapes that you can then edit, fill, and stroke just as you do objects you create with the shape tools (explored in Chapter 14). Alternatively, you can convert text to a work path.

✦ Rasterize the text so that you can apply any filters or tools applicable to ordinary image layers.

As you can see, the changes to type rank among the largest upgrades in Photoshop 6. And because Adobe implemented these features using controls similar to those found in page layout, illustration, and even advanced word processing programs, you should be able to make them a regular part of your text routine in no time.

Note I don't cover the Photoshop 6 options for formatting Chinese, Korean, and Japanese text, which become available when you select the Show Asian Text Options check box on the General panel of the Preference dialog box (Ctrl+K). Like the rest of the Photoshop 6 type controls, these options should be familiar to you if you work regularly with type in these languages. But if you're not sure what each control does, check the Photoshop online help system for details.

The five flavors of text

As I mentioned a few paragraphs ago, the type tool now produces vector type. But you also can create a text-based selection outline or work path, convert each character to a separate vector object, or create a bitmap version of your text. Here's a rundown of your type choices:

✦ To create regular text, click the Text Layer button on the Options bar, click in the image window, and type away. Or, to create paragraph text, drag to create a text frame and then type your text in the frame. You then can choose from a smorgasbord of type formatting options, apply layer effects, and more. The only thing you can't do is apply the effects in the Filter menu or use the standard selection tools. As for that last one, there's no need to use the selection tools anyway — you can select characters simply by dragging over them, as you do in a word processor.

✦ To produce a text-based selection outline, click the Type Mask button on the Options bar and create your text, as I explain in the section "Character Masks and Layer Effects," toward the end of this chapter. All formatting options available for regular type work on type masks as well.

✦ After creating text, choose Layer ➪ Type ➪ Convert to Shape to turn each character to an individual vector shape that works just like those you create with the new shape tools (also covered in Chapter 14). You then can edit the shape of individual characters, an option explored in "Editing text as shapes," later in this chapter.

✦ Choose Layer ➪ Type ➪ Create Work Path to generate a work path from text. One reason to use this option is to create a clipping path based on your text.

✦ Finally, you can convert text to bitmapped type by choosing Layer ➪ Rasterize ➪ Type. After rasterizing the text, you can apply Photoshop's filters and other pixel-based features to it.

After you rasterize text or convert it to a shape or work path, you can't go back and fix typos or change the text formatting as you can while working with vector text or type masks. So be sure that you're happy with those aspects of your text before you convert it. You may even want to save a copy of the vector text in a new layer so that you can get it back if needed.

Also note that when you save images in formats that offer the Include Vector Data option, you must select that option to retain the vector properties of your text. If you turn off the check box or save in a format that doesn't support vectors, Photoshop rasterizes your text. Again, saving a backup copy of the image in the native Photoshop format is a good idea.

Text as art

Before I get into the nitty-gritty of creating text, I want to share a few ideas to inspire you to see text for the creative playground that it can be. Combine the new powers of the Photoshop 6 type tool with the program's effects, filters, paint and edit tools, and layering features, and you can create an almost unlimited array of text effects to enhance your images — even produce text that stands alone as a powerful image in its own right.

With that flowery speech out of the way, allow me to provide some examples of the kind of things you can do with your text:

✦ **Create translucent type:** Because Photoshop automatically creates type on a new layer, you can change the translucency of type simply by adjusting the Opacity value for the type layer in the Layers palette. Using this technique, you can merge type and images to create subtle overlay effects, as illustrated in Figure 15-1.

✦ **Use type as a selection:** By creating a type mask, you can use type to select a portion of an image and then move, copy, or transform it. To create Figure 15-2, for example, I used my text to select the vintage photo. Then I dragged it into a different stock photo background and applied the Multiply blend mode from the Layers palette. You'd be hard-pressed to tell that there's a parade inside those letters, but it serves as an interesting texture.

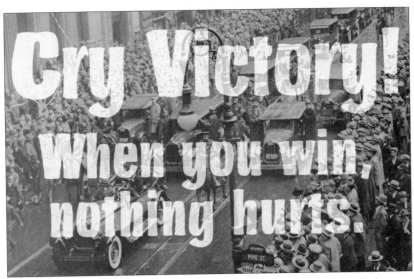

Figure 15-1: After creating some white type layered against a vintage photo, I lowered the type opacity to 70 percent. Though child's play in Photoshop, this effect is virtually impossible to create in most drawing programs.

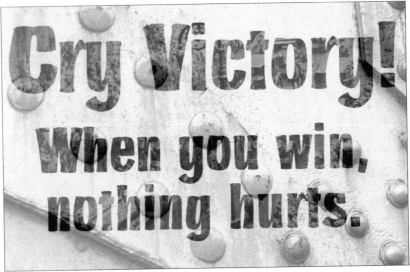

Figure 15-2: Photoshop is virtually unique in permitting you to select an image using type. Here I selected the image from Figure 15-1 and dragged the selection into a different background.

✦ **Apply layer effects:** Photoshop's layer effects are fully applicable to type. In Figure 15-3, I replaced the industrial background from Figure 15-2 with a background texture created with the Clouds and Emboss filters (see Chapter 11). Then I applied a pillow emboss effect to the text layer using Layer ➪ Layer Style ➪ Bevel and Emboss.

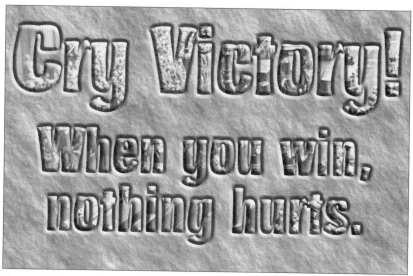

Figure 15-3: I used the Bevel and Emboss layer effect to apply a pillow emboss effect.

✦ **Edit type as part of the image:** After rasterizing text (by choosing Layer ➪ Rasterize ➪ Type), you can paint type, erase it, smear it, apply a filter or two, or do anything else that you can do to pixels. In Figure 15-4, I embossed the type, flattened it against its background, applied a few effects filters, and made it sway with the Wave filter.

Using the Type Tool

In a drawing or desktop publishing program, the type tool typically serves two purposes: You can create text with the tool or you can edit existing text by highlighting characters and either replacing them or applying formatting commands. In Photoshop, the type tool not only enables you to create and edit text, but also to create a text-based selection outline.

Figure 15-4: This image is the result of going nuts for 15 minutes or so using the commands in the Filter menu. I used Emboss, Radial Blur, Colored Pencil, Craquelure, and Wave.

Adobe completely revamped the type tool in Photoshop 6, as I mentioned earlier. The following steps show you the basics of using the new tool and its accompanying options. Note that these steps assume that you're creating text for the first time in your image (more about adding to existing text later).

STEPS: Creating Text in Photoshop 6

1. **Select the type tool by clicking its icon in the toolbox or pressing T.** Photoshop activates the type tool, displays the text cursor in the image window, and displays type controls on the Options bar. You can access additional formatting options by displaying the new Character and Paragraph palettes, shown in Figure 15-5. Don't bother hunting for the old Type Tool dialog box — all its controls are now found on the Options bar or in the palettes.

2. **Click the Text Layer button (labeled in Figure 15-5) if it's not already selected.** When the button is selected, the type tool creates regular, filled text (the default setting). If you choose the Type Mask button instead, you create a text-based selection outline.

3. **Click a type orientation button (also labeled in the figure).** When the left button is selected, you create ordinary, horizontal text. Click the other button to lay down characters vertically. (See the next section for more details.)

Text layer

Type mask   Insertion marker

Horizontal type

Vertical type   Text palettes

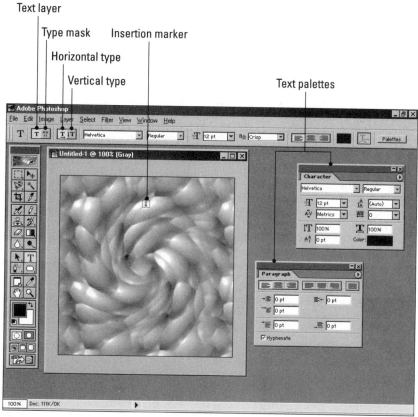

Figure 15-5: Photoshop 6 provides a full complement of text creation and formatting options, which you access from the Options bar, Character palette, and Paragraph palette.

4. **Select the font, type size, and other formatting attributes from the Options bar and palettes.** The upcoming sections explain your options.

5. **Click or drag in the image window.** If you click, Photoshop places the first character you type at the location of the blinking insertion marker, just as when you type in a word-processing program. Adobe calls this creating *point text*. Each line of type operates as an independent entity. Press Enter to begin a new line of text.

Alternatively, you can create paragraph text by dragging with the type tool to draw a frame—called a *bounding box*—to hold the text. Now your text flows within the frame, wrapping to the next line automatically when you reach the edge of the bounding box.

If you create your text this way, you can apply standard paragraph formatting attributes, such as justification, paragraph spacing, and so on. In other words, everything works pretty much like it does in every other program in which you create text in a frame. Pressing Enter starts a new paragraph within the bounding box.

6. **Type your text.** If you mess up, press Backspace to delete the character to the left of the insertion marker. Press Delete to wipe out the character to the right of the insertion marker.

7. **Edit the text, if necessary.** To alter the character formatting, select the characters you want to change by dragging over them or using the selection shortcuts listed in the upcoming Table 15-1. Then choose the new formatting attributes from the Options bar, Character palette, or Paragraph palette. If you don't select any text, paragraph formatting affects all text in the bounding box. Otherwise, only the selected paragraph responds to your commands.

8. **Click the Commit (check mark) button on the right end of the Options bar to commit the text.** Don't worry — "committing the text" simply takes you out of text-editing mode. As long as you don't convert the text to a regular image layer, work path, or shape, you can edit it at any time.

Tip

If the Options bar is hidden or you just don't like reaching to click the button, you can commit text by selecting any other tool, clicking any palette but the Character or Paragraph palette, or pressing Ctrl+Enter.

Note

While you're in text edit mode, most menu commands are unavailable. You must commit the text or cancel the current type operation to regain access to them. To abandon your type operation, click the Cancel button — the large X at the right end of the Options bar — or press Esc.

When you create the first bit of type in an image, Photoshop creates a new layer to hold the text. After you commit the type, clicking or dragging with the type tool has one of two outcomes. If Photoshop finds any text near the spot where you click or drag, it assumes that you want to edit that text and, therefore, selects the text layer and puts the type tool into edit mode. For paragraph text, the paragraph is selected as well. If no text is in the vicinity of the spot you click, the program decides that you must want to create a brand new text layer, and responds accordingly. You can force Photoshop to take this second route by Shift-clicking or Shift-dragging with the type tool, which comes in handy if you want to create one block of text on top of another.

Tip

Photoshop automatically uses the first characters you type as the layer name. You can change the layer name by Alt-double-clicking on the layer name in the Layers palette to bring up the Layer Properties dialog box.

Creating vertical type

By default, the type tool places characters horizontally across the image. But you can create a column of vertical type as well. In Photoshop 6, you don't use a separate type tool as you did in recent versions. Instead, just click the vertical type button on the Options bar (labeled back in Figure 15-5). To return to normal left-to-right text orientation, click the adjacent horizontal type button.

In truth, the vertical type option is nothing more than the standard type tool lifted from the Japanese version of Photoshop. As shown in the first example of Figure 15-6, it creates vertical columns of type that read right to left, as in Japan. If you want to make columns of type that read left to right, you have to create each column as an independent text block.

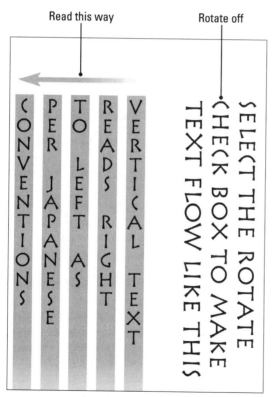

Figure 15-6: By default, vertical type reads right to left, as shown in the first example. If you deselect the Rotate Character option in the Character palette menu, your characters appear like those on the right.

After you click in the image, you have access to the Rotate Character command in the Character palette menu. (If the palette isn't open, press Ctrl+T or click the Palettes button on the Options bar.) By default, the option is turned on, which gives you upright characters like those on the left side of Figure 15-6. Choose the command again to rotate 90 degrees clockwise and flip characters on their side, as shown in the right side of the figure.

If you want to rotate the type to some other degree, wait until after you commit the text to the layer (by clicking the check-mark button on the Options bar) and then use the Edit ➪ Free Transform command, which I describe in Chapter 12, to rotate the text layer.

You also can choose Layer ➪ Type ➪ Horizontal and Layer ➪ Type ➪ Horizontal to change vertically oriented type to horizontally oriented type, and vice versa.

Creating and manipulating text in a frame

By dragging in your image with the type tool, you create paragraph text. As you drag, Photoshop draws a frame to hold your text, as shown in Figure 15-7. Photoshop calls this frame a *bounding box.* If you want to create a text frame that's a specific size, Alt-click with the type tool instead of dragging. Photoshop displays the Paragraph Text Size dialog box, in which you can specify the width and height of the box. Press Enter, and Photoshop creates the bounding box, placing the top-left corner of the box at the spot you clicked.

Origin point

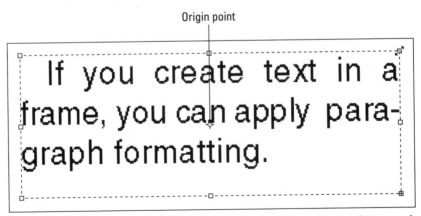

Figure 15-7: Drag the box handles to transform the frame alone or frame and text together.

The bounding box looks just like the one that appears when you choose Edit ⇨ Free Transform, and some of its functions are the same:

✦ Drag a corner handle to resize the box. Shift-drag to retain the original proportions of the box. The text reflows to fit the new dimensions of the box.

✦ Ctrl-drag a corner handle to scale the text and box together. Ctrl+Shift-drag to scale proportionally. To scale text alone, use the character formatting controls on the Options bar or in the Character palette (explained next). Either way, you can scale up or down as much as you want without degrading the text quality, thanks to the new vector-orientation of the type tool.

✦ To rotate both box and text, move the cursor outside the box and drag, just as you do when transforming selections, crop boundaries, and layers. Shift-drag to rotate in 15-degree increments. The rotation occurs respective to the origin point, which you can relocate by dragging, as usual.

Using the bounding-box approach to type has more benefits than being able to use the transformation techniques I just described, however. You also can apply all sorts of paragraph formatting options to control how the text flows within the bounding box, as described in the upcoming section "Applying paragraph formatting."

Note

Keep in mind that you also can scale, skew, rotate, and otherwise transform the text layer after you commit the text to the layer. In addition, you can size, distort, and rotate text using the options in the new Character palette, as explained later in this chapter.

If you ever decide that you'd like to work with your text as regular text instead of paragraph text, cancel out of text edit mode by clicking the Commit or Cancel buttons on the Options bar (the check mark and X buttons). Then select the text layer and choose Layer ⇨ Type ⇨ Convert to Point Text. Photoshop splits the paragraph text into individual lines. To go back to paragraph text, select the text layer and choose Layer ⇨ Type ⇨ Convert to Paragraph Text.

Selecting text

Before you can modify a single character of type, you have to select it. You can select all text on a text layer by simply clicking the layer name in the Layers palette. You can select individual characters by dragging over them with the type tool, as in any word processing program. You also have access to a range of keyboard tricks, listed in Table 15-1.

Table 15-1	
Selecting Text from the Keyboard	
Text Selection	*Keystrokes*
Select character to left or right	Shift-left or right arrow
Select whole word	Double-click on word
Select entire line	Triple-click the line
Move left or right one word	Ctrl+left or right arrow
Select word to left or right	Ctrl+Shift+left or right arrow
Select to end of line	Shift+End
Select to beginning of line	Shift+Home
Select one line up or down	Shift+up or down arrow
Select range of characters	Click at one point, Shift-click at another
Select all text	Ctrl+A

After selecting type, you can replace it by entering new text from the keyboard. You can likewise cut, copy, or paste text by pressing the standard keyboard shortcuts (Ctrl+X, C, and V) or by choosing commands from the Edit menu. You can undo a text modification by pressing Ctrl+Z or choosing Edit ➪ Undo. However, if you type a few characters and then choose Undo, you wipe out all the new characters, not just the most recently typed one.

If things go terribly wrong, press Esc or click the Cancel button on the Options bar (the big X) to cancel out of the current type operation.

When you select text by clicking its layer name in the Layers palette, the text appearance doesn't change on screen. If you use any other selection method, selected text appears highlighted, as is the convention. If the highlight gets in your way, press Ctrl+H to hide it. In Photoshop 6, this shortcut hides all on-screen helpers, including guides.

Applying character formatting

After you click your image with the type tool, the text orientation, Type Mask, and Text Layer buttons disappear, leaving you with the collection of formatting controls shown in Figure 15-8. The Character palette and its palette menu, also shown in the figure, offer some of these same controls plus a few additional options. If you use Adobe InDesign, the palette should look familiar to you—with a few exceptions, it's a virtual twin of the InDesign Character palette.

To open the palette and its partner, the Paragraph palette, click the Palettes button on the Options bar. Or choose View ➪ Show Character or press Ctrl+T to display the Character palette by its lonesome.

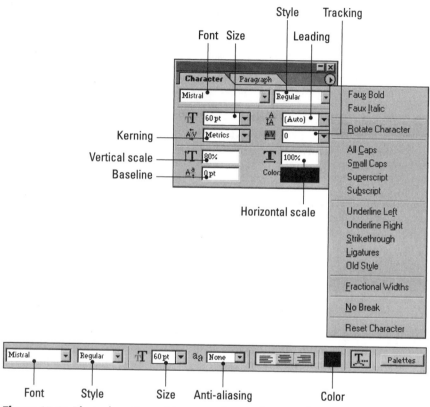

Figure 15-8: Photoshop 6 provides several new character-formatting options; look for them on the Options bar and in the Character palette.

In Photoshop 6, you can apply formatting on a per-character basis. For example, you can type one letter, change the font color, and then type the next letter in the new color. You can even change fonts from letter to letter.

The next several sections explain the character formatting options. All apply to both paragraph and regular text. You can specify formatting before you type or reformat existing type by selecting it first.

Tip

If you ever want to return the settings in the Character palette to the defaults, make sure that no type is selected. Then choose Reset Character from the bottom of the palette menu.

Font

Select the typeface and type style you want to use from the Font and Style pop-up menus. Rather than offering lowest-common-denominator Bold and Italic check boxes (as was the case for Photoshop 4), Photoshop now is smart enough to present a full list of designer style options. For example, while Times is limited to Bold and Italic, the Helvetica family may yield such stylistic variations as Oblique, Light, Black, Condensed, Inserat, and Ultra Compressed.

The Character palette menu contains a bunch of additional style options, which you can see in Figure 15-8. Click these options in the menu to toggle them on and off. A check mark next to the style name means that it's active.

✦ Faux Bold and Faux Italic enable you to apply bold and italic effects to the letters when the font designer doesn't include them as a type style. Use these options *only* if the Style pop-up menu doesn't offer bold and italic settings; you get better looking type by applying the font designer's own bold and italic versions of the characters.

✦ Choose All Caps and Small Caps to convert the case of the type. You can't convert capital letters to Small Caps if you created those capitals by pressing Shift or Caps Lock on the keyboard.

Tip

Pressing Ctrl+Shift+K toggles selected text from uppercase to lowercase, as it does in QuarkXPress and InDesign. Remember that this shortcut works only when text is selected. If you're working with the type tool and haven't selected text, the shortcut affects any new text you create after the insertion marker; with any other tool, it brings up the Color Settings dialog box.

✦ Superscript and Subscript shrink the selected characters and move them above or below the text baseline, as you might want to do when typing mathematical equations. If Superscript and Subscript don't position characters as you want them, use the Baseline option to control them, as I explain in the upcoming section "Baseline."

✦ Underline Left and Underline Right apply to vertical type only and enable you to add a line to the left or right of the selected characters, respectively. When you work with horizontal type, the option changes to Underline and does just what its name implies. Strikethrough draws a line that slices right through the middle of your letters.

Tip

Keep in mind that you can always produce these styles manually by using the pencil or paintbrush — a choice that I prefer because it enables me to control the thickness, color, and opacity of the line and even play with blend modes.

✦ The Ligatures and Old Style options become available only if you select an OpenType font and only if the font designer included the required type variations. A ligature is a special character that produces a stylized version of a pair of characters, such as *a* and *e,* tying the two characters together with no space between, like so: æ. Old Style creates numbers at a reduced size, which may extend below the baseline.

Size

You can measure type in Photoshop 6 in points, pixels, or millimeters. To make your selection, press Ctrl+K and then Ctrl+5 to open the Units and Rulers panel of the Preferences dialog box. (You must exit text mode to do so.) Select the unit you want to use from the Type pop-up menu.

You can enter values in any of the acceptable units of measurement, and Photoshop automatically converts the value to the unit you select in the Preferences dialog box. Just type the number followed by the unit's abbreviation ("in" for inches, for example). After you press Enter, Photoshop makes the conversion for you. See Chapter 2 for more information about measurement units in Photoshop 6.

If the resolution of your image is 72 ppi, points and pixels are equal. There are 72 points in an inch, so 72 ppi means only 1 pixel per point. If the resolution is higher, however, a single point may include many pixels. The moral is to select the point option when you want to scale text according to image resolution; select pixels when you want to map text to an exact number of pixels in an image. (If you prefer, you can use millimeters instead of points; 1 millimeter equals 0.039 inch, which means 25.64 mm equals 72 points.)

Whatever unit you choose, type is measured from the top of its *ascenders* — letters like *b, d,* and *h* that rise above the level of most lowercase characters — to the bottom of its *descenders* — letters like *g, p,* and *q* that sink below the baseline. That's the way it's supposed to work, anyway. But throughout history, designers have played pretty loose and free with type size. To illustrate, Figure 15-9 shows the two standards, Times and Helvetica, along with a typical display font and a typical script. Each line is set to a type size of 180 pixels and then placed inside a 180-pixel box. The dotted horizontal lines indicate the baselines. As you can see, the only font that comes close to measuring the full 180 pixels is Tekton. The Brush Script sample is relatively minuscule (and Brush Script is husky compared with most scripts). So if you're looking to fill a specific space, be prepared to experiment. The only thing you can be sure of is that the type *won't* measure the precise dimensions you enter into the Size option box.

You can change type size by selecting a size from the Size pop-up menu or double-clicking the Size value, typing a new size, and pressing Enter. But the quickest option is to use the following keyboard shortcuts: To increase the type size in 2-point (or pixel) increments, press Ctrl+Shift+greater than (>). To similarly decrease the size, press Ctrl+Shift+less than (<). Add Alt to raise or lower the type size in 10-point (or pixel) increments. If you select millimeters as your unit of measurement, Photoshop raises or lowers the type size by 0.71 mm, which is the equivalent of 2 points.

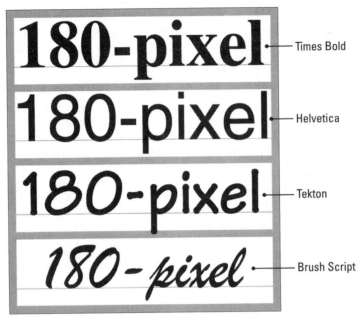

Figure 15-9: Four samples of 180-pixel type set inside 180-pixel boxes. As you can see, type size is an art, not a science.

Leading

Also called line spacing, *leading* is the vertical distance between the baseline of one line of type and the baseline of the next line of type, as illustrated in Figure 15-10. In Photoshop 6, you set leading via the Leading pop-up menu in the Character palette, labeled in Figure 15-8. Again, either select one of the menu options or double-click the current value, type a new value, and press Enter. Leading is measured in the unit you select from the Type pop-up menu in the Preferences dialog box.

If you choose the Auto setting, Photoshop automatically applies a leading equal to 120 percent of the type size. The 120 percent value isn't set in stone, however. To change the value, open the Paragraph palette menu and choose Justification to display the Justification dialog box. Enter the value you want to use in the Auto Leading option box and press Enter.

Tip

The easiest way to change the distance between one line and another is like so: First, when adjusting the space between a pair of lines, select the bottom of the two. Then press Alt+up arrow to decrease the leading in 2-point (pixel) increments and move the lines closer together. Press Alt+down arrow to increase the leading and spread the lines apart. To work in 10-point (pixel) increments, press Ctrl+Alt+up or down arrow. (Again, if you work in millimeters, the leading value changes by 0.71 mm and 3.53 mm—the equivalent of 2 points and 10 points, respectively.)

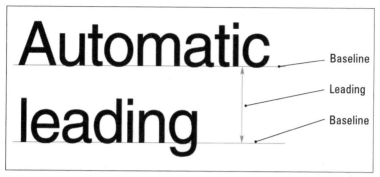

Figure 15-10: Leading is the distance between any two baselines in a single paragraph of text. Here, the type size is 120 pixels and the leading is 150 pixels.

Kerning

Technically, *kern* is the predetermined amount of space that surrounds each character of type and separates it from its immediate neighbors. (Some type-heads also call it *side bearing*.) But as is so frequently the case with our molten magma of a language, kern has found new popularity in recent years as a verb. So if a friend says, "Let's kern!" don't reach for your rowing oars. Get psyched to adjust the amount of room between characters of type. (Yes, there are people who love to kern and, yes, it is sad.)

You establish kerning via the Kerning pop-up menu in the Character palette, labeled earlier, in Figure 15-8. Select 0 to use the amount of side bearing indicated by the specifications in the font file on your hard drive. This setting gives you the same result as turning off the Auto Kern check box in earlier versions of Photoshop.

Some character combinations, however, don't look right when subjected to the default bearing. The spacing that separates a *T* and an *h* doesn't look so good when you scrap the *h* and insert an *r*. Therefore, the character combination *T* and *r* is a special-needs pair, a typographic marriage that requires kern counseling. If you select Metrics from the Kerning pop-up menu, Photoshop digs farther into the font specifications and pulls out a list of special-needs letter pairs. Then it applies a prescribed amount of spacing compensation, as illustrated by the second line in Figure 15-11. In former versions of Photoshop, turning on the Auto Kern check box performed the same function as the Metrics option.

In most cases, you'll want to select Metrics and trust in the designers' pair-kerning expertise. But there may be times when the prescribed kerning isn't to your liking. To establish your own kerning, click between two badly spaced characters of type. Then select any value other than 0 from the Kerning pop-up menu. Or double-click the current kerning value, type a value (in whole numbers from –1000 to 1000), and press Enter. Enter a negative value to shift the letters closer together. Enter a positive value to kern them farther apart. The last line in Figure 15-11 shows examples of my tighter manual kerns.

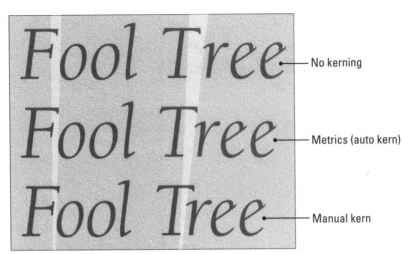

Figure 15-11: Three examples of the kerning options in
Photoshop 6. I've added wedges to track the ever-decreasing
space between the difficult pairs *Fo* and *Tr.*

Tip

To decrease the Kerning value (and thereby tighten the spacing) in increments of
20, press Alt+left arrow. To increase the Kerning value by 20, press Alt+right arrow.
You can also modify the kerning in increments of 100 by pressing Ctrl+Alt+left or
right arrow.

Incidentally, the Kerning and Tracking values (explained next) are measured in
$\frac{1}{1000}$ em, where an *em* (or *em space*) is the width of the letter *m* in the current font
at the current size. This may sound weird, but it's actually very helpful. Working in
ems ensures that your character spacing automatically updates to accommodate
changes in font and type size.

Fractional Widths

If kerning gives you fits, try turning off this option, found in the Character palette
menu. (Click the option name to toggle the feature on and off.) When type gets
very small, the spacing between letters may vary by fractions of a single pixel.
Photoshop has to split the difference in favor of one pixel or the other, and
50 percent of the time the visual effect is wrong. Better to turn the feature off
and avoid the problem entirely.

Tip

Enabling Fractional Widths is handy when you set the Kerning pop-up menu to 0
(which results in auto kerning) and set antialiasing to none, as demonstrated by the
10-point type in Figure 15-12. Macintosh users will find Fractional Widths especially
useful, particularly when working with preset screen font sizes such as 9-point
Geneva.

This is 10-point Arial with Auto kerning and Fractional Widths turned on. The letter spacing is a mess.

Turning off Auto kerning solves some of the spacing weirdness.

But turning off Fractional Widths produces the best effect.

Figure 15-12: Examples of how automatic kerning and the Fractional Widths option work together to correct the appearance of small type when antialiasing is turned off.

Tracking

The Tracking value, which you set using the pop-up menu to the right of the Kerning pop-up (see Figure 15-8), is virtually identical to Kerning. It affects character spacing, as measured in em spaces. It even reacts to the same keyboard shortcuts. The only differences are that you can apply Tracking to multiple characters at a time. And Photoshop permits you to apply a Tracking value on top of either automatic or manual kerning. (For folks experienced with Photoshop 4 and earlier, Tracking is more or less the equivalent of the old Spacing option, but measured in ems.)

Horizontal and vertical scaling

The Size pop-up menu scales text proportionally. But using the two scaling options highlighted in Figure 15-13, you can scale the width and height of letters individually. A value of 100 percent equals no change to the width and height. Enter a value larger than 100 percent to enlarge the character or lower than 100 percent to shrink it.

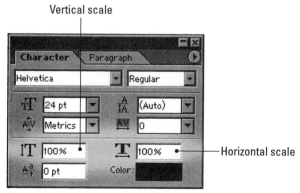

Figure 15-13: Change the Horizontal and Vertical scale values to change the height or width of text.

Photoshop applies horizontal and vertical scaling with respect to the baseline. If you're creating vertical type, then the Vertical value affects the width of the column of letters and the Horizontal value changes the height of each character.

Tip

You also can distort text after you create it by applying the Edit ➪ Free Transform command to the text layer. If you go that route and then decide you want the letters back at their original proportions, just open the Character palette and enter scaling values of 100 percent.

By converting text to shapes, as explained a little later in this chapter, you can reshape characters with even more flexibility, dragging points and line segments as you do when reshaping paths and objects created with the shape tools.

Baseline

The Baseline value, which you set using the option box in the bottom-left corner of the Character palette, raises or lowers selected text with respect to the baseline. In type parlance, this is called *baseline shift*. Raising type results in a superscript. Lowering type results in a subscript. An example of each appears in Figure 15-14.

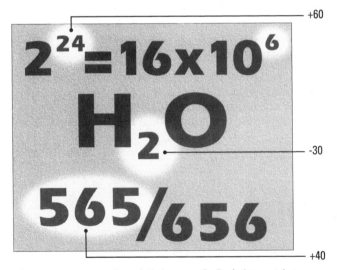

Figure 15-14: Baseline shift frequently finds its way into the worlds of math and science. The labels show the Baseline values.

You can also raise type to create a built fraction. Select the number before the slash (the *numerator*) and enter a positive value into the Baseline option box. Reduce the type size of the number after the slash (the *denominator*) but leave the Baseline value set to 0. That's all I did to get the fraction at the bottom of Figure 15-14.

Press Alt+up arrow to raise the Baseline value by 1 or Shift+Alt+down arrow to lower the value by 1. To change the value in increments of 10, add in the Ctrl key.

Of course, now that Photoshop offers both a superscript and subscript type style, which you toggle on and off from the Character palette menu, you can use those options to create your fractions, too. But using the Baseline option gives you more control over how much your characters move up or down from the baseline.

Color

Click the Color swatch on the Options bar or in the Character palette to display the Color Picker dialog box. In Photoshop 6, you can apply color on a per-character basis. The color you select affects the next character you type and selected text. This new approach to color makes creating multihued lines of text much easier than it was in the past, when you had to create your text in a single color, select the colors you wanted to change, and then fill those characters by using Alt+Delete.

When applying color to selected text, you can't preview the new color accurately because the selection highlight interferes with the display. Press Ctrl+H to toggle the selection highlight (as well as all other on-screen guides) on and off so that you can better judge your color choice.

Antialiasing

The anti-aliasing pop-up menu, found on the Options bar in Photoshop 6 (refer back to Figure 15-8), offers four choices. Whichever option you choose, the entire layer gets the effect. You can't apply antialiasing to individual characters on a layer, as you can other formatting options.

Choose None from the pop-up menu to turn off antialiasing (softening) and give characters hard, choppy edges, which is good for very small type. Crisp adds a slight amount of antialiasing, thus retaining sharp contrast. If you notice jagged edges, try applying the Smooth setting. If antialiasing seems to rob the text of its weight, you can thicken it up a bit with the Strong setting. Crisp, Strong, and Smooth produce more dramatic effects at small type sizes, as shown in Figure 15-15.

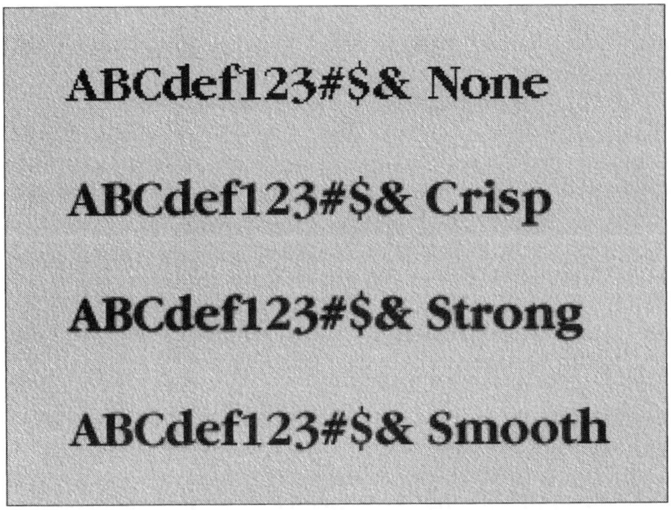

Figure 15-15: The results of the four antialias settings, which you choose from a pop-up menu on the Options bar in Photoshop 6

Applying paragraph formatting

Photoshop 6 brings the addition of paragraph formatting options, including justification, alignment, hyphenation, line spacing, indent, and even first-line indent. With the exception of the alignment option, all these options appear only in the new Paragraph palette and affect text that you create inside a bounding box. (See the section "Creating and manipulating text in a frame," earlier in this chapter, for information about this method of adding text.)

Figure 15-16 provides a field guide to the Paragraph palette and also shows the palette menu. Like the Character palette menu, this one offers additional choices related to paragraph formatting.

Note Photoshop can apply formatting to each paragraph in a bounding box independently of the others. Click with the type tool inside a paragraph to alter the formatting of that paragraph only. To format multiple paragraphs, drag over them. If you want to format all paragraphs in the bounding box, click the type layer in the Layers palette, which selects the whole shebang. You also can click the type and then press Ctrl+A.

Tip When no text is selected, you can restore the palette's default paragraph settings by choosing Reset Paragraph from the Paragraph palette menu.

Indent options

Alignment buttons

Justification buttons

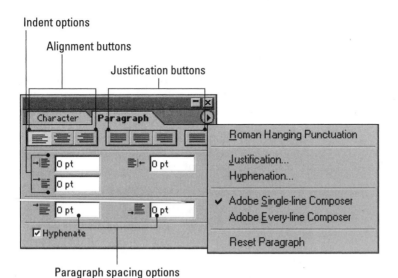

Paragraph spacing options

Figure 15-16: If you create text in a bounding box, you can control how text flows inside the box by using the options in the new Paragraph palette.

Alignment

The alignment options, found both in the Paragraph palette and on the Options bar, let you control how lines of type align with each other. Photoshop lets you align text left, center, or right. Figure 15-17 labels the alignment options along with the justification options, explained next. The lines on the alignment buttons indicate what each option does, and they change depending on whether you're formatting vertical or horizontal type.

Align left

Align center

Align right

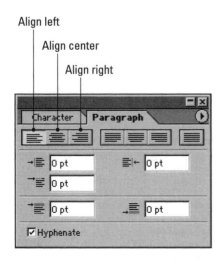

Figure 15-17: In addition to aligning individual lines of type with each other, you can apply paragraph justification to text in Photoshop 6.

If you create bounding-box text, Photoshop aligns text with respect to the boundaries of the box. For example, if you draw a bounding box with the right alignment option selected, the text cursor appears at the right edge of the box and moves to the left as you type. For vertical type, the right-align and left-align options align text to the bottom and top of the bounding box, respectively. You must choose a different alignment option to relocate the cursor; you can't simply click at another spot in the bounding box.

When you create point text — that is, by simply clicking in the image window instead of drawing a bounding box — the alignment occurs with respect to the first spot you click and affects all lines on the current text layer.

You can change the alignment using standard keyboard tricks. Press Ctrl+Shift+L to align selected lines to the left. Ctrl+Shift+C centers text, and Ctrl+Shift+R aligns it to the right.

Roman Hanging Punctuation

One additional alignment option controls the alignment of punctuation marks. You can choose to have punctuation marks fall outside the bounding box so that the first and last characters in all lines of type are letters or numbers. This setup can create a cleaner-looking block of text. Choose Roman Hanging Punctuation from the Paragraph palette menu to toggle the option on and off.

Justification

The justification options adjust text so that it stretches from one edge of the bounding box to another. The different options, labeled in Figure 15-18, affect the way Photoshop deals with the last line in a paragraph.

Choose left justify to align the line to the left edge of the box; right justify to align to the right edge; and center to put the line smack dab between the left and right edges. With force justify, Photoshop adjusts the spacing of the last line of text so that it, too, fills the entire width of the bounding box. This option typically produces ugly results, especially with very short lines, because you wind up with huge gullies between words. However, if you want to space a word evenly across an area of your image, you can use force justify to your advantage. Drag the bounding box to match the size of the area you want to cover, type the word, and then choose the force justify option. If you later change the size of the bounding box, the text shifts accordingly.

You can further control how Photoshop justifies text by using the spacing options in the Justification dialog box, also shown in Figure 15-18. To open the dialog box, choose Justification from the Paragraph palette menu. You can adjust the amount of space allowed between words and characters, and you can specify whether you want to alter the width of *glyphs* — a fancy word meaning the individual characters in a font. Here's what you need to know:

✦ The values reflect a percentage of default spacing. The default word spacing is 100 percent, which gives you a normal space character between words. You can increase word spacing to 1,000 percent of the norm or reduce it to 0 percent.

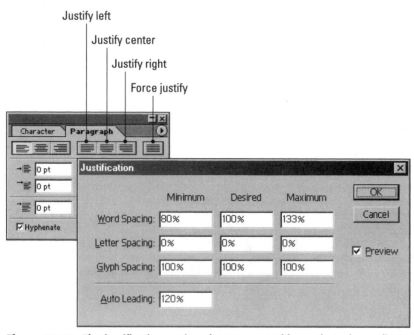

Figure 15-18: The justification options let you control how Photoshop adjusts your text when justifying it.

✦ The default letter spacing is 0 percent, which means no space between characters. The maximum letter spacing value is 500 percent; the minimum is –100 percent.

✦ For glyphs, the default value is 100 percent, which leaves the characters at their original width. You can stretch the characters to 200 percent of their original width or squeeze them to 50 percent.

Enter your ideal value for each option into the Desired box. Whenever possible, Photoshop uses these values. The Minimum and Maximum options tell Photoshop how much it can alter the spacing or character width when justifying text. If you wind up with text that's crammed too tightly into the bounding box, raise the Minimum values. Similarly, if the text looks too far apart, lower the Maximum values. Enter negative values to set a value lower than 0 percent.

Note

You can't enter a Minimum value that's larger than the Desired value or a Maximum value that's smaller than the Desired value. Nor can you enter a Desired value that's larger than Maximum or smaller than Minimum.

Tip

If you want a specific character width used consistently throughout your text, use the Horizontal scale option in the Character palette rather than the Glyph spacing option. You can apply Horizontal scaling to regular text as well as paragraph text.

As for that Auto Leading option at the bottom of the Justification dialog box, it determines the amount of leading that's used when you select Auto from the Leading pop-up menu in the Character palette. For information on additional paragraph spacing controls, keep reading.

Indents and paragraph spacing

The five option boxes in the Paragraph palette control the amount of space between individual paragraphs in a bounding box and between the text and the edges of the bounding box. Figure 15-19 labels each option.

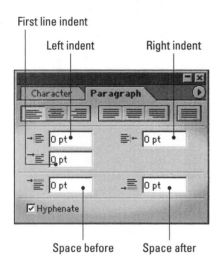

First line indent

Left indent   Right indent

Space before   Space after

Figure 15-19: Enter values into the top three option boxes to adjust the paragraph indent; use the bottom options to change spacing before and after a paragraph.

Photoshop's indent options work the same as their counterparts in just about every program on the planet. But just to cover all bases, here's the drill:

✦ Enter values in the top two option boxes to indent the entire paragraph from the left edge or right edge of the box.

✦ To indent the first line of the paragraph only, enter a value into the first-line indent option box, which sits all alone on the second row of option boxes. Enter a positive value to shove the first line to the right; enter a negative value to push it leftward, so that it extends beyond the left edge of the other lines in the paragraph.

✦ Use the bottom option boxes to increase the space before a paragraph (left box) and after a paragraph (right box).

Note

In all cases, you must press Enter to apply the change. To set the unit of measurement for these options, use the Type pop-up menu in the Preferences dialog box; you can choose from pixels, points, and millimeters. As is the case with options in the

Character palette, however, you can enter the value using some other unit of measurement by typing the value followed by the unit's abbreviation ("in" for inches, for example). When you press Enter, Photoshop converts the value to the unit you selected in the Preferences dialog box. (Chapter 2 explains other pertinent facts about units preferences in Photoshop 6.)

Hyphenation

In most cases, you probably won't be entering text that requires hyphenation to an image. I mean, if you're entering that much text, you're better off doing it in your page-layout program and then importing the image into the layout.

But just to cover all bases, Photoshop offers the Hyphenate check box in the Paragraph palette. When you select this option, the program automatically hyphenates your text using the limits set in the Hyphenation dialog box, shown in Figure 15-20. Choose Hyphenation from the Paragraph palette menu to open the dialog box.

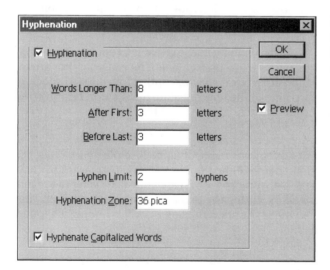

Figure 15-20: If you ever want to hyphenate text, set the hyphenation controls here.

This dialog box, like several others related to text formatting, comes straight from Adobe InDesign and Illustrator. In case you're not familiar with the controls, they work as follows:

 ✦ Enter a value into the Words Longer Than option box to specify the number of characters required before Photoshop can hyphenate a word.

 ✦ Use the After First and Before Last options to control the minimum number of characters before a hyphen and after a hyphen, respectively.

✦ Enter a number into the Hyphen Limit option box to tell Photoshop how many consecutive lines can contain hyphens.

✦ Finally, specify how far from the edge of the bounding box Photoshop can place a hyphen by entering a value into the Hyphenation Zone box.

✦ Turn off the Hyphenate Capitalized Words check box if you want Photoshop to keep its mitts off words that start with an uppercase letter. Hope I didn't insult your intelligence on this one.

Line breaks and composition methods

When you create paragraph text that includes several lines, you may not like the way that Photoshop breaks text from line to line. You may be able to improve the situation by changing the equation that Photoshop uses to determine where lines break.

If you choose Adobe Every-line Composer from the Paragraph palette, the program evaluates the lines of text as a group and figures out the best place to break lines. In doing so, Photoshop takes into account the Hyphenation and Justification settings. Typically, this option results in more evenly spaced text and fewer hyphens.

Adobe Single-line Composer takes a line-by-line approach to your text, using a few basic rules to determine the best spot to break a line. The program first attempts to fit all words on the line by adjusting word spacing, opting for reduced spacing over expanded spacing where possible. If the spacing adjustments don't do the trick, Photoshop hyphenates the last word on the line and breaks the line after the hyphen.

As I've mentioned before, these options may not come into play very often because most people don't create long blocks of text in Photoshop. If you want to control line breaks for a few lines of text, you can just create your text using the regular, text-at-a-point method instead of putting the text in a bounding box. Then you can just press Enter at the spot where you want the line to break, adding a hyphen to the end of the line if needed.

Warping text

For all its glories, text in Photoshop has always lacked an option widely used by designers creating type in drawing programs: the ability to fit text to a path. You were limited to creating straight lines of text only—no wrapping type around a circle or otherwise bending your words.

You still can't fit text to a path in Photoshop 6, but you may be able to get close to the effect you want by using the new Warp Text feature. Similar to the text art features that have been available in word processing programs for some time, Warp Text bends and distorts text to simulate the effect of fitting text to a path. You can choose from 15 different path shapes and choose to curve type, distort it, or both.

Tip

You can warp paragraph text or regular text, but the warp always affects all existing text on the layer. So if you want to reshape just a part of a line of text—for example, to make the last few letters in a word bend upward—put that bit of text on its own layer.

Note

In addition, note that you can't warp type to which you've applied the faux styles that reside on the Character palette menu. Nor can you warp bitmap fonts or fonts for which the designer hasn't provided the paths, or outlines, that make up the font characters.

After selecting a text layer, click the Warp Text button on the Options bar, labeled in Figure 15-21, or choose Layer ➪ Type ➪ Warp Text. Photoshop displays the Warp Text dialog box, also shown in the figure.

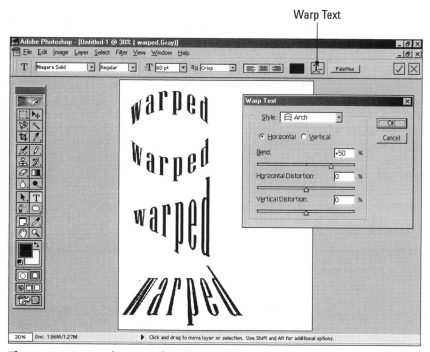

Figure 15-21: Use the controls in the Warp Text dialog box to simulate the effect of fitting text to a path.

After choosing a warp design from the Style pop-up menu, set the orientation of the warp by clicking the Horizontal or Vertical radio button. Then adjust the Bend, Horizontal Distortion, and Vertical Distortion sliders until you get an effect that fits your needs. You can preview your changes in the image window.

I'm sure you could easily figure out how this dialog box works, but a few hints may speed you on your way:

✦ When you select the Horizontal radio button, the warp occurs as the shape in the Style pop-up menu suggests. If you choose Vertical, the warp is applied as if you turned the shape on its side.

✦ Use the Bend value to change the direction of the curve. For the warp style selected in Figure 15-21, for example, a positive Bend value curves the text upward, as shown in the top example in Figure 15-21, and a negative value curves the text in the opposite direction, as shown in the second example.

✦ You can use the Horizontal and Vertical Distortion options to create perspective effects. Horizontal Distortion puts the origin point of the perspective to the left if you enter a positive value and to the right if you enter a negative value. I used a positive value to create the third line of text in Figure 15-21.

Vertical Distortion, as you can probably guess, places the origin point above the text if you enter a positive value and below the text if you enter a negative value. I created the bottom line of type in Figure 15-21 by entering a positive Vertical Distortion value.

✦ If you edit warped text, Photoshop reapplies the original warp to the layer.

Tip   After warping the text, you can often improve the effect by tweaking the tracking, kerning, and other character spacing and scaling formatting. If you have trouble achieving the distortion or perspective effect you're after, bypass the Warp Text dialog box and instead use Edit ➪ Free Transform to manipulate the text layer. (You must get out of text edit mode to access the command.) The steps in the next section offer an example of this technique.

Editing text as shapes

Way back near the beginning of this chapter, I mentioned that you can convert each letter in a text layer to individual shapes by choosing Layer ➪ Type ➪ Convert to Shape. The command converts all text on a layer; you can't convert part of the text on a layer and leave the rest alone. If the command is grayed out, you're in text edit mode; click the Commit (check mark) or Cancel (X) button on the Options bar to exit edit mode.

After you make the conversion, each character works just like a shape that you create with the new shape tools. Photoshop creates points and line segments as it sees fit for each letter, as shown in Figure 15-22. This enables you to fool with the shape of each letter by dragging points and segments, as I'm doing in the right example in the figure. And you can apply all the same effects to your new text shapes as you can to any shape. (Chapter 14 provides a complete rundown of your options.)

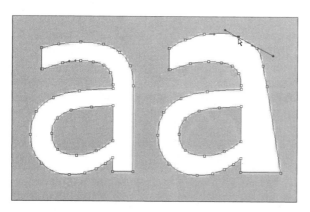

Figure 15-22: Converting text to shapes enables you to drag line segments and handles to reshape individual characters, as I did here.

Before you convert text to shapes, however, make sure that you don't need to make further changes to character or paragraph formatting or add or delete letters. Photoshop sees your text purely as shapes after the conversion so you can't edit the text using the type tool anymore. For safety's sake, save the text to a new layer or image before choosing Convert to Shape.

As do regular shapes, type shapes appear jagged around the edges because of the tiny outline that Photoshop displays around the shape. To hide the outline and smooth out the on-screen appearance of the text, press Ctrl+H. Of course, in Photoshop 6, this command also hides the marching ants, guides, and other on-screen aids. The View ➪ Show ➪ Target Path command enables you to toggle just the shape outlines.

Character Masks and Layer Effects

In Photoshop 6, you can create a text-based selection outline or mask using one of two methods: Enter text with the type tool set to type mask mode or convert existing text to a work path. The next two sections explain both options.

Creating a text mask

In past editions of Photoshop, you used special type mask tools to create text-shaped selection outlines. Now you use the ordinary type tool (press T to select it) and set the tool to mask mode by clicking the Type Mask button on the Options bar, labeled in Figure 15-23. Be sure to click the button *before* you create your text.

Type mask

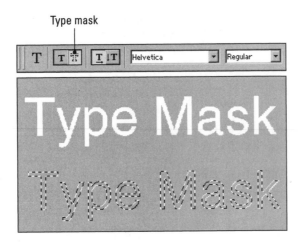

Figure 15-23: When you work in type mask mode, white areas (top row) indicate unmasked portions of the image, just as in quick mask mode.

After you click in the image, Photoshop covers it with a translucent overlay, as when you work in quick mask mode. The overlay appears in whatever color, and at whatever opacity, you set for the quick mask overlay (by double-clicking the quick mask icon in the toolbox).

As you type, you create white characters, as shown in the top example in the figure, giving you the same result as when you paint with white in quick mask mode—that is, to unmask areas of the image. Only this time, Photoshop dumps the white paint on for you. You can apply all of the same text formatting options that are available when you work with ordinary text.

Tip If you move your cursor away from the text while you're in text edit mode, the move cursor appears. You can then drag the mask around the image window to position it without exiting text mode. When you commit the text (by pressing Ctrl+Enter or clicking the check-mark button on the Options bar), the overlay disappears and your selection outline appears, as shown in the bottom of Figure 15-23, just as when you switch from quick mask mode back to marching ants mode.

Tip After you create your first selection outline, you can Shift-click with the type tool to redisplay the overlay and create a second text mask, just as you Shift-click with standard selection outlines to add to an existing selection.

Converting type to a path

To convert existing type to a work path, choose Layer ➪ Type ➪ Create Work Path. You see the path outline around the characters, as when you convert text to shapes, and the new text-based path item appears in the Paths palette. All the standard path-editing techniques apply. You can edit, stroke, and fill the path, export it as a clipping path, or convert the path to a selection outline. Chapter 8 provides a full explanation of working with paths.

Note After you create a work path, Photoshop does not trash the original text layer. You can continue to edit the type as usual or delete the layer if you want to keep only the path.

Type masks on the march

The most obvious use for a type-based selection is to select a portion of an image. In a matter of seconds, you get type filled with photographic imagery. While nifty in theory, finding a use for photographic type is another matter. In the following steps, I created a type mask to select a portion of an image, send it to a new layer, and then modify brightness values to distinguish the text from its background. Though very easy, this technique yields some interesting results.

STEPS: Selecting Part of an Image Using Character Outlines

1. **Assemble the image you want to mask.** In my case, I start with the classic eel erupting from a clock pictured in Figure 15-24. I know, you're thinking, "Deke, how do you come up with such attractive stuff?" It's a knack, I guess. Try not to be jealous.

Figure 15-24: I created this image by selecting an eel, layering it against a clock, and using a layer mask to blend the two images. Then I flattened the image and saved it.

Photoshop 6

2. **Create your text.** Select the type tool, click the Type Mask button, and click in the image window. Enter and format your type as usual. To reposition the mask, move the cursor away from the type until you see the move cursor and then drag in the image window. When you're happy with the mask, press Ctrl+Enter to convert the text mask to a selection outline.

3. **Modify the selection outlines as needed.** I chose Select ➪ Transform Selection and then Ctrl-dragged the corner handles to distort my character outlines, as in Figure 15-25. (The character outlines are hard to see so I've added a translucent white fill to make the text more legible. The fill is there merely for the purpose of the screen shot.)

Figure 15-25: The Transform Selection command enabled me to apply a perspective effect to my character outlines before using them to select the image.

4. **Send the selected text to a separate layer by pressing Ctrl+J.** The selection outlines disappear so the image looks like it did before you started. But rest assured, you have characters filled with imagery on a separate layer.

5. **Return to the background layer and create a new layer by clicking the page icon at the bottom of the Layers palette.** The easiest way to distinguish text from background image is to darken the background image and lighten the text (or vice versa). This new layer is just the ticket.

6. **Fill the layer with a dark color.** Then choose the Multiply mode (Shift+Alt+M) and lower the Opacity value. For my part, I added a black-to-white gradation starting from the lower left and ending in the upper-right portion of the image. Thanks to the Multiply mode, just the area behind the text was darkened, as shown in Figure 15-26. I also lowered the Opacity to 40 percent.

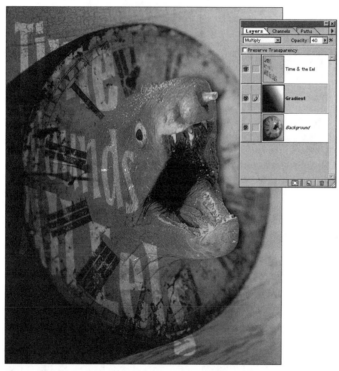

Figure 15-26: To darken the area behind the type, I added a black-to-white gradation on a new layer and set the layer to the Multiply mode.

7. **Switch to the type layer.** Next, we'll make the type a lighter color.

8. **Create a new layer and fill it with a light color.** Set the blend mode to Screen (Shift+Alt+S) and adjust the Opacity value as desired. I filled my layer with white and set the Opacity to 80 percent.

9. **Press Ctrl+G.** This groups the light layer with the type below it, as demonstrated in Figure 15-27. The light area outside the type goes away. Now the type stands out clearly from its background, even though you can see the image both inside and outside the letters.

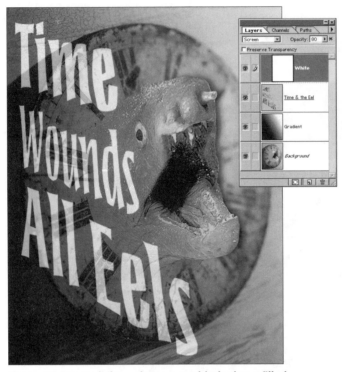

Figure 15-27: To lighten the text, I added a layer filled entirely with white and grouped it with the type layer.

10. **Apply whatever additional effects strike your fancy.** I returned to the type layer and chose Layer ➪ Layer Styles ➪ Bevel and Emboss. Then I selected the Outer Bevel setting to create the letters shown in Figure 15-28. I also applied the Drop Shadow effect to the text in the upper-right corner and the Pillow Emboss effect to the Jelly-Vision logo.

As the enlarged view of the Jelly-Vision logo in Figure 15-29 shows, Photoshop's layer effects can work super-fast miracles on type. In a matter of seconds, I was able to transform the top example in the figure into the bottom one.

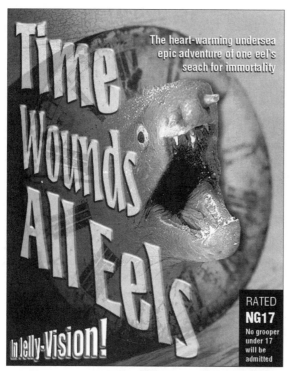

Figure 15-28: I managed to transform a strange, drab composition into this mighty attractive poster art using nothing but text.

Figure 15-29: Creating the Jelly-Vision logo was as simple as distorting the text and applying a Pillow Emboss layer effect.

Layer effects bonanza

You'll have a blast experimenting with layer effects and type. Layer effects are fast, flexible, easy to use, and they were designed largely with editable type in mind. Sure, they get overused. But as with any cool feature, you can stay ahead of the curve by applying your effects creatively.

Figure 15-30 shows three very simple but unusual implementations of layer effects. All three effects rely on character masks, but I created these selection outlines using standard type layers. I clicked with the type tool, entered the words *Shake*, *Murder*, and *Imprint*, and then formatted them. Then I Ctrl-clicked on the layer to draw out the selection outlines as I needed them.

Why use a standard type layer to create selection outlines instead of the type mask option? Simple — because type on a layer is forever editable; a type mask is not. Editing type on a layer doesn't affect an existing character mask, but I can Ctrl-click to generate new masks any time I like. The upshot is that a type layer serves double duty — to create both editable text and type masks. This one tool does everything you need, which is why I for one never change type tools; I always work with layered type.

Figure 15-30: Three examples of childishly simple layer effects applied creatively to character masks

That's really the key to creating cool effects. The rest is just "scribbling and bib-bling" as a dramatized Mozart once said. But because the scribbles and bibbles may prove of minor interest to you, here's how I made each effect:

✦ **Shake:** First, the boring stuff. I extracted the layer mask for the word Shake by Ctrl-clicking on my type layer and Shift+Alt-dragging around the word Shake with the rectangular marquee tool to deselect Murder and Imprint. Then I switched to the background layer and pressed Ctrl+J to send Shake to an inde-pendent layer. Finally I pressed the / key to lock the transparent pixels so I could edit the type and only the type.

Now for the fun stuff. I created a pattern from the embossed texture back in Figure 15-4 using Edit ⇨ Define Pattern. Then I used Edit ⇨ Fill to fill Shake with the pattern. After double-clicking the new layer name to open the Layer Style dialog box, I applied a black drop shadow, setting the blend mode to Multiply, the opacity to 100 percent, and the angle to 45 degrees. Next I applied a white Inner Shadow, setting the blend mode to Screen, opacity to 85 percent, and angle to –135 degrees. The upshot is that the drop shadow darkens the back-ground and the inner shadow lightens the characters.

✦ **Murder:** I filled the background layer behind the word Murder with black. Then I did all the boring stuff that I mentioned two paragraphs ago — Ctrl-clicked the type layer, intersected Murder with the marquee tool, pressed Ctrl+J to send Murder to its own layer, and pressed / to lock the transparent pixels.

I set the foreground color to white and brushed across the Murder layer with the paintbrush set to 40 percent opacity. Because the transparency of the layer was locked, I painted inside the letters only. Finally, I opened the Layer Style dialog box and applied a white drop shadow to the text layer, setting the blend mode to Screen and the Angle value to –126. The result is a directional glow.

✦ **Imprint:** Here I filled the area behind Imprint with the same pattern I defined for Shake, and then I mushed the pattern together using the filters Noise ⇨ Median and Blur ⇨ Gaussian Blur (both explained in Chapter 10). Then, as usual, I did the boring stuff — Ctrl-clicked on the original type layer, inter-sected Imprint with the marquee tool, and pressed Ctrl+J and the / key.

With Imprint on its own layer, I double-clicked the layer name to open the Layer Style dialog box and applied the Bevel and Emboss effect using the Emboss effect style. The result was a bit disappointing. Muted and dark, it didn't have the punch I wanted. To brighten it up, I duplicated the Imprint layer by dragging it onto the page icon at the bottom of the Layers palette. Then I pressed Shift+Alt+S to apply the Screen mode. The final result is the much sharper effect you see in Figure 15-30.

✦   ✦   ✦

Color for Print and the Web

Essential Color Management

Plunging Headlong into Color

Most artists react very warmly to the word *color* and a bit more coolly to the word *management,* especially those of us who have made the mistake of taking on managerial chores ourselves. Put the two words together, however, and you can clear a room. The term *color management* has been known to cause the sturdiest of characters to shriek and sweat like a herd of elephants locked in a sauna.

It's no exaggeration to say that color management is the least understood topic in all of computer imaging. From my experience talking to Photoshop users, most folks expect to calibrate their monitors and achieve reliable if not perfect color. But in point of fact, there's no such thing. So-called *device-dependent color*—that is, synthetic color produced by a piece of hardware—is a moving target. The best Photoshop or any other piece of software can do is to convert from one target to the next.

For what it's worth, most consumer monitors (and video boards, for that matter) are beyond calibration, in the strict sense of the word. You can try your hand at using a hardware calibrator—one of those devices where you plop a little suction cup onto your screen. But calibrators often have less to do with changing screen colors than identifying them. Even if your monitor permits prepress-quality calibration—as in the case of $3,000 devices sold by different vendors over the years, including Radius, Mitsubishi, and LaCie—it's not enough to simply correct the colors on screen; you also have to tell Photoshop what you've done.

Therefore, color management is first and foremost about identifying your monitor. You have to explain your screen's foibles to Photoshop so that it can make every attempt to account for them. In the old days, Photoshop used the screen data to calculate CMYK conversions and that was it. Photoshop 5 went two steps farther, embedding a *profile* that identifies the source of the image and using this information to translate colors from one monitor to another. Photoshop 6 goes a couple of steps farther still, permitting you to work in multiple profile-specific color spaces at the same time — great for artists who alternatively create images for print and the Web — and specify exactly what to do with images that lack profiles.

The new Color Settings command is both wonderful and bewildering. It can just as easily mess up colors as fix them. But if you read this chapter, you and your colors should be able to ride the currents safely from one digital destination to the next. And best of all, color management in Photoshop 6 is consistent with color management found in Illustrator 9 and future Adobe applications. Learn one and the others make a heck of a lot more sense.

A Typical Color-Matching Scenario

Photoshop 6 devotes three features to color management. The first is the Adobe Gamma control panel, which characterizes your monitor. Choose Settings from the Start menu, and then choose Control Panel. After the Control Panel window comes up, double-click the Adobe Gamma icon. The second feature is Edit ➪ Color Settings. Choose this command or press Ctrl+Shift+K to display the Color Settings dialog box, which lets you edit device-dependent color spaces and decide what to do with profile mismatches. Finally, use File ➪ Save As to decide whether to embed a profile into a saved image or include no profile at all.

I could explain each of these features independently and leave it up to you to put them together. But peering into every tree is not always the best way to understand the forest. So rather than explaining so much as a single option, I begin our tour of color management by showing the various control panels, commands, and options in action. In this introductory scenario, I take an RGB image I've created on my Mac and open it up on my PC. The Mac is equipped with a PressView 21SR and the PC is hooked up to a generic Sony Trinitron screen, so I've got both extremes pretty well covered. Yet despite the change of platforms and the even more dramatic change in monitors, Photoshop maintains a high degree of consistency so the image looks the same on both sides of the divide. While the specifics of setting up your system obviously vary, this walk-through should give you an idea of how color management in Photoshop works.

If you're well-versed in Photoshop 5 and you already have a rough idea of how profile-based color management works, skip ahead to the section "Color Conversion Central." There I explain the intricacies of the Color Settings dialog box, which is where the vast majority of the color management process occurs.

Setting up the source monitor

If you own a monitor with calibration capabilities, I recommend that you start off by calibrating it. In the case of the PressView, I launch a utility called ProSense that works with the hardware calibrator to both adjust screen colors and save screen profiles in a variety of formats. For purposes of Photoshop for the Mac, the most important format is ColorSync, which is Apple's system-wide color management extension. I also save a Photoshop Monitor File version of the profile, as shown in Figure 16-1.

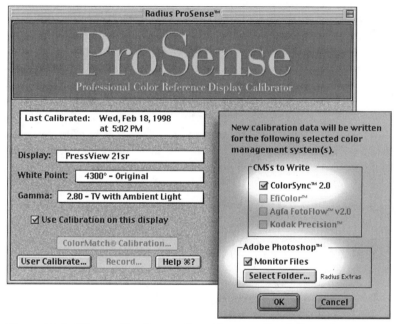

Figure 16-1: When calibrating my PressView monitor, I direct the ProSense utility to save a ColorSync and Photoshop Monitor File version of the screen profile.

The next step is to assign the profile to the monitor. I choose Apple ➪ Control Panels ➪ Monitors. Then I click the Color button to display the scrolling list of ColorSync Profile options shown on the right side of Figure 16-2. The PressView 21sr item turns out to be the profile I just created with the ProSense utility. I select it and move on.

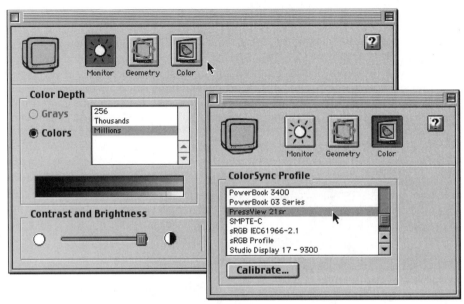

Figure 16-2: On the Mac, choose the Monitors control panel and click the Color button (left) to load a monitor profile that will automatically work with Photoshop.

The Gamma control panel

"Swell," I can hear you say, "But what do those of us with more down-to-earth monitors do?" For everyday people, Photoshop ships with the Adobe Gamma control panel. Choose Start ⇨ Settings ⇨ Control Panel to bring up the Control Panel window. Then double-click the Adobe Gamma icon. (If the control panel displays a warning that your video card doesn't support system-wide color management, don't sweat it. Most video cards don't.) Select the Step By Step (Wizard) option and click the Next button to walk through the setup process one step at a time. If you see a control panel like the one on the right side of Figure 16-3, click the Wizard button to continue.

When using the Adobe Gamma Wizard, all you have to do is answer questions and click the Next button to advance from one screen to another. For example, after adjusting the contrast and brightness settings, Gamma asks you to specify the nature of your screen's red, green, and blue phosphors. If you own a Trinitron or Diamondtron monitor — which you'll know because you paid more for it — select the Trinitron settings. Or select Custom and enter values according to your monitor's documentation. If the documentation does not suggest settings, ignore this screen and click Next to move on. So you don't know your phosphors — that's life. You've got bigger fish to fry.

The next screen, pictured in Figure 16-4, is the most important. It asks you to balance the red, green, and blue display functions of your monitor. But to do so, you need to turn off the View Single Gamma Only check box; this presents you with separate controls over each of the three monitor channels. Then use the sliders to make the inner squares match the outer borders. You are in essence calibrating the monitor according to your unique perceptions of it, making this particular brand of characterization a highly personal one.

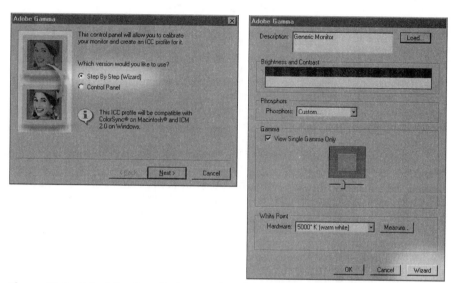

Figure 16-3: Select the Step By Step option (left) or click the Wizard button to advance one step at a time through the monitor setup process.

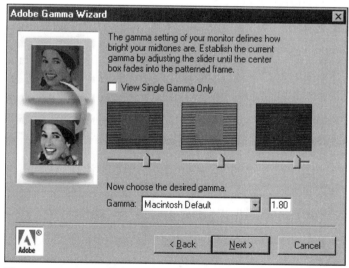

Figure 16-4: Turn off the View Single Gamma Only check box to modify each of the three color channels independently.

The next screen asks you to set the white point, which defines the general color cast of your screen from 5,000 degrees Kelvin for slightly red to 9,300 degrees for slightly blue. A medium value of 6,500 degrees is a happy "daylight" medium. To find the best setting for your monitor, click the Measure button. Then click the gray box that appears the most neutral—neither too warm nor too cool—until you get dumped back into the Gamma Wizard. Then click Next.

When you click the Finish button, the Gamma utility asks you to name your new monitor profile and save it to disk. Name it whatever you want, but don't change the location—it has to go into the Color folder inside the System or System 32 folder to be made available to Photoshop and other applications.

Adobe Gamma generates a custom monitor profile and automatically alerts Photoshop to the change. You don't even have to bring up the ColorSync control panel (though you may want to just to confirm). Your screen may not look any different than it did before you opened Gamma, but you can rest assured that Photoshop is now officially aware of its capabilities and limitations.

Note

Incidentally, the term *gamma* refers to the amount of correction required to convert the color signal generated inside the monitor (let's call it x) to the color display that you see on screen (y). Imagine a simple graph with the input signal x along the bottom and the output y along the side. A gamma of 1.0 would result in a diagonal line from bottom-left to upper-right corner. A higher gamma value tugs at the center of that line and curves it upward. As you tug, more and more of the curve is taken up by darker values, resulting in a darker display. So a typical Mac screen with default gamma of 1.8 is lighter than a typical PC screen with a default gamma of 2.2. For a real-time display of gamma in action, check out the discussion of the Curves dialog box included in Chapter 17.

Selecting the ideal working space

Now that I've identified my monitor, I need to select an RGB *working environment*, which is a color space other than the one identified for the monitor. This is the strangest step, but it's one of the most important as well. Fortunately, all it requires is a bit of imagination to understand fully.

On my Mac, I switch to Photoshop and choose Edit ➪ Color Settings. Photoshop displays the dialog box shown in Figure 16-5. I'm immediately faced with a dizzying array of options—no gradual immersion into the world of color management here— but Photoshop does make a small attempt to simplify the process. The program offers several collections of predefined settings via the Settings pop-up menu. Among the settings are Color Management Off, which deactivates Photoshop's color management entirely; ColorSync Workflow, which is useful in all-Macintosh environments; and Emulate Photoshop 4, which both turns color management off and mimics Version 4's screen display.

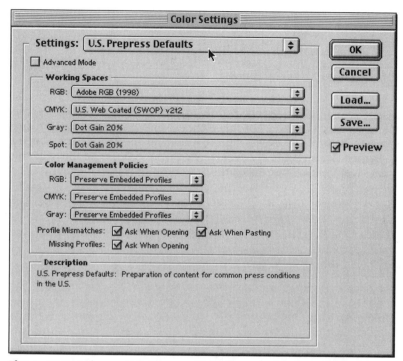

Figure 16-5: I choose U.S. Prepress Defaults to access the Adobe RGB (1998) color space, which affords me a large theoretical RGB spectrum.

Each of these options has its relative advantages in certain settings, but most folks will want to gravitate toward two other options. If you create most of your images for the Web, select the Web Graphics Defaults option. This directs Photoshop's color functions so that they're most amenable to screen display. On the other hand, if most of your artwork finds its way into print, and if you live in the United States or some country that supports U.S. printing standards, select U.S. Prepress Defaults.

For my part, I select U.S. Prepress Defaults, as shown in Figure 16-5. If you have any doubts about whether to favor Web or print graphics, I recommend you do the same. Why? Among its other attractions, the U.S. Prepress option sets the working RGB color space to Adobe RGB (1998), arguably the best environment for viewing 24-bit images on screen.

Adobe RGB includes a wide range of theoretical RGB colors, whether they can truly be displayed on a monitor or not. You may see some *clipping* on screen — where two or more color spaces appear as one — but Photoshop has greater latitude when interpolating and calculating colors.

After selecting U.S. Prepress Defaults, I click the OK button. The source environment is fully prepared. Now to save an image and send it on its way.

Embedding the profile

The final step on the Mac side is to embed the Adobe RGB profile into a test image. (The word *embed* simply means that Photoshop adds a little bit of code to the file stating where it was last edited.) For this, I choose File ➪ Save As, which displays the dialog box in Figure 16-6. After naming the file and specifying a location on disk, I select the Embed Color Profile check box, which embeds the Adobe RGB color profile into the test image. Then I click the Save button to save the file.

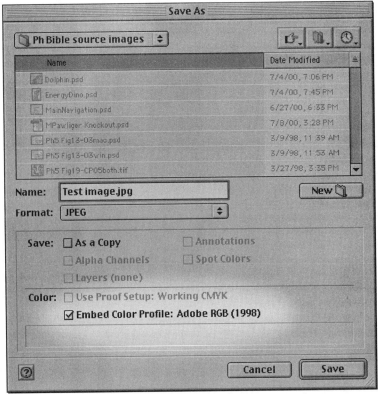

Figure 16-6: I select the Embed Color Profile check box to append the Adobe RGB profile to the image saved on the Mac.

In order to save a profile with an image, you have to select a file format that supports profiles. This includes the native Photoshop (PSD) format, TIFF, JPEG, EPS, and PICT. The two DCS formats also save profiles, but because DCS supports CMYK images only, it converts the RGB image to CMYK and saves a CMYK profile. If you select another format — GIF, PNG, BMP, or the like — the Embed Color Profile check box becomes dimmed.

Note that the Embed Color Profile check box always embeds the device-independent profile defined in the Color Settings dialog box. This is very important — it does *not* embed the monitor profile. Photoshop handles the conversion from monitor space to RGB space internally, without the help of either the Color Settings or Save As commands. This permits Photoshop to accommodate a world of different monitors from a single RGB working space.

Setting up the destination space

After saving the test image with the embedded Adobe RGB profile, I copy it from my Mac to my PC (an Intergraph ExtremeZ equipped with Windows NT) via Miramar's PC MacLAN networking software. But I could just as easily use a different network protocol or even e-mail it from my Mac and download it to my PC. No translation occurs here; this is a simple file copy from one computer to another.

Now before I can open this image and display it properly on my PC, I have to set up my RGB colors. I start by characterizing my monitor. This time I'm using a no-frills, consumer-grade Sony monitor, so I have to perform the calibration using the Adobe Gamma Wizard, as discussed previously in the section "The Gamma control panel."

After I finish with Adobe Gamma, I go into Photoshop and choose Edit ➪ Color Settings or press Ctrl+Shift+K, just as I did on the Mac. Now if I were really trying to calibrate my systems to match up, I would select U.S. Prepress Defaults from the Settings pop-up menu, just as I did on the Mac. But for purposes of this demonstration, I want to force Photoshop to perform a conversion, and a good conversion requires a little dissension. So this time around, I put on my Web artist cap and choose Web Graphics Defaults from the Settings option, as shown in Figure 16-7. This sets the RGB Working Spaces pop-up menu to the utterly indecipherable sRGB IEC and so on and so on.

The truncated name for this working space is *sRGB,* short for *standard RGB,* the ubiquitous monitor space touted by Hewlett-Packard, Microsoft, and a host of others. Although much smaller and drabber than Adobe RGB, the sRGB space is perfect for Web graphics because it represents the colors projected by a run-of-the-mill PC monitor. It also happens to be Photoshop's default setting. Given that many users will never visit this dialog box, sRGB is fast becoming a cross-platform standard.

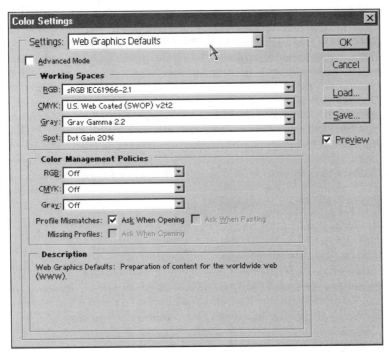

Figure 16-7: On the Windows side, I select Web Graphics Defaults to set my working environment to sRGB. This forces Photoshop to make a conversion.

Defining color management policies

The Color Settings command determines not only how Photoshop projects images on screen, but also how it reads embedded profiles. The three Color Management Policies pop-up menus determine how Photoshop reacts when it tries to open an image whose embedded profiles don't match the active color settings. When Web Graphics Defaults is active, the RGB pop-up menu is set to Off, which tells Photoshop to resist managing colors when it opens an RGB image. Personally, I'm not a big fan of disabling color management entirely, especially when it threatens to ruin my color conversion scenario. So I set the option to Convert to Working RGB, as shown in Figure 16-8.

Finally, Photoshop wants to know how it should behave when it encounters an image garnishing a profile other than sRGB. Should it convert all colors in the image to the sRGB environment? Or should it ask permission before proceeding. Personally, I like my software to be subservient, so I select Ask When Opening from the Profile Mismatches options, as in Figure 16-8.

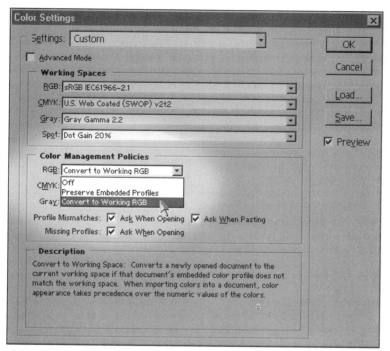

Figure 16-8: Set the first of the Color Management Policies to Convert to Working RGB to convert the image from the Adobe RGB working space to the sRGB space.

Converting the color space

Now I'm ready to open the test image. I choose File ⇨ Open just as I normally would. As Photoshop for Windows opens the test image, it detects the embedded Adobe RGB profile and determines that it does not match the active sRGB profile. Justly troubled by this development, Photoshop displays the alert box shown in Figure 16-9. You can select from three conversion options:

✦ **Use the embedded profile:** Photoshop 6 is perfectly capable of displaying multiple images at a time, each in a different color space. Select this option to tell Photoshop to use the Adobe RGB space instead of sRGB to display the image it's about to open. No colors are converted in the process.

✦ **Convert document's colors to the working space:** This option converts the colors from the Adobe RGB space to sRGB. Because I selected Convert to Working RGB in the previous step, this option is selected by default. Had I not selected the Ask When Opening check box, Photoshop would have performed the conversion without asking me.

✦ **Discard the embedded profile:** Select this option to ignore the embedded profile and to display the image in the sRGB space without any color manipulations. Thanks to the low saturation inherent in sRGB, the result would be a significantly grayer, gloomier image.

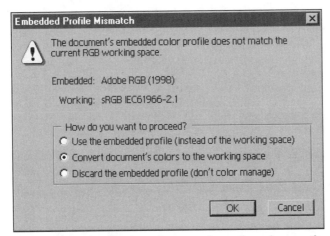

Figure 16-9: The alert box gives you the option of converting the colors from the foreign image or opening the image as is.

I select the Convert Document's Colors radio button and click OK. Photoshop spends a few seconds converting all pixels in the image from Adobe RGB to the smaller sRGB and then displays the converted image on screen. The result is an almost perfect match. Granted the blues demonstrate a slight propensity toward green, as illustrated in Color Plate 16-1. And while I imagine I could address this by finessing the profile for my PC consumer-grade monitor, the match is frankly amazing — much better than the sort of results you could achieve without profile-based color management.

Color Conversion Central

As I mentioned near the outset of this chapter, Color Settings is the command that puts Photoshop's color conversion functions in play. This one dialog box takes the place of Photoshop 5's RGB Setup, CMYK Setup, Grayscale Setup, *and* Profile Setup commands. It at once defines the color space parameters and makes the color conversions happen. The following sections explain the specific options as they're grouped inside the Color Settings dialog box. I also make suggestions for what I consider to be the optimal settings, in case you're interested in a little advice.

Description

This portion of the dialog box comes last, but it's also the most important. It tells you what every one of the Color Settings options does. Just hover the cursor over an option to see a detailed description. To see how an option in a pop-up menu works, select the option and then hover your cursor over it. With help like this, what do you need me for?

No seriously, what *do* you need me for? I think I'll take the rest of the chapter off.

Working spaces

Because every color model except Lab varies according to a piece of hardware — either screen or printer — Photoshop has to tweak the color space to meet your specific needs. There's no such thing as a single, true CMYK color model, for example; instead, there are lots of printer-specific CMYK color models. These color models inside color models are called *working spaces*. You define the default working spaces that Photoshop uses when opening unprofiled images, creating new ones, or converting mismatched images using the four Working Spaces pop-up menus:

✦ **RGB:** The RGB environment defines what you see on screen. Rather than limiting yourself to the circumscribed range of colors that your particular brand of monitor can display — known as the monitor's *gamut* — you can work in a larger, richer color environment, filled with theoretical color options that will serve your image well when projected on other monitors and output from commercial presses. Unless you work strictly on the Web and never create artwork for print, I suggest you select Adobe RGB (1998). Notice that your monitor space also appears in the pop-up menu — this shows that your monitor was correctly tagged with Adobe Gamma.

Tip

If you're a Web artist and you want to preview how an image will look on a different kind of monitor, choose the color space from the View ➪ Proof Setup menu after closing the Color Settings dialog box. For example, choose View ➪ Proof Setup ➪ Windows RGB to see how the image looks on a typical PC monitor. Choose Macintosh RGB for a typical Mac monitor or Monitor RGB to turn off the RGB working space and see the image as it appears without conversion. Then use Ctrl+Y to turn the preview on and off. All these commands work identically regardless of which working space you select, so you might as well use Adobe RGB, the choice most likely to put you in sync with other professionals.

✦ **CMYK:** Use this option to specify the kind of printer you intend to use to print your final CMYK document. This option defines how Photoshop converts an image to the CMYK color space when you choose Image ➪ Mode ➪ CMYK Color. It also governs the performance of the CMYK preview (View ➪ Proof Setup ➪ Working CMYK). Finally, it decides how the colors in a CMYK image are converted for display on your RGB monitor. So any time you open a CMYK image, the RGB working space becomes dormant and this option kicks into gear. For more information about characterizing a CMYK device, see "Custom CMYK Setup" later in this chapter.

✦ **Grayscale:** This command defines how Photoshop displays a grayscale image (created using Image ➪ Mode ➪ Grayscale). You can adjust the gray values in the image to account for a typical Macintosh or PC display (Gray Gamma 1.8 or Gray Gamma 2.2, respectively). Or preview the image according to how it will print, complete with any of several Dot Gain values. (*Dot gain* is the factor by which halftone dots grow when absorbed into paper, as I discuss in the upcoming "Custom CMYK Setup" section.) My preferred setting is Gray Gamma 2.2. It's dark enough to account for dot gains of more than 25 percent, so it accurately reflects the printing conditions typical of grayscale work. Plus it predicts how grays display on a typical PC monitor. Everybody wins.

✦ **Spot:** From a printing perspective, a spot color separation behaves like an extra grayscale print. Specify the dot gain value that correlates to your commercial printer. If you don't know, Dot Gain 20% is a safe bet.

Unlike in previous versions of Photoshop, any open profiled image remains in its working space regardless of how you change the settings in the Color Settings dialog box. Suppose that you open an image in sRGB and then change the working space to Adobe RGB. The open image remains unchanged on screen, safe in its sRGB space. If you'd prefer the image to change to the new space, choose Image ➪ Mode ➪ Assign Profile. Then select the Working RGB radio button, as shown in Figure 16-10. Because Assign Profile leaves the color values of all pixels unchanged, Photoshop merely displays the old pixels in the new space, which permits the colors to shift on screen. So perhaps perversely, not converting pixels results in a visible color shift, whereas converting pixels would not.

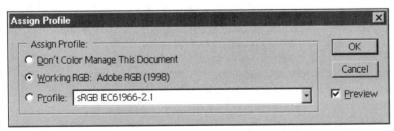

Figure 16-10: Use the Assign Profile command to switch an open image to a different color space without converting pixels. As a result, the image will look different on screen.

Tip

To permit the image to change on the fly according to the active working space, as in Photoshop 5 and 5.5, choose Image ⇨ Mode ⇨ Assign Profile and select the Don't Color Manage This Document option. A pound symbol (#) appears in the title bar to show that the image is no longer tagged with a color profile, as in Figure 16-11. Now whenever you change the image's working space in the Color Settings dialog box, the image updates in kind. Select the Preview check box to view changes without exiting the dialog box.

Figure 16-11: A pound symbol (#) in the title bar shows that the image has not been assigned a color profile. If an asterisk (*) appears, the image uses a profiled space other than the default working space, as when opening an sRGB image in an Adobe RGB environment.

If the Assign Profile command leaves pixels unchanged so they appear to change on screen, there must be a command that converts pixels so they appear consistent on screen. Sure enough, that command is Image ⇨ Mode ⇨ Convert to Profile, which displays the dialog box pictured in Figure 16-12. The options in the lower half of the dialog box—Engine, Intent, and so on—also appear in the Color Settings dialog box when you enter the advanced mode, so you'll be hearing more about them later. For now, just select the color space that you want to convert the image to from the Destination Space pop-up menu and press Enter.

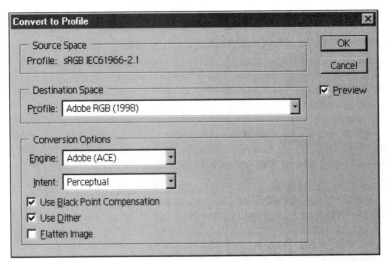

Figure 16-12: Convert to Profile is the complement to Assign Profile. Choose it to both switch an open image to a different color space and convert the pixels. The result is an image that looks the same on screen as it did before.

Tip

On first glance, the Destination Space pop-up menu may seem wildly complicated, offering RGB, CMYK, and grayscale working spaces, and even going so far as to permit you to create your own. But in fact, this dizzying array of options may in some situations lead to less work for you. The Destination Space option is unusual in that it permits you to switch color modes. For example, if you open an RGB image, choose the Convert to Profile command, and select a CMYK space such as U.S. Web Coated (SWOP), Photoshop not only remaps the colors, it converts the RGB channels to CMYK. In this way, Convert to Profile has an edge over Image ⇨ Mode ⇨ CMYK Color — you can switch color modes and nail a specific working space in one operation.

Color management policies

Highlighted in Figure 16-13, the next set of options control how Photoshop reacts when opening an image that either lacks a profile or contains a profile that doesn't match the specified Working Spaces options above. These are the options that are most likely to cause confusion because they're responsible for the error messages Photoshop delivers when opening images. The trick is to keep the error messages to a minimum while keeping control to a maximum. Here are my suggestions for each option with what I hope is enough explanation for you to make your own educated decisions:

✦ **RGB:** The first three pop-up menus establish default policies that Photoshop suggests or implements according to the check boxes that follow. For example, when opening an untagged RGB image, I reckon I might as well tag it with the working RGB profile, which in my case is Adobe RGB. So I select Convert to Working RGB and turn the Missing Profiles check box off. This way, when no profile is evident, Photoshop assigns the Adobe RGB profile without bothering me. However, if the image contains a profile, I might go either way. An image tagged with an sRGB profile is probably a Web image, so I might go ahead and open it in the sRGB space without conversion. However, if I encountered an image tagged with the Apple RGB profile — intended to match a typical Apple Macintosh screen — I'd want to convert it to Adobe RGB. Therefore, I set Profile Mismatches to Ask When Opening. This way, Photoshop will ask me what I want to do every time I open an image with a nonmatching RGB profile. It'll suggest I convert the image to Adobe RGB, but permit me to override if I like.

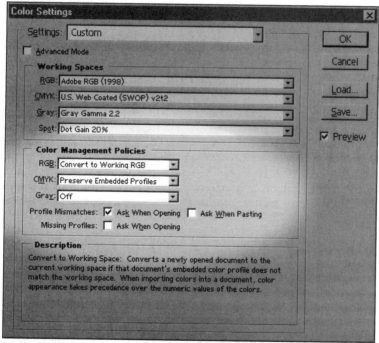

Figure 16-13: Here are my recommended settings for the five Color Management Policies options. They tell Photoshop to ask you when opening images with mismatches, but otherwise proceed automatically.

✦ **CMYK:** Whereas RGB color is a function of your monitor and the RGB working space, accurate CMYK is all about matching colors to a specific output device. Therefore, if you're accepting CMYK images from clients and colleagues, you probably want to be very careful about making arbitrary conversions. By setting CMYK to Preserve Embedded Profiles, I tell Photoshop to open a tagged CMYK image in its own color space and override the default CMYK space specified in the Working Spaces option above. Again, setting Profile Mismatches to Ask When Opening gives me the option to change my mind and convert the image to my working CMYK space if I deem it appropriate. If the image has no profile, Photoshop leaves it untagged, giving me the option of testing out multiple CMYK working spaces and assigning the one that fits best.

✦ **Gray:** Making automatic color manipulations to color images is all very well and good. Clipping is bound to occur, but with millions of theoretical colors at your disposal, the clipping is unlikely to do any visible harm. However, grayscale images are another story. Blessed with just 256 brightness values, they are significantly more fragile than color images. Furthermore, few grayscale images are tagged properly, making Photoshop's automatic adjustments highly suspect. The upshot is that I prefer to correct grayscale images manually (as explained in Chapter 17) and keep Photoshop the heck out of it. Therefore, I set the Gray option to Off.

✦ **Profile Mismatches:** These two check boxes tell Photoshop how to behave when opening an image whose profile does not match the working color space. If you select the Ask When Opening check box, Photoshop asks you permission to perform the conversion suggested in the pop-up menus above. As the top message in Figure 16-14 shows, you also have the option of opening the image in its native color space or leaving the image untagged. Back in the Color Settings dialog box, select Ask When Pasting to tell Photoshop to warn you when you copy an image from one working space and paste it into another. Shown at the bottom of Figure 16-14, this warning is a bit much, in my opinion. In all likelihood, you want Photoshop to convert the colors; so turn off Ask When Pasting and let Photoshop do its work unhindered.

✦ **Missing Profiles:** When Photoshop 5.0 first shipped, it had the regrettable habit of converting images that lacked embedded profiles, even though there was no clearly defined space to serve as the source for the conversion. Photoshop 6 has successfully shaken that habit, but it still likes to ask you whether you want to manage the colors or not. I say turn Ask When Opening off — enough alert messages already! — and let Photoshop take its cues from the RGB, CMYK, and Gray pop-up menus. According to Figure 16-13, this means Photoshop will tag unprofiled RGB images with an Adobe RGB profile and leave unprofiled CMYK and grayscale images alone.

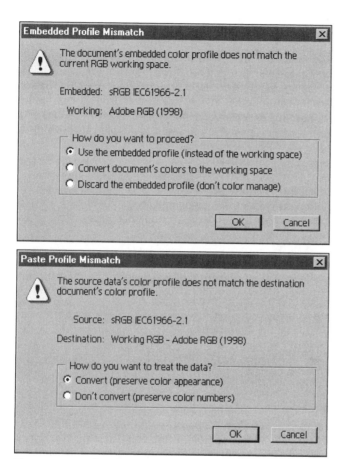

Figure 16-14: The alert message that appears when opening an image with a mismatched profile (top) and then copying part of that image and pasting it into an image that subscribes to the default working space (bottom)

The Color Management Policies options are particularly dense, so I don't blame you if you find yourself reading and rereading my text trying to make sense of it. If you can't for the life of you make heads or tails of what I'm talking about — if it's any consolation, I'm not trying to confuse you, honest — try this instead: Set your options to match the ones I've suggested in Figure 16-13. Then work in Photoshop for a few days or weeks and see how it feels. The good news about my suggestions is that they won't hurt your images, even if you don't know what you're doing. With a little time and practice, you'll get a feel for how the settings work. Then come back, read my text again, and see if it doesn't make more sense. I wouldn't be surprised if it suddenly seems crystal clear.

Advanced mode

Right about now, I picture you scratching your head and thinking, "Wow, this Deke guy really gets off on color management. I mean, dude, give it a rest already!" I have to admit, I do find color management profoundly interesting. It inspires the same twisted feelings I have when watching a highway expansion project. On one hand, I have to admire all that planning and organization. I mean, gee whiz, what a lot of work, all so I can get to the grocery store faster. But at the same time, I think surely there has got to be a better way. If these guys would only put this kind of effort into flying cars, I'd be home by now.

Up to this point, my admiration for Photoshop's color management has outweighed my frustration. But the moment I select the Advanced Mode check box, my patience evaporates. Suddenly, this really is too much. But a book called the *Bible* has a responsibility to cover everything, so I guess I'm stuck with it.

Think of the Advanced Mode check box as the key to the color management underworld. When you select it, you unleash two categories of demonic preference settings: Conversion Options and Advanced Controls. Spotlighted in Figure 16-15, each set of options possesses its own special brand of loathsome and horrible power. For the love of God, dear reader, run away now while you still can.

Okay, perhaps that's a bit of an exaggeration. After all, there is one reason to turn on the Advanced Mode check box, and that's because it permits you to change an ill-advised Intent setting. So what the heck, let's give it a whirl. Even hell can be fun if we only give it a chance:

✦ **Engine:** The first of the Advanced Mode options is Engine, and it does just what it sounds like it does. The force behind the color management process is the *engine*. If you don't like one engine, you can trade it for another. If you work in a Macintosh-centric environment, for example, you might want to select Apple ColorSync. But I recommend you stick with the Adobe Color Engine, or ACE. Not only is ACE a great engine, it ensures compatibility with Illustrator, InDesign, and other Adobe applications.

✦ **Intent:** Whenever you remap colors, a little something gets lost in the translation. The trick is to lose as little as possible, and that's the point of Intent. By default, the option is set to Relative Colorimetric, which converts every color in the source profile to its closest equivalent in the destination profile. But while such a direct transfer of colors may sound attractive, it can create rifts in the image. The closest equivalent for two similar colors in the source profile might be a single color in the destination, or they might be two very different colors. As a result, gradual transitions may become flat or choppy. The better setting is Perceptual, which sacrifices specific colors in favor of retaining the gradual transitions between colors, so important to the success of continuous-tone photographs.

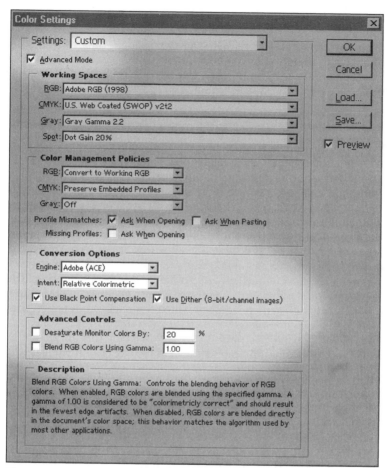

Figure 16-15: Turn on the Advanced Mode check box to display the Conversion Options and Advanced Controls, as well as define your own CMYK working space.

Why should you take my word that Perceptual is better? You shouldn't. To get a second opinion, hover your cursor over the word Perceptual and read the Description text, which tells you that Perceptual "requests a visually pleasing rendering, preserving visual relationships between source colors." The truth is, most folks inside Adobe believe Perceptual to be the better choice. So why is the default setting Relative Colorimetric? Because a direct color translation is the best way to convert object-oriented artwork, like that in Illustrator and InDesign. Because cross-application harmony is very important to the powers that be, Photoshop is stuck towing the line. But don't you get roped in — select Perceptual today.

✦ **Use Black Point Compensation:** Like any other colors, Photoshop wants to convert black and white to new values. Whites are compensated naturally by the Intent setting, which may in many cases map white to a different color in the name of smoother transitions. But if you let black map to a lighter color, you can end up with wimpy gray shadows. To keep your blacks their blackest, turn this check box on.

✦ **Use Dither (8-bit/channel images):** Just so we're all on the same page, a 24-bit image contains 8 bits per channel. So don't think we're talking about 8-bit GIF images here; this option uses *dithering* (random patterns of pixels) to smooth out what might otherwise be harsh color transitions. Ostensibly, it can result in higher file sizes when saving an image in the native PSD format or TIFF with LZW compression. But the effect is usually minimal. Leave this check box turned on.

✦ **Desaturate Monitor Colors By:** The Adobe RGB space in particular has a habit of rendering such vivid colors that the brightest areas in the image flatten out on screen. Because they may or may not have a direct outcome on the appearance of the final image, whether in print or on the Web, such flat areas can be a bit misleading. To better see details in bright areas of color, turn on the Desaturate Monitor Colors check box. Note that this option affects the screen view only; the colors will continue to print as vivid as ever. I recommend you use this option only for running previews from inside the Color Settings dialog box. Leaving this option on for extended periods of time can be more deceiving than turning it off.

✦ **Blend RGB Colors Using Gamma:** When this option is off, as by default, Photoshop blends layers according to the gamma of the working color space. For example, the gamma of Adobe RGB is 2.2, the same as a typical PC screen and a few shades darker than a typical Macintosh screen. On occasion, however, this may result in incongruous highlights around the edges of layers. If you encounter this, try turning on this check box. Photoshop recalculates all blends using a theoretically more desirable gamma value.

To recap, I suggest you turn on the Advanced Mode check box and select Perceptual from the Intent pop-up menu. Then turn off Advanced Mode, click OK, and never set foot inside this dark corner of Photoshop again.

Custom CMYK Setup

To prepare an image for reproduction on a commercial offset or web press, you first need to specify how you want Photoshop to convert the image from the RGB to CMYK color space. This step also affects the conversion from CMYK to RGB, which in turn defines how CMYK images appear on screen.

In Photoshop 6, you specify the CMYK space by choosing Edit ⇨ Color Settings. Then select the color profile you want to use from the CMYK pop-up menu in the Working Spaces section of the dialog box. You can select a predefined color profile. Or define a custom CMYK conversion setup by choosing Custom CMYK from the CMYK pop-up menu. When you choose Custom, Photoshop displays the Custom CMYK dialog box, shown in Figure 16-16.

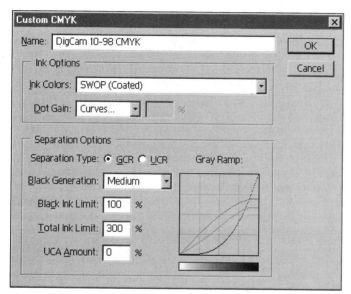

Figure 16-16: Use the options in the Custom CMYK dialog box to prepare an image for printing on a commercial offset or web press.

The following list explains each and every option in the Custom CMYK dialog box. If you're not a print professional, some of these descriptions may seem a little abstruse. After reading this section, you may want to talk with your commercial printer and find out what options, if any, he or she recommends.

✦ **Name:** Okay, so this one's not so abstruse after all. Enter a name for your custom CMYK settings here.

✦ **Ink Colors:** This pop-up menu offers access to a handful of common press inks and paper stocks. Select the option that most closely matches your printing environment. (Your commercial printer can easily help you with this one.) The default setting, SWOP (Coated), represents the most common press type and paper stock used in the United States for magazine and high-end display work. Regardless of which setting you choose, Photoshop automatically changes the Dot Gain value to the most suitable setting.

✦ **Dot Gain:** Enter any value from −10 to 40 percent to specify the amount by which you can expect halftone cells to shrink or expand during the printing process, a variable known as *dot gain*. When printing to uncoated stock, for example, you can expect halftone cells to bleed into the page and expand by about 25 to 30 percent. For newsprint, it varies from 30 to 40 percent. In any case, Photoshop automatically adjusts the brightness of CMYK colors to compensate, lightening the image for high values and darkening it for low values.

Tip

For more control, select Curves from the Dot Gain pop-up menu. As shown in Figure 16-17, this brings up the Dot Gain Curves dialog box, which permits you to specify how much the halftone dots expand on a separation-by-separation basis. If the All Same option is checked, turn it off. Then use the Cyan, Magenta, Yellow, and Black radio buttons in the lower-right corner of the dialog box to switch between the four separations and modify their output independently. To do this, locate the lone point in the center of the curved line in the graph on the left side of the dialog box. Drag this point up to add dot gain, which in turn darkens the display of CMYK colors on screen; drag the point down to lighten the display. If you need more control, you can add points to the graph by clicking on the curved line. Points added to the left side of the curve affect the display of light colors; points added to the right side of the curve affect dark colors.

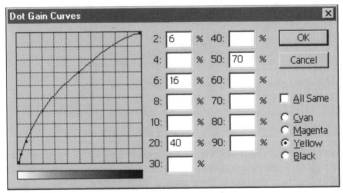

Figure 16-17: Select Curves from the Dot Gain pop-up menu to modify the dot gain values on a separation-by-separation basis. Here, I'm editing the yellow separation.

✦ **Separation Type:** When the densities of cyan, magenta, and yellow inks reach a certain level, they mix to form a muddy brown. The GCR (*gray component replacement*) option avoids this unpleasant effect by overprinting these colors with black to the extent specified with the Black Generation option. If you select the UCR (*under color removal*) option, Photoshop removes cyan, magenta, and yellow inks where they overlap black ink. GCR is almost always the setting of choice except when printing on newsprint.

✦ **Black Generation:** Available only when the GCR option is active, the Black Generation pop-up menu determines how dark the cyan, magenta, and yellow concentrations must be before Photoshop adds black ink. Select Light to use black ink sparingly; select Heavy to apply it liberally. The None option prints no black ink whatsoever, while the Maximum option prints black ink over everything. You may want to use the UCA Amount option to restore cyan, magenta, and yellow ink if you select the Heavy or Maximum option.

✦ **Black Ink Limit:** Enter the maximum amount of black ink that can be applied to the page. By default, this value is 100 percent, which is solid ink coverage. If you raise the UCA Amount value, you'll probably want to lower this value by a similar percentage to prevent the image from overdarkening.

✦ **Total Ink Limit:** This value represents the maximum amount of all four inks permitted on the page. For example, assuming you use the default Black Ink Limit and Total Ink Limit values of 100 and 300 percent, respectively, the darkest printable color contains 100 percent black ink. The sum total of cyan, magenta, and yellow inks, therefore, is the difference between these values: 200 percent. A typical *saturated black* — a mix of inks that results in an absolute pitch-black pigment — is 70 percent cyan, 63 percent magenta, 67 percent yellow, and 100 percent black. And 70 + 63 + 67 + 100 =, you guessed it, 300.

✦ **UCA Amount:** The opposite of UCR, UCA stands for *under color addition,* which enables you to add cyan, magenta, and yellow inks to areas where the concentration of black ink is highest. For example, a value of 20 percent raises the amount of cyan, magenta, and yellow inks applied with black concentrations between 80 and 100 percent. This option is dimmed when the UCR radio button is active.

✦ **Gray Ramp:** The Gray Ramp graph on the right side of the Custom CMYK dialog box shows the effects of your changes. Four lines — one in each color — represent the four inks. Although you can't edit the colored lines in this graph by clicking and dragging them, you can observe the lines to gauge the results of your settings. If you have an urge to grab a curve and yank on it, choose Custom from the Black Generation pop-up menu. The ensuing dialog box lets you edit the black curve directly while you preview its effect on the C, M, and Y curves in the background.

If you're familiar with the color management features in previous versions of Photoshop, you may have noticed that the Custom CMYK dialog box lacks the Preview check box found in earlier versions of the program. To see how your changes affect an open CMYK image in Photoshop 6, do this: Prior to choosing the Color Settings command, choose Image ➪ Mode ➪ Assign Profile and select Don't Color Manage This Document. Then choose Edit ➪ Color Settings and turn on the Preview check box. From then on, the image updates every time you press Enter to accept changes from the Custom CMYK dialog box.

Photoshop

6

Loading CMYK settings from a previous version of Photoshop

Also missing from the Custom CMYK dialog box are the Load and Save buttons. At first glance, you might think this means that Photoshop 6 does not support CMYK setup files created in previous versions of the program. But in fact, Photoshop 6 is ready and able to use setup files from the past — you just have to know how to get there.

Here's how to save a setup file from Photoshop 5 and load it in Photoshop 6:

STEPS: Load a CMYK Setup File Created in Photoshop 5

1. **Launch Photoshop 5.** This technique works in Photoshop 5.5 as well.

2. **Open the CMYK Setup dialog box.** Inside Photoshop 5 or 5.5, choose File ⇨ Color Settings ⇨ CMYK Setup.

3. **Save a CMYK setup file.** Inside the CMYK Setup dialog box, click the Built-in radio button. If the CMYK settings need some tweaking, tweak to your heart's content. Then click the Save button and save the setup file to disk. Note where you save the file so you can find it in Step 6.

4. **Launch Photoshop 6.** You may need to quit Photoshop 5 first.

5. **Choose Color Settings.** Remember that keyboard shortcut, Ctrl+Shift+K.

6. **Load the CMYK setup file.** Choose Load CMYK from the first CMYK pop-up menu (the one in the Working Spaces area). Inside the Load dialog box, choose CMYK Setup (*.API) from the Files of Type pop-up menu. Then locate the CMYK setup file you saved in Step 3 and open it up.

7. **Confirm your selection.** To confirm that you got the right file — and tweak it further if desired — choose Custom CMYK from the CMYK pop-up menu.

That's one way to do it, anyway. In fact, that's the best way to load CMYK settings from Photoshop 5 if you typically work with one commercial printer and that's it. But what if you work with multiple commercial prepress houses? Wouldn't it be nice to be able to select different working spaces from the CMYK pop-up menu without having to constantly open setup files using the Load CMYK option? Yes, it would, and here's how you do it:

STEPS: Create a Profile That Appears in the CMYK Pop-up Menu

1. **Create an ICM file.** If you're saving the CMYK settings from Photoshop 5, choose File ⇨ Color Settings ⇨ CMYK Setup, and then click the Tables radio button. Click the Save button and give the file a name. Don't save the file yet — we do that in the next step.

If you're saving the profile from Photoshop 6, choose Edit ➪ Color Settings, and then choose Save CMYK from the CMYK pop-up menu and give the file a name. Wait to click Save until the next step.

2. **Save the ICM file to the Recommended folder.** For Photoshop 6 to see the CMYK profile, you have to save it to a specific folder. The path for that folder is C:\Program Files\Common Files\Adobe\Color\Profiles\Recommended. This means you open the Program Files folder, then the Common Files folder, then Adobe, then Color, then Profiles, and then Recommended. When you finally arrive inside the Recommended folder, save the ICM file.

3. **Quit Photoshop.** Regardless of which version of Photoshop you're using, quit it by choosing File ➪ Exit.

4. **Launch Photoshop 6.** By starting (or restarting) Photoshop 6, you force the program to load the ICM profile.

5. **Confirm the profile has loaded.** Choose Edit ➪ Color Settings and click the CMYK pop-up menu in the Working Spaces area. You should see the profile you saved in the menu.

Tip

Because the ICM file created in the previous steps resides in the Recommended folder, it appears in the CMYK pop-up menu even when the Advanced Mode check box is turned off. Any ICM files saved in the Profiles folder but outside the Recommended folder appear only when Advanced Mode is turned on.

✦   ✦   ✦

Mapping and Adjusting Colors

What Is Color Mapping?

Color mapping is just a fancy name for shuffling colors around. For example, to map Color A to Color B simply means to take all the A-colored pixels and convert them to B-colored pixels. Photoshop provides several commands that enable you to map entire ranges of colors based on their hues, saturation levels, and most frequently, brightness values.

Color effects and adjustments

Why would you want to change colors around? For one thing, to achieve special effects. You know those psychedelic horror movies that show some guy's hair turning blue while his face turns purple and the palms of his hands glow a sort of cornflower yellow? No? Funny, me neither. But a grayscale version of this very effect appears in the second example of Figure 17-1. Although not the most attractive effect by modern standards — you may be able to harvest more tasteful results if you put your shoulder to the color wheel — psychedelic qualifies as color mapping for the simple reason that each color shifts incrementally to a new color.

But the more common reason to map colors is to enhance the appearance of a scanned image or digital photograph, as demonstrated in the third example in Figure 17-1. In this case, you're not creating special effects; you're just making straightforward repairs, alternatively known as *color adjustments,* or *corrections.* Scans are never perfect, no matter how much money you spend on a scanning device or a service bureau. They can always benefit from tweaking and subtle adjustments, if not outright overhauls, in the color department.

Figure 17-1: Nobody's perfect, and neither is the best of scanned photos (left). You can modify colors in an image to achieve special effects (middle) or simply fix the image with a few well-targeted color corrections (right). Too bad Photoshop hasn't delivered on its promised Remove Excessive Jewelry filter.

Keep in mind, however, that Photoshop can't make something from nothing. In creating the illusion of more and better colors, most of the color-adjustment operations that you perform actually take some small amount of color *away* from the image. Somewhere in your image, two pixels that were two different colors before you started the correction change to the same color. The image may look 10 times better, but it will in fact be less colorful than when you started.

It's important to remember this principle because it demonstrates that color mapping is a balancing act. The first nine operations you perform may make an image look progressively better, but the tenth may send it into decline. There's no magic formula; the amount of color mapping you need to apply varies from image to image. But if you follow my usual recommendations — use the commands in moderation, know when to stop, and save your image to disk before doing anything drastic — you should be fine.

The good, the bad, and the wacky

Photoshop stores all of its color mapping commands under the Image ➪ Adjust submenu. These commands fall into three basic categories:

✦ **Color mappers:** Commands such as Invert and Threshold are quick-and-dirty color mappers. They don't correct images, but they can be useful for creating special effects and adjusting masks.

✦ **Easy color correctors:** Brightness/Contrast and Color Balance are true color correction commands, but they sacrifice functionality for ease of use. If I had my way, these commands would be removed from the Image ➪ Adjust submenu and thrown in the dust heap.

✦ **Expert color correctors:** The third, more complicated variety of color correction commands provides better control, but they take a fair amount of effort to learn. Levels, Curves, and Hue/Saturation are examples of color correcting at its best and most complicated.

This chapter contains little information about the second category of commands for the simple reason that some of them are inadequate and ultimately a big waste of time. There are exceptions, of course — Auto Levels and Auto Contrast are decent quick fixers, and Variations offers deceptively straightforward sophistication — but Brightness/Contrast and Color Balance sacrifice accuracy in their attempt to be straightforward. They are as liable to damage your image as to correct it, making them dangerous in a dull, pedestrian sort of way. I know because I spent my first year with Photoshop relying exclusively on Brightness/Contrast and Color Balance, all the while wondering why I couldn't achieve the effects I wanted. Then, one happy day, I spent about half an hour learning Levels and Curves, and the quality of my images skyrocketed. So wouldn't you just rather learn it correctly in the first place? I hope so, because that's what we're all about to do.

Quick Color Effects

Before we get into all the high-end gunk, however, I take a moment to explain the first category of commands, all of which happen to occupy one of the lower sections in the Image ➪ Adjust submenu. These commands — Invert, Equalize, Threshold, and Posterize — produce immediate effects that are either difficult or require too much effort to duplicate with the more full-featured commands.

Invert

When you choose Image ➪ Adjust ➪ Invert (Ctrl+I), Photoshop converts every color in your image to its exact opposite, as in a photographic negative. As demonstrated in Figure 17-2, black becomes white, white becomes black, fire becomes water, good becomes evil, dogs romance cats, and the brightness value of every primary color component changes to 255 minus the original brightness value.

Note

By itself, the Invert command is not sufficient to convert a scanned color photographic negative to a positive. Negative film produces an orange cast that the Invert command does not address. After inverting, you can use the Variations command to remove the color cast. Or avoid Invert altogether and use the Levels command to invert the image. Both Variations and Levels are explained later in this chapter.

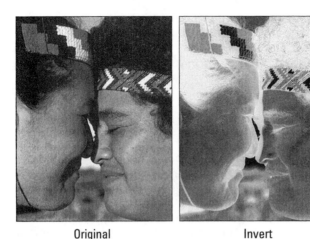

Original   Invert

Figure 17-2: An image before the advent of the Invert command
(left) and after (right).

Image ⇨ Adjust ⇨ Invert is just about the only color mapping command that retains
the rich diversity of color in an image. (The Hue/Saturation command also retains
color diversity under specific conditions.) For example, if you apply the Invert command twice in a row, you arrive at your original image without any loss in quality.

When you're working on a full-color image, the Invert command simply inverts the
contents of each color channel. This means the command produces very different
results when applied to RGB, Lab, and especially CMYK images. Color Plate 17-1
shows the results of inverting a single image in each of these modes. The RGB and
Lab images share some similarities, but you'll find all kinds of subtle differences if
you study the backgrounds and the basic colors of the faces.

Inverting in CMYK is much different. Typically, the Invert command changes most
pixels in a CMYK image to black. Except in rare instances — such as in night scenes —
the black channel contains lots of light shades and few dark shades. So when you
invert the channel, it becomes extremely dark. To reverse this effect, I inverted only
the cyan, magenta, and yellow channels in the right example of Color Plate 17-1. (I did
this by inverting the entire image and then going to the black channel — Ctrl+4 — and
pressing Ctrl+I again.) Although this approach is preferable to inverting the black
channel, it prevents the blacks in the hair and shadows from turning white (which
would be the only portions even remotely light had I inverted the black channel
as well).

Note

Just so you know, when I refer to applying color corrections in the CMYK mode, I
mean applying them after choosing Mode ⇨ CMYK Color. Applying corrections in
the RGB mode when View ⇨ Preview ⇨ CMYK is active produces the same effect as
when CMYK Preview is not selected; the only difference is that the on-screen colors
are curtailed slightly to fit inside the CMYK color space. You're still editing inside
the same old red, green, and blue color channels, so the effects are the same.

Cross-Reference

As I mentioned back in Chapter 12, inverting the contents of the mask channel is the same as applying Select ➪ Inverse to a selection outline in the marching ants mode. In fact, this is one of the most useful applications of the filter. If you're considering inverting a color image, however, I strongly urge you to try out the SuperInvert filter in the Tormentia folder on the CD at the back of this book. It permits you to invert each channel independently and incrementally. Any setting under 128 lessens the contrast of the channel; 128 makes it completely gray; and any value over 128 inverts it to some degree.

Equalize

Equalize is the smartest and at the same time least useful of the Image ➪ Adjust pack. When you invoke this command, Photoshop searches for the lightest and darkest color values in a selection. Then it maps the lightest color in all the color channels to white, maps the darkest color in the channels to black, and distributes the remaining colors to other brightness levels in an effort to evenly distribute pixels over the entire brightness spectrum. This doesn't mean that any one pixel will actually appear white or black after you apply Equalize; rather, one pixel in at least one channel will be white and another pixel in at least one channel will be black. In an RGB image, for example, the red, green, or blue component of one pixel would be white, but the other two components of that same pixel might be black. The result is a higher contrast image with white and black pixels scattered throughout the color channels.

If no portion of the image is selected when you choose Image ➪ Adjust ➪ Equalize, Photoshop automatically maps the entire image across the brightness spectrum, as shown in the upper-right example of Figure 17-3. If you select a portion of the image before choosing the Equalize command, however, Photoshop displays a dialog box containing the following two radio buttons:

✦ **Selected Area Only:** Select this option to apply the Equalize command strictly within the confines of the selection. The lightest pixel in the selection becomes white, the darkest pixel becomes black, and the others remap to shades in between.

✦ **Entire Image Based on Area:** If you select the second radio button, which is the default setting, Photoshop applies the Equalize command to the entire image based on the lightest and darkest colors in the selection. All colors in the image that are lighter than the lightest color in the selection become white and all colors darker than the darkest color in the selection become black.

The bottom two examples in Figure 17-3 show the effects of selecting different parts of the image when the Entire Image Based on Area option is in force. In the left example, I selected a dark portion of the image, which resulted in over-lightening of the entire image. In the right example, I selected an area with both light and dark values, which boosted the amount of contrast between highlights and shadows in the image.

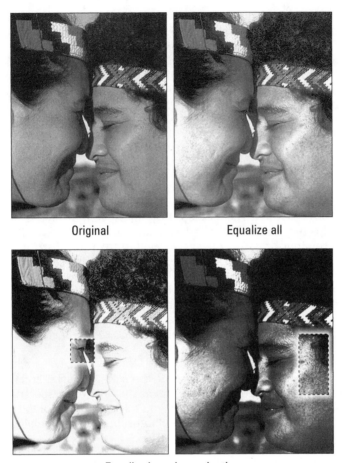

Original   Equalize all

Equalize based on selection

Figure 17-3: An image before (top left) and after (top right)
applying the Equalize command when no portion of the image
is selected. You can also use the brightness values in a selected
region as the basis for equalizing an entire image (bottom left
and right).

The problem with the Equalize command is that it relies too heavily on some bizarre
automation to be of much use as a color correction tool. Certainly, you can create
some interesting special effects. But if you'd prefer to automatically adjust the colors in an image from black to white regardless of the color mode and composition of
the individual channels, choose Image ⇨ Adjust ⇨ Auto Levels (Ctrl+Shift+L). If you
want to adjust the tonal balance manually and therefore with a higher degree of
accuracy, the Levels and Curves commands are tops. I explain all these commands
at length later in this chapter.

Threshold

I touched on the Threshold command a couple of times in previous chapters. As you may recall, Threshold converts all colors to either black or white, based on their brightness values. When you choose Image ⇨ Adjust ⇨ Threshold, Photoshop displays the Threshold dialog box shown in Figure 17-4. The dialog box offers a single option box and a slider bar, either of which you can use to specify the medium brightness value in the image. Photoshop changes any color lighter than the value in the Threshold option box to white and changes any color darker than the value to black.

Histogram

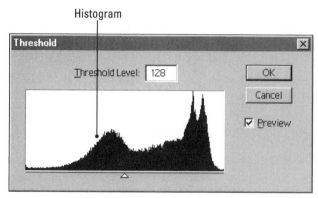

Figure 17-4: The histogram in the Threshold dialog box shows the distribution of brightness values in the selection.

The dialog box also includes a graph of all the colors in the image — even if only a portion of the image is selected. This graph is called a *histogram.* The width of the histogram represents all 256 possible brightness values, starting at black on the left and progressing through white on the right. The height of each vertical line in the graph demonstrates the number of pixels currently associated with that brightness value. Therefore, you can use the histogram to gauge the distribution of lights and darks in your image. It may seem weird at first, but with enough experience, the histogram becomes an invaluable tool, permitting you to corroborate the colors that you see on-screen.

Tip

Generally speaking, you achieve the best effects if you change an equal number of pixels to black as you change to white (and vice versa). So rather than moving the slider bar to 128, which is the medium brightness value, move it to the point at which the area of the vertical lines to the left of the slider triangle looks roughly equivalent to the area of the vertical lines to the right of the slider triangle.

The upper-left example in Figure 17-5 shows the result of applying the Threshold command with a Threshold Level value of 128 (as in Figure 17-4). Although this value evenly distributes black and white pixels, I lost a lot of detail in the dark areas.

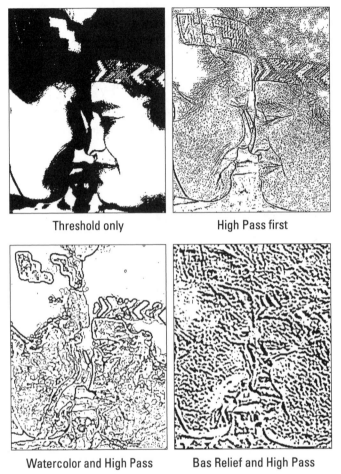

Threshold only   High Pass first

Watercolor and High Pass   Bas Relief and High Pass

Figure 17-5: By itself, the Threshold command tends to deliver
flat results (top left). To better articulate the detail, apply High
Pass and other filters before choosing Threshold.

As you may recall from my "Using the High Pass filter" discussion in Chapter 10, you
can use Filter ⇨ Other ⇨ High Pass before you use the Threshold command to retain
areas of contrast. In the upper-right image in Figure 17-5, I applied the High Pass filter with a radius of 1.0 pixel, followed by the Threshold command with a value of
125. In the two bottom images, I first chose an effects filter — Filter ⇨ Artistic ⇨
Watercolor on the left and Filter ⇨ Sketch ⇨ Bas Relief on the right — and then I
applied High Pass with a radius of 1.0 pixel followed by the Threshold command.

If the Threshold effects in Figure 17-5 are a bit austere, first clone the image to a layer and then mix the layer with the underlying original. Figure 17-6 shows all the effects from Figure 17-5 applied to layers subject to the Overlay blend mode and 50 percent Opacity. In each example, the translucent selection helps to add contrast and reinforce details in the original image.

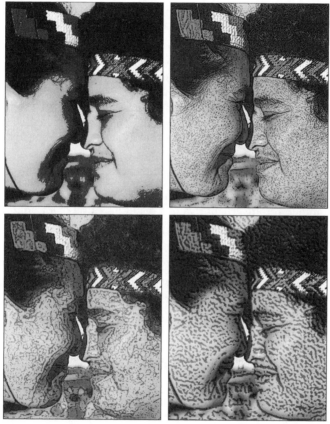

Figure 17-6: The Threshold operations from Figure 17-5 applied to separate layers, blended with the Overlay mode and an Opacity value of 50 percent.

Photoshop 6 adds a new method for speeding up screen previews. Press Ctrl+K, press Ctrl+3, and turn on the Pixel Doubling check box. From now on, whenever you're working in a color correction dialog box, Photoshop will double up pixels so long as you're moving a slider. Release the slider, and the other pixels fill in.

If you want to achieve a colorful Threshold effect, try applying the Threshold command independently to each color channel. In an RGB image, for example, press Ctrl+1 and then apply Image ⇨ Adjust ⇨ Threshold. Then press Ctrl+2 and repeat the command, and press Ctrl+3 and do it again. Color Plate 17-2 shows examples of what happens when I apply High Pass (with a Radius value of 3.0) and Threshold to independent color channels in the RGB, Lab, and CMYK modes. To soften the transitions and avoid trapping problems, I resampled each image up and down a couple of times, as described back in the "Antialiasing an image" section of Chapter 10.

Posterize

The Posterize command is Threshold's rich cousin. Whereas Threshold boils down an image into two colors only, Posterize can retain as many colors as you like. However, you can't control how colors are mapped, as you can when you use Threshold. The Posterize dialog box does not provide a histogram or slider bar. Instead, Posterize automatically divides the full range of 256 brightness values into a specified number of equal increments.

To use this command, choose Image ⇨ Adjust ⇨ Posterize and enter a value in the Levels option box. The Levels value represents the number of brightness values that the Posterize command retains. Higher values result in subtle color adjustments; lower values produce more dramatic effects. The first example in Figure 17-7 shows an image subject to a Levels value of 8.

By now, you may be thinking, "By golly, if Posterize is so similar to Threshold, I wonder how it works when applied after the High Pass filter?" Well, you're in luck, because this is exactly the purpose of the second example in Figure 17-7. Here I chose the High Pass filter and entered 3.0 for the Radius. Then I applied the Posterize command with the same Levels value as before (8).

Now, just in case you've tried this same effect on your full-color image and thought, "Yech, this looks terrible — half the color just disappeared," the key is to apply High Pass and Posterize to a layered version of the image and then mix the effect with the underlying original. Color Plate 17-3 shows the results of applying the High Pass filter with a Radius of 3.0 and the Posterize command with a setting of 8 to the layered clone and then compositing the layer and underlying original using each of three overlay modes from the Layers palette. The Luminosity option applies only the lights and darks in the layered image, allowing the colors in the underlying image to show through; Hard Light strengthens the light and dark shades; and Hue applies the colors from the layer with the saturation and brightness values from the original. After flattening each image, I increase the saturation of the colors using Image ⇨ Adjust ⇨ Hue/Saturation (Ctrl+U), which I discuss in an upcoming section.

 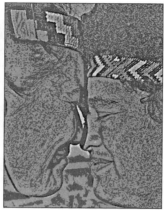

Posterize   High Pass first

Figure 17-7: An image subject to the Posterize command with a Levels value of 8 (left). You can retain more detail in an image by applying the High Pass filter before using Posterize (right).

Quick Corrections

Photoshop offers three quick-correctors under the Image ➪ Adjust submenu that I want to discuss before entering into the larger world of advanced color correction. All are single-shot commands that alter your image without any dialog boxes or special options. The first, Desaturate, sucks the saturation out of a selection and leaves it looking like a grayscale image. The other two, Auto Levels and Auto Contrast, automatically increase the contrast of an image according to what Photoshop deems to be ideal brightness values. Auto Levels examines each color channel independently; Auto Contrast examines the image as a whole.

Sucking saturation

There's little reason to apply the Desaturate command to an entire image; you can just as easily choose Image ➪ Mode ➪ Grayscale to accomplish the same thing and dispose of the extra channels that would otherwise consume room in memory and on disk. I know of only two reasons to sacrifice all colors in the RGB mode:

✦ You want to retain the option of applying RGB-only filters, such as Lens Flare, Lighting Effects, and anything created with the Filter Factory.

✦ You intend to downsize the colors using Image ➪ Mode ➪ Indexed Colors and save the final image in the GIF format for use on the Web (as I discuss in Chapter 19).

But mostly, you'll use Desaturate to rob color from discrete selections or independent layers, neither of which the Grayscale mode can accommodate. For example, in Color Plate 17-4, I used Select ➪ Color Range to select all of the pumpkin except the eyes and mouth and a few speckles here and there. (I could have used the quick mask mode to tweak the selection and get it just right, but it didn't strike me as particularly important in this case.) I then applied Image ➪ Adjust ➪ Desaturate (Ctrl+Shift+U) to achieve the first example. To create the top-right pumpkin, I chose Edit ➪ Fade Desaturate and changed the Opacity value to 50 percent, bringing back some of the original colors from the full-color original and achieving an only slightly desaturated pumpkin.

Tip

In case you missed that last paragraph, you can use Edit ➪ Fade (Ctrl+Shift+F) to back off the effects of any command under the Image ➪ Adjust submenu. As always, the Fade command is available immediately after you apply the color correction; if you so much as alter a selection outline, Fade goes dim.

Desaturate isn't the only way to suck colors out of an image. You can also invert the colors and mix them with their original counterparts to achieve a slightly different effect. The bottom row of Color Plate 17-4 shows what I mean. In the lower-left example, I applied Invert (Ctrl+I) to my same Color Range selection. Then I pressed Ctrl+Shift+F, changed the Opacity setting to 50 percent, and—here's the important part—selected Color from the Mode pop-up menu.

Note that the inverted and mixed colors are slightly different than the desaturated tones in the pumpkin above it. When set to the Color blend mode, the colors in the inverted image should theoretically cancel out the colors in the underlying original. However, the Invert command doesn't change the saturation of the pixels, so the saturation of the inverted and original pixels is the same. As a result, some colors from the underlying image show through, as the bottom-left image shows.

The bottom-right example shows what happened when I changed the Opacity to 70 percent, thus favoring the inverted colors. Why'd I do that? Maybe I just like blue pumpkins. Or more likely, I had a fourth spot to fill in the figure, and a blue pumpkin seemed like the guy to fill it.

Note

By the way, you might be wondering why Adobe selected Ctrl+Shift+U as the keyboard shortcut for Desaturate. Well, Desaturate is actually a renegade element from the Hue/Saturation command, which lets you raise and lower saturation levels to any degree you like. The shortcut for Hue/Saturation is Ctrl+U—for hUe, don't you know—so Desaturate is Ctrl+Shift+U.

The Auto Levels commands

Image ➪ Adjust ➪ Auto Levels (Ctrl+Shift+L) goes through each color channel and changes the lightest pixel to white, changes the darkest pixel to black, and stretches all the shades of gray to fill out the spectrum. In Figure 17-8, I started with a drab and murky image. But when I applied Auto Levels, Photoshop pumped up the lights and darks, bolstering the contrast. Although I would argue that the corrected image is too dark, it's not half bad for an automated, no-brainer command that you just choose and let rip.

Figure 17-8: A grayscale image before (left) and after (right) applying the Auto Levels command.

Unlike the Equalize command, which considers all color channels as a whole, Auto Levels looks at each channel independently. So as with the Invert command, the active color mode has a profound effect on Auto Levels. Color Plate 17-5 shows our friendly jack o' lantern before color corrections, followed by the same image corrected with Auto Levels in the RGB, Lab, and CMYK modes. Frankly, the RGB image is the only one that's acceptable. The Lab image is far too orange, and the CMYK image is too dark, thanks to the exaggeration of the black channel. Auto Levels has also darkened the cyan channel, turning the pumpkin a bright red that one rarely sees in today's sincere pumpkin patches.

Like Invert, Equalize, and other automatic color mappers, Auto Levels is designed for use in the RGB mode. If you use it in CMYK, you're more likely to achieve special effects than color correction.

Cross-Reference The Auto Levels command produces the same effect as the Auto button in the Levels dialog box, as discussed in "The Levels command" section later in this chapter.

The Auto Contrast command

The problem with Image ⇨ Adjust ⇨ Auto Levels is that it modifies values on a channel-by-channel basis, which means it has a habit of upsetting the balance of colors in an image. Consider Color Plate 17-6, for example. The first image is severely washed out. Choosing the Auto Levels command results in a bolder and more vibrant image, but it also changes the cast from sienna to burgundy.

The solution is Image ⇨ Adjust ⇨ Auto Contrast (Ctrl+Shift+Alt+L). The Auto Contrast command adjusts the composite levels, thus preserving the color balance, as in the case of the final image in Color Plate 17-6.

Which should you use when? If a low-contrast image suffers from a color cast that you want to correct, choose Auto Levels. If the image is washed out but the colors are okay, choose Auto Contrast. (When working on a grayscale image, the two commands work the same, so choose whichever is more convenient.) Bear in mind that neither command is perfect, so you'll very likely need to make additional Levels and Variations adjustments.

Hue Shifting and Colorizing

The following sections cover commands designed to change the distribution of colors in an image. You can rotate the hues around the color spectrum, change the saturation of colors, adjust highlights and shadows, and even tint an image. Two of these commands — Hue/Saturation and Selective Color — are applicable exclusively to color images. The other two — Replace Color and Variations — can be applied to grayscale images but are far better suited to color images. If you're more interested in editing grayscale photographs, refer to the Levels and Curves commands, both of which I discuss toward the end of the chapter. For those of you who want to correct colors, however, read on.

Tip

Before I go any further, I should mention one awesome little bit of advice. Remember how Ctrl+Alt+F redisplays the last filter dialog box so that you can tweak the effect? Well, a similar shortcut is available when you apply color corrections. Press Alt when choosing any of the commands described throughout the rest of this chapter to display that command's dialog box with the settings last applied to the image. If the command has a keyboard equivalent, just add Alt to restore the last settings. Ctrl+Alt+U, for example, brings up the Hue/Saturation dialog box with the settings you last used.

Using the Hue/Saturation command

The Hue/Saturation command provides two functions. First, it enables you to adjust colors in an image according to their hues and saturation levels. You can apply the changes to specific ranges of colors or modify all colors equally across the spectrum. And second, the command lets you colorize images by applying new hue and saturation values while retaining the core brightness information from the original image.

This command is perfect for colorizing grayscale images. I know, I know, Woody Allen wouldn't approve, but with some effort, you can make Ted Turner green with envy. Just scan him and change the Hue value to 140 degrees.

When you choose Image ➪ Adjust ➪ Hue/Saturation (Ctrl+U), Photoshop displays the Hue/Saturation dialog box, shown in Figure 17-9. Before I explain how to use this dialog box to produce specific effects, let me briefly introduce the options, starting with the three option boxes:

✦ **Hue:** The Hue slider bar measures colors on the 360-degree color circle, as explained back in the "HSB" section of Chapter 4. You can adjust the Hue value from negative to positive 180 degrees. As you do, Photoshop rotates the colors around the Hue wheel. Consider the example of flesh tones. A Hue value of +30 moves the flesh into the orange range; a value of +100 makes it green. Going in the other direction, a Hue of –30 makes the flesh red and –100 makes it purple.

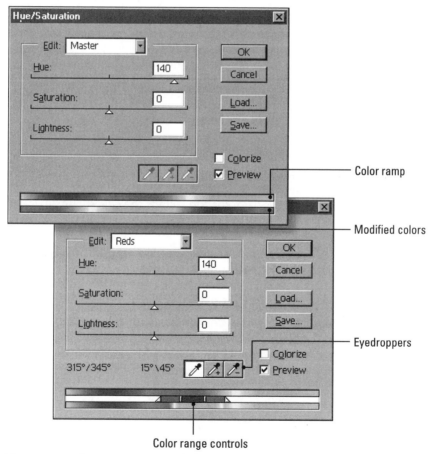

Figure 17-9: The Hue/Saturation dialog box as it appears when editing all colors in a layer (top) or just a specific range of colors (bottom).

When the Colorize check box is selected, Hue becomes an absolute value measured from 0 to 360 degrees. A Hue value of 0 is red, 30 is orange, and so on, as described in Chapter 4.

✦ **Saturation:** The Saturation value changes the intensity of the colors. Normally, the Saturation value varies from –100 for gray to +100 for incredibly vivid hues. The only exception occurs when the Colorize check box is active, in which case saturation becomes an absolute value, measured from 0 for gray to 100 for maximum saturation.

✦ **Lightness:** You can darken or lighten an image by varying the Lightness value from negative to positive 100.

Because this value invariably changes *all* brightness levels in an image to an equal extent—whether or not Colorize is selected—it permanently dulls highlights and shadows. I advise that you avoid this option like the plague and rely instead on the Levels or Curves command to edit brightness and contrast.

✦ **Edit:** The Edit pop-up menu controls which colors in the active selection or layer are affected by the Hue/Saturation command. If you select the Master option, as by default, Hue/Saturation adjusts all colors equally. If you prefer to adjust some colors in the layer differently than others, choose one of the other Edit options or press the keyboard equivalent—Ctrl+1 for Reds, Ctrl+2 for Yellows, and so on.

Each of the Edit options isolates a predefined range of colors inside the image. For example, the Reds option selects the range measured from 345 to 15 degrees on the Hue wheel. Naturally, if you were to modify just the red pixels and left all non-red pixels unchanged, you'd end up with some jagged transitions in your image. So Photoshop softens the edges with 30 degrees of fuzziness at either end of the red spectrum (the same kind of fuzziness described in the "Using the Color Range command" section of Chapter 9).

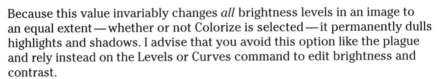

You can apply different Hue, Saturation, and Lightness settings for every one of the color ranges. For example, to change all reds in an image to green and all cyans to gray, do like so: Choose the Reds option and change the Hue value to +50 and then choose Cyans and change the Saturation value to –100.

✦ **Color ramps:** You can track changes made to colors in the Hue/Saturation dialog box in two ways. One way is to select the Preview check box and keep an eye on the changes in the image window. The second way is to observe the color ramps at the bottom of the dialog box. The first ramp shows the 360-degree color spectrum; the second ramp shows what the color ramp looks like after your edits.

✦ **Color range controls:** You can use the color ramps also to broaden or narrow the range of colors affected by Hue/Saturation. When you choose any option other than Master from the Edit pop-up menu, a collection of color range controls appears between the color ramps. The range bar identifies the selected colors and also permits you to edit them.

Figure 17-10 shows the color range controls up close and personal. Here's how they work:

- Drag the central range bar to move the entire color range.

- Drag one of the two lighter-colored fuzziness bars to broaden or narrow the color range without affecting the fuzziness.

- Drag the range control (labeled in Figure 17-10) to change the range while leaving the fuzziness points fixed in place. The result is that you expand the range and condense the fuzziness, or vice versa.

- Drag the triangular fuzziness control to lengthen or contract the fuzziness independently of the color range.

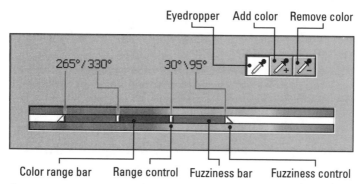

Figure 17-10: After defining a basic range using the Edit pop-up menu, use the color range controls to modify the range or the fuzziness.

By default, red is the central color in the color ramps, with blue at either side. This is great when the range is red or some other warm color. But if you're working with a blue range, the controls get split between the two ends. To move a different color to the central position, Ctrl-drag in the color ramp. The spectrum revolves around the ramp as you drag.

✦ **Eyedroppers:** To lift a color range from the image window, click inside the image window with the eyedropper cursor. (The cursor automatically changes to an eyedropper when you move it outside the Hue/Saturation dialog box.) Photoshop centers the range on the exact color you clicked.

To expand the range to include more colors, Shift-click or drag in the image window. To remove colors from the range, Alt-click or drag in the image. You can also use the alternative plus and minus eyedropper tools, but why bother? Shift and Alt do the job just fine.

✦ **Load/Save:** As in all the best color correction dialog boxes, you can load and save settings to disk in case you want to reapply the options to other images.

These options are especially useful if you find a magic combination of color-correction settings that accounts for most of the color mistakes produced by your scanner.

✦ **Colorize:** Select this check box to apply a single hue and a single saturation level to the entire selection or layer, regardless of how it was previously colored. (Notice that Photoshop 5 sets the Saturation to 25 percent by default, a much more satisfactory setting than the previous overblown default of 100 percent.) All brightness levels remain intact, although you can adjust them incrementally using the Lightness slider bar (a practice that I strongly advise against, as I mentioned earlier).

Color ranges are not permitted when colorizing. The moment you select the Colorize check box, Photoshop dims the Edit pop-up menu and sets it to Master.

✦ **Restore:** You can restore the options in the Hue/Saturation, Levels, and Curves dialog boxes to their original settings by Alt-clicking on the Reset button (the Cancel button changes to Reset when you press Alt).

Tip

To track the behavior of specific colors when using Hue/Saturation or any of Photoshop's other powerful color adjustment commands, display the Info palette (F8) before choosing the Hue/Saturation command. Then move the cursor inside the image window. As shown in Figure 17-11, the Info palette tracks the individual RGB and CMYK values of the pixel beneath the cursor. The number before the slash is the value before the color adjustment; the number after the slash is the value after the adjustment.

Before

After

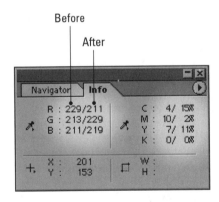

Figure 17-11: When you move the eyedropper outside a color adjustment dialog box and into the image window, the Info palette lists the color values of the pixel beneath the cursor before and after the adjustment.

Remember, you don't have to settle for just one color readout. Shift-click in the image window to add up to four fixed color samples, just like those created with the color sample tool, described in Chapter 4. To move a color sample after you've set it in place, Shift-drag it.

In the case of the Hue/Saturation dialog box, you can set color sample points only when the Edit pop-up menu is set to Master. After you set the samples, select some other options from the pop-up menu to modify a specific range.

Adjusting hue and saturation

All right, now that you know how the copious Hue/Saturation options work, it's time to give them a whirl. I must state one caveat before I launch into things: Grayscale figures won't help you one whit in understanding the Hue/Saturation options, so I refer you to three color plates. You may want to take a moment to slap a Post-it note on the page that contains Color Plates 17-7, 17-8, and 17-9 before you begin reading so that you can easily flip back and forth between text and figures.

Changing hues

When the Colorize check box is inactive, the Hue slider bar shifts colors in an image around the color wheel. It's as if the pixels were playing a colorful game of musical chairs, except that none of the chairs disappear. If you select the Master option and enter a value of +60 degrees, for example, all pixels stand up, march one sixth of the way around the color wheel, and sit down, assuming the colors of their new chairs. A pixel that was red becomes yellow, a pixel that was yellow becomes green, and so on. The top row of Color Plate 17-7 shows the result of applying various Hue values to a single image. Note that in each case, all colors in the image change to an equal degree.

Note

As long as you select only the Master option and edit only the Hue value, Photoshop retains all colors in an image. In other words, after shifting the hues in an image +60 degrees, you can later choose Hue/Saturation and shift the hues –60 degrees to restore the original colors.

If you select any Edit option other than Master, the musical chairs metaphor breaks down a little. All pixels that correspond to the selected color range move while pixels outside the color range remain seated. The pixels that move must sit on the non-moving pixels' laps, meaning that you sacrifice colors in the image.

For example, I edited the images in the second row of Color Plate 17-7 by applying Hue values exclusively while the Cyan option was selected. (In other words, I didn't apply Hue changes in combination with any other color range.) All pixels that fell inside the cyan range shifted to new hues; all non-cyan pixels remained unchanged. Despite the fact that the Hue values in each column of the color plate are identical, the colors in the horse changed less dramatically when Cyan was selected than when I used the Master option. Even the pixels in the primarily cyan areas contain trace amounts of blue and green, which are excluded from the Cyan range.

Changing saturation levels

When I was a little kid, I loved watching my grandmother's television because she kept the Color knob cranked at all times. The images leapt off the screen, like they were radioactive or something. *Way* cool. Well, the Saturation option works just like that Color knob. I don't recommend that you follow my grandmother's example and send the saturation for every image through the roof, but it can prove helpful for enhancing or downplaying the colors in an image. If the image looks washed out, try adding saturation; if colors leap off the screen so that everybody in the image looks like they're wearing neon makeup, subtract saturation.

Note   Just as the Saturation option works like the Color knob on a TV set, the Hue value serves the same purpose as the Tint knob, and the Lightness value works like the Brightness knob. So you see, your mother was quite mistaken when she told you that sitting on your butt and staring at the TV wasn't going to teach you anything. Little did she know, you were getting a head start on electronic art.

The top row of Color Plate 17-8 shows the results of applying Saturation values when the Master option is selected. As you can see, all colors in the image fade or fortify equally. However, by applying the Saturation values to specific color ranges only, you can selectively fade and fortify colors, as demonstrated in the second row of the color plate. The lower-left image in the color plate shows the result of selecting every color range except Cyan and Blue and lowering the Saturation to –100, which translates to no saturation. The result is that all colors outside the cyan and blue ranges turn gray. In the lower-right image, I lowered the Saturation for the Cyan and Blue options to –100 and raised the saturation of all other color ranges to +50, thus eliminating the image's most prominent colors and enhancing the remaining weaker ones.

The Saturation option is especially useful for toning down images captured with low-end scanners and digital cameras, which have a tendency to exaggerate certain colors. Back in the early years, I used to work with an Epson scanner that would digitize flesh tones in varieties of vivid oranges and red. I couldn't, for the life of me, figure out how to peel the colors off the ceiling until I tried the Saturation option in the Hue/Saturation dialog box. By selecting the Red color range and dragging the slider down to about –50, I was usually able to eliminate the problem, and so can you.

Correcting out-of-gamut colors

Another common use for the Saturation option is to prepare RGB images for process-color printing. As I explained in Chapter 4, many colors in the RGB spectrum are considered out-of-gamut, meaning that they fall outside the smaller CMYK color space. Photoshop provides a means for recognizing such colors while remaining inside the RGB color space. Choose View ➪ Gamut Warning (Ctrl+Shift+Y) to color all out-of-gamut colors with gray (or some other color that you specify using the Preferences command). The pixels don't actually change to gray; they just appear gray on-screen as long as the command is active. To turn View ➪ Gamut Warning off, choose the command again.

How do you eliminate such problem colors? Well, you have three options:

✦ Let Photoshop take care of the problem automatically when you convert the image by choosing Image ⇨ Mode ⇨ CMYK Color. This tactic is risky because Photoshop simply cuts off colors outside the gamut and converts them to their nearest CMYK equivalents. What was once an abundant range of differently saturated hues becomes abruptly flattened, like some kind of cruel buzz haircut. Choosing View ⇨ Proof Setup ⇨ Working CMYK gives you an idea of how dramatic the buzz can be while permitting you to continue working in the RGB color space. Sometimes the effect is hardly noticeable, in which case no additional attention may be warranted. Other times, the results can be disastrous.

✦ Another method is to scrub away with the sponge tool. In Chapter 5, I discussed how much I dislike this alternative, and despite the passage of a dozen chapters, I haven't changed my mind. Although it theoretically offers selective control — you just scrub at areas that need attention until the gray pixels created by the Gamut Warning command disappear — the process leaves too much to chance and frequently does more damage than simply choosing Image ⇨ Mode ⇨ CMYK Color.

✦ The third and best solution involves the Saturation option in the Hue/Saturation dialog box.

No doubt that last item comes as a huge surprise, given that I decided to broach the out-of-gamut topic in the middle of examining the Saturation option. But try to scoop your jaw up off the floor long enough to peruse the following steps, which outline the proper procedure for bringing out-of-gamut colors back into the CMYK color space.

STEPS: Eliminating Out-of-Gamut Colors

1. **Create a duplicate of your image to serve as a CMYK preview.** Choose Image ⇨ Duplicate to create a copy of your image. Then choose View ⇨ Proof Setup ⇨ Working CMYK. (Alternatively, you can press Ctrl+Y to invoke color proofing. By default, Photoshop selects the working CMYK space.) This image represents what Photoshop does with your image if you don't make any corrections. It's good to have around for comparison.

2. **Return to your original image and choose Select ⇨ Color Range.** Then select the Out Of Gamut option from the Select pop-up menu and press Enter. You have now selected all nonconformist anti-gamut pixels throughout your image. These radicals must be expunged.

3. **To monitor your progress, choose View ⇨ Gamut Warning to display the gray pixels.** Oh, and don't forget to press Ctrl+H to get rid of those pesky ants.

4. **Press Ctrl+U to display the Hue/Saturation dialog box.**

5. **Lower the saturation of individual color ranges.** Don't change any settings while Master is selected; it's not exacting enough. Rather, experiment with specifying your own color ranges and lowering the Saturation value. Every time you see one of the pixels change from gray to color, it means that another happy pixel has joined the CMYK collective. You may want to state, in your best monotone, "Resistance is futile," if only to make your work more entertaining.

6. **When only a few hundred sporadic gray spots remain on screen, click the OK button to return to the image window.** Bellow imperiously, "You may think you have won, you little gray pixels, but I have a secret weapon!" Then choose Image ⇨ Mode ⇨ CMYK Color and watch as Photoshop forcibly thrusts them into the gamut.

Mind you, the differences between your duplicate image and the one you manually turned away from the evils of RGB excess are subtle, but they may prove enough to produce a better looking image with a more dynamic range of colors.

Avoiding gamut-correction edges

The one problem with the preceding steps is that the Color Range command selects only out-of-gamut pixels without even partially selecting their neighbors. As a result, you desaturate out-of-gamut colors while leaving similar colors fully saturated, an effect that may result in jagged and unnatural edges.

One solution is to insert a step between Steps 2 and 3 in which you do the following: Select the magic wand tool and change the Tolerance value in the Options bar to, say, 12. Next, choose Select ⇨ Similar, which expands the selected area to incorporate all pixels that fall within the Tolerance range. Finally, choose Select ⇨ Feather and enter a Feather Radius value that's about half the Tolerance — in this case, 6.

This solution isn't perfect — ideally, the Color Range option box wouldn't dim the Fuzziness slider when you choose Out Of Gamut — but it does succeed in partially selecting a few neighboring pixels without sacrificing too many of the out-of-gamut bunch.

Colorizing images

When you select the Colorize check box in the Hue/Saturation dialog box, the options perform differently. Returning to that wonderful musical chairs analogy, the pixels no longer walk around a circle of chairs; instead, they all get up and go sit in the same chair. Every pixel in the selection receives the same hue and the same level of saturation. Only the brightness values remain intact to ensure that the image remains recognizable.

The top row of Color Plate 17-9 shows the results of shifting the hues in an image in two different directions around the color wheel. In each case, the Colorize option is turned off. The second row shows similar colors applied separately to the blue and non-blue portions of the image using the Colorize option. (Because you can't specify color ranges in the Hue/Saturation dialog box when Colorize is on, I selected the blue regions using the Color Range command before choosing the Hue/Saturation command.) The colors look similar within each column in the color plate. The Hue values in the shifted images are different than those in the colorized images, however, because the shifted colors are based on relative adjustments while the colorized changes are absolute.

In most cases, you'll only want to colorize grayscale images or bad color scans. After all, colorizing ruins the original color composition of an image. For the best results, you'll want to set the Saturation values to somewhere in the neighborhood of 25 to 75. All the colors in the second-row images in Color Plate 17-9 err on the high side, with Saturation values of 80.

Tip

To touch up the edges of a colorized selection, change the foreground color to match the Hue and Saturation values you used in the Hue/Saturation dialog box. You can do this by choosing the HSB Sliders command from the Color palette menu and entering the values in the H and S option boxes. Set the B (Brightness) value to 100 percent. Next, select the paintbrush tool and change the brush mode to Color (Shift+Alt+C). Then paint away.

Shifting selected colors

The Replace Color command allows you to select an area of related colors and adjust the hue and saturation of that area. When you select Image ➪ Adjust ➪ Replace Color, you get a dialog box much like the Color Range dialog box. The Replace Color dialog box, shown in Figure 17-12, varies in only a few respects: It's missing the Select and Selection Preview pop-up menus and it offers three slider bars, taken right out of the Hue/Saturation dialog box.

In fact, this dialog box works exactly as if you were to select a portion of an image using Select ➪ Color Range and edit it with the Hue/Saturation command. You don't have as many options to work with, but the outcome is the same. The Replace Color and Color Range dialog boxes even share the same default settings. If you change the Fuzziness value in one, the default Fuzziness value of the other changes as well. It's as if they're identical twins or something.

So why does the Replace Color command even exist? Because it allows you to change the selection outline and apply different colors without affecting the image. Just select the Preview check box to see the results of your changes on screen, and you're in business.

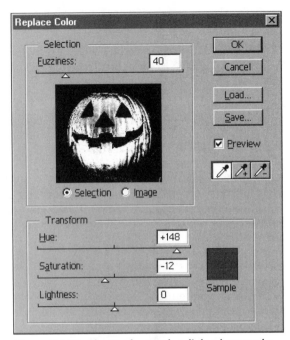

Figure 17-12: The Replace Color dialog box works like the Color Range dialog box described back in Chapter 9, with a few Hue/Saturation options thrown in.

The top row of Color Plate 17-10 shows two effects created by selecting an area and changing the Hue value to +148 and the Saturation value to –12 (as in Figure 17-12). In the first example, I selected the pumpkin face by setting the Fuzziness value to 40 and clicking and Shift-clicking a few times with the eyedropper tool. In the right example, I clicked just once in the area behind the pumpkin and changed the Fuzziness to 200, the maximum setting. I was able to experiment freely without once leaving the dialog box or redrawing the selection outline.

Cross-Reference If you're not clear on how to use all the options in the Replace Color dialog box, read the "Using the Color Range command" section in Chapter 9. It tells you all about the eyedropper tools and the Fuzziness option.

Shifting predefined colors

The Selective Color command permits you to adjust the colors in CMYK images. Although you can use Selective Color also when working on RGB or Lab images, it makes more sense in the CMYK color space because it permits you to adjust the levels of cyan, magenta, yellow, and black inks.

Note

Frankly, I'm not very keen on this command. For general image editing, the Variations command provides better control and more intuitive options. Adobe created the Selective Color command to accommodate traditional press managers who prefer to have direct control over ink levels rather than monkeying around with hue, saturation, and other observational color controls. If Selective Color works for you, great. But don't get hung up on it if it never quite gels. You can accomplish all this and more with the Variations command, described in the next section.

Choosing Image ⇨ Adjust ⇨ Selective Color brings up the dialog box shown in Figure 17-13. To use the dialog box, choose the predefined color that you want to edit from the Colors pop-up menu and then adjust the four process-color slider bars to change the predefined color. When you select the Relative radio button, you add or subtract color, much as if you were moving the color around the musical chairs using the Hue slider bar. When you select Absolute, you change the predefined color to the exact value entered in the Cyan, Magenta, Yellow, and Black option boxes. The Absolute option is therefore very much like the Colorize check box in the Hue/Saturation dialog box.

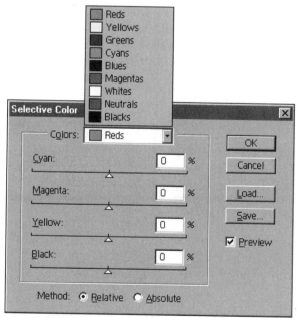

Figure 17-13: Select a predefined color from the Colors pop-up menu and adjust the slider bars to change that color.

If you examine the Selective Color dialog box closely, you'll notice that it is very much like the Hue/Saturation dialog box. You have access to predefined colors in the form of a pop-up menu instead of radio buttons, and you can adjust slider bars to alter the color. The two key differences are that the pop-up menu lets you adjust whites, medium grays (Neutrals), and blacks — options missing from Hue/Saturation — and that the slider bars are always measured in CMYK color space.

The bottom row of Color Plate 17-10 includes two examples that show how the Selective Color dialog box works. To create the first, I chose Red from the Colors pop-up menu and dragged the Cyan slider bar all the way up to +100 percent and the Yellow slider all the way down to –100 percent. I also selected the Relative radio button, which retains a lot of pink in the pumpkin's face. To create the second example, I reapplied the same colors but selected the Absolute radio button, making the entire pumpkin purple. I also chose Black from the Colors pop-up menu and dragged the Black slider to –100 percent.

Tip

As I mentioned at the outset, the Selective Color command produces the most predictable results when you're working on a CMYK image. When you drag the Cyan slider triangle to the right, for example, you're actually transferring brightness values to the cyan channel. However, you have to keep an eye out for a few anomalies, particularly when editing Black. In the CMYK mode, areas of your image that appear black include not only black but also shades of cyan, magenta, and yellow, resulting in what printers call a *rich black* (or *saturated black*). Therefore, to change black to white, as I did in the lower-right example of Color Plate 17-10, you have to set the Black slider to –100 percent and also set the Cyan, Magenta, and Yellow sliders to the same value.

Using the Variations command

The Variations command is Photoshop's most essential color correction function *and* its funkiest.

On one hand, you can adjust hues and luminosity levels based on the brightness values of the pixels, something Hue/Saturation cannot do. You can also see what you're doing by clicking on little thumbnail previews (see Figure 17-14), which takes much of the guesswork out of the correction process.

On the other hand, the Variations dialog box takes over your screen and prevents you from previewing corrections in the image window. Furthermore, you can't see the area outside a selection, which proves disconcerting when making relative color adjustments.

The Variations command is therefore best suited to correcting an image in its entirety. Here's how it works: To infuse color into the image, click one of the thumbnails in the central portion of the dialog box. The thumbnail labeled More Cyan, for example, shifts the colors toward cyan. The thumbnail even shows how the additional cyan will look when added to the image. In case you're interested in seeing how these thumbnails affect a final printed image in the CMYK color space, check out Color Plate 17-11.

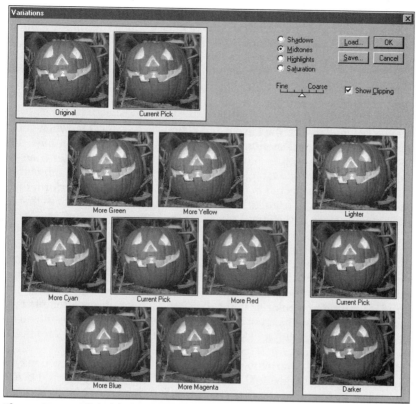

Figure 17-14: Click the thumbnails to shift the colors in an image; adjust the slider bar in the upper-right corner to change the sensitivity of the thumbnails; and use the radio buttons to determine which part of an image is selected.

Now notice that each thumbnail is positioned directly opposite its complementary color. More Cyan is across from More Red, More Blue is across from More Yellow, and so on. In fact, clicking on a thumbnail shifts colors not only toward the named color but also away from the opposite color. For example, if you click More Cyan and then click its opposite, More Red, you arrive at the original image.

Note

Although this isn't exactly how the colors in the additive and subtractive worlds work — cyan is not the empirical opposite of red — the colors are theoretical opposites, and the Variations command makes the theory a practicality. After all, you haven't yet applied the color to the image, so the dialog box can calculate its adjustments in a pure and perfect world. Cyan and red ought to be opposites, so for the moment, they are.

To control the amount of color shifting that occurs when you click a thumbnail, move the slider triangle in the upper-right corner of the dialog box. Fine produces very minute changes; Coarse creates massive changes. Just to give you an idea of the difference between the two, you have to click a thumbnail about 40 times when the slider is set to Fine to equal one click when it's set to Coarse.

The radio buttons at the top control which colors in the image are affected. Select Shadows to change the darkest colors, Highlights to change the lightest colors, and Midtones to change everything in between.

Note

In fact, if you're familiar with the Levels dialog box — as you will be when you read "The Levels command" section later in this chapter — you might have noticed that the first three radio buttons have direct counterparts in the slider triangles in the Levels dialog box. For example, when you click the Lighter thumbnail while the Highlights option is selected in the Variations dialog box, you perform the same action as moving the white triangle in the Levels dialog box to the left — that is, you make the lightest colors in the image even lighter.

The Saturation radio button lets you increase or decrease the saturation of colors in an image. Only one thumbnail appears on each side of the Current Pick image: One that decreases the saturation and another that increases it. The Variations command modifies saturation differently than Hue/Saturation. Hue/Saturation pushes the saturation of a color as far as it will go, but Variations attempts to modify the saturation without changing overall brightness values. As a result, an image saturated with Hue/Saturation looks lighter than one saturated with Variations.

As you click the options — particularly when modifying saturation — you may notice that weird colors spring up inside the thumbnails. These brightly colored pixels are gamut warnings, highlighting colors that exceed the boundaries of the current color space. For example, if you're working in the RGB mode, these colors extend beyond the RGB gamut. Although the colors won't actually appear inverted as they do in the dialog box, it's not a good idea to exceed the color space because it results in areas of flat color, just as when you convert between the RGB and CMYK spaces. To view the thumbnails without the weirdly colored pixels, turn off the Show Clipping check box. (Incidentally, this use of the word *clipping* — Photoshop's third, in case you're counting — has nothing to do with paths or masks.)

Enhancing colors in a compressed image

Now that you know every possible way to adjust hues and saturation levels in Photoshop, it's time to discuss some of the possible stumbling blocks. The danger of rotating colors or increasing the saturation of an image is that you can bring out some very unstable colors. Adjusting the hues can switch ratty pixels from colors that your eyes aren't very sensitive to — particularly blue — into colors your eyes see very well — reds and greens. Drab color can also hide poor detail, which becomes painfully obvious when you make the colors bright and vivid.

Consider the digital photograph featured in Color Plate 17-12. Snapped several years back in Boston's Copley Square using a Kodak DC50 digital camera, the original image at the top of the color plate is drab and lifeless. If I used the Hue/Saturation command to pump up the saturation levels, a world of ugly detail rises out of the muck, as shown in the second example. (Obviously, I've taken the saturation a little too high, but only to demonstrate a point.) The detail would have faired no better if I had used the Variations command to boost the saturation.

Unstable colors may be the result of JPEG compression, as in the case of the digital photo. Or you may have bad scanning or poor lighting to thank. In any case, you can correct the problem using our friends the Median and Gaussian Blur commands, as I explain in the following steps.

If you find yourself working with heavily compressed images on a regular basis, you may want to record these steps with the Actions palette, as explained in Chapter B on the CD-ROM at the back of this book. Unlike the "Adjusting the Focus of Digital Photos" steps back in Chapter 10, you won't want to apply these steps to every digital photograph you take — or even most of them — but they come in handy more often than you might think.

STEPS: Boosting the Saturation of Digital Photos

1. **Select the entire image and copy it to a new layer.** It seems like half of all Photoshop techniques begin with Ctrl+A and Ctrl+J.

2. **Press Ctrl+U to display the Hue/Saturation dialog box.** Then raise the Saturation value to whatever setting you desire. Don't worry if your image starts to fall apart — that's the whole point of these steps. Pay attention to the color and don't worry about the rest. In the second example in Color Plate 17-12, I raised the Saturation to +80.

3. **Choose Filter ➪ Noise ➪ Median.** As you may recall from the last module, Median is the preeminent JPEG image fixer. A Radius value of 4 or 5 pixels works well for most images. You can take it even higher when working with resolutions of 200 ppi or more. I used 5. This destroys the detail, but that's not important. The color is all that matters.

4. **Choose Filter ➪ Blur ➪ Gaussian Blur.** As always, the Median filter introduces its own edges. And this is one case where you don't want to add any edges, so blur the heck out of the layer. I used a Radius of 4.0, just 1 pixel less than my Median Radius value.

5. **Select Color from the blend mode pop-up menu in the Layers palette.** Photoshop mixes the gummy, blurry color with the crisp detail underneath. I also lowered the Opacity to 70 percent to produce the third example in Color Plate 17-12.

My image was still a little soft, so I applied the digital-photo sharpening steps from Chapter 10. After flattening the image, I pressed Ctrl+A and Ctrl+J again to copy it to yet another new layer. Then I applied the Median, Gaussian Blur, and Unsharp Mask filters, flattened the image one last time, and sharpened the image to taste. The finished result appears at the bottom of Color Plate 17-12. Although a tad too colorful—Boston's a lovely city, but it's not quite this resplendent—the edges look every bit as good as they did in the original photograph, and in many ways better.

Making Custom Brightness Adjustments

The Lighter and Darker options in the Variations dialog box are preferable to the Lightness slider bar in the Hue/Saturation dialog box because you can specify whether to edit the darkest, lightest, or medium colors in an image. But neither command is adequate for making precise adjustments to the brightness and contrast of an image. Photoshop provides two expert-level commands for adjusting the brightness levels in both grayscale and color images:

- ✦ **The Levels command is great for most color corrections.** It lets you adjust the darkest values, lightest values, and midrange colors with a minimum of fuss and a generous amount of control.

- ✦ **The Curves command is great for creating special effects and correcting images beyond the help of the Levels command.** Using the Curves command, you can map every brightness value in every color channel to an entirely different brightness value.

Note In the back rooms of some print houses and art shops, a controversy is brewing over which command is better, Levels or Curves. Based on a few letters I've received over the years, it seems that some folks consider Curves to be the command for real men and Levels suitable only for color-correcting wimps.

Naturally, this is a big wad of hooey. Levels provides a histogram, which is absolutely essential for gauging the proper setting for black and white points. Meanwhile, Curves lets you map out a virtually infinite number of significant points on a graph. The point is, both commands have their advantages, and both offer practical benefits for intermediate and advanced users alike.

There's no substitute for a good histogram, so I prefer to use Levels for my day-to-day color correcting. If you can't quite get the effect you want with Levels, or you know that you need to map specific brightness values in an image to other values, use Curves. The Curves command is the more powerful function, but it is likewise more cumbersome.

The Levels command

When you choose Image ➪ Adjust ➪ Levels (Ctrl+L), Photoshop displays the Levels dialog box shown in Figure 17-15. The dialog box offers a histogram, as explained in the "Threshold" section earlier in this chapter, as well as two sets of slider bars with corresponding option boxes and a few automated eyedropper options in the lower-right corner. You can compress and expand the range of brightness values in an image by manipulating the Input Levels options. Then you can map those brightness values to new brightness values by adjusting the Output Levels options.

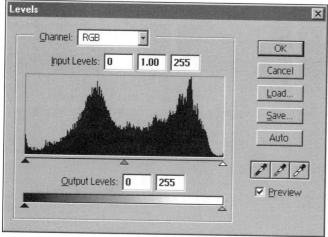

Figure 17-15: Use the Levels dialog box to map brightness values in the image (Input Levels) to new brightness values (Output Levels).

The options in the Levels dialog box work as follows:

✦ **Channel:** Select the color channel that you want to edit from this pop-up menu. You can apply different Input Levels and Output Levels values to each color channel. However, the options along the right side of the dialog box affect all colors in the selected portion of an image regardless of which Channel option is active.

✦ **Input Levels:** Use these options to modify the contrast of the image by darkening the darkest colors and lightening the lightest ones. The Input Levels option boxes correspond to the slider bar immediately below the histogram. You map pixels to black (or the darkest Output Levels value) by entering a number from 0 to 255 in the first option box or by dragging the black slider triangle. For example, if you raise the value to 55, all colors with brightness values of 55 or less in the original image become black, darkening the image as shown in the first example of Figure 17-16.

You can map pixels at the opposite end of the brightness scale to white (or the lightest Output Levels value) by entering a number from 0 to 255 in the last option box or by dragging the white slider triangle. If you lower the value to 200, all colors with brightness values of 200 or greater become white, lightening the image as shown in the second example of Figure 17-16. In the last example of the figure, I raised the first value and lowered the last value, thereby increasing the amount of contrast in the image.

Tip

One of my favorite ways to edit the Input Levels values is to press the up and down arrow keys. Each press of an arrow key raises or lowers the value by 1. Press Shift with an arrow key to change the value in increments of 10.

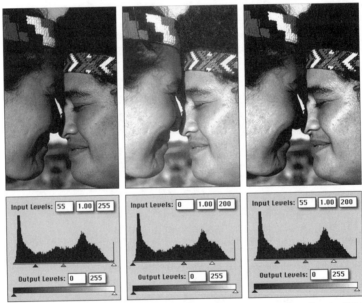

Figure 17-16: The results of raising the first Input Levels value to 55 (left), lowering the last value to 200 (middle), and combining the two (right).

✦ **Gamma:** The middle Input Levels option box and the corresponding gray triangle in the slider bar (shown highlighted in Figure 17-17) represent the gamma value, which is the brightness level of the medium gray value in the image. The gamma value can range from 0.10 to 9.99, with 1.00 being dead-on medium gray. Any change to the gamma value has the effect of decreasing the amount of contrast in the image by lightening or darkening grays without changing shadows and highlights. Increase the gamma value or drag the gray slider triangle to the left to lighten the medium grays (also called *midtones*), as in the first and second examples of Figure 17-18. Lower the gamma value or drag the gray triangle to the right to darken the medium grays, as in the last example in the figure.

You can edit the gamma value also by pressing the up and down arrow keys. Pressing an arrow key changes the value by 0.01; pressing Shift+arrow changes the value by 0.10. I can't stress enough how useful this technique is. I rarely do anything except press arrow keys inside the Levels dialog box anymore.

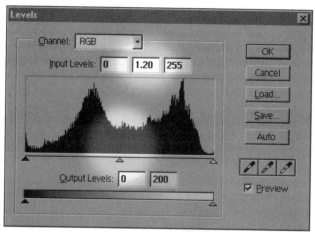

Figure 17-17: To create the spotlighting effects you see here, I selected the circular areas, inversed the selection, and applied the values shown in this very dialog box.

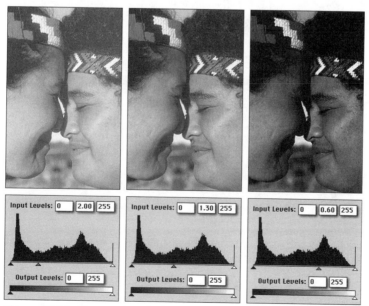

Figure 17-18: The results of raising (left and middle) and lowering (right) the gamma value to lighten and darken the midtones in an image.

✦ **Output Levels:** Use these options to curtail the range of brightness levels in an image by lightening the darkest pixels and darkening the lightest pixels. You adjust the brightness of the darkest pixels — those that correspond to the black Input Levels slider triangle — by entering a number from 0 to 255 in the first option box or by dragging the black slider triangle. For example, if you raise the value to 55, no color can be darker than that brightness level (roughly 80 percent black), which lightens the image as shown in the first example of Figure 17-19. You adjust the brightness of the lightest pixels — those that correspond to the white Input Levels slider triangle — by entering a number from 0 to 255 in the second option box or by dragging the white slider triangle. If you lower the value to 200, no color can be lighter than that brightness level (roughly 20 percent black), darkening the image as shown in the second example of Figure 17-19. In the last example of the figure, I raised the first value and lowered the second value, thereby dramatically decreasing the amount of contrast in the image.

You can fully or partially invert an image using the Output Levels slider triangles. Just drag the black triangle to the right and drag the white triangle to the left past the black triangle. The colors flip, whites mapping to dark colors and blacks mapping to light colors.

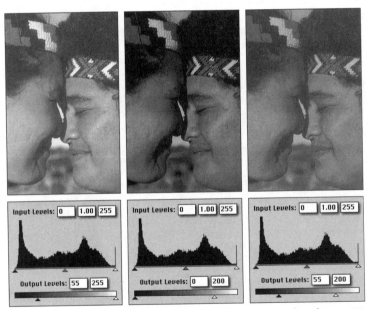

Figure 17-19: The result of raising the first Output Levels value to 55 (left), lowering the second value to 200 (middle), and combining the two (right).

✦ **Load/Save:** You can load and save settings to disk using these buttons.

✦ **Auto:** Click the Auto button to automatically map the darkest pixel in your selection to black and the lightest pixel to white, as if you had chosen Image ➪ Adjust ➪ Auto Levels. Photoshop actually darkens and lightens the image by an extra half a percent just in case the darkest and lightest pixels are statistically inconsistent with the rest of the image.

To enter a percentage of your own, Alt-click the Auto button (the button name changes to Options). This displays two additional options, Black Clip and White Clip. Enter higher values to increase the number of pixels mapped to black and white; decrease the values to lessen the effect. Figure 17-20 compares the effect of the default 0.50 percent values to higher values of 2.50 and 9.99 percent. As you can see, raising the Clip value produces higher contrast effects.

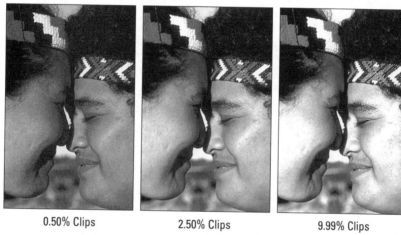

0.50% Clips   2.50% Clips   9.99% Clips

Figure 17-20: The default effect of the Auto button (left) and the effect of the Auto button after raising the Clip values (middle and right).

Any changes made in the Auto Range Options dialog box also affect the performance of the Auto Levels command. At all times, the effects of the Auto button and Auto Levels command are identical.

✦ **Eyedroppers:** Select one of the eyedropper tools in the Levels dialog box and click a pixel in the image window to automatically adjust the color of that pixel. If you click a pixel with the black eyedropper tool (the first of the three), Photoshop maps the color of the pixel and all darker colors to black. If you click a pixel with the white eyedropper tool (the last of the three),

Photoshop maps it and all lighter colors to white. Use the gray eyedropper tool (middle) to change the color you clicked to medium gray and adjust all other colors in accordance. For example, if you click a light pixel, all light pixels change to medium gray and all other pixels change to even darker colors.

One way to use the eyedropper tools is to color-correct scans without a lot of messing around. Include a neutral swatch of gray with the photograph you want to scan. (For those who own a Pantone swatch book, Cool Gray 5 or 6 is your best bet.) After opening the scan in Photoshop, choose the Levels command, select the gray eyedropper tool, and click the neutral gray swatch in the image window. This technique won't perform miracles, but it will help you to distribute lights and darks in the image more evenly. You then can fine-tune the image using the Input Levels and Output Levels options.

By default, the eyedroppers map to white, gray, and black. But you can change that. Double-click any one of the three eyedroppers to display the Color Picker dialog box. For example, suppose you double-click the white eyedropper, set the color values to C:2, M:3, Y:5, K:0, and then click a pixel in the image window. Instead of making the pixel white, Photoshop changes the clicked color — and all colors lighter than it — to C:2, M:3, Y:5, K:0, which is great for avoiding hot highlights and ragged edges.

To give you a sense of how the Levels command works, the following steps describe how to improve the appearance of an overly dark, low-contrast image such as the first example in Color Plate 17-13. Thanks to natural lighting and the dark color of the stone, this statue of Thomas Jefferson is hardly recognizable. Luckily, you can bring out the highlights using Levels.

STEPS: Correcting Brightness and Contrast with the Levels Command

1. **Press Ctrl+L to display the Levels dialog box.** The histogram for the Jefferson image appears superimposed in white in front of the great man's chest. As you can see, most of the colors are clustered on the left side of the graph, showing that there are far more dark colors than light.

2. **Press Ctrl+1 to examine the red channel.** Assuming that you're editing an RGB image, Ctrl+1 displays a histogram for the red channel. The channel-specific histograms appear below Jefferson, colorized for your viewing pleasure.

3. **Edit the black Input Levels value as needed.** Drag the black slider triangle to below the point at which the histogram begins. In the case of Jefferson, you can see a spike in the histogram about a half pica in from the left side of the graph. I dragged the black triangle directly underneath that spike, changing the first Input Levels value to 14, as you can see in the red histogram on the right side of Color Plate 17-13.

4. **Edit the white Input Levels value.** Drag the white slider triangle to below the point at which the histogram ends. In the color plate, the histogram features a tall spike on the far right side. This means a whole lot of pixels are already white. I don't want to create a flat hot spot, so I leave the white triangle alone.

5. **Edit the gamma value.** Drag the gray triangle to the gravitational center of the histogram. Imagine that the histogram is a big mass, and you're trying to balance the mass evenly on top of the gray triangle. Because my histogram is weighted too heavily to the left, I had to drag the gray triangle far to the left until the middle Input Levels value changed to 2.40, which represents a radical shift.

6. **Repeat Steps 2 through 5 for the green and blue channels.** Ctrl+2 takes you to the green channel; Ctrl+3 takes you to blue. Your image probably has a significant preponderance of red about it. To correct this, you need to edit the green and blue channels in kind. The graphs on the right side of Color Plate 17-13 show how I edited my histograms. Feel free to switch back and forth between channels as much as you like to get everything just right.

7. **Press Ctrl+tilde (~) to return to the composite RGB histogram.** After you get the color balance right, you can switch back to the composite mode and further edit the Input Levels. I typically bump up the gamma a few notches — to 1.2 or so — to account for dot gain.

   You may notice that your RGB histogram has changed. Although the histograms in the individual color channels remain fixed, the composite histogram updates to reflect the red, green, and blue modifications. I've superimposed the updated histogram in white on the corrected Jefferson on the right side of Color Plate 17-13. As you can see, the colors are now better distributed across the brightness range.

8. **Press Enter to apply your changes.** Just for fun, press Ctrl+Z a few times to see the before and after shots. Quite the transformation, eh?

Tip

If you decide after looking at the before and after views that you could do a better job, undo the color correction and press Ctrl+Alt+L to bring up the Levels dialog box with the previous settings intact. Now you can take up where you left off.

The Curves command

If you want to be able to map any brightness value in an image to absolutely any other brightness value — no holds barred, as they say — you want the Curves command. When you choose Image ⇨ Adjust ⇨ Curves (Ctrl+M), Photoshop displays the Curves dialog box, shown in Figure 17-21, which offers access to the most complex and powerful color correction options on the planet.

Brightness graph   Brightness curve

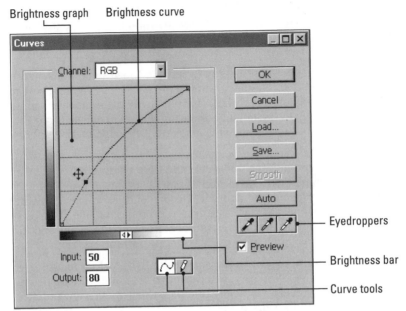

Eyedroppers

Brightness bar

Curve tools

Figure 17-21: The Curves dialog box lets you distribute brightness values by drawing curves on a graph.

Quickly, here's how the options work:

✦ **Channel:** Surely you know how this option works by now. You select the color channel that you want to edit from this pop-up menu. You can apply different mapping functions to different channels by drawing in the graph below the pop-up menu. But, as is always the case, the options along the right side of the dialog box affect all colors in the selected portion of an image regardless of which Channel option is active.

✦ **Brightness graph:** The brightness graph is where you map brightness values in the original image to new brightness values. The horizontal axis of the graph represents input levels; the vertical axis represents output levels. The *brightness curve* charts the relationship between input and output levels. The lower-left corner is the origin of the graph (the point at which both input and output values are 0). Move right in the graph for higher input values and up for higher output values. Because the brightness graph is the core of this dialog box, upcoming sections explain it in more detail.

Tip

By default, a trio of horizontal and vertical dotted lines crisscross the brightness graph, subdividing it into quarters. For added precision, you can divide the graph into horizontal and vertical tenths. Just Alt-click inside the graph to toggle between tenths and quarters.

✦ **Brightness bar:** The horizontal brightness bar shows the direction of light and dark values in the graph. When the dark end of the brightness bar appears on the left — as by default when editing an RGB image — colors are measured in terms of brightness values. The colors in the graph proceed from black on the left to white on the right, as demonstrated in the left example of Figure 17-22. Therefore, higher values produce lighter colors. This is my preferred setting because it measures colors in the same direction as the Levels dialog box.

If you click the brightness bar, white and black switch places, as shown in the second example of the figure. The result is that Photoshop measures the colors in terms of ink coverage, from 0 to 100 percent of the primary color. Higher values now produce darker colors. This is the default setting for grayscale and CMYK images.

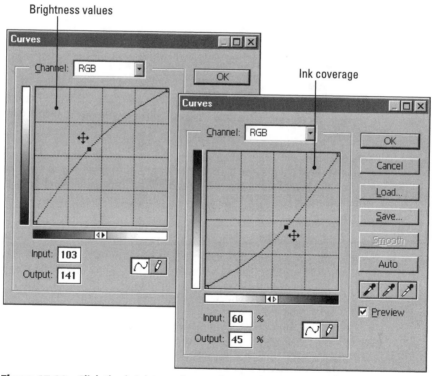

Figure 17-22: Click the brightness bar to change the way in which the graph measures color: by brightness values (left) or by ink coverage (right).

✦ **Curve tools:** Use the curve tools to draw the curve inside the brightness graph. The point tool (labeled in Figure 17-23) is selected by default. Click in the graph with this tool to add a point to the curve. Drag a point to move it. To delete a point, Ctrl-click it.

The pencil tool lets you draw free-form curves simply by dragging inside the graph, as illustrated in Figure 17-23. This pencil works much like Photoshop's standard pencil tool. This means you can draw straight lines by clicking one location in the graph and Shift-clicking a different point.

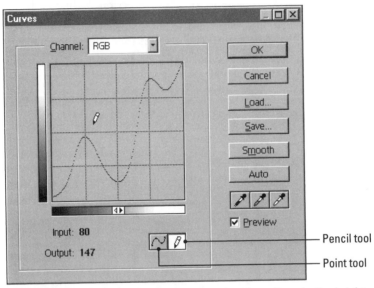

Pencil tool

Point tool

Figure 17-23: Use the pencil tool to draw free-form lines in the brightness graph. If the lines appear rough, you can soften them by clicking on the Smooth button.

✦ **Input and Output values:** The Input and Output values monitor the location of your cursor in the graph according to brightness values or ink coverage, depending on the setting of the brightness bar. You can modify the Input and Output values when working with the point tool. Just click the point on the graph that you want to adjust and then enter new values. The Input number represents the brightness or ink value of the point before you entered the Curves dialog box; the Output number represents the new brightness or ink value.

Tip

You can change the Output value also by using the up and down arrow keys. Click the point you want to modify. Then press the up or down arrow key to raise or lower the Output value by 1. Press Shift+up or down arrow to change the Output value in increments of 10. Note that these techniques — and ones that follow — work only when the point tool is active. (You can't change points with the pencil tool.)

When editing multiple graph points from the keyboard, it's helpful to be able to activate the points from the keyboard as well. To advance from one point to the next, press Ctrl+Tab. To select the previous point, press Ctrl+Shift+Tab. To deselect all points, press Ctrl+D.

✦ **Load/Save:** Use these buttons to load and save settings to disk.

✦ **Smooth:** Click the Smooth button to smooth out curves drawn with the pencil tool. Doing so leads to smoother color transitions in the image window. This button is dimmed except when you use the pencil tool.

✦ **Auto:** Click this button to automatically map the darkest pixel in your selection to black and the lightest pixel to white. Photoshop throws in some additional darkening and lightening according to the Clip percentages, which you can edit by Alt-clicking on the button.

✦ **Eyedroppers:** If you move the cursor out of the dialog box and into the image window, you get the standard eyedropper cursor. Click a pixel in the image to locate the brightness value of that pixel in the graph. A circle appears in the graph, and the Input and Output numbers list the value for as long as you hold down the mouse button, as shown in the first example in Figure 17-24.

The other eyedroppers work as they do in the Levels dialog box, mapping pixels to black, medium gray, or white (or other colors if you double-click the eyedropper icons). For example, the second image in Figure 17-24 shows the white eyedropper tool clicking on a light pixel, thereby mapping that value to white, as shown in the highlighted portion of the graph below the image.

Note

Bear in mind that Photoshop maps the value to each color channel independently. So when editing a full-color image inside the Curves dialog box, you have to switch channels to see the results of clicking with the eyedropper. You can further adjust the brightness value of that pixel by dragging the corresponding point in the graph, as demonstrated in the last example of the figure.

Tip

The eyedropper tools aren't the only way to add points to a curve from the image window. Photoshop offers two more keyboard tricks that greatly simplify the process of pinpointing and adjusting colors inside the Curves dialog box. Bear in mind, both of these techniques work only when the point tool is active:

✦ To add a color as a point along the Curves graph, Ctrl-click a pixel in the image window. Photoshop adds the point to the channel displayed in the dialog box. For example, if the RGB composite channel is visible, the point is added to the RGB composite curve. If the Red channel is visible, Photoshop adds the point to the red graph and leaves the green and blue graphs unchanged.

✦ To add a color to all graphs, regardless of which channel is visible in the Curves dialog box, Ctrl+Shift-click a pixel in the image window. In the case of an RGB image, Photoshop maps the red, green, and blue brightness values for that pixel to each of the red, green, and blue graphs in the Curves dialog box. The RGB composite graph shows no change — switch to the individual channels to see the new point.

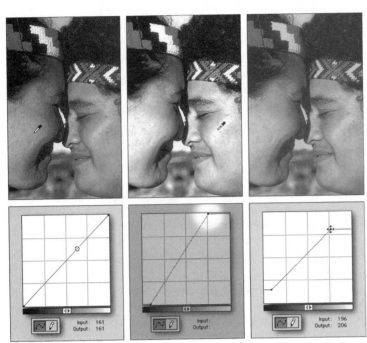

Figure 17-24: Use the standard eyedropper cursor to locate a color in the brightness graph (left). Click with one of the eyedropper tools from the Curves dialog box to map the color of that pixel in the graph (middle). You then can edit the location of the point in the graph by dragging it (right).

Gradient maps

Photoshop has long permitted you to apply a gradation as a Curves map, but Version 6 makes it easier than ever before. Just choose Image ⇨ Adjust ⇨ Gradient Map to display the dialog box pictured in Figure 17-25. Make sure the Preview check box is turned on. Then click the down-pointing arrowhead to the right of the gradient preview to display the familiar gradient drop-down palette. Select a gradient other than Foreground To Background and watch the fireworks.

In the psychedelic Color Plate 17-14, I cloned Constantine to a new layer and applied a heavy dose of Gaussian Blur. Then I used the Gradient Map command to apply each of three custom Curves maps. In the bottom row, I mixed these fantastic images with their underlying originals using the Color blend mode.

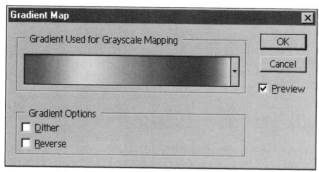

Figure 17-25: Choose the Gradient Map command to apply a preset gradient as a Curves map. Color Plate 17-14 shows examples.

What's going on? As foreign as it may sound, any gradient can be expressed as a Curves graph, progressing through a variety of brightness values in each of the three (RGB) or four (CMYK) color channels. When applied as a gradient map, the beginning of the gradient maps black; the end of the gradient maps white. If you apply the Violet, Orange preset, for example, the dark colors in the image map to violet and the light colors map to orange. Noise-type gradients (introduced in the "Applying Gradient Fills" section of Chapter 6) produce especially interesting effects.

Practical applications: continuous curves

Note

Due to the complex nature and general usefulness of the Curves dialog box, I spend this section and the next exploring practical applications of its many options, concentrating first on the point tool and then on the pencil tool. These discussions assume that the brightness bar is set to edit brightness values, so that the gradation in the bar lightens from left to right. If you set the bar to edit ink coverage — where the bar darkens from left to right — you can still achieve the effects I describe, but you must drag in the opposite direction. For example, if I tell you to lighten colors by dragging upward, you would drag downward.

When you first enter the Curves dialog box, the brightness curve appears as a straight line strung between two points, as shown in the first example of Figure 17-26, mapping every input level from black (the lower-left point) to white (the upper-right point) to an identical output level. If you want to perform seamless color corrections, the point tool is your best bet because it enables you to edit the levels in the brightness graph while maintaining a continuous curve.

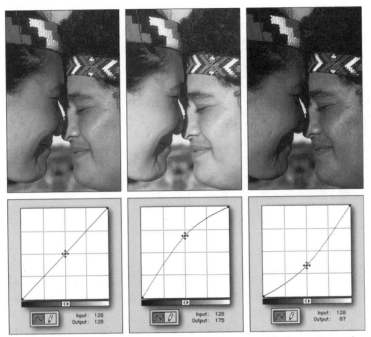

Figure 17-26: Create a single point in the curve with the point tool (left) and then drag it upward (middle) or downward (right) to lighten or darken the image evenly.

To lighten the colors, click near the middle of the curve with the point tool to create a new point and then drag the point upward, as demonstrated in the second example of Figure 17-26. To darken the image, drag the point downward, as in the third example.

Create two points in the curve to boost or lessen the contrast between colors in the image. In the first example of Figure 17-27, I created one point very near the white point in the curve and another point very close to the black point. I then dragged down on the left point and up on the right point to make the dark pixels darker and the light pixels lighter, which translates to higher contrast.

In the second example of the figure, I did just the opposite, dragging up on the left point to lighten the dark pixels and down on the right point to darken the light pixels. As you can see in the second image, this lessens the contrast between colors, making the image more gray.

In the previous example, in Figure 17-27, I bolstered the contrast with a vengeance by dragging the right point down and to the left. This has the effect of springing the right half of the curve farther upward, thus increasing the brightness of the light pixels in the image.

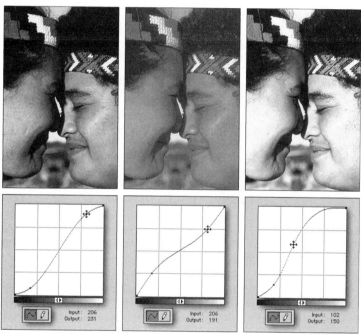

Figure 17-27: Create two points in the curve to change the appearance of contrast in an image, whether by increasing it mildly (left), decreasing it (middle), or boosting it dramatically (right).

Practical applications: arbitrary curves

You can create some mind-numbing color variations by adjusting the brightness curve arbitrarily, mapping light pixels to dark, dark pixels to light, and in-between pixels all over the place. In the first example of Figure 17-28, I used the point tool to achieve an arbitrary curve. By dragging the left point severely upward and the right point severely downward, I caused dark and light pixels alike to soar across the spectrum.

If you're interested in something a little more subtle, try applying an arbitrary curve to a single channel in a color image. Color Plate 17-15, for example, shows an image subject to relatively basic color manipulations in the red and green channels, followed by an arbitrary adjustment to the blue channel.

Although you can certainly achieve arbitrary effects using the point tool, the pencil tool is more versatile and less inhibiting. As shown in the second example of Figure 17-28, I created an effect that would alarm Carlos Castaneda just by zigzagging my way across the graph and clicking on the Smooth button.

Figure 17-28: These arbitrary brightness curves were created using the point tool (left) and the pencil tool (right).

In fact, the Smooth button is an integral part of using the pencil tool. Try this little experiment: Draw a bunch of random lines and squiggles with the pencil tool in the brightness graph. As shown in the first example of Figure 17-29, your efforts will most likely yield an unspeakably hideous and utterly unrecognizable effect.

Next, click the Smooth button. Photoshop automatically connects all portions of the curve, miraculously smoothing out the color-mapping effect and rescuing some semblance of your image, as shown in the second example of the figure. If the effect is still too radical, you can continue to smooth it by clicking the Smooth button additional times. I clicked on the button twice more to create the right image in Figure 17-29. Eventually, the Smooth button restores the curve to a straight line.

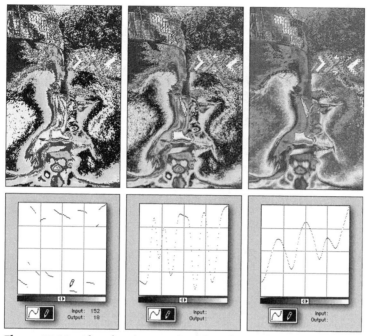

Figure 17-29: After drawing a series of random lines with the pencil tool (left), I clicked on the Smooth button once to connect the lines into a frenetic curve (middle) and then twice more to even out the curve, thus preserving more of the original image (right).

Adjustment Layers

Every one of the commands I've discussed in this chapter is applicable to a single layer at a time. If you want to correct the colors in multiple layers, you have to create a special kind of layer called an *adjustment layer*. Adjustment layers are layers that contain mathematical color correction information. The layer applies its corrections to all layers beneath it, without affecting any layers above.

You can create an adjustment layer in one of two ways:

✦ Choose Layer ➪ New Adjustment Layer. This displays a submenu of color adjustment commands, ranging from Levels and Curves to Invert, Threshold, and Posterize.

✦ Click the half black/half white circle at the bottom of the Layers palette, as shown in Figure 17-30. The first three options — Solid Color, Gradient, and Pattern Layer — are dynamic fill layers, as discussed in Chapter 14. Choose any one of the remaining 11 options to make a new adjustment layer.

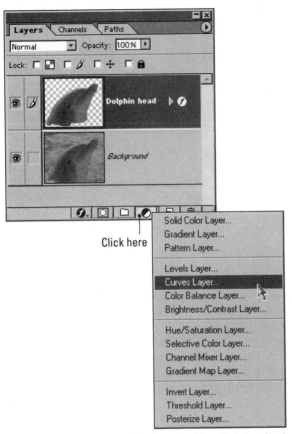

Click here

Solid Color Layer...
Gradient Layer...
Pattern Layer...

Levels Layer...
Curves Layer...
Color Balance Layer...
Brightness/Contrast Layer...

Hue/Saturation Layer...
Selective Color Layer...
Channel Mixer Layer...
Gradient Map Layer...

Invert Layer...
Threshold Layer...
Posterize Layer...

Figure 17-30: Click the black-and-white circle to display a pop-up menu of dynamic fill and adjustment layers.

If you choose a command from the Layer ⇨ New Adjustment Layer submenu, Photoshop displays the New Layer dialog box, which permits you to name the layer, assign a color, and set the blend mode. If you choose an option from the black-and-white circle in the Layers palette (labeled in Figure 17-30), Photoshop bypasses the New Layer dialog box and heads straight to the selected correction. Choosing Curves Layer, for example, displays the Curves dialog box. (Invert Layer is the only option that produces no dialog box whatsoever.) Change the settings as desired and press Enter as you normally would.

Regardless of the color adjustment you select, it appears as a new layer in the Layers palette. In Figure 17-31, for example, I've added a total of three adjustment layers. Photoshop marks adjustment layers with special icons that look like miniature versions of their respective dialog boxes. This way, you can readily tell them apart from image layers.

Adjustment layer icon

Layer mask

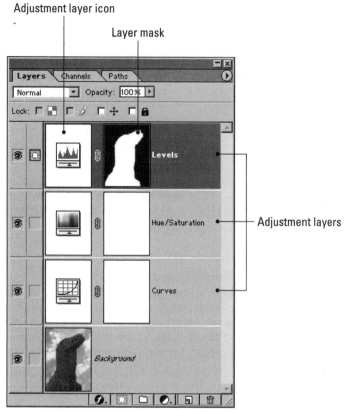

Adjustment layers

Figure 17-31: Here I've created three layers of color correction in front of a single background image.

The advantages of layer-based corrections

At this point, you might think, "Big whoop. You can apply corrections to multiple layers. That doesn't seem like such a great feature." But lest you judge too hastily, here are a few reasons adjustment layers are so great:

✦ **Forever editable:** As long as the adjustment layer remains intact stored in one of the three formats that support layers (native Photoshop PSD, TIFF, or PDF), you can edit the color correction over and over again without damaging the underlying pixels. Unlike standard color corrections, which alter selected pixels directly, adjustment layers have no permanent effect on the pixels. On the slightest whim, double-click the adjustment layer icon to bring up the color correction dialog box, complete with the settings currently in force. Tweak the settings as the mood hits you and press Enter to make changes on the fly. You can't get any more flexible than this.

Caution

When editing the settings for an adjustment layer, be sure to double-click the first icon that precedes the layer name (labeled "Adjustment layer icon" in Figure 17-31). Double-clicking elsewhere displays either the Layer Mask Display Options or Layer Style dialog box, each of which performs a very different function.

✦ **Versatile layer masking:** You can likewise adjust the affected area to your heart's content. An adjustment layer covers the entire image like an adjustable wall-to-wall carpet. You modify the affected area by painting inside the layer. An adjustment layer doesn't contain pixels, so painting inside the layer changes its layer mask. Paint with black to remove the correction from an area; use white to paint the correction back in.

Note

In fact, if a selection is active when you create a new adjustment layer, Photoshop automatically creates a layer mask according to the selection outline. For example, in Color Plate 17-16, I selected the topiary dinosaur before creating the Levels layer. Photoshop thoughtfully converted my selection into a layer mask, as labeled in Figure 17-31. And like any layer mask, I can edit it well into the future without any adverse side effects.

✦ **Reorder your corrections:** As with any layers, you can shuffle adjustment layers up and down in stacking order. For example, if you decide you don't want the correction to affect a specific layer, just drag the adjustment layer to a level in the Layers palette below the layer you want to exclude. If you're juggling multiple adjustment layers, as in Figure 17-31 and Color Plate 17-16, you can shuffle the adjustment layers to change the order in which they're applied. This includes the standard reordering keyboard shortcuts, Ctrl+[and Ctrl+].

✦ **Fade corrections:** You can fade a standard color correction right after you apply it using Edit ➪ Fade. But you can fade a correction applied with an adjustment layer any old time. Just change the blend mode and Opacity settings in the Layers palette.

✦ **Correct with blend modes:** Some folks prefer to correct overly light or dark images using blend modes. Take an image, copy it to a new layer, and apply the Multiply mode to darken the layer or Screen to lighten it. The problem with this trick is that it increases the size of the image in memory. Duplicating the image to a new layer requires Photoshop to double the size of the image in RAM.

Note

Adjustment layers permit you to apply this same technique without adding pixels to RAM. Create a new adjustment layer with the Levels option selected. After the Levels dialog box appears, press Enter to ignore it. Now select Multiply or Screen from the blend mode pop-up menu in the Layers palette. The adjustment layer serves as a surrogate duplicate of the layers below it, mocking every merged pixel. And it doesn't add so much as a K to the file size. It's an image-editing miracle — layers without the pain.

✦ **Change one adjustment to another:** After applying one kind of adjustment layer, you can convert it to another kind of adjustment layer. For example, you could swap an existing Levels adjustment for a Curves adjustment. To do so, choose the desired color adjustment from the Layer ➪ Change Layer Content submenu. Photoshop doesn't try to preserve the prior color adjustment when making the conversion—in other words, it can't convert the Levels information into Curves data—but it does preserve the layer mask, blend mode, and other layer attributes.

Correcting a flat image using layers

Although many artists use adjustment layers to edit multilayer compositions, they are equally applicable to flat photos. Originally printed in the February, 1996 issue of *Macworld* magazine, Color Plate 17-16 shows how I corrected an image shot with a Polaroid PDC-2000 using a total of three color corrections, layered one on top of the other. (Much of the following text also comes from that same article.) At first glance, the original photo on the left side of the color plate is a textbook example of what happens if you ignore backlighting. But as you have probably figured out by now, an image that appears black may actually contain several thousand colors just itching to get out. Adjustment layers make it easier than ever to free these colors and make them fully visible to the world.

Because my image was in such rotten shape, I decided to start with the Curves command. I clicked on the black-and-white circle button and selected Curves Layer from the pop-up menu. Then I used the pencil tool in the Curves dialog box to draw a radical upswing on the left side of the graph, dramatically lightening the blacks right out of the gate. I clicked on the Smooth button a few times to even out the color transitions, as demonstrated in the second example in Color Plate 17-16.

All this lightening resulted in some very washed-out colors (a typical side effect), so I created a second adjustment layer using the Hue/Saturation command. By raising the Saturation value, I quickly breathed a little enthusiasm into these tired old hues—a sufficient amount, in fact, to make it clear how soft the focus was. So I went back to the original image layer and applied the Unsharp Mask filter. Had it not been for the advent of adjustment layers, I would have had to sharpen the image either before color correcting it, making it impossible to accurately gauge the results, or after correcting, which might bring out compression artifacts and other undesirable anomalies. With adjustment layers, however, I can sharpen and correct at the same time, giving no operation precedent over the other.

The hedge monster remained a little dark, so I selected it with the Color Range command and then created a third adjustment layer for the Levels command. Using Levels, I quickly enhanced the brightness and contrast of the green beast, bringing him out into the full light of day. As I mentioned earlier, Photoshop automatically generated a layer mask for my selection, which appears as a tiny white silhouette in the Layers palette.

✦ ✦ ✦

Printing Images

Welcome to Printing

On one hand, printing can be a straightforward topic. You choose the Print command, press Enter, wait for something to come out of your printer, and admire yet another piece of forestry that you've destroyed. On the other hand, printing can be a ridiculously complicated subject, involving dot-gain compensation, hardware calibration, under color removal, toxic processor chemicals, separation table generation, and so many infinitesimal color parameters, you're liable to spend half your life trying to figure out what's happening.

This chapter is about finding a middle ground. Although it is in no way intended to cover every possible facet of printing digitized images, this chapter walks you through the process of preparing and printing the three major categories of output: composites, color separations, and duotones. By the end of the chapter, you'll be familiar with all of Photoshop's printing options. You'll also be prepared to communicate with professionals at your service bureau or at a commercial printer, if need be, and to learn from their input and expertise.

Although most printer manufacturers now offer Windows drivers, those drivers aren't always perfected. Sometimes you must get seriously down and dirty by using an older printer DLL (dynamic link library, a basic component of Windows) with a later printer driver.

If you encounter a Windows-related printing problem, your first cry for help should be to your printer manufacturer's Web site or tech support line. If those sources don't have the answer, check online forums and newsgroups. Your service bureau can also be an excellent source for technical advice. Chances are, you're not the first person to experience the problem and someone, somewhere should have a fix for you.

Understanding Printing Terminology

I'm not a big believer in glossaries. Generally, they contain glib, jargony, out-of-context definitions—about as helpful in gaining understanding of a concept as a seminar in which all the presenters speak pig latin. But before I delve into the inner recesses of printing, I want to introduce, in a semilogical, sort of random order, a smattering of the printing terms you'll encounter. Ood-gay uck-lay.

✦ **Service bureau:** A *service bureau* is a shop filled with earnest, young graphic artists (at least they were young and earnest when *I* worked at one), printer operators, and about a billion dollars' worth of hardware. A small service bureau is usually outfitted with a few laser printers, photocopiers, and self-service computers. Big service bureaus offer scanners, imagesetters, film recorders, and other varieties of professional-quality input and output equipment.

Service bureaus once relied exclusively on the Macintosh. This has changed, but a substantial number of Mac-based service bureaus remain. Most service bureaus are equally ready to help Photoshoppers on both PC and Mac platforms, but many will take your Photoshop file and run it through a Mac. Nothing is wrong with this—Photoshop is nearly identical on the two platforms—but cross-platform problems may crop up. Whenever possible, be sure your service bureau knows how to address cross-platform incompatibilities and has a general working knowledge of Windows.

✦ **Commercial printer:** Generally speaking, a *commercial printer* takes up where the service bureau leaves off. Commercial printers reproduce black-and-white and color pages using offset presses, web presses, and a whole bunch of other age-old technology I don't cover in this miniglossary (or anywhere else in this book, for that matter). The process is less expensive than photocopying when you're dealing with large quantities, say, more than 100 copies, and it delivers professional-quality reproductions.

✦ **Output device:** This is just another way to say *printer*. Rather than writing *Print your image from the printer*, which sounds repetitive and a trifle obvious, I write *Print your image from the output device*. *Output devices* also include laser printers, imagesetters, film recorders, and a whole bunch of other machines.

✦ **Laser printer:** A *laser printer* works much like a photocopier. First, it applies an electric charge to a cylinder, called a *drum*, inside the printer. The charged areas, which correspond to the black portions of the image being printed, attract fine, petroleum-based dust particles called *toner*. The drum transfers the toner to the page, and a heating mechanism fixes the toner in place. Most laser printers have resolutions of at least 300 dots (or *printer pixels*) per inch. The newer printers offer higher resolutions, such as 600 and 1,200 dots per inch (*dpi*).

✦ **Color printers:** *Color printers* fall into three categories. Generally speaking, ink-jet and thermal-wax printers are at the low end, and dye-sublimation printers occupy the high end. *Ink-jet printers* deliver colored dots from disposable ink cartridges. *Thermal-wax* printers apply wax-based pigments to a page in multiple passes. Both kinds of printers mix cyan, magenta, yellow, and, depending on the specific printer, black dots to produce full-color output. If you want photographic quality prints — the kind you'd be proud to hang on your wall — you must migrate up the price ladder to *dye-sublimation printers*. Dye-sub inks permeate the surface of the paper, literally dying it different colors. Furthermore, the cyan, magenta, yellow, and black pigments mix in varying opacities from one dot to the next, resulting in a continuous-tone image that appears nearly as smooth on the page as it does on screen.

✦ **Imagesetter:** A typesetter equipped with a graphics page-description language (most often PostScript) is called an *imagesetter*. Unlike a laser printer, an imagesetter prints photosensitive paper or film by exposing the portions of the paper or film that correspond to the black areas of the image. The process is like exposing film with a camera, but an imagesetter only knows two colors: black and white. The exposed paper or film collects in a lightproof canister. In a separate step, the printer operator develops the film in a processor. Developed paper looks like a typical glossy black-and-white page. Developed film is black where the image is white and transparent where the image is black. Imagesetters typically offer resolutions between 1,200 and 3,600 dpi. But the real beauty of imageset pages is blacks are absolutely black (or transparent), as opposed to the irregular gray you get with laser-printed pages.

✦ **Film recorder:** A *film recorder* transfers images to full-color 35mm and 4 × 5 slides perfect for professional presentations. Slides also can be useful to provide images to publications and commercial printers. Many publications can scan from slides, and commercial printers can use slides to create color separations. So, if you're nervous a color separation printed from Photoshop won't turn out well, ask your service bureau to output the image to a 35mm slide. Then have your commercial printer reproduce the image from the slide.

✦ **PostScript:** The *PostScript* page-description language was the first product developed by Adobe — the same folks who sell Photoshop — and is now a staple of hundreds of brands of laser printers, imagesetters, and film recorders. A *page-description language* is a programming language for defining text and graphics on a page. PostScript specifies the locations of points, draws line segments between them, and fills in areas with solid blacks or *halftone cells* (dot patterns that simulate grays). Some newer printers instead use *stochastic screens* that simulate grays and colors using almost-random patterns.

✦ **Spooling:** Printer *spooling* allows you to work on an image while another image prints. Rather than communicating directly with the output device, Photoshop describes the image to the system software. Under Windows 98, Me, NT, and 2000, set spooling options via the Printer control panel. Choose Settings ⇨ Printers, right-click the icon for your specific printer, and choose Properties from the pop-up menu.

Inside the printer's Properties dialog box, switch to the Details panel and click the Spool Settings button. When Photoshop finishes describing the image — a relatively quick process — you are free to resume working while the system software prints the image in the background.

✦ **Calibration:** Traditionally, *calibrating* a system means synchronizing the machinery. In the context of Photoshop, however, calibrating means to adjust or compensate for the color displays of the scanner, monitor, and printer so what you scan is what you see on screen, which in turn is what you get from the printer. Colors match from one device to the next. Empirically speaking, this is impossible; a yellow image in a photograph won't look exactly like the on-screen yellow or the yellow printed from a set of color separations. But calibrating is designed to make the images look as much alike as possible, taking into account the fundamental differences in hardware technology. Expensive hardware calibration solutions seek to change the configuration of scanner, monitor, and printer. Less expensive software solutions, including those provided by Photoshop, manipulate the image to account for the differences between devices.

✦ **Brightness values/shades:** As described in Chapter 4, there's a fundamental difference between the way your screen and printer create gray values and colors. Your monitor shows colors by lightening an otherwise black screen; the printed page shows colors by darkening an otherwise white piece of paper. On-screen colors, therefore, are measured in terms of *brightness values*. High values equate to light colors; low values equate to dark colors. On the printed page, colors are measured in percentage values called *shades* or, if you prefer, *tints*. High-percentage values result in dark colors, and low-percentage values result in light colors.

✦ **Composite:** A *composite* is a page that shows an image in its entirety. A black-and-white composite printed from a standard laser printer or imagesetter translates all colors in an image to gray values. A color composite printed from a color printer or film recorder shows the colors as they actually appear. Composites are useful any time you want to proof an image or print a final grayscale image from an imagesetter, an overhead projection from a color printer, or a full-color image from a film recorder.

✦ **Proofing:** To *proof* an image is to see how it looks on paper before the final printing. Consumer proofing devices include laser printers and color printers, which provide quality and resolution sufficient only to vaguely predict the appearance of your final output. Professional-level proofing devices include the 3M Rainbow dye-sublimation printer, which prints images of photographic quality, and the IRIS, which uses a special variety of ink-jet technology to create arguably the most accurate electronic proofs in the business.

✦ **Bleeds:** Simply put, a *bleed* is an area that can be printed outside the perimeter of a page. You use a bleed to reproduce an image all the way to the edge of a page, as in a slick magazine ad. For example, this book includes bleeds. Most of the pages — such as the page you're reading — are encircled by a uniform

2-pica margin of white space. This margin keeps the text and figures from spilling off into oblivion. A few pages, however — including the parts pages and the color plates in the middle of the book — print all the way to the edges. In fact, the original artwork goes 2 picas beyond the edges of the paper. This ensures that if the paper shifts when printing — as it invariably does — you won't see any thin white edges around the artwork. This 2 picas of extra artwork is the bleed. In Photoshop, you create a bleed by clicking on the Bleed button in the Page Setup dialog box.

✦ **Color separations:** To output color reproductions, commercial printers require *color separations* (or slides, which they can convert to color separations for a fee). A color-separated image comprises four printouts, one each for the cyan, magenta, yellow, and black primary printing colors. The commercial printer transfers each printout to a *plate*, which is used in the actual reproduction process.

✦ **Duotone:** A grayscale image in Photoshop can contain as many as 256 brightness values, from white on up to black. A printer can convey significantly fewer shades. A laser printer, for example, provides anywhere from 26 to 65 shades. An imagesetter provides from 150 to 200 shades, depending on resolution and screen frequency. And this assumes perfect printing conditions. You can count on at least 30 percent of those shades to get lost in the reproduction process. A *duotone* helps to retain the depth and clarity of detail in a grayscale image by printing with two inks. The number of shades available to you suddenly jumps from 150 to a few thousand. Photoshop also lets you create *tritones* (three inks) and *quadtones* (four inks). Note, using more inks translates to higher printing costs.

✦ **Spot color:** Most color images are printed as a combination of four *process color* inks — cyan, magenta, yellow, and black. But Photoshop also lets you add premixed inks called *spot colors*. As I mentioned in Chapter 4, the most popular purveyor of spot-colors in the United States is Pantone, which provides a library with hundreds of mixings. But many large corporations use custom spot colors for logos and other proprietary emblems. Most spot colors fall outside the CMYK gamut and thus increase the number of colors available to you. In addition to using spot colors in duotones, Photoshop lets you add a spot color channel to any image.

Printing Composites

Now that you've picked up some printer's jargon, you're ready to learn how to put it all together. This section explores the labyrinth of options available for printing composite images. Later in this chapter, I cover color separations and duotones.

Like any Windows application, Photoshop can print composite images to nearly any output device you can hook up to your computer. Assuming your printer is turned on, properly attached, and in working order, printing a composite image from Photoshop is a five-step process, as outlined in the following steps. The sections that follow describe each of these steps in detail.

STEPS: Printing a Composite Image

1. **Choose your printer.** Use the Printers control panel to select the output device to which you want to print. If your computer is not part of a network, you probably rely on a single output device, in which case you can skip this step.

2. **Choose File ➪ Print Options (Ctrl+Alt+P):** This command opens the new Print Options dialog box, where you can position the image on the page, scale the print size of the image, and select a few other options, as discussed later in this chapter.

   Before you select those settings, however, click the Page Setup button to specify the page size and orientation of the image on the page. Then return to the Print Options dialog box and click the Show More Options check box to display and select still more output options.

3. **Adjust the halftone screens, if needed.** Click the Screens button to change the size, angle, and shape of the halftone screen dots. This step is purely optional, useful mostly for creating special effects.

4. **Adjust the transfer function again, if needed.** Click the Transfer button to map brightness values in an image to different shades when printed. This step is also optional, though frequently useful.

5. **Click the Print button to open the Print dialog box.** Depending on your printer, you may also be able to access specialized output functions via a Properties button. When you've tweaked all relevant print settings, click the Print button to send the image to the printer.

If you already have your printer set up to your satisfaction, you can simply choose the File ➪ Print command (Ctrl+P) to skip steps 2 through 4 and go directly to the Print dialog box. Or, to bypass even the Print dialog box, press Ctrl+Alt+Shift+P. You also can Alt-choose the Print command, which becomes Print One whenever you open the File menu while pressing Alt.

At this point, you may be wondering about drag-and-drop printing, where you can drag a file and drop it onto a printer icon at the desktop. Although this approach may seem more convenient, Photoshop still has to launch and access the same functions as when you use the manual process. And in the worst-case scenario, the operating system may print your image from the wrong application. Drag-and-drop printing is great for making quick copies of text files, but when printing photographs and other artwork, don't look for shortcuts.

Choosing a printer

To select a printer, choose Start ⇨ Settings ⇨ Printers. Right-click your printer of choice and select Set As Default on the resulting pop-up menu, as shown in Figure 18-1. If you want to add a printer, double-click the Add Printer icon, and be sure to have either your Windows CD-ROM or a drivers disk from your printer manufacturer.

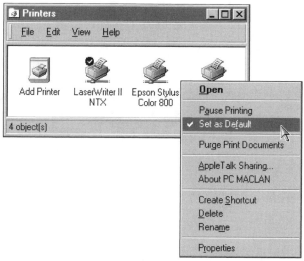

Figure 18-1: Specify your default printer from inside the Printers window.

Printer drivers help the PC hardware, Windows, and Photoshop translate the contents of an image to the printer hardware and the page-description language it uses. You generally want to select the driver for your specific model of printer. But you can, if necessary, prepare an image for output to a printer that isn't currently hooked up to your computer. For example, you can use this technique prior to submitting a document to be output on an imagesetter at a service bureau.

Most high-end Windows graphics applications can take advantage of *PostScript printer description (PPD)* files. A single driver can't account for the myriad differences between different models of PostScript printers, so each PPD serves as a little guidance file, customizing the driver to accommodate a specific printer model. Windows lets you attach a PPD file globally to your PostScript printer, for which you need both the PPD file and the INF file to tell Windows what to install. (Adobe offers its own printer driver called AdobePS — available via *www.adobe.com* — which doesn't require INF files. The setup program works only for Adobe-licensed PostScript printers, however.)

Tip   Windows also lets you switch printers from inside an application. Just choose
File ➪ Page Setup (Ctrl+Shift+P) inside Photoshop and select the printer you want
to use from the Name pop-up menu.

Setting up the page

The next step is to define the relationship between the current image and the page
on which it prints. In Photoshop 6, you handle most aspects of this part of the printing process in the new Print Options dialog box, shown in Figure 18-2. To open the
dialog box, choose File ➪ Print Options or press Ctrl+Alt+P. When you first open
the dialog box, the options shown at the bottom half of the figure aren't visible;
select the More Options check box to display them.

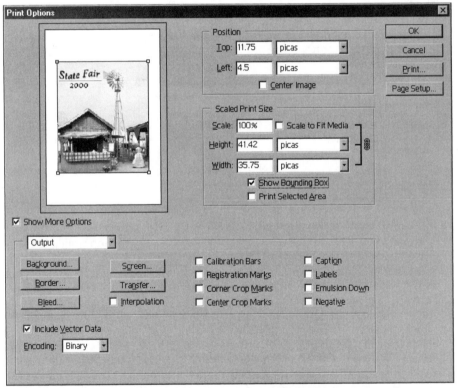

Figure 18-2: The new Print Options dialog box enables you to precisely position the
image, scale the image, and handle almost all other print setup chores.

The settings in the Print Options dialog box, however, relate to the printer, paper
size, and page orientation you select in the Page Setup dialog box. So unless you
want to use Page Setup options that you already established, click the Page Setup

button to transport to that dialog box. Alternatively, you can open the dialog box by choosing File ➪ Page Setup or by pressing Ctrl+Shift+P when the Print Options dialog box isn't open. The next section explains the important choices you need to make in the Page Setup dialog box; after that, I discuss a myriad of other print settings.

Note

Some of Photoshop's print options may appear in several different dialog boxes. For example, you may find image scaling controls in the Page Setup dialog box, as well as in the Print Options dialog box. For most print attributes, Photoshop doesn't care where you specify your print options. But if you want to scale the image for output, use the Scaled Print Size controls in the Print Options dialog box. If you scale the image in the Page Setup dialog box, the Scale, Height, and Width values in the Print Options dialog box may not reflect accurate values.

The Page Setup dialog box

The Page Setup dialog box varies depending on what kind of printer you use. I usually show the Page Setup dialog box for a standard PostScript printer. But this time around, I reckoned a color ink-jet printer might be more in keeping with the current state of the art. Therefore, Figure 18-3 shows the Page Setup options for Epson's Color Stylus 800.

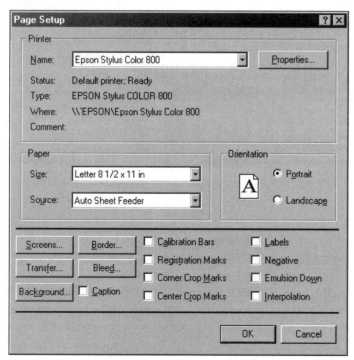

Figure 18-3: Use this dialog box to choose the printer, page size, and image orientation.

Even though the Page Setup dialog box offers different options for different printers, you should always have access to the following (or their equivalents):

✦ **Paper size:** Select the size of the paper loaded into your printer's paper tray. The paper size you select determines the *imageable area* of a page — that is, the amount of the page that Photoshop can use to print the current image. For example, the Letter option calls for a page that measures 8.5 × 11 inches, but only about 7.5 × 10 inches is imageable.

✦ **Source:** Virtually all printers include paper cartridges, but some permit you to manually feed pages or switch between cartridges. Use this option to decide where your paper is coming from.

✦ **Orientation:** You can specify whether an image prints upright on a page (Portrait) or on its side (Landscape) by selecting the corresponding Orientation icon. Use the Landscape setting when an image is wider than it is tall.

Printer-specific options

In addition to the options in the Page Setup dialog box, you may be able to control certain print attributes specific to the selected printer. To explore these options from inside the Page Setup dialog box, click the Properties button to display a multipaneled dialog box of additional choices. In the case of the Color Stylus 800, for example, clicking on the Properties button displays the dialog box shown in Figure 18-4. Here I can modify the print quality, select whether to print in black-and-white or color, and specify the type of paper I'm using.

Figure 18-4: Click the Properties button to access still more settings that are specific to the kind of printer you're using.

Position and scaling options

All of the options I've described so far are constant regardless of what application you're using. However, the settings inside the Print Options dialog box (shown earlier, in Figure 18-2) are unique to Photoshop.

The top half of the dialog box includes controls that are new to Photoshop 6. These welcome additions enable you to position the image on the page and perform a few other handy printing adjustments:

✦ **Position:** Enter values into the Top and Left option boxes to position the image with respect to the top-left corner of the page. You can select from four different measurement units for these options. If you want the image to print smack dab in the middle of the page, as it did in previous versions of Photoshop, select the Center Image check box. And if you're not overly concerned about placing the image exactly at a certain spot, deselect the Center Image check box and then just drag the image in the preview on the left side of the dialog box.

The preview updates to show you the current image position. In the preview, the white area represents the printable region of the paper; shadowed areas indicate the margins required by the selected printer.

✦ **Scaling:** If you want to adjust the image size for the current print job only, use these controls. They have no affect on the actual image file — they merely scale the image for printing. You can enter a scale percentage; anything over 100 percent enlarges the image, and values under 100 percent reduce the image. Or enter a specific size in the Height and Width option boxes. If you want Photoshop to adjust the image automatically to fit the page size, select the Scale to Fit Media check box.

The Show Bounding Box option, when selected, displays handles at the corners of the preview image. For quick and dirty scaling, you can drag the handles until the image is the approximate print size you want.

✦ **Print selection:** If you selected a rectangular area before opening the dialog box, you can print just the selection by turning on the Print Selected Area check box. Any scaling and position settings still apply to the printed output.

Tip

Photoshop prints only visible layers and channels, so you can print select layers or channels in an image by hiding all the other layers or channels. (To hide and display layers and channels, click the eyeball icon next to the layer or channel name in the Layers or Channels palette, respectively.) To print a single layer or channel, Alt-click the eyeball.

Output options

To display the special print options shown at the bottom of Figure 18-2, earlier in this chapter, select the Show More Options check box and then select Output from the pop-up menu immediately below. (If any options are dimmed, your printer doesn't support them.)

The five Output buttons work as follows:

✦ **Background:** To assign a color to the area around the printed image, click this button and select a color from the Color Picker dialog box, described in Chapter 4. This button and the one that follows (Border) are designed specifically to accommodate slides printed from a film recorder. If you select either of these options, Photoshop updates the preview to show them.

✦ **Border:** To print a border around the current image, click this button and enter the thickness of the border into the Width option box. The border automatically appears in black.

✦ **Bleed:** This button lets you print outside the imageable area of the page when outputting to an imagesetter. (Imagesetters print to huge rolls of paper or film, so you can print far outside the confines of standard page sizes. Most other printers use regular old sheets of paper; any bleed — were the printer to acknowledge it — would print off the edge of the page.) Click the Bleed button and enter the thickness of the bleed into the Width option box. Two picas (24 points) is generally a good bet. (Bleeds are defined in the "Understanding Printing Terminology" glossary at the beginning of this chapter.)

✦ **Screen:** Click this button to enter a dialog box that enables you to change the size, angle, and shape of the printed halftone cells, as described in the upcoming "Changing the halftone screen" section.

✦ **Transfer:** The dialog box that appears when you click this button enables you to redistribute shades in the printed image, as explained in the upcoming section, "Specifying a transfer function."

Most of the Output check boxes — all except Negative, Emulsion Down, Interpolation, and Include Vector Data — append special labels and printer marks to the printed version of the image. Figure 18-5 illustrates how they look when printed. For all options except Interpolation and Include Vector Data, Photoshop shows the result of selecting the check box in the image preview.

✦ **Interpolation:** If you own an output device equipped with PostScript Level 2 or later, you can instruct Photoshop to antialias the printed appearance of a low-resolution image by selecting this option. The output device resamples the image up to 200 percent and then reduces the image to its original size using bicubic interpolation (as described in the "General preferences" section of Chapter 2), thereby creating a less-jagged image. This option has no effect on older-model PostScript devices.

✦ **Calibration Bars:** A calibration bar is a 10-step grayscale gradation beginning at 10 percent black and ending at 100 percent black. The function of the calibration bar is to ensure all shades are distinct and on target. If not, the output device isn't properly calibrated, which is a fancy way of saying the printer's colors are out of whack and need realignment by a trained professional armed with a hammer and hacksaw. When you print color separations, the Calibration Bars check box instructs Photoshop to print a gradient tint bar and progressive color bar, also useful to printing professionals.

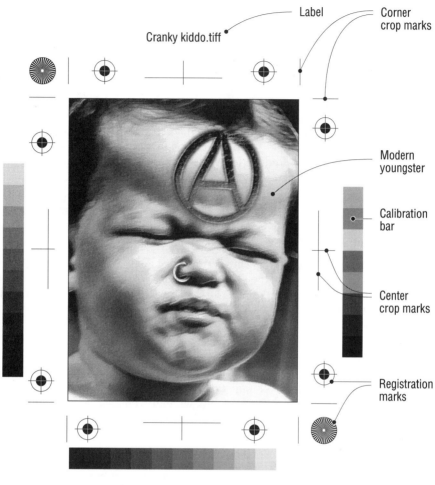

Figure 18-5: An image printed with nearly all the Output check boxes turned on.

✦ **Registration Marks:** Select this option to print eight crosshairs and two star targets near the four corners of the image. Registration marks are imperative when you print color separations; they provide the only reliable means to ensure exact registration of the cyan, magenta, yellow, and black printing plates. When printing a composite image, however, you can ignore this option.

✦ **Corner Crop Marks:** Select this option to print eight hairline crop marks — two in each of the image's four corners — which indicate how to trim the image in case you anticipate engaging in a little traditional paste-up work.

✦ **Center Crop Marks:** Select this option to print four pairs of hairlines that mark the center of the image. Each pair forms a cross. Two pairs are located on the sides of the image, the third pair is above it, and the fourth pair is below the image.

✦ **Caption:** To print a caption beneath the image, select this option. Then press Enter to exit this dialog box, choose File ➪ File Info, and enter a caption into the File Info dialog box. The caption prints in 9-point Helvetica. This is strictly an image-annotation feature, something to help you 17 years down the road, when your brain starts to deteriorate and you can't remember why you printed the darn thing. (You might also use the caption to keep images straight in a busy office where hundreds of folks have access to the same images, but I don't like this alternative as much because I can't make fun of it.)

✦ **Labels:** When you select this check box, Photoshop prints the name of the image and the name of the printed color channel in 9-point Helvetica. If you process many images, you'll find this option extremely useful for associating printouts with documents on disk.

Note

Incidentally, Figure 18-5 shows the actual labels and marks exactly as they print. I started by printing the Photoshop image to disk as an EPS (Encapsulated PostScript) file (as I describe later in the "Printing pages" section). Then I used Illustrator to open the EPS file and assign the callouts. This may not sound like much, but in the old days this would have been impossible. Figure 18-5 represents a practical benefit to Illustrator's (and Photoshop's) ability to open just about any EPS file on the planet.

✦ **Emulsion Down:** The emulsion is the side of a piece of film on which an image is printed. When the Emulsion Down check box is turned off, film prints from an imagesetter emulsion side up; when the check box is turned on, Photoshop flips the image so the emulsion side is down. Like the Negative option, discussed next, this option is useful only when you print film from an imagesetter, and this option should be set in accordance with the preferences of your commercial printer.

✦ **Negative:** When you select this option, Photoshop prints all blacks as white and all whites as black. In-between colors switch accordingly. For example, 20 percent black becomes 80 percent black. Imagesetter operators use this option to print composites and color separations to film negatives.

✦ **Include Vector Data:** If your image contains any vector objects or type for which outline data is available (not outline or protected fonts), select this check box to send the actual vector data to a PostScript printer. Your vector objects then can be scaled to any size without degrading in quality. Including the vector data increases the image file size, which can slow printing and cause other printing problems. But if you turn off the check box, everything in the image is sent to the printer as raster data. This reduces the file size, but you no longer can scale the vector objects or type with impunity. They're subject to the same quality loss that occurs when you enlarge any pixel-based image.

Photoshop
6

✦ **Encoding:** Select an option from this pop-up menu to control the encoding method used to send the image file to the printer. In normal printing situations, leave the option set to the default, Binary. If your network doesn't support binary encoding (highly unlikely in this day and age) or your printer is attached through the local parallel printer port, instead of the network, select the ASCII option to transfer PostScript data in the text-only format. The printing process takes much longer to complete, but at least it's possible. If your printer supports PostScript Level 2 or later, you can also choose to use JPEG compression to reduce the amount of data sent to the printer. (This option is applicable to PostScript printers only.)

Color management options

After you select the Show More Options check box in the Print Options dialog box, you can display color-management settings by selecting Color Management from the pop-up menu, as shown in Figure 18-6. These options enable you to convert the image color space for printing only. You may want to do this to print a proof of the image on a printer other than the printer you'll use for final output. To convert the color space of the actual image file, you need to use the techniques discussed in Chapter 16.

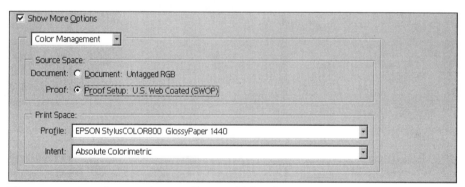

Figure 18-6: Use these options to dictate which color-management settings you want Photoshop to use when printing.

You can select from two Source Space options, Document and Proof. These options tell Photoshop whether you want to print the image according to the color profile officially assigned to the image file or according to the Proof Setup profile (the so-called "soft proofing" profile). Document uses the actual color profile; Proof uses the profile currently selected in the View ➪ Proof Setup submenu.

The Profile options control whether Photoshop converts the image to a different profile during the print process. If you select Same As Source from the Profile pop-up menu, no conversion occurs. To convert to a different profile, select the profile from the pop-up menu. You can then specify the rendering method by selecting it from the Intent pop-up menu.

You can convert to any color space offered by either Photoshop or Kodak's ICC CMS. Ideally, you want to select the specific profile for your brand of printer. If you can't find such a profile, you'll probably want to stick with the RGB Color space (specified with Edit ⇨ Color Settings in Photoshop 6). Another option is to choose Working CMYK, which prints the image just as if you had converted it to the CMYK color space. Unfortunately, most consumer printers are designed to accommodate RGB images and fare pretty badly when printing artwork converted to CMYK. (This is precisely the reason I frequently select RGB Color even when printing a CMYK image — it flat out produces better results.)

Tip

If you own a color printer, I encourage you to take an hour out of your day and conduct a few tests with the other Print Space options. For example, if you select Apple RGB, your printed image will darken several shades. This might throw you. Because the Apple RGB profile features the lightest of the monitor gammas — 1.8 — you might expect the image to print lighter. But what Photoshop is really doing is converting the colors as if the printer were as naturally light as an Apple RGB monitor. In order to maintain consistent color, the conversion therefore darkens the image to account for this unusually light device. Select the Wide Gamut setting and the colors appears lighter and washed out, again accounting for this hyper-saturated Space setting. So think opposite.

Caution

Yet another alternative is to convert an RGB image to the grayscale color space during printing. But it's generally a bad alternative. Asking Photoshop to convert colors on the fly dramatically increases the output time, as well as the likelihood of printing errors. It's better and much faster to simply convert the image to the grayscale mode (Image ⇨ Mode ⇨ Grayscale) and then print it.

Cross-Reference

Again, if you're unfamiliar with any of these terms or just don't know which options are best for your printing situation, review Chapter 16, where I discuss color management in detail.

Changing the halftone screen

Before I explain this option, available when you select Output from the pop-up menu in the Print Options dialog box, I need to explain a bit more about how printing works. To keep costs down, commercial printers use as few inks as possible to create the appearance of a wide variety of colors. Suppose you want to print an image of a pink flamingo wearing a red bow tie. Your commercial printer could print the flamingo in one pass using pink ink, let that color dry, and then load the red ink and print the bow tie. But why go to all this trouble? After all, pink is only a lighter shade of red. Why not imitate the pink by lightening the red ink?

Unfortunately, with the exception of dye-sublimation printers, high-end ink jets, and film recorders, output devices can't print lighter shades of colors. They recognize only solid ink and the absence of ink. So how do you print the lighter shade of red necessary to represent pink?

The answer is *halftoning*. The output device organizes printer pixels into spots called *halftone cells*. Because the cells are so small, your eyes cannot quite focus on them. Instead, the cells appear to blend with the white background of the page to create a lighter shade of an ink. Figure 18-7 shows a detail of an image enlarged to display the individual halftone cells.

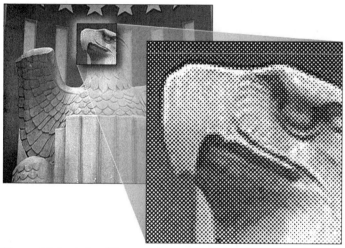

Figure 18-7: A detail from an image (left) is enlarged so that you can see the individual halftone cells (right).

The cells grow and shrink to emulate different shades of color. Large cells result in dark shades; small cells result in light shades. Cell size is measured in printer pixels. The maximum size of any cell is a function of the number of cells in an inch, called the screen frequency.

For example, suppose the default frequency of your printer is 60 halftone cells per linear inch and the resolution is 300 printer pixels per linear inch. Each halftone cell must, therefore, measure 5 pixels wide by 5 pixels tall ($300 \div 60 = 5$), for a total of 25 pixels per cell (5^2). When all pixels in a cell are turned off, the cell appears white; when all pixels are turned on, you get solid ink. By turning on different numbers of pixels — from 0 up to 25 — the printer can create a total of 26 shades, as demonstrated in Figure 18-8.

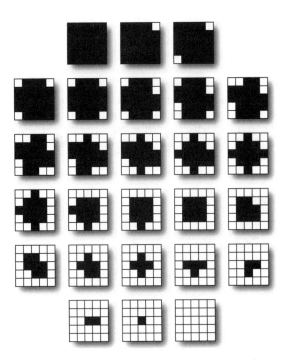

Figure 18-8: 5 × 5-pixel halftone cells with different numbers of pixels activated, ranging from 25 (top left) to 0 (bottom right). Each cell represents a unique shade from 100 to 0 percent black.

Photoshop enables you to change the size, angle, and shape of the individual halftone cells used to represent an image on the printed page. To do so, click the Screen button in the Print Options dialog box (after clicking Show More Options and choosing Output from the pop-up menu). The Halftone Screens dialog box shown in Figure 18-9 appears.

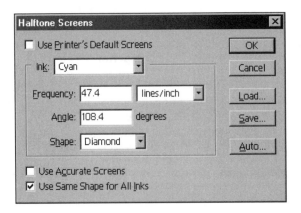

Figure 18-9: Use the Halftone Screens dialog box to edit the size, angle, and shape of the halftone cells for any one ink.

In the dialog box, you can manipulate the following options:

✦ **Use Printer's Default Screens:** Select this check box to accept the default size, angle, and shape settings built into your printer's ROM. All other options in the Halftone Screens dialog box automatically become dimmed to show they are no longer in force.

✦ **Ink:** If the current image is in color, you can select the specific ink you want to adjust from the Ink pop-up menu. When you work with a grayscale image, no pop-up menu is available.

✦ **Frequency:** Enter a new value into this option box to change the number of halftone cells that print per linear inch. A higher value translates to a larger quantity of smaller cells; a smaller value creates fewer, larger cells. Frequency is traditionally measured in *lines-per-inch*, or *lpi* (as in lines of halftone cells), but you can change the measurement to lines per centimeter by selecting Lines/cm from the pop-up menu to the right of the option box.

Higher screen frequencies result in smoother-looking printouts. Raising the Frequency value, however, also decreases the number of shades an output device can print because it decreases the size of each halftone cell and, likewise, decreases the number of printer pixels per cell. Fewer printer pixels mean fewer shades. You can calculate the precise number of printable shades using the following formula:

Number of shades = (printer resolution ÷ frequency)^2 + 1

✦ **Angle:** To change the orientation of the lines of halftone cells, enter a new value into the Angle option box. In the name of accuracy, Photoshop accepts any value between negative and positive 180 degrees.

When printing color composites to ink-jet and thermal-wax printers, and when printing color separations, Photoshop calculates the optimum Frequency and Angle values required to print seamless colors. In such a case, you should change these values only if you know exactly what you're doing. Otherwise, your printout may exhibit weird patterning effects. When printing grayscale images, though, you can edit these values to your heart's content.

✦ **Shape:** By default, most PostScript printers rely on roundish halftone cells. You can change the appearance of all cells for an ink by selecting one of six alternate shapes from the Shape pop-up menu. For a demonstration of four of these shapes, see Figure 4-8 in the "Black and white (bitmap)" section of Chapter 4. If you know how to write PostScript code, you can select the Custom option to display a text-entry dialog box and code away.

✦ **Use Accurate Screens:** If your output device is equipped with PostScript Level 2 or later, select this option to subscribe to the updated screen angles for full-color output. Otherwise, don't worry about this option.

✦ **Use Same Shape for All Inks:** Select this option if you want to apply a single set of size, angle, and shape options to the halftone cells for all inks used to represent the current image. Unless you want to create some sort of special effect, leave this check box deselected. The option is unavailable when you are printing a grayscale image.

✦ **Auto:** Click this button to display the Auto Screens dialog box, which automates the halftone editing process. Enter the resolution of your output device in the Printer option box. Then enter the screen frequency you want to use in the Screen option box. After you press Enter to confirm your change, Photoshop automatically calculates the optimum screen frequencies for all inks. This technique is most useful when you print full-color images — because Photoshop does the work for you, you can't make a mess of things.

✦ **Load/Save:** You can load and save settings to disk in case you want to reapply the options to other images. These buttons are useful if you find a magic combination of halftone settings that results in a really spectacular printout.

You can change the default size, angle, and shape settings Photoshop applies to all future images by Alt-clicking on the Save button. When you press Alt, the Save button changes to read ->Default. To restore the default screen settings at any time, Alt-click the Load button (<-Default).

The Halftone Screens dialog box settings don't apply only to printing images directly from Photoshop. You can export these settings along with the image for placement in QuarkXPress or some other application by saving the image in the Photoshop EPS format. Make sure you turn on the Include Halftone Screen check box in the EPS Format dialog box, as discussed in the "Saving an EPS image" section of Chapter 3. This also applies to transfer function settings, explained in the following section, "Specifying a transfer function."

If you decide to include the halftone screen information with your EPS file, be sure the settings are compatible with your intended output device. You don't want to specify a low Frequency value such as 60 lpi when printing to a state-of-the-art 3,600-dpi imagesetter, for example. If you have any questions, make certain to call your service bureau or commercial printer before saving the image. You don't want both a last-minute surprise and a hefty bill, to boot.

Specifying a transfer function

A *transfer function* enables you to change the way on-screen brightness values translate — or *map* — to printed shades. By default, brightness values print to their nearest shade percentages. A 30 percent gray pixel on screen (which equates to a brightness value of roughly 180) prints as a 30 percent gray value.

Problems arise, however, when your output device prints lighter or darker than it should. For example, in the course of using a LaserWriter NTX over the past seven years or so—I know it's going to die one day but, until then, it keeps chugging along—I've discovered all gray values print overly dark. Dark values fill in and become black; light values appear a dismal gray, muddying up any highlights. The problem increases if I try to reproduce the image on a photocopier.

To compensate for this overdarkening effect, I click the Transfer button in the Print Options dialog box after clicking Show More Options and choosing Output from the pop-up menu, and then I enter the values shown in Figure 18-10. Notice I lighten 20 percent on screen grays to 10 percent printer grays. I also lighten 90 percent screen grays to 80 percent printer grays. The result is a smooth, continuous curve that maps each gray value in an image to a lighter value on paper.

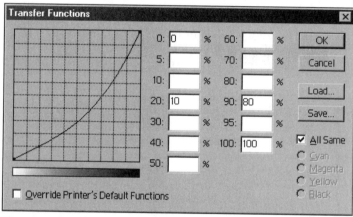

Figure 18-10: The transfer function curve enables you to map on screen brightness values to specific shades on paper.

The options in the Transfer Functions dialog box work as follows:

✦ **Transfer graph:** The *transfer graph* is where you map on-screen brightness values to their printed equivalents. The horizontal axis of the graph represents on-screen brightness values; the vertical axis represents printed shades. The *transfer curve* charts the relationship between on screen and printed colors. The lower-left corner is the origin of the graph—the point at which both on-screen brightness value and printed shade are white. Move to the right in the graph for darker on-screen values; move up for darker printed shades. Click in the graph to add points to the line. Drag up on a point to darken the output; drag down to lighten the output.

Cross-Reference

For a more comprehensive explanation of how to graph colors on a curve, read about the incredibly powerful Curves command, covered in Chapter 17.

✦ **Percentage option boxes:** The option boxes are labeled according to the on-screen brightness values. To lighten or darken the printed brightness values, enter higher or lower percentage values in the option boxes. There is a direct correlation between changes made to the transfer graph and the option boxes. For example, if you enter a value in the 50 percent option box, a new point appears along the middle line of the graph.

✦ **Override Printer's Default Functions:** As an effect of printer calibration, some printers have custom transfer functions built into their read-only memory (ROM). If you have problems making your settings take effect, select this check box to instruct Photoshop to apply the transfer function you specify, regardless of the output device's built-in transfer function.

✦ **Load/Save:** Use these buttons to load and save settings to disk. Alt-click the buttons to retrieve and save default settings.

✦ **Ink controls:** When you print a full-color image, five options appear in the lower-right corner of the Transfer Functions dialog box. These options enable you to apply different transfer functions to different inks. Select the All Same check box to apply a single transfer function to all inks. To apply a different function to each ink, deselect the check box, and then select one of the radio buttons and edit the points in the transfer graph as desired.

Printing pages

When you finish slogging your way through the Page Setup and Print Options dialog boxes, you can initiate the printing process by clicking the Print button in the Print Options dialog box or choosing File ➪ Print (Ctrl+P). The Print dialog box appears, shown in its RGB and CMYK forms in Figure 18-11.

Several options in this dialog box also appear in the Print Options dialog box or the Page Setup dialog box, both discussed earlier in this chapter. The few remaining options you need to understand work as follows:

✦ **Copies:** Enter the number of copies you want to print in this option box. You can print up to 999 copies of a single image, although why you would want to do so is beyond me.

✦ **Print Range:** No such thing as a multipage document exists in Photoshop, so you can ignore these options for the most part. If you selected an image area with the rectangular marquee tool, you can print just the selected area by choosing the Selection radio button or by turning on the Print Selected Area check box in the Print Options dialog box. You may want to use this option to divide an image into pieces when it's too large to fit on a single page.

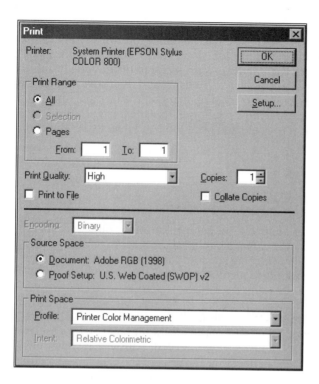

Figure 18-11: The Print dialog box as it appears when printing a color image.

✦ **Print to File:** Exclusively applicable to PostScript printing, this option lets you save a PostScript-language version of the file on disk rather than printing it directly to your printer. Deselect the option to print the image to an output device as usual. Select Print to File to write a PostScript-language version of the image to disk.

Because Photoshop offers its own EPS option via the Save dialog box, you'll probably want to ignore this option. In fact, the only reason to select Print to File is to capture printer's marks, as I did back in Figure 18-5. If you do, a second dialog box appears, asking where you want to save the PostScript file. You can navigate just as in the Open and Save dialog boxes. For the best results, select the Binary radio button.

✦ **Setup:** This button takes you to the Page Setup dialog box, discussed previously.

Press Enter inside the Print dialog box to start the printing process on its merry way. To cancel a print in progress, click the Cancel button. If you neglect to cancel before Photoshop spools the print job, don't worry, you can still cancel. Choose Settings ⇨ Printers from the Windows Start menu to display the Printers dialog box. Right-click the icon for the printer you're using and then select Open. Or you can double-click that tiny printer icon that appears on the far-right side of the taskbar. Either way, Windows shows you a window listing the current print jobs in progress. You can pause or cancel the selected print job by choosing a command from the Document menu.

Creating Color Separations

It's rare that you'll ever have to print color separations directly from Photoshop. You'll more likely import the image into QuarkXPress, PageMaker, InDesign, or a similar application before printing separations. It's even more likely that you'll take the image or page-layout file to a commercial printer and have a qualified technician take care of it.

So why discuss this process? Two reasons. First, it's always a good idea to at least peripherally understand all phases of the computer imaging process, even if you have no intention of becoming directly involved. This way, if something goes wrong on the printer's end, you can decipher the crux of the problem and either propose a solution or strike a compromise that still works in your favor.

Second, before you import your image into another program or submit it to a commercial printer, you'll want to convert the RGB image to the CMYK color space. (You don't absolutely *have* to do this — with Photoshop's improved color matching functions, you can exchange RGB images with greater confidence — but it's always a good idea to prepare your images down to the last detail, and CMYK is invariably the final destination for printed imagery.)

Outputting separations

Accurately converting to CMYK is the trickiest part of printing color separations; the other steps require barely any effort at all. So without further ado, here's how you convert an image to the CMYK color space and print separations. Many of the steps are the same as when printing a grayscale or color composite, others are new and different.

STEPS: Printing CMYK Color Separations

1. **Calibrate your monitor and specify the desired RGB environment.** Use the techniques discussed in the "The Gamma control panel" and "Selecting the ideal working space" sections of Chapter 16.

2. **Identify the final output device.** Again, follow the advice I give in Chapter 16, this time, in the section "Custom CMYK Setup." If you're lucky, your commercial printer may provide a CMYK table that you can load. Otherwise, you'll have to grapple with some weird settings. The good news is that you only need to complete this step once for each time you switch hardware. If you always use the same commercial printer, you can set it up and forget about it.

3. **Convert the image to the CMYK color space.** Choose Image ⇨ Mode ⇨ CMYK Color to convert the image from its present color mode to CMYK.

4. **Adjust the individual color channels.** Switching color modes can dramatically affect the colors in an image. To compensate for color and focus loss, you can edit the individual color channels as described in the "Color Channel Effects" section of Chapter 4.

5. **Trap your image, if necessary.** If your image features many high-contrast elements and you're concerned your printer might not do the best job of registering the cyan, magenta, yellow, and black color plates, you can apply Image ⇨ Trap to prevent your final printout from looking like the color funnies. (When working with typical "continuous-tone" photographs, you can skip this step.)

6. **Choose your printer.** Select the printer you want to use, as described earlier in this chapter in the "Choosing a printer" section.

7. **Turn on a few essential printer marks.** Choose File ⇨ Page Setup (Ctrl+Shift+P) to specify the size of the pages and the size and orientation of the image on the pages, as described in "The Page Setup dialog box" section earlier in this chapter. And in the Print Options dialog box, also introduced earlier, be sure to select the Calibration Bars, Registration Marks, and Labels check boxes, at the very least. (You need to select the Show More Options check box and then select Output from the pop-up menu to display these options.)

8. **Adjust the halftone and transfer functions as needed.** Click the Screen and Transfer buttons in the Print Options dialog box to modify the halftone screen dots and map brightness values for each of the CMYK color channels, as described earlier in the "Changing the halftone screen" and "Specifying a transfer function" sections. This step is entirely optional.

9. **Send the job to the printer.** You can click the Print button in the Print Options dialog box or, if the dialog box isn't open, choose File ⇨ Print (Ctrl+P). Then choose Separations from the Profile pop-up menu in the Print Space section of the dialog box. This tells Photoshop to print each color channel to a separate piece of paper or film.

Note

You also can create color separations by importing an image into a page-layout or drawing program. Instead of choosing your printer in Step 6, save the image in the DCS format, as described in the "QuarkXPress DCS" section of Chapter 3.

Steps 6 through 9 are repeats of concepts explained in previous sections of this chapter. Steps 1, 3, and 4 were covered at length in Chapters 4 and 16. This leaves Steps 2 and 5 — CMYK Setup and trapping — which I explain in the following sections.

Color trapping

If color separations misalign slightly during the reproduction process (a problem called *misregistration*), the final image can exhibit slight gaps between colors. Suppose an image features a 100 percent cyan chicken against a 100 percent magenta background. (Pretty attractive image idea, huh? Go ahead, you can use it if you like.) If the cyan and magenta plates don't line up exactly, you're left with a chicken with a white halo around it. Yuck.

A *trap* is a little extra bit of color that fills in the gap. For example, if you choose Image ⇨ Trap and enter 4 into the Width option box, Photoshop outlines the chicken with an extra 4 pixels of cyan and the background with an extra 4 pixels of magenta. Now the registration can be off a full 8 pixels without any halo occurring.

Continuous-tone images, such as photographs and natural-media painting, don't need trapping because no harsh color transitions occur. In fact, trapping actually harms such images by thickening up the borders and edges, smudging detail, and generally dulling the focus.

One of the primary reasons to use the Trap command, therefore, is to trap rasterized drawings from Illustrator or FreeHand. Some state-of-the-art prepress systems trap documents by first rasterizing them to pixels and then modifying the pixels. Together, Photoshop and Illustrator (or FreeHand) constitute a more rudimentary but, nonetheless, functional trapping system. When you open an illustration in Photoshop, the program converts it into an image according to your size and resolution specifications, as described in the "Rasterizing an Illustrator or FreeHand file" section of Chapter 3. Once the illustration is rasterized, you can apply Image ⇨ Trap to the image as a whole. Despite the command's simplicity, it handles nearly all trapping scenarios, even going so far as to reduce the width of the trap incrementally as the colors of neighboring areas grow more similar.

Caution

If you plan on having a service bureau trap your files for you, do not apply Photoshop's Trap command. You don't want to see what happens when someone traps an image that's already been trapped. If you're paying the extra bucks for professional trapping, leave it to the pros.

Printing Duotones

It's been a few pages since the "Understanding Printing Terminology" section, so here's a quick recap: A *duotone* is a grayscale image printed with two inks. This technique expands the depth of the image by allowing additional shades for highlights, shadows, and midtones. If you've seen a glossy magazine ad for perfume, designer clothing, a car, or just about any other overpriced commodity, you've seen a duotone. Words like *rich, luxurious,* and *palpable* come to mind.

Photoshop also enables you to add a third ink to create a tritone and a fourth ink to create a quadtone. Color Plate 18-1 shows an example of an image printed as a quadtone. Figure 18-12 shows a detail from the image printed in its original grayscale form. See the difference?

Figure 18-12: This salute to all-around athlete Jim Thorpe by artist Mark Collen looks pretty good, but if you want to see great, check out the quadtone in Color Plate 18-1.

Creating a duotone

To convert a grayscale image to a duotone, tritone, or quadtone, choose Image ⇨ Mode ⇨ Duotone. Photoshop displays the Duotone Options dialog box shown in Figure 18-13. By default, Monotone is the active Type option, and the Ink 2, Ink 3, and Ink 4 options are dimmed. To access the Ink 3 option, select Tritone from the Type pop-up menu; to access both Ink 3 and Ink 4, select Quadtone from the pop-up menu.

Specify the color of each ink you want to use by clicking the color box associated with the desired ink option. The first time you define colors, Photoshop displays the Color Picker dialog box. You can either define colors in the Color Picker or click Custom to select a color from the Custom Colors dialog box, as described in the "Predefined colors" section of Chapter 4.

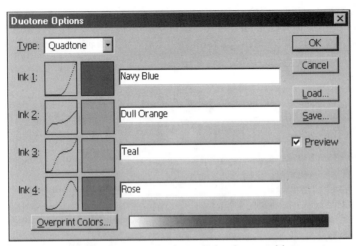

Figure 18-13: The Duotone Options dialog box enables you to apply multiple inks to a grayscale image.

Photoshop takes the guesswork out of creating a duotone by previewing your settings in the image window when the Preview check box is turned on. Keep in mind that the preview may not exactly match your output when using certain Pantone inks. (This is a common problem when previewing Pantone inks in any program, but it's always a good idea to keep in mind, particularly because Photoshop mixes inks to create its duotone effects.)

The next time you create a duotone, Photoshop displays the same colors you defined in your last visit to the Duotone Options dialog box. If you previously defined colors in the Custom Colors dialog box, clicking on a color box brings up that same dialog box (click Picker to get to the Color Picker dialog box).

When creating duotones, tritones, and quadtones, prioritize your inks in order — from darkest at the top to lightest at the bottom — when you specify them in the Duotone Options dialog box. Because Photoshop prints inks in the order they appear in the dialog box, the inks print from darkest to lightest. This ensures rich highlights and shadows and a uniform color range.

After selecting a color, you can use either of two methods to specify how the differently colored inks blend. The first and more dependable way is to click the curve box associated with the desired ink option. Photoshop then displays the Duotone Curve dialog box, which works just like the Transfer Functions dialog box described back in the "Specifying a transfer function" section of this chapter. This method permits you to emphasize specific inks in different portions of the image according to brightness values.

For example, Figure 18-13 shows the inks and curve settings assigned to the quadtone in Color Plate 18-1. The Navy Blue color is associated only with the darkest brightness values in the image; Rose peaks at about 80 percent gray and then descends; Teal covers the midtones in the image; Dull Orange is strongest in the light values. The four colors mix to form an image whose brightness values progress from light orange to olive green to brick red to black.

The second method for controlling the blending of colors is to click the Overprint Colors button. An Overprint Colors dialog box appears, showing how each pair of colors will mix when printed. Other color swatches show how three and four colors mix, if applicable. To change the color swatch, click it to display the Color Picker dialog box.

The problem with this second method is it complicates the editing process. Photoshop doesn't actually change the ink colors or curve settings in keeping with your new specifications; it just applies the new overprint colors without any logical basis. And you lose all changes made with the Overprint Colors dialog box when you adjust any of the ink colors or any of the curves.

To return and change the colors or curves, choose Image ➪ Mode ➪ Duotone again. Instead of reconverting the image, the command now lets you edit the existing duotone, tritone, or quadtone.

Reproducing a duotone

If you want a commercial printer to reproduce a duotone, tritone, or quadtone, you must print the image to color separations, just like a CMYK image. Because you already specified which inks to use and how much of each ink to apply, however, you needn't mess around with all those commands in the Edit ➪ Color Settings dialog box. Just take the following familiar steps:

STEPS: Printing a Duotone, Tritone, or Quadtone

1. **Choose the printer you want to use.** Select a printer as described previously in this chapter.

2. **Set the page size, orientation, and printer marks options.** In the Page Setup dialog box (Ctrl+Shift+P), specify the size of the pages and the size and orientation of the image on the pages, as described in "The Page Setup dialog box" section earlier in this chapter. Then select the Registration Marks option in the Page Setup dialog box or the Print Options dialog box.

3. **Adjust the halftone screens, if desired.** If you're feeling inventive, click the Screens button to change the size, angle, and shape of the halftone screen dots for the individual color plates, as described previously in the "Changing the halftone screen" section.

4. **Choose File ➪ Print (Ctrl+P).** Select the Separations option from the Profile pop-up menu in the Print Space section of the dialog box to print each ink to a separate sheet of paper or film.

To prepare a duotone to be imported into QuarkXPress, Illustrator, or some other application, save the image in the EPS format, as described in the "Saving an EPS image" section of Chapter 3. As listed back in Table 4-1 of Chapter 4, EPS is the only file format other than the native Photoshop format that supports duotones, tritones, and quadtones.

Editing individual duotone plates

If you'll be printing your duotone using CMYK colors and you can't quite get the effect you want inside the Duotone Options dialog box, you can convert the duotone to the CMYK mode by choosing Image ⇨ Mode ⇨ CMYK. Not only will all the duotone shades remain intact, but you'll also have the added advantage of being able to tweak colors and to add color using Photoshop's standard color-correction commands and editing tools. You can even edit individual color channels, as described in Chapter 4.

If your duotone includes Pantone or other spot colors, converting to CMYK is not an option. But you can still access and edit the individual color channels. To separate the duotone inks into channels, choose Image ⇨ Mode ⇨ Multichannel. Each ink appears as a separate spot color inside the Channels palette, as shown in Figure 18-14. You can experiment with different color combinations by turning eyeball icons on and off. In Color Plate 18-2, for example, I turned off one channel in the top row and two channels in the bottom row. You can even switch out one spot color for another by double-clicking on the channel name and then clicking the color swatch.

Figure 18-14: Here I chose Image ⇨ Mode ⇨ Multichannel to separate my quadtone into four independent spot-color channels.

To save a duotone converted to the multichannel mode, you have just two options: native Photoshop (as always) and DCS 2.0. For complete information on the latter, read the "QuarkXPress DCS" section in Chapter 3.

Spot-Color Separations

Photoshop permits you to add spot colors to your images. Although it's unlikely that you'll use spot colors to widen the gamut of your photographs — after all, scanners can't scan spot colors and Photoshop can't automatically lift them out of, say, the RGB color space — you may want to toss in a spot color to highlight a logo, a line of type, and some other special element.

For example, suppose you have a full-color image of a jet ski. The logo along the side of the boat is fully visible, just as the client wants it, but the color is off. Normally, the logo appears in Pantone 265 purple. But the CMYK equivalent for this color looks about three shades darker, four shades redder, and several times muddier. The only solution is to assign the proper spot color — Pantone 265 — to the logo. The following steps tell how:

STEPS: Adding a Spot Color to an Image

1. **Select the logo.** You can use the magic wand tool or a more exacting method, as described in Chapters 8 and 9.

2. **Fill the selection with white.** Press D to get the default foreground and background colors and then press Ctrl+Backspace. It's important that you erase the old logo so that it appears in pure spot color without any mixing with the CMYK inks. But do *not* deselect your selection! It must remain active for Step 5 to work.

3. **Create a new spot channel.** As explained in Chapter 4, the easiest way to do this is to Ctrl-click the page icon at the bottom of the Channels palette. But you can also choose New Spot Channel from the Channels palette menu if you prefer.

4. **Set the color to Pantone 265.** Click the Color swatch in the New Spot Channel dialog box. Then select Pantone 265 from the Custom Colors dialog box. (If the Color Picker comes up instead, click the Custom button.)

5. **Press Enter or click OK twice.** Photoshop adds the new spot color to the Channels palette and automatically fills the selection. Your logo automatically appears in the spot color. (Cool, huh?)

6. **Choose Image ⇨ Trap.** It's a good idea to trap the spot color so that it covers up any gaps that may result from misregistration. Enter a value of 1 or 2 pixels and hit Enter. Photoshop spreads the logo but leaves the CMYK image alone. Very intelligent program, that Photoshop.

7. **Save the image.** You have two choices of formats, native Photoshop or DCS 2.0. If you want to import the image into a different program, use the latter.

Naturally, you don't want to trust Photoshop's on-screen representation of the spot color any more than you would in Illustrator, QuarkXPress, or any other program. The screen version is an approximation, nothing more. So it's a good idea to have a Pantone swatch book on hand so that you know exactly what the color should look like when printed. (If the printed logo doesn't match the swatch book, it's the printer's fault, not Photoshop's.)

Printing Contact Sheets

In the previous edition of this book, I came down pretty hard on Photoshop's Contact Sheet command, and for good reason. At the time I wrote about the command, it was a big mess. Fortunately, my last sentence — "My guess is that we can expect better things from this command in the future" — turned out to be prescient, for now we have Contact Sheet II.

Choose File ➪ Automate ➪ Contact Sheet II to display the dialog box shown in Figure 18-15. These options permit you to take a folder of images and arrange them as thumbnails on a page, greatly expediting the creation of image catalogs. You specify the location of the folder, the number of columns and rows in the grid, and the color mode, and Photoshop does the rest. Contact Sheet II adds the ability to look into folders inside the specified folder (very useful) and label image thumbnails according to their file names (even more useful). You can even select the typeface and type size for the labels from the Font and Font Size pop-up menus.

Contact Sheet II is better than its predecessor, but if you ask me, it still isn't good enough. I'd like control over gutter and spacing, attributes that Contact Sheet II addresses automatically. But until Contact Sheet III comes out, it'll have to do.

In addition to Contact Sheet II, Photoshop offers two other commands under the File ➪ Automate submenu that organize multiple images onto a single page:

✦ **Picture Package:** This command fills a page with multiple copies of a single image, scaled to common print sizes such as 5 × 7 inches, 4 × 5 inches, and wallet snapshots. If you're a photographer, or you simply want to print some pictures of the kids for Grandma, this command does it all.

✦ **Web Photo Gallery:** Again geared toward professional and aspiring photographers, this command assembles a folder of images into a Web site, complete with HTML pages and JPEG images.

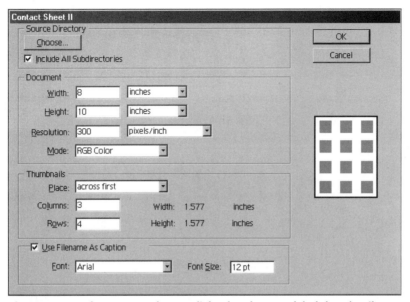

Figure 18-15: The Contact Sheet II dialog box lets you label thumbnails with their corresponding filenames.

In Photoshop 6, you get some design options not previously offered. In the Web Photo Gallery dialog box, shown in Figure 18-16, first select a page style from the Styles pop-up menu. The preview on the right side of the dialog box shows a sample page created using that style. Then you make further design choices by selecting the various items in the Options pop-up menu. For each item, you get a different set of accompanying design options:

- **Banner** enables you to name your page and add the photographer's name and the date. You also can select the font and type size for these items.

- **Gallery Images** provides options for adding a border around your images, resizing images, and applying JPEG compression.

- **Gallery Thumbnails** lets you specify such thumbnail options as the font, type size, thumbnail size, and the number of columns and rows of thumbnails. You can also add borders around the thumbnails and add captions based either on the image filename or the caption entered in the File Info dialog box.

- **Customize Colors** enables you to set the colors for the page background, banner, text, and links.

Web pages created via the Web Photo Gallery command aren't going to win any design awards, but the command is easy to navigate and it gets the job done. And if you know a little HTML, you can use the pages as a jumping off point for a more sophisticated site.

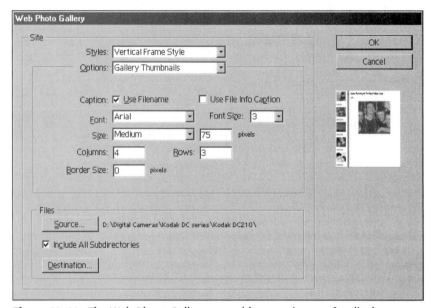

Figure 18-16: The Web Photo Gallery assembles your images for display on a Web page.

Photoshop 6 also lets you define custom Web Photo Gallery page styles. Using an HTML editor, you create a batch of HTML files that contain the instructions for formatting the various elements of the page. To get an idea of how to build your custom style, take a look at the HTML files provided for the Photoshop default styles, found in the Presets/WebContactSheet folder. After creating your custom pages, store them together in a new styles folder in the WebContactSheet folder.

✦　✦　✦

Creating Graphics for the Web

The World of Web Imagery

The Internet may well be the most chaotic, anarchic force ever unleashed on the planet. It has no boundaries, it has no unifying purpose, it is controlled by no one, and it is owned by everyone. It's also incomprehensibly enormous, larger than any single government or business entity on the planet. If the ten richest people in the world pooled their resources, they still couldn't purchase all the computers and cables that keep the Internet alive. In terms of pure size and volume, the Web makes the great thoroughfares of the Roman empire look like a paperboy's route.

As a result, it's impossible to get a bead on the World Wide Web. With several million hands in the pie, and several million more hands groping for a slice, the Web is as subject to casual comprehension as are the depths of the oceans, the infinity of the cosmos, or the meaning of life. And the Web mutates faster than any of those forces. Something just changed while you were reading the last sentence. An important new Web technology hit the market during the sentence you're reading now. It's enough to drive any sane human bonkers.

Fortunately, I'm not altogether sane, so I find the Web quite intriguing. Even so, whatever I write today will very likely change by the time you read this. We may all have the Internet cabled into our homes, animation and video images may rule the day, and the Web as I presently know it may be stone cold dead. All of this will happen gradually, of course — even light-ning-fast changes take some time to occur. And were a new technology to come along that combined the power of Java, the versatility of HTML, and the ease of use of a bar of soap, every one of the untold millions of Web content providers would continue to create their millions of different pages in millions of different ways. The most brilliant of technologies is forever mitigated by the willingness of humans to adapt to it.

I include the preceding by way of a disclaimer for the general thesis of this chapter, which is simply this: Bitmapped graphics rule the Web. Sure, text-based content, file libraries, and hyperlinks are the main stock and trade of the Internet, but the graphics are what make the Web intelligible and invite us to come back for more. Graphics have brought the masses to the Web, images account for 90 percent of all Web graphics, and Photoshop is the world's number one image editor. As a result, Photoshop has become as inextricably linked to the Web as Internet Explorer, Macromedia Dreamweaver, RealAudio, and a hundred other programs. It's just another happy accident in Photoshop's runaway success.

Photoshop and ImageReady

Despite (or perhaps because of) its extraordinary popularity as an online graphics creation tool, Photoshop has been criticized for its relatively paltry collection of Web-savvy features. Adobe used to tell Web designers they were missing the point — Photoshop was for print graphics and ImageReady was for the Web. But most Web designers ignored this advice and continued to grouse, so Adobe did the right thing and caved.

Beginning in Photoshop 5.5, Adobe's engineers started by expropriating a bevy of features from ImageReady 1.0 and hot-wiring them directly into Photoshop. Then midway into the process they said, "Oh to heck with it!" and tossed in ImageReady 2.0 for good measure. It's like a mad scientist who, after creating a half-man half-beast, decides the fellow isn't beasty enough and arms it with a pet wolverine.

Photoshop 6 borrows yet more DNA from ImageReady. You now get tools for creating and editing image slices, so you no longer have to switch programs to take care of that bit of business. You also get broader control over image output through the upgraded Save For Web dialog box.

In this book, I focus on Web features included in Photoshop, as those are the functions most essential to basic Web graphics. But in case you want to move into some advanced Web design, I stray into ImageReady at the end of this chapter to show you how to create image maps, rollovers, and animations.

Rules of Web Imagery

The Web provides an unbelievable outlet for creative expression. How else can you get your work in front of gazillions of people, all over the world? But as is the case with just about everything in life, success on the Web depends not just upon your artistic prowess, but also upon your understanding of the right and wrong ways to prepare your images. To that end, the next few sections discuss the do's and don'ts of Web imagery.

The smaller, the speedier

If you have any experience with the Web, you know that small images are speedy images. By "small," I don't mean small in physical size (although that often helps). I mean small in terms of disk space. A 20K image that fills your screen takes less time to download and display than a 50K file no larger than a sticky note. It's the act of getting the data through the cables and phone lines that takes the time; by comparison, the time it takes your browser software to interpret the data is insignificant.

Therefore, this chapter emphasizes ways to control file size. How can you squish the finest graphics you're capable of creating into the smallest amount of disk space with the least amount of sacrifice? This is the single most important challenge facing Web artists today. And while the Web-wide world is certain to change by the time you read this, I have a sneaking suspicion that small and speedy will remain the watchwords for some time to come.

Mac and PC monitor brightness

Many Web artists come from a background in print media, and while much of what they've learned while preparing printed photographs is equally applicable to online artwork, there are differences. Foremost among the differences, you never need worry about converting images to the CMYK color space. All Web graphics are RGB (or a subset of indexed colors or gray values). This is extremely good news because it means that for once in the history of electronic publishing, what you see on screen is really, truly what you're going to get.

Well, almost. Ignoring the differences in the ways people perceive colors and the variances in ambient light from one office or study to the next, there are measurable differences between monitors. Some monitors produce highly accurate colors, others — especially older screens — are entirely unreliable. But more importantly, some screens display images more brightly than others.

For example, the typical Macintosh user with an Apple-brand monitor is cursed with a very bright screen. Apple monitors — and many non-Apple brands developed for the Mac — are calibrated to a gamma of 1.8. Meanwhile, most PC monitors are calibrated to 2.2, which is roughly equivalent to a standard television.

Higher gamma values translate to darker displays because they indicate degrees of compensation. By compensating less (1.8 versus 2.2), images appear lighter on the Mac.

Figure 19-1 shows a test image subjected to various brightness settings. The upper-left example shows how the image looks when corrected for a typical PC screen. The upper-right example shows that very same image displayed on a typical Macintosh monitor. While it may be safe to assume that most folks who visit your Web page own PCs, the graphics community is still very large and active on the Mac side. So it pays to keep both Mac and PC users in mind when preparing your artwork.

Corrected on PC

Washed out on Mac

Slightly dark for PC

Slightly light for Mac

Figure 19-1: An image corrected for a PC screen lightens up dramatically when viewed on a typical Macintosh monitor.

The solution is to strike a compromise. Choose Image ➪ Adjust ➪ Levels (Ctrl+L) and lower the gamma (the middle Input Levels value) to between 0.8 and 0.75. Although the result will look a tad bit dark on your screen, it strikes a nice balance between PC darkness and Mac brightness. The bottom two examples in Figure 19-1 show what happens when I lower the gamma to 0.75 and display the image on a PC screen (left) and a Mac screen (right). A little dark on one, a little light on the other, but ultimately an equitable compromise.

You can use the Photoshop 6 color management options to preview how your image looks on a foreign monitor. After selecting color profiles and other options in the Color Settings dialog box, as I explain in Chapter 16, choose View ➪ Proof Setup ➪ Macintosh RGB. To switch between the preview and original, press Ctrl+Y, which toggles the Proof Colors command on and off.

More rules of Web imagery

Here are a few more items to remember when creating Web graphics:

✦ **Resolution doesn't matter.** Regardless of the Resolution value you enter into the Image Size dialog box, the Web browser displays one image pixel for every screen pixel (unless you specify an alternative image size in your HTML file). All that counts, therefore, is the pixel measurements — the number of pixels wide by the number of pixels tall.

In the future, however, browsers may end up paying attention to the resolution information, in which case the graphic would get scaled down to the dimension you specify.

✦ **Save in GIF or JPEG.** GIF and JPEG are the file formats of choice for Web graphics. GIF supports just 256 colors, so it's better for high-contrast artwork and text. JPEG applies lossy compression, so it's better for photographs and other continuous-tone images. The upstart format is PNG, which is essentially a 24-bit version of GIF designed for small full-color images that you don't want to compress.

✦ **Index colors with a careful eye.** Before you can save an image in the GIF format, you must reduce the number of colors to 256 or fewer. Photoshop uses a technique called *indexing,* which reassigns colors according to a fixed index, serving much the same purpose as the index in the back of this book. In Photoshop, you can create custom color tables so that the indexing process leaves many of the original image colors intact, thereby improving the appearance of your graphics.

✦ **Save essential data only.** If you save your Web images via the standard Save or Save As command instead of the Save For Web dialog box, you can reduce your file size by turning off all nonessential options — annotations, alpha channels, and so on. Also, for the sake of previews, go into the Saving Files panel of the Preferences dialog box (press Ctrl+K and then Ctrl+2) and set Image Previews to Ask When Saving. Then turn off the previews when saving the files.

By recognizing which formats to use when, and how best to reduce colors, you can better ensure that visitors to your Web site will spend less time sitting on their hands and more time enjoying your site. I explain the fine points of the file formats and color indexing in the following sections.

Saving JPEG Images

When it comes to saving photographic images, no format results in smaller file sizes than JPEG. As explained in gory detail in Chapter 3, the JPEG format decreases the file size by applying a lossy compression scheme that actually redraws details in the image. Inside the JPEG Options dialog box, select lower Quality settings to put the screws to the image and squish it as low as it will go. But in doing so, you also sacrifice image detail. (Revisit the second color plate in this book, Color Plate 3-2, to see an example of JPEG compression at work.)

Just to show you how well the JPEG format works, Figure 19-2 shows a series of images saved in the JPEG and GIF formats, along with their file sizes. The original file consumed 62K in memory. Yet by lowering the Quality setting to Medium, I was able to get the file size down to 28K on disk. To accomplish similar savings using the GIF format, I had to reduce the color palette to 3 bits, or a mere 8 colors. (For the record, this same file saved in the PNG format consumed 63K on disk.) As you can plainly see in the enlarged details, applying JPEG compression has a less destructive effect on the appearance of the image than reducing the color palette.

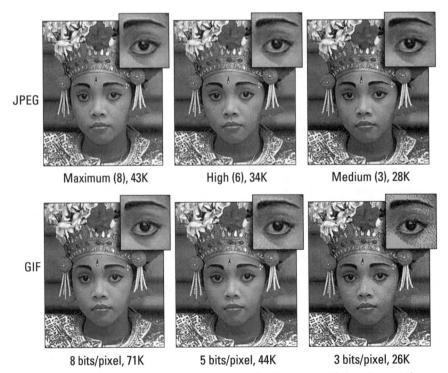

Figure 19-2: JPEG compression produces smaller file sizes with less impact than reducing the color palette and saving in GIF. The number in parentheses indicates the Quality value entered into the JPEG Options dialog box.

Tip

When judging small differences in file size, right-click the file at the desktop level and choose the Properties command. Then check the Size item listed in bytes. For example, the Size item in Figure 19-3 reads 16KB (16,551 bytes), 32,768 bytes used. The value in parentheses is the true reading, accurate to the byte. The second value — in this case, 32,768 bytes — is measured in drive blocks, which are the smallest parcels of disk that the system can write to. This makes for a misleading measurement that is invariably larger than the actual file size and that grows in proportion to the capacity of the hard drive (or drive partition). Whatever you do, don't believe the size listed in the preview box at the far-left end of the status bar. This is the size of the image in memory, but where Web graphics are concerned, all that counts is the size of the file on disk.

Figure 19-3: To gauge the true size of a file — accurate to the byte — right-click it at the desktop level, choose the Properties command, and observe the value in parentheses.

You can save an image to JPEG using either the standard File ➪ Save As command or the Save for Web command, which I explore later in this chapter. When you save via File ➪ Save As, Photoshop displays file size information at the bottom of the dialog box, assuming that you select the Preview check box, as shown in Figure 19-4.

The stated size reflects an approximate indication of the file size you'll get if you use the current JPEG options. What's more, Photoshop estimates how long the file will take to download at a given modem speed, which you select from the Size pop-up menu. Although these values are just approximations, they give you a good idea of how much compression you need to apply to the image to keep it at a reasonable download time.

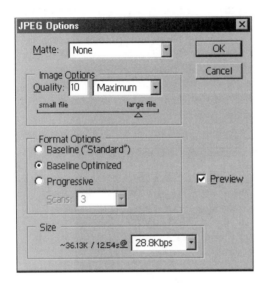

Figure 19-4: If you turn on the Preview check box, Photoshop displays the approximate file size and download time of the image at the current settings.

The other dialog box options work as follows:

✦ **Matte:** Unlike GIF, JPEG does not support transparency. So if your image contains transparent areas, Photoshop needs to know what color to fill them with. Select the desired color from the Matte pop-up menu. Keep an eye on the background image to make sure that you like the effect. Be aware that JPEG compression may cause the actual matte color to differ somewhat from the color you choose from the menu.

✦ **Quality:** If you've ever seen the movie *This Is Spinal Tap*, you may recall the scene in which lead guitarist Nigel Tufnel demonstrates how he can crank up the dials on his amplifier to 11, one beyond the standard maximum of 10. When asked, "Why not just make 10 louder and make 10 the top number?" Nigel blanks for a moment and finally concludes, "This goes to 11!" In that same vein, I present you with the Quality value, which once topped out at 10 and now extends to 12. Why not simply make 10 better quality and make 10 the top number? You don't need a computer science degree to figure out the answer to that question: "This goes to 12!"

At any rate, use the Quality option to specify the amount of compression applied to your image. Lower values mean smaller file sizes and more JPEG compression gook. Many experts say Medium (3) is the best setting for Web graphics, but I think it looks pretty awful, especially on screen. I prefer a Quality value of 5 or better.

✦ **Format Options:** Most Web browsers support two variations on the JPEG format. The so-called *baseline* (or *sequentially displayed*) format displays images in line-by-line passes on screen. The *progressive* JPEG format displays an image on screen in multiple passes, permitting visitors to your page to get an idea of how an image looks right off the bat, without waiting for the entire image to arrive.

To save a baseline image for use on the Web, select Baseline Optimized. This format includes better Huffman encoding that makes the file even smaller than Baseline ("Standard"). You can generally reduce the file size by 5 to 10 percent by using this option.

✦ **Scans:** If you select the Progressive radio button, you can pick a number of passes from the Scans pop-up menu. A higher value results in a faster display of the initial image on your page, but it also takes longer to display completely on screen because of all the incremental refreshing (although some browsers are smart enough not to redisplay individual JPEG scans if they already have received data for subsequent ones). A medium value of 4 is probably best if you choose to create progressive images.

There's a fair amount of debate over whether you should use progressive JPEG (and other incremental display options such as GIF interlacing). I used to be a fan of the option because it gives the viewer the early right of refusal. But I've become aware of enough compatibility issues that I now advise people to turn the option off.

Preparing and Saving GIF Images

So much for JPEG; on to GIF. The GIF format came into being during a time when only the super savvy owned 1200-bps modems. It supports a maximum of 8 bits per pixel (256 colors), and it uses LZW compression, just like TIFF. GIF comes in two varieties, known by the snappy monikers 87a and 89a, with the latter supporting transparent pixels.

Frankly, GIF is getting a little long in the tooth. Most online pundits figure PNG will replace GIF in the next few years. But for the time being, GIF is an extremely popular and widely supported format. And despite its obvious limitations, it has its uses. GIF is a much better format than JPEG for saving high-contrast line art or text. Figure 19-5 shows two versions of the same image; the top image was saved in the JPEG format, and the bottom one was saved in GIF. As you can see, the JPEG compression utterly ruins the image. And I had to reduce the Quality setting to 0—the absolute minimum—to get the file size down to 16K. Meanwhile, saving the image in the GIF format sacrificed no detail whatsoever and resulted in a file size of 18K. GIF's LZW compression is well suited to high-resolution artwork with large areas of flat color.

Figure 19-5: The JPEG format creates weird patterns in high-contrast images (top) and saves relatively little space on disk. Meanwhile, GIF keeps the sharp edges very much intact (bottom).

But before you can save a color image in the GIF format, you have to reduce the number of colors using Image ➪ Mode ➪ Indexed Color. The following section explains how this command works.

Using the Indexed Color command

Choose Image ➪ Mode ➪ Indexed Color to display the dialog box shown in Figure 19-6. This command permits you to strip an image of all but its most essential colors. Photoshop then generates a color look-up table (LUT), which describes the few remaining colors in the image. The LUT serves as an index, which is why the process is called *indexing*.

For some reason, Photoshop doesn't let you apply the Indexed Color command to Lab or CMYK images. And although you can apply Indexed Color to a grayscale image, you don't get any control over the indexing process; Photoshop doesn't let you reduce the image to fewer than 256 colors, for example. So if you want to index a Lab or CMYK image or custom-prepare a grayscale image, choose Image ➪ Mode ➪ RGB to convert the image to the RGB mode and then choose Image ➪ Mode ➪ Indexed Color. Alternatively, you can use Save for Web to save and index your images at the same time. (See the section "Optimizing JPEG and GIF Images," later in this chapter, for more information.)

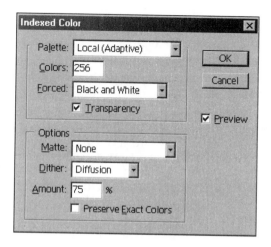

Figure 19-6: Use the Palette options to select the kinds of colors that remain in the image. Use the Colors option to specify how many colors remain.

Tip

Don't expect to be able to edit your image after indexing it. Most of Photoshop's functions — including the gradient tool, all the edit tools, and the filters — refuse to work. Others, like feathering and the paintbrush and airbrush tools, produce undesirable effects. If you plan on editing an 8-bit image much in Photoshop, convert it to the RGB mode, edit it as desired, and then switch back to the indexed color mode when you finish.

Now that I've gotten all the warnings and special advice out of the way, the following sections explain how to use the options inside the Indexed Color dialog box. Adobe gave the dialog box an overhaul in Version 5.5, adding helpful options for locking down important colors, choosing from more naturalistic palettes, and applying transparency.

Specifying the palette

The first pop-up menu — Palette — tells Photoshop how to compute the colors in the look-up table. The following list explains how each of the options works:

✦ **Exact:** If the image already contains fewer than 256 colors, the Exact option appears by default. This only occurs if you've created an extremely high-contrast image — such as a screen shot — or you're working from an image that originally started out as grayscale. If Exact is selected, just press Enter and let the command do its stuff. No sense messing with a good thing.

✦ **System:** Photoshop offers two System options, which are used by the Macintosh and Windows operating systems. The only reason to select either of these options is if you want to add a bit of imagery to the system. For example, it's a good idea to select the System (Windows) option when creating a background pattern, a wallpaper image, or some other item that appears at the desktop level. Color Plate 19-1 shows examples of a 24-bit image downsized to the Mac and Windows system palettes.

✦ **Web:** Just to make things as confusing as possible, Web browsers subscribe to their own variety of color palette. According to folklore, this 216-color LUT is an intersection of colors found in the Mac and Windows system palettes. But in fact, the Web palette includes those 216 colors whose R, G, and B values are divisible by 51. That means each primary color can be set to 0, 51, 102, 153, 204, or 255. Calculate all possible combinations, and you get 216 colors.

When displaying an image on an 8-bit screen, the browser invariably changes all colors to those in the Web palette. Therefore, converting your colors to the Web palette ensures that what you see on your screen is what your guests see as well. But for most folks, I still argue in favor of Adaptive if indexing must be done. An image with an adaptive palette will look far better on 16-bit and better monitors, and these days, high-color screens are in the majority. (The notable exceptions are portables, which often max out at 8-bit screens. But these LCD screens hardly do your color graphics justice, so it seems silly to let such lowest-common-denominator concerns dictate your work.)

✦ **Uniform:** This is the dumbest option of them all. It merely retains a uniform sampling of colors from the spectrum. I've never heard of anyone finding a use for it — but as always, I welcome your suggestions.

✦ **Adaptive:** This option selects the most frequently used colors in your image, which typically delivers the best possible results. Because it ignores all system and Web palettes, images downsized with Adaptive look best on high-color monitors, as I mentioned previously. To demonstrate just how much better they look, the bottom row of Color Plate 19-1 shows three images subject to the Adaptive palette at various Color Depth settings. Even with a mere 64 and 16 colors, the middle and right images look as good or better than the 256-color system-palette images above them.

Tip

In Photoshop 6, Adaptive comes in two flavors, Local and Selective. Choose Local (Adaptive) if you want Photoshop to consider the colors in the current image only. If you have several images open and want to create a palette based on all the images, choose Master (Adaptive).

When you use the Local option, you can influence the performance of the Adaptive option by selecting an area of your image before choosing the Indexed Color command. Photoshop favors the selected area when creating the palette. For example, before indexing the image in Color Plate 19-1 down to the 8-color palette (bottom right), I selected the fellow's face to avoid losing all the flesh tones. If you have more than one image open, Photoshop considers the selection in the active image and the entire palettes in the other images.

✦ **Perceptual and Selective:** These two options, added in Photoshop 5.5, are variations on Adaptive. But where Adaptive maintains the most popular colors, Perceptual is more intelligent, sampling the colors that produce the best transitions. The Selective option tries to maintain key colors, including those in the so-called 216 "Web-safe" palette.

That said, here's some advice: Select Perceptual for images where smooth transitions are more important than color values. Use Selective when an image contains bright colors or sharp, graphic transitions. And if an image contains relatively few colors — and you want to maintain those colors as exactly as possible, go for Adaptive.

As with Adaptive, choose the Local version of Perceptual and Selective if you want the palette created solely on the basis of the current image. The Master versions take all open images into account.

✦ **Custom:** Select this option to travel to the Custom Table dialog box, where you can load a look-up table from disk, or to create and save a custom table. This is useful when creating multimedia content, but rarely serves any purpose for Web graphics. I explain how to save a custom palette later in this chapter, in the section "Editing indexed colors."

✦ **Previous:** This option uses the last look-up table created by the Indexed Color command. If you're trying to create a series of high-contrast graphics that you want to look as homogeneous as possible, use this option. The Previous option is dimmed unless you have used the Indexed Color command at least once during the current session.

Colors

Like all computer programs, Photoshop measures color in terms of *bit depth*. As I've mentioned elsewhere in this book, an 8-bit image translates to 256 colors. Photoshop computes this figure by taking the number 2 and multiplying it by the number of times specified by the bit depth. 24-bit means 2 to the 24th power, which is 16 million; 4-bit means 2 to the 4th power, which is 16.

Before Photoshop 5.5, you controlled the number of colors in the palette by choosing a particular bit depth. Now you simply enter the actual number of colors into the Colors option box. The idea is that scaling colors by an entire bit depth — 8-bit for 256 colors, 7-bit for 128, 6-bit for 64, and so on — isn't really necessary to achieve smaller file sizes, so you might as well free your mind and enter the exact number of colors you deem fit. Still, it was a valuable option, and I would have preferred to see it stay. Sacrificing an entire bit does sometimes make a difference, after all.

As you can guess, fewer colors result in smaller GIF files. I generally start with 64 colors. With the Preview check box turned on, I can see the effect of this palette in the image window. If the image looks okay, I try going even lower. It's all a matter of getting the colors as low as they can go without becoming ugly. The bottom row in Color Plate 19-1 shows examples of the same image with 256, 64, and 16 colors.

Forced

In the past, an Adaptive palette could easily upset extremely important colors. For example, the white background of an image might turn a pale red or blue, even if white was a predominant color. Photoshop 5.5 added the Forced option, which enables you to lock in important colors so that they don't change. Black and White locks in black and white. Primaries protects eight colors — white, red, green, blue, cyan, magenta, yellow, and black. And Web protects the 216 colors in the Web-safe palette.

If you choose Custom, you can select the colors that you want to lock in. When you select Custom, Photoshop opens the Forced Colors dialog box. You see a color swatch for each color locked by the previously selected setting. To add another color, click an empty swatch and then select the color from the Color Picker dialog box. Click an existing swatch to replace it with another color. And to unlock a color, Ctrl-click the swatch. You can save your settings as a color table by clicking the Save button. (Forced colors files use the file extension .act.) Save the file in the Optimized Colors folder, located inside the Presets folder. Load existing settings by clicking the Load button.

Transparency

If an image is set on a layer against a transparent background, selecting this check box maintains that transparency. Bear in mind, however, that transparency in a GIF file is either on or off; there are no soft transitions as in a Photoshop layer.

Note   If you apply the Indexed Color command with the Transparency check box turned on, the familiar checkerboard pattern appears in the transparent portion of the image, as shown in Figure 19-7. What's unusual about this is that Photoshop flattens the file when you first choose the Indexed Color command, as indicated by the single *Background* layer pictured in the figure. Furthermore, you cannot add new layers to the file. This makes an indexed image the only kind of Photoshop document that can accommodate transparency without layers.

Matte

The Matte option works in collaboration with the Transparency check box. (If there is no transparency in an image — that is, all layers cover one another to create a seamless opacity — the Matte option is dimmed.) When you select Transparency, the specified Matte color fills the translucent pixels in the image. When Transparency is turned off, the Matte color fills all translucent and transparent areas. To ensure smooth transitions, select the Matte color that matches the background color of your Web page.

Figure 19-7: An indexed image is unique in that it can accommodate transparency inside a flattened document.

Dither

This option controls how Photoshop mimics the several million colors that you asked it to remove from an image:

✦ **None:** Photoshop maps each color in the image to its closest equivalent in the look-up table, pixel for pixel. This results in the harshest color transitions. But as I explain in a moment, it is frequently the preferable option.

✦ **Diffusion:** This option dithers colors randomly to create a naturalistic effect, as shown in the lower-right example of Figure 19-8 and the last image in Color Plate 19-2.

✦ **Pattern:** Pattern dithers colors in a geometric pattern, which is altogether ugly. Look to the lower-left example of Figure 19-8 and the middle image in Color Plate 19-2 for examples.

✦ **Noise:** Added in Photoshop 5.5, the Noise option mixes pixels throughout the image, not merely in areas of transition.

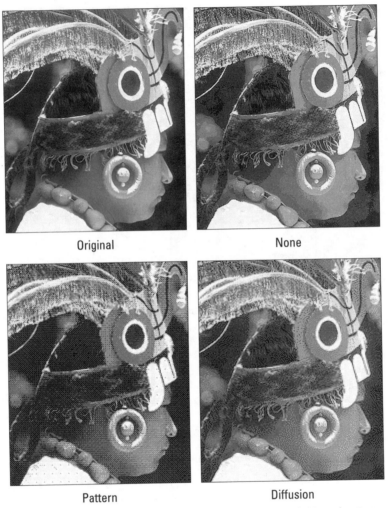

Original

None

Pattern

Diffusion

Figure 19-8: The results of converting an image (upper left) to the System palette using three of the Dither options: None, Pattern, and Diffusion.

After looking at Figure 19-8 and Color Plate 19-2, you may think that Diffusion is the option of choice. And in many cases it is, especially because you can control the amount of dithering using the Amount value, discussed next. But often, None is the better option. First of all, None results in smaller GIF files (as Color Plate 19-2 shows). Because LZW is better suited to compressing uninterrupted expanses of color, harsh transitions mean speedier images. Second, if a guest views your page on an 8-bit monitor, the system dithers the image automatically (assuming that you selected one of the Adaptive options from the Palette pop-up menu). System dithering on top of Diffusion dithering gets incredibly messy; system dithering on its own, however, is acceptable.

Amount

When you choose Diffusion as the dithering mode, you can modify the amount of dithering by raising or lowering this value. Lower values produce harsher color transitions, but lower the file size. It's a trade-off. Keep an eye on the image window to see how low you can go.

Preserve Exact Colors

The Preserve Exact Colors check box is available only when the Diffusion option is selected from the Dither pop-up menu. When turned on, this option turns off dithering inside areas of flat color that exactly match a color in the active palette. Say that you've created some text in a Web-safe color. The text is antialiased, but the letters themselves are flat color. By selecting Web from the palette pop-up menu and selecting the Preserve Exact Colors check box, you tell Photoshop to dither around the edges of the letters but to leave the interiors undithered.

As I mentioned before, you may often get better looking images if you apply no dithering. But if you decide to dither, turn Preserve Exact Colors on. Even if you can't see a difference on your screen, it may show up on another screen.

Editing indexed colors

As I said earlier, Adaptive is generally the best choice when creating Web graphics because it scans each image for its most essential colors. But even the Adaptive option doesn't get things 100-percent right. On occasion, Photoshop selects some colors that look wildly off base.

To replace all occurrences of one color in an indexed image with a different color, choose Image ⇨ Mode ⇨ Color Table. The ensuing Color Table dialog box, shown in Figure 19-9, enables you to selectively edit the contents of the LUT. You can get to this same dialog box by choosing Custom from the Palette pop-up menu in the Indexed Color dialog box, discussed in the preceding sections. The table also appears in the Save For Web dialog box, explored in the upcoming section "Optimizing JPEG and GIF Images."

To edit any color, click it to display the Color Picker dialog box. Then select a different color and press Enter to go back to the Color Table dialog box. Press Enter again to close the Color Table dialog box and change every pixel colored in the old color to the new color.

The Color Table dialog box also enables you to open and save palettes and select predefined palettes from the Table pop-up menu. What the Color Table dialog box doesn't let you do is identify a color from the image. For example, if you're trying to fix a color in your image, you can't display the Color Table dialog box, click the color in the image, and have the dialog box show you the corresponding color in the look-up table.

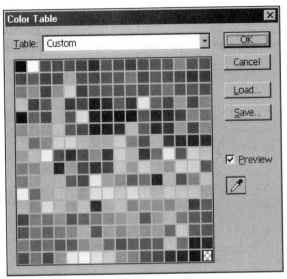

Figure 19-9: Use the Color Table dialog box to modify the colors in an indexed image.

"But," you say, "what about the eyedropper in the dialog box? Doesn't that lift colors?" The answer is yes — but it doesn't add the color you click to the table. Instead, it makes the color transparent, as explained in the next section. The only way to be sure you're editing the correct color — and be forewarned, this is a royal pain in the behind — is to slog through the following steps, which begin *before* you choose Image ➪ Mode ➪ Color Table.

STEPS: Editing a Specific CLUT Color

1. **Use the eyedropper tool to click the offending color in the image.** This makes it the foreground color. Remember, you take this step before opening the Color Table dialog box — you want to work with the eyedropper from the toolbox, not the one in the dialog box.

2. **Click the foreground color icon to display the specs for the color in the Color Picker dialog box.** Or display the Info palette by pressing F8 and then hover the cursor over the foreground color icon. Either way, write down the RGB values on a handy piece of paper, the palm of your hand, or a bald friend's scalp. (Don't edit the color inside the Color Picker dialog box at this time. If you do, you just change the color without changing any pixel in the image associated with that color.) If you're working in the Color Picker, press Esc to close it.

3. **Choose Image ⇨ Mode ⇨ Color Table.** This command becomes available only after you convert the image to Indexed Color mode.

4. **Click a color that looks like it might be the right one.** After the Color Picker appears, compare the color's RGB numbers to those you wrote down. If they match, boy, did you ever luck out. Go ahead and edit the color as desired. If the RGB values don't match, press Esc to return to the Color Table dialog box and try again. And again. And again.

Tip

To create a *color ramp* — that is, a gradual color progression — drag, rather than click, the colors in the palette to select multiple colors at a time. Photoshop then displays the Color Picker dialog box, enabling you to edit the first color in the ramp. After you select the desired color and press Enter, the Color Picker reappears, this time asking you to edit the last color in the ramp. After you specify this color, Photoshop automatically creates the colors between the first and last colors in the ramp in even RGB increments.

Making colors transparent

In the old days, you used File ⇨ Export ⇨ GIF89a Export to save a GIF image with transparent pixels. Now any GIF file can store transparency information. (See the next section for more information.)

After indexing the colors in an image, you can make all occurrences of one of those colors transparent using the Color Table command. Just select the eyedropper tool in the Color Table dialog box, shown in Figure 19-9, and click a color in the palette or in the image itself. Either way, that color becomes transparent.

The Color Table command suffers one limitation, though: You can make just one color transparent at a time. To make a second color transparent, you must press Enter to exit the dialog box and then choose Image ⇨ Mode ⇨ Color Table again.

Cross-Reference

For examples of transparent pixels, you might want to check out my site at *http://www.dekemc.com.* Every single graphic includes some transparent pixels, permitting the drop shadows and other gradual elements to blend in with the background.

Saving (and opening) GIF with transparency

There's really no reason to go on using the GIF89a Export command — the regular GIF format available through the Save As and Save For Web dialog boxes offers all the functions formerly accessible only through GIF89a Export. In addition, GIF89a Export is hard to script from the Actions palette, and you lose your work if you cancel midway through. In fact, the File menu doesn't even offer GIF89a Export anymore — you have to install it separately from the Photoshop 6 program CD.

It's long been rumored that the GIF89a Export command makes files smaller than standard GIF; I even made the mistake of repeating this rumor in the *Photoshop 5 Bible.* (Shame on me.) But after further testing, the rumor turns out to be a misreading of the evidence, as the scientists would say. It's not the GIF89a format *per se,* but rather its automatic exclusion of extraneous data that produces smaller files. When you save to GIF in Photoshop 6, the program automatically disables most options that save nonessential image data.

Here's the new, improved way to save a GIF image with transparency:

1. **Specify the transparency using the Indexed Color command.** You can make additional colors transparent using the Color Table commands, if you like.

2. **Choose File ⇨ Save As and select the As a Copy check box.** This option replaces the Save a Copy command in Photoshop 6.

3. **Select CompuServe GIF from the Format pop-up menu.**

   Be sure to turn off image previews (icons and thumbnails). This assumes that you set the Image Previews option to Ask When Saving inside the Preferences dialog box.

4. **Press Enter.** Photoshop displays the GIF Options dialog box, which offers two options: Normal and Interlaced. If you want the Web browser to display the image in incremental passes — similar to a progressive JPEG image — select the latter. Otherwise, select Normal. (I recommend that you don't interlace GIF images, though, because they can create problems in some browsers.)

5. **Press Enter again.** Photoshop saves the GIF file to disk.

If you save a file to the GIF format before indexing the colors, Photoshop displays the Indexed Color dialog box before showing you the GIF Options dialog box. You can then specify all your indexing preferences as you normally do. So if you forget to index the image before opening the Save As dialog box, don't bother canceling out of the dialog box to go back and choose the Indexed Color command. Just do your indexing as part of the save process. However, note that the on-screen image remains an RGB image; Photoshop doesn't completely convert the image to indexed mode until you close the file.

Regardless, after you create the GIF file, the open image window continues to bear the name and extension it had in the past. This is because you saved a copy of the image; you did not save the open version of the file. If you make any changes to the image, you need to resave the GIF copy to update it.

When you open a GIF file that contains transparency, Photoshop displays the transparency as a checkerboard pattern. No more having to remember which colors are transparent and which are opaque — what you see is what you get.

Optimizing JPEG and GIF Images

Not sure what settings to use when saving a GIF or JPEG file? Wouldn't it be nice to compare a bunch of different settings side-by-side to decide which provided the best trade-off between quality and size? The Save for Web command, introduced in Photoshop 5.5, permits you to do exactly that, and more. File ➪ Save for Web enables you to index colors, add transparency, and save to GIF or JPEG in one operation. So there's no need to use the Indexed Color or Color Table commands — in fact, Save for Web works best if you start from a full-color, RGB image.

Save for Web also enables you to save image slices, which you can create using the slice tool now available directly in Photoshop, as well as ImageReady. When you save the image, Photoshop saves each slice as an individual image file and also generates the HTML file your browser needs to rebuild the image on the Web page.

The Save For Web dialog box can be a little overwhelming at first, but in reality, there's not much more going on than when you save a JPEG or GIF file normally. The following steps provide an overview of the process:

STEPS: Optimizing a Web Image

1. **Choose File ➪ Save for Web or press Ctrl+Shift+Alt+S.** Either way, Photoshop displays the large window shown in Figure 19-10.

2. **Click the tab for the display you want to use.** You have four choices: Original shows you the original image — not much use for that one. Optimized shows the image as it will appear if you save using the current optimization settings. To compare multiple settings at the same time — the real power of the window — click the 2-Up or 4-Up tab in the top-left corner of the window. Figure 19-10 shows the 4-Up view.

   When you choose 2-Up, Photoshop shows you the original and optimized images side by side. With 4-Up view, you get two additional optimized images, which Photoshop generates using settings that create even smaller versions of the file. Photoshop bases the settings for these two additional previews on those you select for the primary optimized view.

   If your image contains slices, you can toggle slice previews on and off by clicking the slice display button, labeled in Figure 19-10.

   To get a closer view of your image in the dialog box previews, zoom and scroll the previews using the zoom and hand tools or use the standard spacebar-based keyboard equivalents. You can also change the zoom ratio via the zoom pop-up menu in the bottom-left corner of the window.

Optimize menu

Preview menu

Slice select tool

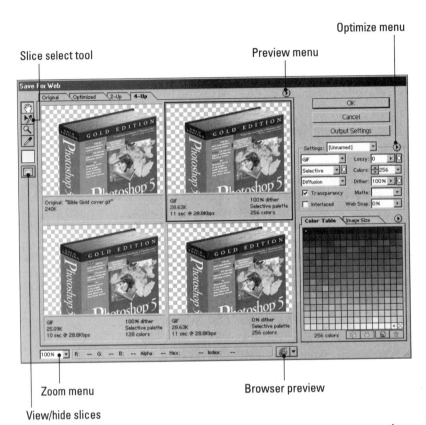

Zoom menu

Browser preview

View/hide slices

Figure 19-10: Click the 4-Up tab at the top of the window to compare the original image to three sets of Web compression settings.

3. **Click a preview and choose the optimization settings you want to apply.** The settings, which run down the right side of the dialog box, change according to the file format that you select. Most options duplicate those found in the JPEG and GIF Options dialog boxes; you can read about the other settings in the next two sections. After you change a setting, Photoshop rebuilds the preview to show you the result. To compare the results with another group of settings, click another preview and apply the new settings. Keep playing around until you arrive at the optimal outcome for your image.

You can also select an option from the Settings pop-up menu to apply a preset collection of optimization settings. Photoshop provides several presets, and you can save your own presets, as well. The upcoming section "The Preview menu" explains how.

If your image contains slices, you can optimize selected slices only. With the slice preview turned on, click the slice select tool, also labeled in the figure, and then click the slice you want to optimize. Shift-click to select additional slices. (For details on how to create slices in the first place, see the section "Slicing Images," later in this chapter.)

4. **If your image contains slices, click the Output Settings button to display the Output Settings dialog box.** You can specify how you want to create the required HTML code, set up automatic naming of the slice files, select the folder where you want all the slices to go, and more. I explore all these options in the "Output settings" section later in this chapter.

Tip

At this point, you may want to preview the image in your Web browser to make sure that you like your settings before you actually save the image. If so, select the browser from the browser preview pop-up menu and then click the browser preview button (labeled in the figure).

5. **Click the preview you like best and then click the OK button or press Enter.** Now you get the dialog box shown in Figure 19-11, which is a variation of the standard Save As dialog box. But instead of selecting the file format — which you've already done — you specify whether you want Photoshop to create just image file(s), the HTML page, or both. Select your choice from the Save as Type pop-up menu. If the image has slices, you can choose to save just the selected slices or all slices; select the option you want from the bottom pop-up menu. Finally, name the image and select a storage location, as usual.

6. **Click Save or press Enter.**

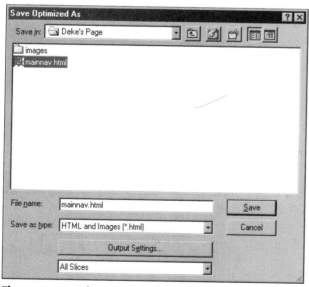

Figure 19-11: When you save the optimized image, you can choose to save just the image(s), just the HTML file, or both.

Now that you've got the basics under your belt, the next few sections get into more detail about the optimization settings and show you a few other features hidden in the preview menu and the optimize menu (both labeled in Figure 19-10).

GIF optimization settings

When you select GIF from the format pop-up menu, labeled in Figure 19-12, you gain access to the options shown in the figure. Most duplicate options found in the Indexed Color and GIF Options dialog boxes, so I won't bore you by explaining them all again. Some of the options aren't named, though, so I label them in Figure 19-12 so that you know what's what. Note that in this dialog box, the option labeled Dither corresponds to the Amount option in the Indexed Color dialog box, while the pop-up menu to the left corresponds to the Dither pop-up menu in the dialog box. Go figure.

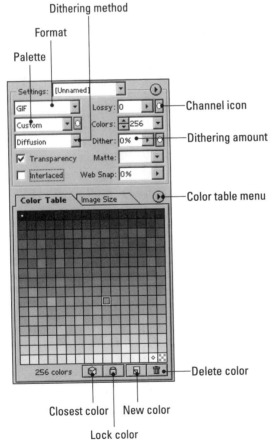

Figure 19-12: Most GIF optimization settings mirror those available through the Indexed Color and GIF Options dialog boxes, but a few are found only in the Save For Web dialog box.

The following list explains the few options that are exclusive to the Save For Web dialog box:

✦ **Lossy:** Technically, GIF relies on "lossless" compression, meaning that no data is sacrificed when saving a file. But by cranking up the Lossy value, you can rearrange the pixels in an image so that they compress better. In my experience, values as high as 30 whittle away the file size while causing little damage to the appearance of an image. Higher values are rarely acceptable. Use this option prudently, and keep an eye on the preview.

✦ **Web Snap:** This ingenious option replaces a specified percentage of colors in an image with members of the 216-color Web-safe palette. It's a way to hedge your bets — you can lock down some colors so they're compatible with older 8-bit monitors and permit other colors to roam free so that the image still looks great on 24-bit screens.

✦ **Color Table:** Clicking on this tab shows all the colors in an image. Below the colors, you'll notice four tiny icons, all labeled in Figure 19-12. The first changes a selected color to the nearest Web-safe equivalent. The second locks the selected color so it can't be changed. The third adds a color selected with the eyedropper to the palette. Here's how it works: Click the original image preview (upper left by default), select the eyedropper, click the color you want to add to the palette, switch back to the preview you want to change, and then click the third Color Table icon. Finally, the fourth icon deletes the selected color.

Double-click a color to display the new and improved Color Picker, with three Web-specific options spotlighted in Figure 19-13. Select the Only Web Colors check box to select exclusively from the 216-color Web-safe palette. When the check box is turned off, the cube icon alerts you that the selected color is not included in the Web-safe palette. Click the color swatch below the cube to replace the color with its nearest Web-safe equivalent. And if you're a hexadecimal geek (and proud of it!), you can enter the desired hexadecimal color value into the # option at the bottom of the dialog box.

✦ **Color Table menu:** When the Color Table tab is active, you can modify selected colors, sort colors, and load and save palettes by choosing commands from this menu. Just click the arrowhead to the right of the tab.

✦ **Image Size:** If an image is physically too large to fit snugly on your Web page, you can make it smaller it by clicking on the Image Size tab and fiddling with the Width, Height, and Percent values. These options work just like those offered by the Image Size command. For complete information, read Chapter 3.

Closest safe color

Web-safe alert

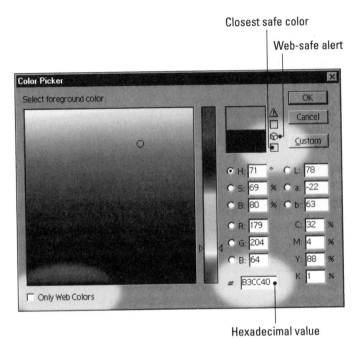

Hexadecimal value

Figure 19-13: The Photoshop Color Picker provides three options specifically for Web designers.

✦ **Channel icons:** When you index an image using Image ⇨ Indexed Color, you can make Photoshop favor a certain area of the image by selecting that area first. In the Save For Web dialog box, you also can selectively optimize a portion of the image when applying your chosen Lossy, Palette, and Dither settings. But in this case, you must save the selection outline as a mask channel before choosing Save for Web. Once inside the Save For Web dialog box, click a channel icon to display a dialog box where you can select a channel and adjust the optimization settings accordingly. If you click the icon next to the palette menu, for example, Photoshop displays the Modify Color Reduction dialog box, shown in Figure 19-14.

After you select a channel, a thumbnail preview of the mask channel appears in the dialog box. Assuming that you turn on the Preview check box, image preview updates to show you how your choice affects the color indexing. Click OK or press Enter if you like what you see; otherwise, click Cancel or select None from the pop-up menu and press Enter.

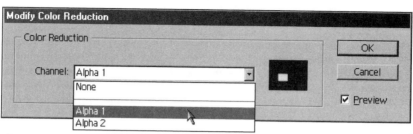

Figure 19-14: Select a mask channel to tell Photoshop to favor a portion of the image when indexing colors.

Note

For the palette menu, the channel optimization works just as when you select an area when indexing via the Indexed Color command. The color table is adjusted so that areas represented by the white portion of the mask channel get preferential treatment. But for Lossy and Dither, things work a little differently. After you select a channel, you can set Minimum and Maximum values for the optimization option. Photoshop again favors the area where the mask is white by applying the value that results in the best image quality — in this case, the Minimum value. Where the mask is black, Photoshop applies the Maximum values. For gray areas, a value somewhere between Maximum and Minimum is applied.

JPEG optimization settings

As you can see from Figure 19-15, most of the JPEG controls in the Save For Web dialog box are also found in the JPEG Options dialog box, covered earlier in this chapter. The following list introduces you to the few options available only if you use Save for Web.

Quality

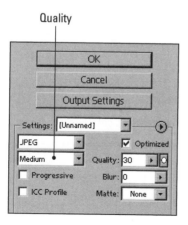

Figure 19-15: You get a few added JPEG options when you work in the Save For Web dialog box.

✦ **ICC Profile:** This check box embeds a color profile with the JPEG image. The color profile adds about 3K to the file size, which means an extra second of download time at 28.8 kilobits per second (Kbps). As I write this, only a few Web browsers can read a color profile without a special plug-in, so the extra 3K usually goes wasted. Leave this option off. Note that when you use File ➪ Save As to save a JPEG image, the Save As dialog box also offers an option for embedding a profile. The story's the same no matter where you find the option: Turn it off.

✦ **Optimized:** This option optimizes the compression built into a JPEG image. It has so little impact on file size—often none whatsoever—that I recommend you turn it off. (This option is unlikely to cause problems with Web browsers, but on rare occasions, it may make the image incompatible with other image editors.)

✦ **Quality:** The Quality pop-up menu and the menu to the immediate left mirror the Quality controls in the JPEG Options dialog box. But while the standard JPEG Options dialog box permits values between 0 and 12, this value ranges from 0 to 100. I can hear Nigel now: "This goes to 100!"

If your image contains a mask channel, you can apply compression selectively by clicking the channel icon to the right of the Quality menu. In the resulting dialog box, shown in Figure 19-16, first select the channel to display the channel thumbnail, as shown in the figure. Then adjust the Minimum and Maximum values, either by entering values into the option boxes or dragging the sliders above. Where the mask is white, Photoshop applies the Maximum quality setting, resulting in the minimum amount of compression. Black areas get the Minimum quality setting, meaning the maximum compression. Gray areas get middle-of-the-road treatment.

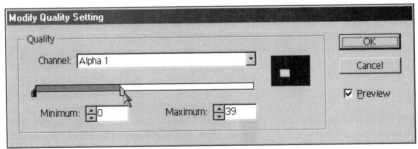

Figure 19-16: Select a mask channel to apply compression selectively to the image.

✦ **Blur:** This option is a dangerous one. The idea is that JPEG's lossy compression scheme is better at compressing soft transitions than hard edges, so it can compress blurry images better than sharp ones. So by blurring an image, you reduce its file size without applying more compression. *But you also destroy the freakin' detail!* Believe me, you're better off applying more compression than blurring the image. Leave this value set to 0.

✦ **Image Size:** You can click the Image Size tab to change the image size and resolution, just as when you work with GIF images.

The Optimization menu

The Optimization menu, shown at the top of Figure 19-17, contains a few additional goodies:

✦ **Save Settings:** Choose this command to save the current optimization settings as a preset. You can then apply the same settings by simply selecting the preset from the Settings pop-up menu.

✦ **Delete Settings:** This one deletes the current preset.

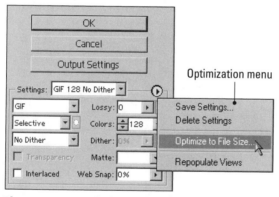

Figure 19-17: Unfurl the Optimization menu and choose Optimize to File Size to automatically choose settings that give you the best results at a given file size.

✦ **Optimize to File Size:** Here's the best reason to open the Optimization menu. Optimize to File Size lets you forgo messing with the options and instead enter a target file size. After you choose the command, Photoshop displays a dialog box in which you can specify whether you want to use the currently selected file format (select the Current Settings button) or let Photoshop pick the best option (Auto Select GIF/JPEG). If the image contains slices, select Current Slice to optimize just the selected slice; All Slices Separately to optimize each slice to the same file size; and All Slices Together to optimize all the slices so that all the slices together add up to the chosen file size.

✦ **Repopulate Views:** As discussed way back in the beginning of this whole Save for Web discussion, Photoshop creates three optimized previews when you're working in 4-Up view. The first preview represents your selected optimization settings; the other two show the image at two other sets of options, each of which results in smaller file sizes than your chosen settings.

If you make changes to your optimization settings, you can update the two alternative previews by selecting Repopulate Views. For example, if the current trio of previews shows you a GIF image at 256, 64, and 32 colors, and you lower the Colors value for the 256-color preview to 64, Photoshop generates the two other previews using Colors values lower than 64.

The Preview menu

One additional dialog box menu, loitering unpretentiously near the top of the Save For Web dialog box, controls the appearance and feedback provided by the previews by using the options on the preview menu shown in Figure 19-18. Click the arrowhead labeled in the figure to display the menu.

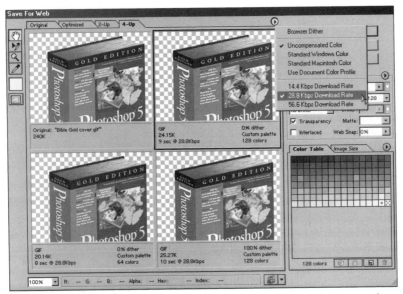

Figure 19-18: Choose a command from the Preview menu to change the appearance of a selected preview.

The commands are divided into three sections:

✦ **Browser Dither:** Select this option to see how a selected preview will look when displayed on an 8-bit monitor. This is an exceedingly useful method for determining whether you need to go with a Web-safe palette and for gauging the performance of the Web Snap value.

✦ **Color Compensation:** Colors shift from one screen to the next and from the Mac to Windows. There's no way to predict exactly how an image will look on another screen, but you can use the four color commands to get a sense. By default, Uncompensated Color is active, so Photoshop makes no attempt at a prediction. Select Standard Windows Color or Standard Macintosh Color to see how the colors might look on another platform. The final color command, Use Document Color Profile, shows the colors as they normally appear when open in your version of Photoshop, using your defined color-profile settings. (See Chapter 16 for details on color profiles.)

✦ **Download Rate:** The final three commands change the modem speed on which Photoshop calculates the estimated download times listed below each preview. These commands are unusual in that they affect all previews, not just the selected one.

Output settings

In addition to all the optimization settings found in the main Save For Web dialog box, you can display a mess of additional options by clicking the Output Settings button, located right underneath the Cancel button. Photoshop displays the Output Settings dialog box, shown in Figure 19-19.

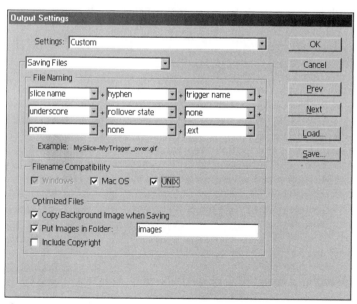

Figure 19-19: Click the Output Settings button in the Save For Web dialog box to uncover additional Web-related options.

If your image contains slices, Photoshop can automatically save each slice as an individual graphics file and generate the HTML page that contains the coding needed to put the slices back together when you open the page in your Web browser. The program also adds code related to links and HTML text that you may have added to slices. (If you're clueless about what I mean by all this stuff, skip ahead and read the "Slicing Images" section, which explains all. Then come back here when you're ready to save your sliced graphic.)

You control how Photoshop does this bit of automatic file generation plus control a few other aspects of the image file by using the options found in the Output Settings dialog box, which is another of Photoshop's multipaneled creatures. This one contains four panels, which you can explore by clicking the Next and Prev buttons on the right side of the dialog box or by choosing the panel you want from the pop-up menu directly underneath the Settings pop-up menu. Here's the short story on each panel:

✦ **HTML:** If you're an experienced HTML type, you can get specific about how you want Photoshop to generate the HTML page on this panel. Otherwise, I recommend that you let Photoshop take the lead and use the default settings.

✦ **Background:** This option enables you to select a background image or solid color to appear behind the selected slice or image on the Web page. If you want to use an image as a background, click the Choose button to select the file. Photoshop automatically creates a tiled background based on the image you select and sets it as the Web page background. For a solid color, select an option from the Color pop-up menu or choose Custom to select a color from the Color Picker.

Tip

You can even select both a background color and image. The color then appears while the image is loading and fills transparent areas afterward.

✦ **Saving Files:** This panel, shown in Figure 19-19, contains a couple of important options:

  • Leave all Filename Compatibility check boxes turned on. When Photoshop names your files, this option ensures that it uses names that can be recognized on Windows, Mac, and UNIX systems.

  • Photoshop automatically names the files it saves for you. But if you want to get specific — *really* specific — about how Photoshop names files, head to this panel. You can use the nine pop-up menus in the File Naming section to specify what image information and punctuation you want Photoshop to use when naming the files.

  • Most people like to keep all images related to an HTML page in a separate subfolder. If you're "most people," select the Put Images in Folder check box and enter the name you want to give the folder. (You specify the main location for the file storage when you actually save the files, as explained in the steps given in the earlier section "Optimizing JPEG and GIF Images.")

- Turn on the Copy Background Image When Saving option if you want to save a copy of the background image you select along with the other images. If you turn off the option, the HTML code for the background points to the original file location. To make copying all files associated with a page easier, I suggest that you leave this option turned on at all times.

- For GIF and PNG images, turning on the Include Copyright option embeds whatever copyright information you enter into the File Info dialog box for the image (File ⇨ File Info). The copyright information isn't visible in a browser, but if others download the image, they can view the data by opening the File Info dialog box.

✦ **Slices:** If you haven't assigned specific names to your slices in the Slice Options dialog box, Photoshop names each slice automatically for you. You can choose how you want the program to generate the names by using the pop-up menus on this panel, as in the Saving Files panel.

If, by this time, you're feeling overwhelmed by all the choices available to you when you use the Save For Web dialog box, you can just select one of the ImageReady Defaults options from the Settings pop-up menu. Or, if someone else saved some custom settings, you can load them by clicking the Load button. And if *you're* the one who did all the work — and don't want to ever do it again — click the Save button to save your choices as a custom setting that you can load the next time you need to save Web graphics.

Saving PNG Images

As I write this, the newest Web image format is the *Portable Network Graphics* format, or PNG (pronounced *ping*). Developed by a panel of independent graphics experts, PNG was designed specifically to outperform and ultimately replace GIF. It supports 24-bit and 48-bit images, it permits you to include mask channels for gradual transparency control, and — perhaps most importantly — PNG is not patented. Starting in 1995, Unisys, the developer of GIF, began to charge royalties to Web software developers. PNG, meanwhile, is free for all, which is why some folks claim PNG unofficially stands for "PNG, Not GIF."

PNG files are typically larger than comparable JPEG or GIF images because a PNG file does not include JPEG's lossy compression, and it can contain more colors than a GIF image. (The exception is when you save a grayscale or indexed PNG file, which is frequently smaller than the same file saved in GIF.) So PNG is generally best suited to small images — buttons and thumbnails — with fine details that you don't want mangled by JPEG compression.

Photoshop supports any RGB, grayscale, or indexed image in the PNG format. PNG doesn't support layers (of course), but it does permit you to include a single mask channel. Assuming the browser supports extra PNG channels, the mask defines the opacity and transparency of the image on the page. PNG graphics can even be translucent (as defined by gray areas in the mask channel), a terrific advantage over GIF and JPEG. When you save a PNG image, Photoshop displays a small dialog box that gives you the option to apply interlacing or not.

Caution

Before you rush out to save an image to the PNG format, however, bear in mind that browser support is thus far spotty. If you want to include a PNG image on your page, your guests may have to install a third-party plug-in, such as Siegel and Gale's PNG Live. I live in hope that this will change. I imagine that PNG support might become more universal by, say, the year 2002. In the meantime, the format is more interesting than practical.

Slicing Images

If you're like most Web designers I talk to, you rough out your pages in Photoshop. If you don't, you should — it's a great way to work. Photoshop lets you assemble all the elements the way that you want them to appear on the final Web page. Then you can slice and dice the elements and save them out to later assemble in HTML.

Consider the rough layout I created for my own Web site, shown as in Figure 19-20. It features a variety of buttons and text labels that I separated into independent GIF files using the Photoshop slicing functions. You can see the slice boundaries in the figure.

Yes, you read that last bit correctly — I said the *Photoshop* slicing functions. You no longer have to switch to ImageReady to create slices; Adobe added the slicing tools and related functions into Photoshop 6. You may still want to visit ImageReady to handle some Web chores, such as adding rollovers and animations, but for simple slicing, no need to stray from Photoshop. The following sections explain how to use the new slice tools.

Creating slices

To draw your slices, press K to select the slice tool. The tool shares a flyout with the slice select tool, as shown in Figure 19-20. You can tell the two apart because the slice select tool includes a little arrow cursor, the universal symbol for selection tool.

Slice tools

Slice number

Selected user slice

Auto slice

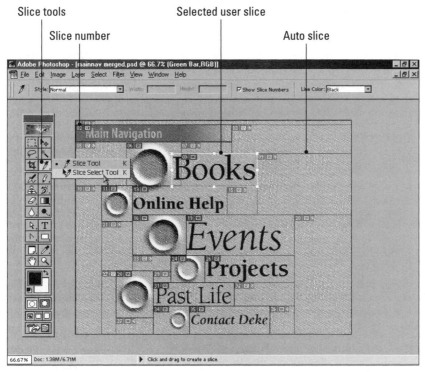

Figure 19-20: A page from my Web site, shown here with the slice previews turned on.

Because images have to be rectangular in shape, it makes sense that all slices are rectangular. Draw a rectangle around the shape that you want to slice; Shift-drag to constrain the slice to a square. For each slice that you create, a slice number appears in the upper-left corner of the slice, as shown in the figure. If the numbers start to annoy you, you can turn them off by deselecting the Show Slice Numbers check box on the Options bar.

Here are a few other points of note relating to slice drawing:

✦ Just as you can constrain the rectangular marquee tool to a fixed size or specific aspect ratio, you can set the slice tool to create a fixed size slice by choosing Fixed Size from the Style pop-up menu on the Options bar and entering values into the Width and Height option boxes. Alternatively, choose Constrained Aspect Ratio to draw a slice using a specific width to height ratio. Again, enter values into the Width and Height options boxes to set the slice ratio.

✦ If you want to base a slice on a selection, draw the selection outline as usual (it must be rectangular, of course). Then select the slice tool and use the selection outline as a guide as you drag to create the slice. Photoshop doesn't clear the selection outline when you activate the slice tool, as it does when you choose other tools. Another convenient option is to drag guidelines into the image to set up your slices and then just follow the guidelines as you drag with the slice tool.

✦ To create a slice that surrounds everything on a particular layer, select the layer in the layers palette and then choose Layer ➪ New Layer Based Slice. If you later change the layer's contents, Photoshop redraws the slice boundary if necessary to include new pixels.

Use this technique when saving slices that contain layer effects, such as drop shadows. This way, you can edit the effect without having to worry about redrawing the slice manually if the new effect takes up more space.

✦ As you draw borders around buttons, graphics, and other page elements, Photoshop automatically fills in the gaps with spacer slices. To differentiate these automatic slices from the so-called "user slices," Photoshop uses dotted lines for borders of the auto slices and a solid line for the user slices. You can set the color for user slices via the Line Color pop-up menu on the Options bar. Photoshop uses this same color scheme on the slice numbers.

✦ To hide and show the slice boundaries, press Ctrl+H, which hides all on-screen aids, including guides and selection outlines, unless you've set up permanent display via the Show Options dialog box. To toggle the slice boundaries on and off independently, choose View ➪ Show ➪ Slices. You also can choose View ➪ Show ➪ Show Options to specify which on-screen aids you want Photoshop to display at all times.

✦ If you draw slice boundaries that overlap, the slices are stacked according to the order in which you drew them, with the most recent slice at the top of the pile. You can edit only the top slice, but you can rearrange the stacking order to get to a lower slice, as explained in the next section.

After you get your slices just so, choose View ➪ Lock Slices to make them uneditable. That way, you won't accidentally alter a slice boundary. View ➪ Unlock unshackles the locked slices.

Editing slices

Need to change to a slice boundary? Grab the slice select tool and click the slice to select it — Shift-click to select additional slices. Then use the editing techniques in the following list to adjust the slices.

You can temporarily access the slice tool while the slice select tool is active by pressing and holding Ctrl. Conversely, if the slice tool is active, holding Ctrl gets you the slice select tool.

✦ To modify the size or shape of a slice boundary, click it to display handles around the slice. Drag a handle to change the shape of the slice. You can also drag inside a selected slice boundary to change its location or press the Backspace to delete it.

Tip

You can drag boundaries in the Save For Web dialog box, as well as in the image window. Click the slice select tool button in the dialog box and drag away.

✦ To duplicate a slice, put the tool cursor on the slice boundary. Then Alt-drag the slice.

✦ To promote an auto slice to a user slice, click the Promote to User Slice button on the Options bar. You can then adjust the boundaries of the slice.

✦ Click the Slice Options button, also on the Options bar, to name the slice, add a link, and set other slice attributes, as covered in the next section. You can also access this dialog box from inside the Save For Web dialog box; select the slice and then double-click the slice select tool icon.

✦ If you created overlapping slices, you can access the topmost one with the slice select tool. Use the four stacking order buttons near the left end of the Options bar, shown in Figure 19-21, to change the stacking order. You can send the selected slice to the bottom of the stack, the top of the stack, or up or down one level.

Figure 19-21: Click a stacking order button to send the selected slice up or down in the stacking order.

Photoshop

6

Setting slice options

After you create a slice, you can give the slice a specific name, create a link to a Web page, and more. Formerly, you had to do this work in ImageReady; now you can enter the data in Photoshop. First, select the slice you want to format and then click the Slice Options button on the Options bar. Or double-click the slice with the slice select tool. Either way, you get the dialog box shown in Figure 19-22.

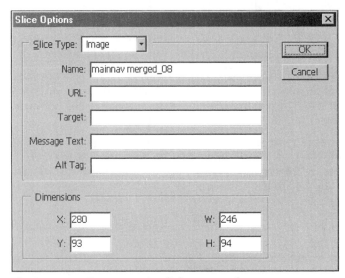

Figure 19-22: You can assign links, create alternate message text, and name individual slices in Photoshop 6.

The dialog box options work like so:

✦ **Slice Type:** You can either fill a slice with an image or with HTML text. Select the No Image option for the latter. The dialog box options change, giving you only a text-entry box into which you can type HTML text. You can format the text using standard HTML tags. But you won't be able to preview the text in Photoshop — you have to use a browser to see it.

The Image option saves the image data for the slice plus any linking data or alternative text that you assign to the graphic.

✦ **Name:** Photoshop automatically names the slices in the order they appear. If you want to override the automatic naming system, enter your slice names here. This option and the four that follow apply only when you select Image as the slice type.

✦ **URL:** To turn the slice into a button, enter the URL for the page you want the button to link to. If you want to link to a page stored in the same folder as the slice, a simple file name will suffice. For files inside other folders, enter the path name. To link to an outside Web page, enter the full URL, such as *http://www.dekemc.com.*

✦ **Target:** If your page includes frames, enter the appropriate frame tag into this option box.

✦ **Message:** Enter a message to appear at the bottom of the browser window when a visitor hovers the cursor over the button. For those familiar with JavaScript, Photoshop handles this using an *onMouseOver="window.status"* tag.

✦ **Alt:** To provide a text alternate for the button, enter the text into this option box.

✦ **Dimensions:** To specify the exact placement and size of a slice boundary, enter the pixel coordinates into the X and Y options and the dimensions into the W and H options. You have access to these options even when you select No Image as the slice type.

When you use the Save For Web dialog box to save your image, you get access to two additional options. Inside the dialog box, double-click the slice with the slice select tool. You get the same options as just described plus these two:

✦ **Background:** If your image contains transparent areas, you can choose to fill them with a color selected from this pop-up menu. Choose Custom to select a color from the Color Picker; choose None to leave transparent areas alone. Again, you can't see the background color in Photoshop; you must use a browser.

✦ **Linked:** That little link icon means that the optimization settings for the slice are linked to another slice. By default, all spacer (automatic) slices are linked together. You can't link slices in Photoshop; you must open the image in ImageReady and choose Slices ➪ Link Slices. You can then apply the same optimization settings to all the linked slices at once, either in ImageReady or in the Save For Web dialog box in Photoshop.

Saving slices

I imagine that by now, your eyes are glazed over and you'd just as soon watch another rerun of *Big Brother*—even though you already know who gets banished from the compound and who gets to stay—so I'll keep this final bit of slice-related data simple.

After you create image slices, you'll want to take one or both of the following saving steps:

✦ To save your original image with all slice information intact, choose File ➪ Save As and select either the Photoshop or TIFF format. Be sure to select the Layers check box, or the slice data gets dumped. When you reopen the image, choose the slice select or slice tool to redisplay the slice boundaries and make any further changes.

✦ To output the image in Web-ready form, choose File ➪ Save for Web. This command enables you to save all the slices as individual image files and to create the HTML page that will reassemble the image in the Web browser. You also can save individual slices, if you like. The preceding thousands of pages in this chapter — okay, so maybe I exaggerate, but just a little — explain this feature.

Doing More in ImageReady

If you like things plain and simple, you can stop reading this chapter right now. You already know everything you need to know to create your basic Web images and sliced graphics. But if you want to add some spice to your Web pages — and really, what's a Web page without a little seasoning? — crack open ImageReady and try your hand at creating the three types of graphics described in this section: image maps, rollovers, and animations.

Creating an image map

Slicing divides a document into several independent graphics. You can turn any of those slices into a button that a viewer clicks to jump to a linked page or frame. By default, each graphic accommodates one and only one button. The upside is simplicity — each slice gets one URL. The downside is that the buttons are rectangular in shape. Even if your button graphic appears circular or some other shape, the browser cursor reacts the second it enters the rectangular boundaries of the sliced graphic.

For complex Web designs — imagine a map of the world in which each country is a separate button — slicing becomes less practical. Each country would have to comprise several graphics, pieced together like colored bricks. The better solution would be one big graphic with irregularly shaped buttons drawn over it. In other words, an image map:

1. **First establish a slice around the entire image.** In the case of my example, the entire map of the world.

2. **Set each area that you want to set as a button on a separate layer.** France would be on one layer, Germany on another, Austria on a third, and so on.

3. **Select the first button's layer in the Layers palette.** If it isn't visible on screen, choose Window ➪ Show Layers. If the layer includes an effect (drop shadow, glow, what have you), make sure that the layer — not the effect — is selected in the Layers palette.

4. **Choose Layer ➪ New Layer Based Image Map Area.** Now display the Image Map palette (Window ➪ Show Image Map), shown in Figure 19-23, and select the shape that you want ImageReady to use to trace the layer outline. In the case of the map, Polygon is the only setting that makes sense, as shown in Figure 19-23.

Image map preview

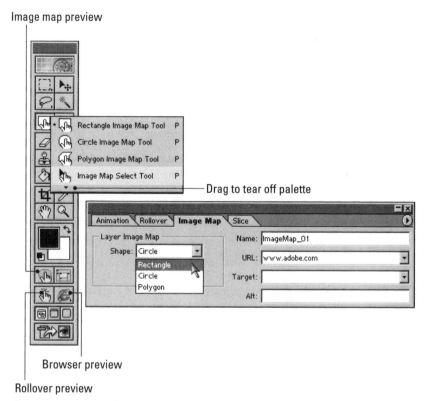

Drag to tear off palette

Browser preview

Rollover preview

Figure 19-23: Use the Image Map palette to specify the URL that you want to associate with an image map button.

5. **Enter the desired file name or address into the URL option box.** To link to an outside Web page, remember to enter the full URL, complete with the *http://* prefix.

6. **Select the next layer that you want to assign as a button and repeat steps 4 and 5.** Keep going until you assign all the button links.

   By using the image map preview button in the toolbox, labeled in Figure 19-23, you can see whether the image map is functioning the way you want. To preview the image map in a browser, click the browser preview button to the right. You can select the browser you want to use from the button's flyout menu.

7. **Choose your optimization settings and then choose File⇨Save Optimized.** You tell ImageReady how to optimize the image map via the Optimize palette (Window⇨Show Optimize). The settings here duplicate those in the Photoshop Save For Web dialog box, explored earlier in this chapter. After you choose File⇨Save Optimized, the Save Optimized dialog box appears. Select HTML and Images from the Format Files of Type pop-up menu. You can control other aspects of the save by clicking the Output Settings button and following the guidelines discussed earlier in this chapter to make your choices.

When you click Save, ImageReady saves both the image and the HMTL code, complete with client-side image map coordinates. If you prefer to create a server-side map, click the Output Settings button in the Save Optimized dialog box and then travel to the HTML panel of the dialog box. Then select the desired setting from the Types pop-up menu. (If in doubt, Client-Side is the way to go.)

As an alternative to creating layer-based image maps, you can draw the boundaries of each button using the new image map tools, shown in Figure 19-23. Drag with the rectangular, circular, or polygonal tools to draw the boundaries of the button. The button automatically appears in the Image Map palette. Add the link information, as usual. Drag again to create the next button.

Tip

You can tear the image map tools off the toolbox to create a tiny floating palette containing just the tools. To do so, drag the down-pointing triangle at the bottom of the flyout menu (see Figure 19-23).

If you ever want to change the button information, click it with the image map selection tool. You see the current data in the Image Map palette. Enter the new data and resave the graphic to finalize the update.

JavaScript rollovers

ImageReady's slicing functions make quick work of creating and assembling HTML buttons. But the program's rollover capabilities are even easier — absolute child's play, in fact. I'm confident you could figure them out without me. But I've already slapped together an introduction, so I might as well keep writing.

For those who aren't familiar with them, a *rollover* is a collection of JavaScript functions that make a button change according to the actions of the mouse cursor. The most common example is a button that highlights when you roll the cursor over it — hence the term "rollover."

The following steps explain how to make a rollover:

1. **Create the different button states, each on its own layer.** For example, Figure 19-24 shows a button created using a series of layers. The first three layers make up the base button, as shown in the top image. A fourth layer, Pink Dent, adds a depression to the button's center, as shown in the bottom image. This dent will be my rollover.

2. **Display those layers that make up the base button state.** In my case, I turn off the Pink Dent layer by clicking on its eyeball icon in the Layers palette.

3. **Display the Rollover palette.** Just click the Rollover tab, or choose Window ➪ Show Rollover.

4. **Select the desired slice that surrounds the button.** Show the slice boundaries if necessary and click the button with the slice select tool. (If you haven't gotten around to drawing a slice yet, by all means, get with it.) The button appears in the Rollover palette, as shown in Figure 19-25.

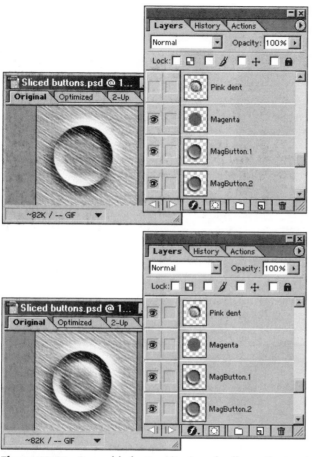

Figure 19-24: Assemble button (top) and rollover (bottom) elements on separate layers.

5. **Click the tiny page icon along the bottom of the Rollover palette.** This adds a new state to the palette. By default, this is the Over state, which changes the button when the cursor moves over it.

6. **Display the alternative button layer.** In my case, I turn on the Pink Dent layer, again by clicking on its eyeball icon in the Layers palette. The state appears in the Over slot, as in Figure 19-26.

Note

For you JavaScripters, there's no need to create another button state for the *onMouseOut* event. ImageReady adds one automatically that restores the normal appearance of the button. (You can, if you wish, override this by creating an Out state, as explained in the next step.)

Figure 19-25: Select the base button with the slice select tool to add it to the Rollover palette.

New rollover state

Figure 19-26: Click the page icon and display the alternative button layer to add a new state to the palette.

7. **If Over isn't the cursor operation you want, click the word Over to select a different one.** You can select from Down, Click, Out, and Up. Down affects the appearance of the graphic when the mouse button is held down. A Click graphic appears when the user clicks and remains in place until the next user action. Out changes the button when the cursor moves away from the button; Up affects the graphic when the mouse button is released. Truly, I can't imagine any reason for using anything but Over — a little bit of rollover goes a long way, after all — but I'm sure a clever reader will come up with something.

To make sure the rollover looks the way you want, select the rollover preview button in the toolbox (labeled in the preceding section, in Figure 19-23). Again, you can preview the effect in your favorite Web browser by clicking the browser preview button, also in the figure. If you want to get rid of the effect, choose Delete Rollover from the Rollover palette menu.

After you finish, select your optimization settings from the Optimize palette and choose File ➪ Save Optimized. Be sure to select the HTML and Images option from the Save as Type pop-up menu in the Save Optimized dialog box.

ImageReady adds comments around its JavaScript functions — in this case, *ImageReady Preload Script* and *End Preload Script* — so that it won't run the risk of upsetting any code you may have added when it updates the HTML file.

Tip If you create many Web graphics, you may want to create styles (presets) for your rollovers. That way, you can easily churn out multiple buttons that all use the same rollover effects.

Creating Web animations

I don't know if you've ever tried to open an animated GIF file in Photoshop, but it's not a pretty sight. Photoshop opens the first frame only and throws the rest away. God forbid you make changes and save the file — if you do, you'll throw away all the frames that Photoshop can't read.

ImageReady is another story. It can read all frames in an animated GIF file and automatically separate each one to an independent layer. Figure 19-27 shows an animated GIF file that I opened in ImageReady. You can see the layers of frames in the Layers palette on the right and the Animation palette, with each layer assigned to a frame, along the bottom. Notice that the Layers and Animation palettes share two buttons, labeled in the figure. These take you backward or forward one frame. Other buttons appear exclusively in the Animation palette: The double-arrow button takes you to the first frame, the single right-pointing arrow button plays, and the square button stops. Note that ImageReady plays the animation at a slower speed than it will play in a Web browser.

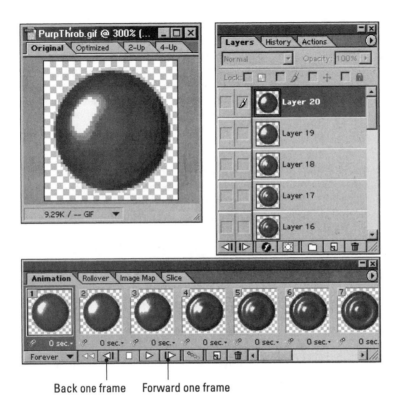

Back one frame   Forward one frame

Figure 19-27: The Layers and Animation palettes permit you to create frames and to assemble animated GIFs.

You can also navigate through frames from the keyboard:

✦ Press Alt+right arrow to advance one frame.

✦ Alt+left arrow backs up a frame.

✦ Shift+Alt+left arrow takes you to the first frame.

✦ Shift+Alt+right arrow advances to the last frame.

Caution   Be careful not to press Ctrl with one of these arrow-key combinations. You'll end up moving or duplicating a layer, which probably isn't something you want to do.

While this gives you a sense of how ImageReady's animation feature works, the fact is, any doofus can open and play an animated GIF file. What you want to do is create an animation of your own, which is why I explain these and other mysteries of the Animation palette in the following sections.

Adding and organizing frames

The Animation palette works like an expanded version of the Rollover palette. Each frame in the palette shows one or more layers and hides others. So every animation effect you add has to be somehow associated with a separate layer.

To add a frame, click the tiny page icon at the bottom of the Animation palette. Then add a layer to the Layers palette and paint or modify the layer as desired. You may find it helpful to duplicate an existing layer to maintain consistency from one frame to the next. For example, if I duplicated one of my purple balls and applied the pinch filter to it, I would create the appearance of a ball getting squished. Feel free to hide and show other layers to get the effect you want.

Tip

If you already created all your image layers, you can automatically dump each layer into a new frame by choosing Make Frames from Layers from the Animation palette menu.

Once a layer is associated with a frame, any changes made to the pixels in that layer affect the frame, as well. This means you can make adjustments to several frames at once by changing a single layer that appears in each one of the frames. An exception occurs if the change does not affect a layer's pixels. For example, changing the opacity of a layer does not change the layer's pixels, nor does setting the blend mode to Multiply or dragging the layer with the move tool. Changes such as these — generally invoked from the Layers palette — affect the active frame only.

You can avoid such intricate and potentially confusing interaction by associating each frame with exactly one layer — no less, no more — just as ImageReady does when it opens a GIF animation. (ImageReady even provides a command that does this for you called Flatten Frames into Layers.) Experiment to find the approach that works best for you.

Once you establish a handful of frames — Web animations may comprise as few as two frames, but rarely contain more than 20 — the Animation palette lets you reorder, delay, and duplicate frames. Here are a few techniques that you should be aware of:

✦ **Selecting:** To select a frame, click it. To select a range of frames, click one and Shift-click another. To select multiple frames out of order, Ctrl+click each frame.

✦ **Reordering:** To change the order of a frame, drag it left or right to a new point in the palette. If necessary, the palette automatically scrolls to keep up.

✦ **Deleting:** Click the trash icon to delete a selected frame. Alt-click to delete the last frame in the bunch. Note that this just deletes the frame. It does not delete any layers from the image, so none of your work is permanently lost.

✦ **Duplicating:** To duplicate one or more selected frames, choose the Copy Frames command from the Animation palette menu, as in Figure 19-28. Then select the frame after which you want the copied frames to appear and choose Paste Frames.

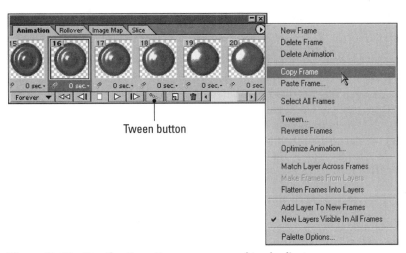

Figure 19-28: Use the Copy Frames command to duplicate one or more selected frames.

✦ **Reversing:** After copying and pasting a series of frames, you can reverse their order by choosing the Reverse Frames command. This is a great way to return the animation to its original appearance so that it repeats (or *loops*) seamlessly when played in a Web browser.

✦ **Tweening:** Like any good animation program, ImageReady provides a *tweening* function that automatically generates transitional frames in between hand-drawn ones. The Tween command affects changes to three attributes: position, opacity, and layer effect. To make a ball move, for example, create a new frame and drag the layer in the image window with the move tool. The image appears to move inside the active frame only.

Next, click the Tween button, now provided in the Animation palette (see Figure 19-28) or choose Tween from the palette menu. In the resulting dialog box, select the Position check box, enter the number of frames that you want ImageReady to insert, and click OK. Tweening is also useful for creating fades between layers and animating glows and shadows.

✦ **Matching effects:** A moment ago, I mentioned how changes made to the opacity or blend mode of a layer affect the active frame only. To override this limitation — and thereby copy a new opacity or blend mode to all frames that contain the affected layer — choose Match Layer Across Frames from the Animation palette menu.

When you choose this command, however, ImageReady also resets the layer position of all frames to match the selected frame. So if you used the Tween command to make a ball bounce, for example, and then match the layers with the final frame of the bounce selected, the ball moves to the same position in all frames.

✦ **Frame disposal:** When you watch a movie, the projector hides one frame before it displays the next. In ImageReady, this is called *frame disposal*. By default, ImageReady automatically determines whether a frame should be hidden or not based on its contents. To make a frame linger, right-click it and choose the Do Not Dispose command. Alternatively, if a frame appears to be lingering when it shouldn't, right-click and choose Restore to Background.

✦ **Adding a delay:** By default, each frame appears for a split second and then gives way to the next frame. But you can make a frame hang for an extended period of time by adding a delay. Click the time listed below the frame thumbnail to display a menu of timing options, as in Figure 19-29. No Delay is the default setting; other settings pause the animation for the specified period of time.

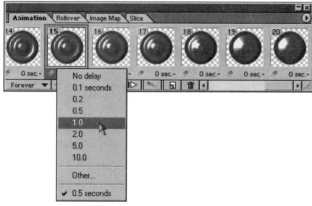

Figure 19-29: To add a delay to a frame, click the time listed below the frame thumbnail.

✦ **Looping:** Web animations aren't Bugs Bunny cartoons — they don't have a plot. Their purpose is to linger and pulsate, like electronic lava lights. Therefore, your typical Web animation is set to play once, buffer in memory, and then loop over and over until your visitor moves on to the next page. But like everything, you can override that. Click the word Forever in the bottom left corner of the palette and choose the number of loops you'd prefer.

Saving the animation

You'd think saving an animation would be a matter of choosing an Export command — and it is if you want to save the animation as a QuickTime movie. But when saving an animated GIF (the more common alternative), saving becomes a bit more elaborate.

Because ImageReady's GIF functions are based on the slicing metaphor, saving your animation becomes a matter of four Optimize features:

1. **Select GIF from the pop-up menu on the left side of the Optimize palette.** Then adjust the other settings according to taste. All settings affect all frames, regardless of which frames are active. To find out more about your options, read the sections that discuss image optimization, earlier in this chapter.

2. **Click the Optimized tab in the image window.** Then click the Play button in the Animation palette to preview the animation in action.

3. **Choose Optimize Animation from the Animation palette menu.** The Bounding Box option crops each frame to make it as small as possible. Redundant Pixel Removal deletes any pixel that hasn't changed since the previous frame. To ensure the smallest animation file possible, both options should be turned on.

4. **Choose File ➪ Save Optimized As.** Select Images Only from the Save as Type pop-up menu. You can also play with the file output options by clicking the Output Settings button. These options work as described in the "Output settings" section earlier in this chapter. After you click OK, ImageReady saves the animated GIF file according to your specifications. (From this point on, you can update the file using the Save Optimize command.)

Remember, that's Optimize, Optimized, Optimize Animation, and Save Optimized As. I think I'm beginning to see a trend. Too bad nobody thought to initiate a little optimization during the software design process.

Tip

To give yourself the freedom to modify your animation file at some later point in time, be sure to also save it in Photoshop's native PSD format. This will likewise permit you to open the file inside Photoshop. ImageReady saves all layers in the RGB color space; the Photoshop format doesn't accommodate layers inside an indexed file.

Animations and rollovers

You'd never know it by looking at them, but the Slice, Rollover, and Animation palettes are inexorably linked. Rollovers occur inside slices and animations occur inside rollovers. One upshot of this is that you can create animated rollovers — animations that begin when the user moves the mouse over the graphic or performs whatever other action you set as the rollover trigger.

Inside the Rollover palette, click the tiny page icon to create a new state, labeled Over by default. Then switch to the Animation palette and create a sequence of frames as explained in the previous sections. The rollover necessitates an HTML file, so after choosing Save Optimized As, be sure to select the Save HTML File check box.

Don't forget that you can preview the effect of your rollover animation right in the image window in ImageReady 3. Just select the rollover preview button (it's labeled in Figure 19-23, earlier in this chapter) and then pass your mouse over the rollover area. Alternatively, click the browser preview button (also labeled in the figure) to see how the rollover behaves in the browser window.

Tip

What if you've already created a GIF animation and you want to make it a rollover after the fact? Simple. With the animation document open, switch to the Rollover palette and click the tiny page icon to make a new Over state. There's your animated rollover. Problem is, you also have an animated base button. To solve that problem, click the Normal thumbnail. Switch to the Animation palette and delete all frames but the first one. Now your base button is a stationary GIF image. To make certain everything's still intact, return to the Rollover palette and click the Over thumbnail. Then go back to the Animation palette. Voila, there's your animation. Now choose File ⇨ Save Optimized to generate the base GIF button, animated GIF rollover, and all necessary HTML code.

✦ ✦ ✦

Using the CD-ROM

The CD-ROM attached to the back cover of this book contains an extensive collection of photographs, artwork, and plug-ins that you can use with Photoshop. The CD-ROM works with both Macs and PCs, regardless of which version of this book you have purchased. On the Mac, you need to be running System 7.5.5 or later. On the PC, you need Windows 95, 98, or NT 4 or later. (The CD-ROM will not function properly under Windows 3.1 or earlier.)

To view the photographs and artwork contained on the CD-ROM, you will need Photoshop or some other image editor. You will also need Photoshop to take advantage of the filters contained in the Plug-Ins folder. The remaining files — including artist biographies and documentation — are provided in one of the following formats:

+ **Text-only (.txt) files:** You can open these in Notepad or a word processor.

+ **Acrobat (.pdf) documents:** To open a .pdf file, you'll need Acrobat Reader or Acrobat Exchange from Adobe. Most folks already have Acrobat Reader, but if you don't, you can find it in the Acrobat Reader folder on the CD-ROM.

+ **Web (.html) pages:** To open these documents, you need access to a Web browser such as Netscape Navigator (*www.netscape.com*) or Microsoft Internet Explorer (*www.microsoft.com*).

+ **QuickTime movies:** To view the Total Training clips, you will need the QuickTime viewer. If you don't have the viewer, you can download it from *www.apple.com*.

The *Photoshop 6 Bible* CD-ROM does not contain all of the software required to read these formats. However, this shouldn't be a problem because most computers come preconfigured with the software you need.

Note One final note before we get underway: This CD-ROM does not contain the Photoshop 6 application. Photoshop sells for about $600 on the street, so it's unrealistic to expect a copy of the software for the $39.99 or less you paid for this book. This book has just two purposes: A) to educate digital artists and, more importantly, B) to prop up youngsters who are too short to reach the table. If you want Photoshop, you have to buy it from Adobe.

Opening the CD

To access the images and artwork included on the CD-ROM, start by inserting the CD into your CD-ROM drive. Next double-click the My Computer icon on your desktop. The CD-ROM drive icon inside the My Computer window changes to Ph6 Bible. Double-click the Ph6 Bible icon to open the CD-ROM. The window pops open and displays the following items:

✦ **PH6 Bible PDFs:** A PDF version of this book, plus a bonus four chapters, is available on this CD-ROM for your convenience. Please don't copy them or post them for friends. They are for your use only.

✦ **Readme.txt:** This file duplicates some of the text from this appendix. But because I'm the kind of person who would pop the CD into the drive before ever cracking open the book, I thought it might be a good idea to include a "read me" file for impatient people like me.

✦ **Artist Gallery:** This folder contains nearly 150MB of original imagery from 16 of the finest artists working with Photoshop today. The artists cover a broad range of styles and techniques, and you can get some great ideas from looking at their work. Note that these images belong to the artists who created them. Feel free to view them on screen, but under no condition should you integrate an image from this folder into your own work, post an image on the Internet, or in any way pass it off as your own. Thanks.

✦ **Total Training**: This folder contains clips of lessons from my Total Photoshop video training series. In addition to training on Photoshop, Total Training provides video lessons for several other graphics applications. To find out more, visit *www.totaltraining.com*.

✦ **PC MacLAN:** Available to Windows users only, this folder contains a demonstration version of Miramar's PC MacLAN, the easiest solution for networking Macintosh and PC computers. This is the software I use in my office, so I can attest that it works great. (If you're viewing the CD-ROM on a Mac, you will not see this folder.)

✦ **Plug-ins:** This folder contains a wide range of Photoshop plug-ins from scads of different vendors, including such luminaries as Alien Skin, and Andromeda. Most of the plug-ins are limited demonstration versions that give you ample chance to try out the software before you buy. But many of the vendors have graciously shared one or two fully functional plug-ins that are exclusive to this book. You can use them right off the CD without paying another dime.

✦ **Stock Photos:** This folder contains a total of 48 high-resolution images from the titans of digital stock photography, PhotoDisc and Digital Stock. Not coincidentally, every one of these photographs is featured in the figures in this book, so you can follow along with the exercises and techniques exactly as I describe them.

PhotoDisc Images courtesy of: PhotoDisc, Inc. 2013 Fourth Ave., Seattle, WA 98121. 1-800-528-3472. www.photodisc.com. All PhotoDisc images: © 1998 PhotoDisc, Inc.

The following sections explain the contents of each of these folders in depth.

Artists Gallery

These folders contain images created by 16 of the finest Photoshop artists working today. I'm hear to tell you, some of this stuff will blow your socks off. In alphabetical order, the artists include Robert Bowen, Ron Chan, Mark Collen, Katrin Eismann, Helen Golden, Wendy Grossman, Dorothy Krause, Bonny Lhotka, Kent Maske, Judith Moncrieff, Bud Peen, Jeff Schewe, Karin Schminke, Gordon Studer, Richard Tuschman, and Nanette Wylde. All images are provided as inspirational material only; they are not for commercial use and the artists retain all copyrights to their work.

Cross-Reference
Each artist folder contains a short biography of the artist. You can open the biography in your favorite word processor. To find out more about how these artists create their work, I recommend you take a look at another book I've written called *Photoshop Studio Secrets, 2nd Edition* (IDG Books Worldwide, 1999). Printed in full color, this book examines the work of 16 artists including many of those included in the Gallery folder—namely Robert Bowen, Ron Chan, Katrin Eismann, Bud Peen, Jeff Schewe, Karin Schminke, and Gordon Studer.

Plug-Ins

The contents of this folder vary depending on whether you're using a Mac or a PC. On the Mac, the Plug-Ins folder contains filters from 12 different vendors. On the Windows side, 11 vendors are represented. This is because two vendors—ImageXpress and Vivid Details—create plug-ins for the Mac only, and another vendor—Ulead—is exclusively Windows. The remaining vendors—Alien Skin, Andromeda, BoxTop Software, Chroma Graphics, Wacom, and Xaos Tools—are cross-platform.

All told, the Plug-Ins folder includes more than 50 pieces of software. Each plug-in includes documentation on the CD that explains what it does and how it works. So rather than itemize each program, here's a quick summary of the highlights to get you started:

+ **Alien Skin:** This folder contains a demo version of Eye Candy 4000, the splendid special-effects suite from Alien Skin.

+ **Andromeda:** Andromeda Software has generously provided samples of five of its special effects and 3D filter collections. Among these is a fully functioning demo of Series 4, Techtures, an excellent texture creation and manipulation laboratory, which also happens to be available exclusively to *Photoshop 6 Bible* readers. Just double-click the Install utilities to add these plug-ins to Photoshop.

+ **BoxTop Software:** BoxTop specializes in plug-ins that export and optimize Web graphics. On the Windows side, you'll find three demo plug-ins. Each program is fully functional for 30 days, and then rather than expiring, it merely slows down. Frankly, that's pretty darn generous. On the Mac side, you'll find several more demos, along with a few freebies, including one—PhotoGIF Lite—which is available exclusively to *Photoshop Bible* readers.

✦ **Chroma Graphics:** This folder contains three traditional demos, no freebies. But I decided to include the filters anyway because they automate one of the most complicated operations in Photoshop, masking. You can't save your work with any of these demos, but at least you can get a sense for how the filters work.

✦ **ImageXpress:** Available on the Mac only, this folder contains a demonstration version of Alius. Alius is a first-rate posterization filter, and is worth a look. The installation is a little tricky, so be sure to read the documentation supplied in the folder. Enter "Trial" as the serial number to use the plug-in free for 7 days.

✦ **Tormentia:** This is the collection of eight filters that I created using the Filter Factory, as explained in Chapter A on the CD-ROM. Every single one of them is fully functional, free, and cross-platform. To install the filters, drag them into Photoshop's Plug-Ins folder. To learn what each of these filters does, read the Torment.txt file included in the Tormentia folder.

✦ **Ulead:** If you Windows folks were starting to feel peeved about the absent filters from BoxTop and ImageXpress, here's your chance to get even. This folder contains a grand total of 14 plug-ins and stand-alone utilities from Ulead, and every one of them is available exclusively for Windows. Many of the plug-ins are fully functioning shareware.

✦ **Vivid Details:** Available only for Macintosh users, this folder contains a demonstration version of Test Strip. This excellent plug-in is ideal for anyone who owns a color proofing or output device and wants to be able to compare side-by-side color variations. Test Strip eliminates the guesswork of printing reliable color and it's extremely easy to use. What more could you ask?

✦ **Xaos Tools:** This folder includes two items. One is a utility that installs Total Xaos (pronounced *chaos*), which is a collection of three demo plug-ins — the brush laboratory Paint Alchemy, the 3D type creation filter Type Caster, and the texture-creation filter Terrazzo. As a special gift to *Photoshop 6 Bible* readers, Xaos has also thrown in 32 "luminous texture" images from the company's commercial Fresco collection. If a bunch of textures strike you as a mite dull, open one or two in Photoshop and you'll quickly change your mind.

Note

Remember, after installing a plug-in from any of the vendors listed above, you must quit Photoshop and relaunch the program in order to load the plug-ins into RAM. Most plug-ins only work if an image is open.

Stock Photos

The idea behind the Stock Photos folder is to provide you access to the original images featured in this book. That way, you can edit the images as you read along. The Stock Photos folder contains two subfolders named after the vendors who contributed photographs to the *Photoshop 6 Bible,* Digital Stock and PhotoDisc. Each subfolder contains another folder called High-rez images. Inside, you'll find 24 high-resolution images from the book.

By way of an endorsement, you can rely on both Digital Stock and PhotoDisc for their vast libraries of high-quality stock photography. If you're looking for an image, one or the other is bound to provide what you need. For more information, or to search for photographs online according to subject, consult the companies' Web sites at *www.digitalstock.com* and *www.photodisc.com.*

✦   ✦   ✦

Index

Continued

Continued

IDG Books Worldwide, Inc.
End-User License Agreement

READ THIS. You should carefully read these terms and conditions before opening the software packet(s) included with this book ("Book"). This is a license agreement ("Agreement") between you and IDG Books Worldwide, Inc. ("IDGB"). By opening the accompanying software packet(s), you acknowledge that you have read and accept the following terms and conditions. If you do not agree and do not want to be bound by such terms and conditions, promptly return the Book and the unopened software packet(s) to the place you obtained them for a full refund.

1. **License Grant.** IDGB grants to you (either an individual or entity) a nonexclusive license to use one copy of the enclosed software program(s) (collectively, the "Software") solely for your own personal or business purposes on a single computer (whether a standard computer or a workstation component of a multiuser network). The Software is in use on a computer when it is loaded into temporary memory (RAM) or installed into permanent memory (hard disk, CD-ROM, or other storage device). IDGB reserves all rights not expressly granted herein.

2. **Ownership.** IDGB is the owner of all right, title, and interest, including copyright, in and to the compilation of the Software recorded on the disk(s) or CD-ROM ("Software Media"). Copyright to the individual programs recorded on the Software Media is owned by the author or other authorized copyright owner of each program. Ownership of the Software and all proprietary rights relating thereto remain with IDGB and its licensers.

3. **Restrictions On Use and Transfer.**

    (a) You may only (i) make one copy of the Software for backup or archival purposes, or (ii) transfer the Software to a single hard disk, provided that you keep the original for backup or archival purposes. You may not (i) rent or lease the Software, (ii) copy or reproduce the Software through a LAN or other network system or through any computer subscriber system or bulletin-hyboard system, or (iii) modify, adapt, or create derivative works based on the Software.

    (b) You may not reverse engineer, decompile, or disassemble the Software. You may transfer the Software and user documentation on a permanent basis, provided that the transferee agrees to accept the terms and conditions of this Agreement and you retain no copies. If the Software is an update or has been updated, any transfer must include the most recent update and all prior versions.

4. **Restrictions on Use of Individual Programs.** You must follow the individual requirements and restrictions detailed for each individual program in the Using the CD-ROM Appendix of this Book. These limitations are also contained

in the individual license agreements recorded on the Software Media. These limitations may include a requirement that after using the program for a specified period of time, the user must pay a registration fee or discontinue use. By opening the Software packet(s), you will be agreeing to abide by the licenses and restrictions for these individual programs that are detailed in the Using the CD-ROM Appendix and on the Software Media. None of the material on this Software Media or listed in this Book may ever be redistributed, in original or modified form, for commercial purposes.

5. **Limited Warranty.**

   (a) IDGB warrants that the Software and Software Media are free from defects in materials and workmanship under normal use for a period of sixty (60) days from the date of purchase of this Book. If IDGB receives notification within the warranty period of defects in materials or workmanship, IDGB will replace the defective Software Media.

   (b) **IDGB AND THE AUTHOR OF THE BOOK DISCLAIM ALL OTHER WARRANTIES, EXPRESS OR IMPLIED, INCLUDING WITHOUT LIMITATION IMPLIED WARRANTIES OF MERCHANTABILITY AND FITNESS FOR A PARTICULAR PURPOSE, WITH RESPECT TO THE SOFTWARE, THE PROGRAMS, THE SOURCE CODE CONTAINED THEREIN, AND/OR THE TECHNIQUES DESCRIBED IN THIS BOOK. IDGB DOES NOT WARRANT THAT THE FUNCTIONS CONTAINED IN THE SOFTWARE WILL MEET YOUR REQUIREMENTS OR THAT THE OPERATION OF THE SOFTWARE WILL BE ERROR FREE.**

   (c) This limited warranty gives you specific legal rights, and you may have other rights that vary from jurisdiction to jurisdiction.

6. **Remedies.**

   (a) IDGB's entire liability and your exclusive remedy for defects in materials and workmanship shall be limited to replacement of the Software Media, which may be returned to IDGB with a copy of your receipt at the following address: Software Media Fulfillment Department, Attn.: *Photoshop 6 for Windows Bible*, IDG Books Worldwide, Inc., 10475 Crosspoint Blvd., Indianapolis, IN 46256, or call 1-800-762-2974. Please allow three to four weeks for delivery. This Limited Warranty is void if failure of the Software Media has resulted from accident, abuse, or misapplication. Any replacement Software Media will be warranted for the remainder of the original warranty period or thirty (30) days, whichever is longer.

   (b) In no event shall IDGB or the author be liable for any damages whatsoever (including without limitation damages for loss of business profits, business interruption, loss of business information, or any other pecuniary loss) arising from the use of or inability to use the Book or the Software, even if IDGB has been advised of the possibility of such damages.

(c) Because some jurisdictions do not allow the exclusion or limitation of liability for consequential or incidental damages, the above limitation or exclusion may not apply to you.

7. **U.S. Government Restricted Rights.** Use, duplication, or disclosure of the Software by the U.S. Government is subject to restrictions stated in paragraph (c)(1)(ii) of the Rights in Technical Data and Computer Software clause of DFARS 252.227-7013, and in subparagraphs (a) through (d) of the Commercial Computer — Restricted Rights clause at FAR 52.227-19, and in similar clauses in the NASA FAR supplement, when applicable.

8. **General.** This Agreement constitutes the entire understanding of the parties and revokes and supersedes all prior agreements, oral or written, between them and may not be modified or amended except in a writing signed by both parties hereto that specifically refers to this Agreement. This Agreement shall take precedence over any other documents that may be in conflict herewith. If any one or more provisions contained in this Agreement are held by any court or tribunal to be invalid, illegal, or otherwise unenforceable, each and every other provision shall remain in full force and effect.

LET THERE BE VIDEOS.

In the beginning, Deke created the *Photoshop Bible*, and behold, it was very good. But Adobe Photoshop® is a visual program. It's about graphics. And the most effective way to learn graphics is by *watching*, not just by reading. That's why Deke McClelland, Photoshop disciple and best-selling author, created *Total Photoshop*.

Deke McClelland's

TOTAL Photoshop

Total Photoshop is a professional interactive training course. *Total Photoshop* combines video lessons with interactive course content; you work with the exact same elements on your computer that Deke works with onscreen. Let's face it, in today's fast-paced, ever-changing graphics world, there is no better investment in yourself than *training*. With *Total Photoshop*, you'll get clear, concise demonstrations of key concepts and techniques. It's like having your own private instructor (the best one in the world!), and most importantly, with videos you can review the materials whenever you need a refresher.

If you're serious about learning Photoshop, there's no better choice than *Total Photoshop!*

TOTAL PHOTOSHOP...

...Takes an Entertaining, Thought-Provoking Approach
- *Enjoy Your Learning Experience!*
- *Retain More Information from a Single Viewing!*
- *Load Up on New Ideas!*
- *If You Need a Recharge, Watch Again and Again!*

...Provides a Thorough Guided Tour
- *Add New Photoshop Skills to Your Arsenal!*
- *Quickly Incorporate Stunning Visual Effects!*
- *Master the Industry's Top Imaging Application!*

...Teaches Valuable Workflow Techniques
- *Streamline Your Image Creation and Editing Process!*
- *Save Time on Your Next Project!*
- *Increase Your Value and Expand Your Career!*

HEAVENLY OFFER:

Buy *Total Photoshop* and we'll credit you the price of the Photoshop Bible!
(Estimated Street Price $50)

Mention offer code (TPS-DPB-6437) when ordering.

Make sure to ask about special discounts on any other Total Training products!

TOTAL TRAINING INC.
www.TotalTraining.com
call (888) DO TOTAL
or (760) 944-3900

Deke McClelland's Look & Learn™

New from the bestselling author of
Photoshop® For Dummies® and *Photoshop® Bible*

Designed and Edited by the
#1 Bestselling Computer
Graphics author

"When you're on a deadline,
no book gives you so much
so quickly."
—Steve Broback, Thunder Lizard Productions

Instant Information
That Sticks In Your Head!

Deke McClelland's
Look & Learn™
Flash™
version **5**

Annotated
screen shots

Step-by-step examples

All text keyed
to images

Unique picture index

look and learn books.com

by Deke McClelland

*"When you're on a deadline,
no other book gives you so
much so quickly"*

—Steve Broback,
Thunder Lizard Productions

Series titles include:

Deke McClelland's Look & Learn™ Photoshop 6

Deke McClelland's Look & Learn™ Flash™ 5

Deke McClelland's Look & Learn™ Windows® Me
Millennium Edition

Available wherever
books are sold

- *The unique, heavily illustrated format lets
  you see how the software works*

- *Each two-color guide explains program
  tools and delivers step-by-step tutorials*

Each book in the *Look & Learn* series is written or edited by
Deke McClelland, a leading digital graphics authority whose
books have sold more than 2 million copies. A seven-time
recipient of the Computer Press Award, he is also host of the
video training series Total Photoshop and a contributing edito
at *Macworld®* and *Publish®* magazines.

© 2000 IDG Books Worldwide, Inc. All rights reserved. Look & Learn, Look & Learn logo and all related designs and trade dress are trademarks of IDG Books Worldwide, Inc.
Flash is a trademark of Macromedia, Inc. FrontPage and Windows are registered trademarks or trademarks of Microsoft Corporation. Photoshop is a registered trademark of Adobe Systems, Inc. All other trademarks are property of their respective owners.

my2cents.idgbooks.com

Register This Book — And Win!

Visit **http://my2cents.idgbooks.com** to register this book and we'll automatically enter you in our fantastic monthly prize giveaway. It's also your opportunity to give us feedback: let us know what you thought of this book and how you would like to see other topics covered.

Discover IDG Books Online!

The IDG Books Online Web site is your online resource for tackling technology — at home and at the office. Frequently updated, the IDG Books Online Web site features exclusive software, insider information, online books, and live events!

10 Productive & Career-Enhancing Things You Can Do at www.idgbooks.com

- Nab source code for your own programming projects.

- Download software.

- Read Web exclusives: special articles and book excerpts by IDG Books Worldwide authors.

- Take advantage of resources to help you advance your career as a Novell or Microsoft professional.

- Buy IDG Books Worldwide titles or find a convenient bookstore that carries them.

- Register your book and win a prize.

- Chat live online with authors.

- Sign up for regular e-mail updates about our latest books.

- Suggest a book you'd like to read or write.

- Give us your 2¢ about our books and about our Web site.

You say you're not on the Web yet? It's easy to get started with IDG Books' *Discover the Internet*, available at local retailers everywhere.

CD-ROM Installation Instructions

To access the images and artwork included on the CD-ROM, start by inserting the CD into your CD-ROM drive. Next double-click the My Computer icon on your desktop. The CD-ROM drive icon inside the My Computer window changes to Ph6 Bible. Double-click the Ph6 Bible icon to open the CD-ROM. The window pops open and displays the following items:

✦ **PH6 Bible PDFs:** a PDF version of this book, plus a bonus four chapters, is available on this CD-ROM for your convenience. Please don't copy them or post them for friends. They are for your use only. Thanks.

✦ **Artist Gallery:** This folder contains nearly 150MB of original imagery from 16 of the finest artists working with Photoshop today. The artists cover a broad range of styles and techniques, and you can get some great ideas from looking at their work.

✦ **Total Training**: This folder contains clips of lessons from my Total Photoshop video training series. In addition to training on Photoshop, Total Training provides video lessons for several other graphics applications. To find out more, visit *www.totaltraining.com.*

✦ **PC MacLAN:** Available to Windows users only, this folder contains a demonstration version of Miramar's PC MacLAN, the easiest solution for networking Macintosh and PC computers. This is the software I use in my office, so I can attest that it works great. (If you're viewing the CD-ROM on a Mac, you will not see this folder.)

✦ **Plug-ins:** This folder contains a wide range of Photoshop plug-ins from scads of different vendors, including such luminaries as Alien Skin, Andromeda, and Extensis. Most of the plug-ins are limited demonstration versions that give you ample chance to try out the software before you buy. But many of the vendors have graciously shared one or two fully functional plug-ins that are exclusive to this book. You can use them right off the CD-ROM without paying another dime.

✦ **Stock Photos:** This folder contains a total of 48 high-resolution images from the titans of digital stock photography, PhotoDisc and Digital Stock.